The Editor

SANDIE BYRNE is Fellow and Tutor in English at Balliol College, Oxford University. She is the author of *Tony Harrison: Loiner, H, v, & O: The Poetry of Tony Harrison,* the *Icon Reader's Guide to the Poetry of Ted Hughes,* and the *Icon Reader's Guide to Mansfield Park.*

W. W. NORTON & COMPANY, INC.
Also Publishes

GEORGE BERNARD SHAW'S PLAYS

MRS WARREN'S PROFESSION • PYGMALION • MAN AND SUPERMAN • MAJOR BARBARA

Contexts and Criticism

SECOND EDITION

Edited by

SANDIE BYRNE
OXFORD UNIVERSITY

First Edition edited by

WARREN SYLVESTER SMITH
LATE OF PENNSYLVANIA STATE UNIVERSITY

W • W • NORTON & COMPANY • *New York* • *London*

Copyright © 2002, 1970 by W. W. Norton & Company, Inc.

Previous edition published as BERNARD SHAW'S PLAYS.

The text of this book is composed in Fairfield Medium
with the display set in Bernhard Modern.
Composition by Binghamton Valley Composition.
Manufacturing by the Maple-Vail Book Manufacturing Group.
Book design by Antonina Krass.

Library of Congress Cataloging-in-Publication Data
Shaw, Bernard, 1856–1950.
[Plays. Selections]
George Bernard Shaw's plays : Mrs. Warren's profession, Pygmalion,
Man and superman, Major Barbara : contexts and criticism /
selected and edited by Sandie Byrne.—2nd ed.
p. cm.—(A Norton critical edition)
Includes bibliographical references.

ISBN 0-393-97753-6 (pbk.)

1. Shaw, Bernard, 1856–1950—Criticism and interpretation.
I. Byrne, Sandie.   II. Title.

PR5361 .B97 2002
822'.912—dc21   2001044733

W. W. Norton & Company, Inc., 500 Fifth Avenue, New York, N.Y. 10110
www.wwnorton.com

W. W. Norton & Company Ltd., Castle House, 75/76 Wells Street, London
W1T 3QT

7 8 9 0

Contents

Preface

Jane Austen has Janeites, George Bernard Shaw has Shavians. The latter, like the rest of the literate and/or play-going world, are in one sense better served, since Shaw left them a far larger and more diverse body of work: over fifty plays; novels; essays; tracts; and reviews. He also left behind far more evidence that he was ever here, and far more clues to his opinions, lifestyle, personality, and personal history: his house; his clothes; his enormous correspondence; authorized biography; interviews; even some autobiographical writing. The latter writing, however, is less revealing than we might expect, and less easily distinguishable from the former, since Shaw was not only mischievous, but manipulative and secretive, so that behind the apparently candid memoirs lie characters every bit as constructed as any of his *dramatis personae*, and behind the ostensible authors of interviews and articles about the great man often lies Shaw himself.

Who was George Bernard Shaw? He hated the name "George," and often signed himself "GBS." He was born in Dublin, and spoke an Irish-inflected English, but left the country when he was twenty, and refused to return for many years. He left school at fifteen, but educated himself through voracious reading. He was an inarticulate young man who turned himself into a brilliant public speaker. Like Oscar Wilde, as much famous as a personality and Great Man as for his publications, Shaw began his writing career as a ghost, producing music criticism for George J. Vandeleur Lee, a man who may have been a Svengali figure to Shaw's mother. Remembered now for his original writing, until the 1890s he earned his living largely as a music journalist (publishing under the name "Corno di Bassetto") and, later, drama critic. He was awarded the Nobel Prize in 1925, but endured widespread opprobrium during the war years for his pacifism, and vilification following the allegedly shocking language of *Pygmalion* (1914) and subject matter of *Man and Superman*. His earliest play, *Widowers' Houses*, was considered too controversial to be passed by the censors, and was initially performed in private.

Shaw conducted lengthy correspondence with some of the most beautiful actresses of the day (such as Ellen Terry, Stella [Mrs. Patrick] Campbell, and Molly Tomkins), yet had intimate relationships

with very few of them, and for very short periods. He pursued a
number of women, bombarding them with amatory correspondence,
yet characteristically shied away once they showed reciprocal interest. He married in 1898, but appears to have had only a companion-
able relationship with his wife, Charlotte Payne-Townshend. He was
much loved and revered by those who worked with and for him, but
could be ferocious, self-centered, and demanding. Of one thing we
can be sure: he was a man of strong opinions, which he articulated
vociferously. He was a supporter of electoral reform and of equal
rights and equal pay for women; he campaigned for reformation of
(British) English spelling and punctuation, and for the abolition of
the English alphabet in favor of a more logical and simpler system.
He was a Fabian and an advocate of the abolition of private property;
he condemned imprisonment as inhumane and pointless, yet advocated painless euthanasia of hopeless cases. He was a teetotal
vegetarian who never drank tea or coffee; wore woolen undergar-
ments and a famous all-wool Jaeger suit, to allow the skin to breathe;
and was obsessively clean in his personal habits, yet who delighted
in driving recklessly and (for the time) fast in a series of motor-cars.
He lived to be 94, finally dying from complications following a fall
in his garden. The paradoxes he loved to dramatize in his work seem
equally engraved on the story of his life.

Fast pacing, rapid-fire dialogue, and Shavian wit keep Shaw's
works from being mere vehicles for his ideas, but critics and the
book-buying and theater-going public took some time to appreciate
the author's genius. Shaw's first five novels were unsuccessful, and
success on the London stage did not come until he was 48, in 1904,
when Harley Granville-Barker and J. E. Vedrenne organized performances of *John Bull's Other Island* at the London Royal Court
Theatre. This was followed in rapid succession by *How He Lied to
Her Husband, Man and Superman, Major Barbara*, and *The Doctor's
Dilemma*. Shaw remained a prolific writer and active social commentator until his death. His plays, like the social problems they
debate, are still much with us in the twenty-first century.

Mrs Warren's Profession

Just as *Widowers' Houses* was a didactic play which instructed the
late—nineteenth century about the realities of capitalism, so *Mrs
Warren's Profession*, in the person of the brothel-keeper Mrs. Warren, taught society about the economic determination and perpetu-
ation of the prostitution which it ostensibly outlawed.

This was Shaw's first "Unpleasant" play, written in 1894 and published in the two-volume *Plays Pleasant and Unpleasant* in 1898.
Public performance having been prohibited by the Lord Chamber-

lain's Examiner, who deemed it immoral, it was first performed by
the Stage Society, which was technically a private club, in 1902. The
first public performance was in the United States, on October 27,
1905, at the Hyperion Theater in New Haven, Connecticut. After
one performance, the police moved in to close the play. It was moved
to the Garrick Theater in New York, but after the October 30 performance, the entire cast was arrested on a charge of disorderly conduct. They were released on bail, and later acquitted.

A notice in the *New York Herald* on the day after the Garrick
performance asserted that the play had reached the limit of stage
indecency, and was "morally rotten"; its characters "wholly immoral
and degenerate."[1] Even the quality of the acting was made matter
for recrimination, since "the better it was acted the more the impurity and degeneracy of the characters, the situations and the lines
were made apparent." More culpable than the play's supposed glo-
rification of debauchery and "besmirching" of a clergyman's calling,
was, allegedly, its flippant discussion of the marriage of brother and
sister and the declaration by Mrs. Warren's daughter that "choice of
shame instead of poverty is eminently right." Shaw's "Author's Apology" for the play was added in a riposte to such critical opinion.

Shaw was to expose the hypocrisy enshrined in contemporary society's treatment of prostitutes and their customers in his journalism,
and was involved in the infamous case of the young girl purchased
for three guineas by the campaigning investigative journalist, William Stead.

Man and Superman

Man and Superman was the first of a group of three plays on which
Shaw's reputation as a serious dramatist was first established. The
other two were *Major Barbara* and *John Bull's Other Island*. It is
possible to read autobiographical elements in the play, in particular
the character of Don Juan, who overcomes his aversion to marriage
only after protracted negotiation. Shaw had remained a bachelor into
middle age, and in spite of a number of passionate attachments,
often conducted largely through correspondence, was practically celibate. He met Charlotte Payne-Townshend through Beatrice and
Sidney Webb in 1895, and debated long and hard the pros and cons
of entering into marriage with her. Among the pros was her large
fortune. After a series of ailments and mishaps, he finally found, or
so he said, that his objection to his own marriage had ceased with
his objection to his own death, and subject to certain grounds
(including non-consummation), agreed to the marriage. On his

1. *New York Herald*, October 31, 1905, 49; reprt. T. F. Evans, ed., *George Bernard Shaw,
The Critical Heritage* (London: Routledge, 1997), p. 139.

recovery, he wrote a sketch, "The Superman, or Don Juan's great grandson's grandson," which he later developed into the dream sequence of *Man and Superman.*

Acts I, II, and IV were performed as a whole and Act III separately at the Court Theatre in 1905 and 1907, but the full version of the play was first staged by Esme Percy at the Lyceum Theatre, Edinburgh, on June 11, 1915. When Percy had asked permission for his company to perform the work in its entirety, Shaw professed to be shocked; he had never conceived the possibility of its being staged in one evening; no one would come, and if they did, no one would stay the full five hours (which was further increased by Percy's commission of a lengthy prelude to the third act). In a letter of 1900, Shaw had predicted that his next play would be "immense" but not for the stage of the current generation. Permission was granted, however, and the play opened to a full house. The prelude to the Hell scene was declaimed from the orchestra pit by an actor dressed as the ghost of Shakespeare.

With this work Shaw enters into his own as a dramatist. Its impetus is not conventional dramatic structure and plot, but ideas, and its dialectic is given force by the balance between male and female characters, principally Ann and Tanner.

Major Barbara

Shaw said that this play might equally have been called *Andrew Undershaft's Profession*, and Undershaft is the characteristically Shavian devil's advocate. Shaw also remarked that even his "cleverest friends confessed that the third act beat them; that their brains simply gave way under it," and the finale can seem something of an anticlimax after the masterful dramatic structure of the second act. It gave GBS some trouble; having completed the rest of the play during the summer, he had to rewrite the last act completely during October 1905, just before rehearsals began. The play was performed first in six matinées at the Royal Court Theatre, then under the management of the famous Vedrenne-Barker partnership, beginning on November 28, 1905. A notice in the *Pall Mall Gazette* of November 29, 1905, acknowledged that the play was witty, and contained a "medley of 'high explosive' characters," but found one line irreverent and even blasphemous.[2] "In the midst of a play largely made up of gibes and pranks, came the words, 'My God, my God, why hast Thou forsaken me?' " The reviewer found Shaw's use of these words, "perhaps the most awful in the world," a betrayal of the playwright's "utter want of religious sense."

---

2. November 29, 1905, vol. 81, 12683, 9; Evans, 142.

Even Shaw's friend and fellow Fabian, Beatrice Webb, was disturbed by the play. A diary entry describes the play as a "dance of devils—amazingly clever, grimly powerful in the second act—but ending, as all his plays [. . .] in an intellectual and moral morass."[3] A few days later, Webb records calling on GBS and finding him perturbed more by the bad acting of Undershaft and all of the cast in the last scene than by the press notices. Webb "found it difficult to sympathize" with Shaw's cogent and earnest argument in defense of the play's message. She could, however, sympathize with Shaw's irritation at the suggested intervention of the censor—"not on account of the upshot of the play, but because Barbara in her despair at the end of the second act utters the cry, 'My God, my God, why hast thou forsaken me.' A wonderful and quite rational climax to the true tragedy of the scene of the Salvation Army Shelter."[4]

Critics have found an imbalance in the dialectic of the third act created by Shaw's fondness for Undershaft, and his unwillingness to give him any really unpleasant or diabolic traits. Cusins' providential fulfillment of the foundling requirement and his financial haggling may seem farcical, and Barbara's movement from despair to resolve and optimism implausibly rapid, but though the play is realistic in mode, it is also an interplay of character types, embodiments of the sides of the political and ethical debate, drawn large for effect.

Lady Britomart is said to have been modeled on the Countess of Carlisle, and to reflect the libertarian Whig principles and personal despotism of her original. The Countess was the mother-in-law of the classicist Gilbert Murray, on whom Adolphus Cusins was modeled, whom Shaw consulted extensively in creating the character and his speeches, and from whose 1902 translation of the *Bacchae* he quotes.

Pygmalion

In his Preface, Shaw playfully suggested that *Pygmalion* was dry and didactic, its subject phonetics rather than the Cinderella transformation of flower-girl to society lady and romantic heroine. It is of course concerned with language, particularly speech as social marker, and of the interaction among language, money, and class.

The play opened at His Majesty's Theatre, London, on April 11, 1914, after a tempestuous rehearsal period characterized by violent disagreements among playwright, actor-manager, and leading actress. The *Daily Express* noted that the combined ages of these was 166: Sir Herbert Beerbohm Tree was 60, George Bernard Shaw was 57, and Stella Campbell (usually referred to as Mrs. Patrick Camp-

3. November 29, 1905; Evans, 147.
4. December 2, 1905; Evans, 148.

bell), who was playing the 18-year-old Eliza, was 49. Tree was playing
Professor Higgins, "a sort of man he had never met and of whom he
had no conception," Shaw was to say.[5] The playwright complained
that Tree "set to work to make this disagreeable and incredible person sympathetic in the character of a lover, for which I had so little
room that he was quite baffled."[6] Tree enraged Shaw by throwing a
bunch of flowers to Eliza at the final curtain, a small but significant
piece of stage business which may have precipitated the epilogue to
the play, which makes clear that Higgins and Eliza are not destined
to become romantically attached. The screenplay to the Gabriel Pascal film version of the play makes this even more explicit: "The producer should bear in mind from the beginning that it is Freddy who
captivates and finally carries off Eliza, and that all suggestion of a
love interest between Eliza and Higgins should be most carefully
avoided."[7]

During rehearsals, Stella Campbell, with whom Shaw had had a
passionate, if unconsummated, affair, played a kind of reverse, ladylike Eliza to Shaw's Higgins, who was trying to coach her into a
Cockney accent. When Shaw demanded that she make her posture
and gestures more coarse, Mrs. Campbell refused to continue until
he had left the theater, later sending word that in future he was to
communicate with her through the assistant stage manager. The play
was a success, nonetheless, partly through the notoriety of Eliza's:
"Not bloody likely!" With ostentatious delicacy reminiscent of the
reception of Gilbert and Sullivan's operetta *Ruddigore* (1887), the
London newspapers printed the word with strategic asterisks, and
many followed the lead of the London *Times* (April 13, 1914), which
put to the "greatly daring Mr Shaw" the question: "You will be able
to boast that you are the first modern dramatist to use this word on
the stage; but really, was it worth while? There is a whole range of
forbidden words in the English language. A little more of your courage, and we suppose they will be heard too; and then good-bye to
the delights of really intimate conversation."

5. Stanley Weintraub, *Journey to Heartbreak* (New York: Weybright and Talley, 1971), p. 3.
6. Ibid., 3–4.
7. Bernard F. Dukore, *The Collected Screenplays of Bernard Shaw* (Athens: University of
   Georgia Press, 1980), p. 226.

The Texts of
THE PLAYS†

---

† The texts of the plays are taken from the editions published by Constable in the early
1920s.

Mrs Warren's Profession[†]

The Author's Apology

Mrs Warren's Profession[1] has been performed at last, after a delay of
only eight years; and I have once more shared with Ibsen the triumphant amusement of startling all but the strongest-headed of the
London theatre critics clean out of the practice of their profession.
No author who has ever known the exultation of sending the Press
into an hysterical tumult of protest, of moral panic, of involuntary
and frantic confession of sin, of a horror of conscience in which the
power of distinguishing between the work of art on the stage and the
real life of the spectator is confused and overwhelmed, will ever care
for the stereotyped compliments which every successful farce or melodrama elicits from the newspapers. Give me that critic who rushed
from my play to declare furiously that Sir George Crofts ought to be
kicked. What a triumph for the actor, thus to reduce a jaded London
journalist to the condition of the simple sailor in the Wapping gallery, who shouts execrations at Iago and warnings to Othello not to
believe him! * * *

Do not suppose, however, that the consternation of the Press
reflects any consternation among the general public. Anybody can
upset the theatre critics, in a turn of the wrist, by substituting for
the romantic commonplaces of the stage the moral commonplaces
of the pulpit, the platform, or the library. Play *Mrs Warren's Profession* to an audience of clerical members of the Christian Social
Union and of women well experienced in Rescue, Temperance, and
Girls' Club work, and no moral panic will arise: every man and
woman present will know that as long as poverty makes virtue hideous and the spare pocket-money of rich bachelordom makes vice
dazzling, their daily hand-to-hand fight against prostitution with
prayer and persuasion, shelters and scanty alms, will be a losing one.
There was a time when they were able to urge that though "the whitelead factory where Anne Jane was poisoned" may be a far more ter-

---

† For consistency, the play has been edited to remove periods from courtesy titles.
1. In a letter of 1893, Shaw suggested that the play blended the plots of *The Second Mrs
  Tanqueray* with P. B. Shelley's *The Cenci.* There may also be a real-life model for Vivie in
  Arabella Susan Lawrence, who read Mathematics at Newnham College, Cambridge, and
  was a suffragist and socialist. Shaw knew her through their mutual political activities.

rible place than Mrs Warren's house, yet hell is still more dreadful. Nowadays they no longer believe in hell; and the girls among whom they are working know that they do not believe in it, and would laugh at them if they did. So well have the rescuers learnt that Mrs Warren's defence of herself and indictment of society is the thing that most needs saying, that those who know me personally reproach me, not for writing this play, but for wasting my energies on "pleasant plays" for the amusement of frivolous people, when I can build up such excellent stage sermons on their own work. *Mrs Warren's Profession* is the one play of mine which I could submit to a censorship without doubt of the result; only, it must not be the censorship of the minor theatre critic, nor of an innocent court official like the Lord Chamberlain's Examiner, much less of people who consciously profit by Mrs Warren's profession, or who personally make use of it, or who hold the widely whispered view that it is an indispensable safety-valve for the protection of domestic virtue, or, above all, who are smitten with a sentimental affection for our fallen sister, and would "take her up tenderly, lift her with care, fashioned so slenderly, young, and *so* fair." Nor am I prepared to accept the verdict of the medical gentlemen who would compulsorily examine and register Mrs Warren, whilst leaving Mrs Warren's patrons, especially her military patrons, free to destroy her health and anybody else's without fear of reprisals. But I should be quite content to have my play judged by, say, a joint committee of the Central Vigilance Society and the Salvation Army. And the sterner moralists the members of the committee were, the better.

Some of the journalists I have shocked reason so unripely that they will gather nothing from this but a confused notion that I am accusing the National Vigilance Association and the Salvation Army of complicity in my own scandalous immorality. It will seem to them that people who would stand this play would stand anything. They are quite mistaken. Such an audience as I have described would be revolted by many of our fashionable plays. They would leave the theatre convinced that the Plymouth Brother who still regards the playhouse as one of the gates of hell is perhaps the safest adviser on the subject of which he knows so little. If I do not draw the same conclusion, it is not because I am one of those who claim that art is exempt from moral obligations, and deny that the writing or performance of a play is a moral act, to be treated on exactly the same footing as theft or murder if it produces equally mischievous consequences. I am convinced that fine art is the subtlest, the most seductive, the most effective instrument of moral propaganda in the world, excepting only the example of personal conduct; and I waive even this exception in favor of the art of the stage, because it works by exhibiting examples of personal conduct made intelligible and moving to crowds of unobservant unreflecting people to whom real life means nothing. I have pointed out again and again that the influence of the theatre in England is growing so great that private conduct, religion, law, science, politics, and morals are becoming more and more theatrical, whilst the theatre itself remains impervious to common sense, religion, science, politics, and morals. That is why I fight the theatre, not with pamphlets and sermons and treatises, but with plays; and so effective do I find the dramatic method that I have no doubt I shall at last persuade even London to take its conscience and its brains with it when it goes to the theatre, instead of leaving them at home with its prayer-book as it does at present. Consequently, I am the last man to deny that if the net effect of performing *Mrs Warren's Profession* were an increase in the number of persons entering that profession or employing it, its performance might well be made an indictable offence.

Now let us consider how such recruiting can be encouraged by the theatre. Nothing is easier. Let the Lord Chamberlain's Examiner of Plays, backed by the Press, make an unwritten but perfectly well understood regulation that members of Mrs Warren's profession shall be tolerated on the stage only when they are beautiful, exquisitely dressed, and sumptuously lodged and fed; also that they shall, at the end of the play, die of consumption to the sympathetic tears of the whole audience, or step into the next room to commit suicide, or at least be turned out by their protectors and passed on to be "redeemed" by old and faithful lovers who have adored them in spite of all their levities. Naturally the poorer girls in the gallery will believe in the beauty, in the exquisite dresses, and the luxurious living, and will see that there is no real necessity for the consumption, the suicide, or the ejectment: mere pious forms, all of them, to save the Censor's face. Even if these purely official catastrophes carried any conviction, the majority of English girls remain so poor, so dependent, so well aware that the drudgeries of such honest work as is within their reach are likely enough to lead them eventually to lung disease, premature death, and domestic desertion or brutality, that they would still see reason to prefer the primrose path to the stony way of virtue, since both, vice at worst and virtue at best, lead to the same end in poverty and overwork. It is true that the Elementary School mistress will tell you that only girls of a certain kind will reason in this way. But alas! that certain kind turns out on inquiry to be simply the pretty, dainty kind: that is, the only kind that gets the chance of acting on such reasoning. Read the first report of the Commission on the Housing of the Working Classes [Bluebook C 4402, 1889]; read the Report on Home Industries (sacred word, Home!) issued by the Women's Industrial Council [Home Industries of Women in London, 1897, 1s.]; and ask yourself whether, if the lot in life therein described were your lot in life, you would not rather be a jewelled Vamp. If you can go deep enough into things to be able to say no, how many ignorant half-starved girls will believe you are speaking sincerely? To them the lot of the stage courtesan is heavenly in comparison with their own. Yet the Lord Chamberlain's Examiner, being an officer of the Royal Household, places the King in the position of saying to the dramatist "Thus, and thus only, shall you present Mrs Warren's profession on the stage, or you shall starve. Witness Shaw, who told the untempting truth about it, and whom We, by the Grace of God, accordingly disallow and suppress, and do what in Us lies to silence." Fortunately, Shaw cannot be silenced. "The harlot's cry from street to street" is louder than the voices of all the kings. I am not dependent on the theatre, and cannot be starved into making my play a standing advertisement of the attractive side of Mrs Warren's business.

Here I must guard myself against a misunderstanding. It is not the fault of their authors that the long string of wanton's tragedies, from *Antony and Cleopatra* to *Iris*, are snares to poor girls, and are objected to on that account by many earnest men and women who consider *Mrs Warren's Profession* an excellent sermon. Pinero is in no way bound to suppress the fact that his Iris is a person to be envied by millions of better women. If he made his play false to life by inventing fictitious disadvantages for her, he would be acting as unscrupulously as any tract-writer. If society chooses to provide for its Irises better than for its working women, it must not expect honest playwrights to manufacture spurious evidence to save its credit. The mischief lies in the deliberate suppression of the other side of the case: the refusal to allow Mrs Warren to expose the drudgery and repulsiveness of plying for hire among coarse tedious drunkards. All that, says the Examiner in effect, is horrifying, loathsome. Precisely: what does he expect it to be? would he have us represent it as beautiful and gratifying? His answer to this question amounts, I fear, to a blunt Yes; for it seems impossible to root out of an Englishman's mind the notion that vice is delightful, and that abstention from it is privation. At all events, as long as the tempting side of it is kept towards the public, and softened by plenty of sentiment and sympathy, it is welcomed by our Censor, whereas the slightest attempt to place it in the light of the policeman's lantern or the Salvation Army shelter is checkmated at once as not merely disgusting, but, if you please, unnecessary.

Everybody will, I hope, admit that this state of things is intolerable; that the subject of Mrs Warren's profession must be either tapu[2]

2. Taboo.

altogether, or else exhibited with the warning side as freely displayed as the tempting side. But many persons will vote for a complete tapu, and an impartial clean sweep from the boards of Mrs Warren and Gretchen and the rest: in short, for banishing the sexual instincts from the stage altogether. Those who think this impossible can hardly have considered the number and importance of the subjects which are actually banished from the stage. Many plays, among them *Lear*, *Hamlet*, *Macbeth*, *Coriolanus*, *Julius Cæsar*, have no sex complications: the thread of their action can be followed by children who could not understand a single scene of *Mrs Warren's Profession* or *Iris*. None of our plays rouse the sympathy of the audience by an exhibition of the pains of maternity, as Chinese plays constantly do. Each nation has its particular set of tapus in addition to the common human stock; and though each of these tapus limits the scope of the dramatist, it does not make drama impossible. If the Examiner were to refuse to license plays with female characters in them, he would only be doing to the stage what our tribal customs already do to the pulpit and the bar. I have myself written a rather entertaining play with only one woman in it, and she quite heartwhole; and I could just as easily write a play without a woman in it at all. I will even go as far as to promise the Examiner my support if he will introduce this limitation for part of the year, say during Lent, so as to make a close season for that dullest of stock dramatic subjects, adultery, and force our managers and authors to find out what all great dramatists find out spontaneously: to wit, that people who sacrifice every other consideration to love are as hopelessly unheroic on the stage as lunatics or dipsomaniacs. Hector and Hamlet are the world's heroes; not Paris and Antony.

But though I do not question the possibility of a drama in which love should be as effectively ignored as cholera is at present, there is not the slightest chance of that way out of the difficulty being taken by the Examiner. If he attempted it there would be a revolt in which he would be swept away, in spite of my singlehanded efforts to defend him. A complete tapu is politically impossible. A complete toleration is equally impossible to the Examiner, because his occupation would be gone if there were no tapu to enforce. He is therefore compelled to maintain the present compromise of a partial tapu, applied, to the best of his judgment, with a careful respect to persons and to public opinion.

*   *   *

All censorships exist to prevent anyone from challenging current conceptions and existing institutions. All progress is initiated by challenging current conceptions, and executed by supplanting existing institutions. Consequently the first condition of progress is the removal of censorships. There is the whole case against censorships in a nutshell.

It will be asked whether theatrical managers are to be allowed to produce what they like, without regard to the public interest. But that is not the alternative. The managers of our London music-halls are not subject to any censorship. They produce their entertainments on their own responsibility, and have no two-guinea certificates to plead if their houses are conducted viciously. They know that if they lose their character, the County Council will simply refuse to renew their license at the end of the year; and nothing in the history of popular art is more amazing than the improvement in music-halls that this simple arrangement has produced within a few years. Place the theatres on the same footing, and we shall promptly have a sim-ilar revolution: a whole class of frankly blackguardly plays, in which unscrupulous low comedians attract crowds to gaze at bevies of girls who have nothing to exhibit but their prettiness, will vanish like the obscene songs which were supposed to enliven the squalid dulness, incredible to the younger generation, of the music-halls fifteen years ago. On the other hand, plays which treat sex questions as problems for thought instead of as aphrodisiacs will be freely performed. Gen-tlemen of the Examiner's way of thinking will have plenty of oppor-tunity of protesting against them in Council; but the result will be that the Examiner will find his natural level; Ibsen and Tolstoy theirs; so no harm will be done.

*　　　*　　　*

I now come to those critics who, intellectually baffled by the problem in *Mrs Warren's Profession*, have made a virtue of running away from it on the gentlemanly ground that the theatre is fre-quented by women as well as by men, and that such problems should not be discussed or even mentioned in the presence of women. With that sort of chivalry I cannot argue: I simply affirm that *Mrs Warren's Profession* is a play for women; that it was written for women; that it has been performed and produced mainly through the determi-nation of women that it should be performed and produced; that the enthusiasm of women made its first performance excitingly success-ful; and that not one of these women had any inducement to support it except their belief in the timeliness and the power of the lesson the play teaches. Those who were "surprised to see ladies present" were men; and when they proceeded to explain that the journals they represented could not possibly demoralize the public by describing such a play, their editors cruelly devoted the space saved by their delicacy to reporting at unusual length an exceptionally abominable police case.

My old Independent Theatre manager, Mr Grein, besides that reproach to me for shattering his ideals, complains that Mrs Warren is not wicked enough, and names several romancers who would have clothed her black soul with all the terrors of tragedy. I have no doubt they would; but that is just what I did not want to do. Nothing would please our sanctimonious British public more than to throw the whole guilt of Mrs Warren's profession on Mrs Warren herself. Now the whole aim of my play is to throw that guilt on the British public itself. Mr Grein may remember that when he produced my first play, *Widowers' Houses*, exactly the same misunderstanding arose. When the virtuous young gentleman rose up in wrath against the slum landlord, the slum landlord very effectually shewed him that slums are the product, not of individual Harpagons,[3] but of the indifference of virtuous young gentlemen to the condition of the city they live in, provided they live at the west end of it on money earned by somebody else's labor. The notion that prostitution is created by the wickedness of Mrs Warren is as silly as the notion—prevalent, nevertheless, to some extent in Temperance circles—that drunkenness is created by the wickedness of the publican. Mrs Warren is not a whit a worse woman than the reputable daughter who cannot endure her. Her indifference to the ultimate social consequences of her means of making money, and her discovery of that means by the ordinary method of taking the line of least resistance to getting it, are too common in English society to call for any special remark. Her vitality, her thrift, her energy, her outspokenness, her wise care of her daughter, and the managing capacity which has enabled her and her sister to climb from the fried fish shop down by the Mint to the establishments of which she boasts, are all high English social virtues. Her defence of herself is so overwhelming that it provokes the *St James's Gazette* to declare that "the tendency of the play is wholly evil" because "it contains one of the boldest and most specious defences of an immoral life for poor women that has ever been penned." Happily the *St James's Gazette* here speaks in its haste. Mrs Warren's defence of herself is not only bold and specious, but valid and unanswerable. But it is no defence at all of the vice which she organizes. It is no defence of an immoral life to say that the alternative offered by society collectively to poor women is a miserable life, starved, overworked, fetid, ailing, ugly. Though it is quite natural and *right* for Mrs Warren to choose what is, according to her lights, the least immoral alternative, it is none the less infamous of society to offer such alternatives. For the alternatives offered are not morality and immorality, but two sorts of immorality. The man who cannot see that starvation, overwork, dirt, and disease are as anti-social as

---

3. Harpagon is the miser in Molière's play *L'Avare* (The Miser).

prostitution—that they are the vices and crimes of a nation, and not merely its misfortunes—is (to put it as politely as possible) a hopelessly Private Person.

The notion that Mrs Warren must be a fiend is only an example of the violence and passion which the slightest reference to sex rouses in undisciplined minds, and which makes it seem natural to our lawgivers to punish silly and negligible indecencies with a ferocity unknown in dealing with, for example, ruinous financial swindling. Had my play been entitled *Mr Warren's Profession*, and Mr Warren been a bookmaker, nobody would have expected me to make him a villain as well. Yet gambling is a vice, and bookmaking an institution, for which there is absolutely nothing to be said. The moral and economic evil done by trying to get other people's money without working for it (and this is the essence of gambling) is not only enormous but uncompensated. There are no two sides to the question of gambling, no circumstances which force us to tolerate it lest its suppression lead to worse things, no consensus of opinion among responsible classes, such as magistrates and military commanders, that it is a necessity, no Athenian records of gambling made splendid by the talents of its professors, no contention that instead of violating morals it only violates a legal institution which is in many respects oppressive and unnatural, no possible plea that the instinct on which it is founded is a vital one. Prostitution can confuse the issue with all these excuses: gambling has none of them. * * *

                    *   *   *

In 1905 Arnold Daly produced *Mrs Warren's Profession* in New York. The press of that city instantly raised a cry that such persons as Mrs Warren are "ordure" and should not be mentioned in the presence of decent people. This hideous repudiation of humanity and social conscience so took possession of the New York journalists that the few among them who kept their feet morally and intellectually could do nothing to check the epidemic of foul language, gross suggestion, and raving obscenity of word and thought that broke out. The writers abandoned all self-restraint under the impression that they were upholding virtue instead of outraging it. They infected each other with their hysteria until they were for all practical purposes indecently mad. They finally forced the police to arrest Daly and his company, and led the magistrate to express his loathing of the duty thus forced upon him of reading an unmentionable and abominable play. Of course the convulsion soon exhausted itself. The magistrate, naturally somewhat impatient when he found that what he had to read was a strenuously ethical play forming part of a book which had been in circulation unchallenged for eight years, and had been received without protest by the whole London and

New York Press, gave the journalists a piece of his mind as to their moral taste in plays. By consent, he passed the case on to a higher court, which declared that the play was not immoral; acquitted Daly; and made an end of the attempt to use the law to declare living women to be "ordure," and thus enforce silence as to the far-reaching fact that you cannot cheapen women in the market for industrial purposes without cheapening them for other purposes as well. I hope *Mrs Warren's Profession* will be played everywhere, in season and out of season, until Mrs Warren has bitten that fact into the public conscience, and shamed the newspapers which support a tariff to keep up the price of every American commodity except American manhood and womanhood.

Unfortunately, Daly had already suffered the usual fate of those who direct public attention to the profits of the sweater or the pleasures of the voluptuary. He was morally lynched side-by-side with me. Months elapsed before the decision of the courts vindicated him; and even then, since his vindication implied the condemnation of the Press, which was by that time sober again, and ashamed of its orgie, his triumph received a rather sulky and grudging publicity. In the meantime he had hardly been able to approach an American city, including even those cities which had heaped applause on him as the defender of hearth and home when he produced *Candida*, without having to face articles discussing whether mothers could allow their daughters to attend such plays as *You Never Can Tell*, written by the infamous author of *Mrs Warren's Profession*, and acted by the monster who produced it. What made this harder to bear was that though no fact is better established in theatrical business than the financial disastrousness of moral discredit, the journalists who had done all the mischief kept paying vice the homage of assuming that it is enormously popular and lucrative, and that Daly and I, being exploiters of vice, must therefore be making colossal fortunes out of the abuse heaped on us, and had in fact provoked it and welcomed it with that express object. Ignorance of real life could hardly go further.

I was deeply disgusted by this unsavory mobbing. And I have certain sensitive places in my soul: I do not like that word "ordure." Apply it to my work, and I can afford to smile, since the world, on the whole, will smile with me. But to apply it to the woman in the street, whose spirit is of one substance with your own and her body no less holy: to look your women folk in the face afterwards and not go out and hang yourself: that is not on the list of pardonable sins.

Shortly after these events a leading New York newspaper, which was among the most abusively clamorous for the suppression of *Mrs Warren's Profession*, was fined heavily for deriving part of its revenue from advertisements of Mrs Warren's houses.

Many people have been puzzled by the fact that whilst stage enter-

tainments which are frankly meant to act on the spectators as aphrodisiacs are everywhere tolerated, plays which have an almost
horrifying contrary effect are fiercely attacked by persons and papers
notoriously indifferent to public morals on all other occasions. The
explanation is very simple. The profits of Mrs Warren's profession
are shared not only by Mrs Warren and Sir George Crofts, but by
the landlords of their houses, the newspapers which advertize them,
the restaurants which cater for them, and, in short, all the trades to
which they are good customers, not to mention the public officials
and representatives whom they silence by complicity, corruption, or
blackmail. Add to these the employers who profit by cheap female
labor, and the shareholders whose dividends depend on it (you find
such people everywhere, even on the judicial bench and in the highest places in Church and State) and you get a large and powerful
class with a strong pecuniary incentive to protect Mrs Warren's profession, and a correspondingly strong incentive to conceal, from their
own consciences no less than from the world, the real sources of
their gain. These are the people who declare that it is feminine vice
and not poverty that drives women to the streets, as if vicious women
with independent incomes ever went there. These are the people
who, indulgent or indifferent to aphrodisiac plays, raise the moral
hue and cry against performances of *Mrs Warren's Profession*, and
drag actresses to the police court to be insulted, bullied, and threatened for fulfilling their engagements. For please observe that the
judicial decision in New York State in favor of the play did not end
the matter. In Kansas City, for instance, the municipality, finding
itself restrained by the courts from preventing the performance, fell
back on a local bye-law against indecency. It summoned the actress
who impersonated Mrs Warren to the police court, and offered her
and her colleagues the alternative of leaving the city or being pros-
ecuted under this bye-law.

Now nothing is more possible than that the city councillors who
suddenly displayed such concern for the morals of the theatre were
either Mrs Warren's landlords, or employers of women at starvation
wages, or restaurant keepers, or newspaper proprietors, or in some
other more or less direct way sharers of the profits of her trade. No
doubt it is equally possible that they were simply stupid men who
thought that indecency consists, not in evil, but in mentioning it. I
have, however, been myself a member of a municipal council, and
have not found municipal councillors quite so simple and inexperienced as this. At all events I do not propose to give the Kansas councillors the benefit of the doubt I therefore advise the public at large,
which will finally decide the matter, to keep a vigilant eye on gentlemen who will stand anything at the theatre except a performance
of *Mrs Warren's Profession*, and who assert in the same breath that

(*a*) the play is too loathsome to be bearable by civilized people, and (*b*) that unless its performance is prohibited the whole town will throng to see it. They may be merely excited and foolish; but I am bound to warn the public that it is equally likely that they may be collected and knavish.

At all events, to prohibit the play is to protect the evil which the play exposes; and in view of that fact, I see no reason for assuming that the prohibitionists are disinterested moralists, and that the author, the managers, and the performers, who depend for their livelihood on their personal reputations and not on rents, advertisements, or dividends, are grossly inferior to them in moral sense and public responsibility.

It is true that in *Mrs Warren's Profession*, Society, and not any individual, is the villain of the piece; but it does not follow that the people who take offence at it are all champions of society. Their credentials cannot be too carefully examined.

PICCARD'S COTTAGE, *January* 1902.

Mrs Warren's Profession

Act I

Summer afternoon in a cottage garden on the eastern slope of a hill a little south of Haslemere in Surrey. Looking up the hill, the cottage is seen in the left–hand corner of the garden, with its thatched roof and porch, and a large latticed window to the left of the porch. Farther back a little wing is built out, making an angle with the right side wall. From the end of this wing a paling curves across and forward, completely shutting in the garden, except for a gate on the right. The common rises uphill beyond the paling to the sky line. Some folded canvas garden chairs are leaning against the side bench in the porch. A lady's bicycle is propped against the wall, under the window. A little to the right of the porch a hammock is slung from two posts. A big canvas umbrella, stuck in the ground, keeps the sun off the hammock, in which a young lady lies reading and making notes, her head towards the cottage and her feet towards the gate. In front of the hammock, and within reach of her hand, is a common kitchen chair, with a pile of serious-looking books and a supply of writing paper upon it.

A gentleman walking on the common comes into sight from behind the cottage. He is hardly past middle age, with something of the artist about him, unconventionally but carefully dressed, and clean-shaven except for a moustache, with an eager, susceptible face and very amiable and considerate manners. He has silky black hair, with waves of grey and white in it. His eyebrows are white, his moustache black. He seems not certain of his way. He looks over the paling; takes stock of the place; and sees the young lady.

THE GENTLEMAN [*Taking off his hat.*]   I beg your pardon. Can you direct me to Hindhead View—Mrs Alison's?

THE YOUNG LADY [*Glancing up from her book.*]   This is Mrs Alison's. [*She resumes her work.*]

THE GENTLEMAN   Indeed! Perhaps—may I ask are you Miss Vivie Warren?

THE YOUNG LADY [*Sharply, as she turns on her elbow to get a good look at him.*]   Yes.

THE GENTLEMAN [*Daunted and conciliatory.*]   I'm afraid I appear intrusive. My name is Praed. [VIVIE *at once throws her books upon the chair, and gets out of the hammock.*] Oh, pray don't let me disturb you.

VIVIE [*Striding to the gate and opening it for him.*]   Come in, Mr Praed. [*He comes in.*] Glad to see you. [*She proffers her hand and takes his with a resolute and hearty grip. She is an attractive specimen of the sensible, able, highly educated young middle-class Englishwoman. Age 22. Prompt, strong, confident, self-possessed. Plain, business-like dress, but not dowdy. She wears a chatelaine at her belt, with a fountain pen and a paper knife among its pendants.*]

PRAED   Very kind of you indeed, Miss Warren. [*She shuts the gate with a vigorous slam: he passes in to the middle of the garden, exercising his fingers, which are slightly numbed by her greeting.*] Has your mother arrived?

VIVIE [*Quickly, evidently scenting aggression.*]   Is she coming?

PRAED [*Surprised.*]   Didn't you expect us?

VIVIE   No.

PRAED   Now, goodness me, I hope I've not mistaken the day. That would be just like me, you know. Your mother arranged that she was to come down from London and that I was to come over from Horsham to be introduced to you.

VIVIE [*Not at all pleased.*]   Did she? H'm! My mother has rather a trick of taking me by surprise—to see how I behave myself when she's away, I suppose. I fancy I shall take my mother very much by surprise one of these days, if she makes arrangements that concern me without consulting me beforehand. She hasn't come.

PRAED [*Embarrassed.*]   I'm really very sorry.

VIVIE [*Throwing off her displeasure.*]   It's not your fault, Mr Praed, is it? And I'm very glad you've come, believe me. You are the only one of my mother's friends I have asked her to bring to see me.

PRAED [*Relieved and delighted.*]   Oh, now this is really very good of you, Miss Warren!

VIVIE   Will you come indoors; or would you rather sit out here whilst we talk?

PRAED   It will be nicer out here, don't you think?

VIVIE   Then I'll go and get you a chair. [*She goes to the porch for a garden chair.*]

PRAED [*Following her.*]   Oh, pray, pray! Allow me. [*He lays hands on the chair.*]

VIVIE [*Letting him take it.*]   Take care of your fingers: they're rather dodgy things, those chairs. [*She goes across to the chair with the books on it; pitches them into the hammock; and brings the chair forward with one swing.*]

PRAED [*Who has just unfolded his chair.*]   Oh, now do let me take that hard chair! I like hard chairs.

VIVIE   So do I. [*She sits down.*] Sit down, Mr Praed. [*This invitation is given with genial peremptoriness, his anxiety to please her clearly striking her as a sign of weakness of character on his part.*]

PRAED   By the way, though, hadn't we better go to the station to meet your mother?

VIVIE [*Coolly.*]   Why? She knows the way. [PRAED *hesitates, and then sits down in the garden chair, rather disconcerted.*] Do you know, you are just like what I expected. I hope you are disposed to be friends with me?

PRAED [*Again beaming.*]   Thank you, my dear Miss Warren; thank you. Dear me! I'm so glad your mother hasn't spoilt you!

VIVIE   How?

PRAED   Well, in making you too conventional. You know, my dear Miss Warren, I am a born anarchist. I hate authority. It spoils the relations between parent and child—even between mother and daughter. Now I was always afraid that your mother would strain her authority to make you very conventional. It's such a relief to find that she hasn't.

VIVIE   Oh! have I been behaving unconventionally?

PRAED   Oh, no: oh, dear no. At least not conventionally unconventionally, you understand. [*She nods. He goes on, with a cordial outburst.*] But it was so charming of you to say that you were disposed to be friends with me! You modern young ladies are splendid—perfectly splendid!

VIVIE [*Dubiously.*]   Eh? [*Watching him with dawning disappointment as to the quality of his brains and character.*]

PRAED   When I was your age, young men and women were afraid of each other: there was no good fellowship—nothing real—only gallantry copied out of novels, and as vulgar and affected as it could be. Maidenly reserve!—gentlemanly chivalry!—always saying no when you meant yes!—simple purgatory for shy and sincere souls!

VIVIE   Yes, I imagine there must have been a frightful waste of time—especially women's time.

PRAED   Oh, waste of life, waste of everything. But things are improving. Do you know, I have been in a positive state of excitement about meeting you ever since your magnificent achievements at Cambridge—a thing unheard of in my day. It was perfectly splendid, your tieing with the third wrangler.[1] Just the right place, you know. The first wrangler is always a dreamy, morbid fellow, in whom the thing is pushed to the length of a disease.

VIVIE   It doesn't pay. I wouldn't do it again for the same money.

PRAED   [Aghast.]   The same money!

VIVIE   I did it for £50.[2] Perhaps you don't know how it was. Mrs Latham, my tutor at Newnham,[3] told my mother that I could distinguish myself in the mathematical tripos if I went for it in earnest. The papers were full just then of Phillipa Summers beating the senior wrangler—you remember about it; and nothing would please my mother but that I should do the same thing. I said flatly that it was not worth my while to face the grind since I was not going in for teaching; but I offered to try for fourth wrangler or thereabouts for £50. She closed with me at that, after a little grumbling; and I was better than my bargain. But I wouldn't do it again for that. £200 would have been nearer the mark.

PRAED   [Much damped.]   Lord bless me! That's a very practical way of looking at it.

VIVIE   Did you expect to find me an unpractical person?

PRAED   No, no. But surely it's practical to consider not only the work these honors cost, but also the culture they bring.

VIVIE   Culture! My dear Mr Praed: do you know what the mathematical[4] tripos means? It means grind, grind, grind, for six to eight hours a day at mathematics, and nothing but mathematics. I'm supposed to know something about science; but I know nothing except the mathematics it involves. I can make calculations for engineers, electricians, insurance companies, and so on; but I know next to nothing about engineering or electricity or insurance. I don't even know arithmetic well. Outside mathematics, lawn-tennis, eating, sleeping, cycling, and walking, I'm a more ignorant barbarian than any woman could possibly be who hadn't gone in for the tripos.

PRAED   [Revolted.]   What a monstrous, wicked, rascally system! I knew it! I felt at once that it meant destroying all that makes womanhood beautiful.

1. A wrangler was someone who took a first-class degree in mathematics at Cambridge University. The senior wrangler was the person with the highest degree. Women could not officially take their degree at Cambridge at this time.
2. Worth about $80.
3. Like Girton, also a Cambridge College, Newnham admitted only women.
4. Tripos are Cambridge University examinations, which are taken in two parts.

VIVIE   I don't object to it on that score in the least. I shall turn it to very good account, I assure you.

PRAED   Pooh! In what way?

VIVIE   I shall set up in chambers in the city and work at actuarial calculations and conveyancing. Under cover of that I shall do some law, with one eye on the Stock Exchange all the time. I've come down here by myself to read law—not for a holiday, as my mother imagines. I hate holidays.

PRAED   You make my blood run cold. Are you to have no romance, no beauty in your life?

VIVIE   I don't care for either, I assure you.

PRAED   You can't mean that.

VIVIE   Oh yes I do. I like working and getting paid for it. When I'm tired of working, I like a comfortable chair, a cigar, a little whisky, and a novel with a good detective story in it.

PRAED [*In a frenzy of repudiation.*]   I don't believe it. I am an artist; and I can't believe it: I refuse to believe it. [*Enthusiastically.*] Ah, my dear Miss Warren, you haven't discovered yet, I see, what a wonderful world art can open up to you.

VIVIE   Yes, I have. Last May I spent six weeks in London with Honoria Fraser. Mamma thought we were doing a round of sightseeing together; but I was really at Honoria's chambers in Chancery Lane every day, working away at actuarial calculations for her, and helping her as well as a greenhorn could. In the evenings we smoked and talked, and never dreamt of going out except for exercise. And I never enjoyed myself more in my life. I cleared all my expenses and got initiated into the business without a fee into the bargain.

PRAED   But bless my heart and soul, Miss Warren, do you call that trying art?

VIVIE   Wait a bit. That wasn't the beginning. I went up to town on an invitation from some artistic people in Fitzjohn's Avenue: one of the girls was a Newnham chum. They took me to the National Gallery, to the Opera, and to a concert where the band played all the evening—Beethoven and Wagner and so on. I wouldn't go through that experience again for anything you could offer me. I held out for civility's sake until the third day; and then I said, plump out, that I couldn't stand any more of it, and went off to Chancery Lane.[5] Now you know the sort of perfectly splendid modern young lady I am. How do you think I shall get on with my mother?

PRAED [*Startled.*]   Well, I hope—er—

VIVIE   It's not so much what you hope as what you believe, that I want to know.

---

5. Legal district of London.

PRAED   Well, frankly, I am afraid your mother will be a little disappointed. Not from any shortcoming on your part—I don't mean
that. But you are so different from her ideal.

VIVIE   What is her ideal like?

PRAED   Well, you must have observed, Miss Warren, that people
who are dissatisfied with their own bringing up generally think that
the world would be all right if everybody were to be brought up
quite differently. Now your mother's life has been—er—I suppose
you know—

VIVIE   I know nothing. [PRAED *is appalled. His consternation grows
as she continues.*] That's exactly my difficulty. You forget, Mr
Praed, that I hardly know my mother. Since I was a child I have
lived in England, at school or college, or with people paid to take
charge of me. I have been boarded out all my life; and my mother
has lived in Brussels or Vienna and never let me go to her. I only
see her when she visits England for a few days. I don't complain:
it's been very pleasant; for people have been very good to me; and
there has always been plenty of money to make things smooth.
But don't imagine I know anything about my mother. I know far
less than you do.

PRAED   [*Very ill at ease.*]   In that case— [*He stops, quite at a loss.
Then, with a forced attempt at gaiety.*] But what nonsense we are
talking! Of course you and your mother will get on capitally. [*He
rises, and looks abroad at the view.*] What a charming little place
you have here!

VIVIE   [*Unmoved.*]   If you think you are doing anything but confirming my worst suspicions by changing the subject like that, you
must take me for a much greater fool than I hope I am.

PRAED   Your worst suspicions! Oh, pray don't say that. Now don't.

VIVIE   Why won't my mother's life bear being talked about?

PRAED   Pray think, Miss Vivie. It is natural that I should have a
certain delicacy in talking to my old friend's daughter about her
behind her back. You will have plenty of opportunity of talking to
her about it when she comes. [*Anxiously.*] I wonder what is keeping her.

VIVIE   No: she won't talk about it either. [*Rising.*] However, I won't
press you. Only mind this, Mr Praed. I strongly suspect there will
be a battle royal when my mother hears of my Chancery Lane
project.

PRAED   [*Ruefully.*]   I'm afraid there will.

VIVIE   I shall win the battle, because I want nothing but my fare
to London to start there to-morrow earning my own living by
devilling for Honoria. Besides, I have no mysteries to keep up;
and it seems she has. I shall use that advantage over her if necessary.

PRAED   [*Greatly shocked.*]   Oh, no. No, pray. You'd not do such a
thing.

VIVIE   Then tell me why not.

PRAED   I really cannot. I appeal to your good feeling. [*She smiles at his sentimentality.*] Besides, you may be too bold. Your mother is not to be trifled with when she's angry.

VIVIE   You can't frighten me, Mr Praed. In that month at Chancery Lane I had opportunities of taking the measure of one or two women, very like my mother who came to consult Honoria. You may back me to win. But if I hit harder in my ignorance than I need, remember that it is you who refuse to enlighten me. Now let us drop the subject. [*She takes her chair and replaces it near the hammock with the same vigorous swing as before.*]

PRAED [*Taking a desperate resolution.*]   One word, Miss Warren. I had better tell you. It's very difficult; but—

   [MRS WARREN *and* SIR GEORGE CROFTS *arrive at the gate.* MRS WARREN *is a woman between 40 and 50, good-looking, showily dressed in a brilliant hat and a gay blouse fitting tightly over her bust and flanked by fashionable sleeves. Rather spoiled and domineering, but, on the whole, a genial and fairly presentable old blackguard of a woman.*

   CROFTS *is a tall, powerfully-built man of about 50, fashionably dressed in the style of a young man. Nasal voice, reedier than might be expected from his strong frame. Clean-shaven, bull-dog jaws, large flat ears, and thick neck, gentlemanly combination of the most brutal types of city man, sporting man, and man about town.*]

VIVIE   Here they are. [*Coming to them as they enter the garden.*] How do, mater.[6] Mr Praed's been here this half hour, waiting for you.

MRS WARREN   Well, if you've been waiting, Praddy, it's your own fault: I thought you'd have had the gumption to know I was coming by the 3:10 train. Vivie, put your hat on, dear: you'll get sunburnt. Oh, forgot to introduce you. Sir George Crofts, my little Vivie.

   [CROFTS *advances to* VIVIE *with his most courtly manner. She nods, but makes no motion to shake hands.*]

CROFTS   May I shake hands with a young lady whom I have known by reputation very long as the daughter of one of my oldest friends?

VIVIE [*Who has been looking him up and down sharply.*]   If you like. [*She takes his tenderly proffered hand and gives it a squeeze that makes him open his eyes; then turns away and says to her mother*] Will you come in, or shall I get a couple more chairs? [*She goes into the porch for the chairs.*]

MRS WARREN   Well, George, what do you think of her?

CROFTS [*Ruefully.*]   She has a powerful fist. Did you shake hands with her, Praed?

PRAED   Yes: it will pass off presently.

---

6. Latin: mother.

CROFTS   I hope so. [VIVIE *reappears with two more chairs. He hurries to her assistance.*] Allow me.

MRS WARREN [*Patronizingly.*]   Let Sir George help you with the chairs, dear.

VIVIE [*Almost pitching two into his arms.*]   Here you are. [*She dusts her hands and turns to* MRS WARREN.] You'd like some tea, wouldn't you?

MRS WARREN [*Sitting in* PRAED's *chair and fanning herself.*]   I'm dying for a drop to drink.

VIVIE   I'll see about it. [*She goes into the cottage.*]

[SIR GEORGE *has by this time managed to unfold a chair and plant it beside* MRS WARREN, *on her left. He throws the other on the grass and sits down, looking dejected and rather foolish, with the handle of his stick in his mouth.* PRAED, *still very uneasy, fidgets about the garden on their right.*]

MRS WARREN [*To* PRAED, *looking at* CROFTS.]   Just look at him, Praddy: he looks cheerful, don't he? He's been worrying my life out these three years to have that little girl of mine shewn to him; and now that I've done it, he's quite out of countenance. [*Briskly.*] Come! sit up, George; and take your stick out of your mouth. [CROFTS *sulkily obeys.*]

PRAED   I think, you know—if you don't mind my saying so—that we had better get out of the habit of thinking of her as a little girl. You see she has really distinguished herself; and I'm not sure, from what I have seen of her, that she is not older than any of us.

MRS WARREN [*Greatly amused.*]   Only listen to him, George! Older than any of us! Well, she has been stuffing you nicely with her importance.

PRAED   But young people are particularly sensitive about being treated in that way.

MRS WARREN   Yes; and young people have to get all that nonsense taken out of them, and a good deal more besides. Don't you interfere, Praddy. I know how to treat my own child as well as you do. [PRAED, *with a grave shake of his head, walks up the garden with his hands behind his back.* MRS WARREN *pretends to laugh, but looks after him with perceptible concern. Then she whispers to* CROFTS.] What's the matter with him? What does he take it like that for?

CROFTS [*Morosely.*]   You're afraid of Praed.

MRS WARREN   What! Me! Afraid of dear old Praddy! Why, a fly wouldn't be afraid of him.

CROFTS   You're afraid of him.

MRS WARREN [*Angry.*]   I'll trouble you to mind your own business, and not try any of your sulks on me. I'm not afraid of you, anyhow. If you can't make yourself agreeable, you'd better go home. [*She gets up, and, turning her back on him, finds herself face to face with*

PRAED.] Come, Praddy, I know it was only your tender-
heartedness. You're afraid I'll bully her.

PRAED   My dear Kitty: you think I'm offended. Don't imagine that:
pray don't. But you know I often notice things that escape you;
and though you never take my advice, you sometimes admit afterwards that you ought to have taken it.

MRS WARREN   Well, what do you notice now?

PRAED   Only that Vivie is a grown woman. Pray, Kitty, treat her with
every respect.

MRS WARREN [*With genuine amazement.*]   Respect! Treat my own
daughter with respect! What next, pray!

VIVIE [*Appearing at the cottage door and calling to* MRS WAR-
REN.]   Mother: will you come up to my room and take your bonnet off before tea?

MRS WARREN   Yes, dearie. [*She laughs indulgently at* PRAED *and pats
him on the cheek as she passes him on her way to the porch. She
follows* VIVIE *into the cottage.*]

CROFTS [*Furtively.*]   I say, Praed.

PRAED   Yes.

CROFTS   I want to ask you a rather particular question.

PRAED   Certainly. [*He takes* MRS WARREN'S *chair and sits close to*
CROFTS.]

CROFTS   That's right: they might hear us from the window. Look
here: did Kitty ever tell you who that girl's father is?

PRAED   Never.

CROFTS   Have you any suspicion of who it might be?

PRAED   None.

CROFTS [*Not believing him.*]   I know, of course, that you perhaps
might feel bound not to tell if she had said anything to you. But
it's very awkward to be uncertain about it now that we shall be
meeting the girl every day. We don't exactly know how we ought
to feel towards her.

PRAED   What difference can that make? We take her on her own
merits. What does it matter who her father was?

CROFTS [*Suspiciously.*]   Then you know who he was?

PRAED [*With a touch of temper.*]   I said no just now. Did you not
hear me?

CROFTS   Look here, Praed. I ask you as a particular favor. If you do
know [*Movement of protest from* PRAED]—I only say, if you know,
you might at least set my mind at rest about her. The fact is I feel
attracted towards her. Oh, don't be alarmed: it's quite an innocent
feeling. That's what puzzles me about it. Why, for all I know, *I*
might be her father.

PRAED   You! Impossible! Oh, no, nonsense!

CROFTS [*Catching him up cunningly.*]   You know for certain that
I'm not?

PRAED   I know nothing about it, I tell you, any more than you. But really, Crofts—oh, no, it's out of the question. There's not the least resemblance.

CROFTS   As to that, there's no resemblance between her and her mother that I can see. I suppose she's not your daughter, is she?

PRAED [*He meets the question with an indignant stare; then recovers himself with an effort and answers gently and gravely.*]   Now listen to me, my dear Crofts. I have nothing to do with that side of Mrs Warren's life, and never had. She has never spoken to me about it; and of course I have never spoken to her about it. Your delicacy will tell you that a handsome woman needs some friends who are not—well, not on that footing with her. The effect of her own beauty would become a torment to her if she could not escape from it occasionally. You are probably on much more confidential terms with Kitty than I am. Surely you can ask her the question yourself.

CROFTS [*Rising impatiently.*]   I have asked her often enough. But she's so determined to keep the child all to herself that she would deny that it ever had a father if she could. No: there's nothing to be got out of her—nothing that one can believe, anyhow. I'm thoroughly uncomfortable about it, Praed.

PRAED [*Rising also.*]   Well, as you are, at all events, old enough to be her father, I don't mind agreeing that we both regard Miss Vivie in a parental way, as a young girl whom we are bound to protect and help. All the more, as the real father, whoever he was, was probably a blackguard. What do you say?

CROFTS [*Aggressively.*]   I'm no older than you, if you come to that.

PRAED   Yes, you are, my dear fellow: you were born old. I was born a boy: I've never been able to feel the assurance of a grown-up man in my life.

MRS WARREN [*Calling from within the cottage.*]   Prad-dee! George! Tea-ea-ea-ea!

CROFTS [*Hastily.*]   She's calling us. [*He hurries in.*]

[PRAED *shakes his head bodingly, and is following slowly when he is hailed by a young gentleman who has just appeared on the common, and is making for the gate. He is a pleasant, pretty, smartly dressed, and entirely good-for-nothing young fellow, not long turned 20, with a charming voice and agreeably disrespectful manner. He carries a very light sporting magazine rifle.*]

THE YOUNG GENTLEMAN   Hallo! Praed!

PRAED   Why, Frank Gardner! [FRANK *comes in and shakes hands cordially.*] What on earth are you doing here?

FRANK   Staying with my father.

PRAED   The Roman father?[7]

---

7. Not "Roman Catholic" (he is a Church of England priest) but a father with a Roman sense of duty. The phrase is used ironically.

FRANK He's rector here. I'm living with my people this autumn for the sake of economy. Things came to a crisis in July: the Roman father had to pay my debts. He's stony broke in consequence; and so am I. What are you up to in these parts? Do you know the people here?

PRAED Yes: I'm spending the day with a Miss Warren.

FRANK [*Enthusiastically.*] What! Do you know Vivie? Isn't she a jolly girl! I'm teaching her to shoot—you see [*Shewing the rifle*]! I'm so glad she knows you: you're just the sort of fellow she ought to know. [*He smiles, and raises the charming voice almost to a singing tone as he exclaims.*] It's ever so jolly to find you here, Praed. Ain't it, now?

PRAED I'm an old friend of her mother's. Mrs Warren brought me over to make her daughter's acquaintance.

FRANK The mother! Is she here?

PRAED Yes—inside at tea.

MRS WARREN [*Calling from within.*] Prad-dee-ee-ee-eee! The tea-cake'll be cold.

PRAED [*Calling.*] Yes, Mrs Warren. In a moment. I've just met a friend here.

MRS WARREN A what?

PRAED [*Louder.*] A friend.

MRS WARREN Bring him up.

PRAED All right. [*To* FRANK.] Will you accept the invitation?

FRANK [*Incredulous, but immensely amused.*] Is that Vivie's mother?

PRAED Yes.

FRANK By Jove! What a lark! Do you think she'll like me?

PRAED I've no doubt you'll make yourself popular, as usual. Come in and try. [*Moving towards the house.*]

FRANK Stop a bit. [*Seriously.*] I want to take you into my confidence.

PRAED Pray don't. It's only some fresh folly, like the barmaid at Redhill.

FRANK It's ever so much more serious than that. You say you've only just met Vivie for the first time?

PRAED Yes.

FRANK [*Rhapsodically.*] Then you can have no idea what a girl she is. Such character! Such sense! And her cleverness! Oh, my eye, Praed, but I can tell you she is clever! And the most loving little heart that—

CROFTS [*Putting his head out of the window.*] I say, Praed: what are you about? Do come along. [*He disappears.*]

FRANK Hallo! Sort of chap that would take a prize at a dog show, ain't he? Who's he?

PRAED Sir George Crofts, an old friend of Mrs Warren's. I think we had better come in.

[*On their way to the porch they are interrupted by a call from the gate. Turning, they see an elderly clergyman looking over it.*]

THE CLERGYMAN [*Calling.*]   Frank!

FRANK   Hallo! [*To* PRAED.] The Roman father. [*To* THE CLERGYMAN] Yes, gov'nor: all right: presently. [*To* PRAED.] Look here, Praed: you'd better go in to tea. I'll join you directly.

PRAED   Very good. [*He raises his hat to the clergyman, who acknowledges the salute distantly.*]

[PRAED *goes into the cottage.* THE CLERGYMAN *remains stiffly outside the gate, with his hands on the top of it.* THE REV SAMUEL GARDNER, *a beneficed clergyman*[8] *of the Established Church, is over 50. He is a pretentious, booming, noisy person, hopelessly asserting himself as a father and a clergyman without being able to command respect in either capacity.*]

REV S   Well, sir. Who are your friends here, if I may ask?

FRANK   Oh, it's all right, gov'nor! Come in.

REV S   No, sir; not until I know whose garden I am entering.

FRANK   It's all right. It's Miss Warren's.

REV S   I have not seen her at church since she came.

FRANK   Of course not: she's a third wrangler—ever so intellectual!— took a higher degree than you did; so why should she go to hear you preach?

REV S   Don't be disrespectful, sir.

FRANK   Oh, it don't matter: nobody hears us. Come in. [*He opens the gate, unceremoniously pulling his father with it into the garden.*] I want to introduce you to her. She and I get on rattling well together: she's charming. Do you remember the advice you gave me last July, gor'nor?

REV S [*Severely.*]   Yes. I advised you to conquer your idleness and flippancy, and to work your way into an honorable profession and live on it and not upon me.

FRANK   No: that's what you thought of afterwards. What you actually said was that since I had neither brains nor money, I'd better turn my good looks to account by marrying somebody with both. Well, look here. Miss Warren has brains: you can't deny that.

REV S   Brains are not everything.

FRANK   No, of course not: there's the money—

REV S [*Interrupting him austerely.*]   I was not thinking of money, sir. I was speaking of higher things—social position, for instance.

FRANK   I don't care a rap about that.

REV S   But I do, sir.

FRANK   Well, nobody wants you to marry her. Anyhow, she has what amounts to a high Cambridge degree; and she seems to have as much money as she wants.

8. I.e., Gardner has a parish with a living.

REV S [*Sinking into a feeble vein of humor.*]   I greatly doubt whether she has as much money as you will want.

FRANK   Oh, come: I haven't been so very extravagant. I live ever so quietly; I don't drink; I don't bet much; and I never go regularly on the razzle-dazzle as you did when you were my age.

REV S [*Booming hollowly.*]   Silence, sir.

FRANK   Well, you told me yourself, when I was making ever such an ass of myself about the barmaid at Redhill, that you once offered a woman £50 for the letters you wrote to her when—

REV S [*Terrified.*]   Sh-sh-sh, Frank, for Heaven's sake! [*He looks round apprehensively. Seeing no one within earshot be plucks up courage to boom again, but more subduedly.*] You are taking an ungentlemanly advantage of what I confided to you for your own good, to save you from an error you would have repented all your life long. Take warning by your father's follies, sir; and don't make them an excuse for your own.

FRANK   Did you ever hear the story of the Duke of Wellington and his letters?

REV S   No, sir; and I don't want to hear it.

FRANK   The old Iron Duke didn't throw away £50—not he. He just wrote: "My dear Jenny: Publish and be damned! Yours affectionately, Wellington." That's what you should have done.

REV S [*Piteously.*]   Frank, my boy: when I wrote those letters I put myself into that woman's power. When I told you about her I put myself, to some extent, I am sorry to say, in your power. She refused my money with these words, which I shall never forget: "Knowledge is power," she said; "and I never sell power."[9] That's more than twenty years ago; and she has never made use of her power or caused me a moment's uneasiness. You are behaving worse to me than she did, Frank.

FRANK   Oh, yes, I dare say! Did you ever preach at her the way you preach at me every day?

REV S [*Wounded almost to tears.*]   I leave you, sir. You are incorrigible. [*He turns towards the gate.*]

FRANK [*Utterly unmoved.*]   Tell them I shan't be home to tea, will you, gov'nor, like a good fellow? [*He goes towards the cottage door and is met by* VIVIE *coming out, followed by* PRAED, CROFTS, *and* MRS WARREN.]

VIVIE [*To* FRANK.]   Is that your father, Frank? I do so want to meet him.

FRANK   Certainly. [*Calling after his father.*] Gov'nor. [THE REV S *turns at the gate, fumbling nervously at his hat.* PRAED *comes down the garden on the opposite side, beaming in anticipation of civilities.* CROFTS *prowls about near the hammock, poking it with his*

9. A Nietzschean sentiment. Shaw was influenced by Nietzsche's theory of the relationship between knowledge and power.

stick to make it swing. MRS WARREN *halts on the threshold, staring hard at the clergyman.*] Let me introduce—my father: Miss Warren.

VIVIE [*Going to* THE CLERGYMAN *and shaking his hand.*]   Very glad to see you here, Mr Gardner. Let me introduce everybody. Mr Gardner—Mr Frank Gardner—Mr Praed—Sir George Crofts, and— [*As the men are raising their hats to one another,* VIVIE *is interrupted by an exclamation from her mother, who swoops down on* THE REVEREND SAMUEL.]

MRS WARREN   Why, it's Sam Gardner, gone into the church! Don't you know us, Sam? This is George Crofts, as large as life and twice as natural. Don't you remember me?

REV S [*Very red.*]   I really—er—

MRS WARREN   Of course you do. Why, I have a whole album of your letters still: I came across them only the other day.

REV S [*Miserably confused.*]   Miss Vavasour, I believe.

MRS WARREN [*Correcting him quickly in a loud whisper.*]   Tch! Nonsense—Mrs Warren: don't you see my daughter there?

Act II

Inside the cottage after nightfall. Looking eastward from within instead of westward from without, the latticed window, with its curtains drawn, is now seen in the middle of the front wall of the cottage, with the porch door to the left of it. In the left-hand side wall is the door leading to the wing. Farther back against the same wall is a dresser with a candle and matches on it, and FRANK's *rifle standing beside them, with the barrel resting in the plate-rack. In the centre a table stands with a lighted lamp on it.* VIVIE's *books and writing materials are on a table to the right of the window, against the wall. The fireplace is on the right, with a settle: there is no fire. Two of the chairs are set right and left of the table.*

The cottage door opens, shewing a fine starlit night without; and MRS WARREN, *her shoulders wrapped in a shawl borrowed from* VIVIE, *enters, followed by* FRANK. *She has had enough of walking, and gives a gasp of relief as she unpins her hat; takes it off; sticks the pin through the crown; and puts it on the table.*

MRS WARREN   O Lord! I don't know which is the worst of the country, the walking or the sitting at home with nothing to do: I could do a whisky and soda now very well, if only they had such a thing in this place.

FRANK [*Helping her to take off her shawl, and giving her shoulders the most delicate possible little caress with his fingers as he does so.*]   Perhaps Vivie's got some.

MRS WARREN [*Glancing back at him for an instant from the corner of her eye as she detects the pressure.*]   Nonsense! What would a young girl like her be doing with such things! Never mind: it don't matter. [*She throws herself wearily into a chair at the table.*] I wonder how she passes her time here! I'd a good deal rather be in Vienna.

FRANK   Let me take you there. [*He folds the shawl neatly; hangs it on the back of the other chair; and sits down opposite* MRS WARREN.]

MRS WARREN   Get out! I'm beginning to think you're a chip of the old block.

FRANK   Like the gov'nor, eh?

MRS WARREN   Never you mind. What do you know about such things? You're only a boy.

FRANK   Do come to Vienna with me? It'd be ever such larks.

MRS WARREN   No, thank you. Vienna is no place for you—at least not until you're a little older. [*She nods at him to emphasize this piece of advice. He makes a mock-piteous face, belied by his laughing eyes. She looks at him; then rises and goes to him.*] Now, look here, little boy [*Taking his face in her hands and turning it up to her*]: I know you through and through by your likeness to your father, better than you know yourself. Don't you go taking any silly ideas into your head about me. Do you hear?

FRANK [*Gallantly wooing her with his voice.*]   Can't help it, my dear Mrs Warren: it runs in the family.

> [*She pretends to box his ears; then looks at the pretty, laughing, upturned face for a moment, tempted. At last she kisses him and immediately turns away, out of patience with herself.*]

MRS WARREN   There! I shouldn't have done that. I am wicked. Never you mind, my dear: it's only a motherly kiss. Go and make love to Vivie.

FRANK   So I have.

MRS WARREN [*Turning on him with a sharp note of alarm in her voice.*]   What!

FRANK   Vivie and I are ever such chums.

MRS WARREN   What do you mean? Now, see here: I won't have any young scamp tampering with my little girl. Do you hear? I won't have it.

FRANK [*Quite unabashed.*]   My dear Mrs Warren: don't you be alarmed. My intentions are honorable—ever so honorable; and your little girl is jolly well able to take care of herself. She don't need looking after half so much as her mother. She ain't so handsome, you know.

MRS WARREN [*Taken aback by his assurance.*]   Well, you have got a nice, healthy two inches thick of cheek all over you. I don't know where you got it—not from your father, anyhow. [*Voices and foot-*

steps in the porch.] Sh! I hear the others coming in. [*She sits down hastily.*] Remember: you've got your warning. [*The* REV SAMUEL *comes in, followed by* CROFTS.] Well, what became of you two? And where's Praddy and Vivie?

CROFTS [*Putting his hat on the settle and his stick in the chimney corner.*]   They went up the hill. We went to the village. I wanted a drink. [*He sits down on the settle, putting his legs up along the seat.*]

MRS WARREN   Well, she oughtn't to go off like that without telling me. [*To* FRANK.] Get your father a chair, Frank: where are your manners? [FRANK *springs up and gracefully offers his father his chair; then takes another from the wall and sits down at the table, in the middle, with his father on his right and* MRS WARREN *on his left.*] George: where are you going to stay to-night? You can't stay here. And what's Praddy going to do?

CROFTS   Gardner'll put me up.

MRS WARREN   Oh, no doubt you've taken care of yourself! But what about Praddy?

CROFTS   Don't know. I suppose he can sleep at the inn.

MRS WARREN   Haven't you room for him, Sam?

REV S   Well, er—you see, as rector here, I am not free to do as I like exactly. Er—what is Mr Praed's social position?

MRS WARREN   Oh, he's all right: he's an architect. What an old-stick-in-the-mud you are, Sam!

FRANK   Yes, it's all right, gov'nor. He built that place down in Monmouthshire for the Duke of Beaufort—Tintern Abbey they call it. You must have heard of it. [*He winks with lightning smartness at* MRS WARREN, *and regards his father blandly.*]

REV S   Oh, in that case, of course we shall only be too happy. I suppose he knows the Duke of Beaufort personally.

FRANK   Oh, ever so intimately! We can stick him in Georgina's old room.

MRS WARREN   Well, that's settled. Now, if those two would only come in and let us have supper. They've no right to stay out after dark like this.

CROFTS [*Aggressively.*]   What harm are they doing you?

MRS WARREN   Well, harm or not, I don't like it.

FRANK   Better not wait for them, Mrs Warren. Praed will stay out as long as possible. He has never known before what it is to stray over the heath on a summer night with my Vivie.

CROFTS [*Sitting up in some consternation.*]   I say, you know. Come!

REV S [*Startled out of his professional manner into real force and sincerity.*]   Frank, once for all, it's out of the question. Mrs Warren will tell you that it's not to be thought of.

CROFTS   Of course not.

FRANK [*With enchanting placidity.*]   Is that so, Mrs Warren?

MRS WARREN [*Reflectively.*]   Well, Sam, I don't know. If the girl wants to get married, no good can come of keeping her unmarried.

REV S [*Astounded.*]   But married to him!—your daughter to my son! Only think: it's impossible.

CROFTS   Of course it's impossible. Don't be a fool, Kitty.

MRS WARREN [*Nettled.*]   Why not? Isn't my daughter good enough for your son?

REV S   But surely, my dear Mrs Warren, you know the reason—

MRS WARREN [*Defiantly.*]   I know no reasons. If you know any, you can tell them to the lad, or to the girl, or to your congregation, if you like.

REV S [*Helplessly.*]   You know very well that I couldn't tell anyone the reasons. But my boy will believe me when I tell him there are reasons.

FRANK   Quite right, Dad: he will. But has your boy's conduct ever been influenced by your reasons?

CROFTS   You can't marry her; and that's all about it. [*He gets up and stands on the hearth, with his back to the fireplace, frowning determinedly.*]

MRS WARREN [*Turning on him sharply.*]   What have you got to do with it, pray?

FRANK [*With his prettiest lyrical cadence.*]   Precisely what I was going to ask, myself, in my own graceful fashion.

CROFTS [*To MRS WARREN.*]   I suppose you don't want to marry the girl to a man younger than herself and without either a profession or twopence to keep her on. Ask Sam, if you don't believe me. [*To THE REV S.*] How much more money are you going to give him?

REV S   Not another penny. He has had his patrimony; and he spent the last of it in July. [MRS WARREN's *face falls.*]

CROFTS [*Watching her.*]   There! I told you. [*He resumes his place on the settle and puts up his legs on the seat again, as if the matter were finally disposed of.*]

FRANK [*Plaintively.*]   This is ever so mercenary. Do you suppose Miss Warren's going to marry for money? If we love one another—

MRS WARREN   Thank you. Your love's a pretty cheap commodity, my lad. If you have no means of keeping a wife, that settles it: you can't have Vivie.

FRANK [*Much amused.*]   What do you say, gov'nor, eh?

REV S   I agree with Mrs Warren.

FRANK   And good old Crofts has already expressed his opinion.

CROFTS [*Turning angrily on his elbow.*]   Look here: I want none of your cheek.

FRANK [*Pointedly.*]   I'm ever so sorry to surprise you, Crofts; but you allowed yourself the liberty of speaking to me like a father a moment ago. One father is enough, thank you.

CROFTS [*Contemptuously.*]   Yah! [*He turns away again.*]

FRANK [*Rising.*]   Mrs Warren: I cannot give my Vivie up even for your sake.

MRS WARREN [*Muttering.*]   Young scamp!

FRANK [*Continuing.*]   And as you no doubt intend to hold out other prospects to her, I shall lose no time in placing my case before her. [*They stare at him; and he begins to declaim gracefully.*]

> He either fears his fate too much,
>   Or his deserts are small,
> That dares not put it to the touch
>   To gain or lose it all.[1]

[*The cottage door opens whilst he is reciting; and* VIVIE *and* PRAED *come in. He breaks off.* PRAED *puts his hat on the dresser. There is an immediate improvement in the company's behaviour.* CROFTS *takes down his legs from the settle and pulls himself together as* PRAED *joins him at the fireplace.* MRS WARREN *loses her ease of manner, and takes refuge in querulousness.*]

MRS WARREN   Wherever have you been, Vivie?

VIVIE [*Taking off her hat and throwing it carelessly on the table.*]   On the hill.

MRS WARREN   Well, you shouldn't go off like that without letting me know. How could I tell what had become of you—and night coming on, too!

VIVIE [*Going to the door of the inner room and opening it, ignoring her mother.*]   Now, about supper? We shall be rather crowded in here, I'm afraid.

MRS WARREN   Did you hear what I said, Vivie?

VIVIE [*Quietly.*]   Yes, mother. [*Reverting to the supper difficulty.*] How many are we? [*Counting.*] One, two, three, four, five, six. Well, two will have to wait until the rest are done: Mrs Alison has only plates and knives for four.

PRAED   Oh, it doesn't matter about me. I—

VIVIE   You have had a long walk and are hungry, Mr Praed: you shall have your supper at once. I can wait myself. I want one person to wait with me. Frank: are you hungry?

FRANK   Not the least in the world—completely off my peck, in fact.

MRS WARREN [*To* CROFTS.]   Neither are you, George. You can wait.

CROFTS   Oh, hang it, I've eaten nothing since tea-time. Can't Sam do it?

FRANK   Would you starve my poor father?

REV S [*Testily.*]   Allow me to speak for myself, sir. I am perfectly willing to wait.

VIVIE [*Decisively.*]   There's no need. Only two are wanted. [*She opens the door of the inner room.*] Will you take my mother in, Mr Gardner. [THE REV S *takes* MRS WARREN; *and they pass into the next*

---

1. Frank loosely quotes "My Dear and Only Love," a poem by James Graham, Marquis of Montrose (1612–1650): "He either fears his fate too much, / Or his deserts are small, / That puts it not unto the touch / To win or lose it all."

room. PRAED *and* CROFTS *follow. All except* PRAED *clearly disapprove of the arrangement, but do not know how to resist it.* VIVIE *stands at the door looking in at them.*] Can you squeeze past to that corner, Mr Praed: it's rather a tight fit. Take care of your coat against the white-wash—that's right. Now, are you all comfortable?

PRAED [*Within.*]   Quite, thank you.

MRS WARREN [*Within.*]   Leave the door open, dearie. [FRANK *looks at* VIVIE: *then steals to the cottage door and softly sets it wide open.*] Oh, Lor', what a draught! You'd better shut it, dear. [VIVIE *shuts it promptly.* FRANK *noiselessly shuts the cottage door.*]

FRANK [*Exulting.*]   Aha! Got rid of 'em. Well, Vivvums: what do you think of my governor!

VIVIE [*Preoccupied and serious.*]   I've hardly spoken to him. He doesn't strike me as being a particularly able person.

FRANK   Well, you know, the old man is not altogether such a fool as he looks. You see, he's rector here; and in trying to live up to it he makes a much bigger ass of himself than he really is. No, the gov'nor ain't so bad, poor old chap; and I don't dislike him as much as you might expect. He means well. How do you think you'll get on with him?

VIVIE [*Rather grimly.*]   I don't think my future life will be much concerned with him, or with any of that old circle of my mother's, except perhaps Praed. What do you think of my mother?

FRANK   Really and truly?

VIVIE   Yes, really and truly.

FRANK   Well, she's ever so jolly. But she's rather a caution, isn't she? And Crofts! Oh, my eye, Crofts!

VIVIE   What a lot, Frank!

FRANK   What a crew!

VIVIE [*With intense contempt for them.*]   If I thought that *I* was like that—that I was going to be a waster, shifting along from one meal to another with no purpose, and no character, and no grit in me, I'd open an artery and bleed to death without one moment's hesitation.

FRANK   Oh, no, you wouldn't. Why should they take any grind when they can afford not to? I wish I had their luck. No: what I object to is their form. It isn't the thing: it's slovenly, ever so slovenly.

VIVIE   Do you think your form will be any better when you're as old as Crofts, if you don't work?

FRANK   Of course I do—ever so much better. Vivvums mustn't lecture: her little boy's incorrigible. [*He attempts to take her face caressingly in his hands.*]

VIVIE [*Striking his hands down sharply.*]   Off with you: Vivvums is not in a humor for petting her little boy this evening.

FRANK   How unkind!

VIVIE [*Stamping at him.*]   Be serious. I'm serious.

FRANK   Good. Let us talk learnedly. Miss Warren: do you know that all the most advanced thinkers are agreed that half the diseases of modern civilization are due to starvation of the affections in the young. Now, I—

VIVIE [*Cutting him short.*]   You are getting tiresome. [*She opens the inner door.*] Have you room for Frank there? He's complaining of starvation.

MRS WARREN [*Within.*]   Of course there is [*clatter of knives and glasses as she moves the things on the table*]. Here: there's room now beside me. Come along, Mr Frank.

FRANK [*Aside to* VIVIE, *as he goes.*]   Her little boy will be ever so even with his Vivvums for this. [*He goes into the other room.*]

MRS WARREN [*Within.*]   Here, Vivie: come on, you too, child. You must be famished. [*She enters, followed by* CROFTS, *who holds the door open for* VIVIE *with marked deference. She goes out without looking at him; and he shuts the door after her.*] Why, George, you can't be done: you've eaten nothing.

CROFTS   Oh, all I wanted was a drink. [*He thrusts his hands in his pockets and begins prowling about the room, restless and sulky.*]

MRS WARREN   Well, I like enough to eat. But a little of that cold beef and cheese and lettuce goes a long way. [*With a sigh of only half repletion she sits down lazily at the table.*]

CROFTS   What do you go encouraging that young pup for?

MRS WARREN [*On the alert at once.*]   Now see here, George: what are you up to about that girl? I've been watching your way of looking at her. Remember: I know you and what your looks mean.

CROFTS   There's no harm in looking at her, is there?

MRS WARREN   I'd put you out and pack you back to London pretty soon if I saw any of your nonsense. My girl's little finger is more to me than your whole body and soul. [CROFTS *receives this with a sneering grin.* MRS WARREN, *flushing a little at her failure to impose on him in the character of a theatrically devoted mother, adds in a lower key*] Make your mind easy: the young pup has no more chance than you have.

CROFTS   Mayn't a man take an interest in a girl?

MRS WARREN   Not a man like you.

CROFTS   How old is she?

MRS WARREN   Never you mind how old she is.

CROFTS   Why do you make such a secret of it?

MRS WARREN   Because I choose.

CROFTS   Well, I'm not fifty yet; and my property is as good as ever it was—

MRS WARREN [*Interrupting him.*]   Yes; because you're as stingy as you're vicious.

CROFTS [*Continuing.*]   And a baronet isn't to be picked up every day. No other man in my position would put up with you for a mother-in-law. Why shouldn't she marry me?

MRS WARREN   You!

CROFTS   We three could live together quite comfortably. I'd die before her and leave her a bouncing widow with plenty of money. Why not? It's been growing in my mind all the time I've been walking with that fool inside there.

MRS WARREN [*Revolted.*]   Yes; it's the sort of thing that would grow in your mind.

[*He halts in his prowling; and the two look at one another, she steadfastly, with a sort of awe behind her contemptuous disgust: he stealthily, with a carnal gleam in his eye and a loose grin, tempting her.*]

CROFTS [*Suddenly becoming anxious and urgent as he sees no sign of sympathy in her.*]   Look here, Kitty: you're a sensible woman: you needn't put on any moral airs. I'll ask no more questions; and you need answer none. I'll settle the whole property on her; and if you want a cheque for yourself on the wedding day, you can name any figure you like—in reason.

MRS WARREN   Faugh! So it's come to that with you, George, like all the other worn out old creatures.

CROFTS [*Savagely.*]   Damn you!

[*She rises and turns fiercely on him; but the door of the inner room is opened just then; and the voices of the others are heard returning.* CROFTS, *unable to recover his presence of mind, hurries out of the cottage.* THE CLERGYMAN *comes back.*]

REV S [*Looking round.*]   Where is Sir George?

MRS WARREN   Gone out to have a pipe. [*She goes to the fireplace, turning her back on him to compose herself.* THE CLERGYMAN *goes to the table for his hat. Meanwhile* VIVIE *comes in, followed by* FRANK, *who collapses into the nearest chair with an air of extreme exhaustion.* MRS WARREN *looks round at* VIVIE *and says, with her affectation of maternal patronage even more forced than usual.*] Well, dearie: have you had a good supper?

VIVIE   You know what Mrs Alison's suppers are. [*She turns to* FRANK *and pets him.*] Poor Frank! was all the beef gone? did it get nothing but bread and cheese and ginger beer? [*Seriously, as if she had done quite enough trifling for one evening.*] Her butter is really awful. I must get some down from the stores.

FRANK   Do, in Heaven's name!

[VIVIE *goes to the writing-table and makes a memorandum to order the butter.* PRAED *comes in from the inner room, putting up his handkerchief, which he has been using as a napkin.*]

REV S   Frank, my boy: it is time for us to be thinking of home. Your mother does not know yet that we have visitors.

PRAED   I'm afraid we're giving trouble.

FRANK   Not the least in the world, Praed: my mother will be delighted to see you. She's a genuinely intellectual, artistic woman; and she sees nobody here from one year's end to another except the gov'nor; so you can imagine how jolly dull it pans out for her. [*To* THE REV S.] You're not intellectual or artistic, are you, pater?[2] So take Praed home at once; and I'll stay here and entertain Mrs Warren. You'll pick up Crofts in the garden. He'll be excellent company for the bull-pup.

PRAED   [*Taking his hat from the dresser, and coming close to* FRANK.]   Come with us, Frank. Mrs Warren has not seen Miss Vivie for a long time; and we have prevented them from having a moment together yet.

FRANK   [*Quite softened, and looking at* PRAED *with romantic admiration.*]   Of course: I forgot. Ever so thanks for reminding me. Perfect gentleman, Praddy. Always were—my ideal through life. [*He rises to go, but pauses a moment between the two older men, and puts his hand on* PRAED's *shoulder.*] Ah, if you had only been my father instead of this unworthy old man! [*He puts his other hand on his father's shoulder.*]

REV S   [*Blustering.*]   Silence, sir, silence: you are profane.

MRS WARREN   [*Laughing heartily.*]   You should keep him in better order, Sam. Good-night. Here: take George his hat and stick with my compliments.

REV S   [*Taking them.*]   Good-night. [*They shake hands.*]
   [*As he passes* VIVIE *he shakes hands with her also and bids her good-night. Then, in booming command, to* FRANK.] Come along, sir, at once. [*He goes out. Meanwhile* FRANK *has taken his cap from the dresser and his rifle from the rack.* PRAED *shakes hands with* MRS WARREN *and* VIVIE *and goes out,* MRS WARREN *accompanying him idly to the door, and looking out after him as he goes across the garden.* FRANK *silently begs a kiss from* VIVIE; *but she, dismissing him with a stern glance, takes a couple of books and some paper from the writing-table, and sits down with them at the middle table, so as to have the benefit of the lamp.*]

FRANK   [*At the door, taking* MRS WARREN's *hand.*]   Good night, dear Mrs Warren.
   [*He squeezes her hand. She snatches it away, her lips tightening, and looks more than half disposed to box his ears. He laughs mischievously and runs off, clapping-to the door behind him.*]

MRS WARREN   [*Coming back to her place at the table, opposite* VIVIE, *resigning herself to an evening of boredom now that the men are gone.*]   Did you ever in your life hear anyone rattle on so? Isn't he a tease? [*She sits down.*] Now that I think of it, dearie, don't

2. Latin: father.

you go encouraging him. I'm sure he's a regular good-for-nothing.

VIVIE   Yes: I'm afraid poor Frank is a thorough good-for-nothing. I shall have to get rid of him; but I shall feel sorry for him, though he's not worth it, poor lad. That man Crofts does not seem to me to be good for much either, is he?

MRS WARREN [*Galled by* VIVIE's *cool tone.*]   What do you know of men, child, to talk that way about them? You'll have to make up your mind to see a good deal of Sir George Crofts, as he's a friend of mine.

VIVIE [*Quite unmoved.*]   Why? Do you expect that we shall be much together—you and I, I mean?

MRS WARREN [*Staring at her.*]   Of course—until you're married. You're not going back to college again.

VIVIE   Do you think my way of life would suit you? I doubt it.

MRS WARREN   Your way of life! What do you mean?

VIVIE [*Cutting a page of her book with the paper knife on her chatelaine.*]   Has it really never occurred to you, mother, that I have a way of life like other people?

MRS WARREN   What nonsense is this you're trying to talk? Do you want to shew your independence, now that you're a great little person at school? Don't be a fool, child.

VIVIE [*Indulgently.*]   That's all you have to say on the subject, is it, mother?

MRS WARREN [*Puzzled, then angry.*]   Don't you keep on asking me questions like that. [*Violently.*] Hold your tongue. [VIVIE *works on, losing no time, and saying nothing.*] You and your way of life, indeed! What next? [*She looks at* VIVIE *again. No reply.*] Your way of life will be what I please, so it will. [*Another pause.*] I've been noticing these airs in you ever since you got that tripos or whatever you call it. If you think I'm going to put up with them you're mistaken; and the sooner you find it out, the better. [*Muttering.*] All I have to say on the subject, indeed! [*Again raising her voice angrily.*] Do you know who you're speaking to, Miss?

VIVIE [*Looking across at her without raising her head from her book.*]   No. Who are you? What are you?

MRS WARREN [*Rising breathless.*]   You young imp!

VIVIE   Everybody knows my reputation, my social standing, and the profession I intend to pursue. I know nothing about you. What is that way of life which you invite me to share with you and Sir George Crofts, pray?

MRS WARREN   Take care. I shall do something I'll be sorry for after, and you, too.

VIVIE [*Putting aside her books with cool decision.*]   Well, let us drop the subject until you are better able to face it. [*Looking critically at her mother.*] You want some good walks and a little lawn tennis to set you up. You are shockingly out of condition: you were not able to manage twenty yards uphill to-day without stopping to pant; and your wrists are mere rolls of fat. Look at mine. [*She holds out her wrists.*]

MRS WARREN [*After looking at her helplessly, begins to whimper.*] Vivie—

VIVIE [*Springing up sharply.*] Now pray don't begin to cry. Anything but that. I really cannot stand whimpering. I will go out of the room if you do.

MRS WARREN [*Piteously.*] Oh, my darling, how can you be so hard on me? Have I no rights over you as your mother?

VIVIE Are you my mother?

MRS WARREN [*Appalled.*] Am I your mother! Oh, Vivie!

VIVIE Then where are our relatives—my father—our family friends? You claim the rights of a mother: the right to call me fool and child; to speak to me as no woman in authority over me at college dare speak to me; to dictate my way of life; and to force on me the acquaintance of a brute whom anyone can see to be the most vicious sort of London man about town. Before I give myself the trouble to resist such claims, I may as well find out whether they have any real existence.

MRS WARREN [*Distracted, throwing herself on her knees.*] Oh, no, no. Stop, stop. I am your mother: I swear it. Oh, you can't mean to turn on me—my own child: it's not natural. You believe me, don't you? Say you believe me.

VIVIE Who was my father?

MRS WARREN You don't know what you're asking. I can't tell you.

VIVIE [*Determinedly.*] Oh, yes, you can, if you like. I have a right to know; and you know very well that I have that right. You can refuse to tell me, if you please; but if you do, you will see the last of me to-morrow morning.

MRS WARREN Oh, it's too horrible to hear you talk like that. You wouldn't—you couldn't leave me.

VIVIE [*Ruthlessly.*] Yes, without a moment's hesitation, if you trifle with me about this. [*Shivering with disgust.*] How can I feel sure that I may not have the contaminated blood of that brutal waster in my veins?

MRS WARREN No, no. On my oath it's not he, nor any of the rest that you have ever met. I'm certain of that, at least. [VIVIE'S *eyes fasten sternly on her mother as the significance of this flashes on her.*]

VIVIE [*Slowly.*] You are certain of that, at least. Ah! You mean that that is all you are certain of. [*Thoughtfully.*] I see. [MRS WARREN *buries her face in her hands.*] Don't do that, mother: you know you don't feel it a bit. [MRS WARREN *takes down her hands and looks up deplorably at* VIVIE, *who takes out her watch and says*] Well, that is enough for to-night. At what hour would you like breakfast? Is half-past eight too early for you?

MRS WARREN [*Wildly.*]   My God, what sort of woman are you?

VIVIE [*Coolly.*]   The sort the world is mostly made of, I should hope. Otherwise I don't understand how it gets its business done. Come [*taking her mother by the wrist, and pulling her up pretty resolutely*]: pull yourself together. That's right.

MRS WARREN [*Querulously.*]   You're very rough with me, Vivie.

VIVIE   Nonsense. What about bed? It's past ten.

MRS WARREN [*Passionately.*]   What's the use of my going to bed? Do you think I could sleep?

VIVIE   Why not? I shall.

MRS WARREN   You! you've no heart. [*She suddenly breaks out vehemently in her natural tongue—the dialect of a woman of the people—with all her affectations of maternal authority and conventional manners gone, and an overwhelming inspiration of true conviction and scorn in her.*] Oh, I won't bear it: I won't put up with the injustice of it. What right have you to set yourself up above me like this? You boast of what you are to me—to me, who gave you the chance of being what you are. What chance had I? Shame on you for a bad daughter and a stuck-up prude!

VIVIE [*Cool and determined, but no longer confident; for her replies, which have sounded convincingly sensible and strong to her so far, now begin to ring rather woodenly and even priggishly against the new tone of her mother.*]   Don't think for a moment I set myself above you in any way. You attacked me with the conventional authority of a mother: I defended myself with the conventional superiority of a respectable woman. Frankly, I am not going to stand any of your nonsense; and when you drop it I shall not expect you to stand any of mine. I shall always respect your right to your own opinions and your own way of life.

MRS WARREN   My own opinions and my own way of life! Listen to her talking! Do you think I was brought up like you—able to pick and choose my own way of life? Do you think I did what I did because I liked it, or thought it right, or wouldn't rather have gone to college and been a lady if I'd had the chance?

VIVIE   Everybody has some choice, mother. The poorest girl alive may not be able to choose between being Queen of England or Principal of Newnham; but she can choose between ragpicking and flowerselling, according to her taste. People are always blaming their circumstances for what they are. I don't believe in circumstances. The people who get on in this world are the people who get up and look for the circumstances they want, and, if they can't find them, make them.

MRS WARREN   Oh, it's easy to talk, very easy, isn't it? Here!—would you like to know what my circumstances were?

VIVIE   Yes: you had better tell me. Won't you sit down?

MRS WARREN   Oh, I'll sit down: don't you be afraid. [*She plants her chair farther forward with brazen energy, and sits down.* VIVIE *is impressed in spite of herself.*] D'you know what your gran'mother was?

VIVIE   No.

MRS WARREN   No, you don't. I do. She called herself a widow and had a fried-fish shop down by the Mint, and kept herself and four daughters out of it. Two of us were sisters: that was me and Liz; and we were both good-looking and well made. I suppose our father was a well-fed man: mother pretended he was a gentleman; but I don't know. The other two were only half sisters—undersized, ugly, starved looking, hard working, honest poor creatures: Liz and I would have half-murdered them if mother hadn't half-murdered us to keep our hands off them. They were the respectable ones. Well, what did they get by their respectability? I'll tell you. One of them worked in a whitelead factory twelve hours a day for nine shillings a week until she died of lead poisoning. She only expected to get her hands a little paralyzed; but she died. The other was always held up to us as a model because she married a Government laborer in the Deptford victualling yard, and kept his room and the three children neat and tidy on eighteen shillings a week—until he took to drink. That was worth being respectable for, wasn't it?

VIVIE   [*Now thoughtfully attentive.*]   Did you and your sister think so?

MRS WARREN   Liz didn't, I can tell you: she had more spirit. We both went to a church school—that was part of the ladylike airs we gave ourselves to be superior to the children that knew nothing and went nowhere—and we stayed there until Liz went out one night and never came back. I know the schoolmistress thought I'd soon follow her example; for the clergyman was always warning me that Lizzie'd end by jumping off Waterloo Bridge. Poor fool: that was all he knew about it! But I was more afraid of the whitelead factory than I was of the river; and so would you have been in my place. That clergyman got me a situation as scullery maid in a temperance restaurant where they sent out for anything you liked. Then I was waitress; and then I went to the bar at Waterloo station—fourteen hours a day serving drinks and washing glasses for four shillings a week and my board. That was considered a great promotion for me. Well, one cold, wretched night, when I was so tired I could hardly keep myself awake, who should come up for a half of Scotch but Lizzie, in a long fur cloak, elegant and comfortable, with a lot of sovereigns in her purse.

VIVIE   [*Grimly.*]   My aunt Lizzie!

MRS WARREN   Yes: and a very good aunt to have, too. She's living down at Winchester now, close to the cathedral, one of the most respectable ladies there—chaperones girls at the county ball, if you please. No river for Liz, thank you! You remind me of Liz a little: she was a first-rate business woman—saved money from the beginning—never let herself look too like what she was—never lost her head or threw away a chance. When she saw I'd grown up good-looking she said to me across the bar: "What are you doing there, you little fool? wearing out your health and your appearance for other people's profit!" Liz was saving money then to take a house for herself in Brussels: and she thought we two could save faster than one. So she lent me some money and gave me a start; and I saved steadily and first paid her back, and then went into business with her as her partner. Why shouldn't I have done it? The house in Brussels was real high class—a much better place for a woman to be in than the factory where Anne Jane got poisoned. None of our girls were ever treated as I was treated in the scullery of that temperance place, or at the Waterloo bar, or at home. Would you have had me stay in them and become a worn out old drudge before I was forty?

VIVIE [*Intensely interested by this time.*]   No; but why did you choose that business? Saving money and good management will succeed in any business.

MRS WARREN   Yes, saving money. But where can a woman get the money to save in any other business? Could you save out of four shillings a week and keep yourself dressed as well? Not you. Of course, if you're a plain woman and can't earn anything more; or if you have a turn for music, or the stage, or newspaper-writing: that's different. But neither Liz nor I had any turn for such things: all we had was our appearance and our turn for pleasing men. Do you think we were such fools as to let other people trade in our good looks by employing us as shopgirls, or barmaids, or waitresses, when we could trade in them ourselves and get all the profits instead of starvation wages? Not likely.

VIVIE   You were certainly quite justified—from the business point of view.

MRS WARREN   Yes; or any other point of view. What is any respectable girl brought up to do but to catch some rich man's fancy and get the benefit of his money by marrying him?—as if a marriage ceremony could make any difference in the right or wrong of the thing! Oh, the hypocrisy of the world makes me sick! Liz and I had to work and save and calculate just like other people; elseways we should be as poor as any good-for-nothing, drunken waster of a woman that thinks her luck will last for ever. [*With great energy.*] I despise such people: they've no character; and if there's a thing I hate in a woman, it's want of character.

VIVIE   Come, now, mother: frankly! Isn't it part of what you call character in a woman that she should greatly dislike such a way of making money?

MRS WARREN   Why, of course. Everybody dislikes having to work and make money; but they have to do it all the same. I'm sure I've often pitied a poor girl, tired out and in low spirits, having to try to please some man that she doesn't care two straws for—some half-drunken fool that thinks he's making himself agreeable when he's teasing and worrying and disgusting a woman so that hardly any money could pay her for putting up with it. But she has to bear with disagreeables and take the rough with the smooth, just like a nurse in a hospital or anyone else. It's not work that any woman would do for pleasure, goodness knows; though to hear the pious people talk you would suppose it was a bed of roses.

VIVIE   Still you consider it worth while. It pays.

MRS WARREN   Of course it's worth while to a poor girl, if she can resist temptation and is good-looking and well conducted and sensible. It's far better than any other employment open to her. I always thought that oughtn't to be. It can't be right, Vivie, that there shouldn't be better opportunities for women. I stick to that: it's wrong. But it's so, right or wrong; and a girl must make the best of it. But, of course, it's not worth while for a lady. If you took to it you'd be a fool; but I should have been a fool if I'd taken to anything else.

VIVIE   [More and more deeply moved.]   Mother: suppose we were both as poor as you were in those wretched old days, are you quite sure that you wouldn't advise me to try the Waterloo bar, or marry a labourer, or even go into the factory?

MRS WARREN [Indignantly.]   Of course not. What sort of mother do you take me for! How could you keep your self-respect in such starvation and slavery? And what's a woman worth? what's life worth? without self-respect! Why am I independent and able to give my daughter a first-rate education, when other women that had just as good opportunities are in the gutter? Because I always knew how to respect myself and control myself. Why is Liz looked up to in a cathedral town? The same reason. Where would we be now if we'd minded the clergyman's foolishness? Scrubbing floors for one and sixpence a day and nothing to look forward to but the workhouse infirmary. Don't you be led astray by people who don't know the world, my girl. The only way for a woman to provide for herself decently is for her to be good to some man that can afford to be good to her. If she's in his own station of life, let her make him marry her; but if she's far beneath him she can't expect it— why should she? It wouldn't be for her own happiness. Ask any lady in London society that has daughters; and she'll tell you the same, except that I tell you straight and she'll tell you crooked. That's all the difference.

VIVIE [Fascinated, gazing at her.]   My dear mother: you are a wonderful woman—you are stronger than all England. And are you really and truly not one wee bit doubtful—or—or—ashamed?

MRS WARREN   Well, of course, dearie, it's only good manners to be ashamed of it; it's expected from a woman. Women have to pre-

tend to feel a great deal that they don't feel. Liz used to be angry
with me for plumping out the truth about it. She used to say that
when every woman could learn enough from what was going on
in the world before her eyes, there was no need to talk about it to
her. But then Liz was such a perfect lady! She had the true instinct
of it; while I was always a bit of a vulgarian. I used to be so pleased
when you sent me your photographs to see that you were growing
up like Liz: you've just her ladylike, determined way. But I can't
stand saying one thing when everyone knows I mean another.
What's the use in such hypocrisy? If people arrange the world that
way for women, there's no good pretending that it's arranged the
other way. I never was a bit ashamed really. I consider that I had
a right to be proud that we managed everything so respectably,
and never had a word against us, and that the girls were so well
taken care of. Some of them did very well: one of them married
an ambassador. But of course now I daren't talk about such things:
whatever would they think of us! [*She yawns.*] Oh, dear! I do
believe I'm getting sleepy after all. [*She stretches herself lazily, thoroughly relieved by her explosion, and placidly ready for her night's
rest.*]

VIVIE   I believe it is I who will not be able to sleep now. [*She goes
to the dresser and lights the candle. Then she extinguishes the lamp,
darkening the room a good deal.*] Better let in some fresh air before
locking up. [*She opens the cottage door, and finds that it is broad
moonlight.*] What a beautiful night! Look!

   [*She draws aside the curtains of the window. The landscape is
   seen bathed in the radiance of the harvest moon rising over
   Blackdown.*]

MRS WARREN [*With a perfunctory glance at the scene.*]   Yes, dear:
but take care you don't catch your death of cold from the night
air.

VIVIE [*Contemptuously.*]   Nonsense.

MRS WARREN [*Querulously.*]   Oh, yes: everything I say is nonsense,
according to you.

VIVIE [*Turning to her quickly.*]   No: really that is not so, mother.
You have got completely the better of me to-night, though I
intended it to be the other way. Let us be good friends now.

MRS WARREN [*Shaking her head a little ruefully.*]   So it has been the
other way. But I suppose I must give in to it. I always got the worst
of it from Liz; and now I suppose it'll be the same with you.

VIVIE   Well, never mind. Come; good-night, dear old mother. [*She
takes her mother in her arms.*]

MRS WARREN [*Fondly.*]   I brought you up well, didn't I, dearie?

VIVIE   You did.

MRS WARREN   And you'll be good to your poor old mother for it,
won't you?

VIVIE   I will, dear. [*Kissing her.*] Good-night.

MRS WARREN [*With unction.*]   Blessings on my own dearie darling—
a mother's blessing!

[*She embraces her daughter protectingly, instinctively looking upward as if to call down a blessing.*]

Act III

In the Rectory garden next morning, with the sun shining and the birds in full song. The garden wall has a five-barred wooden gate, wide enough to admit a carriage, in the middle. Beside the gate hangs a bell on a coiled spring, communicating with a pull outside. The carriage drive comes down the middle of the garden and then swerves to its left, where it ends in a little gravelled circus opposite the rectory porch. Beyond the gate is seen the dusty high road, parallel with the wall, bounded on the farther side by a strip of turf and an unfenced pine wood. On the lawn, between the house and the drive, is a clipped yew tree, with a garden bench in its shade. On the opposite side the garden is shut in by a box hedge; and there is a sundial on the turf, with an iron chair near it. A little path leads off through the box hedge, behind the sundial.

FRANK, seated on the chair near the sundial, on which he has placed the morning papers, is reading the Standard. His father comes from the house, red-eyed and shivery, and meets FRANK's eye with misgiving.

FRANK [*Looking at his watch.*]   Half-past eleven. Nice hour for a rector to come down to breakfast!

REV S   Don't mock, Frank: don't mock. I'm a little—er— [*Shivering.*]——

FRANK   Off colour?

REV S [*Repudiating the expression.*]   No, sir: unwell this morning. Where's your mother?

FRANK   Don't be alarmed: she's not here. Gone to town by the 11:13 with Bessie. She left several messages for you. Do you feel equal to receiving them now, or shall I wait till you've breakfasted?

REV S   I have breakfasted, sir. I am surprised at your mother going to town when we have people staying with us. They'll think it very strange.

FRANK   Possibly she has considered that. At all events, if Crofts is going to stay here, and you are going to sit up every night with him until four, recalling the incidents of your fiery youth, it is clearly my mother's duty, as a prudent housekeeper, to go up to the stores and order a barrel of whisky and a few hundred siphons.

REV S   I did not observe that Sir George drank excessively.

FRANK   You were not in a condition to, gov'nor.

REV S   Do you mean to say that I—

FRANK [*Calmly.*]   I never saw a beneficed clergyman less sober. The anecdotes you told about your past career were so awful that I really don't think Praed would have passed the night under your roof if it hadn't been for the way my mother and he took to one another.

REV S   Nonsense, sir. I am Sir George Crofts' host. I must talk to him about something; and he has only one subject. Where is Mr Praed now?

FRANK   He is driving my mother and Bessie to the station.

REV S   Is Crofts up yet?

FRANK   Oh, long ago. He hasn't turned a hair: he's in much better practice than you—has kept it up ever since, probably. He's taken himself off somewhere to smoke.

> [FRANK *resumes his paper.* THE REV S *turns disconsolately towards the gate; then comes back irresolutely.*]

REV S   Er—Frank.

FRANK   Yes.

REV S   Do you think the Warrens will expect to be asked here after yesterday afternoon?

FRANK   They've been asked already. Crofts informed us at breakfast that *you* told him to bring Mrs Warren and Vivie over here to-day, and to invite them to make this house their home. It was after that communication that my mother found she must go to town by the 11:13 train.

REV S [*With despairing vehemence.*]   I never gave any such invitation. I never thought of such a thing.

FRANK [*Compassionately.*]   How do you know, gov'nor, what you said and thought last night? Hallo! here's Praed back again.

PRAED [*Coming in through the gate.*]   Good morning.

REV S   Good morning. I must apologize for not having met you at breakfast. I have a touch of—of—

FRANK   Clergyman's sore throat, Praed. Fortunately not chronic.

PRAED [*Changing the subject.*]   Well, I must say your house is in a charming spot here. Really most charming.

REV S   Yes: it is indeed. Frank will take you for a walk, Mr Praed, if you like. I'll ask you to excuse me: I must take the opportunity to write my sermon while Mrs Gardner is away and you are all amusing yourselves. You won't mind, will you?

PRAED   Certainly not. Don't stand on the slightest ceremony with me.

REV S   Thank you. I'll—er—er— [*He stammers his way to the porch and vanishes into the house.*]

PRAED [*Sitting down on the turf near* FRANK, *and hugging his ankles.*]   Curious thing it must be writing a sermon every week.

FRANK   Ever so curious, if he did it. He buys 'em. He's gone for some soda water.

PRAED   My dear boy: I wish you would be more respectful to your father. You know you can be so nice when you like.

FRANK   My dear Praddy: you forget that I have to live with the governor. When two people live together—it don't matter whether they're father and son, husband and wife, brother and sister—they can't keep up the polite humbug which comes so easy for ten minutes on an afternoon call. Now the governor, who unites to many admirable domestic qualities the irresoluteness of a sheep and the pompousness and aggressiveness of a jackass—

PRAED   No, pray, pray, my dear Frank, remember! He is your father.

FRANK   I give him due credit for that. But just imagine his telling Crofts to bring the Warrens over here! He must have been ever so drunk. You know, my dear Praddy, my mother wouldn't stand Mrs Warren for a moment. Vivie mustn't come here until she's gone back to town.

PRAED   But your mother doesn't know anything about Mrs Warren, does she?

FRANK   I don't know. Her journey to town looks as if she did. Not that my mother would mind in the ordinary way: she has stuck like a brick to lots of women who had got into trouble. But they were all nice women. That's what makes the real difference. Mrs Warren, no doubt, has her merits; but she's ever so rowdy; and my mother simply wouldn't put up with her. So—hallo! [*This exclamation is provoked by the reappearance of* THE CLERGYMAN, *who comes out of the house in haste and dismay.*]

REV S   Frank: Mrs Warren and her daughter are coming across the heath with Crofts: I saw them from the study windows. What am I to say about your mother?

FRANK [*Jumping up energetically.*]   Stick on your hat and go out and say how delighted you are to see them; and that Frank's in the garden; and that mother and Bessie have been called to the bedside of a sick relative, and were ever so sorry they couldn't stop; and that you hope Mrs Warren slept well; and—and—say any blessed thing except the truth, and leave the rest to Providence.

REV S   But how are we to get rid of them afterwards?

FRANK   There's no time to think of that now. Here! [*He bounds into the porch and returns immediately with a clerical felt hat, which he claps on his father's head.*] Now: off with you. Praed and I'll wait here, to give the thing an unpremeditated air. [THE CLERGYMAN, *dazed, but obedient, hurries off through the gate.* PRAED *gets up from the turf, and dusts himself.*]

FRANK   We must get that old lady back to town somehow, Praed. Come! honestly, dear Praddy, do you like seeing them together— Vivie and the old lady?

PRAED Oh, why not?

FRANK [*His teeth on edge.*]   Don't it make your flesh creep ever so little?—that wicked old devil, up to every villainy under the sun, I'll swear, and Vivie—ugh!

PRAED Hush, pray. They're coming.

[THE CLERGYMAN *and* CROFTS *are seen coming along the road, followed by* MRS WARREN *and* VIVIE *walking affectionately together.*]

FRANK Look: she actually has her arm round the old woman's waist. It's her right arm: she began it. She's gone sentimental, by God! Ugh! ugh! Now do you feel the creeps? [THE CLERGYMAN *opens the gate; and* MRS WARREN *and* VIVIE *pass him and stand in the middle of the garden looking at the house.* FRANK, *in an ecstasy of dissimulation, turns gaily to* MRS WARREN, *exclaiming.*] Ever so delighted to see you, Mrs Warren. This quiet old rectory garden becomes you perfectly.

MRS WARREN Well, I never! Did you hear that, George? He says I look well in a quiet old rectory garden.

REV S [*Still holding the gate for* CROFTS, *who loafs through it, heavily bored.*]   You look well everywhere, Mrs Warren.

FRANK Bravo, gov'nor! Now look here: let's have an awful jolly time of it before lunch. First let's see the church. Everyone has to do that. It's a regular old thirteenth century church, you know: the gov'nor's ever so fond of it, because he got up a restoration fund and had it completely rebuilt six years ago. Praed will be able to show its points.

REV S [*Mooning hospitably at them.*]   I shall be pleased, I'm sure, if Sir George and Mrs Warren really care about it.

MRS WARREN Oh, come along and get it over. It'll do George good: I'll lay he doesn't trouble church much.

CROFTS [*Turning back towards the gate.*]   I've no objection.

REV S Not that way. We go through the fields, if you don't mind. Round here. [*He leads the way by the little path through the box hedge.*]

CROFTS Oh, all right. [*He goes with the parson.*]

[PRAED *follows with* MRS WARREN. VIVIE *does not stir, but watches them until they have gone, with all the lines of purpose in her face marking it strongly.*]

FRANK Ain't you coming.

VIVIE No. I want to give you a warning, Frank. You were making fun of my mother just now when you said that about the rectory garden. That is barred in future. Please treat my mother with as much respect as you treat your own.

FRANK My dear Viv: she wouldn't appreciate it. She's not like my mother: the same treatment wouldn't do for both cases. But what on earth has happened to you? Last night we were perfectly agreed as to your mother and her set. This morning I find you attitudinizing sentimentally with your arm round your parent's waist.

VIVIE [*Flushing.*]   Attitudinizing!

FRANK   That was how it struck me. First time I ever saw you do a second-rate thing.

VIVIE [*Controlling herself.*]   Yes, Frank: there has been a change; but I don't think it a change for the worse. Yesterday I was a little prig.

FRANK   And to-day?

VIVIE [*Wincing; then looking at him steadily.*]   To-day I know my mother better than you do.

FRANK   Heaven forbid!

VIVIE   What do you mean?

FRANK   Viv; there's a freemasonry among thoroughly immoral people that you know nothing of. You've too much character. That's the bond between your mother and me: that's why I know her better than you'll ever know her.

VIVIE   You are wrong: you know nothing about her. If you knew the circumstances against which my mother had to struggle—

FRANK [*Adroitly finishing the sentence for her.*]   I should know why she is what she is, shouldn't I? What difference would that make? Circumstances or no circumstances, Viv, you won't be able to stand your mother.

VIVIE [*Very angry.*]   Why not?

FRANK   Because she's an old wretch, Viv. If you ever put your arm round her waist in my presence again, I'll shoot myself there and then as a protest against an exhibition which revolts me.

VIVIE   Must I choose between dropping your acquaintance and dropping my mother's?

FRANK [*Gracefully.*]   That would put the old lady at ever such a disadvantage. No, Viv: your infatuated little boy will have to stick to you in any case. But he's all the more anxious that you shouldn't make mistakes. It's no use, Viv: your mother's impossible. She may be a good sort; but she's a bad lot, a very bad lot.

VIVIE [*Hotly.*]   Frank—! [*He stands his ground. She turns away and sits down on the bench under the yew tree, struggling to recover her self-command. Then she says*] Is she to be deserted by all the world because she's what you call a bad lot? Has she no right to live?

FRANK   No fear of that, Viv: s h e won't ever be deserted. [*He sits on the bench beside her.*]

VIVIE   But I am to desert her, I suppose.

FRANK [*Babyishly, lulling her and making love to her with his voice.*]   Mustn't go live with her. Little family group of mother and daughter wouldn't be a success. Spoil our little group.

VIVIE [*Falling under the spell.*]   What little group?

FRANK   The babes in the wood: Vivie and little Frank. [*He slips his arm round her waist and nestles against her like a weary child.*] Let's go and get covered up with leaves.

VIVIE [*Rhythmically, rocking him like a nurse.*] Fast asleep, hand in hand, under the trees.

FRANK The wise little girl with her silly little boy.

VIVIE The dear little boy with his dowdy little girl.

FRANK Ever so peaceful, and relieved from the imbecility of the little boy's father and the questionableness of the little girl's—

VIVIE [*Smothering the word against her breast.*] Sh-sh-sh-sh! little girl wants to forget all about her mother. [*They are silent for some moments, rocking one another. Then* VIVIE *wakes up with a shock, exclaiming.*] What a pair of fools we are! Come: sit up. Gracious! your hair. [*She smooths it.*] I wonder do all grown-up people play in that childish way when nobody is looking. I never did it when I was a child.

FRANK Neither did I. You are my first playmate. [*He catches her hand to kiss it, but checks himself to look round first. Very unexpectedly he sees* CROFTS *emerging from the box hedge.*] Oh, damn!

VIVIE Why damn, dear?

FRANK [*Whispering.*] Sh! Here's this brute Crofts. [*He sits farther away from her with an unconcerned air.*]

VIVIE Don't be rude to him, Frank. I particularly wish to be polite to him. It will please my mother. [FRANK *makes a wry face.*]

CROFTS Could I have a few words with you, Miss Vivie?

VIVIE Certainly.

CROFTS [*To* FRANK.] You'll excuse me, Gardner. They're waiting for you in the church, if you don't mind.

FRANK [*Rising.*] Anything to oblige you, Crofts—except church. If you want anything, Vivie, ring the gate bell, and a domestic will appear. [*He goes into the house with unruffled suavity.*]

CROFTS [*Watching him with a crafty air as he disappears, and speaking to* VIVIE *with an assumption of being on privileged terms with her.*] Pleasant young fellow that, Miss Vivie. Pity he has no money, isn't it?

VIVIE Do you think so?

CROFTS Well, what's he to do? No profession, no property. What's he good for?

VIVIE I realize his disadvantages, Sir George.

CROFTS [*A little taken aback at being so precisely interpreted.*] Oh, it's not that. But while we're in this world we're in it; and money's money. [VIVIE *does not answer.*] Nice day, isn't it?

VIVIE [*With scarcely veiled contempt for this effort at conversation.*] Very.

CROFTS [*With brutal good humor, as if he liked her pluck.*] Well, that's not what I came to say. [*Affecting frankness.*] Now listen, Miss Vivie. I'm quite aware that I'm not a young lady's man.

VIVIE Indeed, Sir George?

CROFTS No; and to tell you the honest truth, I don't want to be either. But when I say a thing I mean it; when I feel sentiment I feel it in earnest; and what I value I pay hard money for. That's the sort of man I am.

VIVIE   It does you great credit, I'm sure.

CROFTS   Oh, I don't mean to praise myself. I have my faults, Heaven knows: no man is more sensible of that than I am. I know I'm not perfect: that's one of the advantages of being a middle-aged man; for I'm not a young man, and I know it. But my code is a simple one, and, I think, a good one. Honor between man and man; fidelity between man and woman; and no cant about this religion, or that religion, but an honest belief that things are making for good on the whole.

VIVIE [*With biting irony.*]   "A power, not ourselves, that makes for righteousness," eh?

CROFTS [*Taking her seriously.*]   Oh, certainly, not ourselves, of course. You understand what I mean. [*He sits down beside her; as one who has found a kindred spirit.*] Well, now as to practical matters. You may have an idea that I've flung my money about; but I haven't: I'm richer to-day than when I first came into the property. I've used my knowledge of the world to invest my money in ways that other men have overlooked; and whatever else I may be, I'm a safe man from the money point of view.

VIVIE   It's very kind of you to tell me all this.

CROFTS   Oh, well, come, Miss Vivie: you needn't pretend you don't see what I'm driving at. I want to settle down with a Lady Crofts. I suppose you think me very blunt, eh?

VIVIE   Not at all: I am much obliged to you for being so definite and business-like. I quite appreciate the offer: the money, the position, Lady Crofts, and so on. But I think I will say no, if you don't mind. I'd rather not. [*She rises, and strolls across to the sundial to get out of his immediate neighborhood.*]

CROFTS [*Not at all discouraged, and taking advantage of the additional room left him on the seat to spread himself comfortably, as if a few preliminary refusals were part of the inevitable routine of courtship.*]   I'm in no hurry. It was only just to let you know in case young Gardner should try to trap you. Leave the question open.

VIVIE [*Sharply.*]   My no is final. I won't go back from it. [*She looks authoritatively at him. He grins; leans forward with his elbows on his knees to prod with his stick at some unfortunate insect in the grass; and looks cunningly at her. She turns away impatiently.*]

CROFTS   I'm a good deal older than you—twenty-five years—quarter of a century. I shan't live for ever; and I'll take care that you shall be well off when I'm gone.

VIVIE   I am proof against even that inducement, Sir George. Don't you think you'd better take your answer? There is not the slightest chance of my altering it.

CROFTS [*Rising, after a final slash at a daisy, and beginning to walk to and fro.*]   Well, no matter. I could tell you some things that would change your mind fast enough; but I won't, because I'd rather win you by honest affection. I was a good friend to your mother: ask her whether I wasn't. She'd never have made the money that paid for your education if it hadn't been for my advice and help, not to mention the money I advanced her. There are not many men would have stood by her as I have. I put not less than £40,000[1] into it, from first to last.

VIVIE [*Staring at him.*]   Do you mean to say you were my mother's business partner?

CROFTS   Yes. Now just think of all the trouble and the explanations it would save if we were to keep the whole thing in the family, so to speak. Ask your mother whether she'd like to have to explain all her affairs to a perfect stranger.

VIVIE   I see no difficulty, since I understand that the business is wound up, and the money invested.

CROFTS [*Stopping short, amazed.*]   Wound up! Wind up a business that's paying 35 per cent in the worst years! Not likely. Who told you that?

VIVIE [*Her colour quite gone.*]   Do you mean that it is still—? [*She stops abruptly, and puts her hand on the sundial to support herself. Then she gets quickly to the iron chair and sits down.*] What business are you talking about?

CROFTS   Well, the fact is, it's not what would be considered exactly a high-class business in my set—the county set, you know—our set it will be if you think better of my offer. Not that there's any mystery about it: don't think that. Of course you know by your mother's being in it that it's perfectly straight and honest. I've known her for many years; and I can say of her that she'd cut off her hands sooner than touch anything that was not what it ought to be. I'll tell you all about it if you like. I don't know whether you've found in travelling how hard it is to find a really comfortable private hotel.

VIVIE [*Sickened, averting her face.*]   Yes: go on.

CROFTS   Well, that's all it is. Your mother has a genius for managing such things. We've got two in Brussels, one in Berlin, one in Vienna, and two in Buda-Pesth. Of course there are others besides ourselves in it; but we hold most of the capital; and your mother's indispensable as managing director. You've noticed, I daresay, that she travels a good deal. But you see you can't mention such things in society. Once let out the word hotel and everybody says you keep a public-house. You wouldn't like people to say that of your mother, would you? That's why we're so reserved about it. By the bye, you'll keep it to yourself, won't you? Since it's been a secret so long, it had better remain so.

---

1. Worth approximately $60,000.

VIVIE   And this is the business you invite me to join you in?

CROFTS   Oh, no. My wife shan't be troubled with business. You'll not be in it more than you've always been.

VIVIE   *I* always been! What do you mean?

CROFTS   Only that you've always lived on it. It paid for your education and the dress you have on your back. Don't turn up your nose at business, Miss Vivie: where would your Newnhams and Girtons be without it?

VIVIE   [*Rising, almost beside herself.*]   Take care. I know what this business is.

CROFTS   [*Starting, with a suppressed oath.*]   Who told you?

VIVIE   Your partner—my mother.

CROFTS   [*Black with rage.*]   The old— [VIVIE *looks quickly at him. He swallows the epithet and stands swearing and raging foully to himself. But he knows that his cue is to be sympathetic. He takes refuge in generous indignation.*] She ought to have had more consideration for you. *I'd* never have told you.

VIVIE   I think you would probably have told me when we were married: it would have been a convenient weapon to break me in with.

CROFTS   [*Quite sincerely.*]   I never intended that. On my word as a gentleman I didn't.

  [VIVIE *wonders at him. Her sense of the irony of his protest cools and braces her. She replies with contemptuous self-possession.*]

VIVIE   It does not matter. I suppose you understand that when we leave here to-day our acquaintance ceases.

CROFTS   Why? Is it for helping your mother?

VIVIE   My mother was a very poor woman who had no reasonable choice but to do as she did. You were a rich gentleman; and you did the same for the sake of 35 per cent. You are a pretty common sort of scoundrel, I think. That is my opinion of you.

CROFTS   [*After a stare—not at all displeased, and much more at his ease on these frank terms than on their former ceremonious ones.*]   Ha, ha, ha, ha! Go it, little missie, go it: it doesn't hurt me and it amuses you. Why the devil shouldn't I invest my money that way? I take the interest on my capital like other people: I hope you don't think I dirty my own hands with the work. Come: you wouldn't refuse the acquaintance of my mother's cousin, the Duke of Belgravia, because some of the rents he gets are earned in queer ways. You wouldn't cut the Archbishop of Canterbury, I suppose, because the Ecclesiastical Commissioners have a few publicans and sinners among their tenants? Do you remember your Crofts scholarship at Newnham? Well, that was founded by my brother the M.P. He gets his 22 per cent out of a factory with 600 girls in it, and not one of them getting wages enough to live on. How d'ye suppose most of them manage? Ask your mother. And do you expect me to turn my back on 35 per cent when all the rest are pocketing what they can, like sensible men? No such fool! If you're going to pick and choose your acquaintances on moral principles, you'd better clear out of this country, unless you want to cut yourself out of all decent society.

VIVIE [*Conscience-stricken.*]   You might go on to point out that I myself never asked where the money I spent came from. I believe I am just as bad as you.

CROFTS [*Greatly reassured.*]   Of course you are; and a very good thing, too! What harm does it do after all? [*Rallying her jocularly.*] So you don't think me such a scoundrel now you come to think it over. Eh?

VIVIE   I have shared profits with you; and I admitted you just now to the familiarity of knowing what I think of you.

CROFTS [*With serious friendliness.*]   To be sure you did. You won't find me a bad sort: I don't go in for being superfine intellectually; but I've plenty of honest human feeling; and the old Crofts breed comes out in a sort of instinctive hatred of anything low, in which I'm sure you'll sympathize with me. Believe me, Miss Vivie, the world isn't such a bad place as the croakers make out. So long as you don't fly openly in the face of society, society doesn't ask any inconvenient questions; and it makes precious short work of the cads who do. There are no secrets better kept than the secrets that everybody guesses. In the society I can introduce you to, no lady or gentleman would so far forget themselves as to discuss my business affairs or your mother's. No man can offer you a safer position.

VIVIE [*Studying him curiously.*]   I suppose you really think you're getting on famously with me.

CROFTS   Well, I hope I may flatter myself that you think better of me than you did at first.

VIVIE [*Quietly.*]   I hardly find you worth thinking about at all now. [*She rises and turns towards the gate, pausing on her way to contemplate him and say almost gently, but with intense conviction*] When I think of the society that tolerates you, and the laws that protect you—when I think of how helpless nine out of ten young girls would be in the hands of you and my mother—the unmentionable woman and her capitalist bully—

CROFTS [*Livid.*]   Damn you!

VIVIE   You need not. I feel among the damned already.

[*She raises the latch of the gate to open it and go out. He follows her and puts his hand heavily on the top bar to prevent its opening.*]

CROFTS [*Panting with fury.*]   Do you think I'll put up with this from you, you young devil, you?

VIVIE [*Unmoved.*]   Be quiet. Some one will answer the bell. [*Without flinching a step she strikes the bell with the back of her hand. It clangs harshly; and he starts back involuntarily. Almost immediately* FRANK *appears at the porch with his rifle.*]

FRANK [*With cheerful politeness.*]   Will you have the rifle, Viv; or shall I operate?

VIVIE   Frank: have you been listening?

FRANK   Only for the bell, I assure you; so that you shouldn't have to wait. I think I showed great insight into your character, Crofts.

CROFTS   For two pins I'd take that gun from you and break it across your head.

FRANK [*Stalking him cautiously.*]   Pray don't. I'm ever so careless in handling firearms. Sure to be a fatal accident, with a reprimand from the coroner's jury for my negligence.

VIVIE   Put the rifle away, Frank: it's quite unnecessary.

FRANK   Quite right, Viv. Much more sportsmanlike to catch him in a trap. [CROFTS, *understanding the insult, makes a threatening movement.*] Crofts: there are fifteen cartridges in the magazine here; and I am a dead shot at the present distance at an object of your size.

CROFTS   Oh, you needn't be afraid. I'm not going to touch you.

FRANK   Ever so magnanimous of you under the circumstances! Thank you.

CROFTS   I'll just tell you this before I go. It may interest you, since you're so fond of one another. Allow me, Mister Frank, to introduce you to your half-sister, the eldest daughter of the Reverend Samuel Gardner. Miss Vivie: your half-brother. Good morning. [*He goes out through the gate and along the road.*]

FRANK [*After a pause of stupefaction, raising the rifle.*]   You'll testify before the coroner that it's an accident, Viv. [*He takes aim at the retreating figure of* CROFTS. VIVIE *seizes the muzzle and pulls it round against her breast.*]

VIVIE   Fire now. You may.

FRANK [*Dropping his end of the rifle hastily.*]   Stop! take care. [*She lets it go. It falls on the turf.*] Oh, you've given your little boy such a turn. Suppose it had gone off—ugh! [*He sinks on the garden seat, overcome.*]

VIVIE   Suppose it had: do you think it would not have been a relief to have some sharp physical pain tearing through me?

FRANK [*Coaxingly.*]   Take it ever so easy, dear Viv. Remember: even if the rifle scared that fellow into telling the truth for the first time in his life, that only makes us the babes in the wood in earnest. [*He holds out his arms to her.*] Come and be covered up with leaves again.

VIVIE [*With a cry of disgust.*]   Ah, not that, not that. You make all my flesh creep.

FRANK   Why, what's the matter?

VIVIE   Good-bye. [*She makes for the gate.*]

FRANK [*Jumping up.*]   Hallo! Stop! Viv! Viv! [*She turns in the gateway.*] Where are you going to? Where shall we find you?

VIVIE   At Honoria Fraser's chambers, 67 Chancery Lane, for the rest of my life. [*She goes off quickly in the opposite direction to that taken by* CROFTS.]

FRANK   But I say—wait—dash it! [*He runs after her.*]

Act IV

Honoria Fraser's chambers in Chancery Lane. An office at the top of New Stone Buildings, with a plate-glass window, distempered walls, electric light, and a patent stove. Saturday afternoon. The chimneys of Lincoln's Inn and the western sky beyond are seen through the window. There is a double writing table in the middle of the room, with a cigar box, ash pans, and a portable electric reading lamp almost snowed up in heaps of papers and books. This table has knee holes and chairs right and left and is very untidy. The clerk's desk, closed and tidy, with its high stool, is against the wall, near a door communicating with the inner rooms. In the opposite wall is the door leading to the public corridor. Its upper panel is of opaque glass, lettered in black on the outside, "Fraser and Warren." A baize screen hides the corner between this door and the window.

FRANK, in a fashionable light-colored coaching suit, with his stick, gloves, and white hat in his hands, is pacing up and down the office. Somebody tries the door with a key.

FRANK [*Calling.*]   Come in. It's not locked.

[VIVIE *comes in, in her hat and jacket. She stops and stares at him.*]

VIVIE [*Sternly.*]   What are you doing here?

FRANK   Waiting to see you. I've been here for hours. Is this the way you attend to your business? [*He puts his hat and stick on the table, and perches himself with a vault on the clerk's stool, looking at her with every appearance of being in a specially restless, teasing, flippant mood.*]

VIVIE   I've been away exactly twenty minutes for a cup of tea. [*She takes off her hat and jacket and hangs them up behind the screen.*] How did you get in?

FRANK   The staff had not left when I arrived. He's gone to play football on Primrose Hill. Why don't you employ a woman, and give your sex a chance?

VIVIE   What have you come for?

FRANK [*Springing off the stool and coming close to her.*]   Viv: let's go and enjoy the Saturday half-holiday somewhere, like the staff.

What do you say to Richmond,[1] and then a music hall, and a jolly
supper?

VIVIE   Can't afford it. I shall put in another six hours' work before
I go to bed.

FRANK   Can't afford it, can't we? Aha! Look here. [*He takes out a
handful of sovereigns*[2] *and makes them chink.*] Gold, Viv, gold!

VIVIE   Where did you get it?

FRANK   Gambling, Viv, gambling. Poker.

VIVIE   Pah! It's meaner than stealing it. No: I'm not coming. [*She
sits down to work at the table, with her back to the glass door, and
begins turning over the papers.*]

FRANK [*Remonstrating piteously.*]   But, my dear Viv, I want to talk
to you ever so seriously.

VIVIE   Very well: sit down in Honoria's chair and talk here. I like
ten minutes' chat after tea. [*He murmurs.*] No use groaning: I'm
inexorable. [*He takes the opposite seat disconsolately.*] Pass that
cigar box, will you?

FRANK [*Pushing the cigar box across.*]   Nasty womanly habit. Nice
men don't do it any longer.

VIVIE   Yes: they object to the smell in the office; and we've had to
take to cigarets. See! [*She opens the box and takes out a cigaret,
which she lights. She offers him one; but he shakes his head with a
wry face. She settles herself comfortably in her chair, smoking.*] Go
ahead.

FRANK   Well, I want to know what you've done—what arrangements
you've made.

VIVIE   Everything was settled twenty minutes after I arrived here.
Honoria has found the business too much for her this year; and
she was on the point of sending for me and proposing a partnership
when I walked in and told her I hadn't a farthing[3] in the world. So
I installed myself and packed her off for a fortnight's holiday. What
happened at Haslemere when I left?

FRANK   Nothing at all. I said you'd gone to town on particular business.

VIVIE   Well?

FRANK   Well, either they were too flabbergasted to say anything, or
else Crofts had prepared your mother. Anyhow, she didn't say anything; and Crofts didn't say anything; and Praddy only stared. After
tea they got up and went; and I've not seen them since.

VIVIE [*Nodding placidly with one eye on a wreath of smoke.*]   That's
all right.

FRANK [*Looking round disparagingly.*]   Do you intend to stick in this
confounded place?

VIVIE [*Blowing the wreath decisively away and sitting straight*

---

1. A leafy suburban area on the outskirts of London.
2. Gold coins worth £1 (approximately $1.50).
3. A coin worth 1/4d; less than 1c.

up.]   Yes. These two days have given me back all my strength and self-possession. I will never take a holiday again as long as I live.

FRANK [*With a very wry face.*]   Mps! You look quite happy—and as hard as nails.

VIVIE [*Grimly.*]   Well for me that I am!

FRANK [*Rising.*]   Look here, Viv: we must have an explanation. We parted the other day under a complete misunderstanding.

VIVIE [*Putting away the cigaret.*]   Well: clear it up.

FRANK   You remember what Crofts said?

VIVIE   Yes.

FRANK   That revelation was supposed to bring about a complete change in the nature of our feeling for one another. It placed us on the footing of brother and sister.

VIVIE   Yes.

FRANK   Have you ever had a brother?

VIVIE   No.

FRANK   Then you don't know what being brother and sister feels like? Now I have lots of sisters: Jessie and Georgina and the rest. The fraternal feeling is quite familiar to me; and I assure you my feeling for you is not the least in the world like it. The girls will go their way; I will go mine; and we shan't care if we never see one another again. That's brother and sister. But as to you, I can't be easy if I have to pass a week without seeing you. That's not brother and sister. It's exactly what I felt an hour before Crofts made his revelation. In short, dear Viv, it's love's young dream.

VIVIE [*Bitingly.*]   The same feeling, Frank, that brought your father to my mother's feet. Is that it?

FRANK [*Revolted.*]   I very strongly object, Viv, to have my feelings compared to any which the Reverend Samuel is capable of harboring; and I object still more to a comparison of you to your mother. Besides, I don't believe the story. I have taxed my father with it, and obtained from him what I consider tantamount to a denial.

VIVIE   What did he say?

FRANK   He said he was sure there must be some mistake.

VIVIE   Do you believe him?

FRANK   I am prepared to take his word as against Crofts'.

VIVIE   Does it make any difference? I mean in your imagination or conscience; for of course it makes no real difference.

FRANK [*Shaking his head.*]   None whatever to me.

VIVIE   Nor to me.

FRANK [*Staring.*]   But this is ever so surprising! I thought our whole relations were altered in your imagination and conscience, as you put it, the moment those words were out of that brute's muzzle.

VIVIE   No: it was not that. I didn't believe him. I only wish I could.

FRANK   Eh?

VIVIE   I think brother and sister would be a very suitable relation
for us.

FRANK   You really mean that?

VIVIE   Yes. It's the only relation I care for, even if we could afford
any other. I mean that.

FRANK   [*Raising his eyebrows like one on whom a new light has
dawned, and speaking with quite an effusion of chivalrous sentiment.*]   My dear Viv: why didn't you say so before? I am ever so
sorry for persecuting you. I understand, of course.

VIVIE   [*Puzzled.*]   Understand what?

FRANK   Oh, I'm not a fool in the ordinary sense—only in the Scrip-
tural sense of doing all the things the wise man declared to be
folly, after trying them himself on the most extensive scale. I see
I am no longer Vivvums' little boy. Don't be alarmed: I shall never
call you Vivvums again—at least unless you get tired of your new
little boy, whoever he may be.

VIVIE   My new little boy!

FRANK   [*With conviction.*]   Must be a new little boy. Always happens
that way. No other way, in fact.

VIVIE   None that you know of, fortunately for you. [*Someone knocks
at the door.*]

FRANK   My curse upon yon caller, whoe'er he be!

VIVIE   It's Praed. He's going to Italy and wants to say good-bye. I
asked him to call this afternoon. Go and let him in.

FRANK   We can continue our conversation after his departure for
Italy. I'll stay him out. [*He goes to the door and opens it.*] How are
you, Praddy? Delighted to see you. Come in. [PRAED, *dressed for
travelling, comes in, in high spirits, excited by the beginning of his
journey.*]

PRAED   How do you do, Miss Warren. [*She presses his hand cordially, though a certain sentimentality in his high spirits jars on her.*]
I start in an hour from Holborn Viaduct. I wish I could persuade
you to try Italy.

VIVIE   What for?

PRAED   Why, to saturate yourself with beauty and romance, of
course.

> [VIVIE, *with a shudder, turns her chair to the table, as if the
> work waiting for her there were a consolation and support to
> her.* PRAED *sits opposite to her.* FRANK *places a chair just behind
> VIVIE, and drops lazily and carelessly into it, talking at her over
> his shoulder.*]

FRANK   No use, Praddy. Viv is a little Philistine. She is indifferent
to my romance, and insensible to my beauty.

VIVIE   Mr Praed: once for all, there is no beauty and no romance in
life for me. Life is what it is; and I am prepared to take it as it
is.

PRAED   [*Enthusiastically.*]   You will not say that if you come to

Verona and on to Venice. You will cry with delight at living in such a beautiful world.

FRANK   This is most eloquent, Praddy. Keep it up.

PRAED   Oh, I assure you *I* have cried—I shall cry again, I hope—at fifty! At your age, Miss Warren, you would not need to go so far as Verona. Your spirits would absolutely fly up at the mere sight of Ostend. You would be charmed with the gaiety, the vivacity, the happy air of Brussels. [VIVIE *recoils.*] What's the matter?

FRANK   Hallo, Viv!

VIVIE [*To* PRAED *with deep reproach.*]   Can you find no better example of your beauty and romance than Brussels to talk to me about?

PRAED [*Puzzled.*]   Of course it's very different from Verona. I don't suggest for a moment that—

VIVIE [*Bitterly.*]   Probably the beauty and romance come to much the same in both places.

PRAED [*Completely sobered and much concerned.*]   My dear Miss Warren: I—[*Looking enquiringly at* FRANK] Is anything the matter?

FRANK   She thinks your enthusiasm frivolous, Praddy. She's had ever such a serious call.

VIVIE [*Sharply.*]   Hold your tongue, Frank. Don't be silly.

FRANK [*Calmly.*]   Do you call this good manners, Praed?

PRAED [*Anxious and considerate.*]   Shall I take him away, Miss Warren? I feel sure we have disturbed you at your work. [*He is about to rise.*]

VIVIE   Sit down: I'm not ready to go back to work yet. You both think I have an attack of nerves. Not a bit of it. But there are two subjects I want dropped, if you don't mind. One of them [*to* FRANK] is love's young dream in any shape or form: the other [*to* PRAED] is the romance and beauty of life, especially as exemplified by the gaiety of Brussels. You are welcome to any illusions you may have left to these subjects: I have none. If we three are to remain friends, I must be treated as a woman of business, permanently single [*to* FRANK] and permanently unromantic [*to* PRAED].

FRANK   I also shall remain permanently single until you change your mind. Praddy: change the subject. Be eloquent about something else.

PRAED [*Diffidently.*]   I'm afraid there's nothing else in the world that I can talk about. The Gospel of Art is the only one I can preach. I know Miss Warren is a great devotee of the Gospel of Getting On; but we can't discuss that without hurting your feelings, Frank, since you are determined not to get on.

FRANK   Oh, don't mind my feelings. Give me some improving advice by all means; it does me ever so much good. Have another try to make a successful man of me, Viv. Come: let's have it all: energy, thrift, foresight, self-respect, character. Don't you hate people who have no character, Viv?

VIVIE [*Wincing.*]   Oh, stop: stop: let us have no more of that horrible cant. Mr Praed: if there are really only those two gospels in the world, we had better all kill ourselves; for the same taint is in both, through and through.

FRANK [*Looking critically at her.*]   There is a touch of poetry about you to-day, Viv, which has hitherto been lacking.

PRAED [*Remonstrating.*]   My dear Frank: aren't you a little unsympathetic?

VIVIE [*Merciless to herself.*]   No: it's good for me. It keeps me from being sentimental.

FRANK [*Bantering her.*]   Checks your strong natural propensity that way, don't it?

VIVIE [*Almost hysterically.*]   Oh, yes: go on: don't spare me. I was sentimental for one moment in my life—beautifully sentimental—by moonlight; and now—

FRANK [*Quickly.*]   I say, Viv: take care. Don't give yourself away.

VIVIE   Oh, do you think Mr Praed does not know all about my mother? [*Turning on* PRAED.] You had better have told me that morning, Mr Praed. You are very old-fashioned in your delicacies, after all.

PRAED   Surely it is you who are a little old-fashioned in your prejudices, Miss Warren. I feel bound to tell you, speaking as an artist, and believing that the most intimate human relationships are far beyond and above the scope of the law, that though I know that your mother is an unmarried woman, I do not respect her the less on that account. I respect her more.

FRANK [*Airily.*]   Hear, hear!

VIVIE [*Staring at him.*]   Is that all you know?

PRAED   Certainly that is all.

VIVIE   Then you neither of you know anything. Your guesses are innocence itself compared to the truth.

PRAED [*Startled and indignant, preserving his politeness with an effort.*]   I hope not. [*More emphatically.*] I hope not, Miss Warren. [FRANK's *face shows that he does not share* PRAED's *incredulity.* VIVIE *utters an exclamation of impatience.* PRAED's *chivalry droops before their conviction. He adds, slowly*] If there is anything worse—that is, anything else—are you sure you are right to tell us, Miss Warren?

VIVIE   I am sure that if I had the courage I should spend the rest of my life in telling it to everybody—in stamping and branding it into them until they felt their share in its shame and horror as I feel mine. There is nothing I despise more than the wicked convention that protects these things by forbidding a woman to mention them. And yet I can't tell you. The two infamous words that describe what my mother is are ringing in my ears and struggling on my tongue; but I can't utter them: my instinct is too strong for me. [*She buries her face in her hands. The two men, astonished, stare at one another and then at her. She raises her head again desperately and takes a sheet of paper and a pen.*] Here: let me draft you a prospectus.

FRANK   Oh, she's mad. Do you hear, Viv, mad. Come: pull yourself together.

VIVIE   You shall see. [*She writes.*] "Paid up capital: not less than £40,000 standing in the name of Sir George Crofts, Baronet, the chief shareholder." What comes next?—I forget. Oh, yes: "Premises at Brussels, Berlin, Vienna and Buda-Pesth. Managing director: Mrs Warren"; and now don't let us forget her qualifications: the two words. There! [*She pushes the paper to them.*] Oh, no: don't read it: don't!

> [*She snatches it back and tears it to pieces; then seizes her head in her hands and hides her face on the table.* FRANK, *who has watched the writing carefully over her shoulder, and opened his eyes very widely at it, takes a card from his pocket; scribbles a couple of words; and silently hands it to* PRAED, *who looks at it with amazement.* FRANK *then remorsefully stoops over* VIVIE.]

FRANK [*Whispering tenderly.*]   Viv, dear: that's all right. I read what you wrote: so did Praddy. We understand. And we remain, as this leaves us at present, yours ever so devotedly. [VIVIE *slowly raises her head.*]

PRAED   We do, indeed, Miss Warren. I declare you are the most splendidly courageous woman I ever met.

> [*This sentimental compliment braces* VIVIE. *She throws it away from her with an impatient shake, and forces herself to stand up, though not without some support from the table.*]

FRANK   Don't stir, Viv, if you don't want to. Take it easy.

VIVIE   Thank you. You can always depend on me for two things, not to cry and not to faint. [*She moves a few steps towards the door of the inner rooms, and stops close to* PRAED *to say*] I shall need much more courage than that when I tell my mother that we have come to the parting of the ways. Now I must go into the next room for a moment to make myself neat again, if you don't mind.

PRAED   Shall we go away?

VIVIE   No: I'll be back presently. Only for a moment. [*She goes into the other room,* PRAED *opening the door for her.*]

PRAED   What an amazing revelation! I'm extremely disappointed in Crofts: I am indeed.

FRANK   I'm not in the least. I feel he's perfectly accounted for at last. But what a facer for me, Praddy! I can't marry her now.

PRAED [*Sternly.*]   Frank! [*The two look at one another,* FRANK *unruffled,* PRAED *deeply indignant.*] Let me tell you, Gardner, that if you desert her now you will behave very despicably.

FRANK   Good old Praddy! Ever chivalrous! But you mistake: it's not the moral aspect of the case: it's the money aspect. I really can't bring myself to touch the old woman's money now?

PRAED   And was that what you were going to marry on?

FRANK   What else? *I* haven't any money, nor the smallest turn for making it. If I married Viv now she would have to support me; and I should cost her more than I am worth.

PRAED   But surely a clever, bright fellow like you can make something by your own brains.

FRANK   Oh, yes, a little. [*He takes out his money again.*] I made all that yesterday—in an hour and a half. But I made it in a highly speculative business. No, dear Praddy: even if Jessie and Georgina marry millionaires and the governor dies after cutting them off with a shilling,[4] I shall have only four hundred a year. And he won't die until he's three score and ten: he hasn't originality enough. I shall be on short allowance for the next twenty years. No short allowance for Viv, if I can help it. I withdraw gracefully and leave the field to the gilded youth of England. So that's settled. I shan't worry her about it: I'll just send her a little note after we're gone. She'll understand.

PRAED   [*Grasping his hand.*]   Good fellow, Frank! I heartily beg your pardon. But must you never see her again?

FRANK   Never see her again! Hang it all, be reasonable. I shall come along as often as possible, and be her brother. I cannot understand the absurd consequences you romantic people expect from the most ordinary transactions. [*A knock at the door.*] I wonder who this is. Would you mind opening the door? If it's a client it will look more respectable than if I appeared.

PRAED   Certainly. [*He goes to the door and opens it.* FRANK *sits down in* VIVIE'S *chair to scribble a note.*] My dear Kitty: come in, come in.

[MRS WARREN *comes in, looking apprehensively round for* VIVIE. *She has done her best to make herself matronly and dignified. The brilliant hat is replaced by a sober bonnet, and the gay blouse covered by a costly black silk mantle. She is pitiably anxious and ill at ease—evidently panic-stricken.*]

MRS WARREN   [*To* FRANK.]   What! You're here, are you?

FRANK   [*Turning in his chair from his writing, but not rising.*]   Here, and charmed to see you. You come like a breath of spring.

MRS WARREN   Oh, get out with your nonsense. [*In a low voice.*] Where's Vivie?

[*Frank points expressively to the door of the inner room, but says nothing.*]

MRS WARREN   [*Sitting down suddenly and almost beginning to cry.*]   Praddy: won't she see me, don't you think?

PRAED   My dear Kitty: don't distress yourself. Why should she not?

---

4. A coin worth 12d (1/20 of a pound); about 7c.

MRS WARREN   Oh, you never can see why not: you're too amiable. Mr Frank: did she say anything to you?

FRANK [*Folding his note.*]   She must see you, if [*very expressively*] you wait until she comes in.

MRS WARREN [*Frightened.*]   Why shouldn't I wait?

[FRANK *looks quizzically at her; puts his note carefully on the ink-bottle, so that* VIVIE *cannot fail to find it when next she dips her pen; then rises and devotes his attention entirely to her.*]

FRANK   My dear Mrs Warren: suppose you were a sparrow—ever so tiny and pretty a sparrow hopping in the roadway—and you saw a steam roller coming in your direction, would you wait for it?

MRS WARREN   Oh, don't bother me with your sparrows. What did she run away from Haslemere like that for?

FRANK   I'm afraid she'll tell you if you wait until she comes back.

MRS WARREN   Do you want me to go away?

FRANK   No. I always want you to stay. But I advise you to go away.

MRS WARREN   What! And never see her again!

FRANK   Precisely.

MRS WARREN [*Crying again.*]   Praddy: don't let him be cruel to me. [*She hastily checks her tears and wipes her eyes.*] She'll be so angry if she sees I've been crying.

FRANK [*With a touch of a real compassion in his airy tenderness.*]   You know that Praddy is the soul of kindness, Mrs Warren. Praddy: what do you say? Go or stay?

PRAED [*To* MRS WARREN.]   I really should be very sorry to cause you unnecessary pain; but I think perhaps you had better not wait. The fact is— [VIVIE *is heard at the inner door.*]

FRANK   Sh! Too late. She's coming.

MRS WARREN   Don't tell her I was crying. [VIVIE *comes in. She stops gravely on seeing* MRS WARREN, *who greets her with hysterical cheerfulness.*] Well, dearie. So here you are at last.

VIVIE   I am glad you have come: I want to speak to you. You said you were going, Frank, I think.

FRANK   Yes. Will you come with me, Mrs Warren? What do you say to a trip to Richmond, and the theatre in the evening? There is safety in Richmond. No steam roller there.

VIVIE   Nonsense, Frank. My mother will stay here.

MRS WARREN [*Scared.*]   I don't know: perhaps I'd better go. We're disturbing you at your work.

VIVIE [*With quiet decision.*]   Mr Praed: please take Frank away. Sit down, mother. [MRS WARREN *obeys helplessly.*]

PRAED   Come, Frank. Good-bye, Miss Vivie.

VIVIE [*Shaking hands.*]   Good-bye. A pleasant trip.

PRAED   Thank you: thank you. I hope so.

FRANK [*To* MRS WARREN.]   Good-bye: you'd ever so much better have taken my advice. [*He shakes hands with her. Then airily to* VIVIE.] Bye-bye, Viv.

VIVIE   Good-bye.

> [*He goes out gaily without shaking hands with her.* PRAED *follows.* VIVIE, *composed and extremely grave, sits down in Honoria's chair, and waits for her mother to speak.* MRS WARREN, *dreading a pause, loses no time in beginning.*]

MRS WARREN   Well, Vivie, what did you go away like that for without saying a word to me? How could you do such a thing! And what have you done to poor George? I wanted him to come with me; but he shuffled out of it. I could see that he was quite afraid of you. Only fancy: he wanted me not to come. As if [*trembling*] I should be afraid of you, dearie. [VIVIE'S *gravity deepens.*] But of course I told him it was all settled and comfortable between us, and that we were on the best of terms. [*She breaks down.*] Vivie: what's the meaning of this? [*She produces a paper from an envelope; comes to the table; and hands it across.*] I got it from the bank this morning.

VIVIE   It is my month's allowance. They sent it to me as usual the other day. I simply sent it back to be placed to your credit, and asked them to send you the lodgment receipt. In future I shall support myself.

MRS WARREN [*Not daring to understand.*]   Wasn't it enough? Why didn't you tell me? [*With a cunning gleam in her eye.*] I'll double it: I was intending to double it. Only let me know how much you want.

VIVIE   You know very well that that has nothing to do with it. From this time I go my own way in my own business and among my own friends. And you will go yours. [*She rises.*] Good-bye.

MRS WARREN [*Appalled.*]   Good-bye?

VIVIE   Yes: good-bye. Come: don't let us make a useless scene: you understand perfectly well. Sir George Crofts has told me the whole business.

MRS WARREN [*Angrily.*]   Silly old— [*She swallows an epithet, and turns white at the narrowness of her escape from uttering it.*] He ought to have his tongue cut out. But I explained it all to you; and you said you didn't mind.

VIVIE [*Steadfastly.*]   Excuse me: I do mind. You explained how it came about. That does not alter it.

> [MRS WARREN, *silenced for a moment, looks forlornly at* VIVIE, *who waits like a statue, secretly hoping that the combat is over. But the cunning expression comes back into* MRS WARREN's *face; and she bends across the table, sly and urgent, half whispering.*]

MRS WARREN   Vivie: do you know how rich I am?

VIVIE   I have no doubt you are very rich.

MRS WARREN   But you don't know all that that means: you're too young. It means a new dress every day; it means theatres and balls every night; it means having the pick of all the gentlemen in Europe at your feet; it means a lovely house and plenty of servants; it means the choicest of eating and drinking; it means everything you like, everything you want, everything you can think of. And what are you here? A mere drudge, toiling and moiling early and late for your bare living and two cheap dresses a year. Think over it. [*Soothingly.*] You're shocked, I know. I can enter into your feelings; and I think they do you credit; but trust me, nobody will blame you: you may take my word for that. I know what young girls are; and I know you'll think better of it when you've turned it over in your mind.

VIVIE   So that's how it's done, is it? You must have said all that to many a woman, mother, to have it so pat.

MRS WARREN [*Passionately.*]   What harm am I asking you to do? [VIVIE *turns away contemptuously.* MRS WARREN *follows her desperately.*] Vivie: listen to me: you don't understand: you've been taught wrong on purpose: you don't know what the world is really like.

VIVIE [*Arrested.*]   Taught wrong on purpose! What do you mean?

MRS WARREN   I mean that you're throwing away all your chances for nothing. You think that people are what they pretend to be—that the way you were taught at school and college to think right and proper is the way things really are. But it's not: it's all only a pretence, to keep the cowardly, slavish, common run of people quiet. Do you want to find that out, like other women, at forty, when you've thrown yourself away and lost your chances; or won't you take it in good time now from your own mother, that loves you and swears to you that it's truth—gospel truth? [*Urgently.*] Vivie: the big people, the clever people, the managing people, all know it. They do as I do, and think what I think. I know plenty of them. I know them to speak to, to introduce you to, to make friends of for you. I don't mean anything wrong: that's what you don't understand: your head is full of ignorant ideas about me. What do the people that taught you know about life or about people like me? When did they ever meet me, or speak to me, or let anyone tell them about me?—the fools! Would they ever have done anything for you if I hadn't paid them? Haven't I told you that I want you to be respectable? Haven't I brought you up to be respectable? And how can you keep it up without my money and my influence and Lizzie's friends? Can't you see that you're cutting your own throat as well as breaking my heart in turning your back on me?

VIVIE   I recognise the Crofts philosophy of life, mother. I heard it all from him that day at the Gardners'.

MRS WARREN   You think I want to force that played-out old sot on you! I don't, Vivie: on my oath I don't.

VIVIE   It would not matter if you did: you would not succeed. [MRS

WARREN *winces, deeply hurt by the implied indifference towards her affectionate intention.* VIVIE, *neither understanding this nor concerning herself about it, goes on calmly.*] Mother: you don't at all know the sort of person I am. I don't object to Crofts more than to any other coarsely built man of his class. To tell you the truth, I rather admire him for being strong-minded enough to enjoy himself in his own way and make plenty of money instead of living the usual shooting, hunting, dining-out, tailoring, loafing life of his set merely because all the rest do it. And I'm perfectly aware that if I'd been in the same circumstances as my aunt Liz, I'd have done exactly what she did. I don't think I'm more prejudiced or strait-laced than you: I think I'm less. I'm certain I'm less sentimental. I know very well that fashionable morality is all a pretence: and that if I took your money and devoted the rest of my life to spending it fashionably, I might be as worthless and vicious as the silliest woman could possibly want to be without having a word said to me about it. But I don't want to be worthless. I shouldn't enjoy trotting about the park to advertise my dressmaker and carriage builder, or being bored at the opera to show off a shop windowful of diamonds.

MRS WARREN [*Bewildered.*]   But—

VIVIE   Wait a moment: I've not done. Tell me why you continue your business now that you are independent of it. Your sister, you told me, has left all that behind her. Why don't you do the same?

MRS WARREN   Oh, it's all very easy for Liz: she likes good society, and has the air of being a lady. Imagine me in a cathedral town! Why, the very rooks in the trees would find me out even if I could stand the dulness of it. I must have work and excitement, or I should go melancholy mad. And what else is there for me to do? The life suits me: I'm fit for it and not for anything else. If I didn't do it, somebody else would; so I don't do any real harm by it. And then it brings in money; and I like making money. No: it's no use: I can't give it up—not for anybody. But what need you know about it? I'll never mention it. I'll keep Crofts away. I'll not trouble you much: you see I have to be constantly running about from one place to another. You'll be quit of me altogether when I die.

VIVIE   No: I am my mother's daughter. I am like you: I must have work, and must make more money than I spend. But my work is not your work, and my way not your way. We must part. It will not make much difference to us: instead of meeting one another for perhaps a few months in twenty years, we shall never meet: that's all.

MRS WARREN [*Her voice stifled in tears.*]   Vivie: I meant to have been more with you: I did indeed.

VIVIE   It's no use, mother: I am not to be changed by a few cheap tears and entreaties any more than you are, I dare say.

MRS WARREN [*Wildly.*]   Oh, you call a mother's tears cheap.

VIVIE   They cost you nothing; and you ask me to give you the peace and quietness of my whole life in exchange for them. What use would my company be to you if you could get it? What have we two in common that could make either of us happy together?

MRS WARREN [*Lapsing recklessly into her dialect.*]   We're mother and daughter. I want my daughter. I've a right to you. Who is to care for me when I'm old? Plenty of girls have taken to me like daughters and cried at leaving me; but I let them all go because I had you to look forward to. I kept myself lonely for you. You've no right to turn on me now and refuse to do your duty as a daughter.

VIVIE [*Jarred and antagonized by the echo of the slums in her mother's voice.*]   My duty as a daughter! I thought we should come to that presently. Now once for all, mother, you want a daughter and Frank wants a wife. I don't want a mother; and I don't want a husband. I have spared neither Frank nor myself in sending him about his business. Do you think I will spare you?

MRS WARREN [*Violently.*]   Oh, I know the sort you are—no mercy for yourself or anyone else. *I* know. My experience has done that for me anyhow: I can tell the pious, canting, hard, selfish woman when I meet her. Well, keep yourself to yourself: *I* don't want you. But listen to this. Do you know what I would do with you if you were a baby again—aye, as sure as there's a Heaven above us?

VIVIE   Strangle me, perhaps.

MRS WARREN   No: I'd bring you up to be a real daughter to me, and not what you are now, with your pride and your prejudices and the college education you stole from me—yes, stole: deny it if you can: what was it but stealing? I'd bring you up in my own house, so I would.

VIVIE [*Quietly.*]   In one of your own houses.

MRS WARREN [*Screaming.*]   Listen to her! listen to how she spits on her mother's grey hairs! Oh, may you live to have your own daughter tear and trample on you as you have trampled on me. And you will: you will. No woman ever had luck with a mother's curse on her.

VIVIE   I wish you wouldn't rant, mother. It only hardens me. Come: I suppose I am the only young woman you ever had in your power that you did good to. Don't spoil it all now.

MRS WARREN   Yes. Heaven forgive me, it's true; and you are the only one that ever turned on me. Oh, the injustice of it, the injustice, the injustice! I always wanted to be a good woman. I tried honest work; and I was slave-driven until I cursed the day I ever heard of honest work. I was a good mother; and because I made my daughter a good woman she turns me out as if I was a leper. Oh, if I only had my life to live over again! I'd talk to that lying clergyman in the school. From this time forth, so help me Heaven in my last hour, I'll do wrong and nothing but wrong. And I'll prosper on it.

VIVIE   Yes: it's better to choose your line and go through with it. If

I had been you, mother, I might have done as you did; but I should not have lived one life and believed in another. You are a conventional woman at heart. That is why I am bidding you good-bye now. I am right, am I not?

MRS WARREN [*Taken aback.*]   Right to throw away all my money!

VIVIE   No: right to get rid of you? I should be a fool not to? Isn't that so?

MRS WARREN [*Sulkily.*]   Oh, well, yes, if you come to that, I suppose you are. But Lord help the world if everybody took to doing the right thing! And now I'd better go than stay where I'm not wanted. [*She turns to the door.*]

VIVIE [*Kindly.*]   Won't you shake hands?

MRS WARREN [*After looking at her fiercely for a moment with a savage impulse to strike her.*]   No, thank you. Good-bye.

VIVIE [*Matter-of-factly.*]   Good-bye. [MRS WARREN *goes out, slamming the door behind her. The strain on* VIVIE'S *face relaxes; her grave expression breaks up into one of joyous content; her breath goes out in a half sob, half laugh of intense relief. She goes buoyantly to her place at the writing-table; pushes the electric lamp out of the way; pulls over a great sheaf of papers; and is in the act of dipping her pen in the ink when she finds* FRANK'S *note. She opens it unconcernedly and reads it quickly, giving a little laugh at some quaint turn of expression in it.*] And good-bye, Frank. [*She tears the note up and tosses the pieces into the wastepaper basket without a second thought. Then she goes at her work with a plunge, and soon becomes absorbed in her figures.*]

Man and Superman[†]

To Arthur Bingham Walkley

My dear Walkley

You once asked me why I did not write a Don Juan play. The levity with which you assumed this frightful responsibility has probably by this time enabled you to forget it; but the day of reckoning has arrived: here is your play! I say your play, because qui facit per alium facit per se.[1] Its profits, like its labor, belong to me: its morals, its manners, its philosophy, its influence on the young, are for you to justify. You were of mature age when you made the suggestion; and you knew your man. It is hardly fifteen years since, as twin pioneers of the New Journalism of that time, we two, cradled in the same new sheets, began an epoch in the criticism of the theatre and the opera house by making it the pretext for a propaganda of our own views of life. So you cannot plead ignorance of the character of the force you set in motion. You meant me to épater le bourgeois;[2] and if he protests, I hereby refer him to you as the accountable party.

I warn you that if you attempt to repudiate your responsibility, I shall suspect you of finding the play too decorous for your taste. The fifteen years have made me older and graver. In you I can detect no such becoming change. Your levities and audacities are like the loves and comforts prayed for by Desdemona: they increase, even as your days do grow. No mere pioneering journal dares meddle with them now: the stately *Times* itself is alone sufficiently above suspicion to act as your chaperone; and even the *Times* must sometimes thank its stars that new plays are not produced every day, since after each such event its gravity is compromised, its platitude turned to epigram, its portentousness to wit, its propriety to elegance, and even its decorum

---

[†] The title comes from the philosopher Friedrich William Nietzsche's distinction between man and superman (Übermensch); the superman would impose his will upon the weak. See also *Sprach Zarathustra* (Thus Spoke Zarathustra) (1883–92). Shaw was influenced by Nietzsche's ideas, but also drew upon Richard Wagner's Siegfried, an archetypal hero whom he connected to the idea of the "life force." Discussion of the life force in *Man and Superman* articulates a major Shavian theme: that man is the spiritual creator, whereas woman is the biological life force which will always, because it must, triumph over him.
1. A legal principle: that which one does through an agent, one does oneself.
2. French: shock the middle class.

into naughtiness by criticisms which the traditions of the paper do not allow you to sign at the end, but which you take care to sign with the most extravagant flourishes between the lines. I am not sure that this is not a portent of Revolution. In eighteenth-century France the end was at hand when men bought the Encyclopedia and found Diderot there. When I buy the *Times* and find you there, my prophetic ear catches a rattle of twentieth century tumbrils.

However, that is not my present anxiety. The question is, will you not be disappointed with a Don Juan play in which not one of that hero's *mille e tre*[3] adventures is brought upon the stage? To propitiate you, let me explain myself. You will retort that I never do anything else: it is your favorite jibe at me that what I call drama is nothing but explanation. But you must not expect me to adopt your inexplicable, fantastic, petulant, fastidious ways: you must take me as I am, a reasonable, patient, consistent, apologetic, laborious person, with the temperament of a schoolmaster and the pursuits of a vestryman. No doubt that literary knack of mine which happens to amuse the British public distracts attention from my character; but the character is there none the less, solid as bricks. I have a conscience; and conscience is always anxiously explanatory. You, on the contrary, feel that a man who discusses his conscience is much like a woman who discusses her modesty. The only moral force you condescend to parade is the force of your wit: the only demand you make in public is the demand of your artistic temperament for symmetry, elegance, style, grace, refinement, and the cleanliness which comes next to godliness if not before it. But my conscience is the genuine pulpit article: it annoys me to see people comfortable when they ought to be uncomfortable; and I insist on making them think in order to bring them to conviction of sin. If you dont like my preaching you must lump it. I really cannot help it.

In the preface to my *Plays for Puritans* I explained the predicament of our contemporary English drama, forced to deal almost exclusively with cases of sexual attraction, and yet forbidden to exhibit the incidents of that attraction or even to discuss its nature. Your suggestion that I should write a Don Juan play was virtually a challenge to me to treat this subject myself dramatically. The challenge was difficult enough to be worth accepting, because, when you come to think of it, though we have plenty of dramas with heroes and heroines who are in love and must accordingly marry or perish at the end of the play, or about people whose relations with one another have been complicated by the marriage laws, not to mention the looser sort of plays which trade on the tradition that illicit love affairs are at once vicious and delightful, we have no modern English plays in which

3. A thousand and three (according to tradition, the number of women seduced by Don Juan).

the natural attraction of the sexes for one another is made the main-spring of the action. That is why we insist on beauty in our performers, differing herein from the countries our friend William Archer holds up as examples of seriousness to our childish theatres. There the Juliets and Isoldes, the Romeos and Tristans, might be our mothers and fathers. Not so the English actress. The heroine she impersonates is not allowed to discuss the elemental relations of men and women: all her romantic twaddle about novelet-made love, all her purely legal dilemmas as to whether she was married or "betrayed," quite miss our hearts and worry our minds. To console ourselves we must just look at her. We do so; and her beauty feeds our starving emotions. Sometimes we grumble ungallantly at the lady because she does not act as well as she looks. But in a drama which, with all its preoccupation with sex, is really void of sexual interest, good looks are more desired than histrionic skill.

Let me press this point on you, since you are too clever to raise the fool's cry of paradox whenever I take hold of a stick by the right instead of the wrong end. Why are our occasional attempts to deal with the sex problem on the stage so repulsive and dreary that even those who are most determined that sex questions shall be held open and their discussion kept free, cannot pretend to relish these joyless attempts at social sanitation? Is it not because at bottom they are utterly sexless? What is the usual formula for such plays? A woman has, on some past occasion, been brought into conflict with the law which regulates the relations of the sexes. A man, by falling in love with her, or marrying her, is brought into conflict with the social convention which discountenances the woman. Now the conflicts of individuals with law and convention can be dramatized like all other human conflicts; but they are purely judicial; and the fact that we are much more curious about the suppressed relations between the man and the woman than about the relations between both and our courts of law and private juries of matrons, produces that sensation of evasion, of dissatisfaction, of fundamental irrelevance, of shallowness, of useless disagreeableness, of total failure to edify and partial failure to interest, which is as familiar to you in the theatres as it was to me when I, too, frequented those uncomfortable buildings, and found our popular playwrights in the mind to (as they thought) emulate Ibsen.

I take it that when you asked me for a Don Juan play you did not want that sort of thing. Nobody does: the successes such plays sometimes obtain are due to the incidental conventional melodrama with which the experienced popular author instinctively saves himself from failure. But what did you want? Owing to your unfortunate habit—you now, I hope, feel its inconvenience—of not explaining yourself, I have had to discover this for myself. First, then, I have had to ask myself, what is a Don Juan? Vulgarly, a libertine. But your dislike of vulgarity is pushed to the length of a defect (universality of character is impossible without a share of vulgarity); and even if you could acquire the taste, you would find yourself overfed from ordinary sources without troubling me. So I took it that you demanded a Don Juan in the philosophic sense.

Philosophically, Don Juan is a man who, though gifted enough to be exceptionally capable of distinguishing between good and evil, follows his own instincts without regard to the common, statute, or canon law; and therefore, whilst gaining the ardent sympathy of our rebellious instincts (which are flattered by the brilliances with which Don Juan associates them) finds himself in mortal conflict with existing institutions, and defends himself by fraud and force as unscrupulously as a farmer defends his crops by the same means against vermin. The prototypic Don Juan, invented early in the XVI century by a Spanish monk, was presented, according to the ideas of that time, as the enemy of God, the approach of whose vengeance is felt throughout the drama, growing in menace from minute to minute. No anxiety is caused on Don Juan's account by any minor antagonist: he easily eludes the police, temporal and spiritual; and when an indignant father seeks private redress with the sword, Don Juan kills him without an effort. Not until the slain father returns from heaven as the agent of God, in the form of his own statue, does he prevail against his slayer and cast him into hell. The moral is a monkish one: repent and reform now; for tomorrow it may be too late. This is really the only point on which Don Juan is sceptical; for he is a devout believer in an ultimate hell, and risks damnation only because, as he is young, it seems so far off that repentance can be postponed until he has amused himself to his heart's content.

But the lesson intended by an author is hardly ever the lesson the world chooses to learn from his book.

*   *   *

Now it is all very well for you at the beginning of the XX century to ask me for a Don Juan play; but you will see from the foregoing survey that Don Juan is a full century out of date for you and for me; and if there are millions of less literate people who are still in the eighteenth century, have they not Molière and Mozart, upon whose art no human hand can improve? * * *

* * * Man is no longer, like Don Juan, victor in the duel of sex. Whether he has ever really been may be doubted: at all events the enormous superiority of Woman's natural position in this matter is telling with greater and greater force. As to pulling the Nonconformist Conscience by the beard as Don Juan plucked the beard of the Commandant's statue in the convent of San Francisco, that is out

of the question nowadays: prudence and good manners alike forbid
it to a hero with any mind. Besides, it is Don Juan's own beard that
is in danger of plucking. Far from relapsing into hypocrisy, as Sgan-
arelle[4] feared, he has unexpectedly discovered a moral in his immorality. The growing recognition of his new point of view is heaping
responsibility on him. His former jests he has had to take as seriously
as I have had to take some of the jests of Mr W. S. Gilbert.[5] His
scepticism, once his least tolerated quality, has now triumphed so
completely that he can no longer assert himself by witty negations,
and must, to save himself from cipherdom, find an affirmative position. His thousand and three affairs of gallantry, after becoming, at
most, two immature intrigues leading to sordid and prolonged complications and humiliations, have been discarded altogether as
unworthy of his philosophic dignity and compromising to his newly
acknowledged position as the founder of a school. Instead of pretending to read Ovid he does actually read Schopenhaur and Nietzsche, studies Westermarck, and is concerned for the future of the
race instead of for the freedom of his own instincts.[6] Thus his prof-
ligacy and his dare-devil airs have gone the way of his sword and
mandoline into the rag shop of anachronisms and superstitions. In
fact, he is now more Hamlet than Don Juan; for though the lines
put into the actor's mouth to indicate to the pit that Hamlet is a
philosopher are for the most part mere harmonious platitude which,
with a little debasement of the word-music, would be properer to
Pecksniff,[7] yet if you separate the real hero, inarticulate and unintelligible to himself except in flashes of inspiration, from the performer who has to talk at any cost through five acts; and if you also
do what you must always do in Shakespear's tragedies: that is, dissect
out the absurd sensational incidents and physical violence of the
borrowed story from the genuine Shakespearian tissue, you will get
a true Promethean foe of the gods, whose instinctive attitude towards
women much resembles that to which Don Juan is now driven. From
this point of view Hamlet was a developed Don Juan whom Shakespear palmed off as a reputable man just as he palmed poor Macbeth off as a murderer. To-day the palming off is no longer necessary
(at least on your plane and mine) because Don Juanism is no longer
misunderstood as mere Casanovism. Don Juan himself is almost
ascetic in his desire to avoid that misunderstanding; and so my
attempt to bring him up to date by launching him as a modern Englishman into a modern English environment has produced a figure
superficially quite unlike the hero of Mozart.

4. Don Juan's pusillanimous servant.
5. Gilbert and his associate Sullivan produced some of the most popular and successful
   comic operettas of the nineteenth century.
6. I.e., he reads serious philosophical works.
7. Unctuous and hypocritical architect in Charles Dickens's *Martin Chuzzlewit* (1844).

And yet I have not the heart to disappoint you wholly of another glimpse of the Mozartian *dissoluto punito* and his antagonist the statue. I feel sure you would like to know more of that statue—to draw him out when he is off duty, so to speak. To gratify you, I have resorted to the trick of the strolling theatrical manager who advertizes the pantomime of *Sinbad the Sailor* with a stock of second-hand picture posters designed for *Ali Baba*. He simply thrusts a few oil jars into the valley of diamonds, and so fulfils the promise held out by the hoardings to the public eye. I have adapted this easy device to our occasion by thrusting into my perfectly modern three-act play a totally extraneous act in which my hero, enchanted by the air of the Sierra, has a dream in which his Mozartian ancestor appears and philosophizes at great length in a Shavio-Socratic dialogue with the lady, the statue, and the devil.

But this pleasantry is not the essence of the play. Over this essence I have no control. You propound a certain social substance, sexual attraction to wit, for dramatic distillation; and I distil it for you. I do not adulterate the product with aphrodisiacs nor dilute it with romance and water; for I am merely executing your commission, not producing a popular play for the market. You must therefore (unless, like most wise men, you read the play first and the preface afterwards) prepare yourself to face a trumpery story of modern London life, a life in which, as you know, the ordinary man's main business is to get means to keep up the position and habits of a gentleman, and the ordinary woman's business is to get married. In 9,999 cases out of 10,000, you can count on their doing nothing, whether noble or base, that conflicts with these ends; and that assurance is what you rely on as their religion, their morality, their principles, their patriotism, their reputation, their honor and so forth.

On the whole, this is a sensible and satisfactory foundation for society. Money means nourishment and marriage means children; and that men should put nourishment first and women [and] children first is, broadly speaking, the law of Nature and not the dictate of personal ambition. The secret of the prosaic man's success, such as it is, is the simplicity with which he pursues these ends: the secret of the artistic man's failure, such as that is, is the versatility with which he strays in all directions after secondary ideals. The artist is either a poet or a scallawag: as poet, he cannot see, as the prosaic man does, that chivalry is at bottom only romantic suicide: as scallawag, he cannot see that it does not pay to spunge and beg and lie and brag and neglect his person. Therefore do not misunderstand my plain statement of the fundamental constitution of London society as an Irishman's reproach to your nation. From the day I first set foot on this foreign soil I knew the value of the prosaic qualities of which Irishmen teach Englishmen to be ashamed as well as I knew the vanity of the poetic qualities of which Englishmen teach Irishmen to be proud. For the Irishman instinctively disparages the quality which makes the Englishman dangerous to him; and the Englishman instinctively flatters the fault that makes the Irishman harmless and amusing to him. What is wrong with the prosaic Englishman is what is wrong with the prosaic men of all countries: stupidity. The vitality which places nourishment and children first, heaven and hell a somewhat remote second, and the health of society as an organic whole nowhere, may muddle successfully through the comparatively tribal stages of gregariousness; but in nineteenth century nations and twentieth century empires the determination of every man to be rich at all costs, and of every woman to be married at all costs, must, without a highly scientific social organization, produce a ruinous development of poverty, celibacy, prostitution, infant mortality, adult degeneracy, and everything that wise men most dread. In short, there is no future for men, however brimming with crude vitality, who are neither intelligent nor politically educated enough to be Socialists. So do not misunderstand me in the other direction either: if I appreciate the vital qualities of the Englishman as I appreciate the vital qualities of the bee, I do not guarantee the Englishman against being, like the bee (or the Canaanite) smoked out and unloaded of his honey by beings inferior to himself in simple acquisitiveness, combativeness, and fecundity, but superior to him in imagination and cunning.

The Don Juan play, however, is to deal with sexual attraction, and not with nutrition, and to deal with it in a society in which the serious business of sex is left by men to women, as the serious business of nutrition is left by women to men. That the men, to protect themselves against a too aggressive prosecution of the women's business, have set up a feeble romantic convention that the initiative in sex business must always come from the man, is true; but the pretence is so shallow that even in the theatre, that last sanctuary of unreality, it imposes only on the inexperienced. In Shakespear's plays the woman always takes the initiative. In his problem plays and his popular plays alike the love interest is the interest of seeing the woman hunt the man down. * * * I find in my own plays that Woman, projecting herself dramatically by my hands (a process over which I assure you I have no more real control than I have over my wife), behaves just as Woman did in the plays of Shakespear.

And so your Don Juan has come to birth as a stage projection of the tragi-comic love chase of the man by the woman; and my Don Juan is the quarry instead of the huntsman. Yet he is a true Don Juan, with a sense of reality that disables convention, defying to the last the fate which finally overtakes him. The woman's need of him to enable her to carry on Nature's most urgent work, does not prevail against him until his resistance gathers her energy to a climax at which she dares to throw away her customary exploitations of the conventional affectionate and dutiful poses, and claim him by natural right for a purpose that far transcends their mortal personal purposes.

Among the friends to whom I have read this play in manuscript are some of our own sex who are shocked at the "unscrupulousness," meaning the total disregard of masculine fastidiousness, with which the woman pursues her purpose. It does not occur to them that if women were as fastidious as men, morally or physically, there would be an end of the race. Is there anything meaner than to throw necessary work upon other people and then disparage it as unworthy and indelicate. We laugh at the haughty American nation because it makes the negro clean its boots and then proves the moral and physical inferiority of the negro by the fact that he is a shoeblack; but we ourselves throw the whole drudgery of creation on one sex, and then imply that no female of any womanliness or delicacy would initiate any effort in that direction. There are no limits to male hypocrisy in this matter. No doubt there are moments when man's sexual immunities are made acutely humiliating to him. When the terrible moment of birth arrives, its supreme importance and its superhuman effort and peril, in which the father has no part, dwarf him into the meanest insignificance: he slinks out of the way of the humblest petticoat, happy if he be poor enough to be pushed out of the house to outface his ignominy by drunken rejoicings. But when the crisis is over he takes his revenge, swaggering as the breadwinner, and speaking of Woman's "sphere" with condescension, even with chivalry, as if the kitchen and the nursery were less important than the office in the city. When his swagger is exhausted he drivels into erotic poetry or sentimental uxoriousness; and the Tennysonian King Arthur posing at Guinevere becomes Don Quixote grovelling before Dulcinea. You must admit that here Nature beats Comedy out of the field: the wildest hominist or feminist farce is insipid after the most commonplace "slice of life." The pretence that woman do not take the initiative is part of the farce. Why, the whole world is strewn with snares, traps, gins and pitfalls for the capture of men by women. Give women the vote, and in five years there will be a crushing tax on bachelors. Men, on the other hand, attach penalties to marriage, depriving women of property, of the franchise, of the free use of their limbs, of that ancient symbol of immortality, the right to make oneself at home in the house of God by taking off the hat, of everything that he can force Woman to dispense with without compelling himself to dispense with her. All in vain. Woman must marry because the race must perish without her travail: if the risk of death and the certainty of pain, danger and unutterable discomforts cannot deter her, slavery and swaddled ankles will not. And yet we assume that the force that carries women through all these perils and hardships, stops abashed before the primnesses of our behavior for young ladies. It is assumed that the woman must wait, motionless, until she is wooed. Nay, she often does wait motionless. That is how the spider waits for the fly. But the spider spins her web. And if the fly, like my hero, shews a strength that promises to extricate him, how swiftly does she abandon her pretence of passiveness, and openly fling coil about him until he is secured for ever!

If the really impressive books and other art-works of the world were produced by ordinary men, they would express more fear of women's pursuit than love of their illusory beauty. But ordinary men cannot produce really impressive art-works. Those who can are men of genius: that is, men selected by Nature to carry on the work of building up an intellectual consciousness of her own instinctive purpose. Accordingly, we observe in the man of genius all the unscrupulousness and all the "self-sacrifice" (the two things are the same) of Woman. He will risk the stake and the cross; starve, when necessary, in a garret all his life; study women and live on their work and care as Darwin studied worms and lived upon sheep; work his nerves into rags without payment, a sublime altruist in his disregard of himself, an atrocious egotist in his disregard of others. Here Woman meets a purpose as impersonal, as irresistible as her own; and the clash is sometimes tragic. When it is complicated by the genius being a woman, then the game is one for a king of critics: your George Sand becomes a mother to gain experience for the novelist and to develop her, and gobbles up men of genius, Chopins, Mussets and the like, as mere hors d'œuvres.

I state the extreme case, of course; but what is true of the great man who incarnates the philosophic consciousness of Life and the woman who incarnates its fecundity, is true in some degree of all geniuses and all women. Hence it is that the world's books get written, its pictures painted, its statues modelled, its symphonies composed, by people who are free from the otherwise universal dominion of the tyranny of sex. Which leads us to the conclusion, astonishing to the vulgar, that art, instead of being before all things the expression of the normal sexual situation, is really the only department in which sex is a superseded and secondary power, with its consciousness so confused and its purpose so perverted, that its ideas are mere fantasy to common men. Whether the artist becomes poet or philosopher, moralist or founder of a religion, his sexual doctrine is nothing but a barren special pleading for pleasure, excitement, and knowledge when he is young, and for contemplative tranquillity when he is old and satiated. Romance and Asceticism, Amorism and Puritanism are equally unreal in the great Philistine world. The world shewn us in books, whether the books be confessed epics or professed gospels, or in codes, or in political orations, or in philosophic systems, is not the main world at all: it is only the self-consciousness of certain abnormal people who have the specific artistic talent and temperament. A serious matter this for you and me, because the man whose consciousness does not correspond to that of the majority is a madman; and the old habit of worshipping madmen is giving way to the new habit of locking them up. And since what we call education and culture is for the most part nothing but the substitution of reading for experience, of literature for life, of the obsolete fictitious for the contemporary real, education, as you no doubt observed at Oxford, destroys, by supplantation, every mind that is not strong enough to see through the imposture and to use the great Masters of Arts as what they really are and no more: that is, patentees of highly questionable methods of thinking, and manufacturers of highly questionable, and for the majority but half valid representations of life. The schoolboy who uses his Homer to throw at his fellow's head makes perhaps the safest and most rational use of him; and I observe with reassurance that you occasionally do the same, in your prime, with your Aristotle.

*   *   *

But I hear you asking me in alarm whether I have actually put all this tub thumping into a Don Juan comedy. I have not. I have only made my Don Juan a political pamphleteer, and given you his pamphlet in full by way of appendix. You will find it at the end of the book. I am sorry to say that it is a common practice with romancers to announce their hero as a man of extraordinary genius, and then leave his works entirely to the reader's imagination; so that at the end of the book you whisper to yourself ruefully that but for the author's solemn preliminary assurance you should hardly have given the gentleman credit for ordinary good sense. You cannot accuse me of this pitiable barrenness, this feeble evasion. I not only tell you that my hero wrote a revolutionists' handbook: I give you the handbook at full length for your edification if you care to read it. And in that handbook you will find the politics of the sex question as I conceive Don Juan's descendant to understand them. Not that I disclaim the fullest responsibility for his opinions and for those of all my characters, pleasant and unpleasant. They are all right from their several points of view; and their points of view are, for the dramatic moment, mine also. This may puzzle the people who believe that there is such a thing as an absolutely right point of view, usually their own. It may seem to them that nobody who doubts this can be in a state of grace. However that may be, it is certainly true that nobody who agrees with them can possibly be a dramatist, or indeed anything else that turns upon a knowledge of mankind. Hence it has been pointed out that Shakespear had no conscience. Neither have I, in that sense.

* * *

I should make formal acknowledgment to the authors whom I have pillaged in the following pages if I could recollect them all. The theft of the brigand-poetaster from Sir Arthur Conan Doyle is deliberate; and the metamorphosis of Leporello into Enry Straker, motor engineer and New Man, is an intentional dramatic sketch of the contemporary embryo of Mr H. G. Wells's anticipation of the efficient engineering class which will, he hopes, finally sweep the jabberers out of the way of civilization. Mr Barrie has also, whilst I am correcting my proofs, delighted London with a servant who knows more than his masters. The conception of Mendoza Limited I trace back to a certain West Indian colonial secretary, who, at a period when he and I and Mr Sidney Webb were sowing our political wild oats as a sort of Fabian Three Musketeers, without any prevision of the surprising respectability of the crop that followed, recommended Webb, the encyclopedic and inexhaustible, to form himself into a company for the benefit of the shareholders. Octavius I take over unaltered from Mozart; and I hereby authorize any actor who impersonates him, to sing *"Dalla sua pace"* (if he can) at any convenient moment during the representation. Ann was suggested to me by the fifteenth century Dutch morality called Everyman, which Mr William Poel has lately resuscitated so triumphantly. I trust he will work that vein further, and recognize that Elizabethan Renascence fustian is no more bearable after medieval poesy than Scribe after Ibsen. As I sat watching Everyman at the Charterhouse, I said to myself Why not Everywoman? Ann was the result: every woman is not Ann; but Ann is Everywoman.

* * *

Man and Superman

Act I

ROEBUCK RAMSDEN *is in his study, opening the morning's letters. The study, handsomely and solidly furnished, proclaims the man of means. Not a speck of dust is visible: it is clear that there are at least two housemaids and a parlormaid downstairs, and a housekeeper upstairs who does not let them spare elbow-grease. Even the top of* ROEBUCK's *head is polished: on a sunshiny day he could helio-*

*graph his orders to distant camps by merely nodding. In
no other respect, however, does he suggest the military
man. It is in active civil life that men get his broad air of
importance, his dignified expectation of deference, his
determinate mouth disarmed and refined since the hour of
his success by the withdrawal of opposition and the con-
cession of comfort and precedence and power. He is more
than a highly respectable man: he is marked out as a president of highly respectable men, a chairman among directors, an alderman among councillors, a mayor among
aldermen. Four tufts of iron-grey hair, which will soon be
as white as isinglass,[1] and are in other respects not at all
unlike it, grow in two symmetrical pairs above his ears and
at the angles of his spreading jaws. He wears a black frock
coat, a white waistcoat (it is bright spring weather), and
trousers, neither black nor perceptibly blue, of one of those
indefinitely mixed hues which the modern clothier has
produced to harmonize with the religions of respectable
men. He has not been out of doors yet to-day; so he still
wears his slippers, his boots being ready for him on the
hearthrug. Surmising that he has no valet, and seeing that
he has no secretary with a shorthand notebook and a type-
writer, one meditates on how little our great burgess
domesticity has been disturbed by new fashions and methods, or by the enterprise of the railway and hotel companies
which sell you a Saturday to Monday of life at Folkestone
as a real gentleman for two guineas, first class fares both
ways included.*

How old is ROEBUCK? *The question is important on the
threshold of a drama of ideas; for under such circumstances everything depends on whether his adolescence
belonged to the sixties or to the eighties. He was born, as
a matter of fact, in 1839, and was a Unitarian and Free
Trader from his boyhood, and an Evolutionist from the
publication of the* Origin of Species.[2] *Consequently he has
always classed himself as an advanced thinker and fear-
lessly outspoken reformer.*

*Sitting at his writing table, he has on his right the win-
dows giving on Portland Place.[3] Through these, as through
a proscenium, the curious spectator may contemplate his
profile as well as the blinds will permit. On his left is the
inner wall, with a stately bookcase, and the door not quite*

---

1. Derived from the spurgeon, isinglass is a gelatin which sets stiff and white.
2. Charles Darwin's seminal work on evolution and the "survival of the fittest."
3. A respectable area of London.

*in the middle, but somewhat further from him. Against
the wall opposite him are two busts on pillars: one, to his
left, of John Bright; the other, to his right, of Mr Herbert
Spencer. Between them hang an engraved portrait of
Richard Cobden; enlarged photographs of Martineau,
Huxley, and George Eliot; autotypes of allegories by Mr
G. F. Watts (for* ROEBUCK *believes in the fine arts with all
the earnestness of a man who does not understand them),
and an impression of Dupont's engraving of Delaroche's
Beaux Arts hemicycle, representing the great men of all
ages.*[4] *On the wall behind him, above the mantelshelf, is a
family portrait of impenetrable obscurity.*

*A chair stands near the writing table for the convenience
of business visitors. Two other chairs are against the wall
between the busts.*

A PARLORMAID *enters with a visitor's card.* ROEBUCK
takes it, and nods, pleased. Evidently a welcome caller.

RAMSDEN   Shew him up.

[*The* PARLORMAID *goes out and returns with the visitor.*]

THE MAID   Mr Robinson.

[MR ROBINSON *is really an uncommonly nice looking young
fellow. He must, one thinks, be the jeune premier; for it is not
in reason to suppose that a second such attractive male figure
should appear in one story. The slim, shapely frame, the elegant
suit of new mourning, the small head and regular features, the
pretty little moustache, the frank clear eyes, the wholesome
bloom on the youthful complexion, the well brushed glossy hair,
not curly, but of fine texture and good dark color, the arch of
good nature in the eyebrows, the erect forehead and neatly
pointed chin, all announce the man who will love and suffer
later on. And that he will not do so without sympathy is guaranteed by an engaging sincerity and eager modest serviceable-
ness which stamp him as a man of amiable nature. The moment
he appears,* RAMSDEN'S *face expands into fatherly liking and
welcome, an expression which drops into one of decorous grief
as the young man approaches him with sorrow in his face as
well as in his black clothes.* RAMSDEN *seems to know the nature
of the bereavement. As the visitor advances silently to the writing table, the old man rises and shakes his hand across it without a word: a long, affectionate shake which tells the story of a
recent sorrow common to both.*]

4. Roebuck's possessions represent him as a liberal interested in all branches of art. His
name could refer ironically to the character of Roebuck, an impecunious rake, in George
Farquhar's Restoration comedy *Love and a Bottle.*

RAMSDEN [*Concluding the handshake and cheering up*]   Well, well,
Octavius, it's the common lot. We must all face it some day. Sit
down.

> [OCTAVIUS *takes the visitor's chair.* RAMSDEN *replaces himself
> in his own.*]

OCTAVIUS   Yes: we must face it, Mr Ramsden. But I owed him a
great deal. He did everything for me that my father could have
done if he had lived.

RAMSDEN   He had no son of his own, you see.

OCTAVIUS   But he had daughters; and yet he was as good to my sister
as to me. And his death was so sudden! I always intended to thank
him—to let him know that I had not taken all his care of me as a
matter of course, as any boy takes his father's care. But I waited
for an opportunity; and now he is dead—dropped without a
moment's warning. He will never know what I felt. [*He takes out
his handkerchief and cries unaffectedly.*]

RAMSDEN   How do we know that, Octavius? He may know it: we
cannot tell. Come! dont grieve. [OCTAVIUS *masters himself and puts
up his handkerchief.*] Thats right. Now let me tell you something
to console you. The last time I saw him—it was in this very room—
he said to me: "Tavy is a generous lad and the soul of honor; and
when I see how little consideration other men get from their sons,
I realize how much better than a son hes been to me." There!
Doesnt that do you good?

OCTAVIUS   Mr Ramsden: he used to say to me that he had met only
one man in the world who was the soul of honor, and that was
Roebuck Ramsden.

RAMSDEN   Oh, that was his partiality: we were very old friends, you
know. But there was something else he used to say about you. I
wonder whether I ought to tell you or not!

OCTAVIUS   You know best.

RAMSDEN   It was something about his daughter.

OCTAVIUS [*Eagerly*]   About Ann! Oh, do tell me that, Mr Ramsden.

RAMSDEN   Well, he said he was glad, after all, you were not his son,
because he thought that someday Annie and you— [OCTAVIUS
blushes vividly.] Well, perhaps I shouldnt have told you. But he
was in earnest.

OCTAVIUS   Oh, if only I thought I had a chance! You know, Mr
Ramsden, I dont care about money or about what people call position; and I cant bring myself to take an interest in the business of
struggling for them. Well, Ann has a most exquisite nature; but
she is so accustomed to be in the thick of that sort of thing that
she thinks a man's character incomplete if he is not ambitious.
She knows that if she married me she would have to reason herself
out of being ashamed of me for not being a big success of some
kind.

RAMSDEN [*Getting up and planting himself with his back to the fire-*

place] Nonsense, my boy, nonsense! Youre too modest. What does she know about the real value of men at her age? [*More seriously.*] Besides, shes a wonderfully dutiful girl. Her father's wish would be sacred to her. Do you know that since she grew up to years of discretion, I dont believe she has ever once given her own wish as a reason for doing anything or not doing it. It's always "Father wishes me to," or "Mother wouldnt like it." It's really almost a fault in her. I have often told her she must learn to think for herself.

OCTAVIUS [*Shaking his head*]   I couldnt ask her to marry me because her father wished it, Mr Ramsden.

RAMSDEN   Well, perhaps not. No: of course not. I see that. No: you certainly couldnt. But when you win her on your own merits, it will be a great happiness to her to fulfil her father's desire as well as her own. Eh? Come! youll ask her, wont you?

OCTAVIUS [*With sad gaiety*]   At all events I promise you I shall never ask anyone else.

RAMSDEN   Oh, you shant need to. She'll accept you, my boy—although [*Here he suddenly becomes very serious indeed*] you have one great drawback.

OCTAVIUS [*Anxiously*]   What drawback is that, Mr Ramsden? I should rather say which of my many drawbacks?

RAMSDEN   I'll tell you, Octavius. [*He takes from the table a book bound in red cloth.*] I have in my hand a copy of the most infamous, the most scandalous, the most mischievous, the most blackguardly book that ever escaped burning at the hands of the common hangman. I have not read it: I would not soil my mind with such filth; but I have read what the papers say of it. The title is quite enough for me. [*He reads it.*] The Revolutionist's Handbook and Pocket Companion. By John Tanner, M.I.R.C., Member of the Idle Rich Class.

OCTAVIUS [*Smiling*]   But Jack—

RAMSDEN [*Testily*]   For goodness' sake, dont call him Jack under my roof. [*He throws the book violently down on the table. Then, somewhat relieved, he comes past the table to* OCTAVIUS, *and addresses him at close quarters with impressive gravity*] Now, Octavius, I know that my dead friend was right when he said you were a generous lad. I know that this man was your schoolfellow, and that you feel bound to stand by him because there was a boyish friendship between you. But I ask you to consider the altered circumstances. You were treated as a son in my friend's house. You lived there; and your friends could not be turned from the door. This man Tanner was in and out there on your account almost from his childhood. He addresses Annie by her Christian name as freely as you do. Well, while her father was alive, that was her father's business, not mine. This man Tanner was only a boy to him: his opinions were something to be laughed at, like a man's hat on a child's head. But now Tanner is a grown man and Annie a grown woman. And her father is gone. We dont as yet know the exact terms of his will; but he often talked it over with me; and I have no more doubt than I have that youre sitting there that the will appoints me Annie's trustee and guardian. [*Forcibly.*] Now I tell you, once for all, I cant and I wont have Annie placed in such a position that she must, out of regard for you, suffer the intimacy of this fellow Tanner. It's not fair: it's not right: it's not kind. What are you going to do about it?

OCTAVIUS   But Ann herself has told Jack that whatever his opinions are, he will always be welcome because he knew her dear father.

RAMSDEN [*Out of patience*]   That girl's mad about her duty to her parents. [*He starts off like a goaded ox in the direction of John Bright, in whose expression there is no sympathy for him. As he speaks he fumes down to Herbert Spencer, who receives him still more coldly.*] Excuse me, Octavius; but there are limits to social toleration. You know that I am not a bigoted or prejudiced man. You know that I am plain Roebuck Ramsden when other men who have done less have got handles to their names, because I have stood for equality and liberty of conscience while they were truckling to the Church and to the aristocracy. Whitefield and I lost chance after chance through our advanced opinions. But I draw the line at Anarchism and Free Love and that sort of thing. If I am to be Annie's guardian, she will have to learn that she has a duty to me. I wont have it: I will not have it. She must forbid John Tanner the house; and so must you.

   [*The* PARLORMAID *returns.*]

OCTAVIUS   But—

RAMSDEN [*Calling his attention to the servant*]   Ssh! Well?

THE MAID   Mr Tanner wishes to see you, sir.

RAMSDEN   Mr Tanner!

OCTAVIUS   Jack!

RAMSDEN   How dare Mr Tanner call on me! Say I cannot see him.

OCTAVIUS [*Hurt*]   I am sorry you are turning my friend from your door like that.

THE MAID [*Calmly*]   Hes not at the door, sir. Hes upstairs in the drawingroom with Miss Ramsden. He came with Mrs Whitefield and Miss Ann and Miss Robinson, sir.

   [RAMSDEN'*s feelings are beyond words.*]

OCTAVIUS [*Grinning*]   Thats very like Jack, Mr Ramsden. You must see him, even if it's only to turn him out.

RAMSDEN [*Hammering out his words with suppressed fury*]   Go upstairs and ask Mr Tanner to be good enough to step down here. [*The* PARLORMAID *goes out; and* RAMSDEN *returns to the fireplace, as to a fortified position.*] I must say that of all the confounded pieces of impertinence—well, if these are Anarchist manners, I hope you like them. And Annie with him! Annie! A— [*He chokes.*]

OCTAVIUS   Yes: thats what surprises me. Hes so desperately afraid
of Ann. There must be something the matter.

[MR JOHN TANNER *suddenly opens the door and enters. He is
too young to be described simply as a big man with a beard. But
it is already plain that middle life will find him in that category.
He has still some of the slimness of youth; but youthfulness is
not the effect he aims at: his frock coat would befit a prime
minister; and a certain high chested carriage of the shoulders,
a lofty pose of the head, and the Olympian majesty with which
a mane, or rather a huge wisp, of hazel colored hair is thrown
back from an imposing brow, suggest Jupiter rather than
Apollo. He is prodigiously fluent of speech, restless, excitable
(mark the snorting nostril and the restless blue eye, just the
thirty-secondth of an inch too wide open), possibly a little mad.
He is carefully dressed, not from the vanity that cannot resist
finery, but from a sense of the importance of everything he does
which leads him to make as much of paying a call as other men
do of getting married or laying a foundation stone. A sensitive,
susceptible, exaggerative, earnest man: a megalomaniac, who
would be lost without a sense of humor.*

*Just at present the sense of humor is in abeyance. To say that
he is excited is nothing: all his moods are phases of excitement.
He is now in the panic-stricken phase; and he walks straight
up to* RAMSDEN *as if with the fixed intention of shooting him
on his own hearthrug. But what he pulls from his breast pocket
is not a pistol, but a foolscap document which he thrusts under
the indignant nose of* RAMSDEN *as he exclaims—*]

TANNER   Ramsden: do you know what that is?

RAMSDEN [*Loftily*]   No, sir.

TANNER   It's a copy of Whitefield's will. Ann got it this morning.

RAMSDEN   When you say Ann, you mean, I presume, Miss Whitefield.

TANNER   I mean our Ann, your Ann, Tavy's Ann, and now, Heaven
help me, my Ann!

OCTAVIUS [*Rising, very pale*]   What do you mean?

TANNER   Mean! [*He holds up the will.*] Do you know who is
appointed Ann's guardian by this will?

RAMSDEN [*Coolly*]   I believe I am.

TANNER   You! You and I, man. I! I!! I!!! Both of us! [*He flings the
will down on the writing table.*]

RAMSDEN   You! Impossible.

TANNER   It's only too hideously true. [*He throws himself into* OCTAV-
IUS*'s chair.*] Ramsden: get me out of it somehow. You dont know
Ann as well as I do. She'll commit every crime a respectable
woman can; and she'll justify everyone of them by saying that it
was the wish of her guardians. She'll put everything on us; and we

shall have no more control over her than a couple of mice over a cat.

OCTAVIUS　Jack: I wish you wouldnt talk like that about Ann.

TANNER　This chap's in love with her: that's another complication. Well, she'll either jilt him and say I didnt approve of him, or marry him and say you ordered her to. I tell you, this is the most staggering blow that has ever fallen on a man of my age and temperament.

RAMSDEN　Let me see that will, sir. [*He goes to the writing table and picks it up.*] I cannot believe that my old friend Whitefield would have shewn such a want of confidence in me as to associate me with— [*His countenance falls as he reads.*]

TANNER　It's all my own doing: thats the horrible irony of it. He told me one day that you were to be Ann's guardian; and like a fool I began arguing with him about the folly of leaving a young woman under the control of an old man with obsolete ideas.

RAMSDEN [*Stupended*]　My ideas obsolete!!!!!!!

TANNER　Totally. I had just finished an essay called Down with Government by the Greyhaired; and I was full of arguments and illustrations. I said the proper thing was to combine the experience of an old hand with the vitality of a young one. Hang me if he didnt take me at my word and alter his will—it's dated only a fortnight after that conversation—appointing me as joint guardian with you!

RAMSDEN [*Pale and determined*]　I shall refuse to act.

TANNER　Whats the good of that? Ive been refusing all the way from Richmond; but Ann keeps on saying that of course shes only an orphan; and that she cant expect the people who were glad to come to the house in her father's time to trouble much about her now. Thats the latest game. An orphan! It's like hearing an ironclad talk about being at the mercy of the winds and waves.

OCTAVIUS　This is not fair, Jack. She is an orphan. And you ought to stand by her.

TANNER　Stand by her! What danger is she in? She has the law on her side; she has popular sentiment on her side; she has plenty of money and no conscience. All she wants with me is to load up all her moral responsibilities on me, and do as she likes at the expense of my character. I cant control her; and she can compromise me as much as she likes. I might as well be her husband.

RAMSDEN　You can refuse to accept the guardianship. *I* shall certainly refuse to hold it jointly with you.

TANNER　Yes; and what will she say to that? what does she say to it? Just that her father's wishes are sacred to her, and that she shall always look up to me as her guardian whether I care to face the responsibility or not. Refuse! You might as well refuse to accept the embraces of a boa constrictor when once it gets round your neck.

OCTAVIUS　This sort of talk is not kind to me, Jack.

TANNER [*Rising and going to* OCTAVIUS *to console him, but still lamenting*]   If he wanted a young guardian, why didnt he appoint Tavy?

RAMSDEN   Ah! why indeed?

OCTAVIUS   I will tell you. He sounded me about it; but I refused the trust because I loved her. I had no right to let myself be forced on her as a guardian by her father. He spoke to her about it; and she said I was right. You know I love her, Mr Ramsden; and Jack knows it too. If Jack loved a woman, I would not compare her to a boa constrictor in his presence, however much I might dislike her [*He sits down between the busts and turns his face to the wall.*]

RAMSDEN   I do not believe that Whitefield was in his right senses when he made that will. You have admitted that he made it under your influence.

TANNER   You ought to be pretty well obliged to me for my influence. He leaves you two thousand five hundred for your trouble. He leaves Tavy a dowry for his sister and five thousand for himself.

OCTAVIUS [*His tears flowing afresh*]   Oh, I cant take it. He was too good to us.

TANNER   You wont get it, my boy, if Ramsden upsets the will.

RAMSDEN   Ha! I see. You have got me in a cleft stick.

TANNER   He leaves me nothing but the charge of Ann's morals, on the ground that I have already more money than is good for me. That shews that he had his wits about him, doesnt it?

RAMSDEN [*Grimly*]   I admit that.

OCTAVIUS [*Rising and coming from his refuge by the wall*]   Mr Ramsden: I think you are prejudiced against Jack. He is a man of honor, and incapable of abusing—

TANNER   Dont, Tavy: youll make me ill. I am not a man of honor: I am a man struck down by a dead hand. Tavy: you must marry her after all and take her off my hands. And I had set my heart on saving you from her!

OCTAVIUS   Oh, Jack, you talk of saving me from my highest happiness.

TANNER   Yes, a lifetime of happiness. If it were only the first half hour's happiness, Tavy, I would buy it for you with my last penny. But a lifetime of happiness! No man alive could bear it: it would be hell on earth.

RAMSDEN [*Violently*]   Stuff, sir. Talk sense; or else go and waste someone else's time: I have something better to do than listen to your fooleries [*He positively kicks his way to his table and resumes his seat*].

TANNER   You hear him, Tavy! Not an idea in his head later than eighteensixty. We cant leave Ann with no other guardian to turn to.

RAMSDEN   I am proud of your contempt for my character and opinions, sir. Your own are set forth in that book, I believe.

TANNER [*Eagerly going to the table*]   What! Youve got my book! What do you think of it?

RAMSDEN   Do you suppose I would read such a book, sir?

TANNER   Then why did you buy it?

RAMSDEN   I did not buy it, sir. It has been sent me by some foolish lady who seems to admire your views. I was about to dispose of it when Octavius interrupted me. I shall do so now, with your permission. [*He throws the book into the waste paper basket with such vehemence that* TANNER *recoils under the impression that it is being thrown at his head.*]

TANNER   You have no more manners than I have myself. However, that saves ceremony between us. [*He sits down again.*] What do you intend to do about this will?

OCTAVIUS   May I make a suggestion?

RAMSDEN   Certainly, Octavius.

OCTAVIUS   Arnt we forgetting that Ann herself may have some wishes in this matter?

RAMSDEN   I quite intend that Annie's wishes shall be consulted in every reasonable way. But she is only a woman, and a young and inexperienced woman at that.

TANNER   Ramsden: I begin to pity you.

RAMSDEN [*Hotly*]   I dont want to know how you feel towards me, Mr Tanner.

TANNER   Ann will do just exactly what she likes. And whats more, she'll force us to advise her to do it; and she'll put the blame on us if it turns out badly. So, as Tavy is longing to see her—

OCTAVIUS [*Shyly*]   I am not, Jack.

TANNER   You lie, Tavy: you are. So lets have her down from the drawingroom and ask her what she intends us to do. Off with you, Tavy, and fetch her. [TAVY *turns to go.*] And dont be long; for the strained relations between myself and Ramsden will make the interval rather painful. [RAMSDEN *compresses his lips, but says nothing.*]

OCTAVIUS   Never mind him, Mr Ramsden. He's not serious. [*He goes out.*]

RAMSDEN [*Very deliberately*]   Mr Tanner: you are the most impudent person I have ever met.

TANNER [*Seriously*]   I know it, Ramsden. Yet even I cannot wholly conquer shame. We live in an atmosphere of shame. We are ashamed of everything that is real about us; ashamed of ourselves, of our relatives, of our incomes, of our accents, of our opinions, of our experience, just as we are ashamed of our naked skins. Good Lord, my dear Ramsden, we are ashamed to walk, ashamed to ride in an omnibus, ashamed to hire a hansom instead of keeping a carriage, ashamed of keeping one horse instead of two and a groom-gardener instead of a coachman and footman. The more things a man is ashamed of, the more respectable he is. Why, youre ashamed to buy my book, ashamed to read it: the only thing youre not ashamed of is to judge me for it without having read it; and even that only means that youre ashamed to have heterodox opinions. Look at the effect I produce because my fairy godmother withheld from me this gift of shame. I have every possible virtue that a man can have except—

RAMSDEN   I am glad you think so well of yourself.

TANNER   All you mean by that is that you think I ought to be ashamed of talking about my virtues. You dont mean that I havnt got them: you know perfectly well that I am as sober and honest a citizen as yourself, as truthful personally, and much more truthful politically and morally.

RAMSDEN [*Touched on his most sensitive point*]   I deny that. I will not allow you or any man to treat me as if I were a mere member of the British public. I detest its prejudices; I scorn its narrowness; I demand the right to think for myself. You pose as an advanced man. Let me tell you that I was an advanced man before you were born.

TANNER   I knew it was a long time ago.

RAMSDEN   I am as advanced as ever I was. I defy you to prove that I have ever hauled down the flag. I am more advanced than ever I was. I grow more advanced every day.

TANNER   More advanced in years, Polonius.

RAMSDEN   Polonius! So you are Hamlet, I suppose.

TANNER   No: I am only the most impudent person youve ever met. Thats your notion of a thoroughly bad character. When you want to give me a piece of your mind, you ask yourself, as a just and upright man, what is the worst you can fairly say of me. Thief, liar, forger, adulterer, perjurer, glutton, drunkard? Not one of these names fit me. You have to fall back on my deficiency in shame. Well, I admit it. I even congratulate myself; for if I were ashamed of my real self, I should cut as stupid a figure as any of the rest of you. Cultivate a little impudence, Ramsden; and you will become quite a remarkable man.

RAMSDEN   I have no—

TANNER   You have no desire for that sort of notoriety. Bless you, I knew that answer would come as well as I know that a box of matches will come out of an automatic machine when I put a penny in the slot: you would be ashamed to say anything else.

[*The crushing retort for which* RAMSDEN *has been visibly collecting his forces is lost for ever; for at this point* OCTAVIUS *returns with* MISS ANN WHITEFIELD *and her mother; and* RAMSDEN *springs up and hurries to the door to receive them. Whether* ANN *is good-looking or not depends upon your taste; also and perhaps chiefly on your age and sex. To* OCTAVIUS *she is an enchantingly beautiful woman, in whose presence the world becomes transfigured, and the puny limits of individual*

consciousness are suddenly made infinite by a mystic memory
of the whole life of the race to its beginnings in the east, or even
back to the paradise from which it fell. She is to him the reality
of romance, the inner good sense of nonsense, the unveiling of
his eyes, the freeing of his soul, the abolition of time, place and
circumstance, the etherealization of his blood into rapturous
rivers of the very water of life itself, the revelation of all the
mysteries and the sanctification of all the dogmas. To her
mother she is, to put it as moderately as possible, nothing whatever of the kind. Not that OCTAVIUS's admiration is in any way
ridiculous or discreditable. ANN is a well-formed creature, as
far as that goes; and she is perfectly ladylike, graceful, and
comely, with ensnaring eyes and hair. Besides, instead of making herself an eyesore, like her mother, she has devised a mourning costume of black and violet silk which does honor to her
late father and reveals the family tradition of brave unconven-
tionality by which RAMSDEN sets such store.

But all this is beside the point as an explanation of ANN's
charm. Turn up her nose, give a cast to her eye, replace her
black and violet confection by the apron and feathers of a flower
girl, strike all the aitches out of her speech, and ANN would still
make men dream. Vitality is as common as humanity; but, like
humanity, it sometimes rises to genius; and ANN is one of the
vital geniuses. Not at all, if you please, an oversexed person:
that is a vital defect, not a true excess. She is a perfectly respectable, perfectly self-controlled woman, and looks it; though her
pose is fashionably frank and impulsive. She inspires confidence
as a person who will do nothing she does not mean to do; also
some fear, perhaps, as a woman who will probably do everything
she means to do without taking more account of other people
than may be necessary and what she calls right. In short, what
the weaker of her own sex sometimes call a cat.

Nothing can be more decorous than her entry and her reception by RAMSDEN, whom she kisses. The late Mr Whitefield
would be gratified almost to impatience by the long faces of the
men (except TANNER, who is fidgety), the silent handgrasps, the
sympathetic placing of chairs, the sniffing of the widow, and
the liquid eye of the daughter, whose heart, apparently, will not
let her control her tongue to speech. RAMSDEN and OCTAVIUS
take the two chairs from the wall, and place them for the two
ladies; but ANN comes to TANNER and takes his chair, which he
offers with a brusque gesture, subsequently relieving his irritation by sitting down on the corner of the writing table with
studied indecorum. OCTAVIUS gives MRS WHITEFIELD a chair
next ANN, and himself takes the vacant one which RAMSDEN

has placed under the nose of the effigy of Mr Herbert Spencer.
MRS WHITEFIELD, *by the way, is a little woman, whose faded
flaxen hair looks like straw on an egg. She has an expression of
muddled shrewdness, a squeak of protest in her voice, and an
odd air of continually elbowing away some larger person who
is crushing her into a corner. One guesses her as one of those
women who are conscious of being treated as silly and negligible, and who, without having strength enough to assert themselves effectually, at any rate never submit to their fate. There
is a touch of chivalry in* OCTAVIUS's *scrupulous attention to her,
even whilst his whole soul is absorbed by* ANN.

    RAMSDEN *goes solemnly back to his magisterial seat at the
writing table, ignoring* TANNER, *and opens the proceedings.*]
RAMSDEN   I am sorry, Annie, to force business on you at a sad time
like the present. But your poor dear father's will has raised a very
serious question. You have read it, I believe?
    [ANN *assents with a nod and a catch of her breath, too much
affected to speak.*]
    I must say I am surprised to find Mr Tanner named as joint
guardian and trustee with myself of you and Rhoda. [*A pause. They
all look portentous; but they have nothing to say.* RAMSDEN, *a little
ruffled by the lack of any response, continues*] I dont know that I
can consent to act under such conditions. Mr Tanner has, I understand, some objection also; but I do not profess to understand its
nature: he will no doubt speak for himself. But we are agreed that
we can decide nothing until we know your views. I am afraid I
shall have to ask you to choose between my sole guardianship and
that of Mr Tanner; for I fear it is impossible for us to undertake a
joint arrangement.
ANN [*In a low musical voice*]   Mamma—
MRS WHITEFIELD [*Hastily*]   Now, Ann, I do beg you not to put it on
me. I have no opinion on the subject; and if I had, it would probably not be attended to. I am quite content with whatever you
three think best.
    [TANNER *turns his head and looks fixedly at* RAMSDEN, *who
angrily refuses to receive this mute communication.*]
ANN [*Resuming in the same gentle voice, ignoring her mother's bad
taste*]   Mamma knows that she is not strong enough to bear the
whole responsibility for me and Rhoda without some help and
advice. Rhoda must have a guardian; and though I am older, I do
not think any young unmarried woman should be left quite to her
own guidance. I hope you agree with me, Granny?
TANNER [*Starting*]   Granny! Do you intend to call your guardians
Granny?
ANN   Dont be foolish, Jack. Mr Ramsden has always been Grand-
papa Roebuck to me: I am Granny's Annie; and he is Annie's

Granny. I christened him so when I first learned to speak.

RAMSDEN [*Sarcastically*]   I hope you are satisfied, Mr Tanner. Go on, Annie: I quite agree with you.

ANN   Well, if I am to have a guardian, can I set aside anybody whom my dear father appointed for me?

RAMSDEN [*Biting his lip*]   You approve of your father's choice, then?

ANN   It is not for me to approve or disapprove. I accept it. My father loved me and knew best what was good for me.

RAMSDEN   Of course I understand your feeling, Annie. It is what I should have expected of you; and it does you credit. But it does not settle the question so completely as you think. Let me put a case to you. Suppose you were to discover that I had been guilty of some disgraceful action—that I was not the man your poor dear father took me for! Would you still consider it right that I should be Rhoda's guardian?

ANN   I cant imagine you doing anything disgraceful, Granny.

TANNER [*To* RAMSDEN]   You havnt done anything of the sort, have you?

RAMSDEN [*Indignantly*]   No sir.

MRS WHITEFIELD [*Placidly*]   Well, then, why suppose it?

ANN   You see, Granny, Mamma would not like me to suppose it.

RAMSDEN [*Much perplexed*]   You are both so full of natural and affectionate feeling in these family matters that it is very hard to put the situation fairly before you.

TANNER   Besides, my friend, you are not putting the situation fairly before them.

RAMSDEN [*Sulkily*]   Put it yourself, then.

TANNER   I will. Ann: Ramsden thinks I am not fit to be your guardian; and I quite agree with him. He considers that if your father had read my book, he wouldnt have appointed me. That book is the disgraceful action he has been talking about. He thinks it's your duty for Rhoda's sake to ask him to act alone and to make me withdraw. Say the word; and I will.

ANN   But I havent read your book, Jack.

TANNER [*Diving at the waste-paper basket and fishing the book out for her*]   Then read it at once and decide.

RAMSDEN [*Vehemently*]   If I am to be your guardian, I positively forbid you to read that book, Annie. [*He smites the table with his fist and rises.*]

ANN   Of course not if you dont wish it. [*She puts the book on the table.*]

TANNER   If one guardian is to forbid you to read the other guardian's book, how are we to settle it? Suppose I order you to read it! What about your duty to me?

ANN [*Gently*]   I am sure you would never purposely force me into a painful dilemma, Jack.

RAMSDEN [*Irritably*]   Yes, yes, Annie: this is all very well, and, as I said, quite natural and becoming. But you must make a choice one way or the other. We are as much in a dilemma as you.

ANN   I feel that I am too young, too inexperienced, to decide. My father's wishes are sacred to me.

MRS WHITEFIELD   If you two men wont carry them out I must say it is rather hard that you should put the responsibility on Ann. It seems to me that people are always putting things on other people in this world.

RAMSDEN   I am sorry you take it in that way.

ANN [*Touchingly*]   Do you refuse to accept me as your ward, Granny?

RAMSDEN   No: I never said that. I greatly object to act with Mr Tanner: thats all.

MRS WHITEFIELD   Why? What's the matter with poor Jack?

TANNER   My views are too advanced for him.

RAMSDEN [*Indignantly*]   They are not. I deny it.

ANN   Of course not. What nonsense! Nobody is more advanced than Granny. I am sure it is Jack himself who has made all the difficulty. Come, Jack! be kind to me in my sorrow. You dont refuse to accept me as your ward, do you?

TANNER [*Gloomily*]   No. I let myself in for it; so I suppose I must face it. [*He turns away to the bookcase, and stands there, moodily studying the titles of the volumes.*]

ANN [*Rising and expanding with subdued but gushing delight*]   Then we are all agreed; and my dear father's will is to be carried out. You dont know what a joy that is to me and to my mother! [*She goes to* RAMSDEN *and presses both his hands, saying*] And I shall have my dear Granny to help and advise me. [*She casts a glance at* TANNER *over her shoulder.*] And Jack the Giant Killer. [*She goes past her mother to* OCTAVIUS.] And Jack's inseparable friend Ricky-ticky-tavy [*He blushes and looks inexpressibly foolish*].

MRS WHITEFIELD [*Rising and shaking her widow's weeds straight*]   Now that you are Ann's guardian, Mr Ramsden, I wish you would speak to her about her habit of giving people nicknames. They cant be expected to like it. [*She moves towards the door.*]

ANN   How can you say such a thing, Mamma! [*Glowing with affectionate remorse.*] Oh, I wonder can you be right! Have I been inconsiderate? [*She turns to* OCTAVIUS, *who is sitting astride his chair with his elbows on the back of it. Putting her hand on his forehead she turns his face up suddenly*] Do you want to be treated like a grown up man? Must I call you Mr Robinson in future?

OCTAVIUS [*Earnestly*]   Oh please call me Ricky-ticky-tavy. "Mr Robinson" would hurt me cruelly. [*She laughs and pats his cheek with her finger; then comes back to* RAMSDEN.] You know I'm beginning to think that Granny is rather a piece of impertinence. But I never dreamt of its hurting you.

RAMSDEN [*Breezily, as he pats her affectionately on the back*]   My dear Annie, nonsense. I insist on Granny. I wont answer to any other name than Annie's Granny.

ANN [*Gratefully*]   You all spoil me, except Jack.

TANNER [*Over his shoulder, from the bookcase*]   I think you ought to call me Mr Tanner.

ANN [*Gently*]   No you dont, Jack. Thats like the things you say on purpose to shock people: those who know you pay no attention to them. But, if you like, I'll call you after your famous ancestor Don Juan.

RAMSDEN   Don Juan!

ANN [*Innocently*]   Oh, is there any harm in it? I didnt know. Then I certainly wont call you that. May I call you Jack until I can think of something else?

TANNER   Oh, for Heaven's sake dont try to invent anything worse. I capitulate. I consent to Jack. I embrace Jack. Here endeth my first and last attempt to assert my authority.

ANN   You see, Mamma, they all really like to have pet names.

MRS WHITEFIELD   Well, I think you might at least drop them until we are out of mourning.

ANN [*Reproachfully, stricken to the soul*]   Oh, how could you remind me, mother? [*She hastily leaves the room to conceal her emotion.*]

MRS WHITEFIELD   Of course. My fault as usual! [*She follows* ANN.]

TANNER [*Coming from the bookcase*]   Ramsden: we're beaten— smashed—nonentitized, like her mother.

RAMSDEN   Stuff, sir. [*He follows* MRS WHITEFIELD *out of the room.*]

TANNER [*Left alone with* OCTAVIUS, *stares whimsically at him.*]   Tavy: do you want to count for something in the world?

OCTAVIUS   I want to count for something as a poet: I want to write a great play.

TANNER   With Ann as the heroine?

OCTAVIUS   Yes: I confess it.

TANNER   Take care, Tavy. The play with Ann as the heroine is all right; but if youre not very careful, by Heaven she'll marry you.

OCTAVIUS [*Sighing*]   No such luck, Jack!

TANNER   Why, man, your head is in the lioness's mouth: you are half swallowed already—in three bites—Bite One, Ricky; Bite Two, Ticky; Bite Three, Tavy; and down you go.

OCTAVIUS   She is the same to everybody, Jack: you know her ways.

TANNER   Yes: she breaks everybody's back with the stroke of her paw; but the question is, which of us will she eat? My own opinion is that she means to eat you.

OCTAVIUS [*Rising, pettishly*]   It's horrible to talk like that about her when she is upstairs crying for her father. But I do so want her to eat me that I can bear your brutalities because they give me hope.

TANNER Tavy; thats the devilish side of a woman's fascination: she makes you will your own destruction.

OCTAVIUS But it's not destruction: it's fulfilment.

TANNER Yes, of her purpose; and that purpose is neither her happiness nor yours, but Nature's. Vitality in a woman is a blind fury of creation. She sacrifices herself to it: do you think she will hesitate to sacrifice you?

OCTAVIUS Why, it is just because she is self-sacrificing that she will not sacrifice those she loves.

TANNER That is the profoundest of mistakes, Tavy. It is the self-sacrificing women that sacrifice others most recklessly. Because they are unselfish, they are kind in little things. Because they have a purpose which is not their own purpose, but that of the whole universe, a man is nothing to them but an instrument of that purpose.

OCTAVIUS Dont be ungenerous, Jack. They take the tenderest care of us.

TANNER Yes, as a soldier takes care of his rifle or a musician of his violin. But do they allow us any purpose or freedom of our own? Will they lend us to one another? Can the strongest man escape from them when once he is appropriated? They tremble when we are in danger, and weep when we die; but the tears are not for us, but for a father wasted, a son's breeding thrown away. They accuse us of treating them as a mere means to our pleasure; but how can so feeble and transient a folly as a man's selfish pleasure enslave a woman as the whole purpose of Nature embodied in a woman can enslave a man?

OCTAVIUS What matter, if the slavery makes us happy?

TANNER No matter at all if you have no purpose of your own, and are, like most men, a mere breadwinner. But you, Tavy, are an artist: that is, you have a purpose as absorbing and as unscrupulous as a woman's purpose.

OCTAVIUS Not unscrupulous.

TANNER Quite unscrupulous. The true artist will let his wife starve, his children go barefoot, his mother drudge for his living at seventy, sooner than work at anything but his art. To women he is half vivisector, half vampire. He gets into intimate relations with them to study them, to strip the mask of convention from them, to surprise their inmost secrets, knowing that they have the power to rouse his deepest creative energies, to rescue him from his cold reason, to make him see visions and dream dreams, to inspire him, as he calls it. He persuades women that they may do this for their own purpose whilst he really means them to do it for his. He steals the mother's milk and blackens it to make printer's ink to scoff at her and glorify ideal women with. He pretends to spare her the pangs of child-bearing so that he may have for himself the tenderness and fostering that belong of right to her children. Since marriage began, the great artist has been known as a bad husband. But he is worse: he is a child-robber, a blood-sucker, a hypocrite and a cheat. Perish the race and wither a thousand women if only the sacrifice of them enable him to act Hamlet better, to paint a finer picture, to write a deeper poem, a greater play, a profounder philosophy! For mark you, Tavy, the artist's work is to shew us ourselves as we really are. Our minds are nothing but this knowledge of ourselves; and he who adds a jot to such knowledge creates new mind as surely as any woman creates new men. In the rage of that creation he is as ruthless as the woman, as dangerous to her as she to him, and as horribly fascinating. Of all human struggles there is none so treacherous and remorseless as the struggle between the artist man and the mother woman. Which shall use up the other? that is the issue between them. And it is all the deadlier because, in your romanticist cant, they love one another.

OCTAVIUS   Even if it were so—and I dont admit it for a moment—it is out of the deadliest struggles that we get the noblest characters.

TANNER   Remember that the next time you meet a grizzly bear or a Bengal tiger, Tavy.

OCTAVIUS   I meant where there is love, Jack.

TANNER   Oh, the tiger will love you. There is no love sincerer than the love of food. I think Ann loves you that way: she patted your cheek as if it were a nicely under-done chop.

OCTAVIUS   You know, Jack, I should have to run away from you if I did not make it a fixed rule not to mind anything you say. You come out with perfectly revolting things sometimes.

[RAMSDEN *returns, followed by* ANN. *They come in quickly, with their former leisurely air of decorous grief changed to one of genuine concern, and, on* RAMSDEN's *part, of worry. He comes between the two men, intending to address* OCTAVIUS, *but pulls himself up abruptly as he sees* TANNER.]

RAMSDEN   I hardly expected to find you still here, Mr Tanner.

TANNER   Am I in the way? Good morning, fellow guardian [*he goes towards the door*].

ANN   Stop, Jack. Granny: he must know, sooner or later.

RAMSDEN   Octavius: I have a very serious piece of news for you. It is of the most private and delicate nature—of the most painful nature too, I am sorry to say. Do you wish Mr Tanner to be present whilst I explain?

OCTAVIUS [*Turning pale*]   I have no secrets from Jack.

RAMSDEN   Before you decide that finally, let me say that the news concerns your sister, and that it is terrible news.

OCTAVIUS   Violet! What has happened? Is she—dead?

RAMSDEN   I am not sure that it is not even worse than that.

OCTAVIUS   Is she badly hurt? Has there been an accident?

RAMSDEN   No: nothing of that sort.

TANNER   Ann: will you have the common humanity to tell us what the matter is?

ANN [*Half whispering*]   I cant. Violet has done something dreadful. We shall have to get her away somewhere. [*She flutters to the writing table and sits in* RAMSDEN's *chair, leaving the three men to fight it out between them.*]

OCTAVIUS [*Enlightened*]   Is that what you meant, Mr Ramsden?

RAMSDEN   Yes. [OCTAVIUS *sinks upon a chair, crushed.*] I am afraid there is no doubt that Violet did not really go to Eastbourne three weeks ago when we thought she was with the Parry Whitefields. And she called on a strange doctor yesterday with a wedding ring on her finger. Mrs Parry Whitefield met her there by chance; and so the whole thing came out.

OCTAVIUS [*Rising with his fists clenched*]   Who is the scoundrel?

ANN   She wont tell us.

OCTAVIUS [*Collapsing into the chair again*]   What a frightful thing!

TANNER [*With angry sarcasm*]   Dreadful. Appalling. Worse than death, as Ramsden says. [*He comes to* OCTAVIUS.] What would you not give, Tavy, to turn it into a railway accident, with all her bones broken, or something equally respectable and deserving of sympathy?

OCTAVIUS   Dont be brutal, Jack.

TANNER   Brutal! Good Heavens, man, what are you crying for? Here is a woman whom we all supposed to be making bad water color sketches, practising Grieg and Brahms, gadding about to concerts and parties, wasting her life and her money. We suddenly learn that she has turned from these sillinesses to the fulfilment of her highest purpose and greatest function—to increase, multiply and replenish the earth. And instead of admiring her courage and rejoicing in her instinct; instead of crowning the completed womanhood and raising the triumphal strain of "Unto us a child is born: unto us a son is given," here you are—you who have been as merry as grigs in your mourning for the dead—all pulling long faces and looking as ashamed and disgraced as if the girl had committed the vilest of crimes.

RAMSDEN [*Roaring with rage*]   I will not have these abominations uttered in my house [*He smites the writing table with his fist*].

TANNER   Look here: if you insult me again I'll take you at your word and leave your house. Ann: where is Violet now?

ANN   Why? Are you going to her?

TANNER   Of course I am going to her. She wants help; she wants money; she wants respect and congratulation; she wants every chance for her child. She does not seem likely to get it from you: she shall from me. Where is she?

ANN   Dont be so headstrong, Jack. She's upstairs.

TANNER   What! Under Ramsden's sacred roof! Go and do your miserable duty, Ramsden. Hunt her out into the street. Cleanse your threshold from her contamination. Vindicate the purity of your English home. I'll go for a cab.

ANN [*Alarmed*]   Oh, Granny, you mustnt do that.

OCTAVIUS [*Broken-heartedly, rising*]   I'll take her away, Mr Ramsden. She had no right to come to your house.

RAMSDEN [*Indignantly*]   But I am only too anxious to help her. [*Turning on* TANNER] How dare you, sir, impute such monstrous intentions to me? I protest against it. I am ready to put down my last penny to save her from being driven to run to you for protection.

TANNER [*Subsiding*]   It's all right, then. He's not going to act up to his principles. It's agreed that we all stand by Violet.

OCTAVIUS   But who is the man? He can make reparation by marrying her; and he shall, or he shall answer for it to me.

RAMSDEN   He shall, Octavius. There you speak like a man.

TANNER   Then you dont think him a scoundrel, after all?

OCTAVIUS   Not a scoundrel! He is a heartless scoundrel.

RAMSDEN   A damned scoundrel. I beg your pardon, Annie; but I can say no less.

TANNER   So we are to marry your sister to a damned scoundrel by way of reforming her character! On my soul, I think you are all mad.

ANN   Dont be absurd, Jack. Of course you are quite right, Tavy; but we dont know who he is: Violet wont tell us.

TANNER   What on earth does it matter who he is? He's done his part; and Violet must do the rest.

RAMSDEN [*Beside himself*]   Stuff! lunacy! There is a rascal in our midst, a libertine, a villain worse than a murderer; and we are not to learn who he is! In our ignorance we are to shake him by the hand; to introduce him into our homes; to trust our daughters with him; to—to—

ANN [*Coaxingly*]   There, Granny, dont talk so loud. It's most shocking: we must all admit that; but if Violet wont tell us, what can we do? Nothing. Simply nothing.

RAMSDEN   Hmph! I'm not so sure of that. If any man has paid Violet any special attention, we can easily find that out. If there is any man of notoriously loose principles among us—

TANNER   Ahem!

RAMSDEN [*Raising his voice*]   Yes sir, I repeat, if there is any man of notoriously loose principles among us—

TANNER   Or any man notoriously lacking in self-control.

RAMSDEN [*Aghast*]   Do you dare to suggest that *I* am capable of such an act?

TANNER   My dear Ramsden, this is an act of which every man is capable. That is what comes of getting at cross purposes with Nature. The suspicion you have just flung at me clings to us all. It's a sort of mud that sticks to the judge's ermine or the cardinal's robe as fast as to the rags of the tramp. Come, Tavy! dont look so bewildered: it might have been me: it might have been Ramsden; just as it might have been anybody. If it had, what could we do but lie and protest—as Ramsden is going to protest.

RAMSDEN [*Choking*]   I—I—I—

TANNER   Guilt itself could not stammer more confusedly. And yet you know perfectly well hes innocent, Tavy.

RAMSDEN [*Exhausted*]   I am glad you admit that, sir. I admit, myself, that there is an element of truth in what you say, grossly as you may distort it to gratify your malicious humor. I hope, Octavius, no suspicion of me is possible in your mind.

OCTAVIUS   Of you! No, not for a moment.

TANNER [*Drily*]   I think he suspects me just a little.

OCTAVIUS   Jack: you couldnt—you wouldnt—

TANNER   Why not?

OCTAVIUS [*Appalled*]   Why not!

TANNER   Oh, well, I'll tell you why not. First, you would feel bound to quarrel with me. Second, Violet doesnt like me. Third, if I had the honor of being the father of Violet's child, I should boast of it instead of denying it. So be easy: our friendship is not in danger.

OCTAVIUS   I should have put away the suspicion with horror if only you would think and feel naturally about it. I beg your pardon.

TANNER   My pardon! nonsense! And now lets sit down and have a family council. [*He sits down. The rest follow his example, more or less under protest.*] Violet is going to do the State a service; consequently she must be packed abroad like a criminal until it's over. Whats happening upstairs?

ANN   Violet is in the housekeeper's room—by herself, of course.

TANNER   Why not in the drawing-room?

ANN   Dont be absurd, Jack. Miss Ramsden is in the drawing-room with my mother, considering what to do.

TANNER   Oh! the housekeeper's room is the penitentiary, I suppose; and the prisoner is waiting to be brought before her judges. The old cats!

ANN   Oh, Jack!

RAMSDEN   You are at present a guest beneath the roof of one of the old cats, sir. My sister is the mistress of this house.

TANNER   She would put me in the housekeeper's room, too, if she dared, Ramsden. However, I withdraw cats. Cats would have more sense. Ann: as your guardian, I order you to go to Violet at once and be particularly kind to her.

ANN   I have seen her, Jack. And I am sorry to say I am afraid she is going to be rather obstinate about going abroad. I think Tavy ought to speak to her about it.

OCTAVIUS   How can I speak to her about such a thing? [*He breaks down.*]

ANN   Dont break down, Ricky. Try to bear it for all our sakes.

RAMSDEN   Life is not all plays and poems, Octavius. Come! face it like a man.

TANNER [*Chafing again*]   Poor dear brother! Poor dear friends of the family! Poor dear Tabbies and Grimalkins! Poor dear everybody except the woman who is going to risk her life to create another life! Tavy: dont you be a selfish ass. Away with you and talk to Violet; and bring her down here if she cares to come. [OCTAVIUS *rises*] Tell her we'll stand by her.

RAMSDEN [*Rising*]   No, sir—

TANNER [*Rising also and interrupting him*]   Oh, we understand: it's against your conscience; but still youll do it.

OCTAVIUS   I assure you all, on my word, I never meant to be selfish. It's so hard to know what to do when one wishes earnestly to do right.

TANNER   My dear Tavy, your pious English habit of regarding the world as a moral gymnasium built expressly to strengthen your character in, occasionally leads you to think about your own confounded principles when you should be thinking about other people's necessities. The need of the present hour is a happy mother and a healthy baby. Bend your energies on that; and you will see your way clearly enough.

[OCTAVIUS, *much perplexed, goes out.*]

RAMSDEN [*Facing* TANNER *impressively*]   And Morality, sir? What is to become of that?

TANNER   Meaning a weeping Magdalen and an innocent child branded with her shame. Not in our circle, thank you. Morality can go to its father the devil.

RAMSDEN   I thought so, sir. Morality sent to the devil to please our libertines, male and female. That is to be the future of England, is it?

TANNER   Oh, England will survive your disapproval. Meanwhile, I understand that you agree with me as to the practical course we are to take?

RAMSDEN   Not in your spirit, sir. Not for your reasons.

TANNER   You can explain that if anybody calls you to account, here or hereafter. [*He turns away, and plants himself in front of Mr Herbert Spencer, at whom he stares gloomily.*]

ANN [*Rising and coming to* RAMSDEN]   Granny: hadnt you better go up to the drawing room and tell them what we intend to do?

RAMSDEN [*Looking pointedly at* TANNER.]   I hardly like to leave you alone with this gentleman. Will you not come with me?

ANN   Miss Ramsden would not like to speak about it before me, Granny. I ought not to be present.

RAMSDEN   You are right: I should have thought of that. You are a good girl, Annie.

[*He pats her on the shoulder. She looks up at him with beaming eyes; and he goes out, much moved. Having disposed of him, she looks at* TANNER. *His back being turned to her, she gives a moment's attention to her personal appearance, then softly goes to him and speaks almost into his ear.*]

ANN   Jack [*He turns with a start*]: are you glad that you are my guardian? You dont mind being made responsible for me, I hope.

TANNER   The latest addition to your collection of scapegoats, eh?

ANN   Oh, that stupid old joke of yours about me! Do please drop it. Why do you say things that you know must pain me? I do my best to please you, Jack: I suppose I may tell you so now that you are my guardian. You will make me so unhappy if you refuse to be friends with me.

TANNER [*Studying her as gloomily as he studied the bust*]   You need not go begging for my regard. How unreal our moral judgments are! You seem to me to have absolutely no conscience—only hypocrisy; and you cant see the difference—yet there is a sort of fascination about you. I always attend to you, somehow. I should miss you if I lost you.

ANN [*Tranquilly slipping her arm into his and walking about with him*]   But isnt that only natural, Jack? We have known each other since we were children. Do you remember—

TANNER [*Abruptly breaking loose*]   Stop! I remember everything.

ANN   Oh, I daresay we were often very silly; but—

TANNER   I wont have it, Ann. I am no more that schoolboy now than I am the dotard of ninety I shall grow into if I live long enough. It is over: let me forget it.

ANN   Wasnt it a happy time? [*She attempts to take his arm again.*]

TANNER   Sit down and behave yourself. [*He makes her sit down in the chair next the writing table.*] No doubt it was a happy time for you. You were a good girl and never compromised yourself. And yet the wickedest child that ever was slapped could hardly have had a better time. I can understand the success with which you bullied the other girls: your virtue imposed on them. But tell me this: did you ever know a good boy?

ANN   Of course. All boys are foolish sometimes; but Tavy was always a really good boy.

TANNER [*Struck by this*]   Yes: youre right. For some reason you never tempted Tavy.

ANN   Tempted! Jack!

TANNER   Yes, my dear Lady Mephistopheles, tempted. You were insatiably curious as to what a boy might be capable of, and diabolically clever at getting through his guard and surprising his inmost secrets.

ANN   What nonsense! All because you used to tell me long stories of the wicked things you had done—silly boy's tricks! And you call such things inmost secrets! Boy's secrets are just like men's; and you know what they are!

TANNER [*Obstinately*]   No I dont. What are they, pray?

ANN   Why, the things they tell everybody, of course.

TANNER   Now I swear I told you things I told no one else. You lured me into a compact by which we were to have no secrets from one another. We were to tell one another everything. I didnt notice that you never told me anything.

ANN   You didnt want to talk about me, Jack. You wanted to talk about yourself.

TANNER   Ah, true, horribly true. But what a devil of a child you must have been to know that weakness and to play on it for the satisfaction of your own curiosity! I wanted to brag to you, to make myself interesting. And I found myself doing all sorts of mischievous things simply to have something to tell you about. I fought with boys I didnt hate; I lied about things I might just as well have told the truth about; I stole things I didnt want; I kissed little girls I didn't care for. It was all bravado: passionless and therefore unreal.

ANN   I never told of you, Jack.

TANNER   No; but if you had wanted to stop me you would have told of me. You wanted me to go on.

ANN   [*Flashing out*]   Oh, thats not true: it's not true, Jack. I never wanted you to do those dull, disappointing, brutal, stupid, vulgar things. I always hoped that it would be something really heroic at last. [*Recovering herself*] Excuse me, Jack; but the things you did were never a bit like the things I wanted you to do. They often gave me great uneasiness; but I could not tell on you and get you into trouble. And you were only a boy. I knew you would grow out of them. Perhaps I was wrong.

TANNER   [*Sardonically*]   Do not give way to remorse, Ann. At least nineteen twentieths of the exploits I confessed to you were pure lies. I soon noticed that you didnt like the true stories.

ANN   Of course I knew that some of the things couldnt have happened. But—

TANNER   You are going to remind me that some of the most disgraceful ones did.

ANN   [*Fondly, to his great terror*]   I dont want to remind you of anything. But I knew the people they happened to, and heard about them.

TANNER   Yes; but even the true stories were touched up for telling. A sensitive boy's humiliations may be very good fun for ordinary thickskinned grown-ups; but to the boy himself they are so acute, so ignominious, that he cannot confess them—cannot but deny them passionately. However, perhaps it was as well for me that I romanced a bit; for, on the one occasion when I told you the truth, you threatened to tell of me.

ANN   Oh, never. Never once.

TANNER   Yes, you did. Do you remember a dark-eyed girl named Rachel Rosetree? [ANN's *brows contract for an instant involuntar-*

ily.] I got up a love affair with her; and we met one night in the garden and walked about very uncomfortably with our arms round one another, and kissed at parting, and were most conscientiously romantic. If that love affair had gone on, it would have bored me to death; but it didnt go on; for the next thing that happened was that Rachel cut me because she found out that I had told you. How did she find it out? From you. You went to her and held the guilty secret over her head, leading her a life of abject terror and humiliation by threatening to tell on her.

ANN   And a very good thing for her, too. It was my duty to stop her misconduct; and she is thankful to me for it now.

TANNER   Is she?

ANN   She ought to be, at all events.

TANNER   It was not your duty to stop my misconduct, I suppose.

ANN   I did stop it by stopping her.

TANNER   Are you sure of that? You stopped my telling you about my adventures; but how do you know that you stopped the adventures?

ANN   Do you mean to say that you went on in the same way with other girls?

TANNER   No. I had enough of that sort of romantic tomfoolery with Rachel.

ANN [*Unconvinced*]   Then why did you break off our confidences and become quite strange to me?

TANNER [*Enigmatically*]   It happened just then that I got something that I wanted to keep all to myself instead of sharing it with you.

ANN   I am sure I shouldnt have asked for any of it if you had grudged it.

TANNER   It wasnt a box of sweets, Ann. It was something youd never have let me call my own.

ANN [*Incredulously*]   What?

TANNER   My soul.

ANN   Oh, do be sensible, Jack. You know youre talking nonsense.

TANNER   The most solemn earnest, Ann. You didnt notice at that time that you were getting a soul too. But you were. It was not for nothing that you suddenly found you had a moral duty to chastise and reform Rachel. Up to that time you had traded pretty extensively in being a good child; but you had never set up a sense of duty to others. Well, I set one up too. Up to that time I had played the boy buccaneer with no more conscience than a fox in a poultry farm. But now I began to have scruples, to feel obligations, to find that veracity and honor were no longer goody-goody expressions in the mouths of grown up people, but compelling principles in myself.

ANN [*Quietly*]   Yes, I suppose youre right. You were beginning to be a man, and I to be a woman.

TANNER   Are you sure it was not that we were beginning to be something more? What does the beginning of manhood and womanhood mean in most people's mouths? You know: it means the beginning of love. But love began long before that for me. Love played its part in the earliest dreams and follies and romances I can remember—may I say the earliest follies and romances we can remember?—though we did not understand it at the time. No: the change that came to me was the birth in me of moral passion; and I declare that according to my experience moral passion is the only real passion.

ANN   All passions ought to be moral, Jack.

TANNER   Ought! Do you think that anything is strong enough to impose oughts on a passion except a stronger passion still?

ANN   Our moral sense controls passion, Jack. Dont be stupid.

TANNER   Our moral sense! And is that not a passion? Is the devil to have all the passions as well as all the good tunes? If it were not a passion—if it were not the mightiest of the passions, all the other passions would sweep it away like a leaf before a hurricane. It is the birth of that passion that turns a child into a man.

ANN   There are other passions, Jack. Very strong ones.

TANNER   All the other passions were in me before; but they were idle and aimless—mere childish greedinesses and cruelties, curiosities and fancies, habits and superstitions, grotesque and ridiculous to the mature intelligence. When they suddenly began to shine like newly lit flames it was by no light of their own, but by the radiance of the dawning moral passion. That passion dignified them, gave them conscience and meaning, found them a mob of appetites and organized them into an army of purposes and principles. My soul was born of that passion.

ANN   I noticed that you got more sense. You were a dreadfully destructive boy before that.

TANNER   Destructive! Stuff! I was only mischievous.

ANN   Oh Jack, you were very destructive. You ruined all the young fir trees by chopping off their leaders with a wooden sword. You broke all the cucumber frames with your catapult. You set fire to the common: the police arrested Tavy for it because he ran away when he couldnt stop you. You—

TANNER   Pooh! pooh! pooh! these were battles, bombardments, stratagems to save our scalps from the red Indians. You have no imagination, Ann. I am ten times more destructive now than I was then. The moral passion has taken my destructiveness in hand and directed it to moral ends. I have become a reformer, and, like all reformers, an iconoclast. I no longer break cucumber frames and burn gorse bushes: I shatter creeds and demolish idols.

ANN [Bored]   I am afraid I am too feminine to see any sense in destruction. Destruction can only destroy.

TANNER   Yes. That is why it is so useful. Construction cumbers the ground with institutions made by busybodies. Destruction clears it and gives us breathing space and liberty.

ANN Its no use, Jack. No woman will agree with you there.

TANNER Thats because you confuse construction and destruction with creation and murder. Theyre quite different: I adore creation and abhor murder. Yes: I adore it in tree and flower, in bird and beast, even in you. [*A flush of interest and delight suddenly chases the growing perplexity and boredom from her face.*] It was the creative instinct that led you to attach me to you by bonds that have left their mark on me to this day. Yes, Ann: the old childish compact between us was an unconscious love compact—

ANN Jack!

TANNER Oh, dont be alarmed—

ANN I am not alarmed.

TANNER [*Whimsically*] Then you ought to be: where are your principles?

ANN Jack: are you serious or are you not?

TANNER Do you mean about the moral passion?

ANN No, no; the other one. [*Confused*] Oh! you are so silly: one never knows how to take you.

TANNER You must take me quite seriously. I am your guardian; and it is my duty to improve your mind.

ANN The love compact is over, then, is it? I suppose you grew tired of me?

TANNER No; but the moral passion made our childish relations impossible. A jealous sense of my new individuality arose in me—

ANN You hated to be treated as a boy any longer. Poor Jack!

TANNER Yes, because to be treated as a boy was to be taken on the old footing. I had become a new person; and those who knew the old person laughed at me. The only man who behaved sensibly was my tailor: he took my measure anew every time he saw me, whilst all the rest went on with their old measurements and expected them to fit me.

ANN You became frightfully self-conscious.

TANNER When you go to heaven, Ann, you will be frightfully conscious of your wings for the first year or so. When you meet your relatives there, and they persist in treating you as if you were still a mortal, you will not be able to bear them. You will try to get into a circle which has never known you except as an angel.

ANN So it was only your vanity that made you run away from us after all?

TANNER Yes, only my vanity, as you call it.

ANN You need not have kept away from me on that account.

TANNER From you above all others. You fought harder than anybody against my emancipation.

ANN [*Earnestly*] Oh, how wrong you are! I would have done anything for you.

TANNER   Anything except let me get loose from you. Even then you had acquired by instinct that damnable woman's trick of heaping obligations on a man, of placing yourself so entirely and helplessly at his mercy that at last he dare not take a step without running to you for leave. I know a poor wretch whose one desire in life is to run away from his wife. She prevents him by threatening to throw herself in front of the engine of the train he leaves her in. That is what all women do. If we try to go where you do not want us to go there is no law to prevent us; but when we take the first step your breasts are under our foot as it descends: your bodies are under our wheels as we start. No woman shall ever enslave me in that way.

ANN   But, Jack, you cannot get through life without considering other people a little.

TANNER   Ay; but what other people? It is this consideration of other people—or rather this cowardly fear of them which we call consideration—that makes us the sentimental slaves we are. To consider you, as you call it, is to substitute your will for my own. How if it be a baser will than mine? Are women taught better than men or worse? Are mobs of voters taught better than statesmen or worse? Worse, of course, in both cases. And then what sort of world are you going to get, with its public men considering its voting mobs, and its private men considering their wives? What does Church and State mean nowadays? The Woman and the Ratepayer.

ANN [*Placidly*]   I am so glad you understand politics, Jack: it will be most useful to you if you go into parliament [*He collapses like a pricked bladder*]. But I am sorry you thought my influence a bad one.

TANNER   I dont say it was a bad one. But bad or good, I didnt choose to be cut to your measure. And I wont be cut to it.

ANN   Nobody wants you to, Jack. I assure you—really on my word— I dont mind your queer opinions one little bit. You know we have all been brought up to have advanced opinions. Why do you persist in thinking me so narrow minded?

TANNER   Thats the danger of it. I know you dont mind, because youve found out that it doesnt matter. The boa constrictor doesnt mind the opinions of a stag one little bit when once she has got her coils round it.

ANN [*Rising in sudden enlightenment*]   O-o-o-o-oh! now I understand why you warned Tavy that I am a boa constrictor. Granny told me. [*She laughs and throws her boa round his neck.*] Doesnt it feel nice and soft, Jack?

TANNER [*In the toils*]   You scandalous woman, will you throw away even your hypocrisy?

ANN   I am never hypocritical with you, Jack. Are you angry? [*She*

withdraws the boa and throws it on a chair.] Perhaps I shouldnt
have done that.

TANNER [*Contemptuously*]   Pooh, prudery! Why should you not, if
it amuses you?

ANN [*Shyly*]   Well, because—because I suppose what you really
meant by the boa constrictor was this [*she puts her arms round
his neck*].

TANNER [*Staring at her*]   Magnificent audacity! [*She laughs and pats
his cheeks.*] Now just to think that if I mentioned this episode not
a soul would believe me except the people who would cut me for
telling, whilst if you accused me of it nobody would believe my
denial!

ANN [*Taking her arms away with perfect dignity*]   You are incorrigible, Jack. But you should not jest about our affection for one
another. Nobody could possibly misunderstand it. You do not misunderstand it, I hope.

TANNER   My blood interprets for me, Ann. Poor Ricky Ticky Tavy!

ANN [*Looking quickly at him as if this were a new light*]   Surely you
are not so absurd as to be jealous of Tavy.

TANNER   Jealous! Why should I be? But I dont wonder at your grip
of him. I feel the coils tightening round my very self, though you
are only playing with me.

ANN   Do you think I have designs on Tavy?

TANNER   I know you have.

ANN [*Earnestly*]   Take care, Jack. You may make Tavy very unhappy
if you mislead him about me.

TANNER   Never fear: he will not escape you.

ANN   I wonder are you really a clever man!

TANNER   Why this sudden misgiving on the subject?

ANN   You seem to understand all the things I dont understand; but
you are a perfect baby in the things I do understand.

TANNER   I understand how Tavy feels for you, Ann: you may depend
on that, at all events.

ANN   And you think you understand how I feel for Tavy, dont
you?

TANNER   I know only too well what is going to happen to poor Tavy.

ANN   I should laugh at you, Jack, if it were not for poor papa's death.
Mind! Tavy will be very unhappy.

TANNER   Yes; but he wont know it, poor devil. He is a thousand
times too good for you. Thats why he is going to make the mistake
of his life about you.

ANN   I think men make more mistakes by being too clever than by
being too good [*She sits down, with a trace of contempt for the
whole male sex in the elegant carriage of her shoulders*].

TANNER   Oh, I know you dont care very much about Tavy. But there
is always one who kisses and one who only allows the kiss. Tavy

will kiss; and you will only turn the cheek. And you will throw him over if anybody better turns up.

ANN [*Offended*] You have no right to say such things, Jack. They are not true, and not delicate. If you and Tavy choose to be stupid about me, that is not my fault.

TANNER [*Remorsefully*] Forgive my brutalities, Ann. They are levelled at this wicked world, not at you. [*She looks up at him, pleased and forgiving. He becomes cautious at once.*] All the same, I wish Ramsden would come back. I never feel safe with you: there is a devilish charm—or no: not a charm, a subtle interest [*She laughs*]—Just so: you know it; and you triumph in it. Openly and shamelessly triumph in it!

ANN What a shocking flirt you are, Jack!

TANNER A flirt!! I!!!

ANN Yes, a flirt. You are always abusing and offending people; but you never really mean to let go your hold of them.

TANNER I will ring the bell. This conversation has already gone further than I intended.

> [RAMSDEN *and* OCTAVIUS *come back with* MISS RAMSDEN, *a hardheaded old maiden lady in a plain brown silk gown, with enough rings, chains, and brooches to shew that her plainness of dress is a matter of principle, not of poverty. She comes into the room very determinedly: the two men, perplexed and downcast, following her.* ANN *rises and goes eagerly to meet her.* TANNER *retreats to the wall between the busts and pretends to study the pictures.* RAMSDEN *goes to his table as usual; and* OCTAVIUS *clings to the neighborhood of* TANNER.]

MISS RAMSDEN [*Almost pushing* ANN *aside as she comes to* MRS WHITEFIELD's *chair and plants herself there resolutely*] I wash my hands of the whole affair.

OCTAVIUS [*Very wretched*] I know you wish me to take Violet away, Miss Ramsden. I will. [*He turns irresolutely to the door.*]

RAMSDEN No no—

MISS RAMSDEN What is the use of saying no, Roebuck? Octavius knows that I would not turn any truly contrite and repentant woman from your doors. But when a woman is not only wicked, but intends to go on being wicked, she and I part company.

ANN Oh, Miss Ramsden, what do you mean? What has Violet said?

RAMSDEN Violet is certainly very obstinate. She wont leave London. I dont understand her.

MISS RAMSDEN I do. It's as plain as the nose on your face, Roebuck, that she wont go because she doesnt want to be separated from this man, whoever he is.

ANN Oh, surely, surely! Octavius: did you speak to her?

OCTAVIUS She wont tell us anything. She wont make any arrangement until she has consulted somebody. It cant be anybody else than the scoundrel who has betrayed her.

TANNER [*To* OCTAVIUS]   Well, let her consult him. He will be glad enough to have her sent abroad. Where is the difficulty?

MISS RAMSDEN [*Taking the answer out of* OCTAVIUS's *mouth.*]   The difficulty, Mr Jack, is that when I offered to help her I didn't offer to become her accomplice in her wickedness. She either pledges her word never to see that man again, or else she finds some new friends; and the sooner the better.

> [*The* PARLORMAID *appears at the door.* ANN *hastily resumes her seat, and looks as unconcerned as possible.* OCTAVIUS *instinctively imitates her.*]

THE MAID   The cab is at the door, maam.

MISS RAMSDEN   What cab?

THE MAID   For Miss Robinson.

MISS RAMSDEN   Oh! [*Recovering herself*] All right. [*The* MAID *withdraws*] She has sent for a cab.

TANNER   I wanted to send for that cab half an hour ago.

MISS RAMSDEN   I am glad she understands the position she has placed herself in.

RAMSDEN   I dont like her going away in this fashion, Susan. We had better not do anything harsh.

OCTAVIUS   No: thank you again and again; but Miss Ramsden is quite right. Violet cannot expect to stay.

ANN   Hadnt you better go with her, Tavy?

OCTAVIUS   She wont have me.

MISS RAMSDEN   Of course she wont. Shes going straight to that man.

TANNER   As a natural result of her virtuous reception here.

RAMSDEN [*Much troubled*]   There, Susan! You hear! and theres some truth in it. I wish you could reconcile it with your principles to be a little patient with this poor girl. Shes very young; and theres a time for everything.

MISS RAMSDEN   Oh, she will get all the sympathy she wants from the men. I'm surprised at you, Roebuck.

TANNER   So am I, Ramsden, most favorably.

> [VIOLET *appears at the door. She is as impenitent and self-possessed a young lady as one would desire to see among the best behaved of her sex. Her small head and tiny resolute mouth and chin; her haughty crispness of speech and trimness of carriage; the ruthless elegance of her equipment, which includes a very smart hat with a dead bird in it, mark a personality which is as formidable as it is exquisitely pretty. She is not a siren, like* ANN: *admiration comes to her without any compulsion or even interest on her part; besides, there is some fun in* ANN, *but in this woman none, perhaps no mercy either: if anything restrains her, it is intelligence and pride, not compassion. Her voice might be the voice of a schoolmistress addressing a class of girls*

*who had disgraced themselves, as she proceeds with complete
composure and some disgust to say what she has come to say.*]

VIOLET   I have only looked in to tell Miss Ramsden that she will
find her birthday present to me, the filagree bracelet, in the housekeeper's room.

TANNER   Do come in, Violet, and talk to us sensibly.

VIOLET   Thank you: I have had quite enough of the family conversation this morning. So has your mother, Ann: she has gone home
crying. But at all events, I have found out what some of my pretended friends are worth. Good bye.

TANNER   No, no: one moment. I have something to say which I beg
you to hear. [*She looks at him without the slightest curiosity, but
waits, apparently as much to finish getting her glove on as to hear
what he has to say.*] I am altogether on your side in this matter. I
congratulate you, with the sincerest respect, on having the courage
to do what you have done. You are entirely in the right; and the
family is entirely in the wrong.

> [*Sensation.* ANN *and* MISS RAMSDEN *rise and turn towards the
> two.* VIOLET, *more surprised than any of the others, forgets her
> glove, and comes forward into the middle of the room, both
> puzzled and displeased.* OCTAVIUS *alone does not move or raise
> his head: he is overwhelmed with shame.*]

ANN [*Pleading to* TANNER *to be sensible*]   Jack!

MISS RAMSDEN [*Outraged*]   Well, I must say!

VIOLET [*Sharply to* TANNER]   Who told you?

TANNER   Why, Ramsden and Tavy of course. Why should they not?

VIOLET   But they dont know.

TANNER   Dont know what?

VIOLET   They dont know that I am in the right, I mean.

TANNER   Oh, they know it in their hearts, though they think themselves bound to blame you by their silly superstitions about morality and propriety and so forth. But I know, and the whole world
really knows, though it dare not say so, that you were right to
follow your instinct; that vitality and bravery are the greatest qualities a woman can have, and motherhood her solemn initiation
into womanhood; and that the fact of your not being legally married matters not one scrap either to your own worth or to our real
regard for you.

VIOLET [*Flushing with indignation*]   Oh! You think me a wicked
woman, like the rest. You think I have not only been vile, but that
I share your abominable opinions. Miss Ramsden: I have borne
your hard words because I knew you would be sorry for them when
you found out the truth. But I wont bear such a horrible insult as
to be complimented by Jack on being one of the wretches of whom
he approves. I have kept my marriage a secret for my husband's
sake. But now I claim my right as a married woman not to be
insulted.

OCTAVIUS [*Raising his head with inexpressible relief*]   You are married!

VIOLET   Yes; and I think you might have guessed it. What business had you all to take it for granted that I had no right to wear my wedding ring? Not one of you even asked me: I cannot forget that.

TANNER [*In ruins*]   I am utterly crushed. I meant well. I apologize—abjectly apologize.

VIOLET   I hope you will be more careful in future about the things you say. Of course one does not take them seriously; but they are very disagreeable, and rather in bad taste, I think.

TANNER [*Bowing to the storm*]   I have no defence: I shall know better in future than to take any woman's part. We have all disgraced ourselves in your eyes, I am afraid, except Ann. She befriended you. For Ann's sake, forgive us.

VIOLET   Yes: Ann has been very kind; but then Ann knew.

TANNER   Oh!

MISS RAMSDEN [*Stiffly*]   And who, pray, is the gentleman who does not acknowledge his wife?

VIOLET [*Promptly*]   That is my business, Miss Ramsden, and not yours. I have my reasons for keeping my marriage a secret for the present.

RAMSDEN   All I can say is that we are extremely sorry, Violet. I am shocked to think of how we have treated you.

OCTAVIUS [*Awkwardly*]   I beg your pardon, Violet. I can say no more.

MISS RAMSDEN [*Still loth to surrender*]   Of course what you say puts a very different complexion on the matter. All the same, I owe it to myself—

VIOLET [*Cutting her short*]   You owe me an apology, Miss Ramsden: thats what you owe both to yourself and to me. If you were a married woman you would not like sitting in the housekeeper's room and being treated like a naughty child by young girls and old ladies without any serious duties and responsibilities.

TANNER   Dont hit us when we're down, Violet. We seem to have made fools of ourselves; but really it was you who made fools of us.

VIOLET   It was no business of yours, Jack, in any case.

TANNER   No business of mine! Why, Ramsden as good as accused me of being the unknown gentleman.

[RAMSDEN *makes a frantic demonstration; but* VIOLET's *cool keen anger extinguishes it.*]

VIOLET   You! Oh, how infamous! how abominable! how disgracefully you have all been talking about me! If my husband knew it he would never let me speak to any of you again. [*To* RAMSDEN.] I think you might have spared me that, at least.

RAMSDEN   But I assure you I never—at least it is a monstrous perversion of something I said that—

MISS RAMSDEN You neednt apologize, Roebuck. She brought it all on herself. It is for her to apologize for having deceived us.

VIOLET I can make allowances for you, Miss Ramsden: you cannot understand how I feel on this subject, though I should have expected rather better taste from people of greater experience. However, I quite feel that you have all placed yourselves in a very painful position; and the most truly considerate thing for me to do is to go at once. Good morning.

[*She goes, leaving them staring.*]

MISS RAMSDEN Well, I must say!

RAMSDEN [*Plaintively*] I dont think she is quite fair to us.

TANNER You must cower before the wedding ring like the rest of us, Ramsden. The cup of our ignominy is full.

Act II

On the carriage drive in the park of a country house near Richmond a motor car has broken down. It stands in front of a clump of trees round which the drive sweeps to the house, which is partly visible through them: indeed TAN-NER, *standing in the drive with the car on his right hand, could get an unobstructed view of the west corner of the house on his left were he not far too much interested in a pair of supine legs in blue serge trousers which protrude from beneath the machine. He is watching them intently with bent back and hands supported on his knees. His leathern overcoat and peaked cap proclaim him one of the dismounted passengers.*

THE LEGS Aha! I got him.

TANNER All right now?

THE LEGS Aw right now.

[TANNER *stoops and takes the legs by the ankles, drawing their owner forth like a wheelbarrow, walking on his hands, with a hammer in his mouth. He is a young man in a neat suit of blue serge, clean shaven, dark eyed, square fingered, with short well brushed black hair and rather irregular scept-ically turned eyebrows. When he is manipulating the car his movements are swift and sudden, yet attentive and deliberate. With* TANNER *and* TANNER's *friends his manner is not in the least deferential, but cool and reticent, keeping them quite effectually at a distance whilst giving them no excuse for complaining of him. Nevertheless he has a vigilant eye on them always, and that, too, rather cynically, like a man who knows the world well from its seamy side. He speaks slowly*

*and with a touch of sarcasm; and as he does not at all affect
the gentleman in his speech, it may be inferred that his smart
appearance is a mark of respect to himself and his own class,
not to that which employs him.*

*He now gets into the car to test his machinery and put his
cap and overcoat on again.* TANNER *takes off his leathern overcoat and pitches it into the car. The chauffeur (or automobilist
or motoreer or whatever England may presently decide to call
him) looks round inquiringly in the act of stowing away his
hammer.*]

THE CHAUFFEUR   Had enough of it, eh?

TANNER   I may as well walk to the house and stretch my legs and
calm my nerves a little. [*Looking at his watch*] I suppose you know
that we have come from Hyde Park Corner to Richmond in
twenty-one minutes.

THE CHAUFFEUR   I'd ha done it under fifteen if I'd had a clear road
all the way.

TANNER   Why do you do it? Is it for love of sport or for the fun of
terrifying your unfortunate employer?

THE CHAUFFEUR   What are you afraid of?

TANNER   The police, and breaking my neck.

THE CHAUFFEUR   Well, if you like easy going, you can take a bus,
you know. Its cheaper. You pay me to save your time and give you
the value of your thousand pound car. [*He sits down calmly.*]

TANNER   I am the slave of that car and of you too. I dream of the
accursed thing at night.

THE CHAUFFEUR   Youll get over that. If youre going up to the house,
may I ask how long youre goin to stay there? Because if you mean
to put in the whole morning talkin to the ladies, I'll put the car in
the stables and make myself comfortable. If not, I'll keep the car
on the go about here til you come.

TANNER   Better wait here. We shant be long. Theres a young American gentleman, a Mr Malone, who is driving Mr Robinson down
in his new American steam car.

THE CHAUFFEUR [*Springing up and coming hastily out of the car to
TANNER*]   American steam car! Wot! racin us down from London!

TANNER   Perhaps theyre here already.

THE CHAUFFEUR   If I'd known it! [*With deep reproach*] Why didnt
you tell me, Mr Tanner?

TANNER   Because Ive been told that this car is capable of 84 miles
an hour; and I already know what you are capable of when there
is a rival car on the road. No, Henry: there are things it is not good
for you to know; and this was one of them. However, cheer up:
we are going to have a day after your own heart. The American is
to take Mr Robinson and his sister and Miss Whitefield. We are
to take Miss Rhoda.

THE CHAUFFEUR [*Consoled, and musing on another matter*]   Thats Miss Whitefield's sister, isnt it?

TANNER   Yes.

THE CHAUFFEUR   And Miss Whitefield herself is goin in the other car? Not with you?

TANNER   Why the devil should she come with me? Mr Robinson will be in the other car. [THE CHAUFFEUR *looks at* TANNER *with cool incredulity, and turns to the car, whistling a popular air softly to himself.* TANNER, *a little annoyed, is about to pursue the subject when he hears the footsteps of* OCTAVIUS *on the gravel.* OCTAVIUS *is coming from the house, dressed for motoring, but without his over-coat.*] Weve lost the race, thank Heaven: heres Mr Robinson. Well, Tavy, is the steam car a success?

OCTAVIUS   I think so. We came from Hyde Park Corner here in seventeen minutes. [THE CHAUFFEUR, *furious, kicks the car with a groan of vexation.*] How long were you?

TANNER   Oh, about three quarters of an hour or so.

THE CHAUFFEUR [*Remonstrating*]   Now, now, Mr Tanner, come now! We could ha done it easy under fifteen.

TANNER   By the way, let me introduce you. Mr Octavius Robinson: Mr Enry Straker.

STRAKER   Pleased to meet you, sir. Mr Tanner is gittin at you with is Enry Straker, you know. You call it Henery. But I dont mind, bless you.

TANNER   You think it's simply bad taste in me to chaff him, Tavy. But youre wrong. This man takes more trouble to drop his aitches than ever his father did to pick them up. It's a mark of caste to him. I have never met anybody more swollen with the pride of class than Enry is.

STRAKER   Easy, easy! A little moderation, Mr Tanner.

TANNER   A little moderation, Tavy, you observe. You would tell me to draw it mild. But this chap has been educated. Whats more, he knows that we havnt. What was that Board School[1] of yours, Straker?

STRAKER   Sherbrooke Road.

TANNER   Sherbrooke Road! Would any of us say Rugby! Harrow! Eton! in that tone of intellectual snobbery? Sherbrooke Road is a place where boys learn something: Eton is a boy farm where we are sent because we are nuisances at home, and because in after life, whenever a Duke is mentioned, we can claim him as an old school-fellow.

STRAKER   You dont know nothing about it, Mr Tanner. It's not the Board School that does it: it's the Polytechnic.[2]

TANNER   His university, Octavius. Not Oxford, Cambridge, Durham, Dublin or Glasgow. Not even those Nonconformist holes in

1. Board schools were state-run and provided free education.
2. Polytechnics provided vocational education for those entering skilled trades.

Wales. No, Tavy. Regent Street, Chelsea, the Borough—I dont
know half their confounded names: these are his universities, not
mere shops for selling class limitations like ours. You despise
Oxford, Enry, dont you?

STRAKER   No, I dont. Very nice sort of place, Oxford, I should think,
for people that like that sort of place. They teach you to be a
gentleman there. In the Polytechnic they teach you to be an engineer or such like. See?

TANNER   Sarcasm, Tavy, sarcasm! Oh, if you could only see into
Enry's soul, the depth of his contempt for a gentleman, the arrogance of his pride in being an engineer, would appal you. He positively likes the car to break down because it brings out my
gentlemanly helplessness and his workmanlike skill and resource.

STRAKER   Never you mind him, Mr Robinson. He likes to talk. We
know him, dont we?

OCTAVIUS [*Earnestly*]   But theres a great truth at the bottom of what
he says. I believe most intensely in the dignity of labor.

STRAKER [*Unimpressed*]   Thats because you never done any, Mr
Robinson. My business is to do away with labor. Youll get more
out of me and a machine than you will out of twenty laborers, and
not so much to drink either.

TANNER   For Heaven's sake, Tavy, dont start him on political economy. He knows all about it; and we dont. Youre only a poetic
Socialist, Tavy: hes a scientific one.

STRAKER [*Unperturbed*]   Yes. Well, this conversation is very
improvin; but Ive got to look after the car; and you two want to
talk about your ladies. *I* know. [*He retires to busy himself about the
car; and presently saunters off towards the house.*]

TANNER   Thats a very momentous social phenomenon.

OCTAVIUS   What is?

TANNER   Straker is. Here have we literary and cultured persons
been for years setting up a cry of the New Woman whenever some
unusually old fashioned female came along; and never noticing
the advent of the New Man. Straker's the New Man.

OCTAVIUS   I see nothing new about him, except your way of chaffing
him. But I dont want to talk about him just now. I want to speak
to you about Ann.

TANNER   Straker knew even that. He learnt it at the Polytechnic,
probably. Well, what about Ann? Have you proposed to her?

OCTAVIUS [*Self-reproachfully*]   I was brute enough to do so last
night.

TANNER   Brute enough! What do you mean?

OCTAVIUS [*Dithyrambically*][3]   Jack: we men are all coarse: we never
understand how exquisite a woman's sensibilities are. How could
I have done such a thing!

---

3. Speaking as though declaiming enthusiastically or even wildly.

TANNER　Done what, you maudlin idiot?

OCTAVIUS　Yes, I am an idiot. Jack: if you had heard her voice! if you had seen her tears! I have lain awake all night thinking of them. If she had reproached me, I could have borne it better.

TANNER　Tears! thats dangerous. What did she say?

OCTAVIUS　She asked me how she could think of anything now but her dear father. She stifled a sob— [*he breaks down*].

TANNER　[*Patting him on the back.*]　Bear it like a man, Tavy, even if you feel it like an ass. It's the old game: shes not tired of playing with you yet.

OCTAVIUS　[*Impatiently*]　Oh, dont be a fool, Jack. Do you suppose this eternal shallow cynicism of yours has any real bearing on a nature like hers?

TANNER　Hm! Did she say anything else?

OCTAVIUS　Yes; and that is why I expose myself and her to your ridicule by telling you what passed.

TANNER　[*Remorsefully*]　No, dear Tavy, not ridicule, on my honor! However, no matter. Go on.

OCTAVIUS　Her sense of duty is so devout, so perfect, so—

TANNER　Yes: I know. Go on.

OCTAVIUS　You see, under this new arrangement, you and Ramsden are her guardians; and she considers that all her duty to her father is now transferred to you. She said she thought I ought to have spoken to you both in the first instance. Of course she is right; but somehow it seems rather absurd that I am to come to you and formally ask to be received as a suitor for your ward's hand.

TANNER　I am glad that love has not totally extinguished your sense of humor, Tavy.

OCTAVIUS　That answer wont satisfy her.

TANNER　My official answer is, obviously, Bless you, my children: may you be happy!

OCTAVIUS　I wish you would stop playing the fool about this. If it is not serious to you, it is to me, and to her.

TANNER　You know very well that she is as free to choose as you are.

OCTAVIUS　She does not think so.

TANNER　Oh, doesnt she! just! However, say what you want me to do?

OCTAVIUS　I want you to tell her sincerely and earnestly what you think about me. I want you to tell her that you can trust her to me—that is, if you feel you can.

TANNER　I have no doubt that I can trust her to you. What worries me is the idea of trusting you to her. Have you read Maeterlinck's book about the bee?

OCTAVIUS　[*Keeping his temper with difficulty*]　I am not discussing literature at present.

TANNER　Be just a little patient with me. *I* am not discussing literature: the book about the bee is natural history. It's an awful lesson to mankind. You think that you are Ann's suitor; that you are the pursuer and she the pursued; that it is your part to woo, to persuade, to prevail, to overcome. Fool: it is you who are the pursued, the marked down quarry, the destined prey. You need not sit looking longingly at the bait through the wires of the trap: the door is open, and will remain so until it shuts behind you for ever.

OCTAVIUS   I wish I could believe that, vilely as you put it.

TANNER   Why, man, what other work has she in life but to get a husband? It is a woman's business to get married as soon as possible, and a man's to keep unmarried as long as he can. You have your poems and your tragedies to work at: Ann has nothing.

OCTAVIUS   I cannot write without inspiration. And nobody can give me that except Ann.

TANNER   Well, hadnt you better get it from her at a safe distance? Petrarch didnt see half as much of Laura, nor Dante of Beatrice, as you see of Ann now; and yet they wrote first-rate poetry—at least so Im told. They never exposed their idolatry to the test of domestic familiarity; and it lasted them to their graves. Marry Ann; and at the end of a week youll find no more inspiration in her than in a plate of muffins.

OCTAVIUS   You think I shall tire of her!

TANNER   Not at all: you dont get tired of muffins. But you dont find inspiration in them; and you wont in her when she ceases to be a poet's dream and becomes a solid eleven-stone wife. Youll be forced to dream about somebody else; and then there will be a row.

OCTAVIUS   This sort of talk is no use, Jack. You dont understand. You have never been in love.

TANNER   I! I have never been out of it. Why, I am in love even with Ann. But I am neither the slave of love nor its dupe. Go to the bee, thou poet: consider her ways and be wise. By Heaven, Tavy, if women could do without our work, and we ate their children's bread instead of making it, they would kill us as the spider kills her mate or as the bees kill the drone. And they would be right if we were good for nothing but love.

OCTAVIUS   Ah, if we were only good enough for Love! There is nothing like Love: there is nothing else but Love: without it the world would be a dream of sordid horror.

TANNER   And this—this is the man who asks me to give him the hand of my ward! Tavy: I believe we were changed in our cradles, and that you are the real descendant of Don Juan.

OCTAVIUS   I beg you not to say anything like that to Ann.

TANNER   Dont be afraid. She has marked you for her own; and nothing will stop her now. You are doomed. [STRAKER *comes back with a newspaper.*] Here comes the New Man, demoralizing himself with a halfpenny paper[4] as usual.

4. A halfpenny (pronounced "ha'penny") was worth 1/2d and less than 1c. Straker is holding a cheap tabloid newspaper.

STRAKER   Now would you believe it, Mr Robinson, when we're out motoring we take in two papers, the *Times* for him, the *Leader* or the *Echo* for me. And do you think I ever see my paper? Not much. He grabs the *Leader* and leaves me to stodge myself with his *Times*.

OCTAVIUS   Are there no winners in the *Times*?

TANNER   Enry dont old with bettin, Tavy. Motor records are his weakness. Whats the latest?

STRAKER   Paris to Biskra at forty mile an hour average, not countin the Mediterranean.

TANNER   How many killed?

STRAKER   Two silly sheep. What does it matter? Sheep dont cost such a lot: they were glad to ave the price without the trouble o sellin em to the butcher. All the same, d'y'see, therell be a clamor agin it presently; and then the French Government'll stop it; an our chance'll be gone, see? Thats what makes me fairly mad: Mr Tanner wont do a good run while he can.

TANNER   Tavy: do you remember my uncle James?

OCTAVIUS   Yes. Why?

TANNER   Uncle James had a first rate cook: he couldnt digest anything except what she cooked. Well, the poor man was shy and hated society. But his cook was proud of her skill, and wanted to serve up dinners to princes and ambassadors. To prevent her from leaving him, that poor old man had to give a big dinner twice a month, and suffer agonies of awkwardness. Now here am I; and here is this chap Enry Straker, the New Man. I loathe travelling; but I rather like Enry. He cares for nothing but tearing along in a leather coat and goggles, with two inches of dust all over him, at sixty miles an hour and the risk of his life and mine. Except, of course, when he is lying on his back in the mud under the machine trying to find out where it has given way. Well, if I dont give him a thousand-mile run at least once a fortnight I shall lose him. He will give me the sack and go to some American millionaire; and I shall have to put up with a nice respectful groom-gardener-amateur, who will touch his hat and know his place. I am Enry's slave, just as Uncle James was his cook's slave.

STRAKER [*Exasperated*]   Garn! I wish I had a car that would go as fast as you can talk, Mr Tanner. What I say is that you lose money by a motor car unless you keep it workin. Might as well ave a pram and a nussmaid to wheel you in it as that car and me if you dont git the last inch out of us both.

TANNER [*Soothingly*]   All right, Henry, all right. We'll go out for half an hour presently.

STRAKER [*In disgust*]   Arf an ahr! [*He returns to his machine; seats himself in it; and turns up a fresh page of his paper in search of more news.*]

OCTAVIUS   Oh, that reminds me. I have a note for you from Rhoda. [*He gives* TANNER *a note.*]

TANNER [*Opening it*]   I rather think Rhoda is heading for a row with Ann. As a rule there is only one person an English girl hates more than she hates her mother; and thats her eldest sister. But Rhoda positively prefers her mother to Ann. She— [*Indignantly*] Oh, I say!

OCTAVIUS   Whats the matter?

TANNER   Rhoda was to have come with me for a ride in the motor car. She says Ann has forbidden her to go out with me.

> [STRAKER *suddenly begins whistling his favorite air with remarkable deliberation. Surprised by this burst of larklike melody, and jarred by a sardonic note in its cheerfulness, they turn and look inquiringly at him. But he is busy with his paper; and nothing comes of their movement.*]

OCTAVIUS [*Recovering himself*]   Does she give any reason?

TANNER   Reason! An insult is not a reason. Ann forbids her to be alone with me on any occasion. Says I am not a fit person for a young girl to be with. What do you think of your paragon now?

OCTAVIUS   You must remember that she has a very heavy responsibility now that her father is dead. Mrs Whitefield is too weak to control Rhoda.

TANNER [*Staring at him*]   In short, you agree with Ann.

OCTAVIUS   No; but I think I understand her. You must admit that your views are hardly suited for the formation of a young girl's mind and character.

TANNER   I admit nothing of the sort. I admit that the formation of a young lady's mind and character usually consists in telling her lies; but I object to the particular lie that I am in the habit of abusing the confidence of girls.

OCTAVIUS   Ann doesnt say that, Jack.

TANNER   What else does she mean?

STRAKER [*Catching sight of* ANN *coming from the house*]   Miss Whitefield, gentlemen. [*He dismounts and strolls away down the avenue with the air of a man who knows he is no longer wanted.*]

ANN [*Coming between* OCTAVIUS *and* TANNER]   Good morning, Jack. I have come to tell you that poor Rhoda has got one of her headaches and cannot go out with you to-day in the car. It is a cruel disappointment to her, poor child!

TANNER   What do you say now, Tavy?

OCTAVIUS   Surely you cannot misunderstand, Jack. Ann is shewing you the kindest consideration, even at the cost of deceiving you.

ANN   What do you mean?

TANNER   Would you like to cure Rhoda's headache, Ann?

ANN   Of course.

TANNER   Then tell her what you said just now; and add that you arrived about two minutes after I had received her letter and read it.

ANN   Rhoda has written to you!

TANNER   With full particulars.

OCTAVIUS   Never mind him, Ann. You were right—quite right. Ann was only doing her duty, Jack; and you know it. Doing it in the kindest way, too.

ANN [*Going to* OCTAVIUS]   How kind you are, Tavy! How helpful! How well you understand!

[OCTAVIUS *beams.*]

TANNER   Ay: tighten the coils. You love her, Tavy, dont you?

OCTAVIUS   She knows I do.

ANN   Hush. For shame, Tavy!

TANNER   Oh, I give you leave. I am your guardian; and I commit you to Tavy's care for the next hour. I am off for a turn in the car.

ANN   No, Jack. I must speak to you about Rhoda. Ricky: will you go back to the house and entertain your American friend. Hes rather on Mamma's hands so early in the morning. She wants to finish her housekeeping.

OCTAVIUS   I fly, dearest Ann. [*He kisses her hand.*]

ANN [*Tenderly*]   Ricky Ticky Tavy!

[*He looks at her with an eloquent blush, and runs off.*]

TANNER [*Bluntly*]   Now look here, Ann. This time youve landed yourself; and if Tavy were not in love with you past all salvation he'd have found out what an incorrigible liar you are.

ANN   You misunderstand, Jack. I didnt dare tell Tavy the truth.

TANNER   No: your daring is generally in the opposite direction. What the devil do you mean by telling Rhoda that I am too vicious to associate with her? How can I ever have any human or decent relations with her again, now that you have poisoned her mind in that abominable way?

ANN   I know you are incapable of behaving badly—

TANNER   Then why did you lie to her?

ANN   I had to.

TANNER   Had to!

ANN   Mother made me.

TANNER [*His eye flashing*]   Ha! I might have known it. The mother! Always the mother!

ANN   It was that dreadful book of yours. You know how timid mother is. All timid women are conventional: we must be conventional, Jack, or we are so cruelly, so vilely misunderstood. Even you, who are a man, cannot say what you think without being misunderstood and vilified—yes: I admit it: I have had to vilify you. Do you want to have poor Rhoda misunderstood and vilified in the same way? Would it be right for mother to let her expose herself to such treatment before she is old enough to judge for herself?

TANNER   In short, the way to avoid misunderstanding is for every-body to lie and slander and insinuate and pretend as hard as they can. That is what obeying your mother comes to.

ANN   I love my mother, Jack.

TANNER [*Working himself up into a sociological rage*]   Is that any reason why you are not to call your soul your own? Oh, I protest against this vile abjection of youth to age! Look at fashionable society as you know it. What does it pretend to be? An exquisite dance of nymphs. What is it? A horrible procession of wretched girls, each in the claws of a cynical, cunning, avaricious, disillu-sioned, ignorantly experienced, foul-minded old woman whom she calls mother, and whose duty it is to corrupt her mind and sell her to the highest bidder. Why do these unhappy slaves marry any-body, however old and vile, sooner than not marry at all? Because marriage is their only means of escape from these decrepit fiends who hide their selfish ambitions, their jealous hatreds of the young rivals who have supplanted them, under the mask of maternal duty and family affection. Such things are abominable: the voice of nature proclaims for the daughter a father's care and for the son a mother's. The law for father and son and mother and daughter is not the law of love: it is the law of revolution, of emancipation, of final supersession of the old and worn-out by the young and capable. I tell you, the first duty of manhood and womanhood is a Declaration of Independence: the man who pleads his father's authority is no man: the woman who pleads her mother's authority is unfit to bear citizens to a free people.

ANN [*Watching him with quiet curiosity*]   I suppose you will go in seriously for politics some day, Jack.

TANNER [*Heavily let down*]   Eh? What? Wh—? [*Collecting his scat-tered wits*] What has that got to do with what I have been saying?

ANN   You talk so well.

TANNER   Talk! Talk! It means nothing to you but talk. Well, go back to your mother, and help her to poison Rhoda's imagination as she has poisoned yours. It is the tame elephants who enjoy capturing the wild ones.

ANN   I am getting on. Yesterday I was a boa constrictor: to-day I am an elephant.

TANNER   Yes. So pack your trunk and begone: I have no more to say to you.

ANN   You are so utterly unreasonable and impracticable. What can I do?

TANNER   Do! Break your chains. Go your way according to your own conscience and not according to your mother's. Get your mind clean and vigorous; and learn to enjoy a fast ride in a motor car instead of seeing nothing in it but an excuse for a detestable intrigue. Come with me to Marseilles and across to Algiers and to Biskra, at sixty miles an hour. Come right down to the Cape if you

like. That will be a Declaration of Independence with a vengeance.
You can write a book about it afterwards. That will finish your
mother and make a woman of you.

ANN [*Thoughtfully*]   I dont think there would be any harm in that,
Jack. You are my guardian: you stand in my father's place, by his
own wish. Nobody could say a word against our travelling together.
It would be delightful: thank you a thousand times, Jack. I'll come.

TANNER [*Aghast*]   Youll come!!!

ANN   Of course.

TANNER   But— [*He stops, utterly appalled; then resumes feebly*] No:
look here, Ann: if theres no harm in it theres no point in doing
it.

ANN   How absurd you are! You dont want to compromise me, do
you?

TANNER   Yes: thats the whole sense of my proposal.

ANN   You are talking the greatest nonsense; and you know it. You
would never do anything to hurt me.

TANNER   Well, if you dont want to be compromised, dont come.

ANN [*With simple earnestness*]   Yes, I will come, Jack, since you wish
it. You are my guardian; and I think we ought to see more of one
another and come to know one another better. [*Gratefully.*] It's
very thoughtful and very kind of you, Jack, to offer me this lovely
holiday, especially after what I said about Rhoda. You really are
good—much better than you think. When do we start?

TANNER   But—

[*The conversation is interrupted by the arrival of* MRS WHITE-
FIELD *from the house. She is accompanied by the American
gentleman, and followed by* RAMSDEN *and* OCTAVIUS.

HECTOR MALONE *is an Eastern American; but he is not at
all ashamed of his nationality. This makes English people of
fashion think well of him, as of a young fellow who is manly
enough to confess to an obvious disadvantage without any
attempt to conceal or extenuate it. They feel that he ought not
to be made to suffer for what is clearly not his fault, and make
a point of being specially kind to him. His chivalrous manners
to women, and his elevated moral sentiments, being both gra-
tuitous and unusual, strike them as being a little unfortunate;
and though they find his vein of easy humor rather amusing
when it has ceased to puzzle them (as it does at first) they have
had to make him understand that he really must not tell anecdotes unless they are strictly personal and scandalous, and also
that oratory is an accomplishment which belongs to a cruder
stage of civilization than that in which his migration has landed
him. On these points* HECTOR *is not quite convinced: he still
thinks that the British are apt to make merits of their stupidities,
and to represent their various incapacities as points of good*

breeding. English life seems to him to suffer from a lack of edifying rhetoric (which he calls moral tone); English behavior to shew a want of respect for womanhood; English pronunciation to fail very vulgarly in tackling such words as world, girl, bird, etc.; English society to be plain spoken to an extent which stretches occasionally to intolerable coarseness; and English intercourse to need enlivening by games and stories and other pastimes; so he does not feel called upon to acquire these defects after taking great pains to cultivate himself in a first rate manner before venturing across the Atlantic. To this culture he finds English people either totally indifferent, as they very commonly are to all culture, or else politely evasive, the truth being that HECTOR's *culture is nothing but a state of saturation with our literary exports of thirty years ago, reimported by him to be unpacked at a moment's notice and hurled at the head of English literature, science and art, at every conversational opportunity. The dismay set up by these sallies encourages him in his belief that he is helping to educate England. When he finds people chattering harmlessly about Anatole France and Nietzsche, he devastates them with Matthew Arnold, the Autocrat of the Breakfast Table, and even Macaulay; and as he is devoutly religious at bottom, he first leads the unwary, by humorous irreverence, to leave popular theology out of account in discussing moral questions with him, and then scatters them in confusion by demanding whether the carrying out of his ideals of conduct was not the manifest object of God Almighty in creating honest men and pure women. The engaging freshness of his personality and the dumbfoundering staleness of his culture make it extremely difficult to decide whether he is worth knowing; for whilst his company is undeniably pleasant and enlivening, there is intellectually nothing new to be got out of him, especially as he despises politics, and is careful not to talk commercial shop, in which department he is probably much in advance of his English capitalist friends. He gets on best with romantic Christians of the amoristic sect: hence the friendship which has sprung up between him and* OCTAVIUS.

In appearance HECTOR *is a neatly built young man of twenty-four, with a short, smartly trimmed black beard, clear, well shaped eyes, and an ingratiating vivacity of expression. He is, from the fashionable point of view, faultlessly dressed. As he comes along the drive from the house with* MRS WHITEFIELD *he is sedulously making himself agreeable and entertaining, and thereby placing on her slender wit a burden it is unable to bear. An Englishman would let her alone, accepting boredom and*

*indifference as their common lot; and the poor lady wants to be
either let alone or let prattle about the things that interest her.*

RAMSDEN *strolls over to inspect the motor car.* OCTAVIUS
joins HECTOR.]

ANN [*Pouncing on her mother joyously*]   Oh, mama, what do you
think! Jack is going to take me to Nice in his motor car. Isnt it
lovely? I am the happiest person in London.

TANNER [*Desperately*]   Mrs Whitefield objects. I am sure she
objects. Doesnt she, Ramsden?

RAMSDEN   I should think it very likely indeed.

ANN   You dont object, do you, mother?

MRS WHITEFIELD   *I* object! Why should I? I think it will do you good,
Ann. [*Trotting over to* TANNER] I meant to ask you to take Rhoda
out for a run occasionally: she is too much in the house; but it
will do when you come back.

TANNER   Abyss beneath abyss of perfidy!

ANN [*Hastily, to distract attention from this outburst*]   Oh, I forgot:
you have not met Mr Malone. Mr Tanner, my guardian: Mr Hector
Malone.

HECTOR   Pleased to meet you, Mr Tanner. I should like to suggest
an extension of the travelling party to Nice, if I may.

ANN   Oh, we're all coming. That's understood, isnt it?

HECTOR   I also am the mawdest possessor of a motor car. If Miss
Rawbnsn will allow me the privilege of taking her, my car is at her
service.

OCTAVIUS   Violet!

[*General constraint.*]

ANN [*Subduedly*]   Come, mother: we must leave them to talk over
the arrangements. I must see to my travelling kit.

[MRS WHITEFIELD *looks bewildered; but* ANN *draws her discreetly away; and they disappear round the corner towards the
house.*]

HECTOR   I think I may go so far as to say that I can depend on Miss
Rawbnsn's consent.

[*Continued embarrassment.*]

OCTAVIUS   I'm afraid we must leave Violet behind. There are circumstances which make it impossible for her to come on such an
expedition.

HECTOR [*Amused and not at all convinced*]   Too American, eh?
Must the young lady have a chaperone?

OCTAVIUS   It's not that, Malone—at least not altogether.

HECTOR   Indeed! May I ask what other objection applies?

TANNER [*Impatiently*]   Oh, tell him, tell him. We shall never be able
to keep the secret unless everybody knows what it is. Mr Malone:
if you go to Nice with Violet, you go with another man's wife. She
is married.

HECTOR [*Thunderstruck*]   You dont tell me so!

TANNER   We do. In confidence.

RAMSDEN [*With an air of importance, lest* MALONE *should suspect a misalliance.*]   Her marriage has not yet been made known: she desires that it shall not be mentioned for the present.

HECTOR   I shall respect the lady's wishes. Would it be indiscreet to ask who her husband is, in case I should have an opportunity of cawnsulting him about this trip?

TANNER   We dont know who he is.

HECTOR [*Retiring into his shell in a very marked manner*]   In that case, I have no more to say.

   [*They become more embarrassed than ever.*]

OCTAVIUS   You must think this very strange.

HECTOR   A little singular. Pardn mee for saying so.

RAMSDEN [*Half apologetic, half huffy*]   The young lady was married secretly; and her husband has forbidden her, it seems, to declare his name. It is only right to tell you, since you are interested in Miss—er—in Violet.

OCTAVIUS [*Sympathetically*]   I hope this is not a disappointment to you.

HECTOR [*Softened, coming out of his shell again*]   Well: it is a blow. I can hardly understand how a man can leave his wife in such a position. Surely it's not custoMary.[5] It's not manly. It's not considerate.

OCTAVIUS   We feel that, as you may imagine, pretty deeply.

RAMSDEN [*Testily*]   It is some young fool who has not enough experience to know what mystifications of this kind lead to.

HECTOR [*With strong symptoms of moral repugnance*]   I hope so. A man need be very young and pretty foolish too to be excused for such conduct. You take a very lenient view, Mr Ramsden. Too lenient to my mind. Surely marriage should ennoble a man.

TANNER [*Sardonically*]   Ha!

HECTOR   Am I to gather from that cacchination[6] that you dont agree with me, Mr Tanner?

TANNER [*Drily*]   Get married and try. You may find it delightful for a while: you certainly wont find it ennobling. The greatest common measure of a man and a woman is not necessarily greater than the man's single measure.

HECTOR   Well, we think in America that a woman's morl number is higher than a man's, and that the purer nature of a woman lifts a man right out of himself, and makes him better than he was.

OCTAVIUS [*With conviction*]   So it does.

TANNER   No wonder American women prefer to live in Europe! Its more comfortable than standing all their lives on an altar to be worshipped. Anyhow, Violet's husband has not been ennobled. So whats to be done?

5. Shaw intended the capital M to emphasize Hector's American pronunciation.
6. Loud or prolonged laughter.

HECTOR [*Shaking his head*]   I cant dismiss that man's cawnduct as lightly as you do, Mr Tanner. However, I'll say no more. Whoever he is, he's Miss Rawbnsn's husband; and I should be glad for her sake to think better of him.

OCTAVIUS [*Touched; for he divines a secret sorrow*]   I'm very sorry, Malone. Very sorry.

HECTOR [*Gratefully*]   Youre a good fellow, Rawbnsn. Thank you.

TANNER   Talk about something else. Violet's coming from the house.

HECTOR   I should esteem it a very great favor, gentlemen, if you would take the opportunity to let me have a few words with the lady alone. I shall have to cry off this trip; and it's rather a dullicate—

RAMSDEN [*Glad to escape*]   Say no more. Come, Tanner. Come, Tavy. [*He strolls away into the park with* OCTAVIUS *and* TANNER, *past the motor car.*]

[VIOLET *comes down the avenue to* HECTOR.]

VIOLET   Are they looking?

HECTOR   No.
         [*She kisses him.*]

VIOLET   Have you been telling lies for my sake?

HECTOR   Lying! Lying hardly describes it. I overdo it. I get carried away in an ecstacy of mendacity. Violet: I wish youd let me own up.

VIOLET [*Instantly becoming serious and resolute*]   No, no, Héctor: you promised me not to.

HECTOR   I'll keep my prawmise until you release me from it. But I feel mean, lying to those men, and denying my wife. Just dastardly.

VIOLET   I wish your father were not so unreasonable.

HECTOR   Hes not unreasonable. Hes right from his point of view. He has a prejudice against the English middle class.

VIOLET   It's too ridiculous. You know how I dislike saying such things to you, Hector; but if I were to—oh, well, no matter.

HECTOR   I know. If you were to marry the son of an English manufacturer of awffice furniture, your friends would consider it a misalliance. And here's my silly old dad, who is the biggest awffice furniture man in the world, would shew me the door for marrying the most perfect lady in England merely because she has no handle to her name. Of course it's just absurd. But I tell you, Violet, I dont like deceiving him. I feel as if I was stealing his money. Why wont you let me own up?

VIOLET   We cant afford it. You can be as romantic as you please about love, Hector; but you mustnt be romantic about money.

HECTOR [*Divided between his uxoriousness and his habitual elevation of moral sentiment*]   Thats very English. [*Appealing to her impulsively.*] Violet: dad's bound to find us out someday.

VIOLET   Oh yes, later on of course. But dont let's go over this every time we meet, dear. You promised—

HECTOR   All right, all right, I—

VIOLET   [*Not to be silenced*]   It is I and not you who suffer by this concealment; and as to facing a struggle and poverty and all that sort of thing I simply will not do it. It's too silly.

HECTOR   You shall not. I'll sort of borrow the money from my dad until I get on my own feet; and then I can own up and pay up at the same time.

VIOLET   [*Alarmed and indignant*]   Do you mean to work? Do you want to spoil our marriage?

HECTOR   Well, I dont mean to let marriage spoil my character. Your friend Mr Tanner has got the laugh on me a bit already about that; and—

VIOLET   The beast! I hate Jack Tanner.

HECTOR   [*Magnanimously*]   Oh, hes all right: he only needs the love of a good woman to ennoble him. Besides, hes proposed a motoring trip to Nice; and I'm going to take you.

VIOLET   How jolly!

HECTOR   Yes; but how are we going to manage? You see, theyve warned me off going with you, so to speak. Theyve told me in cawnfidnce that youre married. Thats just the most overwhelming cawnfidnce Ive ever been honored with.

        [TANNER *returns with* STRAKER, *who goes to his car.*]

TANNER   Your car is a great success, Mr Malone. Your engineer is showing it off to Mr Ramsden.

HECTOR   [*Eagerly—forgetting himself*]   Lets come, Vi.

VIOLET   [*Coldly, warning him with her eyes*]   I beg your pardon, Mr Malone, I did not quite catch—

HECTOR   [*Recollecting himself*]   I ask to be allowed the pleasure of shewing you my little American steam car, Miss Rawbnsn.

VIOLET   I shall be very pleased. [*They go off together down the avenue.*]

TANNER   About this trip, Straker.

STRAKER   [*Preoccupied with the car*]   Yes?

TANNER   Miss Whitefield is supposed to be coming with me.

STRAKER   So I gather.

TANNER   Mr Robinson is to be one of the party.

STRAKER   Yes.

TANNER   Well, if you can manage so as to be a good deal occupied with me, and leave Mr Robinson a good deal occupied with Miss Whitefield, he will be deeply grateful to you.

STRAKER   [*Looking round at him*]   Evidently.

TANNER   "Evidently"! Your grandfather would have simply winked.

STRAKER   My grandfather would have touched his at.

TANNER   And I should have given your good nice respectful grandfather a sovereign.

STRAKER   Five shillins, more likely.[7] [*He leaves the car and approaches* TANNER.] What about the lady's views?

TANNER   She is just as willing to be left to Mr Robinson as Mr Robinson is to be left to her. [STRAKER *looks at his principal with cool scepticism; then turns to the car whistling his favorite air.*] Stop that aggravating noise. What do you mean by it? [STRAKER *calmly resumes the melody and finishes it.* TANNER *politely hears it out before he again addresses* STRAKER, *this time with elaborate seriousness*] Enry: I have ever been a warm advocate of the spread of music among the masses; but I object to your obliging the company whenever Miss Whitefield's name is mentioned. You did it this morning, too.

STRAKER [*Obstinately*]   It's not a bit o use. Mr Robinson may as well give it up first as last.

TANNER   Why?

STRAKER   Garn! You know why. Course it's not my business; but you neednt start kiddin me about it.

TANNER   I am not kidding. I dont know why.

STRAKER [*Cheerfully sulky*]   Oh, very well. All right. It aint my business.

TANNER [*Impressively*]   I trust, Enry, that, as between employer and engineer, I shall always know how to keep my proper distance, and not intrude my private affairs on you. Even our business arrangements are subject to the approval of your Trade Union. But dont abuse your advantages. Let me remind you that Voltaire said that what was too silly to be said could be sung.

STRAKER   It wasnt Voltaire: it was Bow Mar Shay.

TANNER   I stand corrected: Beaumarchais[8] of course. Now you seem to think that what is too delicate to be said can be whistled. Unfortunately your whistling, though melodious, is unintelligible. Come! there's nobody listening: neither my genteel relatives nor the secretary of your confounded Union. As man to man, Enry, why do you think that my friend has no chance with Miss Whitefield?

STRAKER   Cause shes arter summun else.

TANNER   Bosh! who else?

STRAKER   You.

TANNER   Me!!!

STRAKER   Mean to tell me you didnt know? Oh, come, Mr Tanner!

TANNER [*In fierce earnest*]   Are you playing the fool, or do you mean it?

STRAKER [*With a flash of temper*]   I'm not playin no fool. [*More coolly.*] Why, it's as plain as the nose on your face. If you aint spotted that, you dont know much about these sort of things.

---

7. A sovereign was a gold coin worth one pound. Five shillings is worth about 40c.
8. Pierre-Augustin Caron de Beaumarchais, French author of two comedies, *The Barber of Seville* (1776) and *The Marriage of Figaro* (1784), on which Mozart based his operas.

[*Serene again*] Ex-cuse me, you know, Mr Tanner; but you asked me as man to man; and I told you as man to man.

TANNER [*Wildly appealing to the heavens*]   Then I—I am the bee, the spider, the marked down victim, the destined prey.

STRAKER   I dunno about the bee and the spider. But the marked down victim, thats what you are and no mistake; and a jolly good job for you, too, I should say.

TANNER [*Momentously*]   Henry Straker: the golden moment of your life has arrived.

STRAKER   What d'y'mean?

TANNER   That record to Biskra.

STRAKER [*Eagerly*]   Yes?

TANNER   Break it.

STRAKER [*Rising to the height of his destiny*]   D'y'mean it?

TANNER   I do.

STRAKER   When?

TANNER   Now. Is that machine ready to start?

STRAKER [*Quailing*]   But you cant—

TANNER [*Cutting him short by getting into the car.*]   Off we go. First to the bank for money; then to my rooms for my kit; then to your rooms for your kit; then break the record from London to Dover or Folkestone; then across the channel and away like mad to Marseilles, Gibraltar, Genoa, any port from which we can sail to a Mahometan country where men are protected from women.

STRAKER   Garn! youre kiddin.

TANNER [*Resolutely*]   Stay behind then. If you wont come I'll do it alone. [*He starts the motor.*]

STRAKER [*Running after him*]   Here! Mister! arf a mo! steady on! [*He scrambles in as the car plunges forward.*]

Act III

Evening in the Sierra Nevada. Rolling slopes of brown, with olive trees instead of apple trees in the cultivated patches, and occasional prickly pears instead of gorse and bracken in the wilds. Higher up, tall stone peaks and precipices, all handsome and distinguished. No wild nature here: rather a most aristocratic mountain landscape made by a fastidious artist-creator. No vulgar profusion of vegetation: even a touch of aridity in the frequent patches of stones: Spanish magnificence and Spanish economy everywhere.

Not very far north of a spot at which the high road over one of the passes crosses a tunnel on the railway from Malaga to Granada, is one of the mountain amphitheatres of the Sierra. Looking at it from the wide end of the horse-

shoe, one sees, a little to the right, in the face of the cliff, a romantic cave which is really an abandoned quarry, and towards the left a little hill, commanding a view of the road, which skirts the amphitheatre on the left, maintaining its higher level on embankments and an occasional stone arch. On the hill, watching the road, is a man who is either a Spaniard or a Scotchman. Probably a Spaniard, since he wears the dress of a Spanish goatherd and seems at home in the Sierra Nevada, but very like a Scotchman for all that. In the hollow, on the slope leading to the quarry-cave, are about a dozen men who, as they recline at their ease round a heap of smouldering white ashes of dead leaf and brushwood, have an air of being conscious of themselves as picturesque scoundrels honoring the Sierra by using it as an effective pictorial background. As a matter of artistic fact they are not picturesque; and the mountains tolerate them as lions tolerate lice. An English policeman or Poor Law Guardian would recognize them as a selected band of tramps and ablebodied paupers.

This description of them is not wholly contemptuous. Whoever has intelligently observed the tramp, or visited the ablebodied ward of a workhouse, will admit that our social failures are not all drunkards and weaklings. Some of them are men who do not fit the class they were born into. Precisely the same qualities that make the educated gentleman an artist may make an uneducated manual laborer an ablebodied pauper. There are men who fall helplessly into the workhouse because they are good for nothing; but there are also men who are there because they are strongminded enough to disregard the social convention (obviously not a disinterested one on the part of the ratepayer) which bids a man live by heavy and badly paid drudgery when he has the alternative of walking into the workhouse, announcing himself as a destitute person, and legally compelling the Guardians to feed, clothe and house him better than he could feed, clothe and house himself without great exertion. When a man who is born a poet refuses a stool in a stockbroker's office, and starves in a garret, spunging on a poor landlady or on his friends and relatives sooner than work against his grain; or when a lady, because she is a lady, will face any extremity of parasitic dependence rather than take a situation as cook or parlormaid, we make large allowances for them. To such allowances the ablebodied pauper, and his nomadic variant the tramp, are equally entitled.

Further, the imaginative man, if his life is to be tolerable
to him, must have leisure to tell himself stories, and a position which lends itself to imaginative decoration. The
ranks of unskilled labor offer no such positions. We misuse
our laborers horribly; and when a man refuses to be mis-
used, we have no right to say that he is refusing honest
work. Let us be frank in this matter before we go on with
our play; so that we may enjoy it without hypocrisy. If we
were reasoning, farsighted people, four fifths of us would
go straight to the Guardians for relief, and knock the whole
social system to pieces with most beneficial reconstructive
results. The reason we do not do this is because we work
like bees or ants, by instinct or habit, not reasoning about
the matter at all. Therefore when a man comes along who
can and does reason, and who, applying the Kantian test
to his conduct, can truly say to us, If everybody did as I do,
the world would be compelled to reform itself industrially,
and abolish slavery and squalor, which exist only because
everybody does as you do, let us honor that man and seriously consider the advisability of following his example.
Such a man is the able-bodied, able-minded pauper. Were
he a gentleman doing his best to get a pension or a sinecure
instead of sweeping a crossing, nobody would blame him
for deciding that so long as the alternative lies between
living mainly at the expense of the community and allowing the community to live mainly at his, it would be folly
to accept what is to him personally the greater of the two
evils.

We may therefore contemplate the tramps of the Sierra
without prejudice, admitting cheerfully that our objects—
briefly, to be gentlemen of fortune—are much the same as
their's, and the difference in our position and methods
merely accidental. One or two of them, perhaps, it would
be wiser to kill without malice in a friendly and frank
manner; for there are bipeds, just as there are quadrupeds,
who are too dangerous to be left unchained and unmuz-
zled; and these cannot fairly expect to have other men's
lives wasted in the work of watching them. But as society
has not the courage to kill them, and, when it catches
them, simply wreaks on them some superstitious expiatory
rites of torture and degradation, and then lets them loose
with heightened qualifications for mischief, it is just as
well that they are at large in the Sierra, and in the hands
of a chief who looks as if he might possibly, on provocation,
order them to be shot.

This CHIEF, *seated in the centre of the group on a squared block of stone from the quarry, is a tall strong man, with a striking cockatoo nose, glossy black hair, pointed beard, upturned moustache, and a Mephistophelean affectation which is fairly imposing, perhaps because the scenery admits of a larger swagger than Piccadilly, perhaps because of a certain sentimentality in the man which gives him that touch of grace which alone can excuse deliberate picturesqueness. His eyes and mouth are by no means rascally; he has a fine voice and a ready wit; and whether he is really the strongest man in the party or not, he looks it. He is certainly the best fed, the best dressed, and the best trained. The fact that he speaks English is not unexpected, in spite of the Spanish landscape; for with the exception of one man who might be guessed as a bullfighter ruined by drink, and one unmistakable Frenchman, they are all cockney or American; therefore, in a land of cloaks and sombreros, they mostly wear seedy overcoats, woollen mufflers, hard hemispherical hats, and dirty brown gloves. Only a very few dress after their leader, whose broad sombrero with a cock's feather in the band, and voluminous cloak descending to his high boots, are as un-English as possible. None of them are armed; and the ungloved ones keep their hands in their pockets because it is their national belief that it must be dangerously cold in the open air with the night coming on. (It is as warm an evening as any reasonable man could desire.)*

Except the bullfighting inebriate there is only one person in the company who looks more than, say, thirty-three. He is a small man with reddish whiskers, weak eyes, and the anxious look of a small tradesman in difficulties. He wears the only tall hat visible: it shines in the sunset with the sticky glow of some sixpenny patent hat reviver, often applied and constantly tending to produce a worse state of the original surface than the ruin it was applied to remedy. He has a collar and cuffs of celluloid; and his brown Chesterfield overcoat, with velvet collar, is still presentable. He is pre-eminently the respectable man of the party, and is certainly over forty, possibly over fifty. He is the corner man on the leader's right, opposite three men in scarlet ties on his left. One of these three is the FRENCHMAN. Of the remaining two, who are both English, one is argumentative, solemn, and obstinate; the other rowdy and mischievous.

THE CHIEF, *with a magnificent fling of the end of his*

cloak across his left shoulder, rises to address them. The
applause which greets him shews that he is a favorite ora-
tor.

THE CHIEF   Friends and fellow brigands. I have a proposal to make
to this meeting. We have now spent three evenings in discussing
the question Have Anarchists or Social-Democrats the most personal courage? We have gone into the principles of Anarchism and
Social-Democracy at great length. The cause of Anarchy has been
ably represented by our one Anarchist, who doesnt know what
Anarchism means [*Laughter*]—

THE ANARCHIST [*Rising*]   A point of order, Mendoza—

MENDOZA [*Forcibly*]   No, by thunder: your last point of order took
half an hour. Besides, Anarchists dont believe in order.

THE ANARCHIST [*Mild, polite but persistent: he is, in fact, the respect-*
able-looking elderly man in the celluloid collar and cuffs.]   That
is a vulgar error. I can prove—

MENDOZA   Order, order.

THE OTHERS [*Shouting*]   Order, order. Sit down. Chair! Shut up.
        [THE ANARCHIST *is suppressed.*]

MENDOZA   On the other hand we have three Social-Democrats
among us. They are not on speaking terms; and they have put
before us three distinct and incompatible views of Social-
Democracy.

THE THREE MEN IN SCARLET TIES   1. Mr Chairman, I protest. A
personal explanation. 2. It's a lie. I never said so. Be fair, Mendoza.
3. Je demande la parole. C'est absolument faux. C'est faux! faux!!
faux!!![1] Assas-s-s-s-sin!!!!!!

MENDOZA   Order, order.

THE OTHERS.   Order, order, order! Chair!
        [THE SOCIAL-DEMOCRATS *are suppressed.*]

MENDOZA   Now, we tolerate all opinions here. But after all, comrades, the vast majority of us are neither Anarchists nor Socialists,
but gentlemen and Christians.

THE MAJORITY [*Shouting assent*]   Hear, hear! So we are. Right.

THE ROWDY SOCIAL-DEMOCRAT [*Smarting under suppression.*]   You
aint no Christian. Youre a Sheeny,[2] you are.

MENDOZA [*With crushing magnanimity*]   My friend: *I* am an exception to all rules. It is true that I have the honor to be a Jew; and
when the Zionists need a leader to reassemble our race on its
historic soil of Palestine, Mendoza will not be the last to volunteer
[*Sympathetic applause—hear, hear. &c.*]. But I am not a slave to
any superstition. I have swallowed all the formulas, even that of
Socialism; though, in a sense, once a Socialist, always a Socialist.

1. I demand to speak. It's absolutely false. It's false! false!! false!!!
2. Jew.

THE SOCIAL-DEMOCRATS   Hear, hear!

MENDOZA   But I am well aware that the ordinary man—even the ordinary brigand, who can scarcely be called an ordinary man [*Hear, hear!*]—is not a philosopher. Common sense is good enough for him; and in our business affairs common sense is good enough for me. Well, what is our business here in the Sierra Nevada, chosen by the Moors as the fairest spot in Spain? Is it to discuss abstruse questions of political economy? No: it is to hold up motor cars and secure a more equitable distribution of wealth.

THE SULKY SOCIAL-DEMOCRAT   All made by labor, mind you.

MENDOZA [*Urbanely*]   Undoubtedly. All made by labor, and on its way to be squandered by wealthy vagabonds in the dens of vice that disfigure the sunny shores of the Mediterranean. We intercept that wealth. We restore it to circulation among the class that produced it and that chiefly needs it—the working class. We do this at the risk of our lives and liberties, by the exercise of the virtues of courage, endurance, foresight, and abstinence—especially abstinence. I myself have eaten nothing but prickly pears and broiled rabbit for three days.

THE SULKY SOCIAL-DEMOCRAT [*Stubbornly*]   No more aint we.

MENDOZA [*Indignantly*]   Have I taken more than my share?

THE SULKY SOCIAL-DEMOCRAT [*Unmoved*]   Why should you?

THE ANARCHIST   Why should he not? To each according to his needs: from each according to his means.

THE FRENCHMAN [*Shaking his fist at the* ANARCHIST]   Fumiste!

MENDOZA [*Diplomatically*]   I agree with both of you.

THE GENUINELY ENGLISH BRIGANDS   Hear, hear! Bravo Mendoza!

MENDOZA   What I say is, let us treat one another as gentlemen, and strive to excel in personal courage only when we take the field.

THE ROWDY SOCIAL-DEMOCRAT [*Derisively*]   Shikespear.

[*A whistle comes from* THE GOATHERD *on the hill. He springs up and points excitedly forward along the road to the north.*]

THE GOATHERD   Automobile! Automobile! [*He rushes down the hill and joins the rest, who all scramble to their feet.*]

MENDOZA [*In ringing tones*]   To arms! Who has the gun?

THE SULKY SOCIAL-DEMOCRAT [*Handing a rifle to* MENDOZA]   Here.

MENDOZA   Have the nails been strewn in the road?

THE ROWDY SOCIAL-DEMOCRAT   Two ahnces of em.

MENDOZA   Good! [*To* THE FRENCHMAN] With me, Duval. If the nails fail, puncture their tires with a bullet. [*He gives the rifle to* DUVAL, *who follows him up the hill.* MENDOZA *produces an opera glass. The others hurry across to the road and disappear to the north.*]

MENDOZA [*On the hill, using his glass*]   Two only, a capitalist and his chauffeur. They look English.

DUVAL   Angliche! Aoh yess. Cochons! [*Handling the rifle*] Faut tirer, n'est-ce-pas?[3]

3. "Cochons": pigs; "Shall we shoot?"

MENDOZA   No: the nails have gone home. Their tire is down: they stop.

DUVAL [*Shouting to the others*]   Fondez sur eux, nom de Dieu![4]

MENDOZA [*Rebuking his excitement*]   Du calme, Duval: keep your hair on. They take it quietly. Let us descend and receive them.

> [MENDOZA *descends, passing behind the fire and coming forward, whilst* TANNER *and* STRAKER, *in their motoring goggles, leather coats, and caps, are led in from the road by the brigands.*]

TANNER   Is this the gentleman you describe as your boss? Does he speak English?

THE ROWDY SOCIAL-DEMOCRAT   Course he does. Y' downt suppowz we Hinglishmen luts ahrselves be bossed by a bloomin Spenniard, do you?

MENDOZA [*With dignity*]   Allow me to introduce myself: Mendoza, President of the League of the Sierra! [*Posing loftily.*] I am a brigand: I live by robbing the rich.

TANNER [*Promptly*]   I am a gentleman: I live by robbing the poor. Shake hands.

THE ENGLISH SOCIAL-DEMOCRATS   Hear, hear!

> [*General laughter and good humor.* TANNER *and* MENDOZA *shake hands.* THE BRIGANDS *drop into their former places.*]

STRAKER   Ere! where do I come in?

TANNER [*Introducing*]   My friend and chauffeur.

THE SULKY SOCIAL-DEMOCRAT [*Suspiciously*]   Well, which is he? friend or show-for? It makes all the difference, you know.

MENDOZA [*Explaining*]   We should expect ransom for a friend. A professional chauffeur is free of the mountains. He even takes a trifling percentage of his principal's ransom if he will honor us by accepting it.

STRAKER   I see. Just to encourage me to come this way again. Well, I'll think about it.

DUVAL [*Impulsively rushing across to* STRAKER]   Mon frère![5] [*He embraces him rapturously and kisses him on both cheeks.*]

STRAKER [*Disgusted*]   Ere, git out: dont be silly. Who are you, pray?

DUVAL   Duval: Social-Democrat.

STRAKER   Oh, youre a Social-Democrat, are you?

THE ANARCHIST   He means that he has sold out to the parliamentary humbugs and the bourgeoisie. Compromise! that is his faith.

DUVAL [*Furiously*]   I understand what he say. He say Bourgeois. He say Compromise. Jamais de la vie! Misérable menteur—[6]

STRAKER   See here, Captain Mendoza, ow much o this sort o thing do you put up with here? Are we avin a pleasure trip in the mountains, or are we at a Socialist meetin?

---

4. Literally, "Melt on them, in the name of God!" i.e., fall on them.
5. My brother!
6. Never in my life! Miserable liar—.

THE MAJORITY   Hear, hear! Shut up. Chuck it. Sit down, &c. &c.
[THE SOCIAL-DEMOCRATS *and* THE ANARCHIST *are hustled into the background.* STRAKER, *after superintending this proceeding with satisfaction, places himself on* MENDOZA'*s left,* TANNER *being on his right.*]

MENDOZA   Can we offer you anything? Broiled rabbit and prickly pears—

TANNER   Thank you: we have dined.

MENDOZA [*To his followers*]   Gentlemen: business is over for the day. Go as you please until morning.

[THE BRIGANDS *disperse into groups lazily. Some go into the cave. Others sit down or lie down to sleep in the open. A few produce a pack of cards and move off towards the road; for it is now starlight; and they know that motor cars have lamps which can be turned to account for lighting a card party.*]

STRAKER [*Calling after them*]   Dont none of you go fooling with that car, d'ye hear?

MENDOZA   No fear, Monsieur le Chauffeur. The first one we captured cured us of that.

STRAKER [*Interested*]   What did it do?

MENDOZA   It carried three brave comrades of ours, who did not know how to stop it, into Granada, and capsized them opposite the police station. Since then we never touch one without sending for the chauffeur. Shall we chat at our ease?

TANNER   By all means.

[TANNER, MENDOZA, *and* STRAKER *sit down on the turf by the fire.* MENDOZA *delicately waives his presidential dignity, of which the right to sit on the squared stone block is the appanage, by sitting on the ground like his guests, and using the stone only as a support for his back.*]

MENDOZA   It is the custom in Spain always to put off business until to-morrow. In fact, you have arrived out of office hours. However, if you would prefer to settle the question of ransom at once, I am at your service.

TANNER   To-morrow will do for me. I am rich enough to pay anything in reason.

MENDOZA [*Respectfully, much struck by this admission*]   You are a remarkable man, sir. Our guests usually describe themselves as miserably poor.

TANNER   Pooh! Miserably poor people dont own motor cars.

MENDOZA   Precisely what we say to them.

TANNER   Treat us well: we shall not prove ungrateful.

STRAKER   No prickly pears and broiled rabbits, you know. Dont tell me you cant do us a bit better than that if you like.

MENDOZA   Wine, kids, milk, cheese and bread can be procured for ready money.

STRAKER [*Graciously*]   Now youre talking.

TANNER   Are you all Socialists here, may I ask?

MENDOZA [*Repudiating this humiliating misconception*]   Oh no, no, no: nothing of the kind, I assure you. We naturally have modern views as to the justice of the existing distribution of wealth: otherwise we should lose our self-respect. But nothing that you could take exception to, except two or three faddists.

TANNER   I had no intention of suggesting anything discreditable. In fact, I am a bit of a Socialist myself.

STRAKER [*Drily*]   Most rich men are, I notice.

MENDOZA   Quite so. It has reached us, I admit. It is in the air of the century.

STRAKER   Socialism must be lookin up a bit if your chaps are taking to it.

MENDOZA   That is true, sir. A movement which is confined to philosophers and honest men can never exercise any real political influence: there are too few of them. Until a movement shews itself capable of spreading among brigands, it can never hope for a political majority.

TANNER   But are your brigands any less honest than ordinary citizens?

MENDOZA   Sir: I will be frank with you. Brigandage is abnormal. Abnormal professions attract two classes: those who are not good enough for ordinary bourgeois life and those who are too good for it. We are dregs and scum, sir: the dregs very filthy, the scum very superior.

STRAKER   Take care! some o the dregs'll hear you.

MENDOZA   It does not matter: each brigand thinks himself scum, and likes to hear the others called dregs.

TANNER   Come! you are a wit. [MENDOZA *inclines his head, flattered*] May one ask you a blunt question?

MENDOZA   As blunt as you please.

TANNER   How does it pay a man of your talent to shepherd such a flock as this on broiled rabbit and prickly pears? I have seen men less gifted, and I'll swear less honest, supping at the Savoy on foie gras and champagne.

MENDOZA   Pooh! they have all had their turn at the broiled rabbit, just as I shall have my turn at the Savoy. Indeed, I have had a turn there already—as waiter.

TANNER   A waiter! You astonish me!

MENDOZA [*Reflectively*]   Yes: I, Mendoza of the Sierra, was a waiter. Hence, perhaps, my cosmopolitanism. [*With sudden intensity.*] Shall I tell you the story of my life?

STRAKER [*Apprehensively*]   If it aint too long, old chap—

TANNER [*Interrupting him.*]   Tsh-sh: you are a Philistine, Henry: you have no romance in you. [*To* MENDOZA] You interest me extremely, President. Never mind Henry: he can go to sleep.

MENDOZA   The woman I loved—

STRAKER   Oh, this is a love story, is it? Right you are. Go on: I was only afraid you were going to talk about yourself.

MENDOZA   Myself! I have thrown myself away for her sake: that is why I am here. No matter: I count the world well lost for her. She had, I pledge you my word, the most magnificent head of hair I ever saw. She had humor; she had intellect; she could cook to perfection; and her highly strung temperament made her uncertain, incalculable, variable, capricious, cruel, in a word, enchanting.

STRAKER   A six shillin novel sort o woman, all but the cookin. Er name was Lady Gladys Plantagenet, wasnt it?

MENDOZA   No, sir: she was not an earl's daughter. Photography, reproduced by the half-tone process, has made me familiar with the appearance of the daughters of the English peerage; and I can honestly say that I would have sold the lot, faces, dowries, clothes, titles, and all, for a smile from this woman. Yet she was a woman of the people, a worker: otherwise—let me reciprocate your bluntness—I should have scorned her.

TANNER   Very properly. And did she respond to your love?

MENDOZA   Should I be here if she did? She objected to marry a Jew.

TANNER   On religious grounds?

MENDOZA   No: she was a freethinker. She said that every Jew considers in his heart that English people are dirty in their habits.

TANNER [Surprised.]   Dirty!

MENDOZA   It shewed her extraordinary knowledge of the world; for it is undoubtedly true. Our elaborate sanitary code makes us unduly contemptuous of the Gentile.

TANNER   Did you ever hear that, Henry?

STRAKER   Ive heard my sister say so. She was cook in a Jewish family once.

MENDOZA   I could not deny it; neither could I eradicate the impression it made on her mind. I could have got round any other objection; but no woman can stand a suspicion of indelicacy as to her person. My entreaties were in vain: she always retorted that she wasnt good enough for me, and recommended me to marry an accursed barmaid named Rebecca Lazarus, whom I loathed. I talked of suicide: she offered me a packet of beetle poison to do it with. I hinted at murder: she went into hysterics; and as I am a living man I went to America so that she might sleep without dreaming that I was stealing upstairs to cut her throat. In America I went out west and fell in with a man who was wanted by the police for holding up trains. It was he who had the idea of holding up motor cars in the South of Europe: a welcome idea to a desperate and disappointed man. He gave me some valuable introductions to capitalists of the right sort. I formed a syndicate; and the present enterprise is the result. I became leader, as the Jew always becomes leader, by his brains and imagination. But with all my pride of race I would give everything I possess to be an Englishman. I am like a boy: I cut her name on the trees and her initials on the sod. When I am alone I lie down and tear my wretched hair and cry Louisa—

STRAKER [*Startled*]   Louisa!

MENDOZA   It is her name—Louisa—Louisa Straker—

TANNER   Straker!

STRAKER [*Scrambling up on his knees most indignantly.*]   Look here: Louisa Straker is my sister, see? Wot do you mean by gassin about her like this? Wotshe got to do with you?

MENDOZA   A dramatic coincidence! You are Enry, her favorite brother!

STRAKER   Oo are you callin Enry? What call have you to take a liberty with my name or with hers? For two pins I'd punch your fat ed, so I would.

MENDOZA [*With grandiose calm.*]   If I let you do it, will you promise to brag of it afterwards to her? She will be reminded of her Mendoza: that is all I desire.

TANNER   This is genuine devotion, Henry. You should respect it.

STRAKER [*Fiercely.*]   Funk,[7] more likely.

MENDOZA [*Springing to his feet.*]   Funk! Young man: I come of a famous family of fighters; and as your sister well knows, you would have as much chance against me as a perambulator against your motor car.

STRAKER [*Secretly daunted, but rising from his knees with an air of reckless pugnacity.*]   I aint afraid of you. With your Louisa! Louisa! Miss Straker is good enough for you, I should think.

MENDOZA   I wish you could persuade her to think so.

STRAKER [*Exasperated.*]   Here—

TANNER [*Rising quickly and interposing.*]   Oh come, Henry: even if you could fight the President you cant fight the whole League of the Sierra. Sit down again and be friendly. A cat may look at a king; and even a President of brigands may look at your sister. All this family pride is really very old fashioned.

STRAKER [*Subdued, but grumbling*]   Let him look at her. But wot does he mean by makin out that she ever looked at im? [*Reluctantly resuming his couch on the turf.*] Ear him talk, one ud think she was keepin company with him. [*He turns his back on them and composes himself to sleep.*]

MENDOZA [*To* TANNER, *becoming more confidential as he finds himself virtually alone with a sympathetic listener in the still starlight of the mountains; for all the rest are asleep by this time*]   It was just so with her, sir. Her intellect reached forward into the twentieth century: her social prejudices and family affections reached back into the dark ages. Ah, sir, how the words of Shakespear seem to fit every crisis in our emotions!

7. Failure of nerve.

> I loved Louisa: 40,000 brothers
> Could not with all their quantity of love
> Make up my sum.[8]

And so on. I forget the rest. Call it madness if you will—infatuation. I am an able man, a strong man: in ten years I should have owned a first-class hotel. I met her; and—you see!—I am a brigand, an outcast. Even Shakespear cannot do justice to what I feel for Louisa. Let me read you some lines that I have written about her myself. However slight their literary merit may be, they express what I feel better than any casual words can. [*He produces a packet of hotel bills scrawled with manuscript, and kneels at the fire to decipher them, poking it with a stick to make it glow.*]

TANNER [*Slapping him rudely on the shoulder*]   Put them in the fire, President.

MENDOZA [*Startled*]   Eh?

TANNER   You are sacrificing your career to a monomania.

MENDOZA   I know it.

TANNER   No you dont. No man would commit such a crime against himself if he really knew what he was doing. How can you look round at these august hills, look up at this divine sky, taste this finely tempered air, and then talk like a literary hack on a second floor in Bloomsbury?[9]

MENDOZA [*Shaking his head*]   The Sierra is no better than Bloomsbury when once the novelty has worn off. Besides, these mountains make you dream of women—of women with magnificent hair.

TANNER   Of Louisa, in short. They will not make me dream of women, my friend: I am heartwhole.

MENDOZA   Do not boast until morning, sir. This is a strange country for dreams.

TANNER   Well, we shall see. Goodnight. [*He lies down and composes himself to sleep.*]

> [MENDOZA, *with a sigh, follows his example; and for a few moments there is peace in the Sierra. Then* MENDOZA *sits up suddenly and says pleadingly to* TANNER—]

MENDOZA   Just allow me to read a few lines before you go to sleep. I should really like your opinion of them.

TANNER [*Drowsily*]   Go on. I am listening.

MENDOZA   I saw thee first in Whitsun week
            Louisa, Louisa—

TANNER [*Rousing himself*]   My dear President, Louisa is a very pretty name; but it really doesnt rhyme well to Whitsun week.

8. See *Hamlet* 6.1.291: "I loved Ophelia . . ."
9. Area of London near the British Museum.

MENDOZA   Of course not. Louisa is not the rhyme, but the refrain.

TANNER [*Subsiding*]   Ah, the refrain. I beg your pardon. Go on.

MENDOZA   Perhaps you do not care for that one: I think you will like this better. [*He recites, in rich soft tones, and in slow time*]

> Louisa, I love thee.
> I love thee, Louisa.
> Louisa, Louisa, Louisa, I love thee.
> One name and one phrase make my music, Louisa.
> Louisa, Louisa, Louisa, I love thee.
>
> Mendoza thy lover,
> Thy lover, Mendoza,
> Mendoza adoringly lives for Louisa.
> There's nothing but that in the world for Mendoza.
> Louisa, Louisa, Mendoza adores thee.

[*Affected*] There is no merit in producing beautiful lines upon such a name. Louisa is an exquisite name, is it not?

TANNER [*All but asleep, responds with a faint groan.*]

MENDOZA   O wert thou, Louisa,
> The wife of Mendoza,
> Mendoza's Louisa, Louisa Mendoza,
> How blest were the life of Louisa's Mendoza!
> How painless his longing of love for Louisa!

That is real poetry—from the heart—from the heart of hearts. Dont you think it will move her?

[*No answer.*]

[*Resignedly*] Asleep, as usual. Doggrel to all the world: heavenly music to me! Idiot that I am to wear my heart on my sleeve! [*He composes himself to sleep, murmuring.*] Louisa, I love thee; I love thee, Louisa; Louisa, Louisa, Louisa, I—

[STRAKER *snores; rolls over on his side; and relapses into sleep. Stillness settles on the Sierra; and the darkness deepens. The fire has again buried itself in white ash and ceased to glow. The peaks shew unfathomably dark against the starry firmament; but now the stars dim and vanish; and the sky seems to steal away out of the universe. Instead of the Sierra there is nothing; omnipresent nothing. No sky, no peaks, no light, no sound, no time nor space, utter void. Then somewhere the beginning of a pallor, and with it a faint throbbing buzz as of a ghostly violoncello palpitating on the same note endlessly. A couple of ghostly violins presently take advantage of this bass*]

and therewith the pallor reveals a man in the void, an incorporeal but visible man, seated, absurdly enough, on nothing. For a moment he raises his head as the music passes him by. Then, with a heavy sigh, he droops in utter dejection; and the violins, discouraged, retrace their melody in despair and at last give it up, extinguished by wailings from uncanny wind instruments, thus:—

It is all very odd. One recognizes the Mozartian strain; and on this hint, and by the aid of certain sparkles of violet light in the pallor, the man's costume explains itself as that of a Spanish nobleman of the XV–XVI century. DON JUAN, of course; but where? why? how? Besides, in the brief lifting of his face, now hidden by his hat brim, there was a curious suggestion of TANNER. A more critical, fastidious, handsome face, paler and colder, without TANNER's impetuous credulity and enthusiasm, and without a touch of his modern plutocratic vulgarity, but still a resemblance, even an identity. The name too: DON JUAN TENORIA, JOHN TANNER. Where on earth—or elsewhere—have we got to from the XX century and the Sierra?

Another pallor in the void, this time not violet, but a disagreeable smoky yellow. With it, the whisper of a ghostly clarionet turning this tune into infinite sadness:

The yellowish pallor moves: there is an OLD CRONE wandering in the void, bent and toothless; draped, as well as one can guess, in the coarse brown frock of some religious order. She wanders *and wanders in her slow hopeless way, much as a wasp flies in its rapid busy way, until she blunders against the thing she seeks: companionship. With a sob of relief the poor old creature clutches at the presence of the man and addresses him in her dry unlovely voice, which can still express pride and resolution as well as suffering.*]

THE OLD WOMAN   Excuse me; but I am so lonely; and this place is so awful.

DON JUAN   A new comer?

THE OLD WOMAN   Yes: I suppose I died this morning. I confessed; I had extreme unction; I was in bed with my family about me and my eyes fixed on the cross. Then it grew dark; and when the light came back it was this light by which I walk seeing nothing. I have wandered for hours in horrible loneliness.

DON JUAN [*Sighing*] Ah! you have not yet lost the sense of time. One soon does, in eternity.

THE OLD WOMAN   Where are we?

DON JUAN   In hell.

THE OLD WOMAN [*Proudly*]   Hell! I in hell! How dare you?

DON JUAN [*Unimpressed*]   Why not, Señora?

THE OLD WOMAN   You do not know to whom you are speaking. I am a lady, and a faithful daughter of the Church.

DON JUAN   I do not doubt it.

THE OLD WOMAN   But how then can I be in hell? Purgatory, per-haps: I have not been perfect: who has? But hell! oh, you are lying.

DON JUAN   Hell, Señora, I assure you; hell at its best: that is, its most solitary—though perhaps you would prefer company.

THE OLD WOMAN   But I have sincerely repented; I have confessed—

DON JUAN   How much?

THE OLD WOMAN   More sins than I really committed. I loved con-fession.

DON JUAN   Ah, that is perhaps as bad as confessing too little. At all events, Señora, whether by oversight or intention, you are cer-tainly damned, like myself; and there is nothing for it now but to make the best of it.

THE OLD WOMAN [*Indignantly*]   Oh! and I might have been so much wickeder! All my good deeds wasted! It is unjust.

DON JUAN   No: you were fully and clearly warned. For your bad deeds, vicarious atonement, mercy without justice. For your good deeds, justice without mercy. We have many good people here.

THE OLD WOMAN   Were you a good man?

DON JUAN   I was a murderer.

THE OLD WOMAN   A murderer! Oh, how dare they send me to herd with murderers! I was not as bad as that: I was a good woman. There is some mistake: where can I have it set right?

DON JUAN   I do not know whether mistakes can be corrected here. Probably they will not admit a mistake even if they have made one.

THE OLD WOMAN   But whom can I ask?

DON JUAN   I should ask the Devil, Señora: he understands the ways of this place, which is more than I ever could.

THE OLD WOMAN   The Devil! *I* speak to the Devil!

DON JUAN   In hell, Señora, the Devil is the leader of the best society.

THE OLD WOMAN   I tell you, wretch, I know I am not in hell.

DON JUAN   How do you know?

THE OLD WOMAN   Because I feel no pain.

DON JUAN   Oh, then there is no mistake: you are intentionally damned.

THE OLD WOMAN   Why do you say that?

DON JUAN   Because hell, Señora, is a place for the wicked. The wicked are quite comfortable in it: it was made for them. You tell me you feel no pain. I conclude you are one of those for whom hell exists.

THE OLD WOMAN   Do you feel no pain?

DON JUAN   I am not one of the wicked, Señora; therefore it bores me, bores me beyond description, beyond belief.

THE OLD WOMAN   Not one of the wicked! You said you were a murderer.

DON JUAN   Only a duel. I ran my sword through an old man who was trying to run his through me.

THE OLD WOMAN   If you were a gentleman, that was not a murder.

DON JUAN   The old man called it murder, because he was, he said, defending his daughter's honor. By this he meant that because I foolishly fell in love with her and told her so, she screamed; and he tried to assassinate me after calling me insulting names.

THE OLD WOMAN   You were like all men. Libertines and murderers all, all, all!

DON JUAN   And yet we meet here, dear lady.

THE OLD WOMAN   Listen to me. My father was slain by just such a wretch as you, in just such a duel, for just such a cause. I screamed: it was my duty. My father drew on my assailant: his honor demanded it. He fell: that was the reward of honor. I am here: in hell, you tell me: that is the reward of duty. Is there justice in heaven?

DON JUAN   No; but there is justice in hell: heaven is far above such idle human personalities. You will be welcome in hell, Señora. Hell is the home of honor, duty, justice, and the rest of the seven deadly virtues. All the wickedness on earth is done in their name: where else but in hell should they have their reward? Have I not told you that the truly damned are those who are happy in hell?

THE OLD WOMAN   And are you happy here?

DON JUAN [*Springing to his feet*]   No; and that is the enigma on which I ponder in darkness. Why am I here? I, who repudiated all duty, trampled honor underfoot, and laughed at justice!

THE OLD WOMAN   Oh, what do I care why you are here? Why am *I* here? I, who sacrificed all my inclinations to womanly virtue and propriety!

DON JUAN   Patience, lady: you will be perfectly happy and at home here. As saith the poet, "Hell is a city much like Seville."[1]

THE OLD WOMAN   Happy! here! where I am nothing! where I am nobody!

DON JUAN   Not at all: you are a lady; and wherever ladies are is hell. Do not be surprised or terrified: you will find everything here that a lady can desire, including devils who will serve you from sheer love of servitude, and magnify your importance for the sake of dignifying their service—the best of servants.

THE OLD WOMAN   My servants will be devils!

DON JUAN   Have you ever had servants who were not devils?

THE OLD WOMAN   Never: they were devils, perfect devils, all of them. But that is only a manner of speaking. I thought you meant that my servants here would be real devils.

DON JUAN   No more real devils than you will be a real lady. Nothing is real here. That is the horror of damnation.

THE OLD WOMAN   Oh, this is all madness. This is worse than fire and the worm.

DON JUAN   For you, perhaps, there are consolations. For instance: how old were you when you changed from time to eternity?

THE OLD WOMAN   Do not ask me how old I was—as if I were a thing of the past. I am 77.

DON JUAN   A ripe age, Señora. But in hell old age is not tolerated. It is too real. Here we worship Love and Beauty. Our souls being entirely damned, we cultivate our hearts. As a lady of 77, you would not have a single acquaintance in hell.

THE OLD WOMAN   How can I help my age, man?

DON JUAN   You forget that you have left your age behind you in the realm of time. You are no more 77 than you are 7 or 17 or 27.

THE OLD WOMAN   Nonsense!

DON JUAN   Consider, Señora: was not this true even when you lived on earth? When you were 70, were you really older underneath your wrinkles and your grey hairs than when you were 30?

THE OLD WOMAN   No, younger: at 30 I was a fool. But of what use is it to feel younger and look older?

DON JUAN   You see, Señora, the look was only an illusion. Your wrinkles lied, just as the plump smooth skin of many a stupid girl of 17, with heavy spirits and decrepit ideas, lies about her age? Well, here we have no bodies: we see each other as bodies only because we learnt to think about one another under that aspect when we were alive; and we still think in that way, knowing no other. But we can appear to one another at what age we choose. You have but to will any of your old looks back, and back they will come.

1. See Percy Bysshe Shelley, *Peter Bell the 3rd* (1819): "Hell is a city much like London . . ."

THE OLD WOMAN   It cannot be true.

DON JUAN   Try.

THE OLD WOMAN   Seventeen!

DON JUAN   Stop. Before you decide, I had better tell you that these
things are a matter of fashion. Occasionally we have a rage for 17;
but it does not last long. Just at present the fashionable age is
40—or say 37; but there are signs of a change. If you were at all
good-looking at 27, I should suggest your trying that, and setting
a new fashion.

THE OLD WOMAN   I do not believe a word you are saying. However,
27 be it. [*Whisk! the old woman becomes a young one, and so handsome that in the radiance into which her dull yellow halo has suddenly lightened one might almost mistake her for* ANN WHITEFIELD.]

DON JUAN   Doña Ana de Ulloa!

ANA   What? You know me!

DON JUAN   And you forget me!

ANA   I cannot see your face. [*He raises his hat.*] Don Juan Tenorio!
Monster! You who slew my father! even here you pursue me.

DON JUAN   I protest I do not pursue you. Allow me to withdraw
[*Going*].

ANA [*Seizing his arm*]   You shall not leave me alone in this dreadful
place.

DON JUAN   Provided my staying be not interpreted as pursuit.

ANA [*Releasing him*]   You may well wonder how I can endure your
presence. My dear, dear father!

DON JUAN   Would you like to see him?

ANA   My father here!!!

DON JUAN   No: he is in heaven.

ANA   I knew it. My noble father! He is looking down on us now.
What must he feel to see his daughter in this place, and in conversation with his murderer!

DON JUAN   By the way, if we should meet him—

ANA   How can we meet him? He is in heaven.

DON JUAN   He condescends to look in upon us here from time to
time. Heaven bores him. So let me warn you that if you meet him
he will be mortally offended if you speak of me as his murderer!
He maintains that he was a much better swordsman than I, and
that if his foot had not slipped he would have killed me. No doubt
he is right: I was not a good fencer. I never dispute the point; so
we are excellent friends.

ANA   It is no dishonor to a soldier to be proud of his skill in arms.

DON JUAN   You would rather not meet him, probably.

ANA   How dare you say that?

DON JUAN   Oh, that is the usual feeling here. You may remember
that on earth—though of course we never confessed it—the death
of anyone we knew, even those we liked best, was always mingled
with a certain satisfaction at being finally done with them.

ANA   Monster! Never, never.

DON JUAN [*Placidly*]   I see you recognize the feeling. Yes: a funeral was always a festivity in black, especially the funeral of a relative. At all events, family ties are rarely kept up here. Your father is quite accustomed to this: he will not expect any devotion from you.

ANA   Wretch: I wore mourning for him all my life.

DON JUAN   Yes: it became you. But a life of mourning is one thing: an eternity of it quite another. Besides, here you are as dead as he. Can anything be more ridiculous than one dead person mourning for another? Do not look shocked, my dear Ana; and do not be alarmed: there is plenty of humbug in hell (indeed there is hardly anything else); but the humbug of death and age and change is dropped because here we are all dead and all eternal. You will pick up our ways soon.

ANA   And will all the men call me their dear Ana?

DON JUAN   No. That was a slip of the tongue. I beg your pardon.

ANA [*Almost tenderly*]   Juan: did you really love me when you behaved so disgracefully to me?

DON JUAN [*Impatiently*]   Oh, I beg you not to begin talking about love. Here they talk of nothing else but love—its beauty, its holiness, its spirituality, its devil knows what!—excuse me; but it does so bore me. They dont know what they're talking about: I do. They think they have achieved the perfection of love because they have no bodies. Sheer imaginative debauchery! Faugh!

ANA   Has even death failed to refine your soul, Juan? Has the terrible judgment of which my father's statue was the minister taught you no reverence?

DON JUAN   How is that very flattering statue, by the way? Does it still come to supper with naughty people and cast them into this bottomless pit?

ANA   It has been a great expense to me. The boys in the monastery school would not let it alone: the mischievous ones broke it; and the studious ones wrote their names on it. Three new noses in two years, and fingers without end. I had to leave it to its fate at last; and now I fear it is shockingly mutilated. My poor father!

DON JUAN   Hush! Listen! [*Two great chords rolling on syncopated waves of sound break forth: D minor and its dominant: a sound of dreadful joy to all musicians.*] Ha! Mozart's statue music. It is your father. You had better disappear until I prepare him. [*She vanishes.*]

> [*From the void comes a living* STATUE *of white marble, designed to represent a majestic old man. But he waives his majesty with infinite grace; walks with a feather-like step; and makes every wrinkle in his war worn visage brim over with holiday joyousness. To his sculptor he owes a perfectly trained figure, which he carries erect and trim; and the ends of his moustache curl*]

up, elastic as watchsprings, giving him an air which, but for its Spanish dignity, would be called jaunty. He is on the pleasantest terms with DON JUAN. *His voice, save for a much more distinguished intonation, is so like the voice of* ROEBUCK RAMSDEN *that it calls attention to the fact that they are not unlike one another in spite of their very different fashions of shaving.*]

DON JUAN   Ah, here you are, my friend. Why dont you learn to sing the splendid music Mozart has written for you?

THE STATUE   Unluckily he has written it for a bass voice. Mine is a counter tenor. Well: have you repented yet?

DON JUAN   I have too much consideration for you to repent, Don Gonzalo. If I did, you would have no excuse for coming from Heaven to argue with me.

THE STATUE   True. Remain obdurate, my boy. I wish I had killed you, as I should have done but for an accident. Then I should have come here; and you would have had a statue and a reputation for piety to live up to. Any news?

DON JUAN   Yes: your daughter is dead.

THE STATUE [*Puzzled*]   My daughter? [*Recollecting*] Oh! the one you were taken with. Let me see: what was her name?

DON JUAN   Ana.

THE STATUE   To be sure: Ana. A good-looking girl, if I recollect aright. Have you warned Whatshisname—her husband?

DON JUAN   My friend Ottavio? No: I have not seen him since Ana arrived.

[ANA *comes indignantly to light.*]

ANA   What does this mean? Ottavio here and your friend! And you, father, have forgotten my name. You are indeed turned to stone.

THE STATUE   My dear: I am so much more admired in marble than I ever was in my own person that I have retained the shape the sculptor gave me. He was one of the first men of his day: you must acknowledge that.

ANA   Father! Vanity! personal vanity! from you!

THE STATUE   Ah, you outlived that weakness, my daughter: you must be nearly 80 by this time. I was cut off (by an accident) in my 64th year, and am considerably your junior in consequence. Besides, my child, in this place, what our libertine friend here would call the farce of parental wisdom is dropped. Regard me, I beg, as a fellow creature, not as a father.

ANA   You speak as this villain speaks.

THE STATUE   Juan is a sound thinker, Ana. A bad fencer, but a sound thinker.

ANA [*Horror creeping upon her*]   I begin to understand. These are devils, mocking me. I had better pray.

THE STATUE [*Consoling her*]   No, no, no, my child: do not pray. If you do, you will throw away the main advantage of this place.

Written over the gate here are the words "Leave every hope behind, ye who enter." Only think what a relief that is! For what is hope? A form of moral responsibility. Here there is no hope, and consequently no duty, no work, nothing to be gained by praying, nothing to be lost by doing what you like. Hell, in short, is a place where you have nothing to do but amuse yourself. [DON JUAN *sighs deeply.*] You sigh, friend Juan; but if you dwell in heaven, as I do, you would realize your advantages.

DON JUAN   You are in good spirits to-day, Commander. You are positively brilliant. What is the matter?

THE STATUE   I have come to a momentous decision, my boy. But first, where is our friend the Devil? I must consult him in the matter. And Ana would like to make his acquaintance, no doubt.

ANA   You are preparing some torment for me.

DON JUAN   All that is superstition, Ana. Reassure yourself. Remember: the devil is not so black as he is painted.

THE STATUE   Let us give him a call.

[*At the wave of* THE STATUE's *hand the great chords roll out again; but this time Mozart's music gets grotesquely adulterated with Gounod's. A scarlet halo begins to glow; and into it* THE DEVIL *rises, very Mephistophelean, and not at all unlike* MENDOZA, *though not so interesting. He looks older; is getting prematurely bald; and, in spite of an effusion of goodnature and friendliness, is peevish and sensitive when his advances are not reciprocated. He does not inspire much confidence in his powers of hard work or endurance, and is, on the whole, a disagreeably self-indulgent looking person; but he is clever and plausible, though perceptibly less well bred than the two other men, and enormously less vital than the woman.*]

THE DEVIL [*Heartily*]   Have I the pleasure of again receiving a visit from the illustrious Commander of Calatrava? [*Coldly*] Don Juan, your servant. [*Politely*] And a strange lady? My respects, Señora.

ANA   Are you—

THE DEVIL [*Bowing*]   Lucifer, at your service.

ANA   I shall go mad.

THE DEVIL [*Gallantly*]   Ah, Señora, do not be anxious. You come to us from earth, full of the prejudices and terrors of that priest-ridden place. You have heard me ill spoken of; and yet, believe me, I have hosts of friends there.

ANA   Yes: you reign in their hearts.

THE DEVIL [*Shaking his head*]   You flatter me, Señora; but you are mistaken. It is true that the world cannot get on without me; but it never gives me credit for that: in its heart it mistrusts and hates me. Its sympathies are all with misery, with poverty, with starvation of the body and of the heart. I call on it to sympathize with joy, with love, with happiness, with beauty—

DON JUAN [*Nauseated*]   Excuse me: I am going. You know I cannot stand this.

THE DEVIL [*Angrily*]   Yes: I know that you are no friend of mine.

THE STATUE   What harm is he doing you, Juan? It seems to me that he was talking excellent sense when you interrupted him.

THE DEVIL [*Warmly shaking the statue's hand*]   Thank you, my friend: thank you. You have always understood me: he has always disparaged and avoided me.

DON JUAN   I have treated you with perfect courtesy.

THE DEVIL   Courtesy! What is courtesy? I care nothing for mere courtesy. Give me warmth of heart, true sincerity, the bond of sympathy with love and joy—

DON JUAN   You are making me ill.

THE DEVIL   There! [*Appealing to the statue*] You hear, sir! Oh, by what irony of fate was this cold selfish egotist sent to my kingdom, and you taken to the icy mansions of the sky!

THE STATUE   I cant complain. I was a hypocrite; and it served me right to be sent to heaven.

THE DEVIL   Why, sir, do you not join us, and leave a sphere for which your temperament is too sympathetic, your heart too warm, your capacity for enjoyment too generous?

THE STATUE   I have this day resolved to do so. In future, excellent Son of the Morning, I am yours. I have left heaven for ever.

THE DEVIL [*Again grasping his hand*]   Ah, what an honor for me! What a triumph for our cause! Thank you, thank you. And now, my friend—I may call you so at last—could you not persuade him to take the place you have left vacant above?

THE STATUE [*Shaking his head*]   I cannot conscientiously recommend anybody with whom I am on friendly terms to deliberately make himself dull and uncomfortable.

THE DEVIL   Of course not; but are you sure he would be uncomfortable? Of course you know best: you brought him here originally; and we had the greatest hopes of him. His sentiments were in the best taste of our best people. You remember how he sang? [*He begins to sing in a nasal operatic baritone, tremulous from an eternity of misuse in the French manner*]

> Vivan le femmine!
> Viva il buon vino!

THE STATUE [*Taking up the tune an octave higher in his counter tenor*]

> Sostegno e gloria
> D'umanità.[2]

---

2. Long live the feminine!
   Long live the good wine!
   Mainstay and glory
   Of humanity.

THE DEVIL   Precisely. Well, he never sings for us now.

DON JUAN   Do you complain of that? Hell is full of musical amateurs: music is the brandy of the damned. May not one lost soul
be permitted to abstain?

THE DEVIL   You dare blaspheme against the sublimest of the arts!

DON JUAN [*With cold disgust*]   You talk like a hysterical woman
fawning on a fiddler.

THE DEVIL   I am not angry. I merely pity you. You have no soul; and
you are unconscious of all that you lose. Now you, Señor Commander, are a born musician. How well you sing! Mozart would
be delighted if he were still here; but he moped and went to
heaven. Curious how these clever men, whom you would have
supposed born to be popular here, have turned out social failures,
like Don Juan!

DON JUAN   I am really very sorry to be a social failure.

THE DEVIL   Not that we dont admire your intellect, you know. We
do. But I look at the matter from your own point of view. You dont
get on with us. The place doesnt suit you. The truth is, you have—I
wont say no heart; for we know that beneath all your affected
cynicism you have a warm one—

DON JUAN [*Shrinking*]   Dont, please dont.

THE DEVIL [*Nettled*]   Well, youve no capacity for enjoyment. Will
that satisfy you?

DON JUAN   It is a somewhat less insufferable form of cant than the
other. But if youll allow me, Ill take refuge, as usual, in solitude.

THE DEVIL   Why not take refuge in heaven? Thats the proper place
for you. [*To* ANA] Come, Señora! could you not persuade him for
his own good to try change of air?

ANA   But can he go to heaven if he wants to?

THE DEVIL   Whats to prevent him?

ANA   Can anybody—can *I* go to heaven if I want to?

THE DEVIL [*Rather contemptuously*]   Certainly, if your taste lies that
way.

ANA   But why doesnt everybody go to heaven, then?

THE STATUE [*Chuckling*]   *I* can tell you that, my dear. It's because
heaven is the most angelically dull place in all creation: thats why.

THE DEVIL   His excellency the Commander puts it with military
bluntness; but the strain of living in heaven is intolerable. There
is a notion that I was turned out of it; but as a matter of fact
nothing could have induced me to stay there. I simply left it and
organized this place.

THE STATUE   I dont wonder at it. Nobody could stand an eternity of
heaven.

THE DEVIL   Oh, it suits some people. Let us be just, Commander:
it is a question of temperament. I dont admire the heavenly temperament: I dont understand it: I dont know that I particularly
want to understand it; but it takes all sorts to make a universe.

There is no accounting for tastes: there are people who like it. I think Don Juan would like it.

DON JUAN But—pardon my frankness—could you really go back there if you desired to; or are the grapes sour?

THE DEVIL Back there! I often go back there. Have you never read the book of Job? Have you any canonical authority for assuming that there is any barrier between our circle and the other one?

ANA But surely there is a great gulf fixed.

THE DEVIL Dear lady: a parable must not be taken literally. The gulf is the difference between the angelic and the diabolic temperament. What more impassable gulf could you have? Think of what you have seen on earth. There is no physical gulf between the philosopher's class room and the bull ring; but the bull fighters do not come to the class room for all that. Have you ever been in the country where I have the largest following—England? There they have great racecourses, and also concert rooms where they play the classical compositions of his Excellency's friend Mozart. Those who go to the racecourses can stay away from them and go to the classical concerts instead if they like: there is no law against it; for Englishmen never will be slaves: they are free to do whatever the Government and public opinion allow them to do. And the classical concert is admitted to be a higher, more cultivated, poetic, intellectual, ennobling place than the racecourse. But do the lovers of racing desert their sport and flock to the concert room? Not they. They would suffer there all the weariness the Commander has suffered in heaven. There is the great gulf of the parable between the two places. A mere physical gulf they could bridge; or at least I could bridge it for them (the earth is full of Devil's Bridges); but the gulf of dislike is impassable and eternal. And that is the only gulf that separates my friends here from those who are invidiously called the blest.

ANA I shall go to heaven at once.

THE STATUE My child: one word of warning first. Let me complete my friend Lucifer's similitude of the classical concert. At every one of those concerts in England you will find rows of weary people who are there, not because they really like classical music, but because they think they ought to like it. Well, there is the same thing in heaven. A number of people sit there in glory, not because they are happy, but because they think they owe it to their position to be in heaven. They are almost all English.

THE DEVIL Yes: the Southerners give it up and join me just as you have done. But the English really do not seem to know when they are thoroughly miserable. An Englishman thinks he is moral when he is only uncomfortable.

THE STATUE In short, my daughter, if you go to heaven without being naturally qualified for it, you will not enjoy yourself there.

ANA And who dares say that I am not naturally qualified for it? The

most distinguished princes of the Church have never questioned
it. I owe it to myself to leave this place at once.

THE DEVIL [*Offended*]   As you please, Señora. I should have
expected better taste from you.

ANA   Father: I shall expect you to come with me. You cannot stay
here. What will people say?

THE STATUE   People! Why, the best people are here—princes of the
church and all. So few go to heaven, and so many come here, that
the blest, once called a heavenly host, are a continually dwindling
minority. The saints, the fathers, the elect of long ago are the
cranks, the faddists, the outsiders of to-day.

THE DEVIL   It is true. From the beginning of my career I knew that
I should win in the long run by sheer weight of public opinion, in
spite of the long campaign of misrepresentation and calumny
against me. At bottom the universe is a constitutional one; and
with such a majority as mine I cannot be kept permanently out of
office.

DON JUAN   I think, Ana, you had better stay here.

ANA [*Jealously*]   You do not want me to go with you.

DON JUAN   Surely you do not want to enter heaven in the company
of a reprobate like me.

ANA   All souls are equally precious. You repent, do you not?

DON JUAN   My dear Ana, you are silly. Do you suppose heaven is
like earth, where people persuade themselves that what is done
can be undone by repentance; that what is spoken can be unspoken by withdrawing it; that what is true can be annihilated by a
general agreement to give it the lie? No: heaven is the home of the
masters of reality: that is why I am going thither.

ANA   Thank you: I am going to heaven for happiness. I have had
quite enough of reality on earth.

DON JUAN   Then you must stay here; for hell is the home of the
unreal and of the seekers for happiness. It is the only refuge from
heaven, which is, as I tell you, the home of the masters of reality,
and from earth, which is the home of the slaves of reality. The
earth is a nursery in which men and women play at being heros
and heroines, saints and sinners; but they are dragged down from
their fool's paradise by their bodies: hunger and cold and thirst,
age and decay and disease, death above all, make them slaves of
reality: thrice a day meals must be eaten and digested: thrice a
century a new generation must be engendered: ages of faith, of
romance, and of science are all driven at last to have but one prayer
"Make me a healthy animal." But here you escape this tyranny of
the flesh; for here you are not an animal at all: you are a ghost, an
appearance, an illusion, a convention, deathless, ageless: in a
word, bodiless. There are no social questions here, no political
questions, no religious questions, best of all, perhaps, no sanitary
questions. Here you call your appearance beauty, your emotions

love, your sentiments heroism, your aspirations virtue, just as you did on earth; but here there are no hard facts to contradict you, no ironic contrast of your needs with your pretensions, no human comedy, nothing but a perpetual romance, a universal melodrama. As our German friend[3] put it in his poem, "the poetically nonsensical here is good sense; and the Eternal Feminine draws us ever upward and on"—without getting us a step farther. And yet you want to leave this paradise!

ANA   But if Hell be so beautiful as this, how glorious must heaven be!

    [THE DEVIL, THE STATUE, *and* DON JUAN *all begin to speak at once in violent protest; then stop, abashed.*]

DON JUAN   I beg your pardon.

THE DEVIL   Not at all. I interrupted you.

THE STATUE   You were going to say something.

DON JUAN   After you, gentlemen.

THE DEVIL [*To* DON JUAN]   You have been so eloquent on the advantages of my dominions that I leave you to do equal justice to the drawbacks of the alternative establishment.

DON JUAN   In heaven, as I picture it, dear lady, you live and work instead of playing and pretending. You face things as they are; you escape nothing but glamor; and your steadfastness and your peril are your glory. If the play still goes on here and on earth, and all the world is a stage, heaven is at least behind the scenes. But heaven cannot be described by metaphor. Thither I shall go presently, because there I hope to escape at last from lies and from the tedious, vulgar pursuit of happiness, to spend my eons in contemplation—

THE STATUE   Ugh!

DON JUAN   Señor Commander: I do not blame your disgust: a picture gallery is a dull place for a blind man. But even as you enjoy the contemplation of such romantic mirages as beauty and pleasure; so would I enjoy the contemplation of that which interests me above all things: namely, Life: the force that ever strives to attain greater power of contemplating itself. What made this brain of mine, do you think? Not the need to move my limbs; for a rat with half my brains moves as well as I. Not merely the need to do, but the need to know what I do, lest in my blind efforts to live I should be slaying myself.

THE STATUE   You would have slain yourself in your blind efforts to fence but for my foot slipping, my friend.

DON JUAN   Audacious ribald: your laughter will finish in hideous boredom before morning.

THE STATUE   Ha ha! Do you remember how I frightened you when

3. Johann Wolfgang von Goethe (1749–1832); the quotation is from *Faust*, part 2.

I said something like that to you from my pedestal in Seville? It sounds rather flat without my trombones.

DON JUAN   They tell me it generally sounds flat with them, Commander.

ANA   Oh, do not interrupt with these frivolities, father. Is there nothing in heaven but contemplation, Juan?

DON JUAN   In the heaven I seek, no other joy. But there is the work of helping Life in its struggle upward. Think of how it wastes and scatters itself, how it raises up obstacles to itself and destroys itself in its ignorance and blindness. It needs a brain, this irresistible force, lest in its ignorance it should resist itself. What a piece of work is man! says the poet. Yes: but what a blunderer! Here is the highest miracle of organization yet attained by life, the most intensely alive thing that exists, the most conscious of all the organisms; and yet, how wretched are his brains! Stupidity made sordid and cruel by the realities learnt from toil and poverty: Imagination resolved to starve sooner than face these realities, piling up illusions to hide them, and calling itself cleverness, genius! And each accusing the other of its own defect: Stupidity accusing Imagination of folly, and Imagination accusing Stupidity of ignorance: whereas, alas! Stupidity has all the knowledge, and Imagination all the intelligence.

THE DEVIL   And a pretty kettle of fish they make of it between them. Did I not say, when I was arranging that affair of Faust's, that all Man's reason has done for him is to make him beastlier than any beast. One splendid body is worth the brains of a hundred dyspeptic, flatulent philosophers.

DON JUAN   You forget that brainless magnificence of body has been tried. Things immeasurably greater than man in every respect but brain have existed and perished. The megatherium, the icthyosaurus have paced the earth with seven-league steps and hidden the day with cloud vast wings. Where are they now? Fossils in museums, and so few and imperfect at that, that a knuckle bone or a tooth of one of them is prized beyond the lives of a thousand soldiers. These things lived and wanted to live; but for lack of brains they did not know how to carry out their purpose, and so destroyed themselves.

THE DEVIL   And is Man any the less destroying himself for all this boasted brain of his? Have you walked up and down upon the earth lately? I have; and I have examined Man's wonderful inventions. And I tell you that in the arts of life man invents nothing; but in the arts of death he outdoes Nature herself, and produces by chemistry and machinery all the slaughter of plague, pestilence and famine. The peasant I tempt to-day eats and drinks what was eaten and drunk by the peasants of ten thousand years ago; and the house he lives in has not altered as much in a thousand centuries as the fashion of a lady's bonnet in a score of weeks. But when he goes out to slay, he carries a marvel of mechanism that lets loose at the touch of his finger all the hidden molecular energies, and leaves the javelin, the arrow, the blowpipe of his fathers far behind. In the arts of peace Man is a bungler. I have seen his cotton factories and the like, with machinery that a greedy dog could have invented if it had wanted money instead of food. I know his clumsy typewriters and bungling locomotives and tedious bicycles: they are toys compared to the Maxim gun, the submarine torpedo boat. There is nothing in Man's industrial machinery but his greed and sloth: his heart is in his weapons. This marvellous force of Life of which you boast is a force of Death: Man measures his strength by his destructiveness. What is his religion? An excuse for hating me. What is his law? An excuse for hanging *you*. What is his morality? Gentility! an excuse for consuming without producing. What is his art? An excuse for gloating over pictures of slaughter. What are his politics? Either the worship of a despot because a despot can kill, or parliamentary cockfighting. I spent an evening lately in a certain celebrated legislature, and heard the pot lecturing the kettle for its blackness, and ministers answering questions. When I left I chalked up on the door the old nursery saying "Ask no questions and you will be told no lies." I bought a sixpenny family magazine, and found it full of pictures of young men shooting and stabbing one another. I saw a man die: he was a London bricklayer's laborer with seven children. He left seventeen pounds club money; and his wife spent it all on his funeral and went into the workhouse with the children next day. She would not have spent sevenpence on her children's schooling: the law had to force her to let them be taught gratuitously; but on death she spent all she had. Their imagination glows, their energies rise up at the idea of death, these people: they love it; and the more horrible it is the more they enjoy it. Hell is a place far above their comprehension: they derive their notion of it from two of the greatest fools that ever lived, an Italian and an Englishman.[4] The Italian described it as a place of mud, frost, filth, fire, and venomous serpents: all torture. This ass, when he was not lying about me, was maundering about some woman whom he saw once in the street. The Englishman described me as being expelled from heaven by cannons and gunpowder; and to this day every Briton believes that the whole of his silly story is in the Bible. What else he says I do not know; for it is all in a long poem which neither I nor anyone else ever succeeded in wading through. It is the same in everything. The highest form of literature is the tragedy, a play in which everybody is murdered at the end. In the old chronicles you read of earthquakes and pestilences, and are told that these

---

4. That is, Dante Alighieri (1265–1321), author of *The Divine Comedy*, and John Milton (1608–1674), author of *Paradise Lost*.

shewed the power and majesty of God and the littleness of Man. Nowadays the chronicles describe battles. In a battle two bodies of men shoot at one another with bullets and explosive shells until one body runs away, when the others chase the fugitives on horseback and cut them to pieces as they fly. And this, the chronicle concludes, shews the greatness and majesty of empires, and the littleness of the vanquished. Over such battles the people run about the streets yelling with delight, and egg their Governments on to spend hundreds of millions of money in the slaughter, whilst the strongest Ministers dare not spend an extra penny in the pound against the poverty and pestilence through which they themselves daily walk. I could give you a thousand instances; but they all come to the same thing: the power that governs the earth is not the power of Life but of Death; and the inner need that has nerved Life to the effort of organizing itself into the human being is not the need for higher life but for a more efficient engine of destruction. The plague, the famine, the earthquake, the tempest were too spasmodic in their action; the tiger and crocodile were too easily satiated and not cruel enough: something more constantly, more ruthlessly, more ingeniously destructive was needed; and that something was Man, the inventor of the rack, the stake, the gallows, and the electrocutor; of the sword and gun; above all, of justice, duty, patriotism and all the other isms by which even those who are clever enough to be humanely disposed are persuaded to become the most destructive of all the destroyers.

DON JUAN   Pshaw! all this is old. Your weak side, my diabolic friend, is that you have always been a gull: you take Man at his own valuation. Nothing would flatter him more than your opinion of him. He loves to think of himself as bold and bad. He is neither one nor the other: he is only a coward. Call him tyrant, murderer, pirate, bully; and he will adore you, and swagger about with the consciousness of having the blood of the old sea kings in his veins. Call him liar and thief; and he will only take an action against you for libel. But call him coward; and he will go mad with rage: he will face death to outface that stinging truth. Man gives every reason for his conduct save one, every excuse for his crimes save one, every plea for his safety save one; and that one is his cowardice. Yet all his civilization is founded on his cowardice, on his abject tameness, which he calls his respectability. There are limits to what a mule or an ass will stand; but Man will suffer himself to be degraded until his vileness becomes so loathsome to his oppressors that they themselves are forced to reform it.

THE DEVIL   Precisely. And these are the creatures in whom you discover what you call a Life Force!

DON JUAN   Yes; for now comes the most surprising part of the whole business.

THE STATUE   Whats that?

DON JUAN   Why, that you can make any of these cowards brave by simply putting an idea into his head.

THE STATUE   Stuff! As an old soldier I admit the cowardice: it's as universal as sea sickness, and matters just as little. But that about putting an idea into a man's head is stuff and nonsense. In a battle all you need to make you fight is a little hot blood and the knowledge that it's more dangerous to lose than to win.

DON JUAN   That is perhaps why battles are so useless. But men never really overcome fear until they imagine they are fighting to further a universal purpose—fighting for an idea, as they call it. Why was the Crusader braver than the pirate? Because he fought, not for himself, but for the Cross. What force was it that met him with a valor as reckless as his own? The force of men who fought, not for themselves, but for Islam. They took Spain from us, though we were fighting for our very hearths and homes; but when we, too, fought for that mighty idea, a Catholic Church, we swept them back to Africa.

THE DEVIL [*Ironically*]   What! you a Catholic, Señor Don Juan! A devotee! My congratulations.

THE STATUE [*Seriously*]   Come come! as a soldier, I can listen to nothing against the Church.

DON JUAN   Have no fear, Commander: this idea of a Catholic Church will survive Islam, will survive the Cross, will survive even that vulgar pageant of incompetent schoolboyish gladiators which you call the Army.

THE STATUE   Juan: you will force me to call you to account for this.

DON JUAN   Useless: I cannot fence. Every idea for which Man will die will be a Catholic idea. When the Spaniard learns at last that he is no better than the Saracen, and his prophet no better than Mahomet, he will arise, more Catholic than ever, and die on a barricade across the filthy slum he starves in, for universal liberty and equality.

THE STATUE   Bosh!

DON JUAN   What you call bosh is the only thing men dare die for. Later on, Liberty will not be Catholic enough: men will die for human perfection, to which they will sacrifice all their liberty gladly.

THE DEVIL   Ay: they will never be at a loss for an excuse for killing one another.

DON JUAN   What of that? It is not death that matters, but the fear of death. It is not killing and dying that degrades us, but base living, and accepting the wages and profits of degradation. Better ten dead men than one live slave or his master. Men shall yet rise up, father against son and brother against brother, and kill one another for the great Catholic idea of abolishing slavery.

THE DEVIL   Yes, when the Liberty and Equality of which you prate shall have made free white Christians cheaper in the labor market than black heathen slaves sold by auction at the block.

DON JUAN   Never fear! the white laborer shall have his turn too. But I am not now defending the illusory forms the great ideas take. I am giving you examples of the fact that this creature Man, who in his own selfish affairs is a coward to the backbone, will fight for an idea like a hero. He may be abject as a citizen; but he is dangerous as a fanatic. He can only be enslaved whilst he is spiritually weak enough to listen to reason. I tell you, gentlemen, if you can shew a man a piece of what he now calls God's work to do, and what he will later on call by many new names, you can make him entirely reckless of the consequences of himself personally.

ANA   Yes: he shirks all his responsibilities, and leaves his wife to grapple with them.

THE STATUE   Well said, daughter. Do not let him talk you out of your common sense.

THE DEVIL   Alas! Señor Commander, now that we have got on to the subject of Woman, he will talk more than ever. However, I confess it is for me the one supremely interesting subject.

DON JUAN   To a woman, Señora, man's duties and responsibilities begin and end with the task of getting bread for her children. To her, Man is only a means to the end of getting children and rearing them.

ANA   Is that your idea of a woman's mind? I call it cynical and disgusting materialism.

DON JUAN   Pardon me, Ana: I said nothing about a woman's whole mind. I spoke of her view of Man as a separate sex. It is no more cynical than her view of herself as above all things a Mother. Sexually, Woman is Nature's contrivance for perpetuating its highest achievement. Sexually, Man is Woman's contrivance for fulfilling Nature's behest in the most economical way. She knows by instinct that far back in the evolutionary process she invented him, differentiated him, created him in order to produce something better than the single-sexed process can produce. Whilst he fulfils the purpose for which she made him, he is welcome to his dreams, his follies, his ideals, his heroisms, provided that the keystone of them all is the worship of woman, of motherhood, of the family, of the hearth. But how rash and dangerous it was to invent a separate creature whose sole function was her own impregnation! For mark what has happened. First, Man has multiplied on her hands until there are as many men as women; so that she has been unable to employ for her purposes more than a fraction of the immense energy she has left at his disposal by saving him the exhausting labor of gestation. This superfluous energy has gone to his brain and to his muscle. He has become too strong to be controlled by her bodily, and too imaginative and mentally vigorous to be content with mere self-reproduction. He has created civilization without consulting her, taking her domestic labor for granted as the foundation of it.

ANA   That is true, at all events.

THE DEVIL   Yes; and this civilization! what is it, after all?

DON JUAN   After all, an excellent peg to hang your cynical commonplaces on; but before all, it is an attempt on Man's part to make himself something more than the mere instrument of Woman's purpose. So far, the result of Life's continual effort not only to maintain itself, but to achieve higher and higher organization and completer self-consciousness, is only, at best, a doubtful campaign between its forces and those of Death and Degeneration. The battles in this campaign are mere blunders, mostly won, like actual military battles, in spite of the commanders.

THE STATUE   That is a dig at me. No matter: go on, go on.

DON JUAN   It is a dig at a much higher power than you, Commander. Still, you must have noticed in your profession that even a stupid general can win battles when the enemy's general is a little stupider.

THE STATUE [*Very seriously*]   Most true, Juan, most true. Some donkeys have amazing luck.

DON JUAN   Well, the Life Force is stupid; but it is not so stupid as the forces of Death and Degeneration. Besides, these are in its pay all the time. And so Life wins, after a fashion. What mere copiousness of fecundity can supply and mere greed preserve, we possess. The survival of whatever form of civilization can produce the best rifle and the best fed riflemen is assured.

THE DEVIL   Exactly! the survival, not of the most effective means of Life but of the most effective means of Death. You always come back to my point, in spite of your wrigglings and evasions and sophistries, not to mention the intolerable length of your speeches.

DON JUAN   Oh come! who began making long speeches? However, if I overtax your intellect, you can leave us and seek the society of love and beauty and the rest of your favorite boredoms.

THE DEVIL [*Much offended*]   This is not fair, Don Juan, and not civil. I am also on the intellectual plane. Nobody can appreciate it more than I do. I am arguing fairly with you, and, I think, utterly refuting you. Let us go on for another hour if you like.

DON JUAN   Good: let us.

THE STATUE   Not that I see any prospect of your coming to any point in particular, Juan. Still, since in this place, instead of merely killing time we have to kill eternity, go ahead by all means.

DON JUAN [*Somewhat impatiently*]   My point, you marble-headed old masterpiece, is only a step ahead of you. Are we agreed that Life is a force which has made innumerable experiments in organizing itself, that the mammoth and the man, the mouse and the megatherium, the flies and the fleas and the Fathers of the Church, are all more or less successful attempts to build up that raw force into higher and higher individuals, the ideal individual being omnipotent, omniscient, infallible, and withal completely, unilludedly self-conscious: in short, a god?

THE DEVIL   I agree, for the sake of argument.

THE STATUE   I agree, for the sake of avoiding argument.

ANA   I most emphatically disagree as regards the Fathers of the Church; and I must beg you not to drag them into the argument.

DON JUAN   I did so purely for the sake of alliteration, Ana; and I shall make no further allusion to them. And now, since we are, with that exception, agreed so far, will you not agree with me further that Life has not measured the success of its attempts at godhead by the beauty or bodily perfection of the result, since in both these respects the birds, as our friend Aristophanes long ago pointed out, are so extraordinarily superior, with their power of flight and their lovely plumage, and, may I add, the touching poetry of their loves and nestings, that it is inconceivable that Life, having once produced them, should, if love and beauty were her object, start off on another line and labor at the clumsy elephant and the hideous ape, whose grandchildren we are?

ANA   Aristophanes was a heathen; and you, Juan, I am afraid, are very little better.

THE DEVIL   You conclude, then, that Life was driving at clumsiness and ugliness?

DON JUAN   No, perverse devil that you are, a thousand times no. Life was driving at brains—at its darling object: an organ by which it can attain not only self-consciousness but self-understanding.

THE STATUE   This is metaphysics, Juan. Why the devil should— [*To* THE DEVIL] I beg your pardon.

THE DEVIL   Pray dont mention it. I have always regarded the use of my name to secure additional emphasis as a high compliment to me. It is quite at your service, Commander.

THE STATUE   Thank you: thats very good of you. Even in heaven, I never quite got out of my old military habits of speech. What I was going to ask Juan was why Life should bother itself about getting a brain. Why should it want to understand itself? Why not be content to enjoy itself?

DON JUAN   Without a brain, Commander, you would enjoy yourself without knowing it, and so lose all the fun.

THE STATUE   True, most true. But I am quite content with brain enough to know that I'm enjoying myself. I dont want to understand why. In fact, I'd rather not. My experience is that ones pleasures dont bear thinking about.

DON JUAN   That is why intellect is so unpopular. But to Life, the force behind the Man, intellect is a necessity, because without it he blunders into death. Just as Life, after ages of struggle, evolved that wonderful bodily organ the eye, so that the living organism could see where it was going and what was coming to help or threaten it, and thus avoid a thousand dangers that formerly slew it, so it is evolving to-day a mind's eye that shall see, not the physical world, but the purpose of Life, and thereby enable the individual to work for that purpose instead of thwarting and baffling it by setting up shortsighted personal aims as at present. Even as it is, only one sort of man has ever been happy, has ever been universally respected among all the conflicts of interests and illusions.

THE STATUE   You mean the military man.

DON JUAN   Commander: I do not mean the military man. When the military man approaches, the world locks up its spoons and packs off its womankind. No: I sing, not arms and the hero, but the philosophic man: he who seeks in contemplation to discover the inner will of the world, in invention to discover the means of fulfilling that will, and in action to do that will by the so-discovered means. Of all other sorts of men I declare myself tired. They are tedious failures. When I was on earth, professors of all sorts prowled round me feeling for an unhealthy spot in me on which they could fasten. The doctors of medicine bade me consider what I must do to save my body, and offered me quack cures for imaginary diseases. I replied that I was not a hypochondriac; so they called me Ignoramus and went their way. The doctors of divinity bade me consider what I must do to save my soul; but I was not a spiritual hypochondriac any more than a bodily one, and would not trouble myself about that either; so they called me Atheist and went their way. After them came the politician, who said there was only one purpose in Nature, and that was to get him into parliament. I told him I did not care whether he got into parliament or not; so he called me Mugwump and went his way. Then came the romantic man, the Artist, with his love songs and his paintings and his poems; and with him I had great delight for many years, and some profit; for I cultivated my senses for his sake; and his songs taught me to hear better, his paintings to see better, and his poems to feel more deeply. But he led me at last into the worship of Woman.

ANA   Juan!

DON JUAN   Yes: I came to believe that in her voice was all the music of the song, in her face all the beauty of the painting, and in her soul all the emotion of the poem.

ANA   And you were disappointed, I suppose. Well, was it her fault that you attributed all these perfections to her?

DON JUAN   Yes, partly. For with a wonderful instinctive cunning, she kept silent and allowed me to glorify her; to mistake my own visions, thoughts, and feelings for hers. Now my friend the romantic man was often too poor or too timid to approach those women who were beautiful or refined enough to seem to realize his ideal; and so he went to his grave believing in his dream. But I was more favored by nature and circumstance. I was of noble birth and rich; and when my person did not please, my conversation flattered, though I generally found myself fortunate in both.

THE STATUE   Coxcomb!

DON JUAN   Yes; but even my coxcombry pleased. Well, I found that when I had touched a woman's imagination, she would allow me to persuade myself that she loved me; but when my suit was granted she never said "I am happy: my love is satisfied": she always said, first, "At last, the barriers are down," and second, "When will you come again?"

ANA   That is exactly what men say.

DON JUAN   I protest I never said it. But all women say it. Well, these two speeches always alarmed me; for the first meant that the lady's impulse had been solely to throw down my fortifications and gain my citadel; and the second openly announced that henceforth she regarded me as her property, and counted my time as already wholly at her disposal.

THE DEVIL   That is where your want of heart came in.

THE STATUE [*Shaking his head*]   You shouldnt repeat what a woman says, Juan.

ANA [*Severely*]   It should be sacred to you.

THE STATUE   Still, they certainly do say it. I never minded the barriers; but there was always a slight shock about the other, unless one was very hard hit indeed.

DON JUAN   Then the lady, who had been happy and idle enough before, became anxious, preoccupied with me, always intriguing, conspiring, pursuing, watching, waiting, bent wholly on making sure of her prey—I being the prey, you understand. Now this was not what I had bargained for. It may have been very proper and very natural; but it was not music, painting, poetry and joy incarnated in a beautiful woman. I ran away from it. I ran away from it very often: in fact I became famous for running away from it.

ANA   Infamous, you mean.

DON JUAN   I did not run away from you. Do you blame me for running away from the others?

ANA   Nonsense, man. You are talking to a woman of 77 now. If you had had the chance, you would have run away from me too—if I had let you. You would not have found it so easy with me as with some of the others. If men will not be faithful to their home and their duties, they must be made to be. I daresay you all want to marry lovely incarnations of music and painting and poetry. Well, you cant have them, because they dont exist. If flesh and blood is not good enough for you you must go without: thats all. Women have to put up with flesh-and-blood husbands—and little enough of that too, sometimes; and you will have to put up with flesh-and-blood wives. [THE DEVIL *looks dubious.* THE STATUE *makes a wry face.*] I see you dont like that, any of you; but its true, for all that; so if you don't like it you can lump it.

DON JUAN   My dear lady, you have put my whole case against romance into a few sentences. That is just why I turned my back on the romantic man with the artist nature, as he called his infatuation. I thanked him for teaching me to use my eyes and ears; but I told him that his beauty worshipping and happiness hunting and woman idealizing was not worth a dump as a philosophy of life; so he called me Philistine and went his way.

ANA   It seems that Woman taught you something, too, with all her defects.

DON JUAN   She did more: she interpreted all the other teaching for me. Ah, my friends, when the barriers were down for the first time, what an astounding illumination! I had been prepared for infatuation, for intoxication, for all the illusions of love's young dream; and lo! never was my perception clearer, nor my criticism more ruthless. The most jealous rival of my mistress never saw every blemish in her more keenly than I. I was not duped: I took her without chloroform.

ANA   But you did take her.

DON JUAN   That was the revelation. Up to that moment I had never lost the sense of being my own master; never consciously taken a single step until my reason had examined and approved it. I had come to believe that I was a purely rational creature: a thinker! I said, with the foolish philosopher, "I think; therefore I am." It was Woman who taught me to say "I am; therefore I think." And also "I would think more; therefore I must be more."

THE STATUE   This is extremely abstract and metaphysical, Juan. If you would stick to the concrete, and put your discoveries in the form of entertaining anecdotes about your adventures with women, your conversation would be easier to follow.

DON JUAN   Bah! what need I add? Do you not understand that when I stood face to face with Woman, every fibre in my clear critical brain warned me to spare her and save myself. My morals said No. My conscience said No. My chivalry and pity for her said No. My prudent regard for myself said No. My ear, practised on a thousand songs and symphonies; my eye, exercised on a thousand paintings; tore her voice, her features, her color to shreds. I caught all those tell-tale resemblances to her father and mother by which I knew what she would be like in thirty years time. I noted the gleam of gold from a dead tooth in the laughing mouth: I made curious observations of the strange odors of the chemistry of the nerves. The visions of my romantic reveries, in which I had trod the plains of heaven with a deathless, ageless creature of coral and ivory, deserted me in that supreme hour. I remembered them and desperately strove to recover their illusion; but they now seemed the emptiest of inventions: my judgment was not to be corrupted: my brain still said No on every issue. And whilst I was in the act of framing my excuse to the lady, Life seized me and threw me into her arms as a sailor throws a scrap of fish into the mouth of a seabird.

THE STATUE   You might as well have gone without thinking such a lot about it, Juan. You are like all the clever men: you have more brains than is good for you.

THE DEVIL   And were you not the happier for the experience, Señor Don Juan?

DON JUAN   The happier, no: the wiser, yes. That moment introduced me for the first time to myself, and, through myself, to the world. I saw then how useless it is to attempt to impose conditions on the irresistible force of Life; to preach prudence, careful selection, virtue, honor, chastity—

ANA   Don Juan: a word against chastity is an insult to me.

DON JUAN   I say nothing against your chastity, Señora, since it took the form of a husband and twelve children. What more could you have done had you been the most abandoned of women?

ANA   I could have had twelve husbands and no children: thats what I could have done, Juan. And let me tell you that that would have made all the difference to the earth which I replenished.

THE STATUE   Bravo Ana! Juan: you are floored, quelled, annihilated.

DON JUAN   No; for though that difference is the true essential difference—Doña Ana has, I admit, gone straight to the real point— yet it is not a difference of love or chastity, or even constancy; for twelve children by twelve different husbands would have replenished the earth perhaps more effectively. Suppose my friend Ottavio had died when you were thirty, you would never have remained a widow: you were too beautiful. Suppose the successor of Ottavio had died when you were forty, you would still have been irresistible; and a woman who marries twice marries three times if she becomes free to do so. Twelve lawful children borne by one highly respectable lady to three different fathers is not impossible nor condemned by public opinion. That such a lady may be more law abiding than the poor girl whom we used to spurn into the gutter for bearing one unlawful infant is no doubt true; but dare you say she is less self-indulgent?

ANA   She is less virtuous: that is enough for me.

DON JUAN   In that case, what is virtue but the Trade Unionism of the married? Let us face the facts, dear Ana. The Life Force respects marriage only because marriage is a contrivance of its own to secure the greatest number of children and the closest care of them. For honor, chastity and all the rest of your moral figments it cares not a rap. Marriage is the most licentious of human institutions—

ANA   Juan!

THE STATUE [*Protesting*]   Really!—

DON JUAN [*Determinedly*]   I say the most licentious of human institutions: that is the secret of its popularity. And a woman seeking a husband is the most unscrupulous of all the beasts of prey. The confusion of marriage with morality has done more to destroy the conscience of the human race than any other single error. Come, Ana! do not look shocked: you know better than any of us that marriage is a mantrap baited with simulated accomplishments and delusive idealizations. When your sainted mother, by dint of scoldings and punishments, forced you to learn how to play half a dozen pieces on the spinet—which she hated as much as you did—had she any other purpose than to delude your suitors into the belief that your husband would have in his home an angel who would fill it with melody, or at least play him to sleep after dinner? You married my friend Ottavio: well, did you ever open the spinet from the hour when the Church united him to you?

ANA   You are a fool, Juan. A young married woman has something else to do than sit at the spinet without any support for her back; so she gets out of the habit of playing.

DON JUAN   Not if she loves music. No: believe me, she only throws away the bait when the bird is in the net.

ANA [*Bitterly*]   And men, I suppose, never throw off the mask when their bird is in the net. The husband never becomes negligent, selfish, brutal—oh never!

DON JUAN   What do these recriminations prove, Ana? Only that the hero is as gross an imposture as the heroine.

ANA   It is all nonsense: most marriages are perfectly comfortable.

DON JUAN   "Perfectly" is a strong expression, Ana. What you mean is that sensible people make the best of one another. Send me to the galleys and chain me to the felon whose number happens to be next before mine; and I must accept the inevitable and make the best of the companionship. Many such companionships, they tell me, are touchingly affectionate; and most are at least tolerably friendly. But that does not make a chain a desirable ornament nor the galleys an abode of bliss. Those who talk most about the blessings of marriage and the constancy of its vows are the very people who declare that if the chain were broken and the prisoners left free to choose, the whole social fabric would fly asunder. You cannot have the argument both ways. If the prisoner is happy, why lock him in? If he is not, why pretend that he is?

ANA   At all events, let me take an old woman's privilege again, and tell you flatly that marriage peoples the world and debauchery does not.

DON JUAN   How if a time come when this shall cease to be true? Do you not know that where there is a will there is a way—that whatever Man really wishes to do he will finally discover a means of doing? Well, you have done your best, you virtuous ladies, and others of your way of thinking, to bend Man's mind wholly towards honorable love as the highest good, and to understand by honorable love romance and beauty and happiness in the possession of beautiful, refined, delicate, affectionate women. You have taught women to value their own youth, health, shapeliness, and refinement above all things. Well, what place have squalling babies and household cares in this exquisite paradise of the senses and emotions? Is it not the inevitable end of it all that the human will shall say to the human brain: Invent me a means by which I can have love, beauty, romance, emotion, passion without their wretched penalties, their expenses, their worries, their trials, their illnesses and agonies and risks of death, their retinue of servants and nurses and doctors and schoolmasters.

THE DEVIL All this, Señor Don Juan, is realized here in my realm.

DON JUAN Yes, at the cost of death. Man will not take it at that price: he demands the romantic delights of your hell whilst he is still on earth. Well, the means will be found: the brain will not fail when the will is in earnest. The day is coming when great nations will find their numbers dwindling from census to census; when the six-roomed villa will rise in price above the family mansion; when the viciously reckless poor and the stupidly pious rich will delay the extinction of the race only by degrading it; whilst the boldly prudent, the thriftily selfish and ambitious, the imaginative and poetic, the lovers of money and solid comfort, the worshippers of success, of art, and of love, will all oppose to the Force of Life the device of sterility.

THE STATUE That is all very eloquent, my young friend; but if you had lived to Ana's age, or even to mine, you would have learned that the people who get rid of the fear of poverty and children and all the other family troubles, and devote themselves to having a good time of it, only leave their minds free for the fear of old age and ugliness and impotence and death. The childless laborer is more tormented by his wife's idleness and her constant demands for amusement and distraction than he could be by twenty children; and his wife is more wretched than he. I have had my share of vanity; for as a young man I was admired by women; and as a statue I am praised by art critics. But I confess that had I found nothing to do in the world but wallow in these delights I should have cut my throat. When I married Ana's mother—or perhaps, to be strictly correct, I should rather say when I at last gave in and allowed Ana's mother to marry me—I knew that I was planting thorns in my pillow, and that marriage for me, a swaggering young officer thitherto unvanquished, meant defeat and capture.

ANA [*Scandalized*] Father!

THE STATUE I am sorry to shock you, my love; but since Juan has stripped every rag of decency from the discussion I may as well tell the frozen truth.

ANA   Hmf! I suppose I was one of the thorns.

THE STATUE   By no means: you were often a rose. You see, your mother had most of the trouble you gave.

DON JUAN   Then may I ask, Commander, why you have left heaven to come here and wallow, as you express it, in sentimental beatitudes which you confess would once have driven you to cut your throat?

THE STATUE [*Struck by this*]   Egad, thats true.

THE DEVIL [*Alarmed*]   What! You are going back from your word! [*To* DON JUAN] And all your philosophizing has been nothing but a mask for proselytizing! [*To* THE STATUE] Have you forgotten already the hideous dulness from which I am offering you a refuge here? [*To* DON JUAN] And does your demonstration of the approaching sterilization and extinction of mankind lead to anything better than making the most of those pleasures of art and love which you yourself admit refined you, elevated you, developed you?

DON JUAN   I never demonstrated the extinction of mankind. Life cannot will its own extinction either in its blind amorphous state or in any of the forms into which it has organized itself. I had not finished when His Excellency interrupted me.

THE STATUE   I begin to doubt whether you ever will finish, my friend. You are extremely fond of hearing yourself talk.

DON JUAN   True; but since you have endured so much, you may as well endure to the end. Long before this sterilization which I described becomes more than a clearly foreseen possibility, the reaction will begin. The great central purpose of breeding the race, ay, breeding it to heights now deemed superhuman: that purpose which is now hidden in a mephitic cloud of love and romance and prudery and fastidiousness, will break through into clear sunlight as a purpose no longer to be confused with the gratification of personal fancies, the impossible realization of boys' and girls' dreams of bliss, or the need of older people for companionship or money. The plain-spoken marriage services of the vernacular Churches will no longer be abbreviated and half suppressed as indelicate. The sober decency, earnestness and authority of their declaration of the real purpose of marriage will be honored and accepted, whilst their romantic vowings and pledgings and until-death-do-us-partings and the like will be expunged as unbearable frivolities. Do my sex the justice to admit, Señora, that we have always recognized that the sex relation is not a personal or friendly relation at all.

ANA   Not a personal or friendly relation! What relation is more personal? more sacred? more holy?

DON JUAN   Sacred and holy, if you like, Ana, but not personally friendly. Your relation to God is sacred and holy: dare you call it personally friendly? In the sex relation the universal creative

energy, of which the parties are both the helpless agents, over-
rides and sweeps away all personal considerations and dispenses
with all personal relations. The pair may be utter strangers to one
another, speaking different languages, differing in race and color,
in age and disposition, with no bond between them but a possibility of that fecundity for the sake of which the Life Force throws
them into one another's arms at the exchange of a glance. Do we
not recognize this by allowing marriages to be made by parents
without consulting the woman? Have you not often expressed your
disgust at the immorality of the English nation, in which women
and men of noble birth become acquainted and court each other
like peasants? And how much does even the peasant know of his
bride or she of him before he engages himself? Why, you would
not make a man your lawyer or your family doctor on so slight an
acquaintance as you would fall in love with and marry him!

ANA Yes, Juan: we know the libertine's philosophy. Always ignore
the consequences to the woman.

DON JUAN The consequences, yes: they justify her fierce grip of the
man. But surely you do not call that attachment a sentimental
one. As well call the policeman's attachment to his prisoner a love
relation.

ANA You see you have to confess that marriage is necessary,
though, according to you, love is the slightest of all the relations.

DON JUAN How do you know that it is not the greatest of all the
relations? far too great to be a personal matter. Could your father
have served his country if he had refused to kill any enemy of Spain
unless he personally hated him? Can a woman serve her country
if she refuses to marry any man she does not personally love? You
know it is not so: the woman of noble birth marries as the man of
noble birth fights, on political and family grounds, not on personal
ones.

THE STATUE [Impressed] A very clever point that, Juan: I must think
it over. You are really full of ideas. How did you come to think of
this one?

DON JUAN I learnt it by experience. When I was on earth, and made
those proposals to ladies which, though universally condemned,
have made me so interesting a hero of legend, I was not infre-
quently met in some such way as this. The lady would say that she
would countenance my advances, provided they were honorable.
On inquiring what that proviso meant, I found that it meant that
I proposed to get possession of her property if she had any, or to
undertake her support for life if she had not; that I desired her
continual companionship, counsel and conversation to the end of
my days, and would bind myself under penalties to be always
enraptured by them; and, above all, that I would turn my back on
all other women for ever for her sake. I did not object to these
conditions because they were exorbitant and inhuman: it was their

extraordinary irrelevance that prostrated me. I invariably replied with perfect frankness that I had never dreamt of any of these things; that unless the lady's character and intellect were equal or superior to my own, her conversation must degrade and her counsel mislead me; that her constant companionship might, for all I knew, become intolerably tedious to me; that I could not answer for my feelings for a week in advance, much less to the end of my life; that to cut me off from all natural and unconstrained relations with the rest of my fellow creatures would narrow and warp me if I submitted to it, and, if not, would bring me under the curse of clandestinity; that, finally, my proposals to her were wholly unconnected with any of these matters, and were the outcome of a perfectly simple impulse of my manhood towards her womanhood.

ANA   You mean that it was an immoral impulse.

DON JUAN   Nature, my dear lady, is what you call immoral. I blush for it; but I cannot help it. Nature is a pandar, Time a wrecker, and Death a murderer. I have always preferred to stand up to those facts and build institutions on their recognition. You prefer to propitiate the three devils by proclaiming their chastity, their thrift, and their loving kindness; and to base your institutions on these flatteries. Is it any wonder that the institutions do not work smoothly?

THE STATUE   What used the ladies to say, Juan?

DON JUAN   Oh come! Confidence for confidence. First tell me what you used to say to the ladies.

THE STATUE   I! Oh, I swore that I would be faithful to the death; that I should die if they refused me; that no woman could ever be to me what she was—

ANA   She! Who?

THE STATUE   Whoever it happened to be at the time, my dear. I had certain things I always said. One of them was that even when I was eighty, one white hair of the woman I loved would make me tremble more than the thickest gold tress from the most beautiful young head. Another was that I could not bear the thought of anyone else being the mother of my children.

DON JUAN [Revolted]   You old rascal!

THE STATUE [Stoutly]   Not a bit; for I really believed it with all my soul at the moment. I had a heart: not like you. And it was this sincerity that made me successful.

DON JUAN   Sincerity! To be fool enough to believe a ramping, stamping, thumping lie: that is what you call sincerity! To be so greedy for a woman that you deceive yourself in your eagerness to deceive her: sincerity, you call it!

THE STATUE   Oh, damn your sophistries! I was a man in love, not a lawyer. And the women loved me for it, bless them!

DON JUAN   They made you think so. What will you say when I tell you that though I played the lawyer so callously, they made me think so too? I also had my moments of infatuation in which I gushed nonsense and believed it. Sometimes the desire to give pleasure by saying beautiful things so rose in me on the flood of emotion that I said them recklessly. At other times I argued against myself with a devilish coldness that drew tears. But I found it just as hard to escape in the one case as in the others. When the lady's instinct was set on me, there was nothing for it but lifelong servitude or flight.

ANA   You dare boast, before me and my father, that every woman found you irresistible.

DON JUAN   Am I boasting? It seems to me that I cut the most pitiable of figures. Besides, I said "when the lady's instinct was set on me." It was not always so; and then, heavens! what transports of virtuous indignation! what overwhelming defiance to the dastardly seducer! what scenes of Imogen and Iachimo!

ANA   I made no scenes. I simply called my father.

DON JUAN   And he came, sword in hand, to vindicate outraged honor and morality by murdering me.

THE STATUE   Murdering! What do you mean? Did I kill you or did you kill me?

DON JUAN   Which of us was the better fencer?

THE STATUE   I was.

DON JUAN   Of course you were. And yet you, the hero of those scandalous adventures you have just been relating to us, you had the effrontery to pose as the avenger of outraged morality and condemn me to death! You would have slain me but for an accident.

THE STATUE   I was expected to, Juan. That is how things were arranged on earth. I was not a social reformer; and I always did what it was customary for a gentleman to do.

DON JUAN   That may account for your attacking me, but not for the revolting hypocrisy of your subsequent proceedings as a statue.

THE STATUE   That all came of my going to heaven.

THE DEVIL   I still fail to see, Señor Don Juan, that these episodes in your earthly career and in that of the Señor Commander in any way discredit my view of life. Here, I repeat, you have all that you sought without anything that you shrank from.

DON JUAN   On the contrary, here I have everything that disappointed me without anything that I have not already tried and found wanting. I tell you that as long as I can conceive something better than myself I cannot be easy unless I am striving to bring it into existence or clearing the way for it. That is the law of my life. That is the working within me of Life's incessant aspiration to higher organization, wider, deeper, intenser self-consciousness, and clearer self-understanding. It was the supremacy of this purpose that reduced love for me to the mere pleasure of a moment, art for me to the mere schooling of my faculties, religion for me to a mere excuse for laziness, since it had set up a God who looked at the world and saw that it was good, against the instinct in me that looked through my eyes at the world and saw that it could be improved. I tell you that in the pursuit of my own pleasure, my own health, my own fortune, I have never known happiness. It was not love for Woman that delivered me into her hands: it was fatigue, exhaustion. When I was a child, and bruised my head against a stone, I ran to the nearest woman and cried away my pain against her apron. When I grew up, and bruised my soul against the brutalities and stupidities with which I had to strive, I did again just what I had done as a child. I have enjoyed, too, my rests, my recuperations, my breathing times, my very prostrations after strife; but rather would I be dragged through all the circles of the foolish Italian's Inferno than through the pleasures of Europe. That is what has made this place of eternal pleasures so deadly to me. It is the absence of this instinct in you that makes you that strange monster called a Devil. It is the success with which you have diverted the attention of men from their real purpose, which in one degree or another is the same as mine, to yours, that has earned you the name of The Tempter. It is the fact that they are doing your will, or rather drifting with your want of will, instead of doing their own, that makes them the uncomfortable, false, restless, artificial, petulant, wretched creatures they are.

THE DEVIL [*Mortified*]   Señor Don Juan: you are uncivil to my friends.

DON JUAN   Pooh! why should I be civil to them or to you? In this Palace of Lies a truth or two will not hurt you. Your friends are all the dullest dogs I know. They are not beautiful: they are only decorated. They are not clean: they are only shaved and starched. They are not dignified: they are only fashionably dressed. They are not educated: they are only college passmen. They are not religious: they are only pewrenters. They are not moral: they are only conventional. They are not virtuous: they are only cowardly. They are not even vicious: they are only "frail." They are not artistic: they are only lascivious. They are not prosperous: they are only rich. They are not loyal, they are only servile; not dutiful, only sheepish; not public spirited, only patriotic; not courageous, only quarrelsome; not determined, only obstinate; not masterful, only domineering; not self-controlled, only obtuse; not self-respecting, only vain; not kind, only sentimental; not social, only gregarious; not considerate, only polite; not intelligent, only opinionated; not progressive, only factious; not imaginative, only superstitious; not just, only vindictive; not generous, only propitiatory; not disciplined, only cowed; and not truthful at all—liars every one of them, to the very backbone of their souls.

THE STATUE   Your flow of words is simply amazing, Juan. How I wish I could have talked like that to my soldiers.

THE DEVIL   It is mere talk, though. It has all been said before; but what change has it ever made? What notice has the world ever taken of it?

DON JUAN   Yes, it is mere talk. But why is it mere talk? Because, my friend, beauty, purity, respectability, religion, morality, art, patriotism, bravery and the rest are nothing but words which I or anyone else can turn inside out like a glove. Were they realities, you would have to plead guilty to my indictment; but fortunately for your self-respect, my diabolical friend, they are not realities. As you say, they are mere words, useful for duping barbarians into adopting civilization, or the civilized poor into submitting to be robbed and enslaved. That is the family secret of the governing caste; and if we who are of that caste aimed at more Life for the world instead of at more power and luxury for our miserable selves, that secret would make us great. Now, since I, being a nobleman, am in the secret too, think how tedious to me must be your unending cant about all these moralistic figments, and how squalidly disastrous your sacrifice of your lives to them! If you even believed in your moral game enough to play it fairly, it would be interesting to watch; but you dont: you cheat at every trick; and if your opponent outcheats you, you upset the table and try to murder him.

THE DEVIL   On earth there may be some truth in this, because the people are uneducated and cannot appreciate my religion of love and beauty; but here—

DON JUAN   Oh yes: I know. Here there is nothing but love and beauty. Ugh! it is like sitting for all eternity at the first act of a fashionable play, before the complications begin. Never in my worst moments of superstitious terror on earth did I dream that hell was so horrible. I live, like a hairdresser, in the continual contemplation of beauty, toying with silken tresses. I breathe an atmosphere of sweetness, like a confectioner's shopboy. Commander: are there any beautiful women in heaven?

THE STATUE   None. Absolutely none. All dowdies. Not two pennorth of jewellery among a dozen of them. They might be men of fifty.

DON JUAN   I am impatient to get there. Is the word beauty ever mentioned; and are there any artistic people?

THE STATUE   I give you my word they wont admire a fine statue even when it walks past them.

DON JUAN   I go.

THE DEVIL   Don Juan: shall I be frank with you?

DON JUAN   Were you not so before?

THE DEVIL   As far as I went, yes. But I will now go further, and confess to you that men get tired of everything, of heaven no less than of hell; and that all history is nothing but a record of the oscillations of the world between these two extremes. An epoch is but a swing of the pendulum; and each generation thinks the world is progressing because it is always moving. But when you are as old as I am; when you have a thousand times wearied of heaven, like myself and the Commander, and a thousand times wearied of hell, as you are wearied now, you will no longer imagine that every swing from heaven to hell is an emancipation, every swing from hell to heaven an evolution. Where you now see reform, progress, fulfilment of upward tendency, continual ascent by Man on the stepping stones of his dead selves to higher things, you will see nothing but an infinite comedy of illusion. You will discover the profound truth of the saying of my friend Koheleth, that there is nothing new under the sun. Vanitas vanitatum—

DON JUAN [*Out of all patience*] By heaven, this is worse than your cant about love and beauty. Clever dolt that you are, is a man no better than a worm, or a dog than a wolf, because he gets tired of everything? Shall he give up eating because he destroys his appetite in the act of gratifying it? Is a field idle when it is fallow? Can the Commander expend his hellish energy here without accumulating heavenly energy for his next term of blessedness? Granted that the great Life Force has hit on the device of the clockmaker's pendulum, and uses the earth for its bob; that the history of each oscillation, which seems so novel to us the actors, is but the history of the last oscillation repeated; nay more, that in the unthinkable infinitude of time the sun throws off the earth and catches it again a thousand times as a circus rider throws up a ball, and that the total of all our epochs is but the moment between the toss and the catch, has the colossal mechanism no purpose?

THE DEVIL None, my friend. You think, because you have a purpose, Nature must have one. You might as well expect it to have fingers and toes because you have them.

DON JUAN But I should not have them if they served no purpose. And I, my friend, am as much a part of Nature as my own finger is a part of me. If my finger is the organ by which I grasp the sword and the mandoline, my brain is the organ by which Nature strives to understand itself. My dog's brain serves only my dog's purposes; but my brain labors at a knowledge which does nothing for me personally but make my body bitter to me and my decay and death a calamity. Were I not possessed with a purpose beyond my own I had better be a ploughman than a philosopher; for the ploughman lives as long as the philosopher, eats more, sleeps better, and rejoices in the wife of his bosom with less misgiving. This is because the philosopher is in the grip of the Life Force. This Life Force says to him "I have done a thousand wonderful things unconsciously by merely willing to live and following the line of least resistance: now I want to know myself and my destination, and choose my path; so I have made a special brain—a philosopher's brain—to grasp this knowledge for me as the husbandman's hand grasps the plough for me. And this" says the Life Force to the philosopher "must thou strive to do for me until thou diest, when I will make another brain and another philosopher to carry on the work."

THE DEVIL   What is the use of knowing?

DON JUAN   Why, to be able to choose the line of greatest advantage instead of yielding in the direction of the least resistance. Does a ship sail to its destination no better than a log drifts nowhither? The philosopher is Nature's pilot. And there you have our difference: to be in hell is to drift: to be in heaven is to steer.

THE DEVIL   On the rocks, most likely.

DON JUAN   Pooh! which ship goes oftenest on the rocks or to the bottom—the drifting ship or the ship with a pilot on board?

THE DEVIL   Well, well, go your way, Señor Don Juan. I prefer to be my own master and not the tool of any blundering universal force. I know that beauty is good to look at; that music is good to hear; that love is good to feel; and that they are all good to think about and talk about. I know that to be well exercised in these sensations, emotions, and studies is to be a refined and cultivated being. Whatever they may say of me in churches on earth, I know that it is universally admitted in good society that the Prince of Darkness is a gentleman; and that is enough for me. As to your Life Force, which you think irresistible, it is the most resistible thing in the world for a person of any character. But if you are naturally vulgar and credulous, as all reformers are, it will thrust you first into religion, where you will sprinkle water on babies to save their souls from me; then it will drive you from religion into science, where you will snatch the babies from the water sprinkling and inoculate them with disease to save them from catching it accidentally; then you will take to politics, where you will become the catspaw of corrupt functionaries and the henchman of ambitious humbugs; and the end will be despair and decrepitude, broken nerve and shattered hopes, vain regrets for that worst and silliest of wastes and sacrifices, the waste and sacrifice of the power of enjoyment: in a word, the punishment of the fool who pursues the better before he has secured the good.

DON JUAN   But at least I shall not be bored. The service of the Life Force has that advantage, at all events. So fare you well, Señor Satan.

THE DEVIL [Amiably]   Fare you well, Don Juan. I shall often think of our interesting chats about things in general. I wish you every happiness: Heaven, as I said before, suits some people. But if you should change your mind, do not forget that the gates are always open here to the repentant prodigal. If you feel at any time that warmth of heart, sincere unforced affection, innocent enjoyment, and warm, breathing, palpitating reality—

DON JUAN   Why not say flesh and blood at once, though we have left those two greasy commonplaces behind us?

THE DEVIL [*Angrily*]   You throw my friendly farewell back in my teeth, then, Don Juan?

DON JUAN   By no means. But though there is much to be learnt from a cynical devil, I really cannot stand a sentimental one. Señor Commander: you know the way to the frontier of hell and heaven. Be good enough to direct me.

THE STATUE   Oh, the frontier is only the difference between two ways of looking at things. Any road will take you across it if you really want to get there.

DON JUAN   Good. [*Saluting* DOÑA ANA] Señora: your servant.

ANA   But I am going with you.

DON JUAN   I can find my own way to heaven, Ana; but I cannot find yours [*He vanishes*].

ANA   How annoying!

THE STATUE [*Calling after him*]   Bon voyage, Juan! [*He wafts a final blast of his great rolling chords after him as a parting salute. A faint echo of the first ghostly melody comes back in acknowledgment.*] Ah! there he goes. [*Puffing a long breath out through his lips.*] Whew! How he does talk! Theyll never stand it in heaven.

THE DEVIL [*Gloomily*]   His going is a political defeat. I cannot keep these Life Worshippers: they all go. This is the greatest loss I have had since that Dutch painter went—a fellow who would paint a hag of 70 with as much enjoyment as a Venus of 20.

THE STATUE   I remember: he came to heaven. Rembrandt.

THE DEVIL   Ay, Rembrandt. There is something unnatural about these fellows. Do not listen to their gospel, Señor Commander: it is dangerous. Beware of the pursuit of the Superhuman: it leads to an indiscriminate contempt for the Human. To a man, horses and dogs and cats are mere species, outside the moral world. Well, to the Superman, men and women are a mere species too, also outside the moral world. This Don Juan was kind to women and courteous to men as your daughter here was kind to her pet cats and dogs; but such kindness is a denial of the exclusively human character of the soul.

THE STATUE   And who the deuce is the Superman?[5]

THE DEVIL   Oh, the latest fashion among the Life Force fanatics. Did you not meet in Heaven, among the new arrivals, that German Polish madman—what was his name? Nietzsche?

THE STATUE   Never heard of him.

THE DEVIL   Well, he came here first, before he recovered his wits. I had some hopes of him; but he was a confirmed Life Force worshipper. It was he who raked up the Superman, who is as old as Prometheus; and the 20th century will run after this newest of the old crazes when it gets tired of the world, the flesh, and your humble servant.

5. See the note to the title of the play, p. 67.

THE STATUE   Superman is a good cry; and a good cry is half the battle. I should like to see this Nietzsche.

THE DEVIL   Unfortunately he met Wagner here, and had a quarrel with him.

THE STATUE   Quite right, too. Mozart for me!

THE DEVIL   Oh, it was not about music. Wagner once drifted into Life Force worship, and invented a Superman called Siegfried. But he came to his senses afterwards. So when they met here, Nietzsche denounced him as a renegade; and Wagner wrote a pamphlet to prove that Nietzsche was a Jew; and it ended in Nietzsche's going to heaven in a huff. And a good riddance too. And now, my friend, let us hasten to my palace and celebrate your arrival with a grand musical service.

THE STATUE   With pleasure: youre most kind.

THE DEVIL   This way, Commander. We go down the old trap [*He places himself on the grave trap*].

THE STATUE   Good. [*Reflectively*] All the same, the Superman is a fine conception. There is something statuesque about it. [*He places himself on the grave trap beside* THE DEVIL. *It begins to descend slowly. Red glow from the abyss.*] Ah, this reminds me of old times.

THE DEVIL   And me also.

ANA   Stop! [*The trap stops.*]

THE DEVIL   You, Señora, cannot come this way. You will have an apotheosis. But you will be at the palace before us.

ANA   That is not what I stopped you for. Tell me: where can I find the Superman?

THE DEVIL   He is not yet created, Señora.

THE STATUE   And never will be, probably. Let us proceed: the red fire will make me sneeze. [*They descend.*]

ANA   Not yet created! Then my work is not yet done. [*Crossing herself devoutly*] I believe in the Life to Come. [*Crying to the universe*] A father—a father for the Superman!

> She vanishes into the void; and again there is nothing: all existence seems suspended infinitely. Then, vaguely, there is a live human voice crying somewhere. One sees, with a shock, a mountain peak shewing faintly against a lighter background. The sky has returned from afar; and we suddenly remember where we were. The cry becomes distinct and urgent: it says Automobile, Automobile. The complete reality comes back with a rush: in a moment it is full morning in the Sierra; and the brigands are scrambling to their feet and making for the road as THE GOATHERD runs down from the hill, warning them of the approach of another motor. TANNER and MENDOZA rise amazedly and stare at one another with scattered wits. STRAKER

sits up to yawn for a moment before he gets on his feet, making it a point of honor not to shew any undue interest in the excitement of the bandits. MENDOZA *gives a quick look to see that his followers are attending to the alarm; then exchanges a private word with* TANNER.

MENDOZA   Did you dream?

TANNER   Damnably. Did you?

MENDOZA   Yes. I forget what. You were in it.

TANNER   So were you. Amazing!

MENDOZA   I warned you. [*A shot is heard from the road.*] Dolts! they will play with that gun. [*The brigands come running back scared.*] Who fired that shot? [*To* DUVAL] was it you?

DUVAL [*Breathless*]   I have not shoot. Dey shoot first.

ANARCHIST   I told you to begin by abolishing the State. Now we are all lost.

THE ROWDY SOCIAL-DEMOCRAT [*Stampeding across the amphitheatre*]   Run, everybody.

MENDOZA [*Collaring him; throwing him on his back; and drawing a knife*]   I stab the man who stirs. [*He blocks the way. The stampede is checked.*] What has happened?

THE SULKY SOCIAL-DEMOCRAT   A motor—

THE ANARCHIST   Three men—

DUVAL   Deux femmes—

MENDOZA   Three men and two women! Why have you not brought them here? Are you afraid of them?

THE ROWDY ONE [*Getting up*]   Thyve a hescort. Ow, de-ooh luts ook it, Mendowza.

THE SULKY ONE   Two armored cars full o soldiers at the ed o the valley.

ANARCHIST   The shot was fired in the air. It was a signal.

[STRAKER *whistles his favorite air, which falls on the ears of the brigands like a funeral march.*]

TANNER   It is not an escort, but an expedition to capture you. We were advised to wait for it; but I was in a hurry.

THE ROWDY ONE [*In an agony of apprehension*]   And Ow my good Lord, ere we are, wytin for em! Luts tike to the mahntns.

MENDOZA   Idiot, what do you know about the mountains? Are you a Spaniard? You would be given up by the first shepherd you met. Besides, we are already within range of their rifles.

THE ROWDY ONE   Bat—

MENDOZA   Silence. Leave this to me. [*To* TANNER] Comrade: you will not betray us.

STRAKER   Oo are you callin comrade?

MENDOZA   Last night the advantage was with me. The robber of the poor was at the mercy of the robber of the rich. You offered your hand: I took it.

TANNER   I bring no charge against you, comrade. We have spent a pleasant evening with you: that is all.

STRAKER   I gev my and to nobody, sec?

MENDOZA [*Turning on him impressively*]   Young man, if I am tried, I shall plead guilty, and explain what drove me from England, home and duty. Do you wish to have the respectable name of Straker dragged through the mud of a Spanish criminal court? The police will search me. They will find Louisa's portrait. It will be published in the illustrated papers. You blench. It will be your doing, remember.

STRAKER [*With baffled rage*]   I dont care about the court. It's avin our name mixed up with yours that I object to, you blackmailin swine, you.

MENDOZA   Language unworthy of Louisa's brother! But no matter: you are muzzled: that is enough for us. [*He turns to face his own men, who back uneasily across the amphitheatre towards the cave to take refuge behind him, as a fresh party, muffled for motoring, comes from the road in riotous spirits.* ANN, *who makes straight for* TANNER, *comes first; then* VIOLET, *helped over the rough ground by* HECTOR *holding her right hand and* RAMSDEN *her left.* MENDOZA *goes to his presidential block and seats himself calmly with his rank and file grouped behind him, and his Staff, consisting of* DUVAL *and* THE ANARCHIST *on his right and the two* SOCIAL-DEMOCRATS *on his left, supporting him in flank.*]

ANN   It's Jack!

TANNER   Caught!

HECTOR   Why, certainly it is. I said it was you, Tanner. Weve just been stopped by a puncture: the road is full of nails.

VIOLET   What are you doing here with all these men?

ANN   Why did you leave us without a word of warning?

HECTOR   I wawnt that bunch of roses, Miss Whitefield. [*To* TANNER] When we found you were gone, Miss Whitefield bet me a bunch of roses my car would not overtake yours before you reached Monte Carlo.

TANNER   But this is not the road to Monte Carlo.

HECTOR   No matter. Miss Whitefield tracked you at every stopping place: she is a regular Sherlock Holmes.

TANNER   The Life Force! I am lost.

OCTAVIUS [*Bounding gaily down from the road into the amphitheatre, and coming between* TANNER *and* STRAKER]   I am so glad you are safe, old chap. We were afraid you had been captured by brigands.

RAMSDEN [*Who has been staring at* MENDOZA]   I seem to remember the face of your friend here. [MENDOZA *rises politely and advances with a smile between* ANN *and* RAMSDEN.]

HECTOR   Why, so do I.

OCTAVIUS   I know you perfectly well, sir; but I cant think where I have met you.

MENDOZA [*To* VIOLET]   Do you remember me, madam?

VIOLET   Oh, quite well; but I am so stupid about names.

MENDOZA   It was at the Savoy Hotel. [*To* HECTOR] You, sir, used to come with this lady [VIOLET] to lunch. [*To* OCTAVIUS] You, sir, often brought this lady [ANN] and her mother to dinner on your way to the Lyceum Theatre. [*To* RAMSDEN] You, sir, used to come to supper, with [*dropping his voice to a confidential but perfectly audible whisper*] several different ladies.

RAMSDEN [*Angrily*]   Well, what is that to you, pray?

OCTAVIUS   Why, Violet, I thought you hardly knew one another before this trip, you and Malone!

VIOLET [*Vexed*]   I suppose this person was the manager.

MENDOZA   The waiter, madam. I have a grateful recollection of you all. I gathered from the bountiful way in which you treated me that you all enjoyed your visits very much.

VIOLET   What impertinence! [*She turns her back on him, and goes up the hill with* HECTOR.]

RAMSDEN   That will do, my friend. You do not expect these ladies to treat you as an acquaintance, I suppose, because you have waited on them at table.

MENDOZA   Pardon me: it was you who claimed my acquaintance. The ladies followed your example. However, this display of the unfortunate manners of your class closes the incident. For the future, you will please address me with the respect due to a stranger and fellow traveller. [*He turns haughtily away and resumes his presidential seat.*]

TANNER   There! I have found one man on my journey capable of reasonable conversation; and you all instinctively insult him. Even the New Man is as bad as any of you. Enry: you have behaved just like a miserable gentleman.

STRAKER   Gentleman! Not me.

RAMSDEN   Really, Tanner, this tone—

ANN   Dont mind him, Granny: you ought to know him by this time [*She takes his arm and coaxes him away to the hill to join* VIOLET *and* HECTOR. OCTAVIUS *follows her, dog-like*].

VIOLET [*Calling from the hill*]   Here are the soldiers. They are getting out of their motors.

DUVAL [*Panicstricken*]   Oh, nom de Dieu![6]

THE ANARCHIST   Fools: the State is about to crush you because you spared it at the prompting of the political hangers-on of the bourgeoisie.

THE SULKY SOCIAL-DEMOCRAT [*Argumentative to the last*]   On the contrary, only by capturing the State machine—

THE ANARCHIST   It is going to capture you.

THE ROWDY SOCIAL-DEMOCRAT [*His anguish culminating*]   Ow,

---

6. Name of God!

chack it. Wot are we ere for? Wot are we wytin for?

MENDOZA [*Between his teeth*]   Go on. Talk politics, you idiots: nothing sounds more respectable. Keep it up, I tell you.

[*The soldiers line the road, commanding the amphitheatre with
their rifles. The brigands, struggling with an overwhelming
impulse to hide behind one another, look as unconcerned as
they can.* MENDOZA *rises superbly, with undaunted front.* THE
OFFICER *in command steps down from the road into the amphitheatre; looks hard at the brigands; and then inquiringly at* TAN-
NER.]

THE OFFICER   Who are these men, Señor Ingles?

TANNER   My escort.

[MENDOZA, *with a Mephistophelean smile, bows profoundly.
An irrepressible grin runs from face to face among the brigands.
They touch their hats, except* THE ANARCHIST, *who defies the
State with folded arms.*]

Act IV

*The garden of a villa in Granada. Whoever wishes to know
what it is like must go to Granada and see. One may pro-
saically specify a group of hills dotted with villas, the
Alhambra on the top of one of the hills, and a considerable
town in the valley, approached by dusty white roads in
which the children, no matter what they are doing or
thinking about, automatically whine for halfpence and
reach out little clutching brown palms for them; but there
is nothing in this description except the Alhambra, the
begging, and the color of the roads, that does not fit Surrey
as well as Spain. The difference is that the Surrey hills are
comparatively small and ugly, and should properly be
called the Surrey Protuberances; but these Spanish hills
are of mountain stock: the amenity which conceals their
size does not compromise their dignity.*

*This particular garden is on a hill opposite the Alham-
bra; and the villa is as expensive and pretentious as a villa
must be if it is to be let furnished by the week to opulent
American and English visitors. If we stand on the lawn at
the foot of the garden and look uphill, our horizon is the
stone balustrade of a flagged platform on the edge of infinite space at the top of the hill. Between us and this platform is a flower garden with a circular basin and fountain
in the centre, surrounded by geometrical flower beds,
gravel paths, and clipped yew trees in the genteelest order.
The garden is higher than our lawn; so we reach it by a few*

steps in the middle of its embankment. The platform is higher again than the garden, from which we mount a couple more steps to look over the balustrade at a fine view of the town up the valley and of the hills that stretch away beyond it to where, in the remotest distance, they become mountains. On our left is the villa, accessible by steps from the left hand corner of the garden. Returning from the platform through the garden and down again to the lawn (a movement which leaves the villa behind us on our right) we find evidence of literary interests on the part of the tenants in the fact that there is no tennis net nor set of croquet hoops, but, on our left, a little iron garden table with books on it, mostly yellow-backed, and a chair beside it. A chair on the right has also a couple of open books upon it. There are no newspapers, a circumstance which, with the absence of games, might lead an intelligent spectator to the most far reaching conclusions as to the sort of people who live in the villa. Such speculations are checked, however, on this delightfully fine afternoon, by the appearance at a little gate in a paling on our left, of HENRY STRAKER *in his professional costume. He opens the gate for an elderly gentleman, and follows him on to the lawn.*

This elderly gentleman defies the Spanish sun in a black frock coat, tall silk hat, trousers in which narrow stripes of dark grey and lilac blend into a highly respectable color, and a black necktie tied into a bow over spotless linen. Probably therefore a man whose social position needs constant and scrupulous affirmation without regard to climate: one who would dress thus for the middle of the Sahara or the top of Mont Blanc. And since he has not the stamp of the class which accepts as its life-mission the advertizing and maintenance of first rate tailoring and millinery, he looks vulgar in his finery, though in a working dress of any kind he would look dignified enough. He is a bullet cheeked man with a red complexion, stubbly hair, smallish eyes, a hard mouth that folds down at the corners, and a dogged chin. The looseness of skin that comes with age has attacked his throat and the laps of his cheeks; but he is still hard as an apple above the mouth; so that the upper half of his face looks younger than the lower. He has the self-confidence of one who has made money, and something of the truculence of one who has made it in a brutalizing struggle, his civility having under it a perceptible menace that he has other methods in reserve if necessary. Withal, a man to be rather pitied when he is not to be feared; for there is something pathetic about him at times, as if the huge commercial machine which has worked him into his frock coat had allowed him very little of his own way and left his affections hungry and baffled. At the first word that falls from him it is clear that he is an Irishman whose native intonation has clung to him through many changes of place and rank. One can only guess that the original material of his speech was perhaps the surly Kerry brogue; but the degradation of speech that occurs in London, Glasgow, Dublin and big cities generally has been at work on it so long that nobody but an arrant cockney would dream of calling it a brogue now; for its music is almost gone, though its surliness is still perceptible. STRAKER, *being a very obvious cockney, inspires him with implacable contempt, as a stupid Englishman who cannot even speak his own language properly.* STRAKER, *on the other hand, regards the old gentleman's accent as a joke thoughtfully provided by Providence expressly for the amusement of the British race, and treats him normally with the indulgence due to an inferior and unlucky species, but occasionally with indignant alarm when the old gentleman shews signs of intending his Irish nonsense to be taken seriously.*

STRAKER   I'll go tell the young lady. She said youd prefer to stay here [*He turns to go up through the garden to the villa*].

MALONE [*Who has been looking round him with lively curiosity*]   The young lady? That's Miss Violet, eh?

STRAKER [*Stopping on the steps with sudden suspicion*]   Well, you know, dont you?

MALONE   Do I?

STRAKER [*His temper rising*]   Well, do you or dont you?

MALONE   What business is that of yours?

[STRAKER, *now highly indignant, comes back from the steps and confronts the visitor.*]

STRAKER   I'll tell you what business it is of mine. Miss Robinson—

MALONE [*Interrupting*]   Oh, her name is Robinson, is it? Thank you.

STRAKER   Why, you dont know even her name?

MALONE   Yes I do, now that youve told me.

STRAKER [*After a moment of stupefaction at the old man's readiness in repartee*]   Look here: what do you mean by gittin into my car and lettin me bring you here if youre not the person I took that note to?

MALONE   Who else did you take it to, pray?

STRAKER   I took it to Mr Ector Malone, at Miss Robinson's request, see? Miss Robinson is not my principal: I took it to oblige her. I know Mr Malone; and he aint you, not by a long chalk. At the hotel they told me that your name is Ector Malone—

MALONE   *Hector Malone.*

STRAKER [*With calm superiority*]   Hector in your own country: thats what comes o livin in provincial places like Ireland and America. Over here youre Ector: if you avnt noticed it before you soon will. [*The growing strain of the conversation is here relieved by* VIO-LET, *who has sallied from the villa and through the garden to the steps, which she now descends, coming very opportunely between* MALONE *and* STRAKER.]

VIOLET [*To* STRAKER]   Did you take my message?

STRAKER   Yes, miss. I took it to the hotel and sent it up, expecting to see young Mr Malone. Then out walks this gent, and says it's all right and he'll come with me. So as the hotel people said he was Mr Ector Malone, I fetched him. And now he goes back on what he said. But if he isnt the gentleman you meant, say the word: it's easy enough to fetch him back again.

MALONE   I should esteem it a great favor if I might have a short conversation with you, madam. I am Hector's father, as this bright Britisher would have guessed in the course of another hour or so.

STRAKER [*Coolly defiant*]   No, not in another year or so. When weve ad you as long to polish up as weve ad im, perhaps youll begin to look a little bit up to is mark. At present you fall a long way short. Youve got too many aitches, for one thing. [*To* VIOLET, *amiably*] All right, Miss: you want to talk to him: I shant intrude. [*He nods affably to* MALONE *and goes out through the little gate in the paling.*]

VIOLET [*Very civilly*]   I am so sorry, Mr Malone, if that man has been rude to you. But what can we do? He is our chauffeur.

MALONE   Your hwat?

VIOLET   The driver of our automobile. He can drive a motor car at seventy miles an hour, and mend it when it breaks down. We are dependent on our motor cars; and our motor cars are dependent on him; so of course we are dependent on him.

MALONE   Ive noticed, madam, that every thousand dollars an Eng-lishman gets seems to add one to the number of people hes dependent on. However, you neednt apologize for your man: I made him talk on purpose. By doing so I learnt that youre stayin here in Grannida with a party of English, including my son Hector.

VIOLET [*Conversationally*]   Yes. We intended to go to Nice; but we had to follow a rather eccentric member of our party who started first and came here. Wont you sit down? [*She clears the nearest chair of the two books on it.*]

MALONE [*Impressed by this attention*]   Thank you. [*He sits down, examining her curiously as she goes to the iron table to put down the books. When she turns to him again, he says*] Miss Robinson, I believe?

VIOLET [*Sitting down*]   Yes.

MALONE [*Taking a letter from his pocket*]   Your note to Hector runs as follows [VIOLET *is unable to repress a start. He pauses quietly to take out and put on his spectacles, which have gold rims*]: "Dearest: they have all gone to the Alhambra for the afternoon. I have shammed headache and have the garden all to myself. Jump into Jack's motor: Straker will rattle you here in a jiffy. Quick, quick, quick. Your loving Violet." [*He looks at her; but by this time she has recovered herself, and meets his spectacles with perfect composure. He continues slowly*] Now I dont know on hwat terms young people associate in English society; but in America that note would be considered to imply a very considerable degree of affectionate intimacy between the parties.

VIOLET   Yes: I know your son very well, Mr Malone. Have you any objection?

MALONE [*Somewhat taken aback*]   No, no objection exactly. Provided it is understood that my son is altogether dependent on me, and that I have to be consulted in any important step he may propose to take.

VIOLET   I am sure you would not be unreasonable with him, Mr Malone.

MALONE   I hope not, Miss Robinson; but at your age you might think many things unreasonable that dont seem so to me.

VIOLET [*With a little shrug*]   Oh well, I suppose theres no use our playing at cross purposes, Mr Malone. Hector wants to marry me.

MALONE   I inferred from your note that he might. Well, Miss Robinson, he is his own master; but if he marries you he shall not have a rap from me. [*He takes off his spectacles and pockets them with the note.*]

VIOLET [*With some severity*]   That is not very complimentary to me, Mr Malone.

MALONE   I say nothing against you, Miss Robinson: I daresay you are an amiable and excellent young lady. But I have other views for Hector.

VIOLET   Hector may not have other views for himself, Mr Malone.

MALONE   Possibly not. Then he does without me: thats all. I daresay you are prepared for that. When a young lady writes to a young man to come to her quick, quick, quick, money seems nothing and love seems everything.

VIOLET [*Sharply*]   I beg your pardon, Mr Malone: I do not think anything so foolish. Hector must have money.

MALONE [*Staggered*]   Oh, very well, very well. No doubt he can work for it.

VIOLET   What is the use of having money if you have to work for it? [*She rises impatiently.*] It's all nonsense, Mr Malone: you must enable your son to keep up his position. It is his right.

MALONE [*Grimly*]   I should not advise you to marry him on the strength of that right, Miss Robinson.

     [VIOLET, *who has almost lost her temper, controls herself with an effort; unclenches her fingers; and resumes her seat with studied tranquillity and reasonableness.*]

VIOLET   What objection have you to me, pray? My social position is as good as Hector's, to say the least. He admits it.

MALONE [*Shrewdly*]   You tell him so from time to time, eh? Hector's social position in England, Miss Robinson, is just what I choose to buy for him. I have made him a fair offer. Let him pick out the most historic house, castle or abbey that England contains. The day that he tells me he wants it for a wife worthy of its traditions, I buy it for him, and give him the means of keeping it up.

VIOLET   What do you mean by a wife worthy of its traditions? Cannot any well bred woman keep such a house for him?

MALONE   No: she must be born to it.

VIOLET   Hector was not born to it, was he?

MALONE   His granmother was a barefooted Irish girl that nursed me by a turf fire. Let him marry another such, and I will not stint her marriage portion. Let him raise himself socially with my money or raise somebody else: so long as there is a social profit somewhere, I'll regard my expenditure as justified. But there must be a profit for someone. A marriage with you would leave things just where they are.

VIOLET   Many of my relations would object very much to my marrying the grandson of a common woman, Mr Malone. That may be prejudice; but so is your desire to have him marry a title prejudice.

MALONE [*Rising, and approaching her with a scrutiny in which there is a good deal of reluctant respect*]   You seem a pretty straightforward downright sort of a young woman.

VIOLET   I do not see why I should be made miserably poor because I cannot make profits for you. Why do you want to make Hector unhappy?

MALONE   He will get over it all right enough. Men thrive better on disappointments in love than on disappointments in money. I daresay you think that sordid; but I know what I'm talking about. Me father died of starvation in Ireland in the black 47. Maybe youve heard of it.

VIOLET   The Famine?

MALONE [*With smouldering passion*]   No, the starvation. When a country is full o food, and exporting it, there can be no famine. Me father was starved dead; and I was starved out to America in me mother's arms. English rule drove me and mine out of Ireland. Well, you can keep Ireland. Me and me like are coming back to buy England; and we'll buy the best of it. I want no middle class properties and no middle class women for Hector. Thats straightforward, isnt it, like yourself?

VIOLET [*Icily pitying his sentimentality*]   Really, Mr Malone, I am astonished to hear a man of your age and good sense talking in that romantic way. Do you suppose English noblemen will sell their places to you for the asking?

MALONE   I have the refusal of two of the oldest family mansions in England. One historic owner cant afford to keep all the rooms dusted: the other cant afford the death duties. What do you say now?

VIOLET   Of course it is very scandalous; but surely you know that the Government will sooner or later put a stop to all these Socialistic attacks on property.

MALONE [*Grinning*]   D'y'think theyll be able to get that done before I buy the house—or rather the abbey? Theyre both abbeys.

VIOLET [*Putting that aside rather impatiently*]   Oh, well, let us talk sense, Mr Malone. You must feel that we havnt been talking sense so far.

MALONE   I cant say I do. I mean all I say.

VIOLET   Then you dont know Hector as I do. He is romantic and faddy—he gets it from you, I fancy—and he wants a certain sort of wife to take care of him. Not a faddy sort of person, you know.

MALONE   Somebody like you, perhaps?

VIOLET [*Quietly*]   Well, yes. But you cannot very well ask me to undertake this with absolutely no means of keeping up his position.

MALONE [*Alarmed*]   Stop a bit, stop a bit. Where are we getting to? I'm not aware that I'm asking you to undertake anything.

VIOLET   Of course, Mr Malone, you can make it very difficult for me to speak to you if you choose to misunderstand me.

MALONE [*Half bewildered*]   I dont wish to take any unfair advantage; but we seem to have got off the straight track somehow.

[STRAKER, *with the air of a man who has been making haste, opens the little gate, and admits* HECTOR, *who, snorting with indignation, comes upon the lawn, and is making for his father when* VIOLET, *greatly dismayed, springs up and intercepts him.* STRAKER *does not wait; at least he does not remain visibly within earshot.*]

VIOLET   Oh, how unlucky! Now please, Hector, say nothing. Go away until I have finished speaking to your father.

HECTOR [*Inexorably*]   No, Violet: I mean to have this thing out, right away. [*He puts her aside; passes her by; and faces his father, whose cheeks darken as his Irish blood begins to simmer.*] Dad: youve not played this hand straight.

MALONE   Hwat d'y'mean?

HECTOR   Youve opened a letter addressed to me. Youve impersonated me and stolen a march on this lady. Thats disawnerable.

MALONE [*Threateningly*]   Now you take care what youre saying, Hector. Take care, I tell you.

HECTOR   I have taken care. I am taking care. I'm taking care of my honor and my position in English society.

MALONE [*Hotly*]   Your position has been got by my money: do you know that?

HECTOR   Well, youve just spoiled it all by opening that letter. A letter from an English lady, not addressed to you—a cawnfidential letter! a dullicate letter! a private letter! opened by my father! Thats a sort of thing a man cant struggle against in England. The sooner we go back together the better. [*He appeals mutely to the heavens to witness the shame and anguish of two outcasts.*]

VIOLET [*Snubbing him with an instinctive dislike for scene making.*]   Dont be unreasonable, Hector. It was quite natural of Mr Malone to open my letter: his name was on the envelope.

MALONE   There! Youve no common sense, Hector. I thank you, Miss Robinson.

HECTOR   I thank you, too. It's very kind of you. My father knows no better.

MALONE [*Furiously clenching his fists*]   Hector—

HECTOR [*With undaunted moral force*]   Oh, it's no use hectoring me. A private letter's a private letter, dad: you cant get over that.

MALONE [*Raising his voice*]   I won't be talked back to by you, d'y'hear?

VIOLET   Ssh! please, please. Here they all come.

[*Father and son, checked, glare mutely at one another as* TAN-NER *comes in through the little gate with* RAMSDEN, *followed by* OCTAVIUS *and* ANN.]

VIOLET   Back already!

TANNER   The Alhambra is not open this afternoon.

VIOLET   What a sell!

[TANNER *passes on, and presently finds himself between* HEC-TOR *and a strange elder, both apparently on the verge of personal combat. He looks from one to the other for an explanation. They sulkily avoid his eye, and nurse their wrath in silence.*]

RAMSDEN   Is it wise for you to be out in the sunshine with such a headache, Violet?

TANNER   Have you recovered too, Malone?

VIOLET   Oh, I forgot. We have not all met before. Mr Malone: wont you introduce your father?

HECTOR [*With Roman firmness*]   No I will not. He is no father of mine.

MALONE [*Very angry*]   You disown your dad before your English friends, do you?

VIOLET   Oh please dont make a scene.

[ANN *and* OCTAVIUS, *lingering near the gate, exchange an astonished glance, and discreetly withdraw up the steps to the garden, where they can enjoy the disturbance without intruding. On their way to the steps* ANN *sends a little grimace of mute sympathy to* VIOLET, *who is standing with her back to the little table, looking on in helpless annoyance as her husband soars to higher and higher moral eminences without the least regard to the old man's millions.*]

HECTOR   I'm very sorry, Miss Rawbnsn; but I'm contending for a principle. I am a son, and, I hope, a dutiful one; but before everything I'm a Mahn!!! And when dad treats my private letters as his own, and takes it on himself to say that I shant marry you if I am happy and fortunate enough to gain your consent, then I just snap my fingers and go my own way.

TANNER   Marry Violet!

RAMSDEN   Are you in your senses?

TANNER   Do you forget what we told you?

HECTOR [*Recklessly*]   I dont care what you told me.

RAMSDEN [*Scandalized*]   Tut tut, sir! Monstrous! [*He flings away towards the gate, his elbows quivering with indignation.*]

TANNER   Another madman! These men in love should be locked up. [*He gives* HECTOR *up as hopeless, and turns away towards the garden: but* MALONE, *taking offence in a new direction, follows him and compels him, by the aggressiveness of his tone, to stop.*]

MALONE   I dont understand this. Is Hector not good enough for this lady, pray?

TANNER   My dear sir, the lady is married already. Hector knows it; and yet he persists in his infatuation. Take him home and lock him up.

MALONE [*Bitterly*]   So this is the high-born social tone Ive spoilt be me ignorant, uncultivated behavior! Makin love to a married woman! [*He comes angrily between* HECTOR *and* VIOLET, *and almost bawls into* HECTOR's *left ear*] Youve picked up that habit of the British aristocracy, havc you?

HECTOR   Thats all right. Dont you trouble yourself about that. I'll answer for the morality of what I'm doing.

TANNER [*Coming forward to* HECTOR's *right hand with flashing eyes*]   Well said, Malone! You also see that mere marriage laws are not morality! I agree with you; but unfortunately Violet does not.

MALONE   I take leave to doubt that, sir. [*Turning on* VIOLET.] Let me tell you, Mrs Robinson, or whatever your right name is, you had no right to send that letter to my son when you were the wife of another man.

HECTOR [*Outraged*]   This is the last straw. Dad: you have insulted my wife.

MALONE   Your wife!

TANNER   You the missing husband! Another moral impostor! [*He smites his brow, and collapses into* MALONE's *chair.*]

MALONE   Youve married without my consent!

RAMSDEN   You have deliberately humbugged us, sir!

HECTOR   Here: I have had just about enough of being badgered. Violet and I are married: thats the long and the short of it. Now what have you got to say—any of you?

MALONE   I know what Ive got to say. Shes married a beggar.

HECTOR   No; shes married a Worker [*His American pronunciation imparts an overwhelming intensity to this simple and unpopular word*]. I start to earn my own living this very afternoon.

MALONE [*Sneering angrily*]   Yes: youre very plucky now, because you got your remittance from me yesterday or this morning, I reckon. Waitl it's spent. You wont be so full of cheek then.

HECTOR [*Producing a letter from his pocketbook*]   Here it is [*Thrusting it on his father*]. Now you just take your remittance and yourself out of my life. I'm done with remittances; and I'm done with you. I dont sell the privilege of insulting my wife for a thousand dollars.

MALONE [*Deeply wounded and full of concern*]   Hector: you dont know what poverty is.

HECTOR [*Fervidly*]   Well, I wawnt to know what it is. I wawnt'be a Mahn. Violet: you come along with me, to your own home: I'll see you through.

OCTAVIUS [*Jumping down from the garden to the lawn and running to* HECTOR's *left hand.*]   I hope you'll shake hands with me before you go, Hector. I admire and respect you more than I can say. [*He is affected almost to tears as they shake hands.*]

VIOLET [*Also almost in tears, but of vexation.*]   Oh dont be an idiot, Tavy. Hector's about as fit to become a workman as you are.

TANNER [*Rising from his chair on the other side of* HECTOR]   Never fear: there's no question of his becoming a navvy, Mrs Malone. [*To* HECTOR] There's really no difficulty about capital to start with. Treat me as a friend: draw on me.

OCTAVIUS [*Impulsively*]   Or on me.

MALONE [*With fierce jealousy*]   Who wants your durty money? Who should he draw on but his own father? [TANNER *and* OCTAVIUS *recoil,* OCTAVIUS *rather hurt,* TANNER *consoled by the solution of the money difficulty.* VIOLET *looks up hopefully.*] Hector: dont be rash, my boy. I'm sorry for what I said: I never meant to insult Violet: I take it all back. Shes just the wife you want: there!

HECTOR [*Patting him on the shoulder*]   Well, thats all right, dad. Say no more: we're friends again. Only, I take no money from anybody.

MALONE [*Pleading abjectly*]   Dont be hard on me, Hector. I'd rather you quarrelled and took the money than made friends and starved. You dont know what the world is: I do.

HECTOR   No, no, NO. Thats fixed: thats not going to change. [*He passes his father inexorably by, and goes to* VIOLET.] Come, Mrs Malone: youve got to move to the hotel with me, and take your proper place before the world.

VIOLET   But I must go in, dear, and tell Davis to pack. Wont you go

on and make them give you a room overlooking the garden for me?
I'll join you in half an hour.

HECTOR   Very well. Youll dine with us, Dad, wont you?

MALONE [*Eager to conciliate him*]   Yes, yes.

HECTOR   See you all later. [*He waves his hand to* ANN, *who has now
been joined by* TANNER, OCTAVIUS, *and* RAMSDEN *in the garden,
and goes out through the little gate, leaving his father and* VIOLET
together on the lawn.]

MALONE   Youll try to bring him to his senses, Violet: I know you
will.

VIOLET   I had no idea he could be so headstrong. If he goes on like
that, what can I do?

MALONE   Dont be discurridged: domestic pressure may be slow; but
it's sure. Youll wear him down. Promise me you will.

VIOLET   I will do my best. Of course I think it's the greatest nonsense deliberately making us poor like that.

MALONE   Of course it is.

VIOLET [*After a moment's reflection*]   You had better give me the
remittance. He will want it for his hotel bill. I'll see whether I can
induce him to accept it. Not now, of course, but presently.

MALONE [*Eagerly*]   Yes, yes, yes: thats just the thing. [*He hands her
the thousand dollar bill, and adds cunningly*] Y'understand that this
is only a bachelor allowance.

VIOLET [*Coolly*]   Oh, quite. [*She takes it.*] Thank you. By the way,
Mr Malone, those two houses you mentioned—the abbeys.

MALONE   Yes?

VIOLET   Dont take one of them until Ive seen it. One never knows
what may be wrong with these places.

MALONE   I wont. I'll do nothing without consulting you, never fear.

VIOLET [*Politely, but without a ray of gratitude*]   Thanks: that will
be much the best way. [*She goes calmly back to the villa, escorted
obsequiously by* MALONE *to the upper end of the garden.*]

TANNER [*Drawing* RAMSDEN'*s attention to* MALONE'*s cringing attitude
as he takes leave of* VIOLET.]   And that poor devil is a billionaire!
one of the master spirits of the age! Led in a string like a pug dog
by the first girl who takes the trouble to despise him. I wonder will
it ever come to that with me. [*He comes down to the lawn.*]

RAMSDEN [*Following him*]   The sooner the better for you.

MALONE [*Slapping his hands as he returns through the garden*]
Thatll be a grand woman for Hector. I wouldnt exchange her for
ten duchesses. [*He descends to the lawn and comes between* TAN-
NER *and* RAMSDEN.]

RAMSDEN [*Very civil to the billionaire*]   It's an unexpected pleasure
to find you in this corner of the world, Mr Malone. Have you come
to buy up the Alhambra?

MALONE   Well, I dont say I mightnt. I think I could do better with

it than the Spanish government. But thats not what I came about.
To tell you the truth, about a month ago I overheard a deal
between two men over a bundle of shares. They differed about the
price: they were young and greedy, and didnt know that if the
shares were worth what was bid for them they must be worth what
was asked, the margin being too small to be of any account, you
see. To amuse meself, I cut in and bought the shares. Well, to this
day I havnt found out what the business is. The office is in
this town; and the name is Mendoza, Limited. Now whether
Mendoza's a mine, or a steamboat line, or a bank, or a patent
article—

TANNER He's a man. I know him: his principles are thoroughly
commercial. Let us take you round the town in our motor, Mr
Malone, and call on him on the way.

MALONE If youll be so kind, yes. And may I ask who—

TANNER Mr Roebuck Ramsden, a very old friend of your daughter-
in-law.

MALONE Happy to meet you, Mr Ramsden.

RAMSDEN Thank you. Mr Tanner is also one of our circle.

MALONE Glad to know you also, Mr Tanner.

TANNER Thanks. [MALONE *and* RAMSDEN *go out very amicably
through the little gate.* TANNER *calls to* OCTAVIUS, *who is wandering
in the garden with* ANN] Tavy! [TAVY *comes to the steps,* TANNER
whispers loudly to him] Violet has married a financier of brigands.
[TANNER *hurries away to overtake* MALONE *and* RAMSDEN. ANN
strolls to the steps with an idle impulse to torment OCTAVIUS.]

ANN Wont you go with them, Tavy?

OCTAVIUS [*Tears suddenly flushing his eyes*] You cut me to the heart,
Ann, by wanting me to go [*He comes down on the lawn to hide his
face from her. She follows him caressingly*].

ANN Poor Ricky Ticky Tavy! Poor heart!

OCTAVIUS It belongs to you, Ann. Forgive me: I must speak of it. I
love you. You know I love you.

ANN Whats the good, Tavy? You know that my mother is determined that I shall marry Jack.

OCTAVIUS [*Amazed*] Jack!

ANN It seems absurd, doesnt it?

OCTAVIUS [*With growing resentment*] Do you mean to say that Jack
has been playing with me all this time? That he has been urging
me not to marry you because he intends to marry you himself?

ANN [*Alarmed*] No no: you mustnt lead him to believe that I said
that. I dont for a moment think that Jack knows his own mind.
But it's clear from my father's will that he wished me to marry
Jack. And my mother is set on it.

OCTAVIUS But you are not bound to sacrifice yourself always to the
wishes of your parents.

ANN   My father loved me. My mother loves me. Surely their wishes
are a better guide than my own selfishness.

OCTAVIUS   Oh, I know how unselfish you are, Ann. But believe
me—though I know I am speaking in my own interest—there is
another side to this question. Is it fair to Jack to marry him if you
do not love him? Is it fair to destroy my happiness as well as your
own if you can bring yourself to love me?

ANN   [*Looking at him with a faint impulse of pity*]   Tavy, my dear,
you are a nice creature—a good boy.

OCTAVIUS   [*Humiliated*]   Is that all?

ANN   [*Mischievously in spite of her pity*]   Thats a great deal, I assure
you. You would always worship the ground I trod on, wouldnt you?

OCTAVIUS   I do. It sounds ridiculous; but it's no exaggeration. I do;
and I always shall.

ANN   Always is a long word, Tavy. You see, I shall have to live up
always to your idea of my divinity; and I dont think I could do that
if we were married. But if I marry Jack, youll never be disillu-
sioned—at least not until I grow too old.

OCTAVIUS   I too shall grow old, Ann. And when I am eighty, one
white hair of the woman I love will make me tremble more than
the thickest gold trees from the most beautiful young head.

ANN   [*Quite touched*]   Oh, thats poetry, Tavy, real poetry. It gives
me that strange sudden sense of an echo from a former existence
which always seems to me such a striking proof that we have
immortal souls.

OCTAVIUS   Do you believe that it is true?

ANN   Tavy: if it is to come true, you must lose me as well as love
me.

OCTAVIUS   Oh! [*He hastily sits down at the little table and covers his
face with his hands.*]

ANN   [*With conviction*]   Tavy: I wouldnt for worlds destroy your illusions. I can neither take you nor let you go. I can see exactly what
will suit you. You must be a sentimental old bachelor for my sake.

OCTAVIUS   [*Desperately*]   Ann: I'll kill myself.

ANN   Oh no you wont: that wouldnt be kind. You wont have a bad
time. You will be very nice to women; and you will go a good deal
to the opera. A broken heart is a very pleasant complaint for a man
in London if he has a comfortable income.

OCTAVIUS   [*Considerably cooled, but believing that he is only recovering his self-control*]   I know you mean to be kind, Ann. Jack has
persuaded you that cynicism is a good tonic for me. [*He rises with
quiet dignity.*]

ANN   [*Studying him slyly*]   You see, I'm disillusionizing you already.
Thats what I dread.

OCTAVIUS   You do not dread disillusionizing Jack.

ANN   [*Her face lighting up with mischievous ecstasy—whispering*]   I cant: he has no illusions about me. I shall surprise Jack the other way. Getting over an unfavorable impression is ever so much easier than living up to an ideal. Oh, I shall enrapture Jack sometimes!

OCTAVIUS [*Resuming the calm phase of despair, and beginning to enjoy his broken heart and delicate attitude without knowing it*] I dont doubt that. You will enrapture him always. And he—the fool!—thinks you would make him wretched.

ANN Yes: thats the difficulty, so far.

OCTAVIUS [*Heroically*] Shall *I* tell him that you love him?

ANN [*Quickly.*] Oh no: hed run away again.

OCTAVIUS [*Shocked*] Ann: would you marry an unwilling man?

ANN What a queer creature you are, Tavy! Theres no such thing as a willing man when you really go for him. [*She laughs naughtily.*] I'm shocking you, I suppose. But you know you are really getting a sort of satisfaction already in being out of danger yourself.

OCTAVIUS [*Startled*] Satisfaction! [*Reproachfully*] You say that to me!

ANN Well, if it were really agony, would you ask for more of it?

OCTAVIUS Have I asked for more of it?

ANN You have offered to tell Jack that I love him. Thats self-sacrifice, I suppose; but there must be some satisfaction in it. Perhaps its because youre a poet. You are like the bird that presses its breast against the sharp thorn to make itself sing.

OCTAVIUS It's quite simple. I love you; and I want you to be happy. You dont love me; so I cant make you happy myself; but I can help another man to do it.

ANN Yes: it seems quite simple. But I doubt if we ever know why we do things. The only really simple thing is to go straight for what you want and grab it. I suppose I dont love you, Tavy; but sometimes I feel as if I should like to make a man of you somehow. You are very foolish about women.

OCTAVIUS [*Almost coldly*] I am content to be what I am in that respect.

ANN Then you must keep away from them, and only dream about them. I wouldnt marry you for worlds, Tavy.

OCTAVIUS I have no hope, Ann: I accept my ill luck. But I dont think you quite know how much it hurts.

ANN You are so softhearted! It's queer that you should be so different from Violet. Violet's as hard as nails.

OCTAVIUS Oh no. I am sure Violet is thoroughly womanly at heart.

ANN [*With some impatience*] Why do you say that? Is it unwomanly to be thoughtful and businesslike and sensible? Do you want Violet to be an idiot—or something worse, like me?

OCTAVIUS Something worse—like you! What do you mean, Ann?

ANN Oh well, I dont mean that, of course. But I have a great respect for Violet. She gets her own way always.

OCTAVIUS [*Sighing*] So do you.

ANN   Yes; but somehow she gets it without coaxing—without having to make people sentimental about her.

OCTAVIUS [*With brotherly callousness*]   Nobody could get very sentimental about Violet, I think, pretty as she is.

ANN   Oh yes they could, if she made them.

OCTAVIUS   But surely no really nice woman would deliberately practise on men's instincts in that way.

ANN [*Throwing up her hands*]   Oh Tavy, Tavy, Ricky Ticky Tavy, heaven help the woman who marries you!

OCTAVIUS [*His passion reviving at the name*]   Oh why, why, why do you say that? Dont torment me. I dont understand.

ANN   Suppose she were to tell fibs, and lay snares for men?

OCTAVIUS   Do you think I could marry such a woman—I, who have known and loved you?

ANN   Hm! Well, at all events, she wouldnt let you if she were wise. So thats settled. And now I cant talk any more. Say you forgive me, and that the subject is closed.

OCTAVIUS   I have nothing to forgive; and the subject is closed. And if the wound is open, at least you shall never see it bleed.

ANN   Poetic to the last, Tavy. Goodbye, dear. [*She pats his cheek; has an impulse to kiss him and then another impulse of distaste which prevents her; finally runs away through the garden and into the villa.*]

> [OCTAVIUS *again takes refuge at the table, bowing his head on his arms and sobbing softly.* MRS WHITEFIELD, *who has been pottering round the Granada shops, and has a net full of little parcels in her hand, comes in through the gate and sees him.*]

MRS WHITEFIELD [*Running to him and lifting his head*]   Whats the matter, Tavy? Are you ill?

OCTAVIUS   No, nothing, nothing.

MRS WHITEFIELD [*Still holding his head, anxiously*]   But youre crying. Is it about Violet's marriage?

OCTAVIUS   No, no. Who told you about Violet?

MRS WHITEFIELD [*Restoring the head to its owner*]   I met Roebuck and that awful old Irishman. Are you sure youre not ill? What's the matter?

OCTAVIUS [*Affectionately*]   It's nothing—only a man's broken heart. Doesnt that sound ridiculous?

MRS WHITEFIELD   But what is it all about? Has Ann been doing anything to you?

OCTAVIUS   It's not Ann's fault. And dont think for a moment that I blame you.

MRS WHITEFIELD [*Startled*]   For what?

OCTAVIUS [*Pressing her hand consolingly*]   For nothing. I said I didnt blame you.

MRS WHITEFIELD   But I havnt done anything. Whats the matter?

OCTAVIUS [*Smiling sadly*]   Cant you guess? I daresay you are right to prefer Jack to me as a husband for Ann; but I love Ann; and it hurts rather. [*He rises and moves away from her towards the middle of the lawn.*]

MRS WHITEFIELD [*Following him hastily*]   Does Ann say that I want her to marry Jack?

OCTAVIUS   Yes: she has told me.

MRS WHITEFIELD [*Thoughtfully*]   Then I'm very sorry for you, Tavy. It's only her way of saying she wants to marry Jack. Little she cares what *I* say or what *I* want!

OCTAVIUS   But she would not say it unless she believed it. Surely you dont suspect Ann of—of deceit!!

MRS WHITEFIELD   Well, never mind, Tavy. I dont know which is best for a young man: to know too little, like you, or too much, like Jack.

[TANNER *returns.*]

TANNER   Well, Ive disposed of old Malone. Ive introduced him to Mendoza, Limited; and left the two brigands together to talk it out. Hullo, Tavy! anything wrong?

OCTAVIUS   I must go wash my face, I see. [*To* MRS WHITEFIELD] Tell him what you wish. [*To* TANNER] You may take it from me, Jack, that Ann approves of it.

TANNER [*Puzzled by his manner*]   Approves of what?

OCTAVIUS   Of what Mrs Whitefield wishes. [*He goes his way with sad dignity to the villa.*]

TANNER [*To* MRS WHITEFIELD]   This is very mysterious. What is it you wish? It shall be done, whatever it is.

MRS WHITEFIELD [*With snivelling gratitude*]   Thank you, Jack. [*She sits down.* TANNER *brings the other chair from the table and sits close to her with his elbows on his knees, giving her his whole attention.*] I dont know why it is that other people's children are so nice to me, and that my own have so little consideration for me. It's no wonder I dont seem able to care for Ann and Rhoda as I do for you and Tavy and Violet. It's a very queer world. It used to be so straightforward and simple; and now nobody seems to think and feel as they ought. Nothing has been right since that speech that Professor Tyndall made at Belfast.

TANNER   Yes: life is more complicated than we used to think. But what am I to do for you?

MRS WHITEFIELD   Thats just what I want to tell you. Of course youll marry Ann whether I like it or not—

TANNER [*Starting*]   It seems to me that I shall presently be married to Ann whether I like it myself or not.

MRS WHITEFIELD [*Peacefully*]   Oh, very likely you will: you know what she is when she has set her mind on anything. But dont put it on me: thats all I ask. Tavy has just let out that shes been saying that I am making her marry you; and the poor boy is breaking his heart about it; for he is in love with her himself, though what he

sees in her so wonderful, goodness knows: *I* dont. It's no use telling
Tavy that Ann puts things into people's heads by telling them that
I want them when the thought of them never crossed my mind. It
only sets Tavy against me. But you know better than that. So if
you marry her, dont put the blame on me.

TANNER [*Emphatically*]   I havnt the slightest intention of marrying
her.

MRS WHITEFIELD [*Slyly*]   She'd suit you better than Tavy. She'd
meet her match in you, Jack. I'd like to see her meet her match.

TANNER   No man is a match for a woman, except with a poker and
a pair of hobnailed boots. Not always even then. Anyhow, *I* cant
take the poker to her. I should be a mere slave.

MRS WHITEFIELD   No: she's afraid of you. At all events, you would
tell her the truth about herself. She wouldnt be able to slip out of
it as she does with me.

TANNER   Everybody would call me a brute if I told Ann the truth
about herself in terms of her own moral code. To begin with, Ann
says things that are not strictly true.

MRS WHITEFIELD   I'm glad somebody sees she is not an angel.

TANNER   In short—to put it as a husband would put it when exasperated to the point of speaking out—she is a liar. And since she
has plunged Tavy head over ears in love with her without any
intention of marrying him, she is a coquette, according to the standard definition of a coquette as a woman who rouses passions she
has no intention of gratifying. And as she has now reduced you to
the point of being willing to sacrifice me at the altar for the mere
satisfaction of getting me to call her a liar to her face, I may conclude that she is a bully as well. She cant bully men as she bullies
women; so she habitually and unscrupulously uses her personal
fascination to make men give her whatever she wants. That makes
her almost something for which I know no polite name.

MRS WHITEFIELD [*In mild expostulation*]   Well, you cant expect perfection, Jack.

TANNER   I dont. But what annoys me is that Ann does. I know perfectly well that all this about her being a liar and a bully and a
coquette and so forth is a trumped-up moral indictment which
might be brought against anybody. We all lie; we all bully as much
as we dare; we all bid for admiration without the least intention
of earning it; we all get as much rent as we can out of our powers
of fascination. If Ann would admit this I shouldnt quarrel with
her. But she wont. If she has children she'll take advantage of their
telling lies to amuse herself by whacking them. If another woman
makes eyes at me, she'll refuse to know a coquette. She will do
just what she likes herself whilst insisting on everybody else doing
what the conventional code prescribes. In short, I can stand everything except her confounded hypocrisy. Thats what beats me.

MRS WHITEFIELD [*Carried away by the relief of hearing her own opin-*

ion so eloquently expressed]   Oh, she is a hypocrite. She is: she is. Isnt she?

TANNER   Then why do you want to marry me to her?

MRS WHITEFIELD [*Querulously*]   There now! put it on me, of course. I never thought of it until Tavy told me she said I did. But, you know, I'm very fond of Tavy: hes a sort of son to me; and I dont want him to be trampled on and made wretched.

TANNER   Whereas I dont matter, I suppose.

MRS WHITEFIELD   Oh, you are different, somehow: you are able to take care of yourself. Youd serve her out. And anyhow, she must marry somebody.

TANNER   Aha! there speaks the life instinct. You detest her; but you feel that you must get her married.

MRS WHITEFIELD [*Rising, shocked*]   Do you mean that I detest my own daughter! Surely you dont believe me to be so wicked and unnatural as that, merely because I see her faults.

TANNER [*Cynically*]   You love her, then?

MRS WHITEFIELD   Why, of course I do. What queer things you say, Jack! We cant help loving our own blood relations.

TANNER   Well, perhaps it saves unpleasantness to say so. But for my part, I suspect that the tables of consanguinity have a natural basis in a natural repugnance [*He rises*].

MRS WHITEFIELD   You shouldnt say things like that, Jack. I hope you wont tell Ann that I have been speaking to you. I only wanted to set myself right with you and Tavy. I couldnt sit mumchance and have everything put on me.

TANNER [*Politely*]   Quite so.

MRS WHITEFIELD [*Dissatisfied*]   And now Ive only made matters worse. Tavy's angry with me because I dont worship Ann. And when it's been put into my head that Ann ought to marry you, what can I say except that it would serve her right?

TANNER   Thank you.

MRS WHITEFIELD   Now dont be silly and twist what I say into something I dont mean. I ought to have fair play—

[ANN *comes from the villa, followed presently by* VIOLET, *who is dressed for driving.*]

ANN [*Coming to her mother's right hand with threatening suavity*] Well, mamma darling, you seem to be having a delightful chat with Jack. We can hear you all over the place.

MRS WHITEFIELD [*Appalled*]   Have you overheard—

TANNER   Never fear: Ann is only—well, we were discussing that habit of hers just now. She hasnt heard a word.

MRS WHITEFIELD [*Stoutly*]   I dont care whether she has or not: I have a right to say what I please.

VIOLET [*Arriving on the lawn and coming between* MRS WHITEFIELD *and* TANNER]   Ive come to say goodbye. I'm off for my honeymoon.

MRS WHITEFIELD [*Crying*]   Oh dont say that, Violet. And no wedding, no breakfast, no clothes, nor anything.

VIOLET [*Petting her*]   It wont be for long.

MRS WHITEFIELD   Dont let him take you to America. Promise me that you wont.

VIOLET [*Very decidedly*]   I should think not, indeed. Dont cry, dear: I'm only going to the hotel.

MRS WHITEFIELD   But going in that dress, with your luggage, makes one realize— [*She chokes, and then breaks out again*] How I wish you were my daughter, Violet!

VIOLET [*Soothing her*]   There, there: so I am. Ann will be jealous.

MRS WHITEFIELD   Ann doesnt care a bit for me.

ANN   Fie, mother! Come, now: you mustnt cry any more: you know Violet doesnt like it [MRS WHITEFIELD *dries her eyes, and subsides*].

VIOLET   Goodbye, Jack.

TANNER   Goodbye, Violet.

VIOLET   The sooner you get married too, the better. You will be much less misunderstood.

TANNER [*Restively*]   I quite expect to get married in the course of the afternoon. You all seem to have set your minds on it.

VIOLET   You might do worse. [*To* MRS WHITEFIELD: *putting her arm round her*] Let me take you to the hotel with me: the drive will do you good. Come in and get a wrap. [*She takes her towards the villa.*]

MRS WHITEFIELD [*As they go up through the garden.*]   I dont know what I shall do when you are gone, with no one but Ann in the house; and she always occupied with the men! It's not to be expected that your husband will care to be bothered with an old woman like me. Oh, you neednt tell me: politeness is all very well; but I know what people think— [*She talks herself and* VIOLET *out of sight and hearing.*]

> [ANN, *musing on* VIOLET's *opportune advice, approaches* TANNER; *examines him humorously for a moment from toe to top; and finally delivers her opinion.*]

ANN   Violet is quite right. You ought to get married.

TANNER [*Explosively*]   Ann: I will not marry you. Do you hear? I wont, wont, wont, wont, WONT marry you.

ANN [*Placidly*]   Well, nobody axd you, sir she said, sir she said, sir she said.[1] So thats settled.

TANNER   Yes, nobody has asked me; but everybody treats the thing as settled. It's in the air. When we meet, the others go away on absurd pretexts to leave us alone together. Ramsden no longer scowls at me: his eye beams, as if he were already giving you away to me in church. Tavy refers me to your mother and gives me his

---

1. Reference to a nursery rhyme:

   "I won't marry you, my pretty maid."
   "Nobody asked you to, Sir," she said.

blessing. Straker openly treats you as his future employer: it was he who first told me of it.

ANN Was that why you ran away?

TANNER Yes, only to be stopped by a lovesick brigand and run down like a truant schoolboy.

ANN Well, if you dont want to be married, you neednt be [*She turns away from him and sits down, much at her ease.*]

TANNER [*Following her*] Does any man want to be hanged? Yet men let themselves be hanged without a struggle for life, though they could at least give the chaplain a black eye. We do the world's will, not our own. I have a frightful feeling that I shall let myself be married because it is the world's will that you should have a husband.

ANN I daresay I shall, someday.

TANNER But why me—me of all men? Marriage is to me apostasy, profanation of the sanctuary of my soul, violation of my manhood, sale of my birthright, shameful surrender, ignominious capitulation, acceptance of defeat. I shall decay like a thing that has served its purpose and is done with; I shall change from a man with a future to a man with a past; I shall see in the greasy eyes of all the other husbands their relief at the arrival of a new prisoner to share their ignominy. The young men will scorn me as one who has sold out: to the young women I, who have always been an enigma and a possibility, shall be merely somebody else's property—and damaged goods at that: a secondhand man at best.

ANN Well, your wife can put on a cap and make herself ugly to keep you in countenance, like my grandmother.

TANNER So that she may make her triumph more insolent by publicly throwing away the bait the moment the trap snaps on the victim!

ANN After all, though, what difference would it make? Beauty is all very well at first sight; but who ever looks at it when it has been in the house three days? I thought our pictures very lovely when papa bought them; but I havnt looked at them for years. You never bother about my looks: you are too well used to me. I might be the umbrella stand.

TANNER You lie, you vampire: you lie.

ANN Flatterer. Why are you trying to fascinate me, Jack, if you dont want to marry me?

TANNER The Life Force. I am in the grip of the Life Force.

ANN I dont understand in the least: it sounds like the Life Guards.

TANNER Why dont you marry Tavy? He is willing. Can you not be satisfied unless your prey struggles?

ANN [*Turning to him as if to let him into a secret*] Tavy will never marry. Havnt you noticed that that sort of man never marries?

TANNER What! a man who idolizes women! who sees nothing in nature but romantic scenery for love duets! Tavy, the chivalrous, the faithful, the tenderhearted and true! Tavy never marry! Why, he was born to be swept up by the first pair of blue eyes he meets in the street.

ANN   Yes, I know. All the same, Jack, men like that always live in comfortable bachelor lodgings with broken hearts, and are adored by their landladies, and never get married. Men like you always get married.

TANNER [*Smiting his brow*] How frightfully, horribly true! It has been staring me in the face all my life; and I never saw it before.

ANN   Oh, it's the same with women. The poetic temperament's a very nice temperament, very amiable, very harmless and poetic, I daresay; but it's an old maid's temperament.

TANNER   Barren. The Life Force passes it by.

ANN   If thats what you mean by the Life Force, yes.

TANNER   You dont care for Tavy?

ANN [*Looking round carefully to make sure that* TAVY *is not within earshot*] No.

TANNER   And you do care for me?

ANN [*Rising quietly and shaking her finger at him*] Now Jack! Behave yourself.

TANNER   Infamous, abandoned woman! Devil!

ANN   Boa-constrictor! Elephant!

TANNER   Hypocrite!

ANN [*Softly*] I must be, for my future husband's sake.

TANNER   For mine! [*Correcting himself savagely*] I mean for his.

ANN [*Ignoring the correction*] Yes, for yours. You had better marry what you call a hypocrite, Jack. Women who are not hypocrites go about in rational dress and are insulted and get into all sorts of hot water. And then their husbands get dragged in too, and live in continual dread of fresh complications. Wouldnt you prefer a wife you could depend on?

TANNER   No, a thousand times no: hot water is the revolutionist's element. You clean men as you clean milk-pails, by scalding them.

ANN   Cold water has its uses too. It's healthy.

TANNER [*Despairingly*] Oh, you are witty: at the supreme moment the Life Force endows you with every quality. Well, I too can be a hypocrite. Your father's will appointed me your guardian, not your suitor. I shall be faithful to my trust.

ANN [*In low siren tones*] He asked me who would I have as my guardian before he made that will. I chose you!

TANNER   The will is yours then! The trap was laid from the beginning.

ANN [*Concentrating all her magic*] From the beginning—from our childhood—for both of us—by the Life Force.

TANNER   I will not marry you. I will not marry you.

ANN   Oh, you will, you will.

TANNER   I tell you, no, no, no.

ANN   I tell you, yes, yes, yes.

TANNER   No.

ANN   [*Coaxing—imploring—almost exhausted*]   Yes. Before it is too late for repentance. Yes.

TANNER   [*Struck by the echo from the past*]   When did all this happen to me before? Are we two dreaming?

ANN   [*Suddenly losing her courage, with an anguish that she does not conceal*]   No. We are awake; and you have said no: that is all.

TANNER   [*Brutally*]   Well?

ANN   Well, I made a mistake: you do not love me.

TANNER   [*Seizing her in his arms*]   It is false: I love you. The Life Force enchants me: I have the whole world in my arms when I clasp you. But I am fighting for my freedom, for my honor, for my self, one and indivisible.

ANN   Your happiness will be worth them all.

TANNER   You would sell freedom and honor and self for happiness?

ANN   It will not be all happiness for me. Perhaps death.

TANNER   [*Groaning*]   Oh, that clutch holds and hurts. What have you grasped in me? Is there a father's heart as well as a mother's?

ANN   Take care, Jack: if anyone comes while we are like this, you will have to marry me.

TANNER   If we two stood now on the edge of a precipice, I would hold you tight and jump.

ANN   [*Panting, failing more and more under the strain*]   Jack: let me go. I have dared so frightfully—it is lasting longer than I thought. Let me go: I cant bear it.

TANNER   Nor I. Let it kill us.

ANN   Yes: I dont care. I am at the end of my forces. I dont care. I think I am going to faint.

> [*At this moment* VIOLET *and* OCTAVIUS *come from the villa with* MRS WHITEFIELD, *who is wrapped up for driving. Simultaneously* MALONE *and* RAMSDEN, *followed by* MENDOZA *and* STRAKER, *come in through the little gate in the paling.* TANNER *shamefacedly releases* ANN, *who raises her hand giddily to her forehead.*]

MALONE   Take care. Something's the matter with the lady.

RAMSDEN   What does this mean?

VIOLET   [*Running between* ANN *and* TANNER]   Are you ill?

ANN   [*Reeling, with a supreme effort*]   I have promised to marry Jack. [*She swoons.* VIOLET *kneels by her and chafes her hand.* TANNER *runs round to her other hand, and tries to lift her head.* OCTAVIUS *goes to* VIOLET'*s assistance, but does not know what to do.* MRS WHITEFIELD *hurries back into the villa.* OCTAVIUS, MALONE *and* RAMSDEN *run to* ANN *and crowd round her, stooping to assist.* STRAKER *coolly comes to* ANN'*s feet, and* MENDOZA *to her head, both upright and self-possessed.*]

STRAKER   Now then, ladies and gentlemen: she dont want a crowd
round her: she wants air—all the air she can git. If you please,
gents— [MALONE *and* RAMSDEN *allow him to drive them gently past*
ANN *and up the lawn towards the garden, where* OCTAVIUS, *who has
already become conscious of his uselessness, joins them.* STRAKER,
following them up, pauses for a moment to instruct TANNER.] Dont
lift er ed, Mr Tanner: let it go flat so's the blood can run back into
it.

MENDOZA   He is right, Mr Tanner. Trust to the air of the Sierra.
[*He withdraws delicately to the garden steps.*]

TANNER [*Rising*]   I yield to your superior knowledge of physiology,
Henry. [*He withdraws to the corner of the lawn; and* OCTAVIUS
immediately hurries down to him.]

TAVY [*Aside to* TANNER, *grasping his hand*]   Jack: be very happy.

TANNER [*Aside to* TAVY]   I never asked her. It is a trap for me. [*He
goes up the lawn towards the garden.* OCTAVIUS *remains petrified.*]

MENDOZA [*Intercepting* MRS WHITEFIELD, *who comes from the villa
with a glass of brandy*]   What is this, madam? [*He takes it from
her.*]

MRS WHITEFIELD   A little brandy.

MENDOZA   The worst thing you could give her. Allow me. [*He swallows it.*] Trust to the air of the Sierra, madam.

   [*For a moment the men all forget* ANN *and stare at* MENDOZA.]

ANN [*In* VIOLET's *ear, clutching her round the neck*]   Violet: did Jack
say anything when I fainted?

VIOLET   No.

ANN   Ah! [*With a sigh of intense relief she relapses.*]

MRS WHITEFIELD   Oh, shes fainted again.

   [*They are about to rush back to her; but* MENDOZA *stops them
with a warning gesture.*]

ANN [*Supine*]   No I havnt. I'm quite happy.

TANNER [*Suddenly walking determinedly to her, and snatching her
hand from* VIOLET *to feel her pulse*]   Why, her pulse is positively
bounding. Come, get up. What nonsense! Up with you. [*He gets
her up summarily.*]

ANN   Yes: I feel strong enough now. But you very nearly killed me,
Jack, for all that.

MALONE   A rough wooer, eh? Theyre the best sort, Miss Whitefield.
I congratulate Mr Tanner; and I hope to meet you and him as
frequent guests at the Abbey.

ANN   Thank you. [*She goes past* MALONE *to* OCTAVIUS] Ricky Ticky
Tavy: congratulate me. [*Aside to him*] I want to make you cry for
the last time.

TAVY [*Steadfastly*]   No more tears. I am happy in your happiness.
And I believe in you in spite of everything.

RAMSDEN [*Coming between* MALONE *and* TANNER]   You are a happy
man, Jack Tanner. I envy you.

MENDOZA [*Advancing between* VIOLET *and* TANNER]   Sir: there are two tragedies in life. One is not to get your heart's desire. The other is to get it. Mine and yours, sir.

TANNER   Mr Mendoza: I have no heart's desires. Ramsden: it is very easy for you to call me a happy man: you are only a spectator. I am one of the principals; and I know better. Ann: stop tempting Tavy, and come back to me.

ANN [*Complying*]   You are absurd, Jack. [*She takes his proffered arm.*]

TANNER [*Continuing*]   I solemnly say that I am not a happy man. Ann looks happy; but she is only triumphant, successful, victorious. That is not happiness, but the price for which the strong sell their happiness. What we have both done this afternoon is to renounce happiness, renounce freedom, renounce tranquillity, above all, renounce the romantic possibilities of an unknown future, for the cares of a household and a family. I beg that no man may seize the occasion to get half drunk and utter imbecile speeches and coarse pleasantries at my expense. We propose to furnish our own house according to our own taste; and I hereby give notice that the seven or eight travelling clocks, the four or five dressing cases, the salad bowls, the carvers and fish slices, the copy of Tennyson in extra morocco,[2] and all the other articles you are preparing to heap upon us, will be instantly sold, and the proceeds devoted to circulating free copies of the Revolutionist's Handbook.[3] The wedding will take place three days after our return to England, by special license, at the office of the district superintendent registrar, in the presence of my solicitor and his clerk, who, like his clients, will be in ordinary walking dress—

VIOLET [*With intense conviction*]   You are a brute, Jack.

ANN [*Looking at him with fond pride and caressing his arm*]   Never mind her, dear. Go on talking.

TANNER   Talking!

   [*Universal laughter.*]

2. In subsequent versions of the play, Shaw changed this reference from the poetry of Tennyson to *The Angel in the House*, a long poem by Coventry Patmore which dramatized the Victorian ideal of woman as the "angel in the house," i.e., self-sacrificingly ministering to the needs of her husband and family.
3. A prose piece ostensibly written by John Tanner and included with *Man and Superman* by GBS.

Major Barbara

Preface to *Major Barbara*

*   *   *

The Gospel of St Andrew Undershaft.

*   *   *

In the millionaire Undershaft I have represented a man who has become intellectually and spiritually as well as practically conscious of the irresistible natural truth which we all abhor and repudiate: to wit, that the greatest of evils and the worst of crimes is poverty, and that our first duty—a duty to which every other consideration should be sacrificed—is not to be poor. "Poor but honest," "the respectable poor," and such phrases are as intolerable and as immoral as "drunken but amiable," "fraudulent but a good after-dinner speaker," "splendidly criminal," or the like. Security, the chief pretence of civilization, cannot exist where the worst of dangers, the danger of poverty, hangs over everyone's head, and where the alleged protection of our persons from violence is only an accidental result of the existence of a police force whose real business is to force the poor man to see his children starve whilst idle people overfeed pet dogs with the money that might feed and clothe them.

It is exceedingly difficult to make people realize that an evil is an evil. For instance, we seize a man and deliberately do him a malicious injury: say, imprison him for years. One would not suppose that it needed any exceptional clearness of wit to recognize in this an act of diabolical cruelty. But in England such a recognition provokes a stare of surprise, followed by an explanation that the outrage is punishment or justice or something else that is all right, or perhaps by a heated attempt to argue that we should all be robbed and murdered in our beds if such senseless villainies as sentences of imprisonment were not committed daily. It is useless to argue that even if this were true, which it is not, the alternative to adding crimes of our own to the crimes from which we suffer is not helpless submission. Chickenpox is an evil; but if I were to declare that we must either submit to it or else repress it sternly by seizing everyone who suffers from it and punishing them by inoculation with smallpox, I should be

203

laughed at; for though nobody could deny that the result would be to prevent chickenpox to some extent by making people avoid it much more carefully, and to effect a further apparent prevention by making them conceal it very anxiously, yet people would have sense enough to see that the deliberate propagation of smallpox was a creation of evil, and must therefore be ruled out in favor of purely humane and hygienic measures. Yet in the precisely parallel case of a man breaking into my house and stealing my wife's diamonds I am expected as a matter of course to steal ten years of his life, torturing him all the time. If he tries to defeat that monstrous retaliation by shooting me, my survivors hang him. The net result suggested by the police statistics is that we inflict atrocious injuries on the burglars we catch in order to make the rest take effectual precautions against detection; so that instead of saving our wives' diamonds from burglary we only greatly decrease our chances of ever getting them back, and increase our chances of being shot by the robber if we are unlucky enough to disturb him at his work.

But the thoughtless wickedness with which we scatter sentences of imprisonment, torture in the solitary cell and on the plank bed, and flogging, on moral invalids and energetic rebels, is as nothing compared to the stupid levity with which we tolerate poverty as if it were either a wholesome tonic for lazy people or else a virtue to be embraced as St. Francis embraced it. If a man is indolent, let him be poor. If he is drunken, let him be poor. If he is not a gentleman, let him be poor. If he is addicted to the fine arts or to pure science instead of to trade and finance, let him be poor. If he chooses to spend his urban eighteen shillings a week or his agricultural thirteen shillings a week on his beer and his family instead of saving it up for his old age, let him be poor. Let nothing be done for "the undeserving": let him be poor. Serve him right! Also—somewhat inconsistently—blessed are the poor!

Now what does this Let Him Be Poor mean? It means let him be weak. Let him be ignorant. Let him become a nucleus of disease. Let him be a standing exhibition and example of ugliness and dirt. Let him have rickety children. Let him be cheap and let him drag his fellows down to his price by selling himself to do their work. Let his habitations turn our cities into poisonous congeries of slums. Let his daughters infect our young men with the diseases of the streets and his sons revenge him by turning the nation's manhood into scrofula, cowardice, cruelty, hypocrisy, political imbecility, and all the other fruits of oppression and malnutrition. Let the undeserving become still less deserving; and let the deserving lay up for himself, not treasures in heaven, but horrors in hell upon earth. This being so, is it really wise to let him be poor? Would he not do ten times less harm as a prosperous burglar, incendiary, ravisher or murderer, to the utmost limits of humanity's comparatively negligible impulses in these directions? Suppose we were to abolish all penalties for such activities, and decide that poverty is the one thing we will not tolerate—that every adult with less than, say, £365 a year, shall be painlessly but inexorably killed, and every hungry half naked child forcibly fattened and clothed, would not that be an enormous improvement on our existing system, which has already destroyed so many civilizations, and is visibly destroying ours in the same way?

*   *   *

Undershaft, the hero of *Major Barbara*, is simply a man who, having grasped the fact that poverty is a crime, knows that when society offered him the alternative of poverty or a lucrative trade in death and destruction, it offered him, not a choice between opulent villainy and humble virtue, but between energetic enterprise and cowardly infamy. His conduct stands the Kantian test, which Peter Shirley's does not. Peter Shirley is what we call the honest poor man. Undershaft is what we call the wicked rich one: Shirley is Lazarus, Undershaft Dives.[1] Well, the misery of the world is due to the fact that the great mass of men act and believe as Peter Shirley acts and believes. If they acted and believed as Undershaft acts and believes, the immediate result would be a revolution of incalculable beneficence. To be wealthy, says Undershaft, is with me a point of honor for which I am prepared to kill at the risk of my own life. This preparedness is, as he says, the final test of sincerity. Like Froissart's medieval hero, who saw that "to rob and pill was a good life," he is not the dupe of that public sentiment against killing which is propagated and endowed by people who would otherwise be killed themselves, or of the mouth-honor paid to poverty and obedience by rich and insubordinate do-nothings who want to rob the poor without courage and command them without superiority. Froissart's knight, in placing the achievement of a good life before all the other duties— which indeed are not duties at all when they conflict with it, but plain wickednesses—behaved bravely, admirably, and, in the final analysis, public-spiritedly. Medieval society, on the other hand, behaved very badly indeed in organizing itself so stupidly that a good life could be achieved by robbing and pilling. If the knight's contemporaries had been all as resolute as he, robbing and pilling would have been the shortest way to the gallows, just as, if we were all as resolute and clearsighted as Undershaft, an attempt to live by means of what is called "an independent income" would be the shortest way to the lethal chamber. But as, thanks to our political imbecility and personal cowardice (fruits of poverty, both), the best imitation of a

---

1. Dives was a rich man who refused to give alms to the beggar Lazarus. In the next life, Dives, in Hell, was denied respite by Lazarus, who was in Heaven.

good life now procurable is life on an independent income, all sensible people aim at securing such an income, and are, of course, careful to legalize and moralize both it and all the actions and sentiments which lead to it and support it as an institution. What else can they do? They know, of course, that they are rich because others are poor. But they cannot help that: it is for the poor to repudiate poverty when they have had enough of it. The thing can be done easily enough: the demonstrations to the contrary made by the economists, jurists, moralists and sentimentalists hired by the rich to defend them, or even doing the work gratuitously out of sheer folly and abjectness, impose only on the hirers.

*   *   *

* * * "Cease to be slaves, in order that you may become cranks" is not a very inspiring call to arms; nor is it really improved by substituting saints for cranks. Both terms denote men of genius; and the common man does not want to live the life of a man of genius: he would much rather live the life of a pet collie if that were the only alternative. But he does want more money. Whatever else he may be vague about, he is clear about that. He may or may not prefer *Major Barbara* to the Drury Lane pantomime; but he always prefers five hundred pounds to five hundred shillings.

Now to deplore this preference as sordid, and teach children that it is sinful to desire money, is to strain towards the extreme possible limit of impudence in lying, and corruption in hypocrisy. The universal regard for money is the one hopeful fact in our civilization, the one sound spot in our social conscience. Money is the most important thing in the world. It represents health, strength, honor, generosity and beauty as conspicuously and undeniably as the want of it represents illness, weakness, disgrace, meanness and ugliness. Not the least of its virtues is that it destroys base people as certainly as it fortifies and dignifies noble people. It is only when it is cheapened to worthlessness for some, and made impossibly dear to others, that it becomes a curse. In short, it is a curse only in such foolish social conditions that life itself is a curse. For the two things are inseparable: money is the counter that enables life to be distributed socially: it *is* life as truly as sovereigns and bank notes are money. The first duty of every citizen is to insist on having money on reasonable terms; and this demand is not complied with by giving four men three shillings each for ten or twelve hours' drudgery and one man a thousand pounds for nothing. The crying need of the nation is not for better morals, cheaper bread, temperance, liberty, culture, redemption of fallen sisters and erring brothers, nor the grace, love and fellowship of the Trinity, but simply for enough money. And the evil to be attacked is not sin, suffering, greed, priestcraft, kingcraft,

demagogy, monopoly, ignorance, drink, war, pestilence, nor any
other of the scapegoats which reformers sacrifice, but simply poverty.

Once take your eyes from the ends of the earth and fix them on
this truth just under your nose; and Andrew Undershaft's views will
not perplex you in the least. Unless indeed his constant sense that
he is only the instrument of a Will or Life Force which uses him for
purposes wider than his own, may puzzle you. If so, that is because
you are walking either in artificial Darwinian darkness, or in mere
stupidity. All genuinely religious people have that consciousness. To
them Undershaft the Mystic will be quite intelligible, and his perfect
comprehension of his daughter the Salvationist and her lover the
Euripidean republican natural and inevitable. That, however, is not
new, even on the stage. What is new, as far as I know, is that article
in Undershaft's religion which recognizes in Money the first need
and in poverty the vilest sin of man and society.

*   *   *

The Salvation Army.

When *Major Barbara* was produced in London, the second act was
reported in an important northern newspaper as a withering attack
on the Salvation Army, and the despairing ejaculation of Barbara
deplored by a London daily as a tasteless blasphemy. And they were
set right, not by the professed critics of the theatre, but by religious
and philosophical publicists like Sir Oliver Lodge and Dr Stanton
Coit, and strenuous Nonconformist journalists like Mr William
Stead, who not only understood the act as well as the Salvationists
themselves, but also saw it in its relation to the religious life of the
nation, a life which seems to lie not only outside the sympathy of
many of our theatre critics, but actually outside their knowledge of
society.[1] Indeed nothing could be more ironically curious than the
confrontation *Major Barbara* effected of the theatre enthusiasts with
the religious enthusiasts. On the one hand was the playgoer, always
seeking pleasure, paying exorbitantly for it, suffering unbearable discomforts for it, and hardly ever getting it. On the other hand was the
Salvationist, repudiating gaiety and courting effort and sacrifice, yet
always in the wildest spirits, laughing, joking, singing, rejoicing,
drumming, and tambourining: his life flying by in a flash of excitement, and his death arriving as a climax of triumph. And, if you
please, the playgoer despising the Salvationist as a joyless person,
shut out from the heaven of the theatre, self-condemned to a life of
hideous gloom; and the Salvationist mourning over the playgoer as
over a prodigal with vine leaves in his hair, careering outrageously
to hell amid the popping of champagne corks and the ribald laughter

1. See the essay by Tracy C. Davis in this volume, pp. 445–49.

of sirens! Could misunderstanding be more complete, or sympathy worse misplaced?

Fortunately, the Salvationists are more accessible to the religious character of the drama than the playgoers to the gay energy and artistic fertility of religion. They can see, when it is pointed out to them, that a theatre, as a place where two or three are gathered together, takes from that divine presence an inalienable sanctity of which the grossest and profanest farce can no more deprive it than a hypocritical sermon by a snobbish bishop can desecrate Westminster Abbey. But in our professional playgoers this indispensable preliminary conception of sanctity seems wanting. They talk of actors as mimes and mummers, and, I fear, think of dramatic authors as liars and pandars, whose main business is the voluptuous soothing of the tired city speculator when what he calls the serious business of the day is over. Passion, the life of drama, means nothing to them but primitive sexual excitement: such phrases as "impassioned poetry" or "passionate love of truth" have fallen quite out of their vocabulary and been replaced by "passional crime" and the like. They assume, as far as I can gather, that people in whom passion has a larger scope are passionless and therefore uninteresting. Consequently they come to think of religious people as people who are not interesting and not amusing. And so, when Barbara cuts the regular Salvation Army jokes, and snatches a kiss from her lover across his drum, the devotees of the theatre think they ought to appear shocked, and conclude that the whole play is an elaborate mockery of the Army. And then either hypocritically rebuke me for mocking, or foolishly take part in the supposed mockery!

Even the handful of mentally competent critics got into difficulties over my demonstration of the economic deadlock in which the Salvation Army finds itself. Some of them thought that the Army would not have taken money from a distiller and a cannon founder: others thought it should not have taken it: all assumed more or less definitely that it reduced itself to absurdity or hypocrisy by taking it. On the first point the reply of the Army itself was prompt and conclusive. As one of its officers said, they would take money from the devil himself and be only too glad to get it out of his hands and into God's. They gratefully acknowledged that publicans not only give them money but allow them to collect it in the bar—sometimes even when there is a Salvation meeting outside preaching teetotalism. In fact, they questioned the verisimilitude of the play, not because Mrs Baines took the money, but because Barbara refused it.

On the point that the Army ought not to take such money, its justification is obvious. It must take the money because it cannot exist without money, and there is no other money to be had. Practically all the spare money in the country consists of a mass of rent, interest, and profit, every penny of which is bound up with crime,

drink, prostitution, disease, and all the evil fruits of poverty, as inex-
tricably as with enterprise, wealth, commercial probity, and national
prosperity. The notion that you can earmark certain coins as tainted
is an unpractical individualist superstition. None the less the fact
that all our money is tainted gives a very severe shock to earnest
young souls when some dramatic instance of the taint first makes
them conscious of it. When an enthusiastic young clergyman of the
Established Church first realizes that the Ecclesiastical Commissioners receive the rents of sporting public houses, brothels, and
sweating dens; or that the most generous contributor at his last charity sermon was an employer trading in female labor cheapened by
prostitution as unscrupulously as a hotel keeper trades in waiters'
labor cheapened by tips, or commissionaire's labor cheapened by
pensions; or that the only patron who can afford to rebuild his
church or his schools or give his boys' brigade a gymnasium or a
library is the son-in-law of a Chicago meat King, that young clergyman has, like Barbara, a very bad quarter hour. But he cannot help
himself by refusing to accept money from anybody except sweet old
ladies with independent incomes and gentle and lovely ways of life.
He has only to follow up the income of the sweet ladies to its industrial source, and there he will find Mrs Warren's profession and the
poisonous canned meat and all the rest of it. His own stipend has
the same root. He must either share the world's guilt or go to another
planet. He must save the world's honor if he is to save his own. This
is what all the Churches find just as the Salvation Army and Barbara
find it in the play. Her discovery that she is her father's accomplice;
that the Salvation Army is the accomplice of the distiller and the
dynamite maker; that they can no more escape one another than
they can escape the air they breathe; that there is no salvation for
them through personal righteousness, but only through the redemption of the whole nation from its vicious, lazy, competitive anarchy:
this discovery has been made by everyone except the Pharisees and
(apparently) the professional playgoers, who still wear their Tom
Hood[2] shirts and underpay their washer-women without the slightest
misgiving as to the elevation of their private characters, the purity
of their private atmospheres, and their right to repudiate as foreign
to themselves the coarse depravity of the garret and the slum. Not
that they mean any harm: they only desire to be, in their little private
way, what they call gentlemen. They do not understand Barbara's
lesson because they have not, like her, learnt it by taking their part
in the larger life of the nation.

*   *   *

London, June 1906

---

2. Hood's poem "Song of a Shirt" represented the plight of a poor washerwoman.

N.B. The Euripidean[3] verses in the second act of *Major Barbara* are not by me, nor even directly by Euripides. They are by Professor Gilbert Murray, whose English version of the Bacchæ came into our dramatic literature with all the impulsive power of an original work shortly before *Major Barbara* was begun. The play, indeed, stands indebted to him in more ways than one.

GBS.

---

3. Euripides (484–413 B.C.E.) was a high-ranking Athenian and prolific dramatist. His *Bacchae* was written in exile during the last months of his life. The play explores what modern readers might call the psychology of mass violence.

Act I

It is after dinner on a January night, in the library in LADY
BRITOMART UNDERSHAFT's *house in Wilton Crescent. A
large and comfortable settee is in the middle of the room,
upholstered in dark leather. A person sitting on it (it is
vacant at present) would have, on his right,* LADY BRITO-
MART's *writing table, with the lady herself busy at it; a
smaller writing table behind him on his left; the door
behind him on* LADY BRITOMART's *side; and a window with
a window seat directly on his left. Near the window is an
armchair.*

LADY BRITOMART *is a woman of fifty or thereabouts, well
dressed and yet careless of her dress, well bred and quite
reckless of her breeding, well mannered and yet appall-
ingly outspoken and indifferent to the opinion of her inter-
locutors, amiable and yet peremptory, arbitrary, and
high-tempered to the last bearable degree, and withal a
very typical managing matron of the upper class, treated
as a naughty child until she grew into a scolding mother,
and finally settling down with plenty of practical ability
and worldly experience, limited in the oddest way with
domestic and class limitations, conceiving the universe
exactly as if it were a large house in Wilton Crescent,
though handling her corner of it very effectively on that
assumption, and being quite enlightened and liberal as to
the books in the library, the pictures on the walls, the
music in the portfolios, and the articles in the papers.*

Her son, STEPHEN, *comes in. He is a gravely correct
young man under 25, taking himself very seriously, but
still in some awe of his mother, from childish habit and
bachelor shyness rather than from any weakness of character.*

STEPHEN   Whats the matter?
LADY BRITOMART   Presently, Stephen.
    [STEPHEN *submissively walks to the settee and sits down. He
takes up* The Speaker.]
LADY BRITOMART   Dont begin to read, Stephen. I shall require all
your attention.
STEPHEN   It was only while I was waiting—
LADY BRITOMART   Dont make excuses, Stephen. [*He puts down* The
Speaker.] Now! [*She finishes her writing; rises; and comes to the
settee.*] I have not kept you waiting very long, I think.
STEPHEN   Not at all, mother.
LADY BRITOMART   Bring me my cushion. [*He takes the cushion from*

the chair at the desk and arranges it for her as she sits down on the settee.] Sit down. [*He sits down and fingers his tie nervously.*] Dont fiddle with your tie, Stephen: there is nothing the matter with it.

STEPHEN   I beg your pardon. [*He fiddles with his watch chain instead.*]

LADY BRITOMART   Now are you attending to me, Stephen?

STEPHEN   Of course, mother.

LADY BRITOMART   No: it's not of course. I want something much more than your everyday matter-of-course attention. I am going to speak to you very seriously, Stephen. I wish you would let that chain, alone.

STEPHEN [*Hastily relinquishing the chain.*]   Have I done anything to annoy you, mother? If so, it was quite unintentional.

LADY BRITOMART [*Astonished.*]   Nonsense! [*With some remorse.*] My poor boy, did you think I was angry with you?

STEPHEN   What is it, then, mother? You are making me very uneasy.

LADY BRITOMART   [*Squaring herself at him rather aggressively.*]   Stephen: may I ask how soon you intend to realize that you are a grown-up man, and that I am only a woman?

STEPHEN [*Amazed.*]   Only a—

LADY BRITOMART   Dont repeat my words, please: it is a most aggravating habit. You must learn to face life seriously, Stephen. I really cannot bear the whole burden of our family affairs any longer. You must advise me: you must assume the responsibility.

STEPHEN   I!

LADY BRITOMART   Yes, you, of course. You were 24 last June. Youve been at Harrow and Cambridge. Youve been to India and Japan. You must know a lot of things, now; unless you have wasted your time most scandalously. Well, advise me.

STEPHEN [*Much perplexed.*]   You know I have never interfered in the household—

LADY BRITOMART   No: I should think not. I dont want you to order the dinner.

STEPHEN   I mean in our family affairs.

LADY BRITOMART   Well, you must interfere now; for they are getting quite beyond me.

STEPHEN [*Troubled.*]   I have thought sometimes that perhaps I ought; but really, mother, I know so little about them; and what I do know is so painful—it is so impossible to mention some things to you— [*He stops, ashamed.*]

LADY BRITOMART   I suppose you mean your father.

STEPHEN [*Almost inaudibly.*]   Yes.

LADY BRITOMART   My dear: we cant go on all our lives not mentioning him. Of course you were quite right not to open the subject until I asked you to; but you are old enough now to be taken into my confidence, and to help me to deal with him about the girls.

STEPHEN   But the girls are all right. They are engaged.

LADY BRITOMART [*Complacently.*]   Yes: I have made a very good
match for Sarah. Charles Lomax will be a millionaire at 35. But
that is ten years ahead; and in the meantime his trustees cannot
under the terms of his father's will allow him more than £800 a
year.[1]

STEPHEN   But the will says also that if he increases his income by
his own exertions, they may double the increase.

LADY BRITOMART   Charles Lomax's exertions are much more likely
to decrease his income than to increase it. Sarah will have to find
at least another £800 a year for the next ten years; and even then
they will be as poor as church mice. And what about Barbara? I
thought Barbara was going to make the most brilliant career of all
of you. And what does she do? Joins the Salvation Army; dis-
charges her maid; lives on a pound a week; and walks in one evening with a professor of Greek whom she has picked up in the
street, and who pretends to be a Salvationist, and actually plays
the big drum for her in public because he has fallen head over
ears in love with her.

STEPHEN   I was certainly rather taken aback when I heard they were
engaged. Cusins is a very nice fellow, certainly: nobody would ever
guess that he was born in Australia; but—

LADY BRITOMART   Oh, Adolphus Cusins will make a very good husband. After all, nobody can say a word against Greek: it stamps a
man at once as an educated gentleman. And my family, thank
Heaven, is not a pig-headed Tory one. We are Whigs, and believe
in liberty. Let snobbish people say what they please: Barbara shall
marry, not the man they like, but the man *I* like.

STEPHEN   Of course I was thinking only of his income. However,
he is not likely to be extravagant.

LADY BRITOMART   Dont be too sure of that, Stephen. I know your
quiet, simple, refined, poetic people like Adolphus—quite content
with the best of everything! They cost more than your extravagant
people, who are always as mean as they are second rate. No: Barbara will need at least £2000 a year.[2] You see it means two additional households. Besides, my dear, you must marry soon. I dont
approve of the present fashion of philandering bachelors and late
marriages; and I am trying to arrange something for you.

STEPHEN   It's very good of you, mother; but perhaps I had better
arrange that for myself.

LADY BRITOMART   Nonsense! you are much too young to begin
matchmaking: you would be taken in by some pretty little nobody.
Of course I dont mean that you are not to be consulted: you know
that as well as I do. [STEPHEN *closes his lips and is silent.*] Now
dont sulk, Stephen.

1. Approximately $1,200.
2. Approximately $3,500.

STEPHEN   I am not sulking, mother. What has all this got to do with—with—with my father?

LADY BRITOMART   My dear Stephen: where is the money to come from? It is easy enough for you and the other children to live on my income as long as we are in the same house; but I cant keep four families in four separate houses. You know how poor my father is: he has barely seven thousand a year now;[3] and really, if he were not the Earl of Stevenage, he would have to give up society. He can do nothing for us. He says, naturally enough, that it is absurd that he should be asked to provide for the children of a man who is rolling in money. You see, Stephen, your father must be fabulously wealthy, because there is always a war going on somewhere.

STEPHEN   You need not remind me of that, mother. I have hardly ever opened a newspaper in my life without seeing our name in it. The Undershaft torpedo! The Undershaft quick firers! The Undershaft ten inch! the Undershaft disappearing rampart gun! the Undershaft submarine! and now the Undershaft aerial battleship! At Harrow they called me the Woolwich Infant. At Cambridge it was the same. A little brute at King's who was always trying to get up revivals, spoilt my Bible—your first birthday present to me—by writing under my name, "Son and heir to Undershaft and Lazarus, Death and Destruction Dealers: address, Christendom and Judea." But that was not so bad as the way I was kowtowed to everywhere because my father was making millions by selling cannons.

LADY BRITOMART   It is not only the cannons, but the war loans that Lazarus arranges under cover of giving credit for the cannons. You know, Stephen, it's perfectly scandalous. Those two men, Andrew Undershaft and Lazarus, positively have Europe under their thumbs. That is why your father is able to behave as he does. He is above the law. Do you think Bismarck or Gladstone or Disraeli could have openly defied every social and moral obligation all their lives as your father has? They simply wouldnt have dared. I asked Gladstone to take it up. I asked *The Times* to take it up. I asked the Lord Chamberlain to take it up. But it was just like asking them to declare war on the Sultan. They wouldnt. They said they couldnt touch him. I believe they were afraid.

STEPHEN   What could they do? He does not actually break the law.

LADY BRITOMART   Not break the law! He is always breaking the law. He broke the law when he was born: his parents were not married.

STEPHEN   Mother! Is that true?

LADY BRITOMART   Of course it's true: that was why we separated.

STEPHEN   He married without letting you know this!

LADY BRITOMART   [*Rather taken aback by this inference.*]   Oh no. To

---

3. Approximately $12,000, a good income at the time.

do Andrew justice, that was not the sort of thing he did. Besides, you know the Undershaft motto: Unashamed. Everybody knew.

STEPHEN   But you said that was why you separated.

LADY BRITOMART   Yes, because he was not content with being a foundling himself: he wanted to disinherit you for another foundling. That was what I couldnt stand.

STEPHEN [*Ashamed.*]   Do you mean for—for—for—

LADY BRITOMART   Dont stammer, Stephen. Speak distinctly.

STEPHEN   But this is so frightful to me, mother. To have to speak to you about such things!

LADY BRITOMART   It's not pleasant for me, either, especially if you are still so childish that you must make it worse by a display of embarrassment. It is only in the middle classes, Stephen, that people get into a state of dumb helpless horror when they find that there are wicked people in the world. In our class, we have to decide what is to be done with wicked people; and nothing should disturb our self-possession. Now ask your question properly.

STEPHEN   Mother: you have no consideration for me. For Heaven's sake either treat me as a child, as you always do, and tell me nothing at all; or tell me everything and let me take it as best I can.

LADY BRITOMART   Treat you as a child! What do you mean? It is most unkind and ungrateful of you to say such a thing. You know I have never treated any of you as children. I have always made you my companions and friends, and allowed you perfect freedom to do and say whatever you liked, so long as you liked what I could approve of.

STEPHEN [*Desperately.*]   I daresay we have been the very imperfect children of a very perfect mother; but I do beg you to let me alone for once, and tell me about this horrible business of my father wanting to set me aside for another son.

LADY BRITOMART [*Amazed.*]   Another son! I never said anything of the kind. I never dreamt of such a thing. This is what comes of interrupting me.

STEPHEN   But you said—

LADY BRITOMART [*Cutting him short.*]   Now be a good boy, Stephen, and listen to me patiently. The Undershafts are descended from a foundling in the parish of St. Andrew Undershaft in the city. That was long ago, in the reign of James the First. Well, this foundling was adopted by an armorer and gun-maker. In the course of time the foundling succeeded to the business; and from some notion of gratitude, or some vow or something, he adopted another foundling, and left the business to him. And that foundling did the same. Ever since that, the cannon business has always been left to an adopted foundling named Andrew Undershaft.

STEPHEN   But did they never marry? Were there no legitimate sons?

LADY BRITOMART   Oh yes: they married just as your father did; and they were rich enough to buy land for their own children and leave them well provided for. But they always adopted and trained some foundling to succeed them in the business; and of course they always quarrelled with their wives furiously over it. Your father was adopted in that way; and he pretends to consider himself bound to keep up the tradition and adopt somebody to leave the business to. Of course I was not going to stand that. There may have been some reason for it when the Undershafts could only marry women in their own class, whose sons were not fit to govern great estates. But there could be no excuse for passing over my son.

STEPHEN [*Dubiously.*] I am afraid I should make a poor hand of managing a cannon foundry.

LADY BRITOMART Nonsense! you could easily get a manager and pay him a salary.

STEPHEN My father evidently had no great opinion of my capacity.

LADY BRITOMART Stuff, child! you were only a baby: it had nothing to do with your capacity. Andrew did it on principle, just as he did every perverse and wicked thing on principle. When my father remonstrated, Andrew actually told him to his face that history tells us of only two successful institutions: one the Undershaft firm, and the other the Roman Empire under the Antonines. That was because the Antonine emperors all adopted their successors. Such rubbish! The Stevenages are as good as the Antonines, I hope; and you are a Stevenage. But that was Andrew all over. There you have the man! Always clever and unanswerable when he was defending nonsense and wickedness: always awkward and sullen when he had to behave sensibly and decently!

STEPHEN Then it was on my account that your home life was broken up, mother. I am sorry.

LADY BRITOMART Well, dear, there were other differences. I really cannot bear an immoral man. I am not a Pharisee, I hope; and I should not have minded his merely doing wrong things: we are none of us perfect. But your father didn't exactly do wrong things: he said them and thought them: that was what was so dreadful. He really had a sort of religion of wrongness. Just as one doesnt mind men practising immorality so long as they own that they are in the wrong by preaching morality; so I couldnt forgive Andrew for preaching immorality while he practised morality. You would all have grown up without principles, without any knowledge of right and wrong, if he had been in the house. You know, my dear, your father was a very attractive man in some ways. Children did not dislike him; and he took advantage of it to put the wickedest ideas into their heads, and make them quite unmanageable. I did not dislike him myself: very far from it; but nothing can bridge over moral disagreement.

STEPHEN All this simply bewilders me, mother. People may differ about matters of opinion, or even about religion; but how can they differ about right and wrong? Right is right; and wrong is wrong; and if a man cannot distinguish them properly, he is either a fool or a rascal: thats all.

LADY BRITOMART [*Touched.*]   Thats my own boy! [*She pats his cheek.*] Your father never could answer that: he used to laugh and get out of it under cover of some affectionate nonsense. And now that you understand the situation, what do you advise me to do?

STEPHEN   Well, what can you do?

LADY BRITOMART   I must get the money somehow.

STEPHEN   We cannot take money from him. I had rather go and live in some cheap place like Bedford Square or even Hampstead[4] than take a farthing[5] of his money.

LADY BRITOMART   But after all, Stephen, our present income comes from Andrew.

STEPHEN [*Shocked.*]   I never knew that.

LADY BRITOMART   Well, you surely didnt suppose your grandfather had anything to give me. The Stevenages could not do everything for you. We gave you social position. Andrew had to contribute something. He had a very good bargain, I think.

STEPHEN [*Bitterly.*]   We are utterly dependent on him and his cannons, then!

LADY BRITOMART   Certainly not: the money is settled. But he provided it. So you see it is not a question of taking money from him or not: it is simply a question of how much. I dont want any more for myself.

STEPHEN   Nor do I.

LADY BRITOMART   But Sarah does; and Barbara does. That is, Charles Lomax and Adolphus Cusins will cost them more. So I must put my pride in my pocket and ask for it, I suppose. That is your advice, Stephen, is it not?

STEPHEN   No.

LADY BRITOMART [*Sharply.*]   Stephen!

STEPHEN   Of course if you are determined—

LADY BRITOMART   I am not determined: I ask your advice; and I am waiting for it. I will not have all the responsibility thrown on my shoulders.

STEPHEN [*Obstinately.*]   I would die sooner than ask him for another penny.

LADY BRITOMART [*Resignedly.*]   You mean that *I* must ask him. Very well, Stephen: it shall be as you wish. You will be glad to know that your grandfather concurs. But he thinks I ought to ask Andrew to come here and see the girls. After all, he must have some natural affection for them.

STEPHEN   Ask him here!!!

---

4. Middle-class and upper-middle-class areas of London.
5. Small coin, now no longer in use, worth one-quarter of a penny.

LADY BRITOMART   Do not repeat my words, Stephen. Where else
can I ask him?

STEPHEN   I never expected you to ask him at all.

LADY BRITOMART   Now dont tease, Stephen. Come! you see that it
is necessary that he should pay us a visit, dont you?

STEPHEN [*Reluctantly.*]   I suppose so, if the girls cannot do without
his money.

LADY BRITOMART   Thank you, Stephen: I knew you would give me
the right advice when it was properly explained to you. I have asked
your father to come this evening. [STEPHEN *bounds from his seat.*]
Dont jump, Stephen: it fidgets me.

STEPHEN [*In utter consternation.*]   Do you mean to say that my
father is coming here to-night—that he may be here at any
moment?

LADY BRITOMART [*Looking at her watch.*]   I said nine. [*He gasps. She
rises.*] Ring the bell, please. [STEPHEN *goes to the smaller writing
table; presses a button on it; and sits at it with his elbows on the
table and his head in his hands, outwitted and overwhelmed.*] It is
ten minutes to nine yet; and I have to prepare the girls. I asked
Charles Lomax and Adolphus to dinner on purpose that they might
be here. Andrew had better see them in case he should cherish
any delusions as to their being capable of supporting their wives.
[THE BUTLER *enters:* LADY BRITOMART *goes behind the settee to
speak to him.*] Morrison: go up to the drawingroom and tell everybody to come down here at once. [MORRISON *withdraws.* LADY BRI-
TOMART *turns to* STEPHEN.] Now remember, Stephen: I shall need
all your countenance and authority. [*He rises and tries to recover
some vestige of these attributes.*] Give me a chair, dear. [*He pushes
a chair forward from the wall to where she stands, near the smaller
writing table. She sits down; and he goes to the armchair, into which
he throws himself.*] I dont know how Barbara will take it. Ever since
they made her a major in the Salvation Army she has developed a
propensity to have her own way and order people about which
quite cows me sometimes. It's not ladylike: I'm sure I dont know
where she picked it up. Anyhow, Barbara shant bully me; but still
it's just as well that your father should be here before she has time
to refuse to meet him or make a fuss. Dont look nervous, Stephen:
it will only encourage Barbara to make difficulties. *I* am nervous
enough, goodness knows; but I dont shew it.

[SARAH *and* BARBARA *come in with their respective young men,*
CHARLES LOMAX *and* ADOLPHUS CUSINS. SARAH *is slender,
bored, and mundane.* BARBARA *is robuster, jollier, much more
energetic.* SARAH *is fashionably dressed:* BARBARA *is in Salvation
Army uniform.* LOMAX, *a young man about town, is like many
other young men about town. He is afflicted with a frivolous
sense of humor which plunges him at the most inopportune*

moments into paroxysms of imperfectly suppressed laughter.
CUSINS *is a spectacled student, slight, thin haired, and sweet voiced, with a more complex form of* LOMAX'S *complaint. His sense of humor is intellectual and subtle, and is complicated by an appalling temper. The lifelong struggle of a benevolent temperament and a high conscience against impulses of inhuman ridicule and fierce impatience has set up a chronic strain which has visibly wrecked his constitution. He is a most implacable, determined, tenacious, intolerant person who by mere force of character presents himself as—and indeed actually is—considerate, gentle, explanatory, even mild and apologetic, capable possibly of murder, but not of cruelty or coarseness. By the operation of some instinct which is not merciful enough to blind him with the illusions of love, he is obstinately bent on marrying* BARBARA. LOMAX *likes* SARAH *and thinks it will be rather a lark to marry her. Consequently he has not attempted to resist* LADY BRITOMART'S *arrangements to that end.*

All four look as if they had been having a good deal of fun in the drawingroom. The girls enter first, leaving the swains outside. SARAH *comes to the settee.* BARBARA *comes in after her and stops at the door.]*

BARBARA   Are Cholly and Dolly to come in?

LADY BRITOMART [*Forcibly.*]   Barbara: I will not have Charles called Cholly: the vulgarity of it positively makes me ill.

BARBARA   It's all right, mother. Cholly is quite correct nowadays. Are they to come in?

LADY BRITOMART   Yes, if they will behave themselves.

BARBARA [*Through the door.*]   Come in, Dolly, and behave yourself.
    [BARBARA *comes to her mother's writing table.* CUSINS *enters smiling, and wanders towards* LADY BRITOMART.]

SARAH [*Calling.*]   Come in, Cholly.
    [LOMAX *enters, controlling his features very imperfectly, and places himself vaguely between* SARAH *and* BARBARA.]

LADY BRITOMART [*Peremptorily.*]   Sit down, all of you. [*They sit.* CUSINS *crosses to the window and seats himself there.* LOMAX *takes a chair.* BARBARA *sits at the writing table and* SARAH *on the settee.*] I dont in the least know what you are laughing at, Adolphus. I am surprised at you, though I expected nothing better from Charles Lomax.

CUSINS [*In a remarkably gentle voice.*]   Barbara has been trying to teach me the West Ham Salvation March.

LADY BRITOMART   I see nothing to laugh at in that; nor should you if you are really converted.

CUSINS [*Sweetly.*]   You were not present. It was really funny, I believe.

LOMAX Ripping.

LADY BRITOMART Be quiet, Charles. Now listen to me, children. Your father is coming here this evening. [*General stupefaction.*]

LOMAX [*Remonstrating.*] Oh I say!

LADY BRITOMART You are not called on to say anything, Charles.

SARAH Are you serious, mother?

LADY BRITOMART Of course I am serious. It is on your account, Sarah, and also on Charles's. [*Silence.* CHARLES *looks painfully unworthy.*] I hope you are not going to object, Barbara.

BARBARA I! why should I? My father has a soul to be saved like anybody else. Hes quite welcome as far as I am concerned.

LOMAX [*Still remonstrant.*] But really, dont you know! Oh I say!

LADY BRITOMART [*Frigidly.*] What do you wish to convey, Charles?

LOMAX Well, you must admit that this is a bit thick.

LADY BRITOMART [*Turning with ominous suavity to* CUSINS.] Adolphus: you are a professor of Greek. Can you translate Charles Lomax's remarks into reputable English for us?

CUSINS [*Cautiously.*] If I may say so, Lady Brit, I think Charles has rather happily expressed what we all feel. Homer, speaking of Autolycus, uses the same phrase. πυκινὸν δόμον ἐλθεῖν means a bit thick.[6]

LOMAX [*Handsomely.*] Not that I mind, you know, if Sarah dont.

LADY BRITOMART [*Crushingly.*] Thank you. Have I your permission, Adolphus, to invite my own husband to my own house?

CUSINS [*Gallantly.*] You have my unhesitating support in everything you do.

LADY BRITOMART Sarah: have you nothing to say?

SARAH Do you mean that he is coming regularly to live here?

LADY BRITOMART Certainly not. The spare room is ready for him if he likes to stay for a day or two and see a little more of you; but there are limits.

SARAH Well, he cant eat us, I suppose. *I* dont mind.

LOMAX [*Chuckling.*] I wonder how the old man will take it.

LADY BRITOMART Much as the old woman will, no doubt, Charles.

LOMAX [*Abashed.*] I didnt mean—at least—

LADY BRITOMART You didnt think, Charles. You never do; and the result is, you never mean anything. And now please attend to me, children. Your father will be quite a stranger to us.

LOMAX I suppose he hasnt seen Sarah since she was a little kid.

LADY BRITOMART Not since she was a little kid, Charles, as you express it with that elegance of diction and refinement of thought that seem never to desert you. Accordingly—er— [*Impatiently.*] Now I have forgotten what I was going to say. That comes of your

6. "Pukinon domon elthein": translated by Gilbert Murray for GBS as " 'to come into a thick—i.e., a strong or fortified—house' but it would also construe 'It was thick (a bit thick) to come into the house'." (Letter to GBS, October 7, 1905)

provoking me to be sarcastic, Charles. Adolphus: will you kindly tell me where I was.

CUSINS [*Sweetly.*] You were saying that as Mr Undershaft has not seen his children since they were babies, he will form his opinion of the way you have brought them up from their behavior to-night, and that therefore you wish us all to be particularly careful to conduct ourselves well, especially Charles.

LOMAX Look here: Lady Brit didnt say that.

LADY BRITOMART [*Vehemently.*] I did, Charles. Adolphus's recollection is perfectly correct. It is most important that you should be good; and I do beg you for once not to pair off into opposite corners and giggle and whisper while I am speaking to your father.

BARBARA All right, mother. We'll do you credit.

LADY BRITOMART Remember, Charles, that Sarah will want to feel proud of you instead of ashamed of you.

LOMAX Oh I say! theres nothing to be exactly proud of, dont you know.

LADY BRITOMART Well, try and look as if there was.

[MORRISON, *pale and dismayed, breaks into the room in unconcealed disorder.*]

MORRISON Might I speak a word to you, my lady?

LADY BRITOMART Nonsense! Shew him up.

MORRISON Yes, my lady. [*He goes.*]

LOMAX Does Morrison know who it is?

LADY BRITOMART Of course. Morrison has always been with us.

LOMAX It must be a regular corker for him, dont you know.

LADY BRITOMART Is this a moment to get on my nerves, Charles, with your outrageous expressions?

LOMAX But this is something out of the ordinary, really—

MORRISON [*At the door.*] The—er—Mr Undershaft. [*He retreats in confusion.*]

[ANDREW UNDERSHAFT *comes in. All rise.* LADY BRITOMART *meets him in the middle of the room behind the settee.*

ANDREW *is, on the surface, a stoutish, easygoing elderly man, with kindly patient manners, and an engaging simplicity of character. But he has a watchful, deliberate, waiting, listening face, and formidable reserves of power, both bodily and mental, in his capacious chest and long head. His gentleness is partly that of a strong man who has learnt by experience that his natural grip hurts ordinary people unless he handles them very carefully, and partly the mellowness of age and success. He is also a little shy in his present very delicate situation.*]

LADY BRITOMART Good evening, Andrew.

UNDERSHAFT How d'ye do, my dear.

LADY BRITOMART You look a good deal older.

UNDERSHAFT [*Apologetically.*] I am somewhat older. [*With a touch of courtship.*] Time has stood still with you.

LADY BRITOMART [*Promptly.*]   Rubbish! This is your family.

UNDERSHAFT [*Surprised.*]   Is it so large? I am sorry to say my memory is failing very badly in some things.

[*He offers his hand with paternal kindness to* LOMAX.]

LOMAX [*Jerkily shaking his hand.*]   Ahdedoo.

UNDERSHAFT   I can see you are my eldest. I am very glad to meet you again, my boy.

LOMAX [*Remonstrating.*]   No but look here dont you know— [*Overcome.*] Oh I say!

LADY BRITOMART [*Recovering from momentary speechlessness.*] Andrew: do you mean to say that you dont remember how many children you have?

UNDERSHAFT   Well, I am afraid I—. They have grown so much— er. Am I making any ridiculous mistake? I may as well confess: I recollect only one son. But so many things have happened since, of course—er—

LADY BRITOMART [*Decisively.*]   Andrew: you are talking nonsense. Of course you have only one son.

UNDERSHAFT   Perhaps you will be good enough to introduce me, my dear.

LADY BRITOMART   That is Charles Lomax, who is engaged to Sarah.

UNDERSHAFT   My dear sir, I beg your pardon.

LOMAX   Notatall. Delighted, I assure you.

LADY BRITOMART   This is Stephen.

UNDERSHAFT [*Bowing.*]   Happy to make your acquaintance, Mr Stephen. Then [*going to* CUSINS] you must be my son. [*Taking* CUSINS' *hands in his.*] How are you, my young friend? [*To* LADY BRITOMART.] He is very like you, my love.

CUSINS   You flatter me, Mr Undershaft. My name is Cusins: engaged to Barbara. [*Very explicitly.*] That is Major Barbara Undershaft, of the Salvation Army. That is Sarah, your second daughter. This is Stephen Undershaft, your son.

UNDERSHAFT   My dear Stephen, I beg your pardon.

STEPHEN   Not at all.

UNDERSHAFT   Mr Cusins: I am much indebted to you for explaining so precisely. [*Turning to* SARAH.] Barbara, my dear—

SARAH [*Prompting him.*]   Sarah.

UNDERSHAFT   Sarah, of course. [*They shake hands. He goes over to* BARBARA.] Barbara—I am right this time, I hope.

BARBARA   Quite right. [*They shake hands.*]

LADY BRITOMART [*Resuming command.*]   Sit down, all of you. Sit down, Andrew.

[*She comes forward and sits on the settee.* CUSINS *also brings his chair forward on her left.* BARBARA *and* STEPHEN *resume their seats.* LOMAX *gives his chair to* SARAH *and goes for another.*]

UNDERSHAFT Thank you, my love.

LOMAX [*Conversationally, as he brings a chair forward between the writing table and the settee, and offers it to* UNDERSHAFT.] Takes you some time to find out exactly where you are, dont it?

UNDERSHAFT [*Accepting the chair.*] That is not what embarrasses me, Mr Lomax. My difficulty is that if I play the part of a father, I shall produce the effect of an intrusive stranger; and if I play the part of a discreet stranger, I may appear a callous father.

LADY BRITOMART There is no need for you to play any part at all, Andrew. You had much better be sincere and natural.

UNDERSHAFT [*Submissively.*] Yes, my dear: I daresay that will be best. [*Making himself comfortable.*] Well, here I am. Now what can I do for you all?

LADY BRITOMART You need not do anything, Andrew. You are one of the family. You can sit with us and enjoy yourself.

[LOMAX'*s too long suppressed mirth explodes in agonized neighings.*]

LADY BRITOMART [*Outraged.*] Charles Lomax: if you can behave yourself, behave yourself. If not, leave the room.

LOMAX I'm awfully sorry, Lady Brit; but really, you know, upon my soul! [*He sits on the settee between* LADY BRITOMART *and* UNDERSHAFT, *quite overcome.*]

BARBARA Why dont you laugh if you want to, Cholly? It's good for your inside.

LADY BRITOMART Barbara: you have had the education of a lady. Please let your father see that; and dont talk like a street girl.

UNDERSHAFT Never mind me, my dear. As you know, I am not a gentleman; and I was never educated.

LOMAX [*Encouragingly.*] Nobody'd know it, I assure you. You look all right, you know.

CUSINS Let me advise you to study Greek, Mr Undershaft. Greek scholars are privileged men. Few of them know Greek; and none of them know anything else; but their position is unchallengeable. Other languages are the qualifications of waiters and commercial travellers: Greek is to a man of position what the hallmark is to silver.

BARBARA Dolly: dont be insincere. Cholly: fetch your concertina and play something for us.

LOMAX [*Doubtfully to* UNDERSHAFT.] Perhaps that sort of thing isnt in your line, eh?

UNDERSHAFT I am particularly fond of music.

LOMAX [*Delighted.*] Are you? Then I'll get it. [*He goes upstairs for the instrument.*]

UNDERSHAFT Do you play, Barbara?

BARBARA Only the tambourine. But Cholly's teaching me the concertina.

UNDERSHAFT   Is Cholly also a member of the Salvation Army?

BARBARA   No: he says it's bad form to be a dissenter. But I dont despair of Cholly. I made him come yesterday to a meeting at the dock gates, and took the collection in his hat.

LADY BRITOMART   It is not my doing, Andrew. Barbara is old enough to take her own way. She has no father to advise her.

BARBARA   Oh yes she has. There are no orphans in the Salvation Army.

UNDERSHAFT   Your father there has a great many children and plenty of experience, eh?

BARBARA [*Looking at him with quick interest and nodding.*]   Just so. How did you come to understand that? [LOMAX *is heard at the door trying the concertina.*]

LADY BRITOMART   Come in, Charles. Play us something at once.

LOMAX   Righto! [*He sits down in his former place, and preludes.*]

UNDERSHAFT   One moment, Mr Lomax. I am rather interested in the Salvation Army. Its motto might be my own: Blood and Fire.

LOMAX [*Shocked.*]   But not your sort of blood and fire, you know.

UNDERSHAFT   My sort of blood cleanses: my sort of fire purifies.

BARBARA   So do ours. Come down to-morrow to my shelter—the West Ham shelter—and see what we're doing. We're going to march to a great meeting in the Assembly Hall at Mile End.[7] Come and see the shelter and then march with us: it will do you a lot of good. Can you play anything?

UNDERSHAFT   In my youth I earned pennies, and even shillings occasionally, in the streets and in public house parlors by my natural talent for stepdancing. Later on, I became a member of the Undershaft orchestral society, and performed passably on the tenor trombone.

LOMAX [*Scandalized.*]   Oh I say!

BARBARA   Many a sinner has played himself into heaven on the trombone, thanks to the Army.

LOMAX [*To* BARBARA, *still rather shocked.*]   Yes; but what about the cannon business, dont you know? [*To* UNDERSHAFT.] Getting into heaven is not exactly in your line, is it?

LADY BRITOMART   Charles!!!

LOMAX   Well; but it stands to reason, dont it? The cannon business may be necessary and all that: we cant get on without cannons; but it isnt right, you know. On the other hand, there may be a certain amount of tosh about the Salvation Army—I belong to the Established Church myself—but still you cant deny that it's religion; and you cant go against religion, can you? At least unless youre downright immoral, dont you know.

UNDERSHAFT   You hardly appreciate my position, Mr Lomax—

7. Poorer quarters of London.

LOMAX [*Hastily.*]   I'm not saying anything against you personally, you know.

UNDERSHAFT   Quite so, quite so. But consider for a moment. Here I am, a manufacturer of mutilation and murder. I find myself in a specially amiable humor just now because, this morning, down at the foundry, we blew twenty-seven dummy soldiers into fragments with a gun which formerly destroyed only thirteen.

LOMAX [*Leniently.*]   Well, the more destructive war becomes, the sooner it will be abolished, eh?

UNDERSHAFT   Not at all. The more destructive war becomes the more fascinating we find it. No, Mr Lomax: I am obliged to you for making the usual excuse for my trade; but I am not ashamed of it. I am not one of those men who keep their morals and their business in water-tight compartments. All the spare money my trade rivals spend on hospitals, cathedrals and other receptacles for conscience money, I devote to experiments and researches in improved methods of destroying life and property. I have always done so; and I always shall. Therefore your Christmas card moralities of peace on earth and goodwill among men are of no use to me. Your Christianity, which enjoins you to resist not evil, and to turn the other cheek, would make me a bankrupt. My morality—my religion—must have a place for cannons and torpedoes in it.

STEPHEN [*Coldly—almost sullenly.*]   You speak as if there were half a dozen moralities and religions to choose from, instead of one true morality and one true religion.

UNDERSHAFT   For me there is only one true morality; but it might not fit you, as you do not manufacture aerial battleships. There is only one true morality for every man; but every man has not the same true morality.

LOMAX [*Overtaxed.*]   Would you mind saying that again? I didn't quite follow it.

CUSINS   It's quite simple. As Euripides says, one man's meat is another man's poison morally as well as physically.

UNDERSHAFT   Precisely.

LOMAX   Oh, that. Yes, yes, yes. True. True.

STEPHEN   In other words, some men are honest and some are scoundrels.

BARBARA   Bosh. There are no scoundrels.

UNDERSHAFT   Indeed? Are there any good men?

BARBARA   No. Not one. There are neither good men nor scoundrels: there are just children of one Father; and the sooner they stop calling one another names the better. You neednt talk to me: I know them. Ive had scores of them through my hands: scoundrels, criminals, infidels, philanthropists, missionaries, county councillors, all sorts. Theyre all just the same sort of sinner; and theres the same salvation ready for them all.

UNDERSHAFT   May I ask have you ever saved a maker of cannons?

BARBARA   No. Will you let me try?

UNDERSHAFT   Well, I will make a bargain with you. If I go to see you to-morrow in your Salvation Shelter, will you come the day after to see me in my cannon works?

BARBARA   Take care. It may end in your giving up the cannons for the sake of the Salvation Army.

UNDERSHAFT   Are you sure it will not end in your giving up the Salvation Army for the sake of the cannons?

BARBARA   I will take my chance of that.

UNDERSHAFT   And I will take my chance of the other. [*They shake hands on it.*] Where is your shelter?

BARBARA   In West Ham. At the sign of the cross. Ask anybody in Canning Town. Where are your works?

UNDERSHAFT   In Perivale St Andrews. At the sign of the sword. Ask anybody in Europe.

LOMAX   Hadnt I better play something?

BARBARA   Yes. Give us Onward, Christian Soldiers.

LOMAX   Well, thats rather a strong order to begin with, dont you know. Suppose I sing Thourt passing hence, my brother. It's much the same tune.

BARBARA   It's too melancholy. You get saved, Cholly; and youll pass hence, my brother, without making such a fuss about it.

LADY BRITOMART   Really, Barbara, you go on as if religion were a pleasant subject. Do have some sense of propriety.

UNDERSHAFT   I do not find it an unpleasant subject, my dear. It is the only one that capable people really care for.

LADY BRITOMART [*Looking at her watch.*]   Well, if you are determined to have it, I insist on having it in a proper and respectable way. Charles: ring for prayers. [*General amazement.* STEPHEN *rises in dismay.*]

LOMAX [*Rising.*]   Oh I say!

UNDERSHAFT [*Rising.*]   I am afraid I must be going.

LADY BRITOMART   You cannot go now, Andrew: it would be most improper. Sit down. What will the servants think?

UNDERSHAFT   My dear: I have conscientious scruples. May I suggest a compromise? If Barbara will conduct a little service in the drawingroom, with Mr Lomax as organist, I will attend it willingly. I will even take part, if a trombone can be procured.

LADY BRITOMART   Dont mock, Andrew.

UNDERSHAFT [*Shocked—to* BARBARA.]   You dont think I am mocking, my love, I hope.

BARBARA   No, of course not; and it wouldnt matter if you were: half the Army came to their first meeting for a lark. [*Rising.*] Come along. Come, Dolly. Come, Cholly.

[*She goes out with* UNDERSHAFT, *who opens the door for her.* CUSINS *rises.*]

LADY BRITOMART   I will not be disobeyed by everybody. Adolphus: sit down. Charles: you may go. You are not fit for prayers: you cannot keep your countenance.

LOMAX   Oh I say! [*He goes out.*]

LADY BRITOMART [*Continuing.*]   But you, Adolphus, can behave yourself if you choose to. I insist on your staying.

CUSINS   My dear Lady Brit: there are things in the family prayer book that I couldnt bear to hear you say.

LADY BRITOMART   What things, pray?

CUSINS   Well, you would have to say before all the servants that we have done things we ought not to have done, and left undone things we ought to have done, and that there is no health in us. I cannot bear to hear you doing yourself such an unjustice, and Barbara such an injustice. As for myself, I flatly deny it: I have done my best. I shouldnt dare to marry Barbara—I couldnt look you in the face—if it were true. So I must go to the drawingroom.

LADY BRITOMART [*Offended.*]   Well, go. [*He starts for the door.*] And remember this, Adolphus [*He turns to listen*]: I have a very strong suspicion that you went to the Salvation Army to worship Barbara and nothing else. And I quite appreciate the very clever way in which you systematically humbug me. I have found you out. Take care Barbara doesnt. Thats all.

CUSINS [*With unruffled sweetness.*]   Dont tell on me. [*He goes out.*]

LADY BRITOMART   Sarah: if you want to go, go. Anything's better than to sit there as if you wished you were a thousand miles away.

SARAH [*Languidly.*]   Very well, mamma. [*She goes.*]

[LADY BRITOMART, *with a sudden flounce, gives way to a little gust of tears.*]

STEPHEN [*Going to her.*]   Mother: whats the matter?

LADY BRITOMART [*Swishing away her tears with her handkerchief.*]   Nothing. Foolishness. You can go with him, too, if you like, and leave me with the servants.

STEPHEN   Oh, you mustnt think that, mother. I—I dont like him.

LADY BRITOMART   The others do. That is the injustice of a woman's lot. A woman has to bring up her children; and that means to restrain them, to deny them things they want, to set them tasks, to punish them when they do wrong, to do all the unpleasant things. And then the father, who has nothing to do but pet them and spoil them, comes in when all her work is done and steals their affection from her.

STEPHEN   He has not stolen our affection from you. It is only curiosity.

LADY BRITOMART [*Violently.*]   I wont be consoled, Stephen. There is nothing the matter with me. [*She rises and goes towards the door.*]

STEPHEN   Where are you going, mother?

LADY BRITOMART   To the drawingroom, of course. [*She goes out. Onward, Christian Soldiers, on the concertina, with tambourine accompaniment, is heard when the door opens.*] Are you coming, Stephen?

STEPHEN   No. Certainly not.

[*She goes. He sits down on the settee, with compressed lips and an expression of strong dislike.*]

Act II

The yard of the West Ham shelter of the Salvation Army is a cold place on a January morning. The building itself, an old warehouse, is newly whitewashed. Its gabled end projects into the yard in the middle, with a door on the ground floor, and another in the loft above it without any balcony or ladder, but with a pulley rigged over it for hoisting sacks. Those who come from this central gable end into the yard have the gateway leading to the street on their left, with a stone horse-trough just beyond it, and, on the right, a penthouse shielding a table from the weather. There are forms at the table; and on them are seated a MAN *and a* WOMAN, *both much down on their luck, finishing a meal of bread (one thick slice each, with margarine and golden syrup) and diluted milk.*

The MAN, *a workman out of employment, is young, agile, a talker, a poser, sharp enough to be capable of anything in reason except honesty or altruistic considerations of any kind. The* WOMAN *is a commonplace old bundle of poverty and hard-worn humanity. She looks sixty and probably is forty-five. If they were rich people, gloved and muffed and well wrapped up in furs and overcoats, they would be numbed and miserable; for it is a grindingly cold, raw, January day; and a glance at the background of grimy warehouses and leaden sky visible over the whitewashed walls of the yard would drive any idle rich person straight to the Mediterranean. But these two, being no more troubled with visions of the Mediterranean than of the moon, and being compelled to keep more of their clothes in the pawnshop, and less on their persons, in winter than in summer, are not depressed by the cold: rather are they stung into vivacity, to which their meal has just now given an almost jolly turn. The man takes a pull at his mug, and then gets up and moves about the yard with his hands deep in his pockets, occasionally breaking into a stepdance.*

THE WOMAN   Feel better arter your meal, sir?

THE MAN   No. Call that a meal! Good enough for you, praps; but wot is it to me, an intelligent workin man.

THE WOMAN   Workin man! Wot are you?

THE MAN   Painter.

THE WOMAN [*Sceptically.*]   Yus, I dessay.

THE MAN   Yus, you dessay! I know. Every loafer that cant do nothink calls isself a painter. Well, I'm a real painter: grainer, finisher, thirty-eight bob[1] a week when I can get it.

THE WOMAN   Then why dont you go and get it?

THE MAN   I'll tell you why. Fust: I'm intelligent—fffff! it's rotten cold here [*He dances a step or two.*]—yes: intelligent beyond the station o life into which it has pleased the capitalists to call me; and they dont like a man that sees through em. Second, an intelligent bein needs a doo share of appiness; so I drink somethink cruel when I get the chawnce. Third, I stand by my class and do as little as I can so's to leave arf the job for me fellow workers. Fourth, I'm fly enough to know wots inside the law and wots outside it; and inside it I do as the capitalists do: pinch wot I can lay me ands on. In a proper state of society I am sober, industrious and honest: in Rome, so to speak, I do as the Romans do. Wots the consequence? When trade is bad—and it's rotten bad just now—and the employers az to sack arf their men, they generally start on me.

THE WOMAN   Whats your name?

THE MAN   Price. Bronterre O'Brien Price. Usually called Snobby Price, for short.

THE WOMAN   Snobby's a carpenter, aint it? You said you was a painter.

PRICE   Not that kind of snob, but the genteel sort. I'm too uppish, owing to my intelligence, and my father being a Chartist[2] and a reading, thinking man: a stationer, too. I'm none of your common hewers of wood and drawers of water; and dont you forget it. [*He returns to his seat at the table, and takes up his mug.*] Wots your name?

THE WOMAN   Rummy Mitchens, sir.

PRICE [*Quaffing the remains of his milk to her.*]   Your elth, Miss Mitchens.

RUMMY [*Correcting him.*]   Missis Mitchens.

PRICE   Wot! Oh Rummy, Rummy! Respectable married woman, Rummy, gittin rescued by the Salvation Army by pretendin to be a bad un. Same old game!

RUMMY   What am I to do? I cant starve. Them Salvation lasses is dear good girls; but the better you are, the worse they likes to think

---

1. A "bob" is a shilling. Thirty-eight shillings (one pound and eighteen shillings) would have been a high wage for a working man at the time.
2. An English workers' reform movement of the 1840s.

you were before they rescued you. Why shouldnt they av a bit o credit, poor loves? theyre worn to rags by their work. And where would they get the money to rescue us if we was to let on we're no worse than other people? You know what ladies and gentlemen are.

PRICE   Thievin swine! Wish I ad their job, Rummy, all the same. Wot does Rummy stand for? Pet name praps?

RUMMY   Short for Romola.[3]

PRICE   For wot!?

RUMMY   Romola. It was out of a new book. Somebody me mother wanted me to grow up like.

PRICE   We're companions in misfortune, Rummy. Both on us got names that nobody cawnt pronounce. Consequently I'm Snobby and youre Rummy because Bill and Sally wasnt good enough for our parents. Such is life!

RUMMY   Who saved you, Mr Price? Was it Major Barbara?

PRICE   No: I come here on my own. I'm goin to be Bronterre O'Brien Price, the converted painter. I know wot they like. I'll tell em how I blasphemed and gambled and wopped my poor old mother——

RUMMY [Shocked.]   Used you to beat your mother?

PRICE   Not likely. She used to beat me. No matter: you come and listen to the converted painter, and youll hear how she was a pious woman that taught me me prayers at er knee, an how I used to come home drunk and drag her out o bed er snow white airs, an lam into er with the poker.

RUMMY   Thats whats so unfair to us women. Your confessions is just as big lies as ours: you dont tell what you really done no more than us; but you men can tell your lies right out at the meetins and be made much of for it; while the sort o confessions we az to make az to be wispered to one lady at a time. It aint right, spite of all their piety.

PRICE   Right! Do you spose the Army'd be allowed if it went and did right? Not much. It combs our air and makes us good little blokes to be robbed and put upon. But I'll play the game as good as any of em. I'll see somebody struck by lightnin, or hear a voice sayin "Snobby Price: where will you spend eternity?" I'll ave a time of it, I tell you.

RUMMY   You wont be let drink, though.

PRICE   I'll take it out in gorspellin, then. I dont want to drink if I can get fun enough any other way.

[JENNY HILL, a pale, overwrought, pretty Salvation lass of 18, comes in through the yard gate, leading PETER SHIRLEY, a half hardened, half worn-out elderly man, weak with hunger.]

JENNY [Supporting him.]   Come! pluck up. I'll get you something to eat. Youll be all right then.

---

3. The idealistic heroine of George Eliot's novel of this name (1863).

PRICE [*Rising and hurrying officiously to take the old man off* JENNY'S *hands.*]   Poor old man! Cheer up, brother: youll find rest and peace and appiness ere. Hurry up with the food, miss: e's fair done. [JENNY *hurries into the shelter.*] Ere, buck up, daddy! shes fetchin y'a thick slice o breadn treacle, an a mug o skyblue.[4] [*He seats him at the corner of the table.*]

RUMMY [*Gaily.*]   Keep up your old art! Never say die!

SHIRLEY   I'm not an old man. I'm ony 46. I'm as good as ever I was. The grey patch come in my hair before I was thirty. All it wants is three pennorth[5] o hair dye: am I to be turned on the streets to starve for it? Holy God! I've worked ten to twelve hours a day since I was thirteen, and paid my way all through; and now am I to be thrown into the gutter and my job given to a young man that can do it no better than me because Ive black hair that goes white at the first change?

PRICE [*Cheerfully.*]   No good jawrin about it. Youre ony a jumped-up, jerked-off, orspittle-turned-out incurable of an ole workin man: who cares about you? Eh? Make the thievin swine give you a meal: theyve stole many a one from you. Get a bit o your own back. [JENNY *returns with the usual meal.*] There you are, brother. Awsk a blessin an tuck that into you.

SHIRLEY [*Looking at it ravenously but not touching it, and crying like a child.*]   I never took anything before.

JENNY [*Petting him.*]   Come, come! the Lord sends it to you: he wasnt above taking bread from his friends; and why should you be? Besides, when we find you a job you can pay us for it if you like.

SHIRLEY [*Eagerly.*]   Yes, yes: thats true. I can pay you back: it's only a loan. [*Shivering.*] Oh Lord! oh Lord! [*He turns to the table and attacks the meal ravenously.*]

JENNY   Well, Rummy, are you more comfortable now?

RUMMY   God bless you, lovey! youve fed my body and saved my soul, havnt you? [JENNY, *touched, kisses her.*] Sit down and rest a bit: you must be ready to drop.

JENNY   Ive been going hard since morning. But theres more work than we can do. I mustnt stop.

RUMMY   Try a prayer for just two minutes. Youll work all the better after.

JENNY [*Her eyes lighting up.*]   Oh isnt it wonderful how a few minutes prayer revives you! I was quite lightheaded at twelve o'clock, I was so tired; but Major Barbara just sent me to pray for five minutes; and I was able to go on as if I had only just begun. [*To* PRICE.] Did you have a piece of bread?

PRICE [*With unction.*]   Yes, miss; but Ive got the piece that I value more; and thats the peace that passeth hall hannerstennin.

---

4. Molasses and milk.
5. Three old pennies' worth, i.e., about 1c.

RUMMY [*Fervently.*]   Glory Hallelujah!

[BILL WALKER, *a rough customer of about 25, appears at the yard gate and looks malevolently at* JENNY.]

JENNY   That makes me so happy. When you say that, I feel wicked for loitering here. I must get to work again.

[*She is hurrying to the shelter, when the new-comer moves quickly up to the door and intercepts her. His manner is so threatening that she retreats as he comes at her truculently, driving her down the yard.*]

BILL   I know you. Youre the one that took away my girl. Youre the one that set er agen me. Well, I'm goin to av er out. Not that I care a curse for her or you: see? But I'll let er know; and I'll let you know. I'm goin to give er a doin thatll teach er to cut away from me. Now in with you and tell er to come out afore I come in and kick er out. Tell er Bill Walker wants er. She'll know what that means; and if she keeps me waitin itll be worse. You stop to jaw back at me; and I'll start on you: d'ye hear? Theres your way. In you go. [*He takes her by the arm and slings her towards the door of the shelter. She falls on her hand and knee.* RUMMY *helps her up again.*]

PRICE [*Rising, and venturing irresolutely towards* BILL.]   Easy there, mate. She aint doin you no arm.

BILL   Who are you callin mate? [*Standing over him threateningly.*] Youre goin to stand up for her, are you? Put up your ands.

RUMMY [*Running indignantly to him to scold him.*]   Oh, you great brute—

[*He instantly swings his left hand back against her face. She screams and reels back to the trough, where she sits down, covering her bruised face with her hands and rocking herself and moaning with pain.*]

JENNY [*Going to her.*]   Oh God forgive you! How could you strike an old woman like that?

BILL [*Seizing her by the hair so violently that she also screams, and tearing her away from the old woman.*]   You Gawd forgive me again and I'll Gawd forgive you one on the jaw thatll stop you prayin for a week. [*Holding her and turning fiercely on* PRICE.] Av you anything to say agen it? Eh?

PRICE [*Intimidated.*]   No, matey: she aint anything to do with me.

BILL   Good job for you! I'd put two meals into you and fight you with one finger after, you starved cur. [*To* JENNY.] Now are you goin to fetch out Mog Habbijam; or am I to knock your face off you and fetch her myself?

JENNY [*Writhing in his grasp.*]   Oh please someone go in and tell Major Barbara— [*She screams again as he wrenches her head down; and* PRICE *and* RUMMY *flee into the shelter.*]

BILL   You want to go in and tell your Major of me, do you?

JENNY Oh please dont drag my hair. Let me go.

BILL Do you or dont you? [*She stifles a scream.*] Yes or no.

JENNY God give me strength—

BILL [*Striking her with his fist in the face.*] Go and shew her that, and tell her if she wants one like it to come and interfere with me. [JENNY, *crying with pain, goes into the shed. He goes to the form and addresses the old man.*] Here: finish your mess; and get out o my way.

SHIRLEY [*Springing up and facing him fiercely, with the mug in his hand.*] You take a liberty with me, and I'll smash you over the face with the mug and cut your eye out. Aint you satisfied—young whelps like you—with takin the bread out o the mouths of elders that have brought you up and slaved for you, but you must come shovin and cheekin and bullyin in here, where the bread o charity is sickenin in our stummicks?

BILL [*Contemptuously, but backing a little.*] Wot good are you, you old palsy mug?[6] Wot good are you?

SHIRLEY As good as you and better. I'll do a day's work agen you or any fat young soaker of your age. Go and take my job at Horrockses, where I worked for ten year. They want young men there: they cant afford to keep men over forty-five. Theyre very sorry—give you a character and happy to help you to get anything suited to your years—sure a steady man wont be long out of a job. Well, let em try you. Theyll find the differ. What do you know? Not as much as how to beeyave yourself—layin your dirty fist across the mouth of a respectable woman!

BILL Don't provoke me to lay it acrost yours: d'ye hear?

SHIRLEY [*With blighting contempt.*] Yes: you like an old man to hit, dont you, when youve finished with the women. I aint seen you hit a young one yet.

BILL [*Stung.*] You lie, you old soupkitchener, you. There was a young man here. Did I offer to hit him or did I not?

SHIRLEY Was he starvin or was he not? Was he a man or only a crosseyed thief an a loafer? Would you hit my son-in-law's brother?

BILL Who's he?

SHIRLEY Todger Fairmile o Balls Pond. Him that won £20[7] off the Japanese wrastler at the music hall by standin out 17 minutes 4 seconds agen him.

BILL [*Sullenly.*] I'm no music hall wrastler. Can he box?

SHIRLEY Yes: an you cant.

BILL Wot! I cant, cant I? Wots that you say? [*Threatening him.*]

SHIRLEY [*Not budging an inch.*] Will you box Todger Fairmile if I put him on to you? Say the word.

BILL [*Subsiding with a slouch.*] I'll stand up to any man alive, if he

---

6. "Palsy" means a shaking fit, and "mug" is "face." Mug was later corrected to "mag," which is a chatterer.

7. Approximately $35.

was ten Todger Fairmiles. But I dont set up to be a perfessional.

SHIRLEY [*Looking down on him with unfathomable disdain.*] You box! Slap an old woman with the back o your hand! You hadnt even the sense to hit her where a magistrate couldnt see the mark of it, you silly young lump of conceit and ignorance. Hit a girl in the jaw and ony make her cry! If Todger Fairmile'd done it, she wouldnt a got up inside o ten minutes, no more than you would if he got on to you. Yah! I'd set about you myself if I had a week's feedin in me instead o two months starvation. [*He returns to the table to finish his meal.*]

BILL [*Following him and stooping over him to drive the taunt in.*] You lie! you have the bread and treacle in you that you come here to beg.

SHIRLEY [*Bursting into tears.*] Oh God! it's true: I'm only an old pauper on the scrap heap. [*Furiously.*] But youll come to it yourself; and then youll know. Youll come to it sooner than a teetotaller like me, fillin yourself with gin at this hour o the mornin!

BILL I'm no gin drinker, you old liar; but when I want to give my girl a bloomin good idin I like to av a bit o devil in me: see? An here I am, talkin to a rotten old blighter like you sted o givin her wot for. [*Working himself into a rage.*] I'm goin in there to fetch her out. [*He makes vengefully for the shelter door.*]

SHIRLEY Youre goin to the station on a stretcher, more likely; and theyll take the gin and the devil out of you there when they get you inside. You mind what youre about: the major here is the Earl o Stevenage's granddaughter.

BILL [*Checked.*] Garn!

SHIRLEY Youll see.

BILL [*His resolution oozing.*] Well, I aint done nothin to er.

SHIRLEY Spose she said you did! who'd believe you?

BILL [*Very uneasy, skulking back to the corner of the penthouse.*] Gawd! theres no jastice in this country. To think wot them people can do! I'm as good as er.

SHIRLEY Tell her so. It's just what a fool like you would do.

[BARBARA, *brisk and businesslike, comes from the shelter with a note book, and addresses herself to* SHIRLEY. BILL, *cowed, sits down in the corner on a form, and turns his back on them.*]

BARBARA Good morning.

SHIRLEY [*Standing up and taking off his hat.*] Good morning, miss.

BARBARA Sit down: make yourself at home. [*He hesitates; but she puts a friendly hand on his shoulder and makes him obey.*] Now then! since youve made friends with us, we want to know all about you. Names and addresses and trades.

SHIRLEY Peter Shirley. Fitter. Chucked out two months ago because I was too old.

BARBARA [*Not at all surprised.*] Youd pass still. Why didnt you dye your hair?

SHIRLEY   I did. Me age come out at a coroner's inquest on me
daughter.

BARBARA   Steady?

SHIRLEY   Teetotaller. Never out of a job before. Good worker. And
sent to the knackers[8] like an old horse!

BARBARA   No matter: if you did your part God will do his.

SHIRLEY [*Suddenly stubborn.*]   My religion's no concern of anybody
but myself.

BARBARA [*Guessing.*]   I know. Secularist?[9]

SHIRLEY [*Hotly.*]   Did I offer to deny it?

BARBARA   Why should you? My own father's a Secularist, I think.
Our Father—yours and mine—fulfils himself in many ways; and
I daresay he knew what he was about when he made a Secularist
of you. So buck up, Peter! we can always find a job for a steady
man like you. [SHIRLEY, *disarmed, touches his hat. She turns from
him to* BILL.] Whats your name?

BILL [*Insolently.*]   Wots that to you?

BARBARA [*Calmly making a note.*]   Afraid to give his name. Any
trade?

BILL   Who's afraid to give his name? [*Doggedly, with a sense of heroically defying the House of Lords in the person of Lord Stevenage.*]
If you want to bring a charge agen me, bring it. [*She waits, unruffled.*] My name's Bill Walker.

BARBARA [*As if the name were familiar: trying to remember how.*]   Bill
Walker? [*Recollecting.*] Oh, I know: youre the man that Jenny Hill
was praying for inside just now. [*She enters his name in her note
book.*]

BILL   Who's Jenny Hill? And what call has she to pray for me?

BARBARA   I dont know. Perhaps it was you that cut her lip.

BILL [*Defiantly.*]   Yes, it was me that cut her lip. I aint afraid o you.

BARBARA   How could you be, since youre not afraid of God? Youre
a brave man, Mr Walker. It takes some pluck to do our work here;
but none of us dare lift our hand against a girl like that, for fear
of her father in heaven.

BILL [*Sullenly.*]   I want none o your cantin jaw. I suppose you think
I come here to beg from you, like this damaged lot here. Not me.
I dont want your bread and scrape and catlap.[1] I dont believe in
your Gawd, no more than you do yourself.

BARBARA [*Sunnily apologetic and ladylike, as on a new footing with
him.*]   Oh, I beg your pardon for putting your name down, Mr
Walker. I didnt understand. I'll strike it out.

BILL [*Taking this as a slight, and deeply wounded by it.*]   Eah! you
let my name alone. Aint it good enough to be in your book?

8. Buyers and slaughterers of old animals.
9. As a kind of organized atheism, secularism was a thriving movement in London at the
time.
1. Diluted milk; "scrape": thinly spread butter.

BARBARA [*Considering.*]   Well, you see, theres no use putting down
your name unless I can do something for you, is there? Whats your
trade?

BILL [*Still smarting.*]   Thats no concern o yours.

BARBARA   Just so. [*Very businesslike.*] I'll put you down as [*writing*]
the man who—struck—poor little Jenny Hill—in the mouth.

BILL [*Rising threateningly.*]   See here. Ive ad enough o this.

BARBARA [*Quite sunny and fearless.*]   What did you come to us for?

BILL   I come for my girl, see? I come to take her out o this and to
break er jawr for her.

BARBARA [*Complacently.*]   You see I was right about your trade.
[BILL, *on the point of retorting furiously, finds himself, to his great
shame and terror, in danger of crying instead. He sits down again
suddenly.*] Whats her name?

BILL [*Dogged.*]   Er name's Mog Abbijam: thats wot her name is.

BARBARA   Oh, she's gone to Canning Town, to our barracks there.

BILL [*Fortified by his resentment of Mog's perfidy.*]   Is she? [*Vindic-
tively.*] Then I'm goin to Kennintahn arter her. [*He crosses to the
gate; hesitates; finally comes back at* BARBARA.] Are you lyin to me
to get shut o me?

BARBARA   I dont want to get shut of you. I want to keep you here
and save your soul. Youd better stay: youre going to have a bad
time today, Bill.

BILL   Who's goin to give it to me? You, praps.

BARBARA   Someone you dont believe in. But youll be glad afterwards.

BILL [*Slinking off.*]   I'll go to Kennintahn to be out o the reach o
your tongue. [*Suddenly turning on her with intense malice.*] And
if I dont find Mog there, I'll come back and do two years for you,
selp me Gawd if I dont!

BARBARA [*A shade kindlier, if possible.*]   It's no use, Bill. Shes got
another bloke.

BILL   Wot!

BARBARA   One of her own converts. He fell in love with her when
he saw her with her soul saved, and her face clean, and her hair
washed.

BILL [*Surprised.*]   Wottud she wash it for, the carroty slut? It's red.

BARBARA   It's quite lovely now, because she wears a new look in her
eyes with it. It's a pity youre too late. The new bloke has put your
nose out of joint, Bill.

BILL   I'll put his nose out o joint for him. Not that I care a curse for
her, mind that. But I'll teach her to drop me as if I was dirt. And
I'll teach him to meddle with my judy. Wots iz bleedin name?

BARBARA   Sergeant Todger Fairmile.

SHIRLEY [*Rising with grim joy.*]   I'll go with him, miss. I want to see
them two meet. I'll take him to the infirmary when it's over.

BILL [*To* SHIRLEY, *with undissembled misgiving.*]   Is that im you was speakin on?

SHIRLEY   Thats him.

BILL   Im that wrastled in the music all?

SHIRLEY   The competitions at the National Sportin Club was worth nigh a hundred a year to him. Hes gev em up now for religion; so hes a bit fresh for want of the exercise he was accustomed to. He'll be glad to see you. Come along.

BILL   Wots is weight?

SHIRLEY   Thirteen four.[2] [BILL's *last hope expires.*]

BARBARA   Go and talk to him, Bill. He'll convert you.

SHIRLEY   He'll convert your head into a mashed potato.

BILL [*Sullenly.*]   I aint afraid of him. I aint afraid of ennybody. But he can lick me. Shes done me. [*He sits down moodily on the edge of the horse trough.*]

SHIRLEY   You aint goin. I thought not. [*He resumes his seat.*]

BARBARA [*Calling.*]   Jenny!

JENNY [*Appearing at the shelter door with a plaster on the corner of her mouth.*]   Yes, Major.

BARBARA   Send Rummy Mitchens out to clear away here.

JENNY   I think shes afraid.

BARBARA [*Her resemblance to her mother flashing out for a moment.*]   Nonsense! she must do as shes told.

JENNY [*Calling into the shelter.*]   Rummy: the Major says you must come.

> [JENNY *comes to* BARBARA, *purposely keeping on the side next* BILL, *lest he should suppose that she shrank from him or bore malice.*]

BARBARA   Poor little Jenny! Are you tired? [*Looking at the wounded cheek.*] Does it hurt?

JENNY   No: it's all right now. It was nothing.

BARBARA [*Critically.*]   It was as hard as he could hit, I expect. Poor Bill! You dont feel angry with him, do you?

JENNY.   Oh no, no, no: indeed I dont, Major, bless his poor heart! [BARBARA *kisses her; and she runs away merrily into the shelter.* BILL *writhes with an agonizing return of his new and alarming symptoms, but says nothing.* RUMMY MITCHENS *comes from the shelter.*]

BARBARA [*Going to meet* RUMMY.]   Now Rummy, bustle. Take in those mugs and plates to be washed; and throw the crumbs about for the birds.

> [RUMMY *takes the three plates and mugs; but* SHIRLEY *takes back his mug from her, as there is still some milk left in it.*]

RUMMY   There aint any crumbs. This aint a time to waste good bread on birds.

---

2. Thirteen stone, four pounds equal 186 pounds.

PRICE [*Appearing at the shelter door.*]   Gentleman come to see the shelter, Major. Says hes your father.

BARBARA   All right. Coming. [SNOBBY *goes back into the shelter, followed by* BARBARA.]

RUMMY [*Stealing across to* BILL *and addressing him in a subdued voice, but with intense conviction.*]   I'd av the lor of you, you flat eared pignosed potwalloper,[3] if she'd let me. Youre no gentleman, to hit a lady in the face. [BILL, *with greater things moving in him, takes no notice.*]

SHIRLEY [*Following her.*]   Here! in with you and dont get yourself into more trouble by talking.

RUMMY [*With hauteur.*]   I aint ad the pleasure o being hintroduced to you, as I can remember. [*She goes into the shelter with the plates.*]

SHIRLEY   Thats the—

BILL [*Savagely.*]   Dont you talk to me, d'ye hear. You lea me alone, or I'll do you a mischief. I'm not dirt under your feet, anyway.

SHIRLEY [*Calmly.*]   Dont you be afeerd. You aint such prime company that you need expect to be sought after. [*He is about to go into the shelter when* BARBARA *comes out, with* UNDERSHAFT *on her right.*]

BARBARA   Oh there you are, Mr Shirley! [*Between them.*] This is my father: I told you he was a Secularist, didnt I? Perhaps youll be able to comfort one another.

UNDERSHAFT [*Startled.*]   A Secularist! Not the least in the world: on the contrary, a confirmed mystic.

BARBARA   Sorry, I'm sure. By the way, papa, what is your religion— in case I have to introduce you again?

UNDERSHAFT   My religion? Well, my dear, I am a Millionaire. That is my religion.

BARBARA   Then I'm afraid you and Mr Shirley wont be able to comfort one another after all. Youre not a Millionaire, are you, Peter?

SHIRLEY   No; and proud of it.

UNDERSHAFT [*Gravely.*]   Poverty, my friend, is not a thing to be proud of.

SHIRLEY [*Angrily.*]   Who made your millions for you? Me and my like. Whats kep us poor? Keepin you rich. I wouldnt have your conscience, not for all your income.

UNDERSHAFT   I wouldnt have your income, not for all your conscience, Mr Shirley. [*He goes to the penthouse and sits down on a form.*]

BARBARA [*Stopping* SHIRLEY *adroitly as he is about to retort.*]   You wouldnt think he was my father, would you, Peter? Will you go into the shelter and lend the lasses a hand for a while: we're worked off our feet.

---

3. A pot-washer, a menial servant.

SHIRLEY [*Bitterly.*]   Yes: I'm in their debt for a meal, aint I?

BARBARA   Oh, not because youre in their debt; but for love of them, Peter, for love of them. [*He cannot understand, and is rather scandalized.*] There! dont stare at me. In with you; and give that conscience of yours a holiday. [*Bustling him into the shelter.*]

SHIRLEY [*As he goes in.*]   Ah! it's a pity you never was trained to use your reason, miss. Youd have been a very taking lecturer on Secularism.

   [BARBARA *turns to her father.*]

UNDERSHAFT   Never mind me, my dear. Go about your work; and let me watch it for a while.

BARBARA   All right.

UNDERSHAFT   For instance, whats the matter with that out-patient over there?

BARBARA [*Looking at* BILL, *whose attitude has never changed, and whose expression of brooding wrath has deepened.*]   Oh, we shall cure him in no time. Just watch. [*She goes over to* BILL *and waits. He glances up at her and casts his eyes down again, uneasy, but grimmer than ever.*] It would be nice to just stamp on Mog Habbijam's face, wouldnt it, Bill?

BILL [*Starting up from the trough in consternation.*]   It's a lie: I never said so. [*She shakes her head.*] Who told you wot was in my mind?

BARBARA   Only your new friend.

BILL   Wot new friend?

BARBARA   The devil, Bill. When he gets round people they get miserable, just like you.

BILL [*With a heartbreaking attempt at devil-may-care cheerfulness.*]   I aint miserable. [*He sits down again, and stretches his legs in an attempt to seem indifferent.*]

BARBARA   Well, if youre happy, why dont you look happy, as we do?

BILL [*His legs curling back in spite of him.*]   I'm appy enough, I tell you. Why dont you lea me alown? Wot av I done to you? I aint smashed your face, av I?

BARBARA [*Softly: wooing his soul.*]   It's not me thats getting at you, Bill.

BILL   Who else is it?

BARBARA   Somebody that doesnt intend you to smash women's faces, I suppose. Somebody or something that wants to make a man of you.

BILL [*Blustering.*]   Make a man o me! Aint I a man? eh? aint I a man? Who sez I'm not a man?

BARBARA   Theres a man in you somewhere, I suppose. But why did he let you hit poor little Jenny Hill? That wasnt very manly of him, was it?

BILL [*Tormented.*]   Av done with it, I tell you. Chack it. I'm sick of your Jenny Ill and er silly little face.

BARBARA   Then why do you keep thinking about it? Why does it keep coming up against you in your mind? Youre not getting converted, are you?

BILL [*With conviction.*]   Not ME. Not likely. Not arf.

BARBARA   Thats right, Bill. Hold out against it. Put out your strength. Dont lets get you cheap. Todger Fairmile said he wrestled for three nights against his Salvation harder than he ever wrestled with the Jap at the music hall. He gave in to the Jap when his arm was going to break. But he didnt give in to his salvation until his heart was going to break. Perhaps youll escape that. You havnt any heart, have you?

BILL   Wot d'ye mean? Wy aint I got a art the same as ennybody else?

BARBARA   A man with a heart wouldnt have bashed poor little Jenny's face, would he?

BILL [*Almost crying.*]   Ow, will you lea me alown? Av I ever offered to meddle with you, that you come naggin and provowkin me lawk this? [*He writhes convulsively from his eyes to his toes.*]

BARBARA [*With a steady soothing hand on his arm and a gentle voice that never lets him go.*]   It's your soul thats hurting you, Bill, and not me. Weve been through it all ourselves. Come with us, Bill. [*He looks wildly round.*] To brave manhood on earth and eternal glory in heaven. [*He is on the point of breaking down.*] Come. [*A drum is heard in the shelter; and* BILL, *with a gasp, escapes from the spell as* BARBARA *turns quickly.* ADOLPHUS *enters from the shelter with a big drum.*] Oh! there you are, Dolly. Let me introduce a new friend of mine, Mr Bill Walker. This is my bloke, Bill: Mr Cusins. [CUSINS *salutes with his drumstick.*]

BILL   Goin to marry im?

BARBARA   Yes.

BILL [*Fervently.*]   Gord elp im! Gawd elp im!

BARBARA   Why? Do you think he wont be happy with me?

BILL   Ive only ad to stand it for a mornin: e'll av to stand it for a lifetime.

CUSINS   That is a frightful reflection, Mr Walker. But I cant tear myself away from her.

BILL   Well, I can. [*To* BARBARA.] Eah! do you know where I'm goin to, and wot I'm goin to do?

BARBARA   Yes: youre going to heaven; and youre coming back here before the week's out to tell me so.

BILL   You lie. I'm goin to Kennintahn, to spit in Todger Fairmile's eye. I bashed Jenny Ill's face; and now I'll get me own face bashed and come back and shew it to er. E'll it me ardern I it er. Thatll make us square. [*To* ADOLPHUS.] Is that fair or is it not? Youre a genlmn: you oughter know.

BARBARA   Two black eyes wont make one white one, Bill.

BILL   I didnt ast you. Cawnt you never keep your mahth shut? I ast the genlmn.

CUSINS [*Reflectively.*]   Yes: I think youre right, Mr Walker. Yes: I should do it. It's curious: it's exactly what an ancient Greek would have done.

BARBARA   But what good will it do?

CUSINS   Well, it will give Mr Fairmile some exercise; and it will satisfy Mr Walker's soul.

BILL   Rot! there aint no sach a thing as a soul. Ah kin you tell wether Ive a soul or not? You never seen it.

BARBARA   Ive seen it hurting you when you went against it.

BILL [*With compressed aggravation.*]   If you was my girl and took the word out o me mahth lawk thet, I'd give you suthink youd feel urtin, so I would. [*To* ADOLPHUS.] You take my tip, mate. Stop er jawr; or youll die afore your time. [*With intense expression.*] Wore aht: thets wot youll be: wore aht. [*He goes away through the gate.*]

CUSINS [*Looking after him.*]   I wonder!

BARBARA   Dolly! [*Indignant, in her mother's manner.*]

CUSINS   Yes, my dear, it's very wearing to be in love with you. If it lasts, I quite think I shall die young.

BARBARA   Should you mind?

CUSINS   Not at all. [*He is suddenly softened, and kisses her over the drum, evidently not for the first time, as people cannot kiss over a big drum without practice.* UNDERSHAFT *coughs.*]

BARBARA   It's all right, papa, weve not forgotten you. Dolly: explain the place to papa: I havnt time. [*She goes busily into the shelter.*]

[UNDERSHAFT *and* ADOLPHUS *now have the yard to themselves.* UNDERSHAFT, *seated on a form, and still keenly attentive, looks hard at* ADOLPHUS. ADOLPHUS *looks hard at him.*]

UNDERSHAFT   I fancy you guess something of what is in my mind, Mr Cusins. [CUSINS *flourishes his drumsticks as if in the act of beating a lively rataplan, but makes no sound.*] Exactly so. But suppose Barbara finds you out!

CUSINS   You know, I do not admit that I am imposing on Barbara. I am quite genuinely interested in the views of the Salvation Army. The fact is, I am a sort of collector of religions; and the curious thing is that I find I can believe them all. By the way, have you any religion?

UNDERSHAFT   Yes.

CUSINS   Anything out of the common?

UNDERSHAFT   Only that there are two things necessary to Salvation.

CUSINS [*Disappointed, but polite.*]   Ah, the Church Catechism. Charles Lomax also belongs to the Established Church.

UNDERSHAFT   The two things are—

CUSINS   Baptism and—

UNDERSHAFT   No. Money and gunpowder.

CUSINS [*Surprised, but interested.*]   That is the general opinion of our governing classes. The novelty is in hearing any man confess it.

UNDERSHAFT   Just so.

CUSINS   Excuse me: is there any place in your religion for honor, justice, truth, love, mercy and so forth?

UNDERSHAFT   Yes: they are the graces and luxuries of a rich, strong, and safe life.

CUSINS   Suppose one is forced to choose between them and money or gunpowder?

UNDERSHAFT   Choose money and gunpowder; for without enough of both you cannot afford the others.

CUSINS   That is your religion?

UNDERSHAFT   Yes.

[*The cadence of this reply makes a full close in the conversation.* CUSINS *twists his face dubiously and contemplates* UNDER-SHAFT. UNDERSHAFT *contemplates him.*]

CUSINS   Barbara wont stand that. You will have to choose between your religion and Barbara.

UNDERSHAFT   So will you, my friend. She will find out that that drum of yours is hollow.

CUSINS   Father Undershaft: you are mistaken: I am a sincere Salvationist. You do not understand the Salvation Army. It is the army of joy, of love, of courage: it has banished the fear and remorse and despair of the old hell-ridden evangelical sects: it marches to fight the devil with trumpet and drum, with music and dancing, with banner and palm, as becomes a sally from heaven by its happy garrison. It picks the waster out of the public house and makes a man of him: it finds a worm wriggling in a back kitchen, and lo! a woman! Men and women of rank too, sons and daughters of the Highest. It takes the poor professor of Greek, the most artificial and self-suppressed of human creatures, from his meal of roots, and lets loose the rhapsodist in him; reveals the true worship of Dionysos to him; sends him down the public street drumming dithyrambs. [*He plays a thundering flourish on the drum.*][4]

UNDERSHAFT   You will alarm the shelter.

CUSINS   Oh, they are accustomed to these sudden ecstasies of piety. However, if the drum worries you— [*He pockets the drumsticks; unhooks the drum; and stands it on the ground opposite the gateway.*]

UNDERSHAFT   Thank you.

CUSINS   You remember what Euripides says about your money and gunpowder?

UNDERSHAFT   No.

CUSINS [*Declaiming.*]

> One and another
> In money and guns may outpass his brother;
> And men in their millions float and flow

4. See the essay by Margery Morgan, pp. 478–502.

> And seethe with a million hopes as leaven;
> And they win their will; or they miss their will;
> And their hopes are dead or are pined for still;
> > But whoe'er can know
> > As the long days go
> That to live is happy, has found his heaven.

My translation: what do you think of it?

UNDERSHAFT   I think, my friend, that if you wish to know, as the long days go, that to live is happy, you must first acquire money enough for a decent life, and power enough to be your own master.

CUSINS   You are damnably discouraging. [*He resumes his declamation.*]

> > Is it so hard a thing to see
> > That the spirit of God—whate'er it be—
> The Law that abides and changes not, ages long,
> The Eternal and Nature-born: *these* things be strong?
> What else is Wisdom? What of Man's endeavor,
> Or God's high grace so lovely and so great?
> To stand from fear set free? to breathe and wait?
> To hold a hand uplifted over Fate?
> And shall not Barbara be loved for ever?

UNDERSHAFT   Euripides mentions Barbara, does he?

CUSINS   It is a fair translation. The word means Loveliness.

UNDERSHAFT   May I ask—as Barbara's father—how much a year she is to be loved for ever on?

CUSINS   As Barbara's father, that is more your affair than mine. I can feed her by teaching Greek: that is about all.

UNDERSHAFT   Do you consider it a good match for her?

CUSINS [*With polite obstinacy.*]   Mr Undershaft: I am in many ways a weak, timid, ineffectual person; and my health is far from satisfactory. But whenever I feel that I must have anything, I get it, sooner or later. I feel that way about Barbara. I don't like marriage: I feel intensely afraid of it; and I don't know what I shall do with Barbara or what she will do with me. But I feel that I and nobody else must marry her. Please regard that as settled.—Not that I wish to be arbitrary; but why should I waste your time in discussing what is inevitable?

UNDERSHAFT   You mean that you will stick at nothing: not even the conversion of the Salvation Army to the worship of Dionysos.

CUSINS   The business of the Salvation Army is to save, not to wrangle about the name of the pathfinder. Dionysos or another: what does it matter?

UNDERSHAFT [*Rising and approaching him.*]   Professor Cusins: you are a young man after my own heart.

CUSINS   Mr Undershaft: you are, as far as I am able to gather, a most infernal old rascal; but you appeal very strongly to my sense of ironic humor.

[UNDERSHAFT *mutely offers his hand. They shake.*]

UNDERSHAFT [*Suddenly concentrating himself.*]   And now to business.

CUSINS   Pardon me. We were discussing religion. Why go back to such an uninteresting and unimportant subject as business?

UNDERSHAFT   Religion is our business at present, because it is through religion alone that we can win Barbara.

CUSINS   Have you, too, fallen in love with Barbara?

UNDERSHAFT   Yes, with a father's love.

CUSINS   A father's love for a grown-up daughter is the most dangerous of all infatuations. I apologize for mentioning my own pale, coy, mistrustful fancy in the same breath with it.

UNDERSHAFT   Keep to the point. We have to win her; and we are neither of us Methodists.

CUSINS   That doesnt matter. The power Barbara wields here—the power that wields Barbara herself—is not Calvinism, not Presbyterianism, not Methodism—

UNDERSHAFT   Not Greek Paganism either, eh?

CUSINS   I admit that. Barbara is quite original in her religion.

UNDERSHAFT [*Triumphantly.*]   Aha! Barbara Undershaft would be. Her inspiration comes from within herself.

CUSINS   How do you suppose it got there?

UNDERSHAFT [*In towering excitement.*]   It is the Undershaft inheritance. I shall hand on my torch to my daughter. She shall make my converts and preach my gospel—

CUSINS   What! Money and gunpowder!

UNDERSHAFT   Yes, money and gunpowder; freedom and power; command of life and command of death.

CUSINS [*Urbanely: trying to bring him down to earth.*]   This is extremely interesting, Mr Undershaft. Of course you know that you are mad.

UNDERSHAFT [*With redoubled force.*]   And you?

CUSINS   Oh, mad as a hatter. You are welcome to my secret since I have discovered yours. But I am astonished. Can a madman make cannons?

UNDERSHAFT   Would anyone else than a madman make them? And now [*with surging energy*] question for question. Can a sane man translate Euripides?

CUSINS   No.

UNDERSHAFT [*Seizing him by the shoulder.*]   Can a sane woman make a man of a waster or a woman of a worm?

CUSINS [*Reeling before the storm.*]   Father Colossus—Mammoth Millionaire—

UNDERSHAFT [*Pressing him.*]   Are there two mad people or three in this Salvation shelter to-day?

CUSINS   You mean Barbara is as mad as we are!

UNDERSHAFT [*Pushing him lightly off and resuming his equanimity suddenly and completely.*]   Pooh, Professor! let us call things by their proper names. I am a millionaire; you are a poet; Barbara is a savior of souls. What have we three to do with the common mob of slaves and idolaters? [*He sits down again with a shrug of contempt for the mob.*]

CUSINS   Take care! Barbara is in love with the common people. So am I. Have you never felt the romance of that love?

UNDERSHAFT [*Cold and sardonic.*]   Have you ever been in love with Poverty, like St. Francis? Have you ever been in love with Dirt, like St Simeon? Have you ever been in love with disease and suffering, like our nurses and philanthropists? Such passions are not virtues, but the most unnatural of all the vices. This love of the common people may please an earl's granddaughter and a university professor; but I have been a common man and a poor man; and it has no romance for me. Leave it to the poor to pretend that poverty is a blessing: leave it to the coward to make a religion of his cowardice by preaching humility: we know better than that. We three must stand together above the common people: how else can we help their children to climb up beside us? Barbara must belong to us, not to the Salvation Army.

CUSINS   Well, I can only say that if you think you will get her away from the Salvation Army by talking to her as you have been talking to me, you dont know Barbara.

UNDERSHAFT   My friend: I never ask for what I can buy.

CUSINS [*In a white fury.*]   Do I understand you to imply that you can buy Barbara?

UNDERSHAFT   No; but I can buy the Salvation Army.

CUSINS   Quite impossible.

UNDERSHAFT   You shall see. All religious organizations exist by selling themselves to the rich.

CUSINS   Not the Army. That is the Church of the poor.

UNDERSHAFT   All the more reason for buying it.

CUSINS   I dont think you quite know what the Army does for the poor.

UNDERSHAFT   Oh yes I do. It draws their teeth: that is enough for me—as a man of business—

CUSINS   Nonsense! It makes them sober—

UNDERSHAFT   I prefer sober workmen. The profits are larger.

CUSINS   —honest—

UNDERSHAFT   Honest workmen are the most economical.

CUSINS   —attached to their homes—

UNDERSHAFT   So much the better: they will put up with anything sooner than change their shop.

CUSINS   —happy—

UNDERSHAFT   An invaluable safeguard against revolution.

CUSINS   —unselfish—

UNDERSHAFT   Indifferent to their own interests, which suits me exactly.

CUSINS   —with their thoughts on heavenly things—

UNDERSHAFT [*Rising.*]   And not on Trade Unionism nor Socialism. Excellent.

CUSINS [*Revolted.*]   You really are an infernal old rascal.

UNDERSHAFT [*Indicating* PETER SHIRLEY, *who has just come from the shelter and strolled dejectedly down the yard between them.*]   And this is an honest man!

SHIRLEY   Yes; and what av I got by it? [*He passes on bitterly and sits on the form, in the corner of the penthouse.*]

   [SNOBBY PRICE, *beaming sanctimoniously, and* JENNY HILL, with a tambourine full of coppers, come from the shelter and go to the drum, on which JENNY begins to count the money.]

UNDERSHAFT [*Replying to* SHIRLEY.]   Oh, your employers must have got a good deal by it from first to last.

   [*He sits on the table, with one foot on the side form.* CUSINS, *overwhelmed, sits down on the same form nearer the shelter.* BARBARA *comes from the shelter to the middle of the yard. She is excited and a little overwrought.*]

BARBARA   Weve just had a splendid experience meeting at the other gate in Cripps's lane. Ive hardly ever seen them so much moved as they were by your confession, Mr Price.

PRICE   I could almost be glad of my past wickedness if I could believe that it would elp to keep hathers stright.

BARBARA   So it will, Snobby. How much, Jenny?

JENNY   Four and tenpence, Major.[5]

BARBARA   Oh Snobby, if you had given your poor mother just one more kick, we should have got the whole five shillings!

PRICE   If she heard you say that, miss, she'd be sorry I didnt. But I'm glad. Oh what a joy it will be to her when she hears I'm saved!

UNDERSHAFT   Shall I contribute the odd twopence, Barbara? The millionaire's mite, eh? [*He takes a couple of pennies from his pocket.*]

BARBARA   How did you make that twopence?

UNDERSHAFT   As usual. By selling cannons, torpedoes, submarines, and my new patent Grand Duke hand grenade.

BARBARA   Put it back in your pocket. You cant buy your Salvation here for twopence: you must work it out.

UNDERSHAFT   Is twopence not enough? I can afford a little more, if you press me.

BARBARA   Two million millions would not be enough. There is bad

5. Four shillings and ten pence, worth less than 50c.

blood on your hands; and nothing but good blood can cleanse them. Money is no use. Take it away. [*She turns to* CUSINS.] Dolly: you must write another letter for me to the papers. [*He makes a wry face.*] Yes: I know you dont like it; but it must be done. The starvation this winter is beating us: everybody is unemployed. The General says we must close this shelter if we cant get more money. I force the collections at the meetings until I am ashamed: dont I, Snobby?

PRICE   It's a fair treat to see you work it, miss. The way you got them up from three-and-six to four-and-ten with that hymn, penny by penny and verse by verse, was a caution. Not a Cheap Jack on Mile End Waste[6] could touch you at it.

BARBARA   Yes; but I wish we could do without it. I am getting at last to think more of the collection than of the people's souls. And what are those hatfuls of pence and halfpence? We want thousands! tens of thousands! hundreds of thousands! I want to convert people, not to be always begging for the Army in a way I'd die sooner than beg for myself.

UNDERSHAFT [*In profound irony.*]   Genuine unselfishness is capable of anything, my dear.

BARBARA [*Unsuspectingly, as she turns away to take the money from the drum and put it in a cash bag she carries.*]   Yes, isnt it? [UNDER-SHAFT *looks sardonically at* CUSINS.]

CUSINS [*Aside to* UNDERSHAFT.]   Mephistopheles! Machiavelli!

BARBARA [*Tears coming into her eyes as she ties the bag and pockets it.*]   How are we to feed them? I cant talk religion to a man with bodily hunger in his eyes. [*Almost breaking down.*] It's frightful.

JENNY [*Running to her.*]   Major, dear—

BARBARA [*Rebounding.*]   No: dont comfort me. It will be all right. We shall get the money.

UNDERSHAFT   How?

JENNY   By praying for it, of course. Mrs Baines says she prayed for it last night; and she has never prayed for it in vain: never once. [*She goes to the gate and looks out into the street.*]

BARBARA [*Who has dried her eyes and regained her composure.*]   By the way, dad, Mrs Baines has come to march with us to our big meeting this afternoon; and she is very anxious to meet you, for some reason or other. Perhaps she'll convert you.

UNDERSHAFT   I shall be delighted, my dear.

JENNY [*At the gate: excitedly.*]   Major! Major! heres that man back again.

BARBARA   What man?

JENNY   The man that hit me. Oh, I hope hes coming back to join us.

[BILL WALKER, *with frost on his jacket, comes through the gate,*

---

6. A peddler of the bargaining kind, at a familiar spot for gatherings and fairs.

his hands deep in his pockets and his chin sunk between his shoulders, like a cleaned-out gambler. He halts between BARBARA *and the drum.*]

BARBARA   Hullo, Bill! Back already!

BILL [*Nagging at her.*]   Bin talkin ever sence, av you?

BARBARA   Pretty nearly. Well, has Todger paid you out for poor Jenny's jaw?

BILL   No he aint.

BARBARA   I thought your jacket looked a bit snowy.

BILL   So it is snowy. You want to know where the snow come from, dont you?

BARBARA   Yes.

BILL   Well, it come from off the ground in Parkinses Corner in Kennintahn. It got rubbed off be my shoulders: see?

BARBARA   Pity you didnt rub some off with your knees, Bill! That would have done you a lot of good.

BILL [*With sour mirthless humor.*]   I was saving another man's knees at the time. E was kneelin on my ed, so e was.

JENNY   Who was kneeling on your head?

BILL   Todger was. E was prayin for me: prayin comfortable with me as a carpet. So was Mog. So was the ole bloomin meetin. Mog she sez "O Lord break is stubborn spirit; but dont urt is dear art." That was wot she said. "Dont urt is dear art"! An er bloke—thirteen stun four!—kneelin wiv all is weight on me. Funny, aint it?

JENNY   Oh no. We're so sorry, Mr Walker.

BARBARA [*Enjoying it frankly.*]   Nonsense! of course it's funny. Served you right, Bill! You must have done something to him first.

BILL [*Doggedly.*]   I did wot I said I'd do. I spit in is eye. E looks up at the sky and sez, "O that I should be fahnd worthy to be spit upon for the gospel's sake!" e sez; an Mog sez "Glory Allelloolier!"; an then e called me Brother, an dahned me as if I was a kid and e was me mother washin me a Setterda nawt. I adnt just no show wiv im at all. Arf the street prayed; an the tother arf larfed fit to split theirselves. [*To* BARBARA.] There! are you settisfawd nah?

BARBARA [*Her eyes dancing.*]   Wish I'd been there, Bill.

BILL   Yes: youd a got in a hextra bit o talk on me, wouldn't you?

JENNY   I'm so sorry, Mr Walker.

BILL [*Fiercely.*]   Dont you go bein sorry for me: youve no call. Listen ere. I broke your jawr.

JENNY   No, it didnt hurt me: indeed it didnt, except for a moment. It was only that I was frightened.

BILL   I dont want to be forgive be you, or be ennybody. Wot I did I'll pay for. I tried to get me own jawr broke to settisfaw you—

JENNY [*Distressed.*]   Oh no—

BILL [*Impatiently.*]   Tell y'I did: cawnt you listen to wots bein told you? All I got be it was bein made a sight of in the public street for me pains. Well, if I cawnt settisfaw you one way, I can another.

Listen ere! I ad two quid[7] saved agen the frost; an Ive a pahnd of
it left. A mate o mine last week ad words with the judy e's goin to
marry. E give er wot-for; an e's bin fined fifteen bob. E ad a right
to it er because they was goin to be marrid; but I adnt no right to
it you; so put anather fawv bob on an call it a pahnd's worth. [*He
produces a sovereign.*] Eres the money. Take it; and lets av no more
o your forgivin an prayin and your Major jawrin me. Let wot I done
be done and paid for; and let there be a end of it.

JENNY   Oh, I couldn't take it, Mr Walker. But if you would give a
shilling or two to poor Rummy Mitchens! you really did hurt her;
and shes old.

BILL [*Contemptuously.*]   Not likely. I'd give her anather as soon as
look at er. Let her av the lawr o me as she threatened! She aint
forgiven me: not mach. Wot I done to er is not on me mawnd—
wot she [*indicating* BARBARA] might call on me conscience—no
more than stickin a pig. It's this Christian game o yours that I
wont av played agen me: this bloomin forgivin an naggin an jawrin
that makes a man that sore that iz lawf's a burdn to im. I wont av
it, I tell you; so take your money and stop throwin your silly bashed
face hup agen me.

JENNY   Major: may I take a little of it for the Army?

BARBARA   No: the Army is not to be bought. We want your soul,
Bill; and we'll take nothing less.

BILL [*Bitterly.*]   I know. It aint enough. Me an me few shillins is not
good enough for you. Youre a earl's grendorter, you are. Nothin
less than a underd pahnd for you.

UNDERSHAFT   Come, Barbara! you could do a great deal of good
with a hundred pounds. If you will set this gentleman's mind at
ease by taking his pound, I will give the other ninety-nine. [BILL,
astounded by such opulence, instinctively touches his cap.]

BARBARA   Oh, youre too extravagant, papa. Bill offers twenty pieces
of silver. All you need offer is the other ten.[8] That will make the
standard price to buy anybody who's for sale. I'm not; and the
Army's not. [*To* BILL.] Youll never have another quiet moment,
Bill, until you come round to us. You cant stand out against your
salvation.

BILL [*Sullenly.*]   I cawnt stend aht agen music all wrastlers and artful tongued women. Ive offered to pay. I can do no more. Take it
or leave it. There it is. [*He throws the sovereign on the drum, and
sits down on the horse-trough. The coin fascinates* SNOBBY PRICE,
who takes an early opportunity of dropping his cap on it.]

[MRS BAINES *comes from the shelter. She is dressed as a Salvation Army Commissioner. She is an earnest looking woman*

---

7. "Quid" is slang for a pound; "bob" is a shilling, or 1/20 of a pound; a sovereign is a gold
coin worth a pound.
8. Bill's sovereign is twenty silver shillings; thirty "pieces of silver" was Judas's reward for
betraying Jesus.

*of about 40, with a caressing, urgent voice, and an appealing
manner.*]

BARBARA   This is my father, Mrs Baines. [UNDERSHAFT *comes from
the table, taking his hat off with marked civility.*] Try what you can
do with him. He wont listen to me, because he remembers what
a fool I was when I was a baby. [*She leaves them together and chats
with* JENNY.]

MRS BAINES   Have you been shewn over the shelter, Mr Undershaft? You know the work we're doing, of course.

UNDERSHAFT [*Very civilly.*]   The whole nation knows it, Mrs Baines.

MRS BAINES   No, sir: the whole nation does not know it, or we
should not be crippled as we are for want of money to carry our
work through the length and breadth of the land. Let me tell you
that there would have been rioting this winter in London but for
us.

UNDERSHAFT   You really think so?

MRS BAINES   I know it. I remember 1886, when you rich gentlemen
hardened your hearts against the cry of the poor. They broke the
windows of your clubs in Pall Mall.

UNDERSHAFT [*Gleaming with approval of their method.*]   And the
Mansion House Fund went up next day from thirty thousand
pounds to seventy-nine thousand! I remember quite well.

MRS BAINES   Well, wont you help me to get at the people? They
wont break windows then. Come here, Price. Let me shew you to
this gentleman. [PRICE *comes to be inspected.*] Do you remember
the window breaking?

PRICE   My ole father thought it was the revolution, maam.

MRS BAINES   Would you break windows now?

PRICE   Oh no maam. The windows of eaven av bin opened to me. I
know now that the rich man is a sinner like myself.

RUMMY [*Appearing above at the loft door.*]   Snobby Price!

SNOBBY   Wot is it?

RUMMY   Your mother's askin for you at the other gate in Crippses
Lane. She's heard about your confession. [PRICE *turns pale.*]

MRS BAINES   Go, Mr Price; and pray with her.

JENNY   You can go through the shelter, Snobby.

PRICE [*To* MRS BAINES.]   I couldnt face her now, maam, with all the
weight of my sins fresh on me. Tell her she'll find her son at ome,
waitin for her in prayer. [*He skulks off through the gate, incidentally
stealing the sovereign on his way out by picking up his cap from the
drum.*]

MRS BAINES [*With swimming eyes.*]   You see how we take the anger
and the bitterness against you out of their hearts, Mr Undershaft.

UNDERSHAFT   It is certainly most convenient and gratifying to all
large employers of labor, Mrs Baines.

MRS BAINES   Barbara: Jenny: I have good news: most wonderful news. [JENNY *runs to her*.] My prayers have been answered. I told you they would, Jenny, didnt I?

JENNY   Yes, yes.

BARBARA [*Moving nearer to the drum*.]   Have we got money enough to keep the shelter open?

MRS BAINES   I hope we shall have enough to keep all the shelters open. Lord Saxmundham has promised us five thousand pounds—[9]

BARBARA   Hooray!

JENNY   Glory!

MRS BAINES   —if—

BARBARA   "If!" If what?

MRS BAINES   —if five other gentlemen will give a thousand each to make it up to ten thousand.

BARBARA   Who is Lord Saxmundham? I never heard of him.

UNDERSHAFT [*Who has pricked up his ears at the peer's name, and is now watching* BARBARA *curiously*.]   A new creation, my dear. You have heard of Sir Horace Bodger?

BARBARA   Bodger! Do you mean the distiller? Bodger's whisky!

UNDERSHAFT   That is the man. He is one of the greatest of our public benefactors. He restored the cathedral at Hakington. They made him a baronet for that. He gave half a million to the funds of his party: they made him a baron for that.

SHIRLEY   What will they give him for the five thousand?

UNDERSHAFT   There is nothing left to give him. So the five thousand, I should think, is to save his soul.

MRS BAINES   Heaven grant it may! Oh Mr Undershaft, you have some very rich friends. Cant you help us towards the other five thousand? We are going to hold a great meeting this afternoon at the Assembly Hall in the Mile End Road. If I could only announce that one gentleman had come forward to support Lord Saxmundham, others would follow. Dont you know somebody? couldnt you? wouldnt you? [*Her eyes fill with tears*.] oh, think of those poor people, Mr Undershaft: think of how much it means to them, and how little to a great man like you.

UNDERSHAFT [*Sardonically gallant*.]   Mrs Baines: you are irresistible. I cant disappoint you; and I cant deny myself the satisfaction of making Bodger pay up. You shall have your five thousand pounds.

MRS BAINES   Thank God!

UNDERSHAFT   You dont thank me?

MRS BAINES   Oh sir, dont try to be cynical: dont be ashamed of being a good man. The Lord will bless you abundantly; and our prayers will be like a strong fortification round you all the days of your life.

9. Approximately $7,500.

[*With a touch of caution.*] You will let me have the cheque to shew at the meeting, wont you? Jenny: go in and fetch a pen and ink. [JENNY *runs to the shelter door.*]

UNDERSHAFT   Do not disturb Miss Hill: I have a fountain pen. [JENNY *halts. He sits at the table and writes the cheque.* CUSINS *rises to make more room for him. They all watch him silently.*]

BILL   [*Cynically, aside to* BARBARA, *his voice and accent horribly debased.*]   Wot prawce Selvytion nah?

BARBARA   Stop. [UNDERSHAFT *stops writing: they all turn to her in surprise.*] Mrs Baines: are you really going to take this money?

MRS BAINES   [*Astonished.*]   Why not, dear?

BARBARA   Why not! Do you know what my father is? Have you forgotten that Lord Saxmundham is Bodger the whisky man? Do you remember how we implored the County Council to stop him from writing Bodger's Whisky in letters of fire against the sky; so that the poor drinkruined creatures on the embankment could not wake up from their snatches of sleep without being reminded of their deadly thirst by that wicked sky sign? Do you know that the worst thing I have had to fight here is not the devil, but Bodger, Bodger, Bodger, with his whisky, his distilleries, and his tied houses?[1] Are you going to make our shelter another tied house for him, and ask me to keep it?

BILL   Rotten drunken whisky it is too.

MRS BAINES   Dear Barbara: Lord Saxmundham has a soul to be saved like any of us. If heaven has found the way to make a good use of his money, are we to set ourselves up against the answer to our prayers?

BARBARA   I know he has a soul to be saved. Let him come down here; and I'll do my best to help him to his salvation. But he wants to send his cheque down to buy us, and go on being as wicked as ever.

UNDERSHAFT   [*With a reasonableness which* CUSINS *alone perceives to be ironical.*]   My dear Barbara: alcohol is a very necessary article. It heals the sick—

BARBARA   It does nothing of the sort.

UNDERSHAFT   Well, it assists the doctor: that is perhaps a less questionable way of putting it. It makes life bearable to millions of people who could not endure their existence if they were quite sober. It enables Parliament to do things at eleven at night that no sane person would do at eleven in the morning. Is it Bodger's fault that this inestimable gift is deplorably abused by less than one per cent of the poor? [*He turns again to the table; signs the cheque; and crosses it.*]

MRS BAINES   Barbara: will there be less drinking or more if all those poor souls we are saving come to-morrow and find the doors of

---

1. Taverns owned by brewing firms which required the manager to handle only their whisky.

our shelters shut in their faces? Lord Saxmundham gives us the
money to stop drinking—to take his own business from him.

CUSINS [*Impishly.*]   Pure self-sacrifice on Bodger's part, clearly!
Bless dear Bodger! [BARBARA *almost breaks down as* ADOLPHUS, *too,
fails her.*]

UNDERSHAFT [*Tearing out the cheque and pocketing the book as he
rises and goes past* CUSINS *to* MRS BAINES.]   I also, Mrs Baines,
may claim a little disinterestedness. Think of my business! think
of the windows and orphans! the men and lads torn to pieces with
shrapnel and poisoned with lyddite![2] [MRS BAINES *shrinks; but he
goes on remorselessly.*] the oceans of blood, not one drop of which
is shed in a really just cause! the ravaged crops! the peaceful peasants forced, women and men, to till their fields under the fire of
opposing armies on pain of starvation! the bad blood of the fierce
little cowards at home who egg on others to fight for the gratification of their national vanity! All this makes money for me: I am
never richer, never busier than when the papers are full of it. Well,
it is your work to preach peace on earth and goodwill to men. [MRS
BAINES'*s face lights up again.*] Every convert you make is a vote
against war. [*Her lips move in prayer.*] Yet I give you this money
to help you to hasten my own commercial ruin. [*He gives her the
cheque.*]

CUSINS [*Mounting the form in an ecstasy of mischief.*]   The millen-
nium will be inaugurated by the unselfishness of Undershaft and
Bodger. Oh be joyful! [*He takes the drumsticks from his pockets and
flourishes them.*]

MRS BAINES [*Taking the cheque.*]   The longer I live the more proof
I see that there is an Infinite Goodness that turns everything to
the work of salvation sooner or later. Who would have thought
that any good could have come out of war and drink? And yet their
profits are brought today to the feet of salvation to do its blessed
work. [*She is affected to tears.*]

JENNY [*Running to* MRS BAINES *and throwing her arms round
her.*]   Oh dear! how blessed, how glorious it all is!

CUSINS [*In a convulsion of irony.*]   Let us seize this unspeakable
moment. Let us march to the great meeting at once. Excuse me
just an instant. [*He rushes into the shelter.* JENNY *takes her tambourine from the drum head.*]

MRS BAINES   Mr Undershaft: have you ever seen a thousand people
fall on their knees with one impulse and pray? Come with us to
the meeting. Barbara shall tell them that the Army is saved, and
saved through you.

CUSINS [*Returning impetuously from the shelter with a flag and a
trombone, and coming between* MRS BAINES *and* UNDER-
SHAFT.]   You shall carry the flag down the first street, Mrs Baines.

---

2. An explosive.

[*He gives her the flag.*] Mr Undershaft is a gifted trombonist: he shall intone an Olympian diapason to the West Ham Salvation March. [*Aside to* UNDERSHAFT, *as he forces the trombone on him.*] Blow, Machiavelli, blow.

UNDERSHAFT [*Aside to him, as he takes the trombone.*]   The trumpet in Zion! [CUSINS *rushes to the drum, which he takes up and puts on.* UNDERSHAFT *continues, aloud.*] I will do my best. I could vamp a bass if I knew the tune.

CUSINS   It is a wedding chorus from one of Donizetti's operas; but we have converted it. We convert everything to good here, including Bodger. You remember the chorus. "For thee immense rejoicing—immenso giubilo—immenso giubilo." [*With drum obbligato.*] Rum tum ti tum tum, tum tum ti ta—

BARBARA   Dolly: you are breaking my heart.

CUSINS   What is a broken heart more or less here? Dionysos Undershaft has descended. I am possessed.

MRS BAINES   Come, Barbara: I must have my dear Major to carry the flag with me.

JENNY   Yes, yes, Major darling.

CUSINS [*Snatches the tambourine out of* JENNY's *hand and mutely offers it to* BARBARA.]

BARBARA [*Coming forward a little as she puts the offer behind her with a shudder, whilst* CUSINS *recklessly tosses the tambourine back to* JENNY *and goes to the gate.*]   I cant come.

JENNY   Not come!

MRS BAINES [*With tears in her eyes.*]   Barbara: do you think I am wrong to take the money?

BARBARA [*Impulsively going to her and kissing her.*]   No, no: God help you, dear, you must: you are saving the Army. Go; and may you have a great meeting!

JENNY   But arnt you coming?

BARBARA   No. [*She begins taking off the silver* S *brooch from her collar.*]

MRS BAINES   Barbara: what are you doing?

JENNY   Why are you taking your badge off? You cant be going to leave us, Major.

BARBARA [*Quietly.*]   Father: come here.

UNDERSHAFT [*Coming to her.*]   My dear! [*Seeing that she is going to pin the badge on his collar, he retreats to the penthouse in some alarm.*]

BARBARA [*Following him.*]   Dont be frightened. [*She pins the badge on and steps back towards the table, shewing him to the others.*] There! It's not much for £5000, is it?

MRS BAINES   Barbara: if you wont come and pray with us, promise me you will pray for us.

BARBARA   I cant pray now. Perhaps I shall never pray again.

MRS BAINES   Barbara!

JENNY   Major!

BARBARA [*Almost delirious.*]   I cant bear any more. Quick march!

CUSINS [*Calling to the procession in the street outside.*]   Off we go.
Play up, there! Immenso giubilo. [*He gives the time with his
drum; and the band strikes up the march, which rapidly becomes
more distant as the procession moves briskly away.*]

MRS BAINES   I must go, dear. Youre overworked: you will be all right
tomorrow. We'll never lose you. Now Jenny: step out with the old
flag. Blood and Fire! [*She marches out through the gate with her
flag.*]

JENNY   Glory Hallelujah! [*Flourishing her tambourine and marching.*]

UNDERSHAFT [*To* CUSINS, *as he marches out past him easing the slide
of his trombone.*]   "My ducats and my daughter"![3]

CUSINS [*Following him out.*]   Money and gunpowder!

BARBARA   Drunkenness and Murder! My God: why hast thou forsaken me?

[*She sinks on the form with her face buried in her hands. The
march passes away into silence.* BILL WALKER *steals across to
her.*]

BILL [*Taunting.*]   Wot prawce Selvytion nah?

SHIRLEY   Dont you hit her when shes down.

BILL   She it me wen aw wiz dahn. Waw shouldnt I git a bit o me
own back?

BARBARA [*Raising her head.*]   I didnt take your money, Bill. [*She
crosses the yard to the gate and turns her back on the two men to
hide her face from them.*]

BILL [*Sneering after her.*]   Naow, it warnt enough for you. [*Turning
to the drum, he misses the money.*] Ellow! If you aint took it summun else az. Weres it gorn? Blame me if Jenny Ill didnt take it
arter all!

RUMMY [*Screaming at him from the loft.*]   You lie, you dirty blackguard! Snobby Price pinched it off the drum wen e took ap iz cap.
I was ap ere all the time an see im do it.

BILL   Wot! Stowl maw money! Waw didnt you call thief on him, you
silly old mucker you?

RUMMY   To serve you aht for ittin me acrost the fice. It's cost
y'pahnd, that az. [*Raising a pæan of squalid triumph.*] I done you.
I'm even with you. Ive ad it aht o y— [*Bill snatches up Shirley's
mug and hurls it at her. She slams the loft door and vanishes. The
mug smashes against the door and falls in fragments.*]

BILL [*Beginning to chuckle.*]   Tell us, ole man, wot o'clock this mornin was it wen im as they call Snobby Prawce was sived?

BARBARA [*Turning to him more composedly, and with unspoiled sweetness.*]   About half past twelve, Bill. And he pinched your pound

3. Shakespeare, *The Merchant of Venice* 2.8.15.

at a quarter to two. *I* know. Well, you cant afford to lose it. I'll
send it to you.

BILL [*His voice and accent suddenly improving.*] Not if I was to
starve for it. *I* aint to be bought.

SHIRLEY Aint you? Youd sell yourself to the devil for a pint o beer;
ony there aint no devil to make the offer.

BILL [*Unshamed.*] So I would, mate, and often av, cheerful. But
she cawnt buy me. [*Approaching* BARBARA.] You wanted my soul,
did you? Well, you aint got it.

BARBARA I nearly got it, Bill. But weve sold it back to you for ten
thousand pounds.

SHIRLEY And dear at the money!

BARBARA No, Peter: it was worth more than money.

BILL [*Salvationproof.*] It's no good: you cawnt get rahnd me nah. I
dont believe in it; and Ive seen today that I was right. [*Going.*] So
long, old soupkitchener! Ta, ta, Major Earl's Grendorter! [*Turning
at the gate.*] Wot prawce Selvytion nah? Snobby Prawce! Ha! ha!

BARBARA [*Offering her hand.*] Goodbye, Bill.

BILL [*Taken aback, half plucks his cap off: then shoves it on again
defiantly.*] Git aht. [BARBARA *drops her hand, discouraged. He has
a twinge of remorse.*] But thets aw rawt, you knaow. Nathink pasnl.
Naow mellice. So long, Judy. [*He goes.*]

BARBARA No malice. So long, Bill.

SHIRLEY [*Shaking his head.*] You make too much of him, miss, in
your innocence.

BARBARA [*Going to him.*] Peter: I'm like you now. Cleaned out, and
lost my job.

SHIRLEY Youve youth an hope. Thats two better than me.

BARBARA I'll get you a job, Peter. Thats hope for you: the youth will
have to be enough for me. [*She counts her money.*] I have just
enough left for two teas at Lockharts, a Rowton doss[4] for you, and
my tram and bus home. [*He frowns and rises with offended pride.
She takes his arm.*] Dont be proud, Peter: it's sharing between
friends. And promise me youll talk to me and not let me cry. [*She
draws him towards the gate.*]

SHIRLEY Well, I'm not accustomed to talk to the like of you—

BARBARA [*Urgently.*] Yes, yes: you must talk to me. Tell me about
Tom Paine's books and Bradlaugh's[5] lectures. Come along.

SHIRLEY Ah, if you would only read Tom Paine in the proper spirit,
miss! [*They go out through the gate together.*]

---

4. A bed in one of Rowton's cheap rooming houses.
5. A slight anachronism: Charles Bradlaugh, the great secularist, died in 1891.

Act III

Next day after lunch LADY BRITOMART *is writing in the
library in Wilton Crescent.* SARAH *is reading in the armchair near the window.* BARBARA, *in ordinary dress, pale
and brooding, is on the settee.* CHARLES LOMAX *enters.
Coming forward between the settee and the writing table,
he starts on seeing* BARBARA *fashionably attired and in low
spirits.*

LOMAX Youve left off your uniform!

    [BARBARA *says nothing; but an expression of pain passes over
her face.*]

LADY BRITOMART [*Warning him in low tones to be careful.*]   Charles!

LOMAX [*Much concerned, sitting down sympathetically on the settee
beside* BARBARA.]   I'm awfully sorry, Barbara. You know I helped
you all I could with the concertina and so forth. [*Momentously.*]
Still, I have never shut my eyes to the fact that there is a certain
amount of tosh about the Salvation Army. Now the claims of the
Church of England—

LADY BRITOMART Thats enough, Charles. Speak of something
suited to your mental capacity.

LOMAX But surely the Church of England is suited to all our capacities.

BARBARA [*Pressing his hand.*]   Thank you for your sympathy, Cholly.
Now go and spoon[1] with Sarah.

LOMAX [*Rising and going to* SARAH.]   How is my ownest today?

SARAH I wish you wouldnt tell Cholly to do things, Barbara. He
always comes straight and does them. Cholly: we're going to the
works at Perivale St. Andrews this afternoon.

LOMAX What works?

SARAH The cannon works.

LOMAX What! Your governor's shop!

SARAH Yes.

LOMAX Oh I say!

    [CUSINS *enters in poor condition. He also starts visibly when
he sees* BARBARA *without her uniform.*]

BARBARA I expected you this morning, Dolly. Didnt you guess that?

CUSINS [*Sitting down beside her.*]   I'm sorry. I have only just breakfasted.

SARAH But weve just finished lunch.

BARBARA Have you had one of your bad nights?

CUSINS No: I had rather a good night: in fact, one of the most
remarkable nights I have ever passed.

BARBARA The meeting?

---

1. Romance.

CUSINS   No: after the meeting.

LADY BRITOMART   You should have gone to bed after the meeting. What were you doing?

CUSINS   Drinking.

LADY BRITOMART	Adolphus!
SARAH	Dolly!
BARBARA	Dolly!
LOMAX	Oh I say!

LADY BRITOMART   What were you drinking, may I ask?

CUSINS   A most devilish kind of Spanish burgundy, warranted free from added alcohol: a Temperance burgundy in fact. Its richness in natural alcohol made any addition superfluous.

BARBARA   Are you joking, Dolly?

CUSINS [*Patiently.*]   No. I have been making a night of it with the nominal head of this household: that is all.

LADY BRITOMART   Andrew made you drunk!

CUSINS   No: he only provided the wine. I think it was Dionysos who made me drunk. [*To* BARBARA.] I told you I was possessed.

LADY BRITOMART   Youre not sober yet. Go home to bed at once.

CUSINS   I have never before ventured to reproach you, Lady Brit; but how could you marry the Prince of Darkness?

LADY BRITOMART   It was much more excusable to marry him than to get drunk with him. That is a new accomplishment of Andrew's, by the way. He usent to drink.

CUSINS   He doesnt now. He only sat there and completed the wreck of my moral basis, the rout of my convictions, the purchase of my soul. He cares for you, Barbara. That is what makes him so dangerous to me.

BARBARA   That has nothing to do with it, Dolly. There are larger loves and diviner dreams than the fireside ones. You know that, dont you?

CUSINS   Yes: that is our understanding. I know it. I hold to it. Unless he can win me on that holier ground he may amuse me for a while; but he can get no deeper hold, strong as he is.

BARBARA   Keep to that; and the end will be right. Now tell me what happened at the meeting?

CUSINS   It was an amazing meeting. Mrs Baines almost died of emotion. Jenny Hill went stark mad with hysteria. The Prince of Darkness played his trombone like a madman: its brazen roarings were like the laughter of the damned. 117 conversions took place then and there. They prayed with the most touching sincerity and gratitude for Bodger, and for the anonymous donor of the £5000. Your father would not let his name be given.

LOMAX   That was rather fine of the old man, you know. Most chaps would have wanted the advertisement.

CUSINS   He said all the charitable institutions would be down on him like kites on a battle field if he gave his name.

LADY BRITOMART   Thats Andrew all over. He never does a proper thing without giving an improper reason for it.

CUSINS   He convinced me that I have all my life been doing improper things for proper reasons.

LADY BRITOMART   Adolphus: now that Barbara has left the Salvation Army, you had better leave it too. I will not have you playing that drum in the streets.

CUSINS   Your orders are already obeyed, Lady Brit.

BARBARA   Dolly: were you ever really in earnest about it? Would you have joined if you had never seen me?

CUSINS [Disingenuously.]   Well—er—well, possibly, as a collector of religions—

LOMAX [Cunningly.]   Not as a drummer, though, you know. You are a very clearheaded brainy chap, Cholly; and it must have been apparent to you that there is a certain amount of tosh about—

LADY BRITOMART   Charles: if you must drivel, drivel like a grown-up man and not like a schoolboy.

LOMAX [Out of countenance.]   Well, drivel is drivel, dont you know, whatever a man's age.

LADY BRITOMART   In good society in England, Charles, men drivel at all ages by repeating silly formulas with an air of wisdom. Schoolboys make their own formulas out of slang, like you. When they reach your age, and get political private secretaryships and things of that sort, they drop slang and get their formulas out of The Spectator or The Times. You had better confine yourself to The Times. You will find that there is a certain amount of tosh about The Times; but at least its language is reputable.

LOMAX [Overwhelmed.]   You are so awfully strong-minded, Lady Brit—

LADY BRITOMART   Rubbish! [MORRISON comes in.] What is it?

MORRISON   If you please, my lady, Mr Undershaft has just drove up to the door.

LADY BRITOMART   Well, let him in. [MORRISON hesitates.] Whats the matter with you?

MORRISON   Shall I announce him, my lady; or is he at home here, so to speak, my lady?

LADY BRITOMART   Announce him.

MORRISON   Thank you, my lady. You wont mind my asking, I hope. The occasion is in a manner of speaking new to me.

LADY BRITOMART   Quite right. Go and let him in.

MORRISON   Thank you, my lady. [He withdraws.]

LADY BRITOMART   Children: go and get ready. [SARAH and BARBARA go upstairs for their out-of-door wraps.] Charles: go and tell Stephen to come down here in five minutes: you will find him in the drawing room. [CHARLES goes.] Adolphus: tell them to send round the carriage in about fifteen minutes. [ADOLPHUS goes.]

MORRISON [At the door.]   Mr Undershaft.

[UNDERSHAFT *comes in.* MORRISON *goes out.*]

UNDERSHAFT   Alone! How fortunate!

LADY BRITOMART [*Rising.*]   Dont be sentimental, Andrew. Sit down. [*She sits on the settee: he sits beside her, on her left. She comes to the point before he has time to breathe.*] Sarah must have £800 a year until Charles Lomax comes into his property. Barbara will need more, and need it permanently, because Adolphus hasnt any property.

UNDERSHAFT [*Resignedly.*]   Yes, my dear: I will see to it. Anything else? for yourself, for instance?

LADY BRITOMART   I want to talk to you about Stephen.

UNDERSHAFT [*Rather wearily.*]   Dont, my dear. Stephen doesnt interest me.

LADY BRITOMART   He does interest me. He is our son.

UNDERSHAFT   Do you really think so? He has induced us to bring him into the world; but he chose his parents very incongruously, I think. I see nothing of myself in him, and less of you.

LADY BRITOMART   Andrew: Stephen is an excellent son, and a most steady, capable, highminded young man. You are simply trying to find an excuse for disinheriting him.

UNDERSHAFT   My dear Biddy: the Undershaft tradition disinherits him. It would be dishonest of me to leave the cannon foundry to my son.

LADY BRITOMART   It would be most unnatural and improper of you to leave it to anyone else, Andrew. Do you suppose this wicked and immoral tradition can be kept up for ever? Do you pretend that Stephen could not carry on the foundry just as well as all the other sons of the big business houses?

UNDERSHAFT   Yes: he could learn the office routine without understanding the business, like all the other sons; and the firm would go on by its own momentum until the real Undershaft—probably an Italian or a German—would invent a new method and cut him out.

LADY BRITOMART   There is nothing that any Italian or German could do that Stephen could not do. And Stephen at least has breeding.

UNDERSHAFT   The son of a foundling! nonsense!

LADY BRITOMART   My son, Andrew! And even you may have good blood in your veins for all you know.

UNDERSHAFT   True. Probably I have. That is another argument in favor of a foundling.

LADY BRITOMART   Andrew: dont be aggravating. And dont be wicked. At present you are both.

UNDERSHAFT   This conversation is part of the Undershaft tradition, Biddy. Every Undershaft's wife has treated him to it ever since the house was founded. It is mere waste of breath. If the tradition be ever broken it will be for an abler man than Stephen.

LADY BRITOMART [*Pouting.*]   Then go away.

UNDERSHAFT [*Deprecatory.*]   Go away!

LADY BRITOMART   Yes: go away. If you will do nothing for Stephen, you are not wanted here. Go to your foundling, whoever he is; and look after him.

UNDERSHAFT   The fact is, Biddy—

LADY BRITOMART   Dont call me Biddy. I dont call you Andy.

UNDERSHAFT   I will not call my wife Britomart: it is not good sense. Seriously, my love, the Undershaft tradition has landed me in a difficulty. I am getting on in years; and my partner Lazarus has at last made a stand and insisted that the succession must be settled one way or the other; and of course he is quite right. You see, I havnt found a fit successor yet.

LADY BRITOMART [*Obstinately.*]   There is Stephen.

UNDERSHAFT   Thats just it: all the foundlings I can find are exactly like Stephen.

LADY BRITOMART   Andrew!!

UNDERSHAFT   I want a man with no relations and no schooling: that is, a man who would be out of the running altogether if he were not a strong man. And I cant find him. Every blessed foundling nowadays is snapped up in his infancy by Barnardo homes, or School Board officers, or Boards of Guardians; and if he shews the least ability, he is fastened on by schoolmasters; trained to win scholarships like a racehorse; crammed with secondhand ideas; drilled and disciplined in docility and what they call good taste; and lamed for life so that he is fit for nothing but teaching. If you want to keep the foundry in the family, you had better find an eligible foundling and marry him to Barbara.

LADY BRITOMART   Ah! Barbara! Your pet! You would sacrifice Stephen to Barbara.

UNDERSHAFT   Cheerfully. And you, my dear, would boil Barbara to make soup for Stephen.

LADY BRITOMART   Andrew: this is not a question of our likings and dislikings: it is a question of duty. It is your duty to make Stephen your successor.

UNDERSHAFT   Just as much as it is your duty to submit to your husband. Come, Biddy! these tricks of the governing class are of no use with me. I am one of the governing class myself; and it is waste of time giving tracts to a missionary. I have the power in this matter; and I am not to be humbugged into using it for your purposes.

LADY BRITOMART   Andrew: you can talk my head off; but you cant change wrong into right. And your tie is all on one side. Put it straight.

UNDERSHAFT [*Disconcerted.*]   It wont stay unless it's pinned [*He fumbles at it with childish grimaces.*]—
        [STEPHEN *comes in.*]

STEPHEN [*At the door.*]   I beg your pardon. [*About to retire.*]

LADY BRITOMART   No: come in, Stephen. [STEPHEN *comes forward to his mother's writing table.*]

UNDERSHAFT [*Not very cordially.*]   Good afternoon.

STEPHEN [*Coldly.*]   Good afternoon.

UNDERSHAFT [*To* LADY BRITOMART.]   He knows all about the tradition, I suppose?

LADY BRITOMART   Yes. [*To* STEPHEN.] It is what I told you last night, Stephen.

UNDERSHAFT [*Sulkily.*]   I understand you want to come into the cannon business.

STEPHEN   *I* go into trade! Certainly not.

UNDERSHAFT [*Opening his eyes, greatly eased in mind and manner.*]   Oh! in that case—!

LADY BRITOMART   Cannons are not trade, Stephen. They are enterprise.

STEPHEN   I have no intention of becoming a man of business in any sense. I have no capacity for business and no taste for it. I intend to devote myself to politics.

UNDERSHAFT [*Rising.*]   My dear boy: this is an immense relief to me. And I trust it may prove an equally good thing for the country. I was afraid you would consider yourself disparaged and slighted. [*He moves towards* STEPHEN *as if to shake hands with him.*]

LADY BRITOMART [*Rising and interposing.*]   Stephen: I cannot allow you to throw away an enormous property like this.

STEPHEN [*Stiffly.*]   Mother: there must be an end of treating me as a child, if you please. [LADY BRITOMART *recoils, deeply wounded by his tone.*] Until last night I did not take your attitude seriously, because I did not think you meant it seriously. But I find now that you left me in the dark as to matters which you should have explained to me years ago. I am extremely hurt and offended. Any further discussion of my intentions had better take place with my father, as between one man and another.

LADY BRITOMART   Stephen! [*She sits down again; and her eyes fill with tears.*]

UNDERSHAFT [*With grave compassion.*]   You see, my dear, it is only the big men who can be treated as children.

STEPHEN   I am sorry, mother, that you have forced me—

UNDERSHAFT [*Stopping him.*]   Yes, yes, yes, yes: thats all right, Stephen. She wont interfere with you any more: your independence is achieved: you have won your latchkey. Dont rub it in; and above all, dont apologize. [*He resumes his seat.*] Now what about your future, as between one man and another—I beg your pardon, Biddy: as between two men and a woman.

LADY BRITOMART [*Who has pulled herself together strongly.*]   I quite understand, Stephen. By all means go your own way if you feel strong enough. [STEPHEN *sits down magisterially in the chair at the writing table with an air of affirming his majority.*]

UNDERSHAFT   It is settled that you do not ask for the succession to the cannon business.

STEPHEN   I hope it is settled that I repudiate the cannon business.

UNDERSHAFT   Come, come! dont be so devilishly sulky: it's boyish. Freedom should be generous. Besides, I owe you a fair start in life in exchange for disinheriting you. You cant become prime minister all at once. Havnt you a turn for something? What about literature, art and so forth?

STEPHEN   I have nothing of the artist about me, either in faculty or character, thank Heaven!

UNDERSHAFT   A philosopher, perhaps? Eh?

STEPHEN   I make no such ridiculous pretension.

UNDERSHAFT   Just so. Well, there is the army, the navy, the Church, the Bar. The Bar requires some ability. What about the Bar?

STEPHEN   I have not studied law. And I am afraid I have not the necessary push—I believe that is the name barristers give to their vulgarity—for success in pleading.

UNDERSHAFT   Rather a difficult case, Stephen. Hardly anything left but the stage, is there? [STEPHEN *makes an impatient movement*.] Well, come! is there anything you know or care for?

STEPHEN [*Rising and looking at him steadily*.]   I know the difference between right and wrong.

UNDERSHAFT [*Hugely tickled*.]   You dont say so! What! no capacity for business, no knowledge of law, no sympathy with art, no pretension to philosophy; only a simple knowledge of the secret that has puzzled all the philosophers, baffled all the lawyers, muddled all the men of business, and ruined most of the artists: the secret of right and wrong. Why, man, youre a genius, a master of masters, a god! At twenty-four, too!

STEPHEN [*Keeping his temper with difficulty*.]   You are pleased to be facetious. I pretend to nothing more than any honorable English gentleman claims as his birthright. [*He sits down angrily*.]

UNDERSHAFT   Oh, thats everybody's birthright. Look at poor little Jenny Hill, the Salvation lassie! she would think you were laughing at her if you asked her to stand up in the street and teach grammar or geography or mathematics or even drawingroom dancing; but it never occurs to her to doubt that she can teach morals and religion. You are all alike, you respectable people. You cant tell me the bursting strain of a ten-inch gun, which is a very simple matter; but you all think you can tell me the bursting strain of a man under temptation. You darent handle high explosives; but youre all ready to handle honesty and truth and justice and the whole duty of man, and kill one another at that game. What a country! what a world!

LADY BRITOMART [*Uneasily*.]   What do you think he had better do, Andrew?

UNDERSHAFT   Oh, just what he wants to do. He knows nothing; and he thinks he knows everything. That points clearly to a political career. Get him a private secretaryship to someone who can get him an Under Secretaryship; and then leave him alone. He will find his natural and proper place in the end on the Treasury bench.

STEPHEN [*Springing up again.*]　I am sorry, sir, that you force me to forget the respect due to you as my father. I am an Englishman; and I will not hear the Government of my country insulted. [*He thrusts his hands in his pockets, and walks angrily across to the window.*]

UNDERSHAFT [*With a touch of brutality.*]　The government of your country! *I* am the government of your country: I, and Lazarus. Do you suppose that you and half a dozen amateurs like you, sitting in a row in that foolish gabble shop, can govern Undershaft and Lazarus? No, my friend: you will do what pays us. You will make war when it suits us, and keep peace when it doesnt. You will find out that trade requires certain measures when we have decided on those measures. When I want anything to keep my dividends up, you will discover that my want is a national need. When other people want something to keep my dividends down, you will call out the police and military. And in return you shall have the support and applause of my newspapers, and the delight of imagining that you are a great statesman. Government of your country! Be off with you, my boy, and play with your caucuses and leading articles and historic parties and great leaders and burning questions and the rest of your toys. *I* am going back to my counting house to pay the piper and call the tune.

STEPHEN [*Actually smiling, and putting his hand on his father's shoulder with indulgent patronage.*]　Really, my dear father, it is impossible to be angry with you. You dont know how absurd all this sounds to me. You are very properly proud of having been industrious enough to make money; and it is greatly to your credit that you have made so much of it. But it has kept you in circles where you are valued for your money and deferred to for it, instead of in the doubtless very old-fashioned and behind-the-times public school and university where I formed my habits of mind. It is natural for you to think that money governs England; but you must allow me to think I know better.

UNDERSHAFT　And what does govern England, pray?

STEPHEN　Character, father, character.

UNDERSHAFT　Whose character? Yours or mine?

STEPHEN　Neither yours nor mine, father, but the best elements in the English national character.

UNDERSHAFT　Stephen: Ive found your profession for you. Youre a born journalist. I'll start you with a high-toned weekly review. There!

[STEPHEN *goes to the smaller writing table and busies himself with his letters.*

SARAH, BARBARA, LOMAX, *and* CUSINS *come in ready for walking.* BARBARA *crosses the room to the window and looks out.* CUSINS *drifts amiably to the armchair, and* LOMAX *remains near the door, whilst* SARAH *comes to her mother.*]

SARAH   Go and get ready, mamma: the carriage is waiting. [LADY BRITOMART *leaves the room.*]

UNDERSHAFT [*To* SARAH.]   Good day, my dear. Good afternoon, Mr Lomax.

LOMAX [*Vaguely.*]   Ahdedoo.

UNDERSHAFT [*To* CUSINS.]   Quite well after last night, Euripides, eh?

CUSINS   As well as can be expected.

UNDERSHAFT   Thats right. [*To* BARBARA.] So you are coming to see my death and devastation factory, Barbara?

BARBARA [*At the window.*]   You came yesterday to see my salvation factory. I promised you a return visit.

LOMAX [*Coming forward between* SARAH *and* UNDERSHAFT.]   Youll find it awfully interesting. Ive been through the Woolwich Arsenal; and it gives you a ripping feeling of security, you know, to think of the lot of beggars we could kill if it came to fighting. [*To* UNDER-SHAFT, *with sudden solemnity.*] Still, it must be rather an awful reflection for you, from the religious point of view as it were. Youre getting on, you know, and all that.

SARAH   You dont mind Cholly's imbecility, papa, do you?

LOMAX [*Much taken aback.*]   Oh I say!

UNDERSHAFT   Mr Lomax looks at the matter in a very proper spirit, my dear.

LOMAX   Just so. Thats all I meant, I assure you.

SARAH   Are you coming, Stephen?

STEPHEN   Well, I am rather busy—er — [*Magnanimously.*] Oh well, yes: I'll come. That is, if there is room for me.

UNDERSHAFT   I can take two with me in a little motor I am experi-menting with for field use. You wont mind its being rather unfash-ionable. It's not painted yet; but it's bullet proof.

LOMAX [*Appalled at the prospect of confronting Wilton Crescent in an unpainted motor.*]   Oh I say!

SARAH   The carriage for me, thank you. Barbara doesnt mind what shes seen in.

LOMAX   I say, Dolly old chap: do you really mind the car being a guy?[2] Because of course if you do I'll go in it. Still—

CUSINS   I prefer it.

LOMAX   Thanks awfully, old man. Come, Sarah. [*He hurries out to secure his seat in the carriage.* SARAH *follows him.*]

CUSINS [*Moodily walking across to* LADY BRITOMART's *writing*

---

2. Looking foolishly conspicuous.

table.] Why are we two coming to this Works Department of Hell? that is what I ask myself.

BARBARA I have always thought of it as a sort of pit where lost creatures with blackened faces stirred up smoky fires and were driven and tormented by my father. Is it like that, dad?

UNDERSHAFT [*Scandalized.*] My dear! It is a spotlessly clean and beautiful hillside town.

CUSINS With a Methodist chapel? Oh do say theres a Methodist chapel.

UNDERSHAFT There are two: a Primitive one and a sophisticated one. There is even an Ethical Society; but it is not much patronized, as my men are all strongly religious. In the High Explosives Sheds they object to the presence of Agnostics as unsafe.

CUSINS And yet they dont object to you!

BARBARA Do they obey all your orders?

UNDERSHAFT I never give them any orders. When I speak to one of them it is "Well, Jones, is the baby doing well? and has Mrs Jones made a good recovery?" "Nicely, thank you, sir." And thats all.

CUSINS But Jones has to be kept in order. How do you maintain discipline among your men?

UNDERSHAFT I dont. They do. You see, the one thing Jones wont stand is any rebellion from the man under him, or any assertion of social equality between the wife of the man with 4 shillings a week less than himself, and Mrs Jones! Of course they all rebel against me, theoretically. Practically, every man of them keeps the man just below him in his place. I never meddle with them. I never bully them. I dont even bully Lazarus. I say that certain things are to be done; but I dont order anybody to do them. I dont say, mind you, that there is no ordering about and snubbing and even bullying. The men snub the boys and order them about; the carmen snub the sweepers; the artisans snub the unskilled laborers; the foremen drive and bully both the laborers and artisans; the assistant engineers find fault with the foremen; the chief engineers drop on the assistants; the departmental managers worry the chiefs; and the clerks have tall hats and hymnbooks and keep up the social tone by refusing to associate on equal terms with anybody. The result is a colossal profit, which comes to me.

CUSINS [*Revolted.*] You really are a—well, what I was saying yesterday.

BARBARA What was he saying yesterday?

UNDERSHAFT Never mind, my dear. He thinks I have made you unhappy. Have I?

BARBARA Do you think I can be happy in this vulgar silly dress? I! who have worn the uniform. Do you understand what you have done to me? Yesterday I had a man's soul in my hand. I set him in the way of life with his face to salvation. But when we took your money he turned back to drunkenness and derision. [*With intense conviction*.] I will never forgive you that. If I had a child, and you destroyed its body with your explosives—if you murdered Dolly with your horrible guns—I could forgive you if my forgiveness would open the gates of heaven to you. But to take a human soul from me, and turn it into the soul of a wolf! that is worse than any murder.

UNDERSHAFT   Does my daughter despair so easily? Can you strike a man to the heart and leave no mark on him?

BARBARA [*Her face lighting up*.]   Oh, you are right: he can never be lost now: where was my faith?

CUSINS   Oh, clever clever devil!

BARBARA   You may be a devil; but God speaks through you sometimes. [*She takes her father's hands and kisses them*.] You have given me back my happiness: I feel it deep down now, though my spirit is troubled.

UNDERSHAFT   You have learnt something. That always feels at first as if you had lost something.

BARBARA   Well, take me to the factory of death, and let me learn something more. There must be some truth or other behind all this frightful irony. Come, Dolly. [*She goes out*.]

CUSINS   My guardian angel! [*To* UNDERSHAFT.] Avaunt! [*He follows* BARBARA.]

STEPHEN [*Quietly, at the writing table*.]   You must not mind Cusins, father. He is a very amiable good fellow; but he is a Greek scholar and naturally a little eccentric.

UNDERSHAFT   Ah, quite so. Thank you, Stephen. Thank you. [*He goes out*.]

[STEPHEN *smiles patronizingly; buttons his coat responsibly; and crosses the room to the door.* LADY BRITOMART, *dressed for out-of-doors, opens it before he reaches it. She looks round for the others; looks at* STEPHEN; *and turns to go without a word*.]

STEPHEN [*Embarrassed*.]   Mother—

LADY BRITOMART   Dont be apologetic, Stephen. And dont forget that you have outgrown your mother. [*She goes out*.]

Perivale St Andrews lies between two Middlesex hills, half climbing the northern one. It is an almost smokeless town of white walls, roofs of narrow green slates or red tiles, tall trees, domes, campaniles, and slender chimney shafts, beautifully situated and beautiful in itself. The best view of it is obtained from the crest of a slope about half a mile to the east, where the high explosives are dealt with. The foundry lies hidden in the depths between, the tops of its chimneys sprouting like huge skittles into the middle dis-

tance. Across the crest runs a platform of concrete, with a parapet which suggests a fortification, because there is a huge cannon of the obsolete Woolwich Infant pattern peering across it at the town. The cannon is mounted on an experimental gun carriage: possibly the original model of the Undershaft disappearing rampart gun alluded to by STEPHEN. *The parapet has a high step inside which serves as a seat.*

BARBARA *is leaning over the parapet, looking towards the town. On her right is the cannon; on her left the end of a shed raised on piles, with a ladder of three or four steps up to the door, which opens outwards and has a little wooden landing at the threshold, with a fire bucket in the corner of the landing. The parapet stops short of the shed, leaving a gap which is the beginning of the path down the hill through the foundry to the town. Behind the cannon is a trolley carrying a huge conical bombshell, with a red band painted on it. Further from the parapet, on the same side, is a deck chair, near the door of an office, which, like the sheds, is of the lightest possible construction.*

[CUSINS *arrives by the path from the town.*]

BARBARA   Well?

CUSINS   Not a ray of hope. Everything perfect, wonderful, real. It only needs a cathedral to be a heavenly city instead of a hellish one.

BARBARA   Have you found out whether they have done anything for old Peter Shirley.

CUSINS   They have found him a job as gatekeeper and timekeeper. He's frightfully miserable. He calls the timekeeping brainwork, and says he isnt used to it; and his gate lodge is so splendid that hes ashamed to use the rooms, and skulks in the scullery.

BARBARA   Poor Peter!

[STEPHEN *arrives from the town. He carries a fieldglass.*]

STEPHEN [*Enthusiastically.*]   Have you two seen the place? Why did you leave us?

CUSINS   I wanted to see everything I was not intended to see; and Barbara wanted to make the men talk.

STEPHEN   Have you found anything discreditable?

CUSINS   No. They call him Dandy Andy and are proud of his being a cunning old rascal; but it's all horrible, frightfully, immorally, unanswerably perfect.

[SARAH *arrives.*]

SARAH   Heavens! what a place! [*She crosses to the trolley.*] Did you see the nursing home!? [*She sits down on the shell.*]

STEPHEN   Did you see the libraries and schools!?

SARAH   Did you see the ball room and the banqueting chamber in the Town Hall!?

STEPHEN   Have you gone into the insurance fund, the pension fund, the building society, the various applications of co-operation!?

[UNDERSHAFT *comes from the office, with a sheaf of telegrams in his hands.*]

UNDERSHAFT   Well, have you seen everything? I'm sorry I was called away. [*Indicating the telegrams.*] News from Manchuria.

STEPHEN   Good news, I hope.

UNDERSHAFT   Very.

STEPHEN   Another Japanese victory?

UNDERSHAFT   Oh, I dont know. Which side wins does not concern us here. No: the good news is that the aerial battleship is a tremendous success. At the first trial it has wiped out a fort with three hundred soldiers in it.

CUSINS [*From the platform.*]   Dummy soldiers?

UNDERSHAFT   No: the real thing. [CUSINS *and* BARBARA *exchange glances. Then* CUSINS *sits on the step and buries his face in his hands.* BARBARA *gravely lays her hand on his shoulder, and he looks up at her in a sort of whimsical desperation.*] Well, Stephen, what do you think of the place?

STEPHEN   Oh, magnificent. A perfect triumph of organization. Frankly, my dear father, I have been a fool: I had no idea of what it all meant—of the wonderful forethought, the power of organization, the administrative capacity, the financial genius, the colossal capital it represents. I have been repeating to myself as I came through your streets "Peace hath her victories no less renowned than War." I have only one misgiving about it all.

UNDERSHAFT   Out with it.

STEPHEN   Well, I cannot help thinking that all this provision for every want of your workmen may sap their independence and weaken their sense of responsibility. And greatly as we enjoyed our tea at that splendid restaurant—how they gave us all that luxury and cake and jam and cream for threepence I really cannot imagine!—still you must remember that restaurants break up home life. Look at the continent, for instance! Are you sure so much pampering is really good for the men's characters?

UNDERSHAFT   Well you see, my dear boy, when you are organizing civilization you have to make up your mind whether trouble and anxiety are good things or not. If you decide that they are, then, I take it, you simply dont organize civilization; and there you are, with trouble and anxiety enough to make us all angels! But if you decide the other way, you may as well go through with it. However, Stephen, our characters are safe here. A sufficient dose of anxiety is always provided by the fact that we may be blown to smithereens at any moment.

SARAH   By the way, papa, where do you make the explosives?

UNDERSHAFT   In separate little sheds, like that one. When one of them blows up, it costs very little; and only the people quite close to it are killed.

[STEPHEN, *who is quite close to it, looks at it rather scaredly, and moves away quickly to the cannon. At the same moment the door of the shed is thrown abruptly open; and a foreman in overalls and list slippers[3] comes out on the little landing and holds the door open for* LOMAX, *who appears in the doorway.*]

LOMAX [*With studied coolness.*]   My good fellow: you neednt get into a state of nerves. Nothing's going to happen to you; and I suppose it wouldnt be the end of the world if anything did. A little bit of British pluck is what you want, old chap. [*He descends and strolls across to* SARAH.]

UNDERSHAFT [*To the foreman.*]   Anything wrong, Bilton?

BILTON [*With ironic calm.*]   Gentleman walked into the high explosives shed and lit a cigaret, sir: thats all.

UNDERSHAFT   Ah, quite so. [*To* LOMAX.] Do you happen to remember what you did with the match?

LOMAX   Oh come! I'm not a fool. I took jolly good care to blow it out before I chucked it away.

BILTON   The top of it was red hot inside, sir.

LOMAX   Well, suppose it was! I didnt chuck it into any of your messes.

UNDERSHAFT   Think no more of it, Mr Lomax. By the way, would you mind lending me your matches?

LOMAX [*Offering his box.*]   Certainly.

UNDERSHAFT   Thanks. [*He pockets the matches.*]

LOMAX [*Lecturing to the company generally.*]   You know, these high explosives dont go off like gunpowder, except when theyre in a gun. When theyre spread loose, you can put a match to them without the least risk: they just burn quietly like a bit of paper. [*Warming to the scientific interest of the subject.*] Did you know that, Undershaft? Have you ever tried?

UNDERSHAFT   Not on a large scale, Mr Lomax. Bilton will give you a sample of gun cotton when you are leaving if you ask him. You can experiment with it at home. [BILTON *looks puzzled.*]

SARAH   Bilton will do nothing of the sort, papa. I suppose it's your business to blow up the Russians and Japs; but you might really stop short of blowing up poor Cholly. [BILTON *gives it up and retires into the shed.*]

LOMAX   My ownest, there is no danger. [*He sits beside her on the shell.*]

[LADY BRITOMART *arrives from the town with a bouquet.*]

LADY BRITOMART [*Coming impetuously between* UNDERSHAFT *and the*

---

3. Cloth overshoes.

deck chair.]   Andrew: you shouldnt have let me see this place.

UNDERSHAFT   Why, my dear?

LADY BRITOMART   Never mind why: you shouldnt have: thats all. To think of all that [*indicating the town*] being yours! and that you have kept it to yourself all these years!

UNDERSHAFT   It does not belong to me. I belong to it. It is the Undershaft inheritance.

LADY BRITOMART   It is not. Your ridiculous cannons and that noisy banging foundry may be the Undershaft inheritance; but all that plate and linen, all that furniture and those houses and orchards and gardens belong to us. They belong to me: they are not a man's business. I wont give them up. You must be out of your senses to throw them all away; and if you persist in such folly, I will call in a doctor.

UNDERSHAFT [*Stooping to smell the bouquet.*]   Where did you get the flowers, my dear?

LADY BRITOMART   Your men presented them to me in your William Morris Labor Church.[4]

CUSINS [*Springing up.*]   Oh! It needed only that. A Labor Church!

LADY BRITOMART   Yes, with Morris's words in mosaic letters ten feet high round the dome. NO MAN IS GOOD ENOUGH TO BE ANOTHER MAN'S MASTER. The cynicism of it!

UNDERSHAFT   It shocked the men at first, I am afraid. But now they take no more notice of it than of the ten commandments in church.

LADY BRITOMART   Andrew: you are trying to put me off the subject of the inheritance by profane jokes. Well, you shant. I dont ask it any longer for Stephen: he has inherited far too much of your perversity to be fit for it. But Barbara has rights as well as Stephen. Why should not Adolphus succeed to the inheritance? I could manage the town for him; and he can look after the cannons, if they are really necessary.

UNDERSHAFT   I should ask nothing better if Adolphus were a foundling. He is exactly the sort of new blood that is wanted in English business. But hes not a foundling; and theres an end of it.

CUSINS [*Diplomatically.*]   Not quite. [*They all turn and stare at him. He comes from the platform past the shed to* UNDERSHAFT.] I think—Mind! I am not committing myself in any way as to my future course—but I think the foundling difficulty can be got over.

UNDERSHAFT   What do you mean?

CUSINS   Well, I have something to say which is in the nature of a confession.

---

4. The first Labor Church was founded by John Trevor in 1891 in an attempt to transform the Labor movement into a kind of religious organization. The movement did not survive World War I.

SARAH
LADY BRITOMART ⎱ Confession!
BARBARA   ⎰
STEPHEN

LOMAX   Oh I say!

CUSINS   Yes, a confession. Listen, all. Until I met Barbara I thought
  myself in the main an honorable, truthful man, because I wanted
  the approval of my conscience more than I wanted anything else.
  But the moment I saw Barbara, I wanted her far more than the
  approval of my conscience.

LADY BRITOMART   Adolphus!

CUSINS   It is true. You accused me yourself, Lady Brit, of joining
  the Army to worship Barbara; and so I did. She bought my soul
  like a flower at a street corner; but she bought it for herself.

UNDERSHAFT   What! Not for Dionysos or another?

CUSINS   Dionysos and all the others are in herself. I adored what
  was divine in her, and was therefore a true worshipper. But I was
  romantic about her too. I thought she was a woman of the people,
  and that a marriage with a professor of Greek would be far beyond
  the wildest social ambitions of her rank.

LADY BRITOMART   Adolphus!!

LOMAX   Oh I say!!!

CUSINS   When I learnt the horrible truth—

LADY BRITOMART   What do you mean by the horrible truth, pray?

CUSINS   That she was enormously rich; that her grandfather was an
  earl; that her father was the Prince of Darkness—

UNDERSHAFT   Chut!

CUSINS   —and that I was only an adventurer trying to catch a rich
  wife, then I stooped to deceive her about my birth.

BARBARA   Dolly!

LADY BRITOMART   Your birth! Now Adolphus, dont dare to make up
  a wicked story for the sake of these wretched cannons. Remember:
  I have seen photographs of your parents; and the Agent General
  for South Western Australia knows them personally and has
  assured me that they are most respectable married people.

CUSINS   So they are in Australia; but here they are outcasts. Their
  marriage is legal in Australia, but not in England. My mother is
  my father's deceased wife's sister; and in this island I am consequently a foundling. [Sensation.][5] Is the subterfuge good enough,
  Machiavelli?

UNDERSHAFT [Thoughtfully.]   Biddy: this may be a way out of the
  difficulty.

LADY BRITOMART   Stuff! A man cant make cannons any the better
  for being his own cousin instead of his proper self. [She sits down

5. The Deceased Wife's Sister Act, later repealed, forbade marriage of a widower with his
  late wife's sister.

in the deck chair with a bounce that expresses her downright contempt for their casuistry.]

UNDERSHAFT [*To* CUSINS.] You are an educated man. That is against the tradition.

CUSINS Once in ten thousand times it happens that the schoolboy is a born master of what they try to teach him. Greek has not destroyed my mind: it has nourished it. Besides, I did not learn it at an English public school.

UNDERSHAFT Hm! Well, I cannot afford to be too particular: you have cornered the foundling market. Let it pass. You are eligible, Euripides: you are eligible.

BARBARA [*Coming from the platform and interposing between* CUSINS *and* UNDERSHAFT.] Dolly: yesterday morning, when Stephen told us all about the tradition, you became very silent; and you have been strange and excited ever since. Were you thinking of your birth then?

CUSINS When the finger of Destiny suddenly points at a man in the middle of his breakfast, it makes him thoughtful. [BARBARA *turns away sadly and stands near her mother, listening perturbedly.*]

UNDERSHAFT Aha! You have had your eye on the business, my young friend, have you?

CUSINS Take care! There is an abyss of moral horror between me and your accursed aerial battleships.

UNDERSHAFT Never mind the abyss for the present. Let us settle the practical details and leave your final decision open. You know that you will have to change your name. Do you object to that?

CUSINS Would any man named Adolphus—any man called Dolly!— object to be called something else?

UNDERSHAFT Good. Now, as to money! I propose to treat you handsomely from the beginning. You shall start at a thousand a year.

CUSINS [*With sudden heat, his spectacles twinkling with mischief.*] A thousand! You dare offer a miserable thousand to the son-in-law of a millionaire! No, by Heavens, Machiavelli! you shall not cheat me. You cannot do without me; and I can do without you. I must have two thousand five hundred a year for two years. At the end of that time, if I am a failure, I go. But if I am a success, and stay on, you must give me the other five thousand.

UNDERSHAFT What other five thousand.

CUSINS To make the two years up to five thousand a year. The two thousand five hundred is only half pay in case I should turn out a failure. The third year I must have ten per cent on the profits.

UNDERSHAFT [*Taken aback.*] Ten per cent! Why, man, do you know what my profits are?

CUSINS Enormous, I hope: otherwise I shall require twenty-five per cent.

UNDERSHAFT But, Mr Cusins, this is a serious matter of business.

You are not bringing any capital into the concern.

CUSINS   What! no capital! Is my mastery of Greek no capital? Is my access to the subtlest thought, the loftiest poetry yet attained by humanity, no capital? My character! my intellect! my life! my career! what Barbara calls my soul! are these no capital? Say another word; and I double my salary.

UNDERSHAFT   Be reasonable—

CUSINS [*Peremptorily.*]   Mr Undershaft: you have my terms. Take them or leave them.

UNDERSHAFT [*Recovering himself.*]   Very well. I note your terms; and I offer you half.

CUSINS [*Disgusted.*]   Half!

UNDERSHAFT [*Firmly.*]   Half.

CUSINS   You call yourself a gentleman; and you offer me half!!

UNDERSHAFT   I do not call myself a gentleman; but I offer you half.

CUSINS   This to your future partner! your successor! your son-in-law!

BARBARA   You are selling your own soul, Dolly, not mine. Leave me out of the bargain, please.

UNDERSHAFT   Come! I will go a step further for Barbara's sake. I will give you three fifths; but that is my last word.

CUSINS   Done!

LOMAX   Done in the eye. Why, *I* only get eight hundred, you know.

CUSINS   By the way, Mac, I am a classical scholar, not an arithmetical one. Is three fifths more than half or less?

UNDERSHAFT   More, of course.

CUSINS   I would have taken two hundred and fifty. How you can succeed in business when you are willing to pay all that money to a University don who is obviously not worth a junior clerk's wages!—well! What will Lazarus say?

UNDERSHAFT   Lazarus is a gentle romantic Jew who cares for nothing but string quartets and stalls at fashionable theatres. He will get the credit of your rapacity in money matters, as he has hitherto had the credit of mine. You are a shark of the first order, Euripides. So much the better for the firm!

BARBARA   Is the bargain closed, Dolly? Does your soul belong to him now?

CUSINS   No: the price is settled: that is all. The real tug of war is still to come. What about the moral question?

LADY BRITOMART   There is no moral question in the matter at all, Adolphus. You must simply sell cannons and weapons to people whose cause is right and just, and refuse them to foreigners and criminals.

UNDERSHAFT [*Determinedly.*]   No: none of that. You must keep the true faith of an Armorer, or you dont come in here.

CUSINS   What on earth is the true faith of an Armorer?

UNDERSHAFT   To give arms to all men who offer an honest price for them, without respect of persons or principles: to aristocrat and republican, to Nihilist and Tsar, to Capitalist and Socialist, to Protestant and Catholic, to burglar and policeman, to black man white man and yellow man, to all sorts and conditions, all nationalities, all faiths, all follies, all causes and all crimes. The first Undershaft wrote up in his shop IF GOD GAVE THE HAND, LET NOT MAN WITHHOLD THE SWORD. The second wrote up ALL HAVE THE RIGHT TO FIGHT: NONE HAVE THE RIGHT TO JUDGE. The third wrote up TO MAN THE WEAPON: TO HEAVEN THE VICTORY. The fourth had no literary turn; so he did not write up anything; but he sold cannons to Napoleon under the nose of George the Third. The fifth wrote up PEACE SHALL NOT PREVAIL SAVE WITH A SWORD IN HER HAND. The sixth, my master, was the best of all. He wrote up NOTHING IS EVER DONE IN THIS WORLD UNTIL MEN ARE PREPARED TO KILL ONE ANOTHER IF IT IS NOT DONE. After that, there was nothing left for the seventh to say. So he wrote up, simply, UNASHAMED.

CUSINS   My good Machiavelli, I shall certainly write something up on the wall; only, as I shall write it in Greek, you wont be able to read it. But as to your Armorer's faith, if I take my neck out of the noose of my own morality I am not going to put it into the noose of yours. I shall sell cannons to whom I please and refuse them to whom I please. So there!

UNDERSHAFT   From the moment when you become Andrew Undershaft, you will never do as you please again. Dont come here lusting for power, young man.

CUSINS   If power were my aim I should not come here for it. You have no power.

UNDERSHAFT   None of my own, certainly.

CUSINS   I have more power than you, more will. You do not drive this place: it drives you. And what drives the place?

UNDERSHAFT [*Enigmatically.*]   A will of which I am a part.

BARBARA [*Startled.*]   Father! Do you know what you are saying; or are you laying a snare for my soul?

CUSINS   Dont listen to his metaphysics, Barbara. The place is driven by the most rascally part of society, the money hunters, the pleasure hunters, the military promotion hunters; and he is their slave.

UNDERSHAFT   Not necessarily. Remember the Armorer's Faith. I will take an order from a good man as cheerfully as from a bad one. If you good people prefer preaching and shirking to buying my weapons and fighting the rascals, dont blame me. I can make cannons: I cannot make courage and conviction. Bah! You tire me, Euripides, with your morality mongering. Ask Barbara: she understands. [*He suddenly takes* BARBARA's *hands, and looks powerfully into her eyes.*] Tell him, my love, what power really means.

BARBARA [*Hypnotized.*]   Before I joined the Salvation Army, I was in my own power; and the consequence was that I never knew what to do with myself. When I joined it, I had not time enough for all the things I had to do.

UNDERSHAFT [*Approvingly.*] Just so. And why was that, do you suppose?

BARBARA Yesterday I should have said, because I was in the power of God. [*She resumes her self-possession, withdrawing her hands from his with a power equal to his own.*] But you came and shewed me that I was in the power of Bodger and Undershaft. Today I feel—oh! how can I put it into words? Sarah: do you remember the earthquake at Cannes, when we were little children?—how little the surprise of the first shock mattered compared to the dread and horror of waiting for the second? That is how I feel in this place today. I stood on the rock I thought eternal; and without a word of warning it reeled and crumbled under me. I was safe with an infinite wisdom watching me, an army marching to Salvation with me; and in a moment, at a stroke of your pen in a cheque book, I stood alone; and the heavens were empty. That was the first shock of the earthquake: I am waiting for the second.

UNDERSHAFT Come, come, my daughter! dont make too much of your little tinpot tragedy. What do we do here when we spend years of work and thought and thousands of pounds of solid cash on a new gun or an aerial battleship that turns out just a hairsbreadth wrong after all? Scrap it. Scrap it without wasting another hour or another pound on it. Well, you have made for yourself something that you call a morality or a religion or what not. It doesnt fit the facts. Well, scrap it. Scrap it and get one that does fit. That is what is wrong with the world at present. It scraps its obsolete steam engines and dynamos; but it wont scrap its old prejudices and its old moralities and its old religions and its old political constitutions. Whats the result? In machinery it does very well; but in morals and religion and politics it is working at a loss that brings it nearer bankruptcy every year. Dont persist in that folly. If your old religion broke down yesterday, get a newer and a better one for tomorrow.

BARBARA Oh how gladly I would take a better one to my soul! But you offer me a worse one. [*Turning on him with sudden vehemence.*] Justify yourself: shew me some light through the darkness of this dreadful place, with its beautifully clean workshops, and respectable workmen, and model homes.

UNDERSHAFT Cleanliness and respectability do not need justification, Barbara: they justify themselves. I see no darkness here, no dreadfulness. In your Salvation shelter I saw poverty, misery, cold and hunger. You gave them bread and treacle and dreams of heaven. I give from thirty shillings a week to twelve thousand a year. They find their own dreams; but I look after the drainage.

BARBARA And their souls?

UNDERSHAFT I save their souls just as I saved yours.

BARBARA [*Revolted.*]   You saved my soul! What do you mean?

UNDERSHAFT   I fed you and clothed you and housed you. I took care that you should have money enough to live handsomely—more than enough; so that you could be wasteful, careless, generous. That saved your soul from the seven deadly sins.

BARBARA [*Bewildered.*]   The seven deadly sins!

UNDERSHAFT   Yes, the deadly seven. [*Counting on his fingers.*] Food, clothing, firing, rent, taxes, respectability and children. Nothing can lift those seven millstones from Man's neck but money; and the spirit cannot soar until the millstones are lifted. I lifted them from your spirit. I enabled Barbara to become Major Barbara; and I saved her from the crime of poverty.

CUSINS   Do you call poverty a crime?

UNDERSHAFT   The worst of crimes. All the other crimes are virtues beside it: all the other dishonors are chivalry itself by comparison. Poverty blights whole cities; spreads horrible pestilences; strikes dead the very souls of all who come within sight, sound or smell of it. What you call crime is nothing: a murder here and a theft there, a blow now and a curse then: what do they matter? they are only the accidents and illnesses of life: there are not fifty genuine professional criminals in London. But there are millions of poor people, abject people, dirty people, ill fed, ill clothed people. They poison us morally and physically: they kill the happiness of society: they force us to do away with our own liberties and to organize unnatural cruelties for fear they should rise against us and drag us down into their abyss. Only fools fear crime: we all fear poverty. Pah! [*Turning on* BARBARA.] you talk of your half-saved ruffian in West Ham: you accuse me of dragging his soul back to perdition. Well, bring him to me here; and I will drag his soul back again to salvation for you. Not by words and dreams; but by thirty-eight shillings a week, a sound house in a handsome street, and a permanent job. In three weeks he will have a fancy waistcoat; in three months a tall hat and a chapel sitting; before the end of the year he will shake hands with a duchess at a Primrose League meeting, and join the Conservative Party.

BARBARA   And will he be the better for that?

UNDERSHAFT   You know he will. Dont be a hypocrite, Barbara. He will be better fed, better housed, better clothed, better behaved; and his children will be pounds heavier and bigger. That will be better than an American cloth mattress in a shelter, chopping firewood, eating bread and treacle, and being forced to kneel down from time to time to thank heaven for it: knee drill, I think you call it. It is cheap work converting starving men with a Bible in one hand and a slice of bread in the other. I will undertake to convert West Ham to Mahometanism on the same terms. Try your hand on my men: their souls are hungry because their bodies are full.

BARBARA   And leave the east end to starve?

UNDERSHAFT   [*His energetic tone dropping into one of bitter and brooding remembrance.*]   I was an east ender. I moralized and starved until one day I swore that I would be a full-fed free man at all costs—that nothing should stop me except a bullet, neither reason nor morals nor the lives of other men. I said "Thou shalt starve ere I starve"; and with that word I became free and great. I was a dangerous man until I had my will: now I am a useful, beneficent, kindly person. That is the history of most self-made millionaires, I fancy. When it is the history of every Englishman we shall have an England worth living in.

LADY BRITOMART   Stop making speeches, Andrew. This is not the place for them.

UNDERSHAFT   [*Punctured.*]   My dear: I have no other means of conveying my ideas.

LADY BRITOMART   Your ideas are nonsense. You got on because you were selfish and unscrupulous.

UNDERSHAFT   Not at all. I had the strongest scruples about poverty and starvation. Your moralists are quite unscrupulous about both: they make virtues of them. I had rather be a thief than a pauper. I had rather be a murderer than a slave. I dont want to be either; but if you force the alternative on me, then, by Heaven, I'll choose the braver and more moral one. I hate poverty and slavery worse than any other crimes whatsoever. And let me tell you this. Poverty and slavery have stood up for centuries to your sermons and leading articles: they will not stand up to my machine guns. Dont preach at them: dont reason with them. Kill them.

BARBARA   Killing. Is that your remedy for everything?

UNDERSHAFT   It is the final test of conviction, the only lever strong enough to overturn a social system, the only way of saying Must. Let six hundred and seventy fools loose in the street; and three policemen can scatter them. But huddle them together in a certain house in Westminster; and let them go through certain ceremonies and call themselves certain names until at last they get the courage to kill; and your six hundred and seventy fools become a government.[6] Your pious mob fills up ballot papers and imagines it is governing its masters; but the ballot paper that really governs is the paper that has a bullet wrapped up in it.

CUSINS   That is perhaps why, like most intelligent people, I never vote.

UNDERSHAFT   Vote! Bah! When you vote, you only change the names of the cabinet. When you shoot, you pull down governments, inaugurate new epochs, abolish old orders and set up new. Is that historically true, Mr Learned Man, or is it not?

CUSINS   It is historically true. I loathe having to admit it. I repudiate

6. The Houses of Parliament, the home of the British government, are in the Palace of Westminster.

your sentiments. I abhor your nature. I defy you in every possible way. Still, it is true. But it ought not to be true.

UNDERSHAFT Ought, ought, ought, ought, ought! Are you going to spend your life saying ought, like the rest of our moralists? Turn your oughts into shalls, man. Come and make explosives with me. Whatever can blow men up can blow society up. The history of the world is the history of those who had courage enough to embrace this truth. Have you the courage to embrace it, Barbara?

LADY BRITOMART Barbara, I positively forbid you to listen to your father's abominable wickedness. And you, Adolphus, ought to know better than to go about saying that wrong things are true. What does it matter whether they are true if they are wrong?

UNDERSHAFT What does it matter whether they are wrong if they are true?

LADY BRITOMART [Rising.] Children: come home instantly. Andrew: I am exceedingly sorry I allowed you to call on us. You are wickeder than ever. Come at once.

BARBARA [Shaking her head.] It's no use running away from wicked people, mamma.

LADY BRITOMART It is every use. It shews your disapprobation of them.

BARBARA It does not save them.

LADY BRITOMART I can see that you are going to disobey me. Sarah: are you coming home or are you not?

SARAH I daresay it's very wicked of papa to make cannons; but I dont think I shall cut him on that account.

LOMAX [Pouring oil on the troubled waters.] The fact is, you know, there is a certain amount of tosh about this notion of wickedness. It doesn't work. You must look at facts. Not that I would say a word in favor of anything wrong; but then, you see, all sorts of chaps are always doing all sorts of things; and we have to fit them in somehow, dont you know. What I mean is that you cant go cutting everybody; and thats about what it comes to. [Their rapt attention to his eloquence makes him nervous.] Perhaps I don't make myself clear.

LADY BRITOMART You are lucidity itself, Charles. Because Andrew is successful and has plenty of money to give to Sarah, you will flatter him and encourage him in his wickedness.

LOMAX [Unruffled.] Well, where the carcase is, there will the eagles be gathered, dont you know. [To UNDERSHAFT] Eh? What?

UNDERSHAFT Precisely. By the way, may I call you Charles?

LOMAX Delighted. Cholly is the usual ticket.

UNDERSHAFT [To LADY BRITOMART.] Biddy—

LADY BRITOMART [Violently.] Dont dare call me Biddy. Charles Lomax: you are a fool. Adolphus Cusins: you are a Jesuit. Stephen: you are a prig. Barbara: you are a lunatic. Andrew: you are a vulgar tradesman. Now you all know my opinion; and my conscience is clear, at all events [*She sits down again with a vehemence that almost wrecks the chair.*]

UNDERSHAFT   My dear: you are the incarnation of morality. [*She snorts.*] Your conscience is clear and your duty done when you have called everybody names. Come, Euripides! it is getting late; and we all want to get home. Make up your mind.

CUSINS   Understand this, you old demon—

LADY BRITOMART   Adolphus!

UNDERSHAFT   Let him alone, Biddy. Proceed, Euripides.

CUSINS   You have me in a horrible dilemma. I want Barbara.

UNDERSHAFT   Like all young men, you greatly exaggerate the difference between one young woman and another.

BARBARA   Quite true, Dolly.

CUSINS   I also want to avoid being a rascal.

UNDERSHAFT   [*With biting contempt.*]   You lust for personal righteousness, for self-approval, for what you call a good conscience, for what Barbara calls salvation, for what I call patronizing people who are not so lucky as yourself.

CUSINS   I do not: all the poet in me recoils from being a good man. But there are things in me that I must reckon with: pity—

UNDERSHAFT   Pity! The scavenger of misery.

CUSINS   Well, love.

UNDERSHAFT   I know. You love the needy and the outcast: you love the oppressed races, the negro, the Indian ryot,[7] the Pole, the Irishman. Do you love the Japanese? Do you love the Germans? Do you love the English?

CUSINS   No. Every true Englishman detests the English. We are the wickedest nation on earth; and our success is a moral horror.

UNDERSHAFT   That is what comes of your gospel of love, is it?

CUSINS   May I not love even my father-in-law?

UNDERSHAFT   Who wants your love, man? By what right do you take the liberty of offering it to me? I will have your due heed and respect, or I will kill you. But your love! Damn your impertinence!

CUSINS   [*Grinning.*]   I may not be able to control my affections, Mac.

UNDERSHAFT   You are fencing, Euripides. You are weakening: your grip is slipping. Come! try your last weapon. Pity and love have broken in your hand: forgiveness is still left.

CUSINS   No: forgiveness is a beggar's refuge. I am with you there: we must pay our debts.

UNDERSHAFT   Well said. Come! you will suit me. Remember the words of Plato.

CUSINS   [*Starting.*]   Plato! You dare quote Plato to me!

UNDERSHAFT   Plato says, my friend, that society cannot be saved until either the Professors of Greek take to making gunpowder, or

7. Tenant farmer.

else the makers of gunpowder become Professors of Greek.

CUSINS   Oh, tempter, cunning tempter!

UNDERSHAFT   Come! choose, man, choose.

CUSINS   But perhaps Barbara will not marry me if I make the wrong choice.

BARBARA   Perhaps not.

CUSINS [*Desperately perplexed.*]   You hear!

BARBARA   Father: do you love nobody?

UNDERSHAFT   I love my best friend.

LADY BRITOMART   And who is that, pray?

UNDERSHAFT   My bravest enemy. That is the man who keeps me up to the mark.

CUSINS   You know, the creature is really a sort of poet in his way. Suppose he is a great man, after all!

UNDERSHAFT   Suppose you stop talking and make up your mind, my young friend.

CUSINS   But you are driving me against my nature. I hate war.

UNDERSHAFT   Hatred is the coward's revenge for being intimidated. Dare you make war on war? Here are the means: my friend Mr Lomax is sitting on them.

LOMAX [*Springing up.*]   Oh I say! You dont mean that this thing is loaded, do you? My ownest: come off it.

SARAH [*Sitting placidly on the shell.*]   If I am to be blown up, the more thoroughly it is done the better. Dont fuss, Cholly.

LOMAX [*To* UNDERSHAFT, *strongly remonstrant.*]   Your own daughter, you know.

UNDERSHAFT   So I see. [*To* CUSINS.] Well, my friend, may we expect you here at six tomorrow morning?

CUSINS [*Firmly.*]   Not on any account. I will see the whole establishment blown up with its own dynamite before I will get up at five. My hours are healthy, rational hours: eleven to five.

UNDERSHAFT   Come when you please: before a week you will come at six and stay until I turn you out for the sake of your health. [*Calling.*] Bilton! [*He turns to* LADY BRITOMART, *who rises.*] My dear: let us leave these two young people to themselves for a moment. [BILTON *comes from the shed.*] I am going to take you through the gun cotton shed.

BILTON [*Barring the way.*]   You cant take anything explosive in here, sir.

LADY BRITOMART   What do you mean? Are you alluding to me?

BILTON [*Unmoved.*]   No, maam. Mr Undershaft has the other gentleman's matches in his pocket.

LADY BRITOMART [*Abruptly.*]   Oh! I beg your pardon. [*She goes into the shed.*]

UNDERSHAFT   Quite right, Bilton, quite right: here you are. [*He gives* BILTON *the box of matches.*] Come, Stephen. Come, Charles. Bring Sarah. [*He passes into the shed.*]

[BILTON *opens the box and deliberately drops the matches into the fire-bucket.*]

LOMAX   Oh I say! [BILTON *stolidly hands him the empty box.*] Infernal nonsense! Pure scientific ignorance! [*He goes in.*]

SARAH   Am I all right, Bilton?

BILTON   Youll have to put on list slippers, miss: thats all. Weve got em inside. [*She goes in.*]

STEPHEN [*Very seriously to* CUSINS.]   Dolly, old fellow, think. Think before you decide. Do you feel that you are a sufficiently practical man? It is a huge undertaking, an enormous responsibility. All this mass of business will be Greek to you.

CUSINS   Oh, I think it will be much less difficult than Greek.

STEPHEN   Well, I just want to say this before I leave you to yourselves. Dont let anything I have said about right and wrong prejudice you against this great chance in life. I have satisfied myself that the business is one of the highest character and a credit to our country. [*Emotionally.*] I am very proud of my father. I— [*Unable to proceed, he presses* CUSINS' *hand and goes hastily into the shed, followed by* BILTON.]

[BARBARA *and* CUSINS, *left alone together, look at one another silently.*]

CUSINS   Barbara: I am going to accept this offer.

BARBARA   I thought you would.

CUSINS   You understand, dont you, that I had to decide without consulting you. If I had thrown the burden of the choice on you, you would sooner or later have despised me for it.

BARBARA   Yes: I did not want you to sell your soul for me any more than for this inheritance.

CUSINS   It is not the sale of my soul that troubles me: I have sold it too often to care about that. I have sold it for a professorship. I have sold it for an income. I have sold it to escape being imprisoned for refusing to pay taxes for hangmen's ropes and unjust wars and things that I abhor. What is all human conduct but the daily and hourly sale of our souls for trifles? What I am now selling it for is neither money nor position nor comfort, but for reality and for power.

BARBARA   You know that you will have no power, and that he has none.

CUSINS   I know. It is not for myself alone. I want to make power for the world.

BARBARA   I want to make power for the world too; but it must be spiritual power.

CUSINS   I think all power is spiritual: these cannons will not go off by themselves. I have tried to make spiritual power by teaching Greek. But the world can never be really touched by a dead language and a dead civilization. The people must have power; and the people cannot have Greek. Now the power that is made here can be wielded by all men.

BARBARA   Power to burn women's houses down and kill their sons and tear their husbands to pieces.

CUSINS   You cannot have power for good without having power for evil too. Even mother's milk nourishes murderers as well as heroes. This power which only tears men's bodies to pieces has never been so horribly abused as the intellectual power, the imaginative power, the poetic, religious power that can enslave men's souls. As a teacher of Greek I gave the intellectual man weapons against the common man. I now want to give the common man weapons against the intellectual man. I love the common people. I want to arm them against the lawyer, the doctor, the priest, the literary man, the professor, the artist, and the politician, who, once in authority, are the most dangerous, disastrous, and tyrannical of all the fools, rascals, and impostors. I want a democratic power strong enough to force the intellectual oligarchy to use its genius for the general good or else perish.

BARBARA   Is there no higher power than that? [*Pointing to the shell.*]

CUSINS   Yes: but that power can destroy the higher powers just as a tiger can destroy a man: therefore man must master that power first. I admitted this when the Turks and Greeks were last at war. My best pupil went out to fight for Hellas.[8] My parting gift to him was not a copy of Plato's Republic, but a revolver and a hundred Undershaft cartridges. The blood of every Turk he shot—if he shot any—is on my head as well as on Undershaft's. That act committed me to this place for ever. Your father's challenge has beaten me. Dare I make war on war? I dare. I must. I will. And now, is it all over between us?

BARBARA [*Touched by his evident dread of her answer.*]   Silly baby Dolly! How could it be?

CUSINS [*Overjoyed.*]   Then you—you—you— Oh for my drum! [*He flourishes imaginary drumsticks.*]

BARBARA [*Angered by his levity.*]   Take care, Dolly, take care. Oh, if only I could get away from you and from father and from it all! if I could have the wings of a dove and fly away to heaven!

CUSINS   And leave me!

BARBARA   Yes, you, and all the other naughty mischievous children of men. But I cant. I was happy in the Salvation Army for a moment. I escaped from the world into a paradise of enthusiasm and prayer and soul saving; but the moment our money ran short, it all came back to Bodger: it was he who saved our people: he, and the Prince of Darkness, my papa. Undershaft and Bodger: their hands stretch everywhere: when we feed a starving fellow creature, it is with their bread, because there is no other bread; when we tend the sick, it is in the hospitals they endow; if we turn from the churches they build, we must kneel on the stones of the

8. Greece.

streets they pave. As long as that lasts, there is no getting away from them. Turning our backs on Bodger and Undershaft is turning our backs on life.

CUSINS I thought you were determined to turn your back on the wicked side of life.

BARBARA There is no wicked side: life is all one. And I never wanted to shirk my share in whatever evil must be endured, whether it be sin or suffering. I wish I could cure you of middle-class ideas, Dolly.

CUSINS [Gasping.] Middle cl—! A snub! A social snub to me! from the daughter of a foundling!

BARBARA That is why I have no class, Dolly: I come straight out of the heart of the whole people. If I were middle-class I should turn my back on my father's business; and we should both live in an artistic drawingroom, with you reading the reviews in one corner, and I in the other at the piano, playing Schumann: both very superior persons, and neither of us a bit of use. Sooner than that, I would sweep out the guncotton shed, or be one of Bodger's barmaids. Do you know what would have happened if you had refused papa's offer?

CUSINS I wonder!

BARBARA I should have given you up and married the man who accepted it. After all, my dear old mother has more sense than any of you. I felt like her when I saw this place—felt that I must have it—that never, never, never could I let it go; only she thought it was the houses and the kitchen ranges and the linen and china, when it was really all the human souls to be saved: not weak souls in starved bodies, crying with gratitude for a scrap of bread and treacle, but fullfed, quarrelsome, snobbish, uppish creatures, all standing on their little rights and dignities, and thinking that my father ought to be greatly obliged to them for making so much money for him—and so he ought. That is where salvation is really wanted. My father shall never throw it in my teeth again that my converts were bribed with bread. [She is transfigured.] I have got rid of the bribe of bread. I have got rid of the bribe of heaven. Let God's work be done for its own sake: the work he had to create us to do because it cannot be done except by living men and women. When I die, let him be in my debt, not I in his; and let me forgive him as becomes a woman of my rank.

CUSINS Then the way of life lies through the factory of death?

BARBARA Yes, through the raising of hell to heaven and of man to God, through the unveiling of an eternal light in the Valley of The Shadow. [Seizing him with both hands.] Oh, did you think my courage would never come back? did you believe that I was a deserter? that I, who have stood in the streets, and taken my people to my heart, and talked of the holiest and greatest things with them, could ever turn back and chatter foolishly to fashionable people about nothing in a drawingroom? Never, never, never, never: Major Barbara will die with the colors. Oh! and I have my dear little Dolly boy still; and he has found me my place and my work. Glory Hallelujah! [*She kisses him.*]

CUSINS   My dearest: consider my delicate health. I cannot stand as much happiness as you can.

BARBARA   Yes: it is not easy work being in love with me, is it? But it's good for you. [*She runs to the shed, and calls, childlike.*] Mamma! Mamma! [BILTON *comes out of the shed, followed by* UNDERSHAFT.] I want Mamma.

UNDERSHAFT   She is taking off her list slippers, dear. [*He passes on to* CUSINS.] Well? What does she say?

CUSINS   She has gone right up into the skies.

LADY BRITOMART [*Coming from the shed and stopping on the steps, obstructing* SARAH, *who follows with* LOMAX. BARBARA *clutches like a baby at her mother's skirt.*]   Barbara: when will you learn to be independent and to act and think for yourself? I know as well as possible what that cry of "Mamma, Mamma," means. Always running to me!

SARAH [*Touching* LADY BRITOMART's *ribs with her finger tips and imitating a bicycle horn.*]   Pip! pip!

LADY BRITOMART [*Highly indignant.*]   How dare you say Pip! pip! to me, Sarah? You are both very naughty children. What do you want, Barbara?

BARBARA   I want a house in the village to live in with Dolly. [*Dragging at the skirt.*] Come and tell me which one to take.

UNDERSHAFT [*To* CUSINS.]   Six o'clock tomorrow morning, my young friend.

Pygmalion

Preface to *Pygmalion*

A *Professor of Phonetics*.

As will be seen later on, *Pygmalion*[1] needs, not a preface, but a sequel, which I have supplied in its due place.

The English have no respect for their language, and will not teach their children to speak it. They spell it so abominably that no man can teach himself what it sounds like. It is impossible for an Englishman to open his mouth without making some other Englishman hate or despise him. German and Spanish are accessible to foreigners; English is not accessible even to Englishmen. The reformer England needs today is an energetic phonetic enthusiast: that is why I have made such a one the hero of a popular play. There have been heroes of that kind crying in the wilderness for many years past. When I became interested in the subject towards the end of the eighteen-seventies, the illustrious Alexander Melville Bell, the inventor of Visible Speech, had emigrated to Canada, where his son invented the telephone; but Alexander J. Ellis was still a London patriarch, with an impressive head always covered by a velvet skull cap, for which he would apologize to public meetings in a very courtly manner. He and Tito Pagliardini, another phonetic veteran, were men whom it was impossible to dislike. Henry Sweet, then a young man, lacked their sweetness of character: he was about as conciliatory to conventional mortals as Ibsen or Samuel Butler. His great ability as a phonetician (he was, I think, the best of them all at his job) would have entitled him to high official recognition, and perhaps enabled him to popularize his subject, but for his Satanic contempt for all academic dignitaries and persons in general who thought more of Greek than of phonetics. Once, in the days when the Imperial Institute rose in South Kensington, and Joseph Chamberlain was booming the Empire, I induced the editor of a leading monthly review to commission an article from Sweet on the imperial importance of his subject. When it arrived, it contained nothing but a

---

1. In classical legend, Pygmalion was king of Cyprus and a sculptor. He fell in love with a statue which Aphrodite transformed into a living woman, Galatea.

savagely derisive attack on a professor of language and literature whose chair Sweet regarded as proper to a phonetic expert only. The article, being libellous, had to be returned as impossible; and I had to renounce my dream of dragging its author into the limelight. When I met him afterwards, for the first time for many years, I found to my astonishment that he, who had been a quite tolerably presentable young man, had actually managed by sheer scorn to alter his personal appearance until he had become a sort of walking repudiation of Oxford and all its traditions. It must have been largely in his own despite that he was squeezed into something called a Readership of phonetics there. The future of phonetics rests probably with his pupils, who all swore by him; but nothing could bring the man himself into any sort of compliance with the university to which he nevertheless clung by divine right in an intensely Oxonian way. I daresay his papers, if he has left any, include some satires that may be published without too destructive results fifty years hence. He was, I believe, not in the least an illnatured man: very much the opposite, I should say; but he would not suffer fools gladly.

Those who knew him will recognize in my third act the allusion to the patent shorthand in which he used to write postcards, and which may be acquired from a four and six-penny[2] manual published by the Clarendon Press. The postcards which Mrs Higgins describes are such as I have received from Sweet. I would decipher a sound which a cockney would represent by *zerr*, and a Frenchman by *seu*, and then write demanding with some heat what on earth it meant. Sweet, with boundless contempt for my stupidity, would reply that it not only meant but obviously was the word Result, as no other word containing that sound, and capable of making sense with the context, existed in any language spoken on earth. That less expert mortals should require fuller indications was beyond Sweet's patience. Therefore, though the whole point of his "Current Shorthand" is that it can express every sound in the language perfectly, vowels as well as consonants, and that your hand has to make no stroke except the easy and current ones with which you write m, n, and u, l, p, and q, scribbling them at whatever angle comes easiest to you, his unfortunate determination to make this remarkable and quite legible script serve also as a shorthand reduced it in his own practice to the most inscrutable of cryptograms. His true objective was the provision of a full, accurate, legible script for our noble but ill-dressed language; but he was led past that by his contempt for the popular Pitman system of shorthand, which he called the Pitfall system. The triumph of Pitman was a triumph of business organization: there was a weekly paper to persuade you to learn Pitman: there were

2. Four shillings and sixpence, approximately 35c.

cheap textbooks and exercise books and transcripts of speeches for you to copy, and schools where experienced teachers coached you up to the necessary proficiency. Sweet could not organize his market in that fashion. He might as well have been the Sybil who tore up the leaves of prophecy that nobody would attend to. The four and sixpenny manual, mostly in his lithographed handwriting, that was never vulgarly advertized, may perhaps some day be taken up by a syndicate and pushed upon the public as The Times pushed the Encyclopædia Britannica; but until then it will certainly not prevail against Pitman. I have bought three copies of it during my lifetime; and I am informed by the publishers that its cloistered existence is still a steady and healthy one. I actually learned the system two several times; and yet the shorthand in which I am writing these lines is Pitman's. And the reason is, that my secretary cannot transcribe Sweet, having been perforce taught in the schools of Pitman. Therefore, Sweet railed at Pitman as vainly as Thersites railed at Ajax: his raillery, however it may have eased his soul, gave no popular vogue to Current Shorthand.

Pygmalion Higgins is not a portrait of Sweet, to whom the adventure of Eliza Doolittle would have been impossible; still, as will be seen, there are touches of Sweet in the play. With Higgins's physique and temperament Sweet might have set the Thames on fire. As it was, he impressed himself professionally on Europe to an extent that made his comparative personal obscurity, and the failure of Oxford to do justice to his eminence, a puzzle to foreign specialists in his subject. I do not blame Oxford, because I think Oxford is quite right in demanding a certain social amenity from its nurslings (heaven knows it is not exorbitant in its requirements!); for although I well know how hard it is for a man of genius with a seriously underrated subject to maintain serene and kindly relations with the men who underrate it, and who keep all the best places for less important subjects which they profess without originality and sometimes without much capacity for them, still, if he overwhelms them with wrath and disdain, he cannot expect them to heap honors on him.

Of the later generations of phoneticians I know little. Among them towers the Poet Laureate,[3] to whom perhaps Higgins may owe his Miltonic sympathies, though here again I must disclaim all portraiture. But if the play makes the public aware that there are such people as phoneticians, and that they are among the most important people in England at present, it will serve its turn.

I wish to boast that *Pygmalion* has been an extremely successful play all over Europe and North America as well as at home. It is so

3. Robert Bridges, one of the founders of the Society for Pure English, was Poet Laureate at the time of the play's early productions in England.

intensely and deliberately didactic, and its subject is esteemed so dry, that I delight in throwing it at the heads of the wiseacres who repeat the parrot cry that art should never be didactic. It goes to prove my contention that art should never be anything else.

Finally, and for the encouragement of people troubled with accents that cut them off from all high employment, I may add that the change wrought by Professor Higgins in the flower-girl is neither impossible nor uncommon. The modern concierge's daughter who fulfils her ambition by playing the Queen of Spain in Ruy Blas at the Théâtre Français is only one of many thousands of men and women who have sloughed off their native dialects and acquired a new tongue. But the thing has to be done scientifically, or the last state of the aspirant may be worse than the first. An honest and natural slum dialect is more tolerable than the attempt of a phonetically untaught person to imitate the vulgar dialect of the golf club; and I am sorry to say that in spite of the efforts of our Academy of Dramatic Art, there is still too much sham golfing English on our stage, and too little of the noble English of Forbes Robertson.

Pygmalion

Act I

Covent Garden at 11.15 p.m. Torrents of heavy summer rain. Cab whistles blowing frantically in all directions. Pedestrians running for shelter into the market and under the portico of St. Paul's Church, where there are already several people, among them a lady and her daughter in evening dress. They are all peering out gloomily at the rain, except one man with his back turned to the rest, who seems wholly preoccupied with a notebook in which he is writing busily.

The church clock strikes the first quarter.

THE DAUGHTER [*In the space between the central pillars, close to the one on her left.*]   I'm getting chilled to the bone. What can Freddy be doing all this time? Hes been gone twenty minutes.

THE MOTHER [*On her daughter's right.*]   Not so long. But he ought to have got us a cab by this.

A BYSTANDER [*On the lady's right.*]   He wont get no cab not until half-past eleven, missus, when they come back after dropping their theatre fares.

THE MOTHER   But we must have a cab. We cant stand here until half-past eleven. It's too bad.

THE BYSTANDER   Well, it aint my fault, missus.

THE DAUGHTER   If Freddy had a bit of gumption, he would have got one at the theatre door.

THE MOTHER   What could he have done, poor boy?

THE DAUGHTER   Other people got cabs. Why couldnt he?

[FREDDY *rushes in out of the rain from the Southampton Street side, and comes between them closing a dripping umbrella. He is a young man of twenty, in evening dress, very wet round the ankles.*]

THE DAUGHTER   Well, havnt you got a cab?

FREDDY   Theres not one to be had for love or money.

THE MOTHER   Oh, Freddy, there must be one. You cant have tried.

THE DAUGHTER   It's too tiresome. Do you expect us to go and get one ourselves?

FREDDY   I tell you theyre all engaged. The rain was so sudden: nobody was prepared; and everybody had to take a cab. Ive been to Charing Cross one way and nearly to Ludgate Circus the other; and they were all engaged.

THE MOTHER   Did you try Trafalgar Square?

FREDDY   There wasnt one at Trafalgar Square.

THE DAUGHTER   Did you try?

FREDDY   I tried as far as Charing Cross Station. Did you expect me to walk to Hammersmith?

THE DAUGHTER   You havnt tried at all.

THE MOTHER   You really are very helpless, Freddy. Go again; and dont come back until you have found a cab.

FREDDY   I shall simply get soaked for nothing.

THE DAUGHTER   And what about us? Are we to stay here all night in this draught, with next to nothing on. You selfish pig—

FREDDY   Oh, very well: I'll go, I'll go. [*He opens his umbrella and dashes off Strandwards, but comes into collision with a* FLOWER GIRL, *who is hurrying in for shelter, knocking her basket out of her hands. A blinding flash of lightning, followed instantly by a rattling peal of thunder, orchestrates the incident.*]

THE FLOWER GIRL   Nah then, Freddy: look wh'y' gowin, deah.

FREDDY   Sorry [*He rushes off.*]

THE FLOWER GIRL [*Picking up her scattered flowers and replacing them in the basket.*]   Theres menners f'yer! Te-oo banches o voy-lets trod into the mad.

[*She sits down on the plinth of the column, sorting her flowers, on the lady's right. She is not at all an attractive person. She is perhaps eighteen, perhaps twenty, hardly older. She wears a little sailor hat of black straw that has long been exposed to the dust and soot of London and has seldom if ever been brushed. Her hair needs washing rather badly: its mousy color can hardly be natural. She wears a shoddy black coat that reaches nearly*]

*to her knees and is shaped to her waist. She has a brown skirt
with a coarse apron. Her boots are much the worse for wear.
She is no doubt as clean as she can afford to be; but compared
to the ladies she is very dirty. Her features are no worse than
theirs; but their condition leaves something to be desired; and
she needs the services of a dentist.]*

THE MOTHER   How do you know that my son's name is Freddy, pray?

THE FLOWER GIRL   Ow, eez ye-ooa san, is e? Wal, fewd dan y' de-
ooty bawmz a mather should, eed now bettern to spawl a pore gel's
flahrzn than ran awy athaht pyin. Will ye-oo py me f'them? [*Here,
with apologies, this desperate attempt to represent her dialect without a phonetic alphabet must be abandoned as unintelligible outside
London.*]

THE DAUGHTER   Do nothing of the sort, mother. The idea!

THE MOTHER   Please allow me, Clara. Have you any pennies?

THE DAUGHTER   No. Ive nothing smaller than sixpence.[1]

THE FLOWER GIRL [*Hopefully.*]   I can give you change for a tanner,
kind lady.

THE MOTHER [*To* CLARA.]   Give it to me. [CLARA *parts reluctantly.*]
Now [*to the* GIRL.] This is for your flowers.

THE FLOWER GIRL   Thank you kindly, lady.

THE DAUGHTER   Make her give you the change. These things are
only a penny a bunch.

THE MOTHER   Do hold your tongue, Clara. [*To the* GIRL.] You can
keep the change.

THE FLOWER GIRL   Oh, thank you, lady.

THE MOTHER   Now tell me how you know that young gentleman's
name.

THE FLOWER GIRL   I didnt.

THE MOTHER   I heard you call him by it. Dont try to deceive me.

THE FLOWER GIRL [*Protesting.*]   Whos trying to deceive you? I called
him Freddy or Charlie same as you might yourself if you was talking to a stranger and wished to be pleasant. [*She sits down beside
her basket.*]

THE DAUGHTER   Sixpence thrown away! Really, mamma, you might
have spared Freddy that. [*She retreats in disgust behind the pillar.*]
[*An elderly gentleman of the amiable military type rushes into
shelter, and closes a dripping umbrella. He is in the same plight
as* FREDDY, *very wet about the ankles. He is in evening dress,
with a light overcoat. He takes the place left vacant by the
daughter's retirement.*]

THE GENTLEMAN   Phew!

THE MOTHER [*To the* GENTLEMAN.]   Oh, sir, is there any sign of its
stopping?

---

1. A penny (1d) was worth 1/240 of a pound, and 1/12 of a shilling. A shilling is worth
approximately 7c, so sixpence is worth less than 4c.

THE GENTLEMAN   I'm afraid not. It started worse than ever about two minutes ago. [*He goes to the plinth beside* THE FLOWER GIRL; *puts up his foot on it; and stoops to turn down his trouser ends.*]

THE MOTHER   Oh dear! [*She retires sadly and joins her daughter.*]

THE FLOWER GIRL [*Taking advantage of the military gentleman's proximity to establish friendly relations with him.*]   If it's worse, it's a sign it's nearly over. So cheer up, Captain; and buy a flower off a poor girl.

THE GENTLEMAN   I'm sorry. I havnt any change.

THE FLOWER GIRL   I can give you change, Captain.

THE GENTLEMAN   For a sovereign? Ive nothing less.

THE FLOWER GIRL   Garn! Oh do buy a flower off me, Captain. I can change half-a-crown. Take this for tuppence.[2]

THE GENTLEMAN   Now dont be troublesome: theres a good girl. [*Trying his pockets.*] I really havnt any change—Stop: heres three hapence, if thats any use to you. [*He retreats to the other pillar.*]

THE FLOWER GIRL [*Disappointed, but thinking three halfpence better than nothing.*]   Thank you, sir.

THE BYSTANDER [*To the girl.*]   You be careful: give him a flower for it. Theres a bloke here behind taking down every blessed word youre saying. [*All turn to the man who is taking notes.*]

THE FLOWER GIRL [*Springing up terrified.*]   I aint done nothing wrong by speaking to the gentleman. Ive a right to sell flowers if I keep off the kerb. [*Hysterically.*] I'm a respectable girl: so help me, I never spoke to him except to ask him to buy a flower off me. [*General hubbub, mostly sympathetic to* THE FLOWER GIRL, *but deprecating her excessive sensibility. Cries of* Dont start hollerin. Whos hurting you? Nobody's going to touch you. Whats the good of fussing? Steady on. Easy easy, etc., *come from the elderly staid spectators, who pat her comfortingly. Less patient ones bid her shut her head, or ask her roughly what is wrong with her. A remoter group, not knowing what the matter is, crowd in and increase the noise with question and answer:* Whats the row? Whatshe do? Where is he? A tec[3] taking her down. What! him? Yes: him over there: Took money off the gentleman, etc. THE FLOWER GIRL, *distraught and mobbed, breaks through them to the gentleman, crying wildly.*] Oh, sir, dont let him charge me. You dunno what it means to me. Theyll take away my character and drive me on the streets for speaking to gentlemen. They—

THE NOTE TAKER [*Coming forward on her right, the rest crowding after him.*]   There, there, there, there! whos hurting you, you silly girl? What do you take me for?

THE BYSTANDER   It's all right: hes a gentleman: look at his boots.

---

2. A sovereign was a gold coin worth one pound (twenty shillings). Half a crown was a coin worth two shillings and sixpence. Tuppence is two pennies (2d), worth less than 2c.
3. Short for detective.

[*Explaining to* THE NOTE TAKER.] She thought you was a copper's nark,[4] sir.

THE NOTE TAKER [*With quick interest.*]   Whats a copper's nark?

THE BYSTANDER [*Inapt at definition.*]   It's a—well, it's a copper's nark, as you might say. What else would you call it? A sort of informer.

THE FLOWER GIRL [*Still hysterical.*]   I take my Bible oath I never said a word—

THE NOTE TAKER [*Overbearing but good-humored.*]   Oh, shut up, shut up. Do I look like a policeman?

THE FLOWER GIRL [*Far from reassured.*]   Then what did you take down my words for? How do I know whether you took me down right? You just shew me what youve wrote about me. [THE NOTE TAKER *opens his book and holds it steadily under her nose, though the pressure of the mob trying to read it over his shoulders would upset a weaker man.*] Whats that? That aint proper writing. I cant read that.

THE NOTE TAKER   I can. [*Reads, reproducing her pronunciation exactly.*] "Cheer ap, Keptin; n' baw ya flahr orf a pore gel."

THE FLOWER GIRL [*Much distressed.*]   It's because I called him Captain. I meant no harm. [*To* THE GENTLEMAN.] Oh, sir, dont let him lay a charge agen me for a word like that. You—

THE GENTLEMAN   Charge! I make no charge. [*To* THE NOTE TAKER.] Really, sir, if you are a detective, you need not begin protecting me against molestation by young women until I ask you. Anybody could see that the girl meant no harm.

THE BYSTANDERS GENERALLY [*Demonstrating against police espionage.*]   Course they could. What business is it of yours? You mind your own affairs. He wants promotion, he does. Taking down people's words! Girl never said a word to him. What harm if she did? Nice thing a girl cant shelter from the rain without being insulted, etc., etc., etc. [*She is conducted by the more sympathetic demonstrators back to her plinth, where she resumes her seat and struggles with her emotion.*]

THE BYSTANDER   He aint a tec. Hes a blooming busybody: thats what he is. I tell you, look at his boots.

THE NOTE TAKER [*Turning on him genially.*]   And how are all your people down at Selsey?

THE BYSTANDER [*Suspiciously.*]   Who told you my people come from Selsey?

THE NOTE TAKER   Never you mind. They did. [*To* THE GIRL.] How do you come to be up so far east? You were born in Lisson Grove.

THE FLOWER GIRL [*Appalled.*]   Oh, what harm is there in my leaving Lisson Grove? It wasn't fit for a pig to live in; and I had to pay four-and-six a week. [*In tears.*] Oh, boo—hoo—oo—

4. Policeman's informer.

THE NOTE TAKER   Live where you like; but stop that noise.

THE GENTLEMAN [*To* THE GIRL.]   Come, come! he cant touch you: you have a right to live where you please.

A SARCASTIC BYSTANDER [*Thrusting himself between* THE NOTE TAKER *and* THE GENTLEMAN.]   Park Lane,[5] for instance. Id like to go into the Housing Question with you, I would.

THE FLOWER GIRL [*Subsiding into a brooding melancholy over her basket, and talking very low-spiritedly to herself.*]   I'm a good girl, I am.

THE SARCASTIC BYSTANDER [*Not attending to her.*]   Do you know where *I* come from?

THE NOTE TAKER [*Promptly.*]   Hoxton.

[*Titterings. Popular interest in* THE NOTE TAKER's *performance increases.*]

THE SARCASTIC ONE [*Amazed.*]   Well, who said I didn't? Bly me! You know everything, you do.

THE FLOWER GIRL [*Still nursing her sense of injury.*]   Aint no call to meddle with me, he aint.

THE BYSTANDER [*To her.*]   Of course he aint. Dont you stand it from him. [*To* THE NOTE TAKER.] See here: what call have you to know about people what never offered to meddle with you? Wheres your warrant?

SEVERAL BYSTANDERS [*Encouraged by this seeming point of law.*]   Yes: wheres your warrant?

THE FLOWER GIRL   Let him say what he likes. I dont want to have no truck with him.

THE BYSTANDER   You take us for dirt under your feet, dont you? Catch you taking liberties with a gentleman!

THE SARCASTIC BYSTANDER   Yes: tell him where he come from if you want to go fortune-telling.

THE NOTE TAKER   Cheltenham, Harrow, Cambridge, and India.[6]

THE GENTLEMAN   Quite right. [*Great laughter. Reaction in* THE NOTE TAKER's *favor. Exclamations of* He knows all about it. Told him proper. Hear him tell the toff where he come from? etc.] May I ask, sir, do you do this for your living at a music hall?

THE NOTE TAKER   Ive thought of that. Perhaps I shall some day.

[*The rain has stopped; and the persons on the outside of the crowd begin to drop off.*]

THE FLOWER GIRL [*Resenting the reaction.*]   Hes no gentleman, he aint, to interfere with a poor girl.

THE DAUGHTER [*Out of patience, pushing her way rudely to the front and displacing* THE GENTLEMAN, *who politely retires to the other*

---

5. Areas of London. Lisson Grove is a run-down slum area, while Park Lane is exclusive and fashionable.
6. Pickering has followed the conventional route from birth in the home counties to public school, university, and service in the Empire.

side of the pillar.] What on earth is Freddy doing? I shall get pneumonia if I stay in this draught any longer.

THE NOTE TAKER [*To himself, hastily making a note of her pronunciation of "monia."*] Earlscourt.

THE DAUGHTER [*Violently.*] Will you please keep your impertinent remarks to yourself.

THE NOTE TAKER Did I say that out loud? I didnt mean to. I beg your pardon. Your mother's Epsom, unmistakably.

THE MOTHER [*Advancing between* HER DAUGHTER *and* THE NOTE TAKER.] How very curious! I was brought up in Largelady Park, near Epsom.

THE NOTE TAKER [*Uproariously amused.*] Ha! ha! What a devil of a name! Excuse me. [*To* THE DAUGHTER.] You want a cab, do you?

THE DAUGHTER Dont dare speak to me.

THE MOTHER Oh please, please, Clara. [HER DAUGHTER *repudiates her with an angry shrug and retires haughtily.*] We should be so grateful to you, sir, if you found us a cab. [THE NOTE TAKER *produces a whistle.*] Oh, thank you. [*She joins* HER DAUGHTER.]

[THE NOTE TAKER *blows a piercing blast.*]

THE SARCASTIC BYSTANDER There! I knowed he was a plain-clothes copper.

THE BYSTANDER That aint a police whistle: thats a sporting whistle.

THE FLOWER GIRL [*Still preoccupied with her wounded feelings.*] Hes no right to take away my character. My character is the same to me as any lady's.

THE NOTE TAKER I dont know whether youve noticed it; but the rain stopped about two minutes ago.

THE BYSTANDER So it has. Why didnt you say so before? and us losing our time listening to your silliness! [*He walks off towards the Strand.*]

THE SARCASTIC BYSTANDER I can tell where you come from. You come from Anwell. Go back there.

THE NOTE TAKER [*Helpfully.*] Hanwell.

THE SARCASTIC BYSTANDER [*Affecting great distinction of speech.*] Thenk you, teacher. Haw haw! So long. [*He touches his hat with mock respect and strolls off.*]

THE FLOWER GIRL Frightening people like that! How would he like it himself?

THE MOTHER It's quite fine now, Clara. We can walk to a motor bus. Come. [*She gathers her skirts above her ankles and hurries off towards the Strand.*]

THE DAUGHTER But the cab— [HER MOTHER *is out of hearing.*] Oh, how tiresome! [*She follows angrily.*]

[*All the rest have gone except* THE NOTE TAKER, THE GENTLEMAN, *and* THE FLOWER GIRL, *who sits arranging her basket, and still pitying herself in murmurs.*]

THE FLOWER GIRL Poor girl! Hard enough for her to live without being worried and chivied.

THE GENTLEMAN [*Returning to his former place on* THE NOTE TAKER's *left.*] How do you do it, if I may ask?

THE NOTE TAKER Simply phonetics. The science of speech. Thats my profession: also my hobby. Happy is the man who can make a living by his hobby! You can spot an Irishman or a Yorkshireman by his brogue. *I* can place any man within six miles. I can place him within two miles in London. Sometimes within two streets.

THE FLOWER GIRL Ought to be ashamed of himself, unmanly coward!

THE GENTLEMAN But is there a living in that?

THE NOTE TAKER Oh yes. Quite a fat one. This is an age of upstarts. Men begin in Kentish Town with £80 a year, and end in Park Lane with a hundred thousand.[7] They want to drop Kentish Town; but they give themselves away every time they open their mouths. Now I can teach them—

THE FLOWER GIRL Let him mind his own business and leave a poor girl—

THE NOTE TAKER [*Explosively.*] Woman: cease this detestable boohooing instantly; or else seek the shelter of some other place of worship.

THE FLOWER GIRL [*With feeble defiance.*] Ive a right to be here if I like, same as you.

THE NOTE TAKER A woman who utters such depressing and disgusting sounds has no right to be anywhere—no right to live. Remember that you are a human being with a soul and the divine gift of articulate speech: that your native language is the language of Shakespear and Milton and The Bible; and dont sit there crooning like a bilious pigeon.

THE FLOWER GIRL [*Quite overwhelmed, looking up at him in mingled wonder and deprecation without daring to raise her head.*] Ah-ahah-ow-ow-ow-oo!

THE NOTE TAKER [*Whipping out his book.*] Heavens! what a sound! [*He writes; then holds out the book and reads, reproducing her vowels exactly.*] Ah-ah-ah-ow-ow-ow-oo!

THE FLOWER GIRL [*Tickled by the performance, and laughing in spite of herself.*] Garn!

THE NOTE TAKER You see this creature with her kerbstone English: the English that will keep her in the gutter to the end of her days. Well, sir, in three months I could pass that girl off as a duchess at an ambassador's garden party. I could even get her a place as lady's maid or shop assistant, which requires better English. Thats the sort of thing I do for commercial millionaires. And on the

---

7. £80 is approximately $120, and a poor income, while £100,000 was and is a fortune.

profits of it I do genuine scientific work in phonetics, and a little
as a poet on Miltonic lines.

THE GENTLEMAN   I am myself a student of Indian dialects; and—

THE NOTE TAKER [*Eagerly.*]   Are you? Do you know Colonel Pickering, the author of Spoken Sanscrit?

THE GENTLEMAN   I am Colonel Pickering. Who are you?

THE NOTE TAKER   Henry Higgins, author of Higgins's Universal
Alphabet.

PICKERING [*With enthusiasm.*]   I came from India to meet you.

HIGGINS   I was going to India to meet you.

PICKERING   Where do you live?

HIGGINS   27A Wimpole Street. Come and see me tomorrow.

PICKERING   I'm at the Carlton.[8] Come with me now and lets have
a jaw over some supper.

HIGGINS   Right you are.

THE FLOWER GIRL [*To* PICKERING, *as he passes her.*]   Buy a flower,
kind gentleman. I'm short for my lodging.

PICKERING   I really havnt any change. I'm sorry. [*He goes away.*]

HIGGINS [*Shocked at* THE GIRL'*s mendacity.*]   Liar. You said you
could change half-a-crown.

THE FLOWER GIRL [*Rising in desperation.*]   You ought to be stuffed
with nails, you ought. [*Flinging the basket at his feet.*] Take the
whole blooming basket for sixpence.

[*The church clock strikes the second quarter.*]

HIGGINS [*Hearing in it the voice of God, rebuking him for his Pharisaic
want of charity to the poor girl.*]   A reminder. [*He raises his hat
solemnly; then throws a handful of money into the basket and follows
PICKERING.*]

THE FLOWER GIRL [*Picking up a half-crown.*]   Ah-ow-ooh! [*Picking
up a couple of florins.*[9]] Aaah-ow ooh! [*Picking up several coins.*]
Aaaaaah-ow-ooh! [*Picking up a half-sovereign.*] Aaaaaaaaaaaaah-
ow-ooh!!!

FREDDY [*Springing out of a taxicab.*]   Got one at last. Hallo! [*To* THE
GIRL.] Where are the two ladies that were here?

THE FLOWER GIRL   They walked to the bus when the rain stopped.

FREDDY   And left me with a cab on my hands! Damnation!

THE FLOWER GIRL [*With grandeur.*]   Never you mind, young man.
I'm going home in a taxi. [*She sails off to the cab. The driver puts
his hand behind him and holds the door firmly shut against her.
Quite understanding his mistrust, she shews him her handful of
money.*] Eightpence aint no object to me, Charlie. [*He grins and
opens the door.*] Angel Court, Drury Lane, round the corner of
Micklejohn's oil shop. Lets see how fast you can make her hop it.

---

8. A good London hotel.
9. A florin was two shillings and worth about 15c.

[*She gets in and pulls the door to with a slam as the taxicab starts.*]
FREDDY   Well, I'm dashed!

Act II

Next day at 11 a.m. HIGGINS's *laboratory in Wimpole Street. It is a room on the first floor, looking on the street, and was meant for the drawing-room. The double doors are in the middle of the back wall; and persons entering find in the corner to their right two tall file cabinets at right angles to one another against the walls. In this corner stands a flat writing-table, on which are a phonograph, a laryngoscope, a row of tiny organ pipes with a bellows, a set of lamp chimneys for singing flames with burners attached to a gas plug in the wall by an indiarubber tube, several tuning-forks of different sizes, a life-size image of half a human head, shewing in section the vocal organs, and a box containing a supply of wax cylinders for the phonograph.*

Further down the room, on the same side, is a fireplace, with a comfortable leather-covered easy-chair at the side of the hearth nearest the door, and a coal-scuttle. There is a clock on the mantelpiece. Between the fireplace and the phonograph table is a stand for newspapers.

On the other side of the central door, to the left of the visitor, is a cabinet of shallow drawers. On it is a telephone and the telephone directory. The corner beyond, and most of the side wall, is occupied by a grand piano, with the keyboard at the end furthest from the door, and a bench for the player extending the full length of the keyboard. On the piano is a dessert dish heaped with fruit and sweets, mostly chocolates.

The middle of the room is clear. Besides the easy-chair, the piano bench, and two chairs at the phonograph table, there is one stray chair. It stands near the fireplace. On the walls, engravings: mostly Piranesis and mezzotint portraits. No paintings.

PICKERING *is seated at the table, putting down some cards and a tuning-fork which he has been using.* HIGGINS *is standing up near him, closing two or three file drawers which are hanging out. He appears in the morning light as a robust, vital, appetizing sort of man of forty or thereabouts, dressed in a professional-looking black frock-coat with a white linen collar and black silk tie. He is of the energetic, scientific type, heartily, even violently inter-*

*ested in everything that can be studied as a scientific sub-
ject, and careless about himself and other people,
including their feelings. He is, in fact, but for his years and
size, rather like a very impetuous baby "taking notice"
eagerly and loudly, and requiring almost as much watching to keep him out of unintended mischief. His manner
varies from genial bullying when he is in a good humor to
stormy petulance when anything goes wrong; but he is so
entirely frank and void of malice that he remains likeable
even in his least reasonable moments.*

HIGGINS [*As he shuts the last drawer.*]   Well, I think thats the whole
show.

PICKERING   It's really amazing. I havnt taken half of it in, you know.

HIGGINS   Would you like to go over any of it again?

PICKERING [*Rising and coming to the fireplace, where he plants himself with his back to the fire.*]   No, thank you; not now. I'm quite
done up for this morning.

HIGGINS [*Following him, and standing beside him on his left.*]   Tired
of listening to sounds?

PICKERING   Yes. It's a fearful strain. I rather fancied myself because
I can pronounce twenty-four distinct vowel sounds; but your hundred and thirty beat me. I cant hear a bit of difference between
most of them.

HIGGINS [*Chuckling, and going over to the piano to eat sweets.*]   Oh,
that comes with practice. You hear no difference at first; but you
keep on listening, and presently you find theyre all as different as
A from B. [MRS PEARCE *looks in: she is* HIGGINS's *housekeeper.*]
What the matter?

MRS PEARCE [*Hesitating, evidently perplexed.*]   A young woman
wants to see you, sir.

HIGGINS   A young woman! What does she want?

MRS PEARCE   Well, sir, she says youll be glad to see her when you
know what shes come about. Shes quite a common girl, sir. Very
common indeed. I should have sent her away, only I thought perhaps you wanted her to talk into your machines. I hope Ive not
done wrong; but really you see such queer people sometimes—
youll excuse me, I'm sure, sir—

HIGGINS   Oh, thats all right, Mrs Pearce. Has she an interesting
accent?

MRS PEARCE   Oh, something dreadful, sir, really. I dont know how
you can take an interest in it.

HIGGINS [*To* PICKERING.]   Lets have her up. Shew her up, Mrs
Pearce. [*He rushes across to his working table and picks out a cylinder to use on the phonograph.*]

MRS PEARCE [*Only half resigned to it.*]   Very well, sir. It's for you to
say. [*She goes downstairs.*]

HIGGINS   This is rather a bit of luck. I'll shew you how I make records. We'll set her talking; and I'll take it down first in Bell's visible Speech; then in broad Romic; and then we'll get her on the phonograph so that you can turn her on as often as you like with the written transcript before you.

MRS PEARCE [*Returning.*]   This is the young woman, sir.

[THE FLOWER GIRL *enters in state. She has a hat with three ostrich feathers, orange, sky-blue, and red. She has a nearly clean apron, and the shoddy coat has been tidied a little. The pathos of this deplorable figure, with its innocent vanity and consequential air, touches* PICKERING, *who has already straightened himself in the presence of* MRS PEARCE. *But as to* HIGGINS, *the only distinction he makes between men and women is that when he is neither bullying nor exclaiming to the heavens against some featherweight cross, he coaxes women as a child coaxes its nurse when it wants to get anything out of her.*]

HIGGINS [*Brusquely, recognizing her with unconcealed disappointment, and at once, babylike, making an intolerable grievance of it.*]   Why, this is the girl I jotted down last night. Shes no use: Ive got all the records I want of the Lisson Grove lingo; and I'm not going to waste another cylinder on it. [*To* THE GIRL.] Be off with you: I dont want you.

THE FLOWER GIRL   Dont you be so saucy. You aint heard what I come for yet. [*To* MRS PEARCE, *who is waiting at the door for further instructions.*] Did you tell him I come in a taxi?

MRS PEARCE   Nonsense, girl! what do you think a gentleman like Mr Higgins cares what you came in?

THE FLOWER GIRL   Oh, we are proud! He aint above giving lessons, not him: I heard him say so. Well, I aint come here to ask for any compliment; and if my money's not good enough I can go elsewhere.

HIGGINS   Good enough for what?

THE FLOWER GIRL   Good enough for ye-oo. Now you know, dont you? I'm come to have lessons, I am. And to pay for em too: make no mistake.

HIGGINS [*Stupent.*]   Well!!! [*Recovering his breath with a gasp.*] What do you expect me to say to you?

THE FLOWER GIRL   Well, if you was a gentleman, you might ask me to sit down, I think. Dont I tell you I'm bringing you business?

HIGGINS   Pickering: shall we ask this baggage to sit down, or shall we throw her out of the window?

THE FLOWER GIRL [*Running away in terror to the piano, where she turns at bay.*]   Ah-ah-oh-ow-ow-ow-oo! [*Wounded and whimpering.*] I wont be called a baggage when Ive offered to pay like any lady.

[*Motionless, the two men stare at her from the other side of the room, amazed.*]

PICKERING [*Gently.*]   What is it you want, my girl?

THE FLOWER GIRL   I want to be a lady in a flower shop stead of selling at the corner of Tottenham Court Road. But they wont take me unless I can talk more genteel. He said he could teach me. Well, here I am ready to pay him—not asking any favor—and he treats me as if I was dirt.

MRS PEARCE   How can you be such a foolish ignorant girl as to think you could afford to pay Mr Higgins?

THE FLOWER GIRL   Why shouldnt I? I know what lessons cost as well as you do; and I'm ready to pay.

HIGGINS   How much?

THE FLOWER GIRL [*Coming back to him, triumphant.*]   Now youre talking! I thought youd come off it when you saw a chance of getting back a bit of what you chucked at me last night. [*Confidentially.*] Youd had a drop in, hadnt you?

HIGGINS [*Peremptorily.*]   Sit down.

THE FLOWER GIRL   Oh, if youre going to make a compliment of it—

HIGGINS [*Thundering at her.*]   Sit down.

MRS PEARCE [*Severely.*]   Sit down, girl. Do as youre told. [*She places the stray chair near the hearthrug between* HIGGINS *and* PICKERING, *and stands behind it waiting for the girl to sit down.*]

THE FLOWER GIRL   Ah-ah-ah-ow-ow-oo! [*She stands, half rebellious, half bewildered.*]

PICKERING [*Very courteous.*]   Wont you sit down?

LIZA [*Coyly.*]   Dont mind if I do. [*She sits down.* PICKERING *returns to the hearthrug.*]

HIGGINS   Whats your name?

THE FLOWER GIRL   Liza Doolittle.

HIGGINS [*Declaiming gravely.*]
            Eliza, Elizabeth, Betsy and Bess,
            They went to the woods to get a bird's nes':

PICKERING   They found a nest with four eggs in it:

HIGGINS   They took one apiece, and left three in it.

            [*They laugh heartily at their own wit.*]

LIZA   Oh, dont be silly.

MRS PEARCE   You mustnt speak to the gentleman like that.

LIZA   Well, why wont he speak sensible to me?

HIGGINS   Come back to business. How much do you propose to pay me for the lessons?

LIZA   Oh, I know whats right. A lady friend of mine gets French lessons for eighteenpence[1] an hour from a real French gentleman. Well, you wouldnt have the face to ask me the same for teaching

---

1. One shilling and sixpence (1/6), worth about 15c.

me my own language as you would for French; so I wont give more than a shilling. Take it or leave it.

HIGGINS [*Walking up and down the room, rattling his keys and his cash in his pockets.*] You know, Pickering, if you consider a shilling, not as a simple shilling, but as a percentage of this girl's income, it works out as fully equivalent to sixty or seventy guineas[2] from a millionaire.

PICKERING How so?

HIGGINS Figure it out. A millionaire has about £150[3] a day. She earns about half-a-crown.

LIZA [*Haughtily.*] Who told you I only—

HIGGINS [*Continuing.*] She offers me two-fifths of her day's income for a lesson. Two-fifths of a millionaire's income for a day would be somewhere about £60. It's handsome. By George, it's enormous! it's the biggest offer I ever had.

LIZA [*Rising, terrified.*] Sixty pounds! What are you talking about? I never offered you sixty pounds. Where would I get—

HIGGINS Hold your tongue.

LIZA [*Weeping.*] But I aint got sixty pounds. Oh—

MRS PEARCE Dont cry, you silly girl. Sit down. Nobody is going to touch your money.

HIGGINS Somebody is going to touch you, with a broomstick, if you dont stop snivelling. Sit down.

LIZA [*Obeying slowly.*] Ah-ah-ah-ow-oo-o! One would think you was my father.

HIGGINS If I decide to teach you, I'll be worse than two fathers to you. Here! [*He offers her his silk handkerchief.*]

LIZA Whats this for?

HIGGINS To wipe your eyes. To wipe any part of your face that feels moist. Remember: thats your handkerchief; and thats your sleeve. Dont mistake the one for the other if you wish to become a lady in a shop.

[LIZA, *utterly bewildered, stares helplessly at him.*]

MRS PEARCE It's no use talking to her like that, Mr Higgins: she doesnt understand you. Besides, youre quite wrong: she doesnt do it that way at all. [*She takes the handkerchief.*]

LIZA [*Snatching it.*] Here! You give me that handkerchief. He give it to me, not to you.

PICKERING [*Laughing.*] He did. I think it must be regarded as her property, Mrs Pearce.

MRS PEARCE [*Resigning herself.*] Serve you right, Mr Higgins.

PICKERING Higgins: I'm interested. What about the ambassador's garden party? I'll say youre the greatest teacher alive if you make that good. I'll bet you all the expenses of the experiment you cant do it. And I'll pay for the lessons.

2. A guinea is one pound and one shilling.
3. Approximately $225.

LIZA   Oh, you are real good. Thank you, Captain.

HIGGINS [*Tempted, looking at her.*]   It's almost irresistible. Shes so deliciously low—so horribly dirty—

LIZA [*Protesting extremely.*]   Ah-ah-ah-ah-ow-ow-oo-oo!!!   I aint dirty: I washed my face and hands afore I come, I did.

PICKERING   Youre certainly not going to turn her head with flattery, Higgins.

MRS PEARCE [*Uneasy.*]   Oh, dont say that, sir: theres more ways than one of turning a girl's head; and nobody can do it better than Mr Higgins, though he may not always mean it. I do hope, sir, you wont encourage him to do anything foolish.

HIGGINS [*Becoming excited as the idea grows on him.*]   What is life but a series of inspired follies? The difficulty is to find them to do. Never lose a chance: it doesnt come everyday. I shall make a duchess of this draggletailed guttersnipe.

LIZA [*Strongly deprecating this view of her.*]   Ah-ah-ah-ow-ow-oo!

HIGGINS [*Carried away.*]   Yes: in six months—in three if she has a good ear and a quick tongue—I'll take her anywhere and pass her off as anything. We'll start to-day: now! this moment! Take her away and clean her, Mrs Pearce. Monkey Brand, if it wont come off any other way. Is there a good fire in the kitchen?

MRS PEARCE [*Protesting.*]   Yes; but—

HIGGINS [*Storming on.*]   Take all her clothes off and burn them. Ring up Whiteley or somebody for new ones. Wrap her up in brown paper til they come.

LIZA   Youre no gentleman, youre not, to talk of such things. I'm a good girl, I am; and I know what the like of you are, I do.

HIGGINS   We want none of your Lisson Grove prudery here, young woman. Youve got to learn to behave like a duchess. Take her away, Mrs Pearce. If she gives you any trouble, wallop her.

LIZA [*Springing up and running between* PICKERING *and* MRS PEARCE *for protection.*]   No! I'll call the police, I will.

MRS PEARCE   But Ive no place to put her.

HIGGINS   Put her in the dustbin.

LIZA   Ah-ah-ah-ow-ow-oo!

PICKERING   Oh come, Higgins! be reasonable.

MRS PEARCE [*Resolutely.*]   You must be reasonable, Mr Higgins: really you must. You cant walk over everybody like this.

[HIGGINS, *thus scolded, subsides. The hurricane is succeeded by a zephyr of amiable surprise.*]

HIGGINS [*With professional exquisiteness of modulation.*]   I walk over everybody! My dear Mrs Pearce, my dear Pickering, I never had the slightest intention of walking over anyone. All I propose is that we should be kind to this poor girl. We must help her to prepare and fit herself for her new station in life. If I did not express myself clearly it was because I did not wish to hurt her delicacy, or yours.

[LIZA, *reassured, steals back to her chair.*]

MRS PEARCE [*To* PICKERING.]   Well, did you ever hear anything like that, sir?

PICKERING [*Laughing heartily.*]   Never, Mrs Pearce: never.

HIGGINS [*Patiently.*]   Whats the matter?

MRS PEARCE   Well, the matter is, sir, that you cant take a girl up like that as if you were picking up a pebble on the beach.

HIGGINS   Why not?

MRS PEARCE   Why not! But you dont know anything about her. What about her parents? She may be married.

LIZA   Garn!

HIGGINS   There! As the girl very properly says, Garn! Married indeed! Dont you know that a woman of that class looks a worn out drudge of fifty a year after shes married?

LIZA   Whood marry me?

HIGGINS [*Suddenly resorting to the most thrillingly beautiful low tones in his best elocutionary style.*]   By George, Eliza, the streets will be strewn with the bodies of men shooting themselves for your sake before Ive done with you.

MRS PEARCE   Nonsense, sir. You mustnt talk like that to her.

LIZA [*Rising and squaring herself determinedly.*]   I'm going away. He's off his chump, he is. I dont want no balmies teaching me.

HIGGINS [*Wounded in his tenderest point by her insensibility to his elocution.*]   Oh, indeed! I'm mad, am I? Very well, Mrs Pearce: you neednt order the new clothes for her. Throw her out.

LIZA [*Whimpering.*]   Nah-ow. You got no right to touch me.

MRS PEARCE   You see now what comes of being saucy. [*Indicating the door.*] This way, please.

LIZA [*Almost in tears.*]   I didnt want no clothes. I wouldnt have taken them. [*She throws away the handkerchief.*] I can buy my own clothes.

HIGGINS [*Deftly retrieving the handkerchief and intercepting her on her reluctant way to the door.*]   Youre an ungrateful wicked girl. This is my return for offering to take you out of the gutter and dress you beautifully and make a lady of you.

MRS PEARCE   Stop, Mr Higgins. I wont allow it. It's you that are wicked. Go home to your parents, girl; and tell them to take better care of you.

LIZA   I aint got no parents. They told me I was big enough to earn my own living and turned me out.

MRS PEARCE   Wheres your mother?

LIZA   I aint got no mother. Her that turned me out was my sixth stepmother. But I done without them. And I'm a good girl, I am.

HIGGINS   Very well, then, what on earth is all this fuss about? The girl doesnt belong to anybody—is no use to anybody but me. [*He goes to* MRS PEARCE *and begins coaxing.*] You can adopt her, Mrs Pearce: I'm sure a daughter would be a great amusement to you. Now dont make any more fuss. Take her downstairs; and—

MRS PEARCE   But whats to become of her? Is she to be paid anything? Do be sensible, sir.

HIGGINS   Oh, pay her whatever is necessary: put it down in the housekeeping book. [*Impatiently.*] What on earth will she want with money? She'll have her food and her clothes. She'll only drink if you give her money.

LIZA [*Turning on him.*]   Oh you are a brute. It's a lie: nobody ever saw the sign of liquor on me. [*She goes back to her chair and plants herself there defiantly.*]

PICKERING [*In good-humored remonstrance.*]   Does it occur to you, Higgins, that the girl has some feelings?

HIGGINS [*Looking critically at her.*]   Oh no, I don't think so. Not any feelings that we need bother about. [*Cheerily.*] Have you, Eliza?

LIZA   I got my feelings same as anyone else.

HIGGINS [*To PICKERING, reflectively.*]   You see the difficulty!

PICKERING   Eh? What difficulty?

HIGGINS   To get her to talk grammar. The mere pronunciation is easy enough.

LIZA   I dont want to talk grammar. I want to talk like a lady.

MRS PEARCE   Will you please keep to the point, Mr Higgins. I want to know on what terms the girl is to be here. Is she to have any wages? And what is to become of her when youve finished your teaching? You must look ahead a little.

HIGGINS [*Impatiently.*]   Whats to become of her if I leave her in the gutter? Tell me that, Mrs Pearce.

MRS PEARCE   Thats her own business, not yours, Mr Higgins.

HIGGINS   Well, when Ive done with her, we can throw her back into the gutter; and then it will be her own business again; so thats all right.

LIZA   Oh, youve no feeling heart in you: you dont care for nothing but yourself. [*She rises and takes the floor resolutely.*] Here! Ive had enough of this. I'm going. [*Making for the door.*] You ought to be ashamed of yourself, you ought.

HIGGINS [*Snatching a chocolate cream from the piano, his eyes suddenly beginning to twinkle with mischief.*]   Have some chocolates, Eliza.

LIZA [*Halting, tempted.*]   How do I know what might be in them? Ive heard of girls being drugged by the like of you.

> [HIGGINS *whips out his penknife; cuts a chocolate in two; puts one half into his mouth and bolts it; and offers her the other half.*]

HIGGINS   Pledge of good faith, Eliza. I eat one half: you eat the other. [LIZA *opens her mouth to retort: he pops the half chocolate into it.*] You shall have boxes of them, barrels of them, every day. You shall live on them. Eh?

LIZA [*Who has disposed of the chocolate after being nearly choked by it.*]   I wouldnt have ate it, only I'm too ladylike to take it out of my mouth.

HIGGINS   Listen, Eliza. I think you said you came in a taxi.

LIZA   Well, what if I did? Ive as good a right to take a taxi as anyone else.

HIGGINS   You have, Eliza; and in future you shall have as many taxis as you want. You shall go up and down and round the town in a taxi every day. Think of that, Eliza.

MRS PEARCE   Mr Higgins: youre tempting the girl. It's not right. She should think of the future.

HIGGINS   At her age! Nonsense! Time enough to think of the future when you havnt any future to think of. No, Eliza: do as this lady does: think of other people's futures; but never think of your own. Think of chocolates, and taxis, and gold, and diamonds.

LIZA   No: I dont want no gold and no diamonds. I'm a good girl, I am. [*She sits down again, with an attempt at dignity.*]

HIGGINS   You shall remain so, Eliza, under the care of Mrs Pearce. And you shall marry an officer in the Guards,[4] with a beautiful moustache: the son of a marquis, who will disinherit him for marrying you, but will relent when he sees your beauty and goodness—

PICKERING   Excuse me, Higgins; but I really must interfere. Mrs Pearce is quite right. If this girl is to put herself in your hands for six months for an experiment in teaching, she must understand thoroughly what shes doing.

HIGGINS   How can she? Shes incapable of understanding anything. Besides, do any of us understand what we are doing? If we did, would we ever do it?

PICKERING   Very clever, Higgins; but not sound sense. [*To* ELIZA.] Miss Doolittle—

LIZA [*Overwhelmed.*]   Ah-ah-ow-oo!

HIGGINS   There! Thats all youll get out of Eliza. Ah-ah-ow-oo! No use explaining. As a military man you ought to know that. Give her her orders: thats what she wants. Eliza: you are to live here for the next six months, learning how to speak beautifully, like a lady in a florist's shop. If youre good and do whatever youre told, you shall sleep in a proper bedroom, and have lots to eat, and money to buy chocolates and take rides in taxis. If youre naughty and idle you will sleep in the back kitchen among the black beetles, and be walloped by Mrs Pearce with a broomstick. At the end of six months you shall go to Buckingham Palace in a carriage, beautifully dressed. If the King finds out youre not a lady, you will be taken by the police to the Tower of London, where your head will be cut off as a warning to other presumptuous flower girls. If you are not found out, you shall have a present of seven-and-sixpence

---

4. A regiment traditionally formed from the sons of the aristocracy and gentry.

to start life with as a lady in a shop. If you refuse this offer you will be a most ungrateful and wicked girl; and the angels will weep for you. [*To* PICKERING.] Now are you satisfied, Pickering? [*To* MRS PEARCE.] Can I put it more plainly and fairly, Mrs Pearce?

MRS PEARCE [*Patiently.*]   I think youd better let me speak to the girl properly in private. I dont know that I can take charge of her or consent to the arrangement at all. Of course I know you dont mean her any harm; but when you get what you call interested in people's accents, you never think or care what may happen to them or you. Come with me, Eliza.

HIGGINS   Thats all right. Thank you, Mrs Pearce. Bundle her off to the bath-room.

LIZA [*Rising reluctantly and suspiciously.*]   Youre a great bully, you are. I wont stay here if I dont like. I wont let nobody wallop me. I never asked to go to Bucknam Palace, I didnt. I was never in trouble with the police, not me. I'm a good girl—

MRS PEARCE   Dont answer back, girl. You dont understand the gentleman. Come with me. [*She leads the way to the door, and holds it open for* ELIZA.]

LIZA [*As she goes out.*]   Well, what I say is right. I wont go near the king, not if I'm going to have my head cut off. If I'd known what I was letting myself in for, I wouldnt have come here. I always been a good girl; and I never offered to say a word to him; and I dont owe him nothing; and I dont care; and I wont be put upon; and I have my feelings the same as anyone else—

[MRS PEARCE *shuts the door; and* ELIZA's *plaints are no longer audible.* PICKERING *comes from the hearth to the chair and sits astride it with his arms on the back.*]

PICKERING   Excuse the straight question, Higgins. Are you a man of good character where women are concerned?

HIGGINS [*Moodily.*]   Have you ever met a man of good character where women are concerned?

PICKERING   Yes: very frequently.

HIGGINS [*Dogmatically, lifting himself on his hands to the level of the piano, and sitting on it with a bounce.*]   Well, I havnt. I find that the moment I let a woman make friends with me, she becomes jealous, exacting, suspicious, and a damned nuisance. I find that the moment I let myself make friends with a woman, I become selfish and tyrannical. Women upset everything. When you let them into your life, you find that the woman is driving at one thing and youre driving at another.

PICKERING   At what, for example?

HIGGINS [*Coming off the piano restlessly.*]   Oh, Lord knows! I suppose the woman wants to live her own life; and the man wants to live his; and each tries to drag the other on to the wrong track. One wants to go north and the other south; and the result is that both have to go east, though they both hate the east wind. [*He sits down on the bench at the keyboard.*] So here I am, a confirmed old bachelor, and likely to remain so.

PICKERING [*Rising and standing over him gravely.*]   Come, Higgins! You know what I mean. If I'm to be in this business I shall feel responsible for that girl. I hope it's understood that no advantage is to be taken of her position.

HIGGINS   What! That thing! Sacred, I assure you. [*Rising to explain.*] You see, she'll be a pupil; and teaching would be impossible unless pupils were sacred. Ive taught scores of American millionairesses how to speak English: the best looking women in the world. I'm seasoned. They might as well be blocks of wood. *I* might as well be a block of wood. It's—

[MRS PEARCE *opens the door. She has* ELIZA's *hat in her hand.*
PICKERING *retires to the easy chair at the hearth and sits down.*]

HIGGINS [*Eagerly.*]   Well, Mrs Pearce: is it all right?

MRS PEARCE [*At the door.*]   I just wish to trouble you with a word, if I may, Mr Higgins.

HIGGINS   Yes, certainly. Come in. [*She comes forward.*] Dont burn that, Mrs Pearce. I'll keep it as a curiosity. [*He takes the hat.*]

MRS PEARCE   Handle it carefully, sir, please. I had to promise her not to burn it; but I had better put it in the oven for a while.

HIGGINS [*Putting it down hastily on the piano.*]   Oh! thank you. Well, what have you to say to me?

PICKERING   Am I in the way?

MRS PEARCE   Not at all, sir. Mr Higgins: will you please be very particular what you say before the girl?

HIGGINS [*Sternly.*]   Of course. I'm always particular about what I say. Why do you say this to me?

MRS PEARCE [*Unmoved.*]   No, sir: youre not at all particular when youve mislaid anything or when you get a little impatient. Now it doesnt matter before me: I'm used to it. But you really must not swear before the girl.

HIGGINS [*Indignantly.*]   *I* swear! [*Most emphatically.*] I never swear. I detest the habit. What the devil do you mean?

MRS PEARCE [*Stolidly.*]   Thats what I mean, sir. You swear a great deal too much. I dont mind your damning and blasting, and what the devil and where the devil and who the devil—

HIGGINS   Mrs Pearce: this language from your lips! Really!

MRS PEARCE [*Not to be put off.*]   —but there is a certain word I must ask you not to use. The girl has just used it herself because the bath was too hot. It begins with the same letter as bath. She knows no better: she learnt it at her mother's knee. But she must not hear it from your lips.

HIGGINS [*Loftily.*]   I cannot charge myself with having ever uttered it, Mrs Pearce. [*She looks at him steadfastly. He adds, hiding an uneasy conscience with a judicial air.*] Except perhaps in a moment of extreme and justifiable excitement.

MRS PEARCE   Only this morning, sir, you applied it to your boots, to the butter, and to the brown bread.

HIGGINS   Oh, that! Mere alliteration, Mrs Pearce, natural to a poet.

MRS PEARCE   Well, sir, whatever you choose to call it, I beg you not to let the girl hear you repeat it.

HIGGINS   Oh, very well, very well. Is that all?

MRS PEARCE   No, sir. We shall have to be very particular with this girl as to personal cleanliness.

HIGGINS   Certainly. Quite right. Most important.

MRS PEARCE   I mean not to be slovenly about her dress or untidy in leaving things about.

HIGGINS [*Going to her solemnly.*]   Just so. I intended to call your attention to that. [*He passes on to* PICKERING, *who is enjoying the conversation immensely.*] It is these little things that matter, Pickering. Take care of the pence and the pounds will take care of themselves is as true of personal habits as of money. [*He comes to anchor on the hearthrug, with the air of a man in an unassailable position.*]

MRS PEARCE   Yes, sir. Then might I ask you not to come down to breakfast in your dressing-gown, or at any rate not to use it as a napkin to the extent you do, sir. And if you would be so good as not to eat everything off the same plate, and to remember not to put the porridge saucepan out of your hand on the clean table-cloth, it would be a better example to the girl. You know you nearly choked yourself with a fishbone in the jam only last week.

HIGGINS [*Routed from the hearthrug and drifting back to the piano.*]   I may do these things sometimes in absence of mind; but surely I dont do them habitually. [*Angrily.*] By the way: my dressing-gown smells most damnably of benzine.[5]

MRS PEARCE   No doubt it does, Mr Higgins. But if you will wipe your fingers—

HIGGINS [*Yelling.*]   Oh very well, very well: I'll wipe them in my hair in future.

MRS PEARCE   I hope youre not offended, Mr Higgins.

HIGGINS [*Shocked at finding himself thought capable of an unamiable sentiment.*]   Not at all, not at all. Youre quite right, Mrs Pearce: I shall be particularly careful before the girl. Is that all?

MRS PEARCE   No, sir. Might she use some of those Japanese dresses you brought from abroad? I really cant put her back into her old things.

HIGGINS   Certainly. Anything you like. Is that all?

MRS PEARCE   Thank you, sir. Thats all. [*She goes out.*]

---

5. A spirit used as a cleaning agent.

HIGGINS   You know, Pickering, that woman has the most extraordinary ideas about me. Here I am, a shy, diffident sort of man. Ive never been able to feel really grown-up and tremendous, like other chaps. And yet shes firmly persuaded that I'm an arbitrary overbearing bossing kind of person. I cant account for it.

[MRS PEARCE *returns.*]

MRS PEARCE   If you please, sir, the trouble's beginning already. Theres a dustman[6] downstairs, Alfred Doolittle, wants to see you. He says you have his daughter here.

PICKERING [*Rising.*]   Phew! I say! [*He retreats to the hearthrug.*]

HIGGINS [*Promptly.*]   Send the blackguard up.

MRS PEARCE   Oh, very well, sir. [*She goes out.*]

PICKERING   He may not be a blackguard, Higgins.

HIGGINS   Nonsense. Of course hes a blackguard.

PICKERING   Whether he is or not, I'm afraid we shall have some trouble with him.

HIGGINS [*Confidently.*]   Oh no: I think not. If theres any trouble he shall have it with me, not I with him. And we are sure to get something interesting out of him.

PICKERING   About the girl?

HIGGINS   No. I mean his dialect.

PICKERING   Oh!

MRS PEARCE [*At the door.*]   Doolittle, sir. [*She admits* DOOLITTLE *and retires.*]

[ALFRED DOOLITTLE *is an elderly but vigorous dustman, clad in the costume of his profession, including a hat with a back brim covering his neck and shoulders. He has well marked and rather interesting features, and seems equally free from fear and conscience. He has a remarkably expressive voice, the result of a habit of giving vent to his feelings without reserve. His present pose is that of wounded honor and stern resolution.*]

DOOLITTLE [*At the door, uncertain which of the two gentlemen is his man.*]   Professor Higgins?

HIGGINS   Here. Good morning. Sit down.

DOOLITTLE   Morning, Governor. [*He sits down magisterially*.] I come about a very serious matter, Governor.

HIGGINS [*To* PICKERING.]   Brought up in Hounslow. Mother Welsh, I should think. [DOOLITTLE *opens his mouth, amazed.* HIGGINS *continues.*] What do you want, Doolittle?

DOOLITTLE [*Menacingly.*]   I want my daughter: thats what I want. See?

HIGGINS   Of course you do. Youre her father, arnt you? You dont suppose anyone else wants her, do you? I'm glad to see you have some spark of family feeling left. Shes upstairs. Take her away at once.

---

6. Garbage collector.

DOOLITTLE [*Rising, fearfully taken aback.*] What!

HIGGINS Take her away. Do you suppose I'm going to keep your daughter for you?

DOOLITTLE [*Remonstrating.*] Now, now, look here, Governor. Is this reasonable? Is it fairity to take advantage of a man like this? The girl belongs to me. You got her. Where do I come in? [*He sits down again.*]

HIGGINS Your daughter had the audacity to come to my house and ask me to teach her how to speak properly so that she could get a place in a flower-shop. This gentleman and my housekeeper have been here all the time. [*Bullying him*] How dare you come here and attempt to blackmail me? You sent her here on purpose.

DOOLITTLE [*Protesting.*] No, Governor.

HIGGINS You must have. How else could you possibly know that she is here?

DOOLITTLE Dont take a man up like that, Governor.

HIGGINS The police shall take you up. This is a plant—a plot to extort money by threats. I shall telephone for the police. [*He goes resolutely to the telephone and opens the directory.*]

DOOLITTLE Have I asked you for a brass farthing?[7] I leave it to the gentleman here: have I said a word about money?

HIGGINS [*Throwing the book aside and marching down on* DOOLITTLE *with a poser.*] What else did you come for?

DOOLITTLE [*Sweetly.*] Well, what would a man come for? Be human, Governor.

HIGGINS [*Disarmed.*] Alfred: did you put her up to it?

DOOLITTLE So help me, Governor, I never did. I take my Bible oath I aint seen the girl these two months past.

HIGGINS Then how did you know she was here?

DOOLITTLE [*"Most musical, most melancholy."*] I'll tell you, Governor, if youll only let me get a word in. I'm willing to tell you. I'm wanting to tell you. I'm waiting to tell you.

HIGGINS Pickering: this chap has a certain natural gift of rhetoric. Observe the rhythm of his native woodnotes wild. "I'm willing to tell you: I'm wanting to tell you: I'm waiting to tell you." Sentimental rhetoric! thats the Welsh strain in him. It also accounts for his mendacity and dishonesty.

PICKERING Oh, please, Higgins: I'm west country myself. [*To* DOOLITTLE.] How did you know the girl was here if you didnt send her?

DOOLITTLE It was like this, Governor. The girl took a boy in the taxi to give him a jaunt. Son of her landlady, he is. He hung about on the chance of her giving him another ride home. Well, she sent him back for her luggage when she heard you was willing for her

---

7. A farthing was a copper coin worth a quarter of a penny, but a brass farthing would have been worthless.

to stop here. I met the boy at the corner of Long Acre and Endell Street.

HIGGINS   Public house. Yes?

DOOLITTLE   The poor man's club, Governor: why shouldnt I?

PICKERING   Do let him tell his story, Higgins.

DOOLITTLE   He told me what was up. And I ask you, what was my feelings and my duty as a father? I says to the boy, "You bring me the luggage," I says—

PICKERING   Why didnt you go for it yourself?

DOOLITTLE   Landlady wouldnt have trusted me with it, Governor. Shes that kind of woman: you know. I had to give the boy a penny afore he trusted me with it, the little swine. I brought it to her just to oblige you like, and make myself agreeable. Thats all.

HIGGINS   How much luggage?

DOOLITTLE   Musical instrument, Governor. A few pictures, a trifle of jewelry, and a bird-cage. She said she didnt want no clothes. What was I to think from that, Governor? I ask you as a parent what was I to think?

HIGGINS   So you came to rescue her from worse than death, eh?

DOOLITTLE   [Appreciatively: relieved at being so well understood.] Just so, Governor. Thats right.

PICKERING   But why did you bring her luggage if you intended to take her away?

DOOLITTLE   Have I said a word about taking her away? Have I now?

HIGGINS   [Determinedly.] Youre going to take her away, double quick. [He crosses to the hearth and rings the bell.]

DOOLITTLE   [Rising.] No, Governor. Dont say that. I'm not the man to stand in my girl's light. Heres a career opening for her, as you might say; and—

[MRS PEARCE opens the door and awaits orders.]

HIGGINS   Mrs Pearce: this is Eliza's father. He has come to take her away. Give her to him. [He goes back to the piano, with an air of washing his hands of the whole affair.]

DOOLITTLE   No. This is a misunderstanding. Listen here—

MRS PEARCE   He cant take her away, Mr Higgins: how can he? You told me to burn her clothes.

DOOLITTLE   Thats right. I cant carry the girl through the streets like a blooming monkey, can I? I put it to you.

HIGGINS   You have put it to me that you want your daughter. Take your daughter. If she has no clothes go out and buy her some.

DOOLITTLE   [Desperate.] Wheres the clothes she come in? Did I burn them or did your missus here?

MRS PEARCE   I am the housekeeper, if you please. I have sent for some clothes for your girl. When they come you can take her away. You can wait in the kitchen. This way, please.

[DOOLITTLE, much troubled, accompanies her to the door; then hesitates; finally turns confidentially to HIGGINS.]

DOOLITTLE   Listen here, Governor. You and me is men of the world, aint we?

HIGGINS   Oh! Men of the world, are we? Youd better go, Mrs Pearce.

MRS PEARCE   I think so, indeed, sir. [*She goes, with dignity.*]

PICKERING   The floor is yours, Mr Doolittle.

DOOLITTLE [*To* PICKERING.]   I thank you, Governor. [*To* HIGGINS, *who takes refuge on the piano bench, a little overwhelmed by the proximity of his visitor; for* DOOLITTLE *has a professional flavor of dust about him.*] Well, the truth is, Ive taken a sort of fancy to you, Governor; and if you want the girl, I'm not so set on having her back home again but what I might be open to an arrangement. Regarded in the light of a young woman, shes a fine handsome girl. As a daughter shes not worth her keep; and so I tell you straight. All I ask is my rights as a father; and youre the last man alive to expect me to let her go for nothing; for I can see youre one of the straight sort, Governor. Well, whats a five pound note[8] to you? And whats Eliza to me? [*He returns to his chair and sits down judicially.*]

PICKERING   I think you ought to know, Doolittle, that Mr Higgins's intentions are entirely honorable.

DOOLITTLE   Course they are, Governor. If I thought they wasnt, Id ask fifty.

HIGGINS [*Revolted.*]   Do you mean to say, you callous rascal, that you would sell your daughter for £50?

DOOLITTLE   Not in a general way I wouldnt; but to oblige a gentleman like you I'd do a good deal, I do assure you.

PICKERING   Have you no morals, man?

DOOLITTLE [*Unabashed.*]   Cant afford them, Governor. Neither could you if you was as poor as me. Not that I mean any harm, you know. But if Liza is going to have a bit out of this, why not me too?

HIGGINS [*Troubled.*]   I dont know what to do, Pickering. There can be no question that as a matter of morals it's a positive crime to give this chap a farthing. And yet I feel a sort of rough justice in his claim.

DOOLITTLE   Thats it, Governor. Thats all I say. A father's heart, as it were.

PICKERING   Well, I know the feeling; but really it seems hardly right—

DOOLITTLE   Dont say that, Governor. Dont look at it that way. What am I, Governors both? I ask you, what am I? I'm one of the undeserving poor: thats what I am. Think of what that means to a man. It means that hes up agen middle class morality all the time. If theres anything going, and I put in for a bit of it, it's always the

8. Approximately $7.50; known as a "fiver."

same story: "Youre undeserving; so you cant have it." But my needs is as great as the most deserving widow's that ever got money out of six different charities in one week for the death of the same husband. I dont need less than a deserving man: I need more. I dont eat less hearty than him; and I drink a lot more. I want a bit of amusement, cause I'm a thinking man. I want cheerfulness and a song and a band when I feel low. Well, they charge me just the same for everything as they charge the deserving. What is middle class morality? Just an excuse for never giving me anything. Therefore, I ask you, as two gentlemen, not to play that game on me. I'm playing straight with you. I aint pretending to be deserving. I'm undeserving; and I mean to go on being undeserving. I like it; and thats the truth. Will you take advantage of a man's nature to do him out of the price of his own daughter what hes brought up and fed and clothed by the sweat of his brow until shes growed big enough to be interesting to you two gentlemen? Is five pounds unreasonable? I put it to you; and I leave it to you.

HIGGINS [*Rising, and going over to* PICKERING.] Pickering: if we were to take this man in hand for three months, he could choose between a seat in the Cabinet and a popular pulpit in Wales.

PICKERING What do you say to that, Doolittle?

DOOLITTLE Not me, Governor, thank you kindly. Ive heard all the preachers and all the prime ministers—for I'm a thinking man and game for politics or religion or social reform same as all the other amusements—and I tell you it's a dog's life anyway you look at it. Undeserving poverty is my line. Taking one station in society with another, it's—it's—well, it's the only one that has any ginger in it, to my taste.

HIGGINS I suppose we must give him a fiver.

PICKERING He'll make a bad use of it, I'm afraid.

DOOLITTLE Not me, Governor, so help me I wont. Dont you be afraid that I'll save it and spare it and live idle on it. There wont be a penny of it left by Monday: I'll have to go to work same as if I'd never had it. It wont pauperize me, you bet. Just one good spree for myself and the missus, giving pleasure to ourselves and employment to others, and satisfaction to you to think it's not been throwed away. You couldnt spend it better.

HIGGINS [*Taking out his pocket book and coming between* DOOLITTLE *and the piano*.] This is irresistible. Lets give him ten. [*He offers two notes to the dustman.*]

DOOLITTLE No, Governor. She wouldnt have the heart to spend ten; and perhaps I shouldnt neither. Ten pounds is a lot of money: it makes a man feel prudent like; and then goodbye to happiness. You give me what I ask you, Governor: not a penny more, and not a penny less.

PICKERING Why dont you marry that missus of yours? I rather draw the line at encouraging that sort of immorality.

DOOLITTLE   Tell her so, Governor: tell her so. *I*'m willing. It's me
that suffers by it. Ive no hold on her. I got to be agreeable to her.
I got to give her presents. I got to buy her clothes something sinful.
I'm a slave to that woman, Governor, just because I'm not her
lawful husband. And she knows it too. Catch her marrying me!
Take my advice, Governor: marry Eliza while shes young and dont
know no better. If you dont youll be sorry for it after. If you do,
she'll be sorry for it after; but better you than her, because youre
a man, and shes only a woman and dont know how to be happy
anyhow.

HIGGINS   Pickering: if we listen to this man another minute, we
shall have no convictions left. [*To* DOOLITTLE.] Five pounds I think
you said.

DOOLITTLE   Thank you kindly, Governor.

HIGGINS   Youre sure you wont take ten?

DOOLITTLE   Not now. Another time, Governor.

HIGGINS   [*Handing him a five-pound note.*]   Here you are.

DOOLITTLE   Thank you, Governor. Good morning. [*He hurries to the
door, anxious to get away with his booty. When he opens it he is
confronted with a dainty and exquisitely clean young Japanese lady
in a simple blue cotton kimono printed cunningly with small white
jasmine blossoms.* MRS PEARCE *is with her. He gets out of her way
deferentially and apologizes.*] Beg pardon, miss.

THE JAPANESE LADY   Garn! Dont you know your own daughter?

DOOLITTLE	*exclaiming*	Bly me! it's Eliza!
HIGGINS	*simul-*	Whats that! This!
PICKERING	*taneously*	By Jove!

LIZA   Dont I look silly?

HIGGINS   Silly?

MRS PEARCE   [*At the door.*]   Now, Mr Higgins, please dont say anything to make the girl conceited about herself.

HIGGINS   [*Conscientiously.*]   Oh! Quite right, Mrs Pearce. [*To*
ELIZA.] Yes: damned silly.

MRS PEARCE   Please, sir.

HIGGINS   [*Correcting himself.*]   I mean extremely silly.

LIZA   I should look all right with my hat on. [*She takes up her hat;
puts it on; and walks across the room to the fireplace with a fashionable air.*]

HIGGINS   A new fashion, by George! And it ought to look horrible!

DOOLITTLE   [*With fatherly pride.*]   Well, I never thought she'd clean
up as good looking as that, Governor. Shes a credit to me, aint
she?

LIZA   I tell you, it's easy to clean up here. Hot and cold water on
tap, just as much as you like, there is. Woolly towels, there is; and
a towel horse so hot, it burns your fingers. Soft brushes to scrub
yourself, and a wooden bowl of soap smelling like primroses. Now
I know why ladies is so clean. Washing's a treat for them. Wish
they saw what it is for the like of me!

HIGGINS   I'm glad the bath-room met with your approval.

LIZA   It didnt: not all of it; and I dont care who hears me say it. Mrs Pearce knows.

HIGGINS   What was wrong, Mrs Pearce?

MRS PEARCE [*Blandly.*]   Oh, nothing, sir. It doesnt matter.

LIZA   I had a good mind to break it. I didnt know which way to look. But I hung a towel over it, I did.

HIGGINS   Over what?

MRS PEARCE   Over the looking-glass, sir.

HIGGINS   Doolittle: you have brought your daughter up too strictly.

DOOLITTLE   Me! I never brought her up at all, except to give her a lick of a strap now and again. Dont put it on me, Governor. She aint accustomed to it, you see: thats all. But she'll soon pick up your free-and-easy ways.

LIZA   I'm a good girl, I am; and I wont pick up no free and easy ways.

HIGGINS   Eliza: if you say again that youre a good girl, your father shall take you home.

LIZA   Not him. You dont know my father. All he come here for was to touch you for some money to get drunk on.

DOOLITTLE   Well, what else would I want money for? To put into the plate in church, I suppose. [*She puts out her tongue at him. He is so incensed by this that* PICKERING *presently finds it necessary to step between them.*] Dont you give me none of your lip; and dont let me hear you giving this gentleman any of it neither, or youll hear from me about it. See?

HIGGINS   Have you any further advice to give her before you go, Doolittle? Your blessing, for instance.

DOOLITTLE   No, Governor: I aint such a mug as to put up my children to all I know myself. Hard enough to hold them in without that. If you want Eliza's mind improved, Governor, you do it yourself with a strap. So long, gentlemen. [*He turns to go.*]

HIGGINS [*Impressively.*]   Stop. Youll come regularly to see your daughter. It's your duty, you know. My brother is a clergyman; and he could help you in your talks with her.

DOOLITTLE [*Evasively.*]   Certainly. I'll come, Governor. Not just this week, because I have a job at a distance. But later on you may depend on me. Afternoon, gentlemen. Afternoon, maam. [*He takes off his hat to* MRS PEARCE, *who disdains the salutation and goes out. He winks at* HIGGINS, *thinking him probably a fellow-sufferer from* MRS PEARCE's *difficult disposition, and follows her.*]

LIZA   Dont you believe the old liar. He'd as soon you set a bull-dog on him as a clergyman. You wont see him again in a hurry.

HIGGINS   I dont want to, Eliza. Do you?

LIZA   Not me. I dont want never to see him again, I dont. Hes a disgrace to me, he is, collecting dust, instead of working at his trade.

PICKERING   What is his trade, Eliza?

LIZA   Talking money out of other people's pockets into his own. His proper trade's a navvy,[9] and he works at it sometimes too—for exercise—and earns good money at it. Aint you going to call me Miss Doolittle anymore?

PICKERING   I beg your pardon, Miss Doolittle. It was a slip of the tongue.

LIZA   Oh, I dont mind; only it sounded so genteel. I should just like to take a taxi to the corner of Tottenham Court Road and get out there and tell it to wait for me, just to put the girls in their place a bit. I wouldnt speak to them, you know.

PICKERING   Better wait til we get you something really fashionable.

HIGGINS   Besides, you shouldnt cut your old friends now that you have risen in the world. Thats what we call snobbery.

LIZA   You dont call the like of them my friends now, I should hope. Theyve took it out of me often enough with their ridicule when they had the chance; and now I mean to get a bit of my own back. But if I'm to have fashionable clothes, I'll wait. I should like to have some. Mrs Pearce says youre going to give me some to wear in bed at night different to what I wear in the daytime; but it do seem a waste of money when you could get something to shew. Besides, I never could fancy changing into cold things on a winter night.

MRS PEARCE   [*Coming back.*]   Now, Eliza. The new things have come for you to try on.

LIZA   Ah-ow-oo-ooh! [*She rushes out.*]

MRS PEARCE   [*Following her.*]   Oh, dont rush about like that, girl. [*She shuts the door behind her.*]

HIGGINS   Pickering: we have taken on a stiff job.

PICKERING   [*With conviction.*]   Higgins: we have.

Act III

> It is MRS HIGGINS's *at-home day. Nobody has yet arrived. Her drawing-room, in a flat on Chelsea embankment, has three windows looking on the river; and the ceiling is not so lofty as it would be in an older house of the same pretension. The windows are open, giving access to a balcony with flowers in pots. If you stand with your face to the windows, you have the fireplace on your left and the door in the right-hand wall close to the corner nearest the windows.*
>
> MRS HIGGINS *was brought up on Morris and Burne Jones; and her room, which is very unlike her son's room in Wimpole Street, is not crowded with furniture and little*

---

9. Laborer.

tables and nick-nacks.[1] *In the middle of the room there is a big ottoman; and this, with the carpet, the Morris wallpapers, and the Morris chintz window curtains and brocade covers of the ottoman and its cushions, supply all the ornament, and are much too handsome to be hidden by odds and ends of useless things. A few good oil-paintings from the exhibitions in the Grosvenor Gallery thirty years ago (the Burne Jones, not the Whistler side of them) are on the walls. The only landscape is a Cecil Lawson on the scale of a Rubens. There is a portrait of* MRS HIGGINS *as she was when she defied fashion in her youth in one of the beautiful Rossettian costumes which, when caricatured by people who did not understand, led to the absurdities of popular estheticism in the eighteen-seventies.*

In the corner diagonally opposite the door MRS HIGGINS, *now over sixty and long past taking the trouble to dress out of the fashion, sits writing at an elegantly simple writing-table with a bell button within reach of her hand. There is a Chippendale chair further back in the room between her and the window nearest her side. At the other side of the room, further forward, is an Elizabethan chair roughly carved in the taste of Inigo Jones. On the same side a piano in a decorated case. The corner between the fireplace and the window is occupied by a divan cushioned in Morris chintz.*

It is between four and five in the afternoon.

The door is opened violently; and HIGGINS *enters with his hat on.*

MRS HIGGINS [*Dismayed.*]   Henry! [*Scolding him.*] What are you doing here to-day? It is my at-home day: you promised not to come. [*As he bends to kiss her, she takes his hat off, and presents it to him.*]

HIGGINS   Oh bother! [*He throws the hat down on the table.*]

MRS HIGGINS   Go home at once.

HIGGINS [*Kissing her.*]   I know, mother. I came on purpose.

MRS HIGGINS   But you mustnt. I'm serious, Henry. You offend all my friends: they stop coming whenever they meet you.

HIGGINS   Nonsense! I know I have no small talk; but people dont mind. [*He sits on the settee.*]

MRS HIGGINS   Oh! dont they? Small talk indeed! What about your large talk? Really, dear, you mustnt stay.

HIGGINS   I must. Ive a job for you. A phonetic job.

MRS HIGGINS   No use, dear. I'm sorry; but I cant get round your

---

1. The prevailing style of the room is "Arts and Crafts" and Pre-Raphaelite, both fashionable in mid-nineteenth century England.

vowels; and though I like to get pretty postcards in your patent shorthand, I always have to read the copies in ordinary writing you so thoughtfully send me.

HIGGINS   Well, this isnt a phonetic job.

MRS HIGGINS   You said it was.

HIGGINS   Not your part of it. Ive picked up a girl.

MRS HIGGINS   Does that mean that some girl has picked you up?

HIGGINS   Not at all. I dont mean a love affair.

MRS HIGGINS   What a pity!

IIIGGINS   Why?

MRS HIGGINS   Well, you never fall in love with anyone under forty-five. When will you discover that there are some rather nice-looking young women about?

HIGGINS   Oh, I cant be bothered with young women. My idea of a lovable woman is something as like you as possible. I shall never get into the way of seriously liking young women: some habits lie too deep to be changed. [*Rising abruptly and walking about, jingling his money and his keys in his trouser pockets.*] Besides, theyre all idiots.

MRS HIGGINS   Do you know what you would do if you really loved me, Henry?

HIGGINS   Oh bother! What? Marry, I suppose?

MRS HIGGINS   No. Stop fidgeting and take your hands out of your pockets. [*With a gesture of despair, he obeys and sits down again.*] Thats a good boy. Now tell me about the girl.

HIGGINS   Shes coming to see you.

MRS HIGGINS   I dont remember asking her.

HIGGINS   You didnt. *I* asked her. If youd known her you wouldnt have asked her.

MRS HIGGINS   Indeed! Why?

HIGGINS   Well, it's like this. Shes a common flower girl. I picked her off the kerbstone.

MRS HIGGINS   And invited her to my at-home!

HIGGINS [*Rising and coming to her to coax her.*]   Oh, thatll be all right. Ive taught her to speak properly; and she has strict orders as to her behavior. Shes to keep to two subjects: the weather and everybody's health—Fine day and How do you do, you know—and not to let herself go on things in general. That will be safe.

MRS HIGGINS   Safe! To talk about our health! about our insides! perhaps about our outsides! How could you be so silly, Henry?

HIGGINS [*Impatiently.*]   Well, she must talk about something. [*He controls himself and sits down again.*] Oh, She'll be all right: dont you fuss. Pickering is in it with me. Ive a sort of bet on that I'll pass her off as a duchess in six months. I started on her some months ago; and shes getting on like a house on fire. I shall win my bet. She has a quick ear; and shes been easier to teach than my middle-class pupils because shes had to learn a complete new language. She talks English almost as you talk French.

MRS HIGGINS   Thats satisfactory, at all events.

HIGGINS   Well, it is and it isnt.

MRS HIGGINS   What does that mean?

HIGGINS   You see, Ive got her pronunciation all right; but you have to consider not only how a girl pronounces, but what she pronounces; and thats where—

[*They are interrupted by the* PARLOR-MAID, *announcing guests.*]

THE PARLOR-MAID   Mrs and Miss Eynsford Hill. [*She withdraws.*]

HIGGINS   Oh Lord! [*He rises; snatches his hat from the table; and makes for the door; but before he reaches it his mother introduces him.*]

[MRS *and* MISS EYNSFORD HILL *are the mother and daughter who sheltered from the rain in Covent Garden. The mother is well bred, quiet, and has the habitual anxiety of straitened means. The daughter has acquired a gay air of being very much at home in society: the bravado of genteel poverty.*]

MRS EYNSFORD HILL [*To* MRS HIGGINS.]   How do you do? [*They shake hands.*]

MISS EYNSFORD HILL   How d'you do? [*She shakes.*]

MRS HIGGINS [*Introducing.*]   My son Henry.

MRS EYNSFORD HILL   Your celebrated son! I have so longed to meet you, Professor Higgins.

HIGGINS [*Glumly, making no movement in her direction.*]   Delighted. [*He backs against the piano and bows brusquely.*]

MISS EYNSFORD HILL [*Going to him with confident familiarity.*]   How do you do?

HIGGINS [*Staring at her.*]   Ive seen you before somewhere. I havnt the ghost of a notion where; but Ive heard your voice. [*Drearily.*] It doesnt matter. Youd better sit down.

MRS HIGGINS   I'm sorry to say that my celebrated son has no manners. You mustnt mind him.

MISS EYNSFORD HILL [*Gaily.*]   I dont. [*She sits in the Elizabethan chair.*]

MRS EYNSFORD HILL [*A little bewildered.*]   Not at all. [*She sits on the ottoman between her daughter and* MRS HIGGINS, *who has turned her chair away from the writing-table.*]

HIGGINS   Oh, have I been rude? I didnt mean to be.

[*He goes to the central window, through which, with his back to the company, he contemplates the river and the flowers in Battersea Park on the opposite bank as if they were a frozen desert.*

THE PARLOR-MAID *returns, ushering in* PICKERING.]

THE PARLOR-MAID   Colonel Pickering. [*She withdraws.*]

PICKERING   How do you do, Mrs Higgins?

MRS HIGGINS   So glad youve come. Do you know Mrs Eynsford Hill—Miss Eynsford Hill? [*Exchange of bows.* THE COLONEL *brings the Chippendale chair a little forward between* MRS HILL *and* MRS HIGGINS, *and sits down.*]

PICKERING   Has Henry told you what weve come for?

HIGGINS [*Over his shoulder.*]   We were interrupted: damn it!

MRS HIGGINS   Oh Henry, Henry, really!

MRS EYNSFORD HILL [*Half rising.*]   Are we in the way?

MRS HIGGINS [*Rising and making her sit down again.*]   No, no. You couldnt have come more fortunately: we want you to meet a friend of ours.

HIGGINS [*Turning hopefully.*]   Yes, by George! We want two or three people. Youll do as well as anybody else.

[THE PARLOR-MAID *returns, ushering* FREDDY.]

THE PARLOR-MAID   Mr Eynsford Hill.

HIGGINS [*Almost audibly, past endurance.*]   God of Heaven! another of them.

FREDDY [*Shaking hands with* MRS HIGGINS.]   Ahdedo?

MRS HIGGINS   Very good of you to come. [*Introducing.*]   Colonel Pickering.

FREDDY [*Bowing.*]   Ahdedo?

MRS HIGGINS   I dont think you know my son, Professor Higgins.

FREDDY [*Going to* HIGGINS.]   Ahdedo?

HIGGINS [*Looking at him much as if he were a pickpocket.*]   I'll take my oath Ive met you before somewhere. Where was it?

FREDDY   I dont think so.

HIGGINS [*Resignedly.*]   It dont matter, anyhow. Sit down.

[*He shakes* FREDDY's *hand, and almost slings him on to the ottoman with his face to the windows; then comes round to the other side of it.*]

HIGGINS   Well, here we are, anyhow! [*He sits down on the ottoman next* MRS EYNSFORD HILL, *on her left.*] And now, what the devil are we going to talk about until Eliza comes?

MRS HIGGINS   Henry: you are the life and soul of the Royal Society's soirées; but really youre rather trying on more commonplace occasions.

HIGGINS   Am I? Very sorry. [*Beaming suddenly.*] I suppose I am, you know. [*Uproariously.*] Ha, ha!

MISS EYNSFORD HILL [*Who considers* HIGGINS *quite eligible matrimonially.*]   I sympathize. *I* havnt any small talk. If people would only be frank and say what they really think!

HIGGINS [*Relapsing into gloom.*]   Lord forbid!

MRS EYNSFORD HILL [*Taking up her daughter's cue.*]   But why?

HIGGINS   What they think they ought to think is bad enough, Lord knows; but what they really think would break up the whole show. Do you suppose it would be really agreeable if I were to come out now with what I really think?

MISS EYNSFORD HILL [*Gaily.*]   It is so very cynical?

HIGGINS   Cynical! Who the dickens said it was cynical? I mean it wouldnt be decent.

MRS EYNSFORD HILL [*Seriously.*]   Oh! I'm sure you dont mean that, Mr Higgins.

HIGGINS   You see, we're all savages, more or less. We're supposed to be civilized and cultured—to know all about poetry and philosophy and art and science, and so on; but how many of us know even the meanings of these names? [*To* MISS HILL.] What do you know of poetry? [*To* MRS HILL.] What do you know of science? [*Indicating* FREDDY.] What does he know of art or science or anything else? What the devil do you imagine I know of philosophy?

MRS HIGGINS [*Warningly.*]   Or of manners, Henry?

THE PARLOR-MAID [*Opening the door.*]   Miss Doolittle. [*She withdraws.*]

HIGGINS [*Rising hastily and running to* MRS HIGGINS.]   Here she is, mother. [*He stands on tiptoe and makes signs over his mother's head to* ELIZA *to indicate to her which lady is her hostess.*]

[ELIZA, *who is exquisitely dressed, produces an impression of such remarkable distinction and beauty as she enters that they all rise, quite fluttered. Guided by* HIGGINS's *signals, she comes to* MRS HIGGINS *with studied grace.*]

LIZA [*Speaking with pedantic correctness of pronunciation and great beauty of tone.*]   How do you do, Mrs Higgins? [*She gasps slightly in making sure of the H in Higgins, but is quite successful.*] Mr Higgins told me I might come.

MRS HIGGINS [*Cordially.*]   Quite right: I'm very glad indeed to see you.

PICKERING   How do you do, Miss Doolittle?

LIZA [*Shaking hands with him.*]   Colonel Pickering, is it not?

MRS EYNSFORD HILL   I feel sure we have met before, Miss Doolittle. I remember your eyes.

LIZA   How do you do? [*She sits down on the ottoman gracefully in the place just left vacant by* HIGGINS.]

MRS EYNSFORD HILL [*Introducing.*]   My daughter Clara.

LIZA   How do you do?

CLARA [*Impulsively.*]   How do you do? [*She sits down on the ottoman beside* ELIZA, *devouring her with her eyes.*]

FREDDY [*Coming to their side of the ottoman.*]   Ive certainly had the pleasure.

MRS EYNSFORD HILL [*Introducing.*]   My son Freddy.

LIZA   How do you do?

[FREDDY *bows and sits down in the Elizabethan chair, infatuated.*]

HIGGINS [*Suddenly.*]   By George, yes: it all comes back to me! [*They stare at him.*] Covent Garden! [*Lamentably.*] What a damned thing!

MRS HIGGINS   Henry, please! [*He is about to sit on the edge of the table.*] Dont sit on my writing-table: youll break it.

HIGGINS [*Sulkily.*]   Sorry.

[*He goes to the divan, stumbling into the fender and over the fire-irons on his way; extricating himself with muttered imprecations; and finishing his disastrous journey by throwing himself so impatiently on the divan that he almost breaks it.* MRS HIGGINS *looks at him, but controls herself and says nothing.*

A long and painful pause ensues.]

MRS HIGGINS [*At last, conversationally.*]   Will it rain, do you think?

LIZA   The shallow depression in the west of these islands is likely to move slowly in an easterly direction. There are no indications of any great change in the barometrical situation.

FREDDY   Ha! ha! how awfully funny!

LIZA   What is wrong with that, young man? I bet I got it right.

FREDDY   Killing!

MRS EYNSFORD HILL   I'm sure I hope it wont turn cold. Theres so much influenza about. It runs right through our whole family regularly every spring.

LIZA [*Darkly.*]   My aunt died of influenza: so they said.

MRS EYNSFORD HILL [*Clicks her tongue sympathetically.*]   ! ! !

LIZA [*In the same tragic tone.*]   But it's my belief they done the old woman in.

MRS HIGGINS [*Puzzled.*]   Done her in?

LIZA   Y-e-e-e-es, Lord love you! Why should she die of influenza? She come through diphtheria right enough the year before. I saw her with my own eyes. Fairly blue with it, she was. They all thought she was dead; but my father he kept ladling gin down her throat til she came to so sudden that she bit the bowl off the spoon.

MRS EYNSFORD HILL [*Startled.*]   Dear me!

LIZA [*Piling up the indictment.*]   What call would a woman with that strength in her have to die of influenza? What become of her new straw hat that should have come to me? Somebody pinched it; and what I say is, them as pinched it done her in.

MRS EYNSFORD HILL   What does doing her in mean?

HIGGINS [*Hastily.*]   Oh, thats the new small talk. To do a person in means to kill them.

MRS EYNSFORD HILL [*To* ELIZA, *horrified.*]   You surely dont believe that your aunt was killed?

LIZA   Do I not! Them she lived with would have killed her for a hatpin, let alone a hat.

MRS EYNSFORD HILL   But it cant have been right for your father to pour spirits down her throat like that. It might have killed her.

LIZA   Not her. Gin was mother's milk to her. Besides, he'd poured so much down his own throat that he knew the good of it.

MRS EYNSFORD HILL   Do you mean that he drank?

LIZA   Drank! My word! Something chronic.

MRS EYNSFORD HILL   How dreadful for you!

LIZA   Not a bit. It never did him no harm what I could see. But then he did not keep it up regular. [*Cheerfully.*] On the burst, as you might say, from time to time. And always more agreeable when he had a drop in. When he was out of work, my mother used to give him fourpence and tell him to go out and not come back until he'd drunk himself cheerful and loving-like. Theres lots of women has to make their husbands drunk to make them fit to live with. [*Now quite at her ease.*] You see, it's like this. If a man has a bit of a conscience, it always takes him when he's sober; and then it makes him low-spirited. A drop of booze just takes that off and makes him happy. [*To* FREDDY, *who is in convulsions of suppressed laughter.*] Here! what are you sniggering at?

FREDDY   The new small talk. You do it so awfully well.

LIZA   If I was doing it proper, what was you laughing at? [*To* HIGGINS.] Have I said anything I oughtnt?

MRS HIGGINS [*Interposing.*]   Not at all, Miss Doolittle.

LIZA   Well, thats a mercy, anyhow. [*Expansively.*] What I always say is—

HIGGINS [*Rising and looking at his watch.*]   Ahem!

LIZA [*Looking round at him; taking the hint; and rising.*]   Well: I must go. [*They all rise.* FREDDY *goes to the door.*] So pleased to have met you. Good-bye. [*She shakes hands with* MRS HIGGINS.]

MRS HIGGINS   Good-bye.

LIZA   Good-bye, Colonel Pickering.

PICKERING   Good-bye, Miss Doolittle. [*They shake hands.*]

LIZA [*Nodding to the others.*]   Good-bye, all.

FREDDY [*Opening the door for her.*]   Are you walking across the Park, Miss Doolittle? If so—

LIZA   Walk! Not bloody likely. [*Sensation.*] I am going in a taxi. [*She goes out.*]

> [PICKERING *gasps and sits down.* FREDDY *goes out on the balcony to catch another glimpse of* ELIZA.]

MRS EYNSFORD HILL [*Suffering from shock.*]   Well, I really cant get used to the new ways.

CLARA [*Throwing herself discontentedly into the Elizabethan chair.*]   Oh, it's all right, mamma, quite right. People will think we never go anywhere or see anybody if you are so old-fashioned.

MRS EYNSFORD HILL   I daresay I am very old-fashioned; but I do hope you wont begin using that expression, Clara. I have got accustomed to hear you talking about men as rotters, and calling everything filthy and beastly; though I do think it horrible and unladylike. But this last is really too much. Dont you think so, Colonel Pickering?

PICKERING   Dont ask me. Ive been away in India for several years; and manners have changed so much that I sometimes dont know whether I'm at a respectable dinner-table or in a ship's fore-castle.

CLARA   It's all a matter of habit. Theres no right or wrong in it. Nobody means anything by it. And it's so quaint, and gives such a smart emphasis to things that are not in themselves very witty. I find the new small talk delightful and quite innocent.

MRS EYNSFORD HILL [*Rising.*]   Well, after that, I think it's time for us to go.

[PICKERING *and* HIGGINS *rise.*]

CLARA [*Rising.*]   Oh yes: we have three at-homes to go to still. Good-bye, Mrs Higgins. Good-bye, Colonel Pickering. Good-bye, Professor Higgins.

HIGGINS [*Coming grimly at her from the divan, and accompanying her to the door.*]   Good-bye. Be sure you try on that small talk at the three at-homes. Dont be nervous about it. Pitch it in strong.

CLARA [*All smiles.*]   I will. Good-bye. Such nonsense, all this early Victorian prudery!

HIGGINS [*Tempting her.*]   Such damned nonsense!

CLARA   Such bloody nonsense!

MRS EYNSFORD HILL [*Convulsively.*]   Clara!

CLARA   Ha! ha! [*She goes out radiant, conscious of being thoroughly up to date, and is heard descending the stairs in a stream of silvery laughter.*]

FREDDY [*To the heavens at large.*]   Well, I ask you— [*He gives it up, and comes to* MRS HIGGINS.] Good-bye.

MRS HIGGINS [*Shaking hands.*]   Good-bye. Would you like to meet Miss Doolittle again?

FREDDY [*Eagerly.*]   Yes, I should, most awfully.

MRS HIGGINS   Well, you know my days.

FREDDY   Yes. Thanks awfully. Good-bye. [*He goes out.*]

MRS EYNSFORD HILL   Good-bye, Mr Higgins.

HIGGINS   Good-bye. Good-bye.

MRS EYNSFORD HILL [*To* PICKERING.]   It's no use. I shall never be able to bring myself to use that word.

PICKERING   Dont. It's not compulsory, you know. Youll get on quite well without it.

MRS EYNSFORD HILL   Only, Clara is so down on me if I am not positively reeking with the latest slang. Good-bye.

PICKERING   Good-bye. [*They shake hands.*]

MRS EYNSFORD HILL [*To* MRS HIGGINS.]   You mustnt mind Clara. [PICKERING, *catching from her lowered tone that this is not meant for him to hear, discreetly joins* HIGGINS *at the window.*] We're so poor! and she gets so few parties, poor child! She doesnt quite know. [MRS HIGGINS, *seeing that her eyes are moist, takes her hand sympathetically and goes with her to the door.*] But the boy is nice. Dont you think so?

MRS HIGGINS   Oh, quite nice. I shall always be delighted to see him.

MRS EYNSFORD HILL   Thank you, dear. Good-bye. [*She goes out.*]

HIGGINS [*Eagerly.*]   Well? Is Eliza presentable? [*He swoops on his mother and drags her to the ottoman, where she sits down in* ELIZA's *place with her son on her left.*]

[PICKERING *returns to his chair on her right.*]

MRS HIGGINS   You silly boy, of course shes not presentable. Shes a triumph of your art and of her dressmaker's; but if you suppose for a moment that she doesnt give herself away in every sentence she utters, you must be perfectly cracked about her.

PICKERING   But dont you think something might be done? I mean something to eliminate the sanguinary element from her conversation.

MRS HIGGINS   Not as long as she is in Henry's hands.

HIGGINS [*Aggrieved.*]   Do you mean that my language is improper?

MRS HIGGINS   No, dearest: it would be quite proper—say on a canal barge; but it would not be proper for her at a garden party.

HIGGINS [*Deeply injured.*]   Well I must say—

PICKERING [*Interrupting him.*]   Come, Higgins: you must learn to know yourself. I havnt heard such language as yours since we used to review the volunteers in Hyde Park twenty years ago.

HIGGINS [*Sulkily.*]   Oh, well, if you say so, I suppose I dont always talk like a bishop.

MRS HIGGINS [*Quieting* HENRY *with a touch.*]   Colonel Pickering: will you tell me what is the exact state of things in Wimpole Street?

PICKERING [*Cheerfully: as if this completely changed the subject.*]   Well, I have come to live there with Henry. We work together at my Indian Dialects; and we think it more convenient—

MRS HIGGINS   Quite so. I know all about that: it's an excellent arrangement. But where does this girl live?

HIGGINS   With us, of course. Where would she live?

MRS HIGGINS   But on what terms? Is she a servant? If not, what is she?

PICKERING [*Slowly.*]   I think I know what you mean, Mrs Higgins.

HIGGINS   Well, dash me if *I* do! Ive had to work at the girl every day for months to get her to her present pitch. Besides, shes useful. She knows where my things are, and remembers my appointments and so forth.

MRS HIGGINS   How does your housekeeper get on with her?

HIGGINS   Mrs Pearce? Oh, shes jolly glad to get so much taken off her hands; for before Eliza came, she used to have to find things and remind me of my appointments. But shes got some silly bee in her bonnet about Eliza. She keeps saying "You dont think, sir": doesnt she, Pick?

PICKERING   Yes: thats the formula. "You dont think, sir." Thats the end of every conversation about Eliza.

HIGGINS   As if I ever stop thinking about the girl and her confounded vowels and consonants. I'm worn out, thinking about her, and watching her lips and her teeth and her tongue, not to mention her soul, which is the quaintest of the lot.

MRS HIGGINS   You certainly are a pretty pair of babies, playing with your live doll.

HIGGINS   Playing! The hardest job I ever tackled: make no mistake about that, mother. But you have no idea how frightfully interesting it is to take a human being and change her into a quite different human being by creating a new speech for her. It's filling up the deepest gulf that separates class from class and soul from soul.

PICKERING [*Drawing his chair closer to* MRS HIGGINS *and bending over to her eagerly.*]   Yes: it's enormously interesting. I assure you, Mrs Higgins, we take Eliza very seriously. Every week—every day almost—there is some new change. [*Closer again.*] We keep records of every stage—dozens of gramophone disks and photographs—

HIGGINS [*Assailing her at the other ear.*]   Yes, by George: it's the most absorbing experiment I ever tackled. She regularly fills our lives up: doesnt she, Pick?

PICKERING   We're always talking Eliza.

HIGGINS   Teaching Eliza.

PICKERING   Dressing Eliza.

MRS HIGGINS   What!

HIGGINS   Inventing new Elizas.

	[*speaking together.*]	
HIGGINS		You know, she has the most extraordinary quickness of ear:
PICKERING		I assure you, my dear Mrs Higgins, that girl
HIGGINS		just like a parrot. Ive tried her with every
PICKERING		is a genius. She can play the piano quite beautifully.
HIGGINS		possible sort of sound that a human being can make—
PICKERING		We have taken her to classical concerts and to music
HIGGINS		Continental dialects, African dialects, Hottentot
PICKERING		halls; and it's all the same to her: she plays everything
HIGGINS		clicks, things it took me years to get hold of; and
PICKERING		she hears right off when she comes home, whether it's
HIGGINS		she picks them up like a shot, right away, as if she had
PICKERING		Beethoven and Brahms or Lehar and Lionel Monckton;

HIGGINS   been at it all her life.

PICKERING   though six months ago, she'd never as much as touched a piano—

MRS HIGGINS [*Putting her fingers in her ears, as they are by this time shouting one another down with an intolerable noise.*]   Sh-sh-sh—sh! [*They stop.*]

PICKERING   I beg your pardon. [*He draws his chair back apologetically.*]

HIGGINS   Sorry. When Pickering starts shouting nobody can get a word in edgeways.

MRS HIGGINS   Be quiet, Henry. Colonel Pickering: dont you realize that when Eliza walked into Wimpole Street, something walked in with her?

PICKERING   Her father did. But Henry soon got rid of him.

MRS HIGGINS   It would have been more to the point if her mother had. But as her mother didnt something else did.

PICKERING   But what?

MRS HIGGINS [*Unconsciously dating herself by the word.*]   A problem.

PICKERING   Oh, I see. The problem of how to pass her off as a lady.

HIGGINS   I'll solve that problem. Ive half solved it already.

MRS HIGGINS   No, you two infinitely stupid male creatures: the problem of what is to be done with her afterwards.

HIGGINS   I dont see anything in that. She can go her own way, with all the advantages I have given her.

MRS HIGGINS   The advantages of that poor woman who was here just now! The manners and habits that disqualify a fine lady from earning her own living without giving her a fine lady's income! Is that what you mean?

PICKERING [*Indulgently, being rather bored.*]   Oh, that will be all right, Mrs Higgins. [*He rises to go.*]

HIGGINS [*Rising also.*]   We'll find her some light employment.

PICKERING   Shes happy enough. Dont you worry about her. Good-bye. [*He shakes hands as if he were consoling a frightened child, and makes for the door.*]

HIGGINS   Anyhow, theres no good bothering now. The thing's done. Good-bye, mother. [*He kisses her, and follows* PICKERING.]

PICKERING [*Turning for a final consolation.*]   There are plenty of openings. We'll do whats right. Good-bye.

HIGGINS [*To* PICKERING *as they go out together.*]   Let's take her to the Shakespear exhibition at Earls Court.

PICKERING   Yes: lets. Her remarks will be delicious.

HIGGINS   She'll mimic all the people for us when we get home.

PICKERING   Ripping. [*Both are heard laughing as they go downstairs.*]

MRS HIGGINS [*Rises with an impatient bounce, and returns to her work at the writing-table. She sweeps a litter of disarranged papers out of her way; snatches a sheet of paper from her stationery case; and tries resolutely to write. At the third line she gives it up; flings down her pen; grips the table angrily and exclaims.*]   Oh, men! men!! men!!!

Act IV

The Wimpole Street laboratory. Midnight. Nobody in the room. The clock on the mantelpiece strikes twelve. The fire is not alight: it is a summer night.

    Presently HIGGINS *and* PICKERING *are heard on the stairs.*

HIGGINS [*Calling down to* PICKERING.]   I say, Pick: lock up, will you. I shant be going out again.

PICKERING   Right. Can Mrs Pearce go to bed? We dont want anything more, do we?

HIGGINS   Lord, no!

    [ELIZA *opens the door and is seen on the lighted landing in opera cloak, brilliant evening dress, and diamonds, with fan, flowers, and all accessories. She comes to the hearth, and switches on the electric lights there. She is tired: her pallor contrasts strongly with her dark eyes and hair; and her expression is almost tragic. She takes off her cloak; puts her fan and flowers on the piano; and sits down on the bench, brooding and silent.* HIGGINS, *in evening dress, with overcoat and hat, comes in, carrying a smoking jacket which he has picked up downstairs. He takes off the hat and overcoat; throws them carelessly on the newspaper stand; disposes of his coat in the same way; puts on the smoking jacket; and throws himself wearily into the easy-chair at the hearth.* PICKERING, *similarly attired, comes in. He also takes off his hat and overcoat, and is about to throw them on* HIGGINS's *when he hesitates.*]

PICKERING   I say: Mrs Pearce will row if we leave these things lying about in the drawing-room.

HIGGINS   Oh, chuck them over the bannisters into the hall. She'll find them there in the morning and put them away all right. She'll think we were drunk.

PICKERING   We are, slightly. Are there any letters?

HIGGINS   I didnt look. [PICKERING *takes the overcoats and hats and goes downstairs.* HIGGINS *begins half singing half yawning an air from* La Fanciulla del Golden West. *Suddenly he stops and exclaims*] I wonder where the devil my slippers are!

[ELIZA *looks at him darkly; then rises suddenly and leaves the room.*

HIGGINS *yawns again, and resumes his song.*

PICKERING *returns, with the contents of the letter-box in his hand.*]

PICKERING   Only circulars, and this coroneted billet-doux[1] for you. [*He throws the circulars into the fender, and posts himself on the hearthrug, with his back to the grate.*]

HIGGINS [*Glancing at the billet-doux.*]   Money-lender. [*He throws the letter after the circulars.*]

[ELIZA *returns with a pair of large down-at-heel slippers. She places them on the carpet before* HIGGINS, *and sits as before without a word.*]

HIGGINS [*Yawning again.*]   Oh Lord! What an evening! What a crew! What a silly tomfoolery! [*He raises his shoe to unlace it, and catches sight of the slippers. He stops unlacing and looks at them as if they had appeared there of their own accord.*] Oh! theyre there, are they?

PICKERING [*Stretching himself.*]   Well, I feel a bit tired. It's been a long day. The garden party, a dinner party, and the opera! Rather too much of a good thing. But youve won your bet, Higgins. Eliza did the trick, and something to spare, eh?

HIGGINS [*Fervently.*]   Thank God it's over!

[ELIZA *flinches violently; but they take no notice of her; and she recovers herself and sits stonily as before.*]

PICKERING   Were you nervous at the garden party? *I* was. Eliza didnt seem a bit nervous.

HIGGINS   Oh, she wasnt nervous. I knew she'd be all right. No: it's the strain of putting the job through all these months that has told on me. It was interesting enough at first, while we were at the phonetics; but after that I got deadly sick of it. If I hadnt backed myself to do it I should have chucked the whole thing up two months ago. It was a silly notion: the whole thing has been a bore.

PICKERING   Oh come! the garden party was frightfully exciting. My heart began beating like anything.

HIGGINS   Yes, for the first three minutes. But when I saw we were going to win hands down, I felt like a bear in a cage, hanging about doing nothing. The dinner was worse: sitting gorging there for over an hour, with nobody but a damned fool of a fashionable woman to talk to! I tell you, Pickering, never again for me. No more artificial duchesses. The whole thing has been simple purgatory.

PICKERING   Youve never been broken in properly to the social routine. [*Strolling over to the piano.*] I rather enjoy dipping into it

1. Personal or love letter (used ironically).

occasionally myself: it makes me feel young again. Anyhow, it was a great success: an immense success. I was quite frightened once or twice because Eliza was doing it so well. You see, lots of the real people cant do it at all: theyre such fools that they think style comes by nature to people in their position; and so they never learn. Theres always something professional about doing a thing superlatively well.

HIGGINS   Yes: thats what drives me mad: the silly people dont know their own silly business. [*Rising.*] However, it's over and done with; and now I can go to bed at last without dreading tomorrow.

[ELIZA*'s beauty becomes murderous.*]

PICKERING   I think I shall turn in too. Still, it's been a great occasion: a triumph for you. Good-night. [*He goes.*]

HIGGINS [*Following him.*]   Good-night. [*Over his shoulder, at the door.*] Put out the lights, Eliza; and tell Mrs Pearce not to make coffee for me in the morning: I'll take tea. [*He goes out.*]

[ELIZA *tries to control herself and feel indifferent as she rises and walks across to the hearth to switch off the lights. By the time she gets there she is on the point of screaming. She sits down in* HIGGINS's *chair and holds on hard to the arms. Finally she gives way and flings herself furiously on the floor, raging.*]

HIGGINS [*In despairing wrath outside.*]   What the devil have I done with my slippers? [*He appears at the door.*]

LIZA [*Snatching up the slippers, and hurling them at him one after the other with all her force.*]   There are your slippers. And there. Take your slippers; and may you never have a day's luck with them!

HIGGINS [*Astounded.*]   What on earth—! [*He comes to her.*] Whats the matter? Get up. [*He pulls her up.*] Anything wrong?

LIZA [*Breathless.*]   Nothing wrong—with you. Ive won your bet for you, havnt I? Thats enough for you. *I* dont matter, I suppose.

HIGGINS   You won my bet! You! Presumptuous insect! *I* won it. What did you throw those slippers at me for?

LIZA   Because I wanted to smash your face. I'd like to kill you, you selfish brute. Why didnt you leave me where you picked me out of—in the gutter? You thank God it's all over, and that now you can throw me back again there, do you? [*She crisps her fingers frantically.*]

HIGGINS [*Looking at her in cool wonder.*]   The creature is nervous, after all.

ELIZA [*Gives a suffocated scream of fury, and instinctively darts her nails at his face.*]   ! !

HIGGINS [*Catching her wrists.*]   Ah! would you? Claws in, you cat. How dare you shew your temper to me? Sit down and be quiet. [*He throws her roughly into the easy chair.*]

LIZA [*Crushed by superior strength and weight.*]   Whats to become of me? Whats to become of me?

HIGGINS   How the devil do I know whats to become of you? What does it matter what becomes of you?

LIZA   You dont care. I know you dont care. You wouldnt care if I was dead. I'm nothing to you—not so much as them slippers.

HIGGINS [*Thundering.*]   Those slippers.

LIZA [*With bitter submission.*]   Those slippers. I didnt think it made any difference now.

[*A pause.* ELIZA *hopeless and crushed.* HIGGINS *a little uneasy.*]

HIGGINS [*In his loftiest manner.*]   Why have you begun going on like this? May I ask whether you complain of your treatment here?

LIZA   No.

HIGGINS   Has anybody behaved badly to you? Colonel Pickering? Mrs Pearce? Any of the servants?

LIZA   No.

HIGGINS   I presume you dont pretend that *I* have treated you badly?

LIZA   No.

HIGGINS   I am glad to hear it. [*He moderates his tone.*] Perhaps youre tired after the strain of the day. Will you have a glass of champagne? [*He moves towards the door.*]

LIZA   No. [*Recollecting her manners.*] Thank you.

HIGGINS [*Good-humored again.*]   This has been coming on you for some days. I suppose it was natural for you to be anxious about the garden party. But thats all over now. [*He pats her kindly on the shoulder. She writhes.*] Theres nothing more to worry about.

LIZA   No. Nothing more for you to worry about. [*She suddenly rises and gets away from him by going to the piano bench, where she sits and hides her face.*] Oh God! I wish I was dead.

HIGGINS [*Staring after her in sincere surprise.*]   Why? In heaven's name, why? [*Reasonably, going to her.*] Listen to me, Eliza. All this irritation is purely subjective.

LIZA   I dont understand. I'm too ignorant.

HIGGINS   It's only imagination. Low spirits and nothing else. Nobody's hurting you. Nothing's wrong. You go to bed like a good girl and sleep it off. Have a little cry and say your prayers: that will make you comfortable.

LIZA   I heard your prayers. "Thank God it's all over!"

HIGGINS [*Impatiently.*]   Well, dont you thank God it's all over? Now you are free and can do what you like.

LIZA [*Pulling herself together in desperation.*]   What am I fit for? What have you left me fit for? Where am I to go? What am I to do? Whats to become of me?

HIGGINS [*Enlightened, but not at all impressed.*]   Oh, thats whats worrying you, is it? [*He thrusts his hands into his pockets and walks about in his usual manner, rattling the contents of his pockets, as if condescending to a trivial subject out of pure kindness.*] I shouldnt bother about it if I were you. I should imagine you wont have much difficulty in settling yourself somewhere or other, though I hadnt quite realized that you were going away. [*She looks quickly at him: he does not look at her, but examines the dessert stand on the piano and decides that he will eat an apple.*] You might marry, you know. [*He bites a large piece out of the apple and munches it noisily.*] You see, Eliza, all men are not confirmed old bachelors like me and the Colonel. Most men are the marrying sort (poor devils!); and youre not bad-looking: it's quite a pleasure to look at you some-times—not now, of course, because youre crying and looking as ugly as the very devil; but when youre all right and quite yourself, youre what I should call attractive. That is, to the people in the marrying line, you understand. You go to bed and have a good nice rest; and then get up and look at yourself in the glass; and you wont feel so cheap.

[ELIZA *again looks at him, speechless, and does not stir.*

The look is quite lost on him: he eats his apple with a dreamy expression of happiness, as it is quite a good one.]

HIGGINS [*A genial afterthought occurring to him.*]   I daresay my mother could find some chap or other who would do very well.

LIZA   We were above that at the corner of Tottenham Court Road.

HIGGINS [*Waking up.*]   What do you mean?

LIZA   I sold flowers. I didnt sell myself. Now youve made a lady of me I'm not fit to sell anything else. I wish youd left me where you found me.

HIGGINS [*Slinging the core of the apple decisively into the grate.*]   Tosh, Eliza. Dont you insult human relations by dragging all this cant about buying and selling into it. You neednt marry the fellow if you dont like him.

LIZA   What else am I to do?

HIGGINS   Oh, lots of things. What about your old idea of a florist's shop? Pickering could set you up in one: hes lots of money. [*Chuckling.*] He'll have to pay for all those togs you have been wearing to-day; and that, with the hire of the jewellery, will make a big hole in two hundred pounds. Why, six months ago you would have thought it the millennium to have a flower shop of your own. Come! youll be all right. I must clear off to bed: I'm devilish sleepy. By the way, I came down for something: I forget what it was.

LIZA   Your slippers.

HIGGINS   Oh yes, of course. You shied them at me. [*He picks them up, and is going out when she rises and speaks to him.*]

LIZA   Before you go, sir—

HIGGINS [*Dropping the slippers in his surprise at her calling him Sir.*]   Eh?

LIZA   Do my clothes belong to me or to Colonel Pickering?

HIGGINS [*Coming back into the room as if her question were the very climax of unreason.*]   What the devil use would they be to Pick-ering?

LIZA   He might want them for the next girl you pick up to experiment on.

HIGGINS [*Shocked and hurt.*]   Is that the way you feel towards us?

LIZA   I dont want to hear anything more about that. All I want to
know is whether anything belongs to me. My own clothes were
burnt.

HIGGINS   But what does it matter? Why need you start bothering
about that in the middle of the night?

LIZA   I want to know what I may take away with me. I dont want to
be accused of stealing.

HIGGINS [*Now deeply wounded.*]   Stealing! You shouldnt have said
that, Eliza. That shews a want of feeling.

LIZA   I'm sorry. I'm only a common ignorant girl; and in my station
I have to be careful. There cant be any feelings between the like
of you and the like of me. Please will you tell me what belongs to
me and what doesnt?

HIGGINS [*Very sulky.*]   You may take the whole damned houseful if
you like. Except the jewels. Theyre hired. Will that satisfy you?
[*He turns on his heel and is about to go in extreme dudgeon.*]

LIZA [*Drinking in his emotion like nectar, and nagging him to provoke
a further supply.*]   Stop, please. [*She takes off her jewels.*] Will you
take these to your room and keep them safe? I dont want to run
the risk of their being missing.

HIGGINS [*Furious.*]   Hand them over. [*She puts them into his hands.*]
If these belonged to me instead of to the jeweller, I'd ram them
down your ungrateful throat. [*He perfunctorily thrusts them into
his pockets, unconsciously decorating himself with the protruding
ends of the chains.*]

LIZA [*Taking a ring off.*]   This ring isnt the jeweller's: it's the one
you bought me in Brighton. I dont want it now. [HIGGINS *dashes
the ring violently into the fireplace, and turns on her so threateningly
that she crouches over the piano with her hands over her face, and
exclaims*] Dont you hit me.

HIGGINS   Hit you! You infamous creature, how dare you accuse me
of such a thing? It is you who have hit me. You have wounded me
to the heart.

LIZA [*Thrilling with hidden joy.*]   I'm glad. Ive got a little of my own
back, anyhow.

HIGGINS [*With dignity, in his finest professional style.*]   You have
caused me to lose my temper: a thing that has hardly ever happened to me before. I prefer to say nothing more tonight. I am
going to bed.

LIZA [*Pertly.*]   Youd better leave a note for Mrs Pearce about the
coffee; for she wont be told by me.

HIGGINS [*Formally.*]   Damn Mrs Pearce; and damn the coffee; and
damn you; and damn my own folly in having lavished hard-earned
knowledge and the treasure of my regard and intimacy on a heart-

less guttersnipe. [*He goes out with impressive decorum, and spoils it by slamming the door savagely.*]

> [ELIZA *smiles for the first time; expresses her feelings by a wild pantomime in which an imitation of* HIGGINS's *exit is confused with her own triumph; and finally goes down on her knees on the hearthrug to look for the ring.*]

Act V

MRS HIGGINS's *drawing-room. She is at her writing-table as before.* THE PARLOR-MAID *comes in.*

THE PARLOR-MAID [*At the door.*] Mr Henry, mam, is downstairs with Colonel Pickering.

MRS HIGGINS Well, shew them up.

THE PARLOR-MAID Theyre using the telephone, mam. Telephoning to the police, I think.

MRS HIGGINS What!

THE PARLOR-MAID [*Coming further in and lowering her voice.*] Mr Henry is in a state, mam. I thought I'd better tell you.

MRS HIGGINS If you had told me that Mr Henry was not in a state it would have been more surprising. Tell them to come up when theyve finished with the police. I suppose hes lost something.

THE PARLOR-MAID Yes, mam. [*Going.*]

MRS HIGGINS Go upstairs and tell Miss Doolittle that Mr Henry and the Colonel are here. Ask her not to come down til I send for her.

THE PARLOR-MAID Yes, mam.

> [HIGGINS *bursts in. He is, as* THE PARLOR-MAID *has said, in a state.*]

HIGGINS Look here, mother: heres a confounded thing!

MRS HIGGINS Yes, dear. Good-morning. [*He checks his impatience and kisses her, whilst* THE PARLOR-MAID *goes out.*] What is it?

HIGGINS Eliza's bolted.

MRS HIGGINS [*Calmly continuing her writing.*] You must have frightened her.

HIGGINS Frightened her! nonsense! She was left last night, as usual, to turn out the lights and all that; and instead of going to bed she changed her clothes and went right off: her bed wasnt slept in. She came in a cab for her things before seven this morning; and that fool Mrs Pearce let her have them without telling me a word about it. What am I to do?

MRS HIGGINS Do without, I'm afraid, Henry. The girl has a perfect right to leave if she chooses.

HIGGINS [*Wandering distractedly across the room.*] But I cant find anything. I dont know what appointments Ive got. I'm— [PICK-

ERING *comes in.* MRS HIGGINS *puts down her pen and turns away from the writing-table.*]

PICKERING [*Shaking hands.*] Good-morning, Mrs Higgins. Has Henry told you? [*He sits down on the ottoman.*]

HIGGINS What does that ass of an inspector say? Have you offered a reward?

MRS HIGGINS [*Rising in indignant amazement.*] You dont mean to say you have set the police after Eliza.

HIGGINS Of course. What are the police for? What else could we do? [*He sits in the Elizabethan chair.*]

PICKERING The inspector made a lot of difficulties. I really think he suspected us of some improper purpose.

MRS HIGGINS Well, of course he did. What right have you to go to the police and give the girl's name as if she were a thief, or a lost umbrella, or something? Really! [*She sits down again, deeply vexed.*]

HIGGINS But we want to find her.

PICKERING We cant let her go like this, you know, Mrs Higgins. What were we to do?

MRS HIGGINS You have no more sense, either of you, than two children. Why—

[THE PARLOR-MAID *comes in and breaks off the conversation.*]

THE PARLOR-MAID Mr Henry: a gentleman wants to see you very particular. Hes been sent on from Wimpole Street.

HIGGINS Oh, bother! I cant see anyone now. Who is it?

THE PARLOR-MAID A Mr Doolittle, sir.

PICKERING Doolittle! Do you mean the dustman?

THE PARLOR-MAID Dustman! Oh no, sir: a gentleman.

HIGGINS [*Springing up excitedly.*] By George, Pick, it's some relative of hers that shes gone to. Somebody we know nothing about. [*To* THE PARLOR-MAID.] Send him up, quick.

THE PARLOR-MAID Yes, sir. [*She goes.*]

HIGGINS [*Eagerly, going to his mother.*] Genteel relatives! now we shall hear something. [*He sits down in the Chippendale chair.*]

MRS HIGGINS Do you know any of her people?

PICKERING Only her father: the fellow we told you about.

THE PARLOR-MAID [*Announcing.*] Mr Dolittle. [*She withdraws.*]

[DOOLITTLE *enters. He is brilliantly dressed in a new fashionable frock-coat, with white waistcoat and grey trousers. A flower in his buttonhole, a dazzling silk hat, and patent leather shoes complete the effect. He is too concerned with the business he has come on to notice* MRS HIGGINS. *He walks straight to* HIGGINS, *and accosts him with vehement reproach.*]

DOOLITTLE [*Indicating his own person.*] See here! Do you see this? You done this.

HIGGINS Done what, man?

DOOLITTLE   This, I tell you. Look at it. Look at this hat. Look at this coat.

PICKERING   Has Eliza been buying you clothes?

DOOLITTLE   Eliza! not she. Not half. Why would she buy me clothes?

MRS HIGGINS   Good-morning, Mr Doolittle. Wont you sit down?

DOOLITTLE [*Taken aback as he becomes conscious that he has forgotten his hostess.*]   Asking your pardon, maam. [*He approaches her and shakes her proffered hand.*] Thank you. [*He sits down on the ottoman, on* PICKERING's *right.*] I am that full of what has happened to me that I cant think of anything else.

HIGGINS   What the dickens has happened to you?

DOOLITTLE   I shouldnt mind if it had only happened to me: anything might happen to anybody and nobody to blame but Providence, as you might say. But this is something that you done to me: yes, you, Henry Higgins.

HIGGINS   Have you found Eliza? Thats the point.

DOOLITTLE   Have you lost her?

HIGGINS   Yes.

DOOLITTLE   You have all the luck, you have. I aint found her; but she'll find me quick enough now after what you done to me.

MRS HIGGINS   But what has my son done to you, Mr Doolittle?

DOOLITTLE   Done to me! Ruined me. Destroyed my happiness. Tied me up and delivered me into the hands of middle class morality.

HIGGINS [*Rising intolerantly and standing over* DOOLITTLE.]   Youre raving. Youre drunk. Youre mad. I gave you five pounds. After that I had two conversations with you, at half-a-crown an hour. Ive never seen you since.

DOOLITTLE   Oh! Drunk! am I? Mad! am I? Tell me this. Did you or did you not write a letter to an old blighter in America that was giving five millions to found Moral Reform Societies all over the world, and that wanted you to invent a universal language for him?

HIGGINS   What! Ezra D. Wannafeller! Hes dead. [*He sits down again carelessly.*]

DOOLITTLE   Yes: hes dead; and I'm done for. Now did you or did you not write a letter to him to say that the most original moralist at present in England, to the best of your knowledge, was Alfred Doolittle, a common dustman.

HIGGINS   Oh, after your last visit I remember making some silly joke of the kind.

DOOLITTLE   Ah! you may well call it a silly joke. It put the lid on me right enough. Just give him the chance he wanted to shew that Americans is not like us: that they recognize and respect merit in every class of life, however humble. Them words is in his blooming will, in which, Henry Higgins, thanks to your silly joking, he leaves me a share in his Pre-digested Cheese Trust worth three thousand a year on condition that I lecture for his Wannafeller Moral Reform World League as often as they ask me up to six times a year.

HIGGINS   The devil he does! Whew! [*Brightening suddenly.*] What a lark!

PICKERING   A safe thing for you, Doolittle. They wont ask you twice.

DOOLITTLE   It aint the lecturing I mind. I'll lecture them blue in the face, I will, and not turn a hair. It's making a gentleman of me that I object to. Who asked him to make a gentleman of me? I was happy. I was free. I touched pretty nigh everybody for money when I wanted it, same as I touched you, Henry Higgins. Now I am worrited; tied neck and heels; and everybody touches me for money. It's a fine thing for you, says my solicitor. Is it? says I. You mean it's a good thing for you, I says. When I was a poor man and had a solicitor once when they found a pram in the dust cart, he got me off, and got shut of me and got me shut of him as quick as he could. Same with the doctors: used to shove me out of the hospital before I could hardly stand on my legs, and nothing to pay. Now they finds out that I'm not a healthy man and cant live unless they looks after me twice a day. In the house I'm not let do a hand's turn for myself: somebody else must do it and touch me for it. A year ago I hadnt a relative in the world except two or three that wouldnt speak to me. Now Ive fifty, and not a decent week's wages among the lot of them. I have to live for others and not for myself: thats middle class morality. You talk of losing Eliza. Dont you be anxious: I bet shes on my doorstep by this: she that could support herself easy by selling flowers if I wasnt respectable. And the next one to touch me will be you, Henry Higgins. I'll have to learn to speak middle class language from you, instead of speaking proper English. Thats where youll come in; and I daresay thats what you done it for.

MRS HIGGINS   But, my dear Mr Doolittle, you need not suffer all this if you are really in earnest. Nobody can force you to accept this bequest. You can repudiate it. Isnt that so, Colonel Pickering?

PICKERING   I believe so.

DOOLITTLE [*Softening his manner in deference to her sex.*]   Thats the tragedy of it, maam. It's easy to say chuck it; but I havnt the nerve. Which of us has? We're all intimidated. Intimidated, maam: thats what we are. What is there for me if I chuck it but the workhouse in my old age? I have to dye my hair already to keep my job as a dustman. If I was one of the deserving poor, and had put by a bit, I could chuck it; but then why should I, acause the deserving poor might as well be millionaires for all the happiness they ever has. They dont know what happiness is. But I, as one of the undeserving poor, have nothing between me and the pauper's uniform but this here blasted three thousand a year that shoves me into the middle class. (Excuse the expression, maam: youd use it yourself if you had my provocation.) Theyve got you every way you turn: it's a choice between the Skilly of the workhouse and the Char Bydis[1] of the middle class; and I havnt the nerve for the workhouse. Intimidated: thats what I am. Broke. Bought up. Happier men than me will call for my dust, and touch me for their tip; and I'll look on helpless, and envy them. And thats what your son has brought me to. [*He is overcome by emotion.*]

MRS HIGGINS   Well, I'm very glad youre not going to do anything foolish, Mr Doolittle. For this solves the problem of Eliza's future. You can provide for her now.

DOOLITTLE   [*With melancholy resignation.*]   Yes, maam: I'm expected to provide for everyone now, out of three thousand a year.

HIGGINS [*Jumping up.*]   Nonsense! he cant provide for her. He shant provide for her. She doesnt belong to him. I paid him five pounds for her. Doolittle: either youre an honest man or a rogue.

DOOLITTLE [*Tolerantly.*]   A little of both, Henry, like the rest of us: a little of both.

HIGGINS   Well, you took that money for the girl; and you have no right to take her as well.

MRS HIGGINS   Henry: dont be absurd. If you want to know where Eliza is, she is upstairs.

HIGGINS [*Amazed.*]   Upstairs!!! Then I shall jolly soon fetch her downstairs. [*He makes resolutely for the door.*]

MRS HIGGINS [*Rising and following him.*]   Be quiet, Henry. Sit down.

HIGGINS   I—

MRS HIGGINS   Sit down, dear; and listen to me.

HIGGINS   Oh very well, very well, very well. [*He throws himself ungraciously on the ottoman, with his face towards the windows.*] But I think you might have told us this half an hour ago.

MRS HIGGINS   Eliza came to me this morning. She passed the night partly walking about in a rage, partly trying to throw herself into the river and being afraid to, and partly in the Carlton Hotel. She told me of the brutal way you two treated her.

HIGGINS [*Bounding up again.*]   What!

PICKERING [*Rising also.*]   My dear Mrs Higgins, shes been telling you stories. We didnt treat her brutally. We hardly said a word to her; and we parted on particularly good terms. [*Turning on* HIGGINS.] Higgins: did you bully her after I went to bed?

HIGGINS   Just the other way about. She threw my slippers in my face. She behaved in the most outrageous way. I never gave her the slightest provocation. The slippers came bang into my face the

---

1. I.e., In Greek mythology, Scylla is a monster who lives on one side of a narrow strait and Charybdis is an enormous whirlpool on the other. Proverbially, they stand for an impossible situation or a double evil.

moment I entered the room—before I had uttered a word. And used perfectly awful language.

PICKERING [*Astonished.*]   But why? What did we do to her?

MRS HIGGINS   I think I know pretty well what you did. The girl is naturally rather affectionate, I think. Isnt she, Mr Doolittle?

DOOLITTLE   Very tender-hearted, maam. Takes after me.

MRS HIGGINS   Just so. She had become attached to you both. She worked very hard for you, Henry! I dont think you quite realize what anything in the nature of brain work means to a girl like that. Well, it seems that when the great day of trial came, and she did this wonderful thing for you without making a single mistake, you two sat there and never said a word to her, but talked together of how glad you were that it was all over and how you had been bored with the whole thing. And then you were surprised because she threw your slippers at you! *I* should have thrown the fire-irons at you.

HIGGINS   We said nothing except that we were tired and wanted to go to bed. Did we, Pick?

PICKERING [*Shrugging his shoulders.*]   That was all.

MRS HIGGINS [*Ironically.*]   Quite sure?

PICKERING   Absolutely. Really, that was all.

MRS HIGGINS   You didnt thank her, or pet her, or admire her, or tell her how splendid she'd been.

HIGGINS [*Impatiently.*]   But she knew all about that. We didnt make speeches to her, if thats what you mean.

PICKERING [*Conscience stricken.*]   Perhaps we were a little inconsiderate. Is she very angry?

MRS HIGGINS [*Returning to her place at the writing-table.*]   Well, I'm afraid she wont go back to Wimpole Street, especially now that Mr Doolittle is able to keep up the position you have thrust on her; but she says she is quite willing to meet you on friendly terms and to let bygones be bygones.

HIGGINS [*Furious.*]   Is she, by George? Ho!

MRS HIGGINS   If you promise to behave yourself, Henry, I'll ask her to come down. If not, go home; for you have taken up quite enough of my time.

HIGGINS   Oh, all right. Very well. Pick: you behave yourself. Let us put on our best Sunday manners for this creature that we picked out of the mud. [*He flings himself sulkily into the Elizabethan chair.*]

DOOLITTLE [*Remonstrating.*]   Now, now, Henry Higgins! have some consideration for my feelings as a middle class man.

MRS HIGGINS   Remember your promise, Henry. [*She presses the bell-button on the writing-table.*] Mr Doolittle: will you be so good as to step out on the balcony for a moment. I dont want Eliza to have the shock of your news until she has made it up with these two gentlemen. Would you mind?

DOOLITTLE   As you wish, lady. Anything to help Henry to keep her off my hands. [*He disappears through the window.*]

[THE PARLOR-MAID *answers the bell.* PICKERING *sits down in* DOOLITTLE's *place.*]

MRS HIGGINS   Ask Miss Doolittle to come down, please.

THE PARLOR-MAID   Yes, mam. [*She goes out.*]

MRS HIGGINS   Now, Henry: be good.

HIGGINS   I am behaving myself perfectly.

PICKERING   He is doing his best, Mrs Higgins.

[*A pause.* HIGGINS *throws back his head; stretches out his legs; and begins to whistle.*]

MRS HIGGINS   Henry, dearest, you dont look at all nice in that attitude.

HIGGINS [*Pulling himself together.*]   I was not trying to look nice, mother.

MRS HIGGINS   It doesnt matter, dear. I only wanted to make you speak.

HIGGINS   Why?

MRS HIGGINS   Because you cant speak and whistle at the same time.

[HIGGINS *groans. Another very trying pause.*]

HIGGINS [*Springing up, out of patience.*]   Where the devil is that girl? Are we to wait here all day?

[ELIZA *enters, sunny, self-possessed, and giving a staggeringly convincing exhibition of ease of manner. She carries a little work-basket, and is very much at home.* PICKERING *is too much taken aback to rise.*]

LIZA   How do you do, Professor Higgins? Are you quite well?

HIGGINS [*Choking.*]   Am I— [*He can no more.*]

LIZA   But of course you are: you are never ill. So glad to see you again, Colonel Pickering. [*He rises hastily; and they shake hands.*] Quite chilly this morning, isnt it? [*She sits down on his left. He sits beside her.*]

HIGGINS   Dont you dare try this game on me. I taught it to you; and it doesnt take me in. Get up and come home; and dont be a fool.

[ELIZA *takes a piece of needlework from her basket, and begins to stitch at it, without taking the least notice of this outburst.*]

MRS HIGGINS   Very nicely put, indeed, Henry. No woman could resist such an invitation.

HIGGINS   You let her alone, mother. Let her speak for herself. You will jolly soon see whether she has an idea that I havnt put into her head or a word that I havnt put into her mouth. I tell you I have created this thing out of the squashed cabbage leaves of Covent Garden; and now she pretends to play the fine lady with me.

MRS HIGGINS [*Placidly.*]   Yes, dear; but youll sit down, wont you?

[HIGGINS *sits down again, savagely.*]

LIZA [*To* PICKERING, *taking no apparent notice of* HIGGINS, *and work-*

ing away deftly.] Will you drop me altogether now that the experiment is over, Colonel Pickering?

PICKERING   Oh dont. You mustnt think of it as an experiment. It shocks me, somehow.

LIZA   Oh, I'm only a squashed cabbage leaf—

PICKERING [*Impulsively.*]   No.

LIZA [*Continuing quietly.*]   —but I owe so much to you that I should be very unhappy if you forgot me.

PICKERING   It's very kind of you to say so, Miss Doolittle.

LIZA   It's not because you paid for my dresses. I know you are generous to everybody with money. But it was from you that I learnt really nice manners; and that is what makes one a lady, isn't it? You see it was so very difficult for me with the example of Professor Higgins always before me. I was brought up to be just like him, unable to control myself, and using bad language on the slightest provocation. And I should never have known that ladies and gentlemen didnt behave like that if you hadnt been there.

HIGGINS   Well ! !

PICKERING   Oh, thats only his way, you know. He doesnt mean it.

LIZA   Oh, *I* didnt mean it either, when I was a flower girl. It was only my way. But you see I did it; and thats what makes the difference after all.

PICKERING   No doubt. Still, he taught you to speak; and I couldnt have done that, you know.

LIZA [*Trivially.*]   Of course: that is his profession.

HIGGINS   Damnation!

LIZA [*Continuing.*]   It was just like learning to dance in the fashionable way: there was nothing more than that in it. But do you know what began my real education?

PICKERING   What?

LIZA [*Stopping her work for a moment.*]   Your calling me Miss Doolittle that day when I first came to Wimpole Street. That was the beginning of self-respect for me. [*She resumes her stitching.*] And there were a hundred little things you never noticed, because they came naturally to you. Things about standing up and taking off your hat and opening doors—

PICKERING   Oh, that was nothing.

LIZA   Yes: things that shewed you thought and felt about me as if I were something better than a scullery-maid; though of course I know you would have been just the same to a scullery-maid if she had been let into the drawing-room. You never took off your boots in the dining-room when I was there.

PICKERING   You mustnt mind that. Higgins takes off his boots all over the place.

LIZA   I know. I am not blaming him. It is his way, isnt it? But it made such a difference to me that you didnt do it. You see, really and truly, apart from the things anyone can pick up (the dressing and the proper way of speaking, and so on), the difference between a lady and a flower girl is not how she behaves, but how shes treated. I shall always be a flower girl to Professor Higgins, because he always treats me as a flower girl, and always will; but I know I can be a lady to you, because you always treat me as a lady, and always will.

MRS HIGGINS   Please dont grind your teeth, Henry.

PICKERING   Well, this is really very nice of you, Miss Doolittle.

LIZA   I should like you to call me Eliza, now, if you would.

PICKERING   Thank you. Eliza, of course.

LIZA   And I should like Professor Higgins to call me Miss Doolittle.

HIGGINS   I'll see you damned first.

MRS HIGGINS   Henry! Henry!

PICKERING   [*Laughing.*]   Why dont you slang back at him? Dont stand it. It would do him a lot of good.

LIZA   I cant. I could have done it once; but now I cant go back to it. Last night, when I was wandering about, a girl spoke to me; and I tried to get back into the old way with her; but it was no use. You told me, you know, that when a child is brought to a foreign country, it picks up the language in a few weeks, and forgets its own. Well, I am a child in your country. I have forgotten my own language, and can speak nothing but yours. Thats the real break-off with the corner of Tottenham Court Road. Leaving Wimpole Street finishes it.

PICKERING   [*Much alarmed.*]   Oh! but youre coming back to Wimpole Street, arnt you? Youll forgive Higgins?

HIGGINS [*Rising.*]   Forgive! Will she, by George! Let her go. Let her find out how she can get on without us. She will relapse into the gutter in three weeks without me at her elbow.

   [DOOLITTLE *appears at the centre window. With a look of dignified reproach at* HIGGINS, *he comes slowly and silently to his daughter, who, with her back to the window, is unconscious of his approach.*]

PICKERING   Hes incorrigible, Eliza. You wont relapse, will you?

LIZA   No: not now. Never again. I have learnt my lesson. I dont believe I could utter one of the old sounds if I tried. [DOOLITTLE *touches her on her left shoulder. She drops her work, losing her self-possession utterly at the spectacle of her father's splendor.*] A-a-a-a-a-ah-ow-ooh!

HIGGINS [*With a crow of triumph.*]   Aha! Just so. A-a-a-a-ahowooh! A-a-a-a-ahowooh! A-a-a-a-ahowooh! Victory! Victory! [*He throws himself on the divan, folding his arms, and spraddling arrogantly.*]

DOOLITTLE   Can you blame the girl? Dont look at me like that, Eliza. It aint my fault. Ive come into some money.

LIZA   You must have touched a millionaire this time, dad.

DOOLITTLE　I have. But I'm dressed something special today. I'm going to St. George's, Hanover Square. Your stepmother is going to marry me.

LIZA [*Angrily*.]　Youre going to let yourself down to marry that low common woman!

PICKERING [*Quietly*.]　He ought to, Eliza. [*To* DOOLITTLE.] Why has she changed her mind?

DOOLITTLE [*Sadly*.]　Intimidated, Governor. Intimidated. Middle class morality claims its victim. Wont you put on your hat, Liza, and come and see me turned off?

LIZA　If the Colonel says I must, I—I'll [*almost sobbing*] I'll demean myself. And get insulted for my pains, like enough.

DOOLITTLE　Dont be afraid: she never comes to words with anyone now, poor woman! respectability has broke all the spirit out of her.

PICKERING [*Squeezing* ELIZA's *elbow gently*.]　Be kind to them, Eliza. Make the best of it.

LIZA [*Forcing a little smile for him through her vexation*.]　Oh well, just to shew theres no ill feeling. I'll be back in a moment. [*She goes out.*]

DOOLITTLE [*Sitting down beside* PICKERING.]　I feel uncommon nervous about the ceremony, Colonel. I wish youd come and see me through it.

PICKERING　But youve been through it before, man. You were married to Eliza's mother.

DOOLITTLE　Who told you that, Colonel?

PICKERING　Well, nobody told me. But I concluded—naturally—

DOOLITTLE　No: that aint the natural way, Colonel: it's only the middle class way. My way was always the undeserving way. But dont say nothing to Eliza. She dont know: I always had a delicacy about telling her.

PICKERING　Quite right. We'll leave it so, if you dont mind.

DOOLITTLE　And youll come to the church, Colonel, and put me through straight?

PICKERING　With pleasure. As far as a bachelor can.

MRS HIGGINS　May I come, Mr Doolittle? I should be very sorry to miss your wedding.

DOOLITTLE　I should indeed be honored by your condescension, maam; and my poor old woman would take it as a tremenjous compliment. Shes been very low, thinking of the happy days that are no more.

MRS HIGGINS [*Rising*.]　I'll order the carriage and get ready. [*The men rise, except* HIGGINS.] I shant be more than fifteen minutes. [*As she goes to the door* ELIZA *comes in, hatted and buttoning her gloves*.] I'm going to the church to see your father married, Eliza. You had better come in the brougham with me. Colonel Pickering can go on with the bridegroom.

[MRS HIGGINS *goes out.* ELIZA *comes to the middle of the room between the centre window and the ottoman.* PICKERING *joins her.*]

DOOLITTLE   Bridegroom! What a word! It makes a man realize his position, somehow. [*He takes up his hat and goes towards the door.*]

PICKERING   Before I go, Eliza, do forgive him and come back to us.

LIZA   I dont think papa would allow me. Would you, dad?

DOOLITTLE [*Sad but magnanimous.*]   They played you off very cunning, Eliza, them two sportsmen. If it had been only one of them, you could have nailed him. But you see, there was two; and one of them chaperoned the other, as you might say. [*To* PICKERING.] It was artful of you, Colonel; but I bear no malice: I should have done the same myself. I been the victim of one woman after another all my life; and I dont grudge you two getting the better of Eliza. I shant interfere. It's time for us to go, Colonel. So long, Henry. See you in St. George's, Eliza. [*He goes out.*]

PICKERING [*Coaxing.*]   Do stay with us, Eliza. [*He follows* DOOLITTLE.]

[ELIZA *goes out on the balcony to avoid being alone with* HIGGINS. *He rises and joins her there. She immediately comes back into the room and makes for the door; but he goes along the balcony quickly and gets his back to the door before she reaches it.*]

HIGGINS   Well, Eliza, youve had a bit of your own back, as you call it. Have you had enough? and are you going to be reasonable? Or do you want any more?

LIZA   You want me back only to pick up your slippers and put up with your tempers and fetch and carry for you.

HIGGINS   I havnt said I wanted you back at all.

LIZA   Oh, indeed. Then what are we talking about?

HIGGINS   About you, not about me. If you come back I shall treat you just as I have always treated you. I cant change my nature; and I dont intend to change my manners. My manners are exactly the same as Colonel Pickering's.

LIZA   Thats not true. He treats a flower girl as if she was a duchess.

HIGGINS   And I treat a duchess as if she was a flower girl.

LIZA   I see. [*She turns away composedly, and sits on the ottoman, facing the window.*] The same to everybody.

HIGGINS   Just so.

LIZA   Like father.

HIGGINS [*Grinning, a little taken down.*]   Without accepting the comparison at all points, Eliza, it's quite true that your father is not a snob, and that he will be quite at home in any station of life to which his eccentric destiny may call him. [*Seriously.*] The great secret, Eliza, is not having bad manners or good manners or any other particular sort of manners, but having the same manner for all human souls: in short, behaving as if you were in Heaven, where there are no third-class carriages, and one soul is as good as another.

LIZA Amen. You are a born preacher.

HIGGINS [*Irritated.*] The question is not whether I treat you rudely, but whether you ever heard me treat anyone else better.

LIZA [*With sudden sincerity.*] I dont care how you treat me. I dont mind your swearing at me. I dont mind a black eye: Ive had one before this. But [*standing up and facing him*] I wont be passed over.

HIGGINS Then get out of my way; for I wont stop for you. You talk about me as if I were a motor bus.

LIZA So you are a motor bus: all bounce and go, and no consideration for anyone. But I can do without you: dont think I cant.

HIGGINS I know you can. I told you you could.

LIZA [*Wounded, getting away from him to the other side of the ottoman with her face to the hearth.*] I know you did, you brute. You wanted to get rid of me.

HIGGINS Liar.

LIZA Thank you. [*She sits down with dignity.*]

HIGGINS You never asked yourself, I suppose, whether *I* could do without you.

LIZA [*Earnestly.*] Dont you try to get round me. Youll have to do without me.

HIGGINS [*Arrogant.*] I can do without anybody. I have my own soul: my own spark of divine fire. But [*with sudden humility*] I shall miss you, Eliza. [*He sits down near her on the ottoman.*] I have learnt something from your idiotic notions: I confess that humbly and gratefully. And I have grown accustomed to your voice and appearance. I like them, rather.

LIZA Well, you have both of them on your gramophone and in your book of photographs. When you feel lonely without me, you can turn the machine on. It's got no feelings to hurt.

HIGGINS I cant turn your soul on. Leave me those feelings; and you can take away the voice and the face. They are not you.

LIZA Oh, you are a devil. You can twist the heart in a girl as easy as some could twist her arms to hurt her. Mrs Pearce warned me. Time and again she has wanted to leave you; and you always got round her at the last minute. And you dont care a bit for her. And you dont care a bit for me.

HIGGINS I care for life, for humanity; and you are a part of it that has come my way and been built into my house. What more can you or anyone ask?

LIZA I wont care for anybody that doesnt care for me.

HIGGINS Commercial principles, Eliza. Like [*reproducing her Covent Garden pronunciation with professional exactness*] s'yollin voylets [selling violets], isnt it?

LIZA   Dont sneer at me. It's mean to sneer at me.

HIGGINS   I have never sneered in my life. Sneering doesnt become either the human face or the human soul. I am expressing my righteous contempt for Commercialism. I dont and wont trade in affection. You call me a brute because you couldnt buy a claim on me by fetching my slippers and finding my spectacles. You were a fool: I think a woman fetching a man's slippers is a disgusting sight: did I ever fetch your slippers? I think a good deal more of you for throwing them in my face. No use slaving for me and then saying you want to be cared for: who cares for a slave? If you come back, come back for the sake of good fellowship; for youll get nothing else. Youve had a thousand times as much out of me as I have out of you; and if you dare to set up your little dog's tricks of fetching and carrying slippers against my creation of a Duchess Eliza, I'll slam the door in your silly face.

LIZA   What did you do it for if you didnt care for me?

HIGGINS [Heartily.]   Why, because it was my job.

LIZA   You never thought of the trouble it would make for me.

HIGGINS   Would the world ever have been made if its maker had been afraid of making trouble? Making life means making trouble. Theres only one way of escaping trouble; and thats killing things. Cowards, you notice, are always shrieking to have troublesome people killed.

LIZA   I'm no preacher: I dont notice things like that. I notice that you dont notice me.

HIGGINS [Jumping up and walking about intolerantly.]   Eliza: youre an idiot. I waste the treasures of my Miltonic mind by spreading them before you. Once for all, understand that I go my way and do my work without caring twopence what happens to either of us. I am not intimidated, like your father and your stepmother. So you can come back or go to the devil: which you please.

LIZA   What am I to come back for?

HIGGINS [Bouncing up on his knees on the ottoman and leaning over it to her.]   For the fun of it. Thats why I took you on.

LIZA [With averted face.]   And you may throw me out tomorrow if I dont do everything you want me to?

HIGGINS   Yes; and you may walk out tomorrow if I dont do everything you want me to.

LIZA   And live with my stepmother?

HIGGINS   Yes, or sell flowers.

LIZA   Oh! if I only could go back to my flower basket! I should be independent of both you and father and all the world! Why did you take my independence from me? Why did I give it up? I'm a slave now, for all my fine clothes.

HIGGINS   Not a bit. I'll adopt you as my daughter and settle money on you if you like. Or would you rather marry Pickering?

LIZA [Looking fiercely round at him.]   I wouldnt marry you if you asked me; and youre nearer my age than what he is.

HIGGINS [*Gently.*] Than he is: not "than what he is."

LIZA [*Losing her temper and rising.*] I'll talk as I like. Youre not my teacher now.

HIGGINS [*Reflectively.*] I dont suppose Pickering would, though. He's as confirmed an old bachelor as I am.

LIZA Thats not what I want; and dont you think it. Ive always had chaps enough wanting me that way. Freddy Hill writes to me twice and three times a day, sheets and sheets.

HIGGINS [*Disagreeably surprised.*] Damn his impudence! [*He recoils and finds himself sitting on his heels.*]

LIZA He has a right to if he likes, poor lad. And he does love me.

HIGGINS [*Getting off the ottoman.*] You have no right to encourage him.

LIZA Every girl has a right to be loved.

HIGGINS What! By fools like that?

LIZA Freddy's not a fool. And if hes weak and poor and wants me, may be hed make me happier than my betters that bully me and dont want me.

HIGGINS Can he make anything of you? Thats the point.

LIZA Perhaps I could make something of him. But I never thought of us making anything of one another; and you never think of anything else. I only want to be natural.

HIGGINS In short, you want me to be as infatuated about you as Freddy? Is that it?

LIZA No I dont. Thats not the sort of feeling I want from you. And dont you be too sure of yourself or of me. I could have been a bad girl if I'd liked. Ive seen more of some things than you, for all your learning. Girls like me can drag gentlemen down to make love to them easy enough. And they wish each other dead the next minute.

HIGGINS Of course they do. Then what in thunder are we quarrelling about?

LIZA [*Much troubled.*] I want a little kindness. I know I'm a common ignorant girl, and you a book-learned gentleman; but I'm not dirt under your feet. What I done [*correcting herself*] what I did was not for the dresses and the taxis: I did it because we were pleasant together and I come—came—to care for you; not to want you to make love to me, and not forgetting the difference between us, but more friendly like.

HIGGINS Well, of course. Thats just how I feel. And how Pickering feels. Eliza: youre a fool.

LIZA Thats not a proper answer to give me. [*She sinks on the chair at the writing-table in tears.*]

HIGGINS It's all youll get until you stop being a common idiot. If youre going to be a lady, youll have to give up feeling neglected if the men you know dont spend half their time snivelling over you and the other half giving you black eyes. If you cant stand the coldness of my sort of life, and the strain of it, go back to the gutter. Work til you are more a brute than a human being; and then cuddle and squabble and drink til you fall asleep. Oh, it's a fine life, the life of the gutter. It's real: it's warm: it's violent: you can feel it through the thickest skin: you can taste it and smell it without any training or any work. Not like Science and Literature and Classical Music and Philosophy and Art. You find me cold, unfeeling, selfish, dont you? Very well: be off with you to the sort of people you like. Marry some sentimental hog or other with lots of money, and a thick pair of lips to kiss you with and a thick pair of boots to kick you with. If you cant appreciate what youve got, youd better get what you can appreciate.

LIZA [*Desperate.*]   Oh, you are a cruel tyrant. I cant talk to you: you turn everything against me: I'm always in the wrong. But you know very well all the time that youre nothing but a bully. You know I cant go back to the gutter, as you call it, and that I have no real friends in the world but you and the Colonel. You know well I couldnt bear to live with a low common man after you two; and it's wicked and cruel of you to insult me by pretending I could. You think I must go back to Wimpole Street because I have nowhere else to go but father's. But dont you be too sure that you have me under your feet to be trampled on and talked down. I'll marry Freddy, I will, as soon as hes able to support me.

HIGGINS [*Sitting down beside her.*]   Rubbish! you shall marry an ambassador. You shall marry the Governor-General of India or the Lord-Lieutenant of Ireland, or somebody who wants a deputy-queen. I'm not going to have my masterpiece thrown away on Freddy.

LIZA   You think I like you to say that. But I havnt forgot what you said a minute ago; and I wont be coaxed round as if I was a baby or a puppy. If I cant have kindness, I'll have independence.

HIGGINS   Independence? Thats middle class blasphemy. We are all dependent on one another, every soul of us on earth.

LIZA [*Rising determinedly.*]   I'll let you see whether I'm dependent on you. If you can preach, I can teach. I'll go and be a teacher.

HIGGINS   Whatll you teach, in heaven's name?

LIZA   What you taught me. I'll teach phonetics.

HIGGINS   Ha! ha! ha!

LIZA   I'll offer myself as an assistant to Professor Nepean.

HIGGINS [*Rising in a fury.*]   What! That impostor! that humbug! that toadying ignoramus! Teach him my methods! my discoveries! You take one step in his direction and I'll wring your neck. [*He lays hands on her.*] Do you hear?

LIZA [*Defiantly non-resistant.*]   Wring away. What do I care? I knew youd strike me some day. [*He lets her go, stamping with rage at having forgotten himself, and recoils so hastily that he stumbles back into his seat on the ottoman.*] Aha! Now I know how to deal with you. What a fool I was not to think of it before! You cant take away the knowledge you gave me. You said I had a finer ear than you. And I can be civil and kind to people, which is more than you can. Aha! Thats done you, Henry Higgins, it has. Now I dont care that [*snapping her fingers*] for your bullying and your big talk. I'll advertize it in the papers that your duchess is only a flower girl that you taught, and that she'll teach anybody to be a duchess just the same in six months for a thousand guineas. Oh, when I think of myself crawling under your feet and being trampled on and called names, when all the time I had only to lift up my finger to be as good as you, I could just kick myself.

HIGGINS [*Wondering at her.*]   You damned impudent slut, you! But it's better than snivelling; better than fetching slippers and finding spectacles, isn't it? [*Rising.*] By George, Eliza, I said I'd make a woman of you; and I have. I like you like this.

LIZA   Yes: you turn round and make up to me now that I'm not afraid of you, and can do without you.

HIGGINS   Of course I do, you little fool. Five minutes ago you were like a millstone round my neck. Now youre a tower of strength: a consort battleship. You and I and Pickering will be three old bachelors together instead of only two men and a silly girl.

> [MRS HIGGINS *returns, dressed for the wedding.* ELIZA *instantly becomes cool and elegant.*]

MRS HIGGINS   The carriage is waiting, Eliza. Are you ready?

LIZA   Quite. Is the Professor coming?

MRS HIGGINS   Certainly not. He cant behave himself in church. He makes remarks out loud all the time on the clergyman's pronunciation.

LIZA   Then I shall not see you again, Professor. Good-bye. [*She goes to the door.*]

MRS HIGGINS [*Coming to Higgins.*]   Good-bye, dear.

HIGGINS   Good-bye, mother. [*He is about to kiss her, when he recollects something.*] Oh, by the way, Eliza, order a ham and a Stilton cheese, will you? And buy me a pair of reindeer gloves, number eights, and a tie to match that new suit of mine, at Eale & Binman's. You can choose the color. [*His cheerful, careless, vigorous voice shows that he is incorrigible.*]

LIZA [*Disdainfully.*]   Buy them yourself. [*She sweeps out.*]

MRS HIGGINS   I'm afraid youve spoiled that girl, Henry. But never mind, dear: I'll buy you the tie and gloves.

HIGGINS [*Sunnily.*]   Oh, dont bother. She'll buy em all right enough. Good-bye.

> [*They kiss.* MRS HIGGINS *runs out.* HIGGINS, *left alone, rattles his cash in his pocket; chuckles; and disports himself in a highly self-satisfied manner.*]

*   *   *   *   *   *

The rest of the story need not be shewn in action, and indeed, would hardly need telling if our imaginations were not so enfeebled by their lazy dependence on the ready-mades and reach-me-downs of the ragshop in which Romance keeps its stock of "happy endings" to misfit all stories. Now, the history of Eliza Doolittle, though called a romance because the transfiguration it records seems exceedingly improbable, is common enough. Such transfigurations have been achieved by hundreds of resolutely ambitious young women since Nell Gwynne[1] set them the example by playing queens and fascinating kings in the theatre in which she began by selling oranges. Nevertheless, people in all directions have assumed, for no other reason than that she became the heroine of a romance, that she must have married the hero of it. This is unbearable, not only because her little drama, if acted on such a thoughtless assumption, must be spoiled, but because the true sequel is patent to anyone with a sense of human nature in general, and of feminine instinct in particular.

Eliza, in telling Higgins she would not marry him if he asked her, was not coquetting: she was announcing a well-considered decision. When a bachelor interests, and dominates, and teaches, and becomes important to a spinster, as Higgins with Eliza, she always, if she has character enough to be capable of it, considers very seriously indeed whether she will play for becoming that bachelor's wife, especially if he is so little interested in marriage that a determined and devoted woman might capture him if she set herself resolutely to do it. Her decision will depend a good deal on whether she is really free to choose; and that, again, will depend on her age and income. If she is at the end of her youth, and has no security for her livelihood, she will marry him because she must marry anybody who will provide for her. But at Eliza's age a good-looking girl does not feel that pressure: she feels free to pick and choose. She is therefore guided by her instinct in the matter. Eliza's instinct tells her not to marry Higgins. It does not tell her to give him up. It is not in the slightest doubt as to his remaining one of the strongest personal interests in her life. It would be very sorely strained if there was another woman likely to supplant her with him. But as she feels sure of him on that last point, she has no doubt at all as to her course, and would not have any, even if the difference of twenty years in age, which seems so great to youth, did not exist between them.

As our own instincts are not appealed to by her conclusion, let us see whether we cannot discover some reason in it. When Higgins excused his indifference to young women on the ground that they had an irresistible rival in his mother, he gave the clue to his inveterate old-bachelordom. The case is uncommon only to the extent

1. Another poor London girl who worked in Covent Garden (selling oranges at the theater), where she caught the eye of Charles II, whose mistress she became.

that remarkable mothers are uncommon. If an imaginative boy has a sufficiently rich mother who has intelligence, personal grace, dignity of character without harshness, and a cultivated sense of the best art of her time to enable her to make her house beautiful, she sets a standard for him against which very few women can struggle, besides effecting for him a disengagement of his affections, his sense of beauty, and his idealism from his specifically sexual impulses. This makes him a standing puzzle to the huge number of uncultivated people who have been brought up in tasteless homes by commonplace or disagreeable parents, and to whom, consequently, literature, painting, sculpture, music, and affectionate personal relations come as modes of sex if they come at all. The word passion means nothing else to them; and that Higgins could have a passion for phonetics and idealize his mother instead of Eliza, would seem to them absurd and unnatural. Nevertheless, when we look round and see that hardly anyone is too ugly or disagreeable to find a wife or a husband if he or she wants one, whilst many old maids and bachelors are above the average in quality and culture, we cannot help suspecting that the disentanglement of sex from the associations with which it is so commonly confused, a disentanglement which persons of genius achieve by sheer intellectual analysis, is sometimes produced or aided by parental fascination.

Now, though Eliza was incapable of thus explaining to herself Higgins's formidable powers of resistance to the charm that prostrated Freddy at the first glance, she was instinctively aware that she could never obtain a complete grip of him, or come between him and his mother (the first necessity of the married woman). To put it shortly, she knew that for some mysterious reason he had not the makings of a married man in him, according to her conception of a husband as one to whom she would be his nearest and fondest and warmest interest. Even had there been no mother-rival, she would still have refused to accept an interest in herself that was secondary to philosophic interests. Had Mrs Higgins died, there would still have been Milton and the Universal Alphabet. Landor's remark that to those who have the greatest power of loving, love is a secondary affair, would not have recommended Landor to Eliza. Put that along with her resentment of Higgins's domineering superiority, and her mistrust of his coaxing cleverness in getting round her and evading her wrath when he had gone too far with his impetuous bullying, and you will see that Eliza's instinct had good grounds for warning her not to marry her Pygmalion.

And now, whom did Eliza marry? For if Higgins was a predestinate old bachelor, she was most certainly not a predestinate old maid. Well, that can be told very shortly to those who have not guessed it from the indications she has herself given them.

Almost immediately after Eliza is stung into proclaiming her considered determination not to marry Higgins, she mentions the fact that young Mr Frederick Eynsford Hill is pouring out his love for her daily through the post. Now Freddy is young, practically twenty years younger than Higgins: he is a gentleman (or, as Eliza would qualify him, a toff), and speaks like one; he is nicely dressed, is treated by the Colonel as an equal, loves her unaffectedly, and is not her master, nor ever likely to dominate her in spite of his advantage of social standing. Eliza has no use for the foolish romantic tradition that all women love to be mastered, if not actually bullied and beaten. "When you go to women," says Nietzsche, "take your whip with you." Sensible despots have never confined that precaution to women: they have taken their whips with them when they have dealt with men, and been slavishly idealized by the men over whom they have flourished the whip much more than by women. No doubt there are slavish women as well as slavish men; and women, like men, admire those that are stronger than themselves. But to admire a strong person and to live under that strong person's thumb are two different things. The weak may not be admired and hero-worshipped; but they are by no means disliked or shunned; and they never seem to have the least difficulty in marrying people who are too good for them. They may fail in emergencies; but life is not one long emergency: it is mostly a string of situations for which no exceptional strength is needed, and with which even rather weak people can cope if they have a stronger partner to help them out. Accordingly, it is a truth everywhere in evidence that strong people, masculine or feminine, not only do not marry stronger people, but do not shew any preference for them in selecting their friends. When a lion meets another with a louder roar "the first lion thinks the last a bore." The man or woman who feels strong enough for two, seeks for every other quality in a partner than strength.

The converse is also true. Weak people want to marry strong people who do not frighten them too much; and this often leads them to make the mistake we describe metaphorically as "biting off more than they can chew." They want too much for too little; and when the bargain is unreasonable beyond all bearing, the union becomes impossible: it ends in the weaker party being either discarded or borne as a cross, which is worse. People who are not only weak, but silly or obtuse as well, are often in these difficulties.

This being the state of human affairs, what is Eliza fairly sure to do when she is placed between Freddy and Higgins? Will she look forward to a lifetime of fetching Higgins's slippers or to a lifetime of Freddy fetching hers? There can be no doubt about the answer. Unless Freddy is biologically repulsive to her, and Higgins biologically attractive to a degree that overwhelms all her other instincts, she will, if she marries either of them, marry Freddy.

And that is just what Eliza did.

Complications ensued; but they were economic, not romantic. Freddy had no money and no occupation. His mother's jointure, a last relic of the opulence of Largelady Park, had enabled her to struggle along in Earlscourt with an air of gentility, but not to procure any serious secondary education for her children, much less give the boy a profession. A clerkship at thirty shillings a week was beneath Freddy's dignity, and extremely distasteful to him besides. His prospects consisted of a hope that if he kept up appearances somebody would do something for him. The something appeared vaguely to his imagination as a private secretaryship or a sinecure of some sort. To his mother it perhaps appeared as a marriage to some lady of means who could not resist her boy's niceness. Fancy her feelings when he married a flower girl who had become déclassée under extraordinary circumstances which were now notorious!

It is true that Eliza's situation did not seem wholly ineligible. Her father, though formerly a dustman, and now fantastically disclassed, had become extremely popular in the smartest society by a social talent which triumphed over every prejudice and every disadvantage. Rejected by the middle class, which he loathed, he had shot up at once into the highest circles by his wit, his dustmanship (which he carried like a banner), and his Nietzschean transcendence of good and evil. At intimate ducal dinners he sat on the right hand of the Duchess; and in country houses he smoked in the pantry and was made much of by the butler when he was not feeding in the dining-room and being consulted by cabinet ministers. But he found it almost as hard to do all this on four thousand a year as Mrs Eynsford Hill to live in Earlscourt on an income so pitiably smaller that I have not the heart to disclose its exact figure. He absolutely refused to add the last straw to his burden by contributing to Eliza's support.

Thus Freddy and Eliza, now Mr and Mrs Eynsford Hill, would have spent a penniless honeymoon but for a wedding present of £500[2] from the Colonel to Eliza. It lasted a long time because Freddy did not know how to spend money, never having had any to spend, and Eliza, socially trained by a pair of old bachelors, wore her clothes as long as they held together and looked pretty, without the least regard to their being many months out of fashion. Still, £500 will not last two young people for ever; and they both knew, and Eliza felt as well, that they must shift for themselves in the end. She could quarter herself on Wimpole Street because it had come to be her home; but she was quite aware that she ought not to quarter Freddy there, and that it would not be good for his character if she did.

2. About $750.

Not that the Wimpole Street bachelors objected. When she consulted them, Higgins declined to be bothered about her housing problem when that solution was so simple. Eliza's desire to have Freddy in the house with her seemed of no more importance than if she had wanted an extra piece of bedroom furniture. Pleas as to Freddy's character, and the moral obligation on him to earn his own living, were lost on Higgins. He denied that Freddy had any character, and declared that if he tried to do any useful work some competent person would have the trouble of undoing it: a procedure involving a net loss to the community, and great unhappiness to Freddy himself, who was obviously intended by Nature for such light work as amusing Eliza, which, Higgins declared, was a much more useful and honorable occupation than working in the city. When Eliza referred again to her project of teaching phonetics, Higgins abated not a jot of his violent opposition to it. He said she was not within ten years of being qualified to meddle with his pet subject; and as it was evident that the Colonel agreed with him, she felt she could not go against them in this grave matter, and that she had no right, without Higgins's consent, to exploit the knowledge he had given her; for his knowledge seemed to her as much his private property as his watch: Eliza was no communist. Besides, she was superstitiously devoted to them both, more entirely and frankly after her marriage than before it.

It was the Colonel who finally solved the problem, which had cost him much perplexed cogitation. He one day asked Eliza, rather shyly, whether she had quite given up her notion of keeping a flower shop. She replied that she had thought of it, but had put it out of her head, because the Colonel had said, that day at Mrs Higgins's, that it would never do. The Colonel confessed that when he said that, he had not quite recovered from the dazzling impression of the day before. They broke the matter to Higgins that evening. The sole comment vouchsafed by him very nearly led to a serious quarrel with Eliza. It was to the effect that she would have in Freddy an ideal errand boy.

Freddy himself was next sounded on the subject. He said he had been thinking of a shop himself; though it had presented itself to his pennilessness as a small place in which Eliza should sell tobacco at one counter whilst he sold newspapers at the opposite one. But he agreed that it would be extraordinarily jolly to go early every morning with Eliza to Covent Garden and buy flowers on the scene of their first meeting: a sentiment which earned him many kisses from his wife. He added that he had always been afraid to propose anything of the sort, because Clara would make an awful row about a step that must damage her matrimonial chances, and his mother could not be expected to like it after clinging for so many years to that step of the social ladder on which retail trade is impossible.

This difficulty was removed by an event highly unexpected by Freddy's mother. Clara, in the course of her incursions into those artistic circles which were the highest within her reach, discovered that her conversational qualifications were expected to include a grounding in the novels of Mr H. G. Wells.[3] She borrowed them in various directions so energetically that she swallowed them all within two months. The result was a conversion of a kind quite common to-day. A modern Acts of the Apostles would fill fifty whole Bibles if anyone were capable of writing it.

Poor Clara, who appeared to Higgins and his mother as a disagreeable and ridiculous person, and to her own mother as in some inexplicable way a social failure, had never seen herself in either light; for, though to some extent ridiculed and mimicked in West Kensington like everybody else there, she was accepted as a rational and normal—or shall we say inevitable?—sort of human being. At worst they called her The Pusher; but to them no more than to herself had it ever occurred that she was pushing the air, and pushing it in a wrong direction. Still, she was not happy. She was growing desperate. Her one asset, the fact that her mother was what the Epsom greengrocer called a carriage lady, had no exchange value, apparently. It had prevented her from getting educated, because the only education she could have afforded was education with the Earls-court greengrocer's daughter. It had led her to seek the society of her mother's class; and that class simply would not have her, because she was much poorer than the greengrocer, and, far from being able to afford a maid, could not afford even a house-maid, and had to scrape along at home with an illiberally treated general servant. Under such circumstances nothing could give her an air of being a genuine product of Largelady Park. And yet its tradition made her regard a marriage with anyone within her reach as an unbearable humiliation. Commercial people and professional people in a small way were odious to her. She ran after painters and novelists; but she did not charm them; and her bold attempts to pick up and practise artistic and literary talk irritated them. She was, in short, an utter failure, an ignorant, incompetent, pretentious, unwelcome, penniless, useless little snob; and though she did not admit these disqualifications (for nobody ever faces unpleasant truths of this kind until the possibility of a way out dawns on them) she felt their effects too keenly to be satisfied with her position.

Clara had a startling eyeopener when, on being suddenly wakened to enthusiasm by a girl of her own age who dazzled her and produced in her a gushing desire to take her for a model, and gain her friendship, she discovered that this exquisite apparition had graduated

---

3. A popular contemporary writer whose novels often dealt with social issues.

from the gutter in a few months time. It shook her so violently, that
when Mr H. G. Wells lifted her on the point of his puissant pen, and
placed her at the angle of view from which the life she was leading
and the society to which she clung appeared in its true relation to
real human needs and worthy social structure, he effected a conversion and a conviction of sin comparable to the most sensational feats
of General Booth[4] or Gypsy Smith. Clara's snobbery went bang. Life
suddenly began to move with her. Without knowing how or why, she
began to make friends and enemies. Some of the acquaintances to
whom she had been a tedious or indifferent or ridiculous affliction,
dropped her: others became cordial. To her amazement she found
that some "quite nice" people were saturated with Wells, and that
this accessibility to ideas was the secret of their niceness. People she
had thought deeply religious, and had tried to conciliate on that tack
with disastrous results, suddenly took an interest in her, and revealed
a hostility to conventional religion which she had never conceived
possible except among the most desperate characters. They made
her read Galsworthy;[5] and Galsworthy exposed the vanity of Largelady Park and finished her. It exasperated her to think that the dun-
geon in which she had languished for so many unhappy years had
been unlocked all the time, and that the impulses she had so carefully struggled with and stifled for the sake of keeping well with
society, were precisely those by which alone she could have come
into any sort of sincere human contact. In the radiance of these
discoveries, and the tumult of their reaction, she made a fool of
herself as freely and conspicuously as when she so rashly adopted
Eliza's expletive in Mrs Higgins's drawing-room; for the new-born
Wellsian had to find her bearings almost as ridiculously as a baby;
but nobody hates a baby for its ineptitudes, or thinks the worse of it
for trying to eat the matches; and Clara lost no friends by her follies.
They laughed at her to her face this time; and she had to defend
herself and fight it out as best she could.

When Freddy paid a visit to Earlscourt (which he never did when
he could possibly help it) to make the desolating announcement that
he and his Eliza were thinking of blackening the Largelady scutcheon
by opening a shop, he found the little household already convulsed
by a prior announcement from Clara that she also was going to work
in an old furniture shop in Dover Street, which had been started by
a fellow Wellsian. This appointment Clara owed, after all, to her old
social accomplishment of Push. She had made up her mind that,
cost what it might, she would see Mr Wells in the flesh; and she had
achieved her end at a garden party. She had better luck than so rash
an enterprise deserved. Mr Wells came up to her expectations. Age

4. Founder of the Salvation Army.
5. John Galsworthy, popular Edwardian novelist and observer of social minutiae.

had not withered him, nor could custom stale his infinite variety in half an hour. His pleasant neatness and compactness, his small hands and feet, his teeming ready brain, his unaffected accessibility, and a certain fine apprehensiveness which stamped him as susceptible from his topmost hair to his tipmost toe, proved irresistible. Clara talked of nothing else for weeks and weeks afterwards. And as she happened to talk to the lady of the furniture shop, and that lady also desired above all things to know Mr Wells and sell pretty things to him, she offered Clara a job on the chance of achieving that end through her.

And so it came about that Eliza's luck held, and the expected opposition to the flower shop melted away. The shop is in the arcade of a railway station not very far from the Victoria and Albert Museum; and if you live in that neighborhood you may go there any day and buy a buttonhole from Eliza.

Now here is a last opportunity for romance. Would you not like to be assured that the shop was an immense success, thanks to Eliza's charms and her early business experience in Covent Garden? Alas! the truth is the truth: the shop did not pay for a long time, simply because Eliza and her Freddy did not know how to keep it. True, Eliza had not to begin at the very beginning: she knew the names and prices of the cheaper flowers; and her elation was unbounded when she found that Freddy, like all youths educated at cheap, pretentious, and thoroughly inefficient schools, knew a little Latin. It was very little, but enough to make him appear to her a Porson or Bentley,[6] and to put him at his ease with botanical nomenclature. Unfortunately he knew nothing else; and Eliza, though she could count money up to eighteen shillings or so, and had acquired a certain familiarity with the language of Milton from her struggles to qualify herself for winning Higgins's bet, could not write out a bill without utterly disgracing the establishment. Freddy's power of stating in Latin that Balbus built a wall and that Gaul was divided into three parts did not carry with it the slightest knowledge of accounts or business: Colonel Pickering had to explain to him what a cheque book and a bank account meant. And the pair were by no means easily teachable. Freddy backed up Eliza in her obstinate refusal to believe that they could save money by engaging a bookkeeper with some knowledge of the business. How, they argued, could you possibly save money by going to extra expense when you already could not make both ends meet? But the Colonel, after making the ends meet over and over again, at last gently insisted; and Eliza, humbled to the dust by having to beg from him so often, and stung by the uproarious derision of Higgins, to whom the notion of Freddy suc-

6. I.e., a scholar.

ceeding at anything was a joke that never palled, grasped the fact that business, like phonetics, has to be learned.

On the piteous spectacle of the pair spending their evenings in shorthand schools and polytechnic classes, learning bookkeeping and typewriting with incipient junior clerks, male and female, from the elementary schools, let me not dwell. There were even classes at the London School of Economics, and a humble personal appeal to the director of that institution to recommend a course bearing on the flower business. He, being a humorist, explained to them the method of the celebrated Dickensian essay on Chinese Metaphysics by the gentleman who read an article on China and an article on Metaphysics and combined the information. He suggested that they should combine the London School with Kew Gardens.[7] Eliza, to whom the procedure of the Dickensian gentleman seemed perfectly correct (as in fact it was) and not in the least funny (which was only her ignorance) took his advice with entire gravity. But the effort that cost her the deepest humiliation was a request to Higgins, whose pet artistic fancy, next to Milton's verse, was caligraphy, and who himself wrote a most beautiful Italian hand, that he would teach her to write. He declared that she was congenitally incapable of forming a single letter worthy of the least of Milton's words; but she persisted; and again he suddenly threw himself into the task of teaching her with a combination of stormy intensity, concentrated patience, and occasional bursts of interesting disquisition on the beauty and nobility, the august mission and destiny, of human handwriting. Eliza ended by acquiring an extremely uncommercial script which was a positive extension of her personal beauty, and spending three times as much on stationery as anyone else because certain qualities and shapes of paper became indispensable to her. She could not even address an envelope in the usual way because it made the margins all wrong.

Their commercial schooldays were a period of disgrace and despair for the young couple. They seemed to be learning nothing about flower shops. At last they gave it up as hopeless, and shook the dust of the shorthand schools, and the polytechnics, and the London School of Economics from their feet for ever. Besides, the business was in some mysterious way beginning to take care of itself. They had somehow forgotten their objections to employing other people. They came to the conclusion that their own way was the best, and that they had really a remarkable talent for business. The Colonel, who had been compelled for some years to keep a sufficient sum on current account at his bankers to make up their deficits, found that the provision was unnecessary: the young people were prospering. It

7. Famous public botanical gardens on the outskirts of London.

is true that there was not quite fair play between them and their
competitors in trade. Their week-ends in the country cost them nothing, and saved them the price of their Sunday dinners; for the motor
car was the Colonel's; and he and Higgins paid the hotel bills. Mr
F. Hill, florist and greengrocer (they soon discovered that there was
money in asparagus; and asparagus led to other vegetables), had an
air which stamped the business as classy; and in private life he was
still Frederick Eynsford Hill, Esquire. Not that there was any swank
about him: nobody but Eliza knew that he had been christened Frederick Challoner. Eliza herself swanked like anything.

   That is all. That is how it has turned out. It is astonishing how
much Eliza still manages to meddle in the housekeeping at Wimpole
Street in spite of the shop and her own family. And it is notable that
though she never nags her husband, and frankly loves the Colonel
as if she were his favorite daughter, she has never got out of the
habit of nagging Higgins that was established on the fatal night when
she won his bet for him. She snaps his head off on the faintest provocation, or on none. He no longer dares to tease her by assuming an
abysmal inferiority of Freddy's mind to his own. He storms and bullies and derides; but she stands up to him so ruthlessly that the
Colonel has to ask her from time to time to be kinder to Higgins;
and it is the only request of his that brings a mulish expression into
her face. Nothing but some emergency or calamity great enough to
break down all likes and dislikes, and throw them both back on their
common humanity—and may they be spared any such trial!—will
ever alter this. She knows that Higgins does not need her, just as
her father did not need her. The very scrupulousness with which he
told her that day that he had become used to having her there, and
dependent on her for all sorts of little services, and that he should
miss her if she went away (it would never have occurred to Freddy
or the Colonel to say anything of the sort) deepens her inner certainty that she is "no more to him than them slippers"; yet she has
a sense, too, that his indifference is deeper than the infatuation of
commoner souls. She is immensely interested in him. She has even
secret mischievous moments in which she wishes she could get him
alone, on a desert island, away from all ties and with nobody else in
the world to consider, and just drag him off his pedestal and see him
making love like any common man. We all have private imaginations
of that sort. But when it comes to business, to the life that she really
leads as distinguished from the life of dreams and fancies, she likes
Freddy and she likes the Colonel; and she does not like Higgins and
Mr Doolittle. Galatea never does quite like Pygmalion: his relation
to her is too godlike to be altogether agreeable.

CONTEXTS AND CRITICISM

On Shaw

LEON HUGO

From Edwardian Shaw: The Writer and His Age†

*   *   *

[Daly][1] also had an eye for the main chance, the chief beneficiary of such chance being himself rather than the author whose cause he was ostensibly serving; and *Mrs Warren's Profession* caught his eye as a promising source of revenue, even before *Candida*. He appears to have written to Shaw late in 1903 about producing it. Shaw told him flatly that 'There is no money in Mrs Warren; and it ought not to be played for money. But there are other considerations which make it well worth playing.' One consideration was that the actress who had made a great success of the eponymous role in the Stage Society production in 1902, Fanny Brough, was in New York. He encouraged Daly to secure her for the role. If Daly could get *Candida* into the evening bill and then have a few matinees of *Mrs Warren*, he would not be forgotten in a hurry; and his next season would begin in a rush. He also told Daly that 'the scandal would be terrific' but that the play, though startling by its apparent daring, was 'perfectly safe'.[2]

This letter blends encouragement with business-like advice, the essence of which from Shaw's point of view was that Daly should secure Fanny Brough for the main role and introduce the play to New York as quietly as possible; the essence of the letter from Daly's point of view was that there was no money in the enterprise. So he shelved *Mrs Warren* for the next 20 months and, it would seem, took it down and hurriedly put it into rehearsal only when *John Bull's Other Island* failed.

He ignored the advice Shaw had given him about giving a production of the play a low public profile; ignored the clause later written into the contract that the play should be advertised as being suitable

---

† From *Edwardian Shaw: The Writer and His Age* (London: Macmillan, 1999), pp. 75–82.
1. Arnold Daly, an important theatrical manager [*Editor*].
2. Assigned to January 4, 1904. *Collected Letters, 1898–1910*, pp. 398–99.

for representation before serious adult audiences only; and ignored, when it arrived, Shaw's cable withdrawing his permission for the performance. He simply went ahead, and found himself overnight the target of a storm of abuse which would have flattened a less conceited man.

Vanity and the lure of dollars drove him. But there was another cause: envy of Robert Loraine's[3] success with *Man and Superman*, which had opened at the Hudson Theatre on September 5, 1905. Here, suddenly, was an interloper, a rival who threatened to lift from his honest brow the Shavian laurels he had won with *Candida* and *You Never Can Tell*. *John Bull's Other Island*, a month after *Man and Superman*, was calculated to confirm his role as *the* Shavian apostle in the United States, but when it failed and Loraine continued to draw capacity houses, Daly resorted to *Mrs Warren* with all the heedlessness and alacrity of a gambler risking his all on one throw of the dice. In the course of its review of the play, *The New York Times* wondered why Daly had taken the risk: was it a 'blind unreasoning desire to revolutionize the moral state-of-being, or else a wholly unnatural and somewhat disgraceful attempt to win much tainted notoriety'? The critic's own answer is kindly, but Daly's behavior on this occasion and his history as a whole suggests the second alternative.

Act I of our Sutroesque melodrama began a few days before the first performance, when *The New York Times* published correspondence between Anthony Comstock and Daly.[4] Comstock was secretary and special agent of the Society for the Suppression of Vice. A dedicated man, he boasted that since 1873 he had brought 3670 criminals to justice and destroyed 160 tons of 'obscene' literature and pictures.[5] He is immortalized in Shaw's designation of 'Comstockery' as 'the world's standing joke at the expense of the United States'.[6] An anecdote that pre-dates the controversy over *Mrs Warren's Profession* tells that Comstock, when asked about Shaw, replied, 'Shaw? I never heard of him in my life; never saw one of his books; so he can't be much.'[7] On October 20, 1905, however, he had heard of Shaw, if not yet read him, when he wrote to Daly: 'I am informed that you intend to put upon the stage one of Bernard Shaw's filthy products, entitled "Mrs Warren's Profession." ' He darkly warned Daly against pleading ignorance of the law. Daly replied cheekily: 'You call "Mrs Warren's Profession" a "filthy" play. I cannot believe that you have read it; but, if so, your use of the adjective is decorative,

3. The impresario [*Editor*].
4. Unless otherwise indicated, all references pertaining to the controversy are from *The New York Times*, October 25, 1905–November 2, 1905.
5. September 22–23, 1905. *Collected Letters, 1898–1910*, p. 559.
6. Ibid.
7. *Critic* (New York), XLVII, November 1905, p. 388.

but not descriptive.' He invited Comstock to attend a rehearsal of the play the following week. One wonders who leaked these letters to the press: probably Daly.

The next day *The New York Times* dutifully recorded the burgeoning drama, Comstock's response to Daly's invitation. He would not attend a rehearsal of the play. 'Why should I? It is not my purpose to advertise Mr Daly or the works of Mr Shaw.' Had he read the play? 'I have not. I have received a number of letters . . . from people who have read the book, and they tell me that it is quite impossible.' Were the people who wrote to him men of letters? 'Whether they were men of letters or not is not essential. They are men of morality and decency, which is to the point.' Would he be attending the first night? 'The society did its full duty when I wrote a letter of warning to Mr Daly. If the play is put on it is up to the police, and I have not the slightest doubt that Mr McAdoo [the Commissioner of Police] will take the proper steps.'

Daly breezily brushed Comstock aside. 'I do not feel that I need any Comstockian advertising. He is altogether impossible.'

Shaw made his entry on the third day with a special cable. In the usual form of a self-drafted interview, it assumed that Daly was under threat of imprisonment.

> Let [Comstock] imprison Daly, by all means. A few months' rest and quiet would do Daly a great deal of good, and the scandal of his imprisonment would completely defeat Comstock's attempt to hide the fact that Mrs Warren's 'profession' exists because libertines pay women well to be evil, and often show them affection and respect, whilst pious people pay them infamously and drudge their bodies and souls to death at honest labor.

He touched on Comstock's achievement in destroying 93 tons of indecent postcards and the right of every country to have the government it deserves. Then he admitted (although he did not say it in so many words) to having called a retreat. He could not fight Comstock with the American nation at his back and the New York police in his van. Neither could Daly. He had advised Daly to run no risks. 'When this news reached me I had already cabled both Daly and my agent, Miss Marbury, to countermand the performance, because I think New York has had enough of me for one season.'

But—confusingly—he left the field open for Daly:

> Now I am bound to leave Daly free to accept the challenge and throw himself on the good sense of people who want to have the traffic in women stopped . . . He is young and bold; I am elderly and thoroughly intimidated by my knowledge of the appalling weight of stupidity and prejudice, of the unavowed

money interest, direct or indirect, in the exploitation of womanhood, which lies behind his opponent. I cannot save Daly.

This ended Act I of the drama with the audience of thousands
wondering breathlessly whether Daly, now alone, would favour them
with a second act. They had their answer on Sunday morning, October 29. Yes, *Mrs Warren's Profession* had opened on Friday evening
in the New England town of New Haven. New Haven! *The New York
Times* blinked; the mayor himself wondered why Daly had selected
his 'hidebound' town. New Haven was in uproar. Protests came from
all quarters. The mayor, John P. Studley, immediately directed Chief
of Police Wrinn to revoke Daly's licence and to inform him that *Mrs
Warren's Profession* was 'grossly indecent and not fit for public presentation'. Daly was 'beside himself' and spent most of Saturday,
backed by his manager, his press agent and a posse of attorneys,
trying to get the mayor to withdraw his ban. Pressure, part political,
part monetary, was brought to bear when ex-Senator Reynolds of
New York, 'who was interested in the play' (interested because he
owned New York's Garrick Theatre, where the play was scheduled
to open two days later), intervened with an offer to furnish bonds,
but Studley stood firm. So late that Saturday afternoon Daly left New
Haven 'in high dudgeon. . . . saying before he went: "New York will
stand for the play if New Haven will not." ' There is a hint that Daly
was pinning his hopes on political support through Tammany Hall.
If the right kind of pressure came from that body, New York could
well be persuaded to stand for the play. Tammany Hall was as quiet
as a church-mouse during the furor that followed.

Act II, scene ii returned the action to New York with Daly issuing
a statement to the press: he would leave the question of presenting
'Mrs Warren's Profession' to the dramatic critics of the New York
newspapers. If they said on Tuesday morning that the play was unfit,
he would not give another performance. If they said it was fit, he
would continue and run the risk of being arrested. He then spent
what was left of that night and the whole of Sunday 'editing' the text
and rehearsing. Daly's partner, Winchell Smith, evidently a smooth
gentleman, explained. It was true, said he, that Daly had cut and
changed some of the lines, but nowhere had Shaw's meaning been
clouded. 'The changes are purely changes of words, made necessary
by the fact that some of the lines . . . are susceptible of impure construction which were not at all intended.' Daly was also quoted: 'The
play will positively be presented tonight, and if it is condemned by
the jury of critics it will be withdrawn.' So ended Act II—on a high
note of suspense.

Act III opened at the Garrick Theatre that Monday evening (October 31). The scene outside and in the lobby of the theatre was like

a cattle market. People struggled to get into the theatre from as early as 6.30; extra police were ordered out to handle the crowd; between 2000 and 3000 people were turned away. Theatregoers, arriving in carriages, found their way blocked. Ticket speculators were offering orchestra seats at $30.00 and the top gallery at $5.00. *The New York Times* included some telling details in its report:

> . . . Three policemen in the lobby took turns in declaring to the crowds:
> 'There ain't no tickets; there ain't no seats on sale; there ain't no admission nor no standin' room on'y.'
> When the policemen got tired, the man in the box office stopped counting money long enough to emphasize their remarks. He counted money with exasperating coolness, and wrapped up dozens of parcels of it with red strips of paper, on which were printed the inscription, '$100.'

Every seat was taken, standing room was packed, when the curtain went up.

At the end of the third act, in response to repeated calls, Daly came before the curtain and addressed the audience. He mentioned adult men and women who should be allowed to face the problems of life; children, whose cherished illusions should not be shattered; the need for at least one theatre in New York devoted to the Truth. If public opinion forced the theatre to be closed and *Mrs Warren's Profession* to be withdrawn it would be a 'sad commentary on twentieth century so-called civilization and our enlightened new country'.

Silent in his box, Police Commissioner William McAdoo sat through three acts. Afterwards, cornered by the press, he was figurative and non-committal. 'I don't think this is a good test of trying it on the dog. The dog in this instance is rather high bred and the ordinary run of dog may have different ideas.' He left, leaving everyone guessing. Daly's jury, the New York critics, soon followed him into the night.

The next day would provide the climax: the verdict of the critics and the law.

Act IV of our melodrama opened on October 31 with an outraged cry: universal condemnation from the press. The *Herald* said that Shaw had reached the 'limit of indecency' with a play that was 'morally rotten'. The *Tribune* said it was an 'affront to decency and a blot on the theatre'. The *World* said it was a frank, brutal and a wholly nasty justification of prostitution. It had polled the audience the evening before: the result revealed a rather more broad-minded reaction: 576 of the 963 people in the audience had responded; 304 voted 'Fit', 272 'Unfit'. The *American* said the play was 'illuminated gangrene', the 'suppuration of a plague spot', and not permissible on a stage. The *Press* said it was Shaw's best play and in the same breath declared that it glorified the 'Scarlet Woman'. *The New York Times* said *Mrs Warren's Profession* was not only vicious in its tendency but also depressingly stupid, and had to be excluded from the theatre as a moral derelict. The notice pays considerable attention to the acting of Mary Shaw as Mrs Warren. She played the part very broadly and 'reflected to an astonishingly offensive, natural degree the abandoned creatures after whom she has evidently modeled her study'. She was not the Mrs Warren of the text (and certainly not like Fanny Brough of Shaw's London production). If this was so, then it would appear that Daly's sin in 'editing' the lines was compounded by his directing the actress to ignore Shaw's subtly ambiguous delineation of the character.

These reports had scarcely hit the news stands when McAdoo struck. He told Mayor G. B. McClellan that the production was 'revolting, indecent, and nauseating where it was not boring'. He then wrote to Daly, to the owner of the theatre, ex-Senator Reynolds, and the theatre manager, Samuel Gumpertz, telling them that he would prevent a second performance and arrest those participating therein. Later Magistrate Charles Seymour Whitman issued warrants for the arrest of Reynolds, Gumpertz, Daly and the other members of the cast. Gumpertz, the only one immediately taken in custody, appeared in court, pleaded not guilty to the charge of disorderly conduct, asked for an adjournment and was allowed out on his own recognizance on condition he appeared the next day with the other persons named in the warrant.

Daly meanwhile had decided that his jury of critics had returned a favourable verdict: performances would continue. Sales at the Garrick box office continued briskly throughout the morning and by one o'clock more than $10,000 worth of tickets had been sold. At four o'clock the box office was abruptly closed. A notice from Daly was posted on the door of the theatre: 'Further performances of "Mrs Warren's Profession" will be abandoned, owing to the universal condemnation of the press. Theatre closed to-night. Will re-open tomorrow night with "Candida," original cast.' Five hours later Winchell Smith issued a statement which cited the verdict of the press. The sensation that, through no wish of the management, had surrounded the production had drawn the wrong kind of audience on the first night. The management would have cancelled the performance even then, had it not been too late. 'There is no financial or other consideration whatever that could have tempted Mr Daly to give a second performance of the play after last night's experience at the doors, and after seeing the attitude of the papers to-day,' said he, as smooth as ever. He would not say why tickets had been sold until late that afternoon.

Our Sutroesque[8] melodrama as a study of civic humbug (a critic dubbed the whole affair 'Mc'Adoo About Nothing') ends with a nice display of dramatic unity where it began—with Anthony Comstock in his office, adding *Mrs Warren's Profession* to his awesome collection of suppressed smut. His verdict: 'I had full confidence that Mr McAdoo would do his duty.'

There is an epilogue featuring the hero of these scenes: Daly himself. His attorney issued a statement: Mr Daly proposed to fight to the last and was confident the courts would take a liberal view. Daly had been reluctant to appear in court. 'But my dear fellow,' he had told his attorney, ' . . . I have an engagement for luncheon and want to go to the races. Tell the Judge that I would be charmed to come down almost any other day and look at his little jail, but tomorrow it is impossible.' Daly was no stranger to humbug himself.

Eight months later, on July 6, 1906, the Court of Special Sessions acquitted Daly and Gumpertz. The liberal view had prevailed, but by then the damage had been done and Daly himself had failed to regroup and advance on other fronts. *Candida*, rushed in to fill the void left by the banning of *Mrs Warren*, tottered through one week. He continued to present his small repertoire of Shaw's plays, adding *Arms and the Man* in April 1906, but he seemed to have lost momentum. He refused to touch *Mrs Warren's Profession* again, to Shaw's apparent amazement: 'I cannot imagine why you did not stick to poor old Mrs Warren. She is bound to win in the long run.'[9] In the event, it was the Garrick business manager, Samuel Gumpertz, who produced the play in New York once the courts had cleared it, opening at the Manhattan Theatre on March 9, 1907, for 25 performances, and then taking it on tour, not with any great success.

Shaw's role in this affair is ambiguous, a mixture of desire and caution: desire to have the play presented and as much as saying that Daly could carry on with it if he wished, at the same time dissociating himself from the production should Daly proceed. He did not throw Daly to the wolves, but he wanted his cake and he wanted, if possible, to give the appearance of not eating it. When it was over he was convinced that Daly had let him down. He did not drop him precipitately; the association continued for some years, but Shaw gradually loosened the tie. 'Take that excellent young man [Loraine] as your model in future, Arnold. He made my fortune with Man & Superman, and is profoundly grateful to me for it. You ruin me with John Bull and Mrs Warren; and you expect me to be grateful to you for it. Shame!'[1]

The rebuke is deserved. Even so, coming after Mansfield's suc-

8. Alfred Sutro (1863–1933) was a satirical English playwright [*Editor*].
9. December 1907. *Collected Letters, 1898–1910*, p. 739.
1. Ibid., p. 740.

cesses with *Arms and the Man* and *The Devil's Disciple* in the 1890s and preceding Loraine, Daly's productions of *Candida* and *You Never Can Tell* filled the gap at a critical time in Shaw's career and contributed importantly to establishing him in America. Shaw does not appear to have thought so, but infallible and omniscient Shaw was not always right.

NICHOLAS GRENE

Two Models: Wilde and Ibsen†

Without the contribution of Irishmen there would scarcely be a single major comedy in English between 1700 and 1900. Farquhar, Goldsmith, Sheridan, Wilde—the Irish monopoly on eighteenth- and nineteenth-century comedy is remarkable. What is more, these Irish-English comedies have much in common. Each of the comedians was skilled at giving the London audience what they wanted, to some extent even what they expected, but with a cynical stylishness or a cut of satire which made their plays look strikingly original, and differentiated them from their blander English contemporaries. Aimwell in *The Beaux' Stratagem*, for instance, fulfils the ideal of early eighteenth-century tastes in his conversion to marriage for love; but his co-conspirator Archer remains faithful to the tougher ethics of the rake, and the 'happy divorce' of the Sullens, balancing the happy marriage of Aimwell at the end, lends piquancy to the play as a whole. Sheridan, on the other hand, professed to run counter to the tastes of his time in sending up the hypocrisies of sentimentalism in *The School for Scandal*. Yet the ending, with the revelation of Sir Peter's heart of gold reforming an only mildly erring Lady Teazle, is as properly sentimental as can be. Wilde, the last of the line, could produce 'woman with a past' plots of unimpeachable Victorian conventionality, and yet lace them with a series of epigrams which imply a totally cynical disbelief in the values the plots appear to endorse.

It is tempting to define this common quality of creative double-thinking as characteristically Irish. Farquhar, Sheridan, Goldsmith and Wilde may be seen as Irishmen in London out to make their way—aware of their provinciality, eager to succeed in metropolitan terms, but using their sense of distance and self-possession to cultivate a non-English audacity of style.[1] Such generalisations about

---

† From *Bernard Shaw: A Critical View* (London: Macmillan, 1984), pp. 1–13.
1. For a very interesting discussion of the question see Thomas Kilroy, 'Anglo-Irish playwrights and comic tradition', *The Crane Bag*, III, no. 2 (1979): 19–27.

nationality must not be pressed too hard, if only because of the obvious exceptions. Steele, as Irish as the others, produced plays utterly unambiguous in their humourless sentimentality. Sheridan was an orator and entrepreneur in an age of orators and entrepreneurs, and we should not lean too heavily on the idea of him as a fluent Irish actor winning his way to the managership of Drury Lane. However, the concept of the Irishman playing to a foreign market, what Joyce called the role of 'court jester to the English',[2] is genuinely there in the work of all the major Anglo-Irish comedians.

Shaw in many ways fits easily on to the end of this series—Farquhar, Goldsmith, Sheridan, Wilde. Like the rest of them, he came to London from an Anglo-Irish Protestant background, though lower down the social scale than some of the others. Like Wilde, in particular, he made his name as a personality long before he became a playwright. Indeed like so many of his Anglo-Irish comic predecessors, he turned to the writing of plays not as a full-time career, but as the occasional employment of an otherwise busy man. The style, the paradoxes, the wit relate him very obviously to Wilde. And yet his own feelings about Wilde and this whole Irish comic tradition are ambivalent. In some ways if there was one thing of which Shaw was certain at the outset of his career as a dramatist, it was that he would not be another mere Irish jester. He might use his Irish persona, his reputation for cynical iconoclasm, but he would use it to more pointed purpose than the Farquhars, Sheridans and Wildes. Shaw was not just out to conquer London, but to change London. And in this he took as precedent not the part of the Irish jester but that of the Scandinavian prophet. One way of approaching Shaw is by looking at two possible models for his work, the two most significant figures on the theatre scene in the 1890s when he was a reviewer and began writing plays: Wilde and Ibsen.

In a self-drafted interview in the *Star* in 1892, Shaw made clear both his sense of affinity with Wilde and his sense of difference. The interviewer was made to ask whether the public could expect any of Shaw's celebrated humour in *Widowers' Houses*, then about to be produced by the Independent Theatre:

> Certainly not. I have removed with the greatest care every line that could possibly provoke a smile. I have been greatly misunderstood in this matter. Being an Irishman, I do not always see things exactly as an Englishman would: consequently my most serious and blunt statements sometimes raise a laugh and create an impression that I am intentionally jesting. I admit that some Irishmen do take advantage of the public in this way.

---

2. *The Critical Writings of James Joyce*, ed. Ellsworth Mason and Richard Ellmann (London, 1959), p. 202.

Wilde, unquestionably the ablest of our dramatists, has done so
in 'Lady Windermere's Fan'. There are lines in that play which
were put in for no other purpose than to make the audience
laugh."

" 'Widowers' Houses' will be quite free from that sort of thing,
then?

"Absolutely. However, I do not blame Wilde. He wrote for the
stage as an artist. I am simply a propagandist."

(*Collected Plays*, I, 126–7)

A piece of Shaw's deadpan clowning like this has to be recognised
for what it is. Naming Wilde as 'unquestionably the ablest of our
dramatists', at that stage on the strength of *Lady Windermere's Fan*
only, was no doubt intended to outrage and startle. It would be ludi-
crous to take literally Shaw's distinction between Wilde as artist and
himself as propagandist. But from the (nearly simultaneous) beginning of their playwriting careers Shaw stressed the common distinc-
tiveness of their Irish alienation and claimed for himself a greater
responsibility in its use.

Shaw was clearly delighted with the subversion of seriousness
which he found in *An Ideal Husband*, as we can see from his review
of the first production in 1895.

In a certain sense Mr Wilde is to me our only thorough playwright. He plays with everything; with wit, with philosophy,
with drama, with actors and audience, with the whole theatre.
Such a feat scandalises the Englishman, who can no more play
with wit and philosophy than he can with a football or cricket
bat.

Shaw congratulates Wilde on the 'subtle and pervading levity' of *An
Ideal Husband* because it annoys the English. There is no mistaking
the tone of self-identification in his praise for Wilde here:

to the Irishman (and Mr Wilde is almost as acutely Irish an
Irishman as the Iron Duke of Wellington) there is nothing in
the world quite so exquisitely comic as an Englishman's seriousness. It becomes tragic, perhaps, when the Englishman acts
on it; but that occurs too seldom to be taken into account, a
fact which intensifies the humor of the situation, the total result
being the Englishman utterly unconscious of his real self, Mr
Wilde keenly observant of it and playing on the self-
unconsciousness with irresistible humor, and finally, of course,
the Englishman annoyed with himself for being amused at his
own expense, and for being unable to convict Mr Wilde of what
seems an obvious misunderstanding of human nature.[3]

3. Bernard Shaw, *Our Theatres in the Nineties*, I (London, 1931), pp. 10–11.

Shaw's claim for the Irish comedian, for both Wilde and himself, is that they are capable of seeing the truth of English behaviour as the Englishman cannot, that their comedy derives from the tongue-in-cheek observation of the absurdities of the English social scene.

Yet, remarkably, in view of his eloquent review of *An Ideal Husband*, Shaw was disappointed in Wilde's final comic achievement, *The Importance of Being Earnest*. Of course, as always with Shaw's reviewing, we need to allow for an element of perversity. His contention that *The Importance* was an early play—'it must certainly have been written before Lady Windermere's Fan'—is an attempt to make fools of the critics who declared that 'The Importance of Being Earnest is a strained effort of Mr Wilde's at ultra-modernity, and that it could never have been written but for the opening up of entirely new paths in drama last year by Arms and the Man'.[4] But his refusal to join in the chorus of praise for *The Importance* was not just an affectation of singularity. He did not like the play—he was to dislike it all his life—and the reasons why are significant:

> I cannot say that I greatly cared for The Importance of Being Earnest. It amused me, of course; but unless comedy touches me as well as amuses me, it leaves me with a sense of having wasted my evening. I go to the theatre to be moved to laughter, not to be tickled or bustled into it; and that is why, though I laugh as much as anybody at a farcical comedy, I am out of spirits before the end of the second act, and out of temper before the end of the third, my miserable mechanical laughter intensifying these symptoms at every outburst.[5]

It is curious to find Shaw, so often accused of heartless comedy himself, complaining of want of feeling in Wilde. It was Shaw's *Arms and the Man*, produced in 1894, which provoked Yeats's famous dream of the sewing-machine that smiled. But Shaw's belief that comedy should 'move to laughter' is basic to his work. For most modern critics *The Importance* is Wilde's most perfect play, where he finally liberated himself from the need to produce the conventionally sentimental plot to house his farcical vision of the absurd. To Shaw, the complete removal of an emotional strand from comedy, however conventional that emotion might have been, represented a step backwards towards the merely mechanical and unreal.

Shaw and Wilde never became friends. When recalling his memories of Wilde for the benefit of Frank Harris in 1916, Shaw could remember no more than half a dozen occasions on which they met. There was a social dimension to their mutual uneasiness, as Shaw told Harris:

4. Ibid., p. 44.
5. Ibid., p. 44–45.

I was in no way predisposed to like him: he was my fellowtownsman, and a very prime specimen of the sort of fellowtownsman
I most loathed: to wit, the Dublin snob. His Irish charm, potent
with Englishmen, did not exist for me; and on the whole it may
be claimed for him that he got no regard from me that he did
not earn.[6]

It may be that Shaw was hurt by Wilde's famous epigram about him;
at least he answered it with dignity in a letter to Ellen Terry: 'Oscar
Wilde said of me "An excellent man: he has no enemies; and none
of his friends like him." And that's quite true: they don't like me; but
they are my friends, and some of them love me' (Collected Letters, I,
668). The lack of a close relationship between them did not stop
Shaw from supporting Wilde loyally during and after his imprisonment, and his one substantial essay on Wilde, published in German
in the Neue Freie Presse in 1905, accords him generous praise. Yet
in that essay it is clear what he saw as their essential differences and
ultimately Wilde's limitation:

On the whole, Wilde's tastes were basically different from mine.
He loved luxury, and the salon and the atelier were his domain;
while I was a man of the street, an agitator, a vegetarian, a
teetotaler, incapable of enjoying the life of the drawing-room
and the chatter of the studio.[7]

Shaw concludes that 'his originality lay in his superiority to the delusive morality of our time' but that 'he had not, as Nietzsche had,
thought through his own situation sufficiently to understand himself. Without a precisely mapped-out program of life it is impossible,
if not useless, to discard moral concepts.'[8]

Shaw's admiration for Wilde was qualified by his view of him as
essentially an unmodern writer: 'It is difficult to believe that the
author of An Ideal Husband was a contemporary of Ibsen, Strind-
berg, Wagner, Tolstoi, or myself.'[9] In his section on 'Evolution in the
Theatre' in the Preface to Back to Methusaleh, Shaw names Wilde
as the last of a comic tradition which began in the seventeenth century:

From Molière to Oscar Wilde we had a line of comedic playwrights who, if they had nothing fundamentally positive to say,
were at least in revolt against falsehood and imposture, and were
not only, as they claimed, 'chastening morals by ridicule', but,
in Johnson's phrase, clearing our minds of cant, and thereby

6. The Playwright and the Pirate: Bernard Shaw and Frank Harris. A Correspondence, ed.
   Stanley Weintraub (Gerrards Cross, Bucks, 1982), p. 33.
7. Bernard Shaw, The Matter with Ireland, ed. Dan H. Laurence and David H. Greene (New
   York, 1962), p. 31.
8. Ibid., p. 32.
9. Ibid., p. 29.

shewing an uneasiness in the presence of error which is the surest symptom of intellectual vitality. (*CP*, V, 335)

But these negative virtues were not enough:

Ever since Shakespear, playwrights have been struggling with their lack of positive religion. Many of them were forced to become mere pandars and sensation-mongers because, though they had higher ambitions, they could find no better subject matter. From Congreve to Sheridan they were so sterile in spite of their wit that they did not achieve between them the output of Molière's single lifetime; and they were all (not without reason) ashamed of their profession, and preferred to be regarded as mere men of fashion with a rakish hobby. (*CP*, V, 336)

In a passage like this we see expressed the full Puritanism of Shaw which ultimately differentiated him from Wilde, or indeed most other comedians. For all his clowning, he believed that plays and playwrights had to take themselves seriously, that they had to have something positive to say. This was not necessarily to claim that all plays should have a direct social or moral purpose, but that the dramatist should feel himself committed to his work, not a 'mere man of fashion with a rakish hobby'. It is this which made Shaw reject Wilde's dandy-like aestheticism, and it is this which makes all his own plays in some sense plays for Puritans.

The influence of Ibsen on Shaw is well known, and has by now been often and thoroughly discussed.[1] J. L. Wisenthal has collected all of Shaw's writings on Ibsen, including *The Quintessence of Ibsenism*, and has shown in his introductory essay how much more complex Shaw's response was than has generally been imagined.[2] Shaw did not butcher Ibsen to make a Fabian holiday; though *The Quintessence* was avowedly written to show what Ibsen had to offer socialists, it does not mean that it was all Shaw thought Ibsen had to offer. What Shaw rightly detected in *Ibsen*, and was most crucial for him, was a radical belief in artistic truth-telling that went far beyond any party-political platform. Ibsen spent most of his life avoiding identification with any political group and was particularly scornful of so-called progressive parties. His iconoclasm was not to be put to the service of a given set of social objectives. But that it was iconoclasm, and that Shaw was more nearly right about Ibsen than is normally supposed, is evident, for example, from Ibsen's comment in a letter about *Ghosts* before it was published: '*Ghosts* will probably

1. For the significance of Ibsen's work and Shaw's *Quintessence of Ibsenism* in the formation of the Shavian dialectic, see particularly J. L. Wisenthal, *The Marriage of Contraries: Bernard Shaw's Middle Plays* (Toronto, 1974), and Alfred Turco Jr., *Shaw's Moral Vision: The Self and Salvation* (Ithaca, N.Y., 1976).
2. *Shaw and Ibsen: Bernard Shaw's* The Quintessence of Ibsenism and Related Writings, ed. J. L. Wisenthal (Toronto, 1979).

cause alarm in some circles; but there is nothing to be done about
it. If it didn't do that, there would have been no need to write it'.[3]
Ibsen saw his own work, as Shaw saw it, as a contribution to a forward struggle to give people new images of truth, images which at
first they would inevitably be unable to accept.

For Shaw Ibsen was the realist who at last enabled the theatre to
escape from the vapid and meaningless ideals which had dominated
it for so long. In *The Quintessence* he explains the unorthodox use
he makes of the terms realist and idealist. The idealist is the man
who creates self-deceiving myths to make tolerable the reality of a
life which he could not otherwise endure. The realist insists on the
liberation of the human will from the artificial constraints of idealism
which he rejects as deadening and unreal. He is prepared to face life
objectively without the narcotics of the ideal. It can be fairly objected
that this view of Ibsen as realist suits some plays more than others,
and does not take into account Ibsen's deeply ambiguous attitude
towards idealistic self-sacrifice. But it explains why Shaw so constantly stressed the modernity of Ibsen, and saw him as a crucial
revolutionary writer along with Nietzsche or Schopenhauer. In
Shaw's evolutionary concept of human culture Ibsen is one of the
'pioneers of the march to the plains of heaven', moving forward the
ideas of the race by destroying outmoded pieties and beliefs. It is in
this spirit that Shaw celebrated Ibsen's 'plays of nineteenth-century
life with which he overcame Europe, and broke the dusty windows
of every dry-rotten theatre in it from Moscow to Manchester' (*CP*,
V, 336).

If Ibsen is to be seen as a pioneer, a progressive in this suprapol-
itical sense, then the structure of his plays involves a dialectic of
progressive understanding for an audience. Obviously here *A Doll's
House* and *Ghosts* are Shaw's best examples. *A Doll's House* takes
Nora, and us with her, from 'the sweet home, the womanly woman,
the happy family life of the idealist's dream' through disillusionment
to the determination to meet the real world and 'to find out its reality
for herself'. *Ghosts*, which Shaw was one of the first to see as a sequel
to *A Doll's House*, gives a terrifying warning of the consequences of
holding on to the false 'idealist's dream' and refusing to meet reality.
Although the linear synopses of the plays in *The Quintessence* destroy
the emphasis of Ibsen's retrospective technique by which our understanding of the present action involves a growing discovery of the
past shared with the characters, Shaw does demonstrate the essential dramatic movement from stereotype, presupposition and prejudice towards the climactic revelation of truth. We may well feel that
the breezy clarity of his prose is no adequate vehicle for expressing

---

3. Letter to Frederik Hegel, dated November 23, 1881, quoted in *The Oxford Ibsen*, V, trans.
   and ed. James Walter McFarlane (London, 1961), p. 474.

the enigmatic and mysterious form which that truth takes in Ibsen. But Shaw registers the continuous and unresting nature of truth-seeking in Ibsen's work. Within each individual play, from play to play within the canon, Ibsen never allows his audience or readers to settle into the unquestioned assumption that the truth is now before them. The fallacious ideals exposed could include, for example, the apparently Ibsenian ideal of truth-telling represented by Gregers Werle in *The Wild Duck*. Shaw did not, as is sometimes supposed, reduce Ibsen's drama to problem plays with problems which could be solved once and for all by sexual equality, free love, or hygienic drains. The struggle which he saw in Ibsen between idealism and realism was to be a continuing one with no final and unequivocal victory for the latter. The appropriate response to an Ibsen play was open-ended questioning rather than confident enlightenment.

What Shaw admired in Ibsen was his seriousness as an artist, his anti-idealistic stance, and the dialectic structure of his works. In all of these Shaw may be said to have taken Ibsen as his model when he began to write plays himself. Although accusations of influence provoked Shaw into perverse disclaimers—he insisted that *Widowers' Houses* had been started years before he had even heard of Ibsen—no one is likely to miss the obvious Ibsenism of much of Shaw's early work. In fact for generations Shaw was commonly described as the English disciple of Ibsen. But in the unique and distinctive form of comedy of ideas which Shaw developed in the 1890s we must recognise an extraordinary hybrid. There could scarcely be two writers more unlike than Wilde and Ibsen, yet Shaw's plays partake of the nature of both. We could call Shaw, with as much truth as he called Wilde, 'our only thorough playwright. He plays with everything: with wit, with philosophy, with drama, with actors and audience, with the whole theatre.' Ibsen, on the other hand, is the least playful of dramatists. If Shaw at his most Wildean yet reveals characteristics which identify him with Ibsen, at his most Ibsenian he is still not far from the comic mood and manner of Wilde.

A Pleasant and an Unpleasant play may be taken to illustrate the point. *You Never Can Tell* is undoubtedly Shaw's most Wildean play; what is more, it most closely resembles the Wilde play which Shaw professed to dislike, *The Importance of Being Earnest*. The farcical success of both depend on the skill and lightness of touch with which Shaw and Wilde create an absurd world which barely touches on the real. In the spirit of Lady Bracknell's celebrated line—'To lose one parent, Mr Worthing, may be regarded as a misfortune; to lose both looks like carelessness'—is Valentine's benevolent advice to the fatherless Phil and Dolly:

We dont bother much about dress and manners in England, because, as a nation, we dont dress well and weve no manners. But—and now you will excuse my frankness? [*They nod.*] Thank you. Well, in a seaside resort theres one thing you must have before anybody can afford to be seen going about with you; and thats a father, alive or dead. Am I to infer that you have omitted that indispensable part of your social equipment? (*CP*, I, 677)

Margery Morgan suggests that in *You Never Can Tell* Shaw gave comic expression to some of the unhappiness of his own separated family.[4] Perhaps; but more to the point is her observation that the separation and reunion of parents and children is one of the oldest of comic themes. Both Shaw and Wilde stand at the end of the long European tradition of comedy and play knowingly with its familiar conventions. The device of the foundling and the long-lost parent, so standard in Roman comedy, ends up with the absurdity of the lost-property office hero of *The Importance*. The coming together of father and daughter, so moving in *The Winter's Tale* and *Pericles*, becomes deliberate anti-climax in the meeting of Crampton and Gloria in *You Never Can Tell*. The delight of *The Importance* and *You Never Can Tell* is of an elegant and stylised unreality which inverts and parodies the norms of human experience.

It would be absurd to claim that there was much in *You Never Can Tell* to remind us directly of Ibsen. In fact Shaw mischievously portrays Mrs Clandon with her Ibsenite emancipation as already old-fashioned and suggests that the theatre is the only place left where 'her opinions would still pass as advanced'. But Shaw is true to his understanding of Ibsen in showing Gloria as a character who must reject her mother's image of her (however liberally and untraditionally conceived) in order to fulfil her own individuality. In the midst of the caricatures and distortions of farce, Shaw intended to introduce characters and situations of recognisable human reality. The scene between Valentine and Gloria at the end of the second act, he regarded as crucial to the success of the play. He was triumphant when the farce actor Allen Aynesworth, who had been so successful in *The Importance*, was, as he had predicted, unable to perform this scene convincingly.[5] It is not perhaps a very convincing scene in itself, and is one among many which might be used to illustrate Shaw's problems in handling love. But significantly what he wanted to do with it was to show the moment of emotional revelation which shatters the artificial self-images of the two characters. This is in

---

4. Margery M. Morgan, *The Shavian Playground* (London, 1972), pp. 87–89.
5. See Shaw's letter to William Archer of September 7, 1903 (*CL*, II, 362–63), and a chapter contributed by Shaw to Cyril Maude's *The Haymarket Theatre* (reprinted in *CP*, I, 797–803).

some ways closer to the mood of Shakespearean comedy than of Ibsen, but it is consistent with Shaw's complaints against the heartless humour of *The Importance*, and it may remind us that even in a play as fantastic as *You Never Can Tell* he was committed to what he thought of as realism.

I shall be returning to *Mrs Warren's Profession* in more detail in the next chapter, but here it can be conveniently used to demonstrate what is Wildean in Shaw's most Ibsenian manner. In his 'Author's Apology' for the play, written in 1902, Shaw roundly rejected claims of influence: 'I never dreamt of Ibsen or De Maupassant, any more than a blacksmith shoeing a horse thinks of the blacksmith in the next county' (*CP*, I, 271). Maybe, but plays are written more distinctively than horses are shod, and the blacksmith in England worked on strikingly similar lines to the blacksmith in Norway. *Mrs Warren* is Shaw's equivalent to *Ghosts*, a deliberately shocking and provocative attack on the sacred nineteenth-century institution of sexual morality enshrined in marriage. Shaw and Ibsen exploited the then unspeakable aspects of sexuality, prostitution and venereal disease, to provide metaphors for what was wrong with their society, to illustrate the relation between hypocritical ideals and actual degradation. *Mrs Warren* moves, like *Ghosts*, from revelation to revelation, each one taking us further from the comfortable appearances of the first act. It is one of the few plays in which Shaw used Ibsen's characteristic 'strong curtains' to conclude each act. Central to *Mrs Warren* and to *Ghosts* is the misunderstanding and mutual discovery of the parent/child protagonists. The only partially closed gap between Oswald and Mrs Alving matches that between Mrs Warren and Vivie. The extent of Shaw and Ibsen's defiance of conventional attitudes is indicated by their common apparently unblinking acceptance of the possibility of incest.

And yet, and yet, and yet. The 'unpleasantness' of *Mrs Warren* is fresh air and sunshine in comparison with the horrors of *Ghosts*. Representative of the difference is the contrast between the two possibly incestuous relationships. However much Mrs Alving may overcome her squeamishness at the idea of incest, there remains something permanently repulsive in the flirtation between the sickly Oswald and his calculating half-sister. With Vivie and Frank Gardner, the revelation that they might be related only makes them 'babes in the wood in earnest'; their relation ends, as it began, in fairy-tale fantasy. Frank Gardner, above all, is the Wildean joker in *Mrs Warren*. His affectation of complete detachment from moral judgment, his precocious wit, align him with a tradition which runs from Wilde's epigrammatists to Saki's[6] unbearable young men. Frank is

6. Saki was the pseudonym of British writer H. H. Munro (1870–1916). The protagonists of his short stories, such as Clovis and Reginald, were witty, hedonistic dandies [*Editor*].

an idler and proud of it, setting aside the pieties of industry or filial respect with debonair charm. His is a light-hearted immoralism of style and manner. One would not want *Mrs Warren* to be without the deft and deflating humour which he represents, but he makes it a play far from the tone and atmosphere of *Ghosts*. In being like Wilde and Ibsen simultaneously, Shaw is not the least bit like either of them.

Taking Wilde and Ibsen as alternative precedents for Shaw is not to suggest that they were the only two, or even necessarily the major two, influences on his work. When it comes to establishing sources of influence on Shaw, the critic is likely to suffer from an embarrassment of riches. But his attitude to Wilde and Ibsen may stand for coordinates within which his comedy of ideas was developed. Looking at his work in this light may help to explain why, as a playwright, he has suffered from two, apparently incompatible, forms of negative criticism. To some he has seemed the incorrigible clown whose work, amusing and brilliant as it may be, does not finally take itself seriously, the most distinguished example being Tolstoy who found Shaw's levity painful.[7] And yet equally persistent, if not more so, has been the myth of Shaw the preacher rather than the playwright, the writer whose plays were ruined by his intolerable didacticism. But Shaw's attempt to combine the Wildean tradition of manners with the purposefulness of Ibsen's realism is significant not only as it left him open to two forms of misconstruction. It was, I believe, the source of genuine and fundamental problems in his work. It led to certain crucial ambiguities in Shaw's attitude towards the drama and in the tone and substance of the plays themselves.

One example is his use of the high dramatic climax. Shaw refused to take seriously the stock situations of nineteenth-century theatre. More than one critic has ably demonstrated how he used them only to expose them, to turn them on their heads, or to reveal them in a completely new light. Even Ibsen was not exempt from Shaw's reproaches for staginess. In his obituary article in 1906, he denied that Ibsen's theatrical technique was distinctively modern: rather 'Ibsen seems to have succumbed without a struggle to the old notion that a play is not really a play unless it contains a murder, a suicide, or something else out of the Police Gazette.'[8] He stigmatised the use of such events, specifically the death of children, as 'dishonorable . . . artistic devices because they depend on a morbid horror of death and a morbid enjoyment of horror'. He adds that in the final deaths

7. Tolstoy wrote to Shaw reproaching him for the comic tone of *Man and Superman*: 'you are not sufficiently serious. One should not speak jokingly about such a subject as the purpose of human life or the causes of its perversion and of the evil that fills the life of all of us mankind'. *Tolstoy's Letters*, II, ed. and trans. R. F. Christian (New York, 1978), p. 678.
8. Wisenthal, *Shaw and Ibsen*, p. 243.

of *John Gabriel Borkman* or *When We Dead Awaken* the symbolism barely conceals 'the old conventional mortuary ending'. Yet, as Shaw concedes, 'Ibsen turns the Chamber of Horrors to astonishing and illuminating account'. Although we may well agree that the Ibsenian climaxes and catastrophes are stagey and melodramatic, he turns them into a genuine tragic vision by the sheer depth and force of his imagination. He takes them so seriously that he dares his audience to disbelieve in them; as Shaw acutely pointed out, he challenges us to say, with Judge Brack, 'people don't do such things'. But Shaw's instincts of the comedian will never allow him wholly to convince us or himself of the truth of high dramatics. As a result a scene such as the discovery of the murder of Ftatateeta in *Caesar and Cleopatra* seems like a piece of fake sensationalism in a way that Ibsen's stage deaths never do.

More basically the tension within Shaw between the Wildean comedian and the Ibsenian realist sets up difficulties for an audience as to the form of willing suspension of disbelief they are supposed to adopt towards the plays. The comic writer encourages the agreement of a viewpoint for the duration of his comedy which, though often traditional, is not necessarily to be identified with his audience's normal social attitude.[9] The viewpoint may be politically progressive or reactionary, it may be indulgent or satirically censorious, but it bears an oblique and avowedly distorted relation to the reality we know outside the theatre. Comedy contains its own form of truth, which yet cannot be applied directly as truth within an extra-theatrical world. Both the form and effect of comedy are static rather than kinetic; our lives may be enriched but not normally changed by the encounter with great comedy. In this sense a play such as *The Importance of Being Earnest*, though without anything like the depth of the greatest comedy, is true to the tradition of comic form and meaning.

It was Shaw's ambition to harness the energies of comedy, to put them to dynamic use. This was not merely a matter of combining the enjoyment of laughter with a moral, social, or political purpose— a traditional objective of the comedian, in theory at least. His aim was to move forward both his characters and his audience, to bring them to a measurably more advanced stage of self-understanding. His Ibsenian dialectic committed him to a progressive view of truth itself, and in that view comedy had its part to play. By his teasing and his clowning, Shaw believed he could help to make his audience more fully aware of their real situation. But it was not merely obtuseness on the part of the public which so often defeated this purpose in the plays. If they laughed and ignored the message, or objected to

9. See Nicholas Grene, *Shakespeare, Jonson, Molière: The Comic Contract* (London, 1980).

the message as preachiness, it was partly because the status of reality
in the plays was equivocal, the special distorted vision of the comic
fighting the claim to absolute or realistic truth.

T. F. EVANS

The Political Shaw†

At the beginning of the second act of *Man and Superman*, there is
a brief exchange on political themes between Tanner, his friend
Octavius, and his chauffeur, Straker. Tanner warns the would-be
literary man, Octavius, not to start Straker on political economy
because "he knows all about it and we don't." He goes on to explain,
"You're only a poetic Socialist, Tavy: he's a scientific one."[1] The lines
carry a deeper resonance than their significance in the play itself.
First, Shaw was always more concerned with political economy than
with politics in the general sense of the word. Second, the remarks
underline the gulf that Shaw always found between those who, like
Tavy, thought of themselves as poets and dramatists without any
deep concern for the nature of the society to which their art and
literature ought to make some contribution and those who, in contrast, thought of art and politics as indissolubly linked. Shaw himself
might be held to have begun as a "poetic" socialist who made himself
into a "scientific" one. In strictness, however, neither adjective can
be applied without a great deal of qualification or explanation.

Shaw was a socialist, of some kind, throughout the whole of his
adult life. In common with many others on the political Left, he
seems to have spent more of his time pointing out the errors in policy
and practice of those who were theoretically on his own side rather
than the opposing Right, but in this he closely resembled the members of religious factions that sometimes appear to find much greater
satisfaction in drawing attention to the errors of members of other
sects than in pointing out the paths of error being followed by non-
believers. What distinguished Shaw from other politically inclined
writers is how he combined both his political and artistic interests
and activities.

The well-known story told by William Archer of his initial meeting
with Shaw embodies the essential truth. He first glimpsed Shaw in
the reading room of the British Museum with two large volumes

---

† From *Shaw and Politics* (University Park: The Pennsylvania State University Press, 1991),
  pp. 1–19. Copyright 1991 by The Pennsylvania State University. Reprinted by permission
  of the publisher.
1. *Man and Superman, Collected Plays with Their Prefaces*, ed. Dan H. Laurence (London:
   Max Reinhardt, 1970–74), 2:519.

spread out before him on the desk: "Karl Marx's *Das Kapital* (Volume 1, in French), and an orchestral score of *Tristan und Isolde*." Archer added that he did not then know "how exactly this quaint juxtaposition symbolised the main interests of his life."[2] Whether as journalist and critic in his earlier days, or later when he established himself as primarily a dramatist, Shaw was always to combine to an unrivaled extent his literary interests and activities on the one hand and, on the other hand, the closest absorption, practical and theoretical, with the means by which humanity organized itself into societies and managed and governed those societies. Indeed, such a word as "combine" fails to emphasize the true nature of Shaw's joint concerns. For him there was no such thing as art separate from politics or politics separate from art. It may be a useful form of shorthand, but the very term "the political Shaw" must have about it something incomplete and therefore misleading.

Nevertheless, it can be useful to look at Shaw primarily from the political point of view and to try to assess, however loosely, the extent to which his concern with political matters did dominate his life and the part that it played in his artistic creation. Tanner warns Tavy not to start Straker on political economy, not politics more generally. For Shaw, the terms were interchangeable. In fact, while he was for long periods deeply absorbed in political economy, he never had a great deal of time for politics in the limited sense, whether that might mean theories of government or an examination of the day-to-day occupation of party maneuvering or like dealings in Great Britain. For these, Shaw had only a withering contempt. What interested him was the way in which society might be organized in the best interests of all. In a review of *Three Plays for Puritans* in 1901, the novelist Arnold Bennett wrote that Shaw was "the indefatigable champion of social justice, not because he has a passion for social justice but because he has an intellectual perception of it."[3]

Yet, this is a difficult argument to sustain. To refer to Shaw as an "indefatigable champion of social justice," not because he has a passion for social justice but simply because he has an intellectual perception only, is to reduce social justice to pure mathematics or a subtle series of maneuvers in which human motives or concerns play no part. To return to the antithesis in the exchange from *Man and Superman*, it cannot be contended that there was in Shaw himself nothing of the "poetic Socialist," one who is attracted by the emotional or aesthetic appeal of socialism rather than by the merely practical or scientific. To Shaw, such men as Shelley, Ruskin, and Morris were, at different times, among his most influential teachers. To him, Ruskin was not merely an influential critic of art, Shelley not merely

2. William Archer, *World* 963 (December 14, 1892), 14.
3. Arnold Bennett, *Academy* (February 1901), p. 127.

a great lyric poet, Morris not merely a master of art and design. All
three looked forward to a new order of society. Shaw always professed to have become a socialist as a result of the influence of others. It is clear that his socialism was a broad river fed by different
tributaries. After his death, an admirer, but by no means an uncrit-
ical one, summed him up. This was R. Palme Dutt, a Marxist, in an
obituary: "He was a Marxist and an anti-Marxist, a revolutionary and
a reformist, a Fabian and a despiser of Fabianism, a Communist and
a crusader against super-tax."[4]

Shaw paid tribute to an early teacher, Richard Deck. He had met
Deck in 1880 and took lessons in French from him, but, in addition,
Deck introduced his pupil to other subjects, including the ideas of
Proudhon, the French socialist with his ringing declaration that
"Property is theft." Of more immediate importance, said Shaw, Deck
"helped to prepare me for Henry George's 'Progress and Poverty,'
which I read in Sept.–Oct. 1882, and which made me an enthusiast
for 'Nationalization of Land.' "[5] Shaw heard Henry George speak at
the Memorial Hall in Farringdon Street, London, on September 5,
1882. Paradoxically, George was not a socialist himself, and Marx
spoke of him with scorn as a defender of capitalism. Nevertheless,
from the day of the meeting and his subsequent reading of the book,
Shaw realized the importance of "the economic basis" of society and
of human existence itself, and the path of his entire life was given
its direction. Shortly after this he went on to read and study Marx
and to concentrate on mastering economics. At about this time,
Archer found Shaw reading Marx in the British Museum. From then
on, Marx became an important part of Shaw's life. He wrote in 1887
a long review of *Das Kapital* in the *National Reformer*, the weekly
paper of the National Secularist Society.[6]

The review was printed in three parts in successive issues of the
paper. It is more than eight thousand words long. To Shaw, as he
declared in the opening paragraph, the book, first appearing twenty
years before but only recently published in England, was "revelation." He contends, "He that believeth is a true 'scientific Socialist':
he that believeth not is a middle-class self-seeker, a *bourgeois*, an
exploiter of labor, and most likely a police spy." After such a beginning, it comes as something of a surprise that Shaw spent a great
deal of the article pointing out where Marx went wrong. Of course,
he paid him expansive tributes. Marx, according to Shaw, "keeps his
head like a God. . . . The thread of history is in his hand." After reading Marx, said Shaw, students of "the dismal science," however eru-

4. R. Palme Dutt, "George Bernard Shaw," editorial in *Labour Monthly* (London) 32, no. 12
   (1951).
5. *Bernard Shaw, The Diaries 1885–1897*, ed. Stanley Weintraub (University Park: Pennsylvania State University Press, 1986), 1:23.
6. *National Reformer* (London), August 7, 1887, p. 84.

dite they might be, can never be the same. Nevertheless, the extraordinary impression made by Marx, declared Shaw in a lofty tone, does not depend on the soundness of his views but more on "their magnificent scope and on his own imperturbable conviction of their validity." He went on in a long section of the review to point out the fundamental error in Marx.

This took him into a long discussion of Marx's labor theory of value. In very rough terms, the theory is that the value of anything produced consists of the equivalent of the cost of the labor required to produce it. Shaw dissented from this theory and accepted instead the view of the English academic Stanley Jevons. Jevons differed from Marx by declaring that value was determined not by the cost of labor in production but, at the other end of the scale, as it were, by reference to the utility value of the article to the ultimate purchaser. Jevons, who was as much as an academic logician and mathematician as he was an economist, was certainly no socialist either, but Shaw decided that he had the truth of the matter in him and always clung to the Jevonsian theory of value as opposed to the labor theory of Marx.

Not surprisingly, this led to some criticism from the Left, as indicated in the obituary memoir by Palme Dutt, in which the writer declares that "the science of Marx was a closed book to Shaw" and asserts that he

> boggled at the first schoolboy's elementary conundrum over the theory of value, gave up the attempt to think a little further and master the key which unlocked the secrets of the laws of locomotion of capitalist society, and preferred to settle down with the tenth-rate platitudinous commonplaces of a Jevons or a Marshall, without realizing that he had thereby theoretically capitulated to the capitalism which his emotions detested.[7]

There may well be some truth in this harsh comment, but Shaw, no matter how he differed from Marx on questions of faith, doctrine, or theory, declared at the end of the long *National Informer* review that he "never took up a book that proved better worth reading than *Capital*." It was "the extraordinary picture of modern industrialism which gives the book its main force and fascination." It was the devastating criticism of nineteenth-century capitalism combined with the visions of a better world that he found, or was to find, in the writings of Shelley, Ruskin, and Morris that, despite Shaw's labors in the field of political economy, tended to make him, in Tanner's terms, as much a poetic as a scientific socialist.[8]

7. Dutt.
8. Before settling upon Socialist as his political label, Shaw passed through a phase in which he thought of himself as an anarchist. This is examined in *From Radicalism to Socialism: Men and Ideas in the Formation of Fabian Socialist Doctrines, 1881–1889* by Willard Wolfe

The orthodox Socialists and economists of the extreme Left thought Shaw was wrong. In a memorable phrase later to be used by Lenin, his contemporaries who looked for an immediate revolution thought of him as "a good man fallen among Fabians." The Fabian Society had been founded in 1883, and Shaw read the Society's first tract, *Why Are the Many Poor?*, in 1884. The Society appealed to his intelligence and to the need for socialism to make inroads among the intelligentsia of the middle class. Despite the contradiction inherent in Shaw's contempt for orthodox public-school and university education and his being seduced by the classical reference in the name of the Society, he was at once attracted by the idea of a group that, by means of intellectual argument, would succeed in permeating those sections of society in which real power lay. Shaw had already shown himself a great joiner of societies, and he had established himself in such bodies as the Zetetical Society and the Dialectical Society, as well as in such nonspecifically political bodies as the Shelley Society. In all of them, he had developed his powers of exposition and elucidation and his quite remarkable skill as a controversialist, a quality which was later to lead the historian A. J. P. Taylor to describe him as "the greatest arguer there has ever been."[9] As a member of the Fabian Society and, more particularly, as a member of the "Fabian Triumvirate," a loose alliance between himself and the Webbs (Sidney and Beatrice), he made a contribution to the development of the Left in Britain and, indeed, to the pattern of British society that, despite many vicissitudes, may still be seen to have its effect today.[1]

(New Haven and London: Yale University Press, 1975). This aspect of the subject is dealt with also in a concise but informative essay, "Shaw and Anarchism: Among the Leftists," by Richard Nickson in the *Independent Shavian* 26, nos. 1–2 (1988). This issue of the *Independent Shavian* also includes a reprint of "What's in a Name?" by Shaw, which first appeared in the Boston weekly *Liberty* (11 April 1885), the first publication in the United States of anything by Shaw. His thesis is that "we shall never get rid of slavery until we have got rid of authority." Writing some years before he abandoned anarchism and wrote his pamphlet *The Impossibilities of Anarchism* in 1888, Shaw refers to two types of socialists, anarchist and collectivist, and explains that

> the Collectivists would drive the money-changers from Westminster only to replace them with a central administration, committee of public safety, or what not. Instead of "Victoria, by the Grace of God," they would give us "the Superintendent of such and such an Industry, by the authority of the Democratic Federation," or whatever body we are to make our master under the new dispensation.

9. A. J. P. Taylor, *Politicians, Socialism and Historians* (New York: Stein and Day, 1952), p. 131.

1. A full study of the relationship between Shaw and the Webbs has yet to be written. It would provide illumination of both personal and political value. Beatrice was frequently exasperated with Shaw, as may be seen from the comment in her *Diary* for July 13, 1913, a fairly representative sample of her displeasure:

> We are unhappy about Shaw. About five years ago I thought he was going to mellow into deeper thought and feeling, instead of which he wrote *Fanny's First Play*. He used to be a good colleague, genuinely interested in public affairs and a radically kind man.

In inception, the Fabian Society was not a political body in the limited sense of the word—it did not set itself up in opposition to either of the two great parties, the Conservatives and the Liberals. Its aim was to permeate. To this end, it sought to cultivate the leaders and the best brains of both parties (or of none) and, by a process of rational argument and persuasion founded on research and publication, to bring them round to accept the need for basic reform and a new structure for the economy and society. Beatrice Webb was a skillful research worker; Sidney Webb, trained in the civil service, was, in Shaw's words, "the ablest man I ever knew" and an expert draftsman and explainer of political programs. Shaw's great contribution was his flair for publicity and his matchless skill as orator and platform performer, combined with the literary gifts which were put at the disposal of the Society in writing essays and pamphlets and in editing the work of others.

If the 1880s were the decade in which Shaw's political orientation was finally settled, the 1890s were the decade in which he did most of his concentrated political work, chiefly in the Fabian Society. He acted as a kind of general editor for such works as *Fabian Essays*, which appeared in 1889 and which, comprising not only contributions from other pens, but a long introduction by himself and two additional essays on the economic basis of socialism and the transition to socialism, represented one of his most sustained pieces of political writing. For well over a decade, he continued to write and speak regularly for the Fabian Society, and one remarkable feature of his activity at this time was that it was not concentrated on such domestic subjects as, for example, that covered in his booklet *The Common Sense of Municipal Trading*, but extended beyond the boundaries of these islands in his concern for the international aspects of the growth and development of socialism, particularly in its relationship to Britain's imperial responsibilities. The statement issued by the Society entitled *Fabianism and the Empire* impresses not simply as a lucid exposition of a view on an intensely difficult and controversial subject, but perhaps more so because it was produced by Shaw after reading 134 contributions by members of the

Now he is perverse, irate and despotic in his relations, and he is bored with all the old questions. And the quality of his thought is not good . . . poor and petulant reasoning, the lack of accuracy, logic and dignity.

Not six months later, however, she wrote on December 4, 1913,

GBS is making an effort to keep in with the Fabian Society and ourselves and he has attended every one of our six public lectures and taken the chair twice. Also he has been most kind in doing things for the Fabian Society, he no longer writes for the *New Statesman*, though he is quite friendly and asks whether we want more money.

The Diary of Beatrice Webb, ed. Norman and Jeanne MacKenzie (London: Virago Press and the London School of Economics, 1984), 3:190–91.

Society to distill a statement which was accepted as the combined view of the entire Society.

A book which provides an admirable conspectus of Shaw's thoughts on politics and economics during the period of his life when he was most actively concerned with these subjects is *The Road to Equality*, a collection of previously unpublished lectures and essays, edited by Louis Crompton and published in 1971. The ten pieces included were written between 1884 and 1918. The first, "Our Lost Honesty," is the text of a lecture given to the Bedford Debating Society under the chairmanship of the Reverend Stopford Brooke. This was on May 22, 1884, very shortly before Shaw joined the Fabian Society. Briefly, his theme is the effect of capitalism on normal standards of honesty. Even more than in many of his other writings on political and economic themes, this piece develops the relationship between (to use again the formulation in Tanner's remarks to Octavius) the "poetic" and the "scientific." More striking still than the structure of Shaw's argument is the witty tone of voice in which it is expressed. One outstanding example will illustrate this. Shaw presents in his opening a comparison and contrast between the highwayman of old and the present-day capitalist. The highwayman brought romance and color into life, and his existence could be justified economically because, among other things, he gave employment to large numbers, from horse dealers to hangmen. In the course of his activities, he ran enormous risks. Shaw asked, "Will anyone pretend that the risks of the holders of the London and North Western Railway stock are comparable to these? Yet we not only hang the highwayman and reward the shareholder, but we sometimes allege that we reward the shareholder for his risk."[2]

Succeeding lectures include reflections on various different aspects of politics. The last and longest item is the text of a Fabian Society lecture given by Shaw in May 1918. After the cataclysm of the war, Shaw looked at "The Climate and Soil for a Labor Party," but because it covers a wider scope than this title might imply, the editor has called it "Socialism and Culture." The lecture is an odd blend of optimism and pessimism. Nothing could be the same again, but Shaw wanted changes to be fundamental and organic. Thus, he looked for a transformation in the essential economic structure of society rather than for mere political juggling. As in later writings, he recognized the importance and legitimate aspirations of the trade unions but had some misgivings about the precise role that they were to play.

Shaw's activity as a political pamphleteer, general crusader, and persuader during the 1890s would have been remarkable even if it

2. Bernard Shaw, *The Road to Equality: Ten Unpublished Lectures and Essays, 1884–1918*, ed. Louis Crompton (Boston: Beacon Press, 1971), p. 8.

had not been accompanied by other significant work on his part. His activity is even more worthy of praise since, during these years, he embarked on that other career which was to represent his greatest claim to outstanding distinction in the world of the stage and literature. In 1892, his first play, *Widowers' Houses*, was performed, and by the end of the century, he had written nine more plays. That, almost without exception, they failed to attract any great attention is of less importance than that Shaw had now found the means of expression in which he was ultimately to have the greatest effect on the reading and theatergoing public. In addition, for three years, Shaw was a regular dramatic critic, writing a long article each week for the *Saturday Review*. As with the regular music criticism which he had written earlier, first for the *Star* and then for the *World*, Shaw's comments on plays and players were likely to be interspersed with observations on the political or economic situation of the day.

For Shaw, life was never divided into separate and distinct compartments. In a bogus interview which he purported to give to the correspondent of the *Star*, and which was published as part of the advance publicity for *Widowers' Houses*, he declared that the play was, in reality, a lesson in political economy and that he could not guarantee success unless he was allowed to have a blackboard on stage at one point, the better to teach that lesson to the audience. When the play was first published in book form, Shaw concluded his Preface by trying to have it both ways, as it were. The play, he declared, was not only "a work of art as much as any comedy of Molière's is a work of art," but it also dealt with "a burning social question and is deliberately intended to induce people to vote on the Progressive side at the forthcoming County Council election in London."[3]

With this publication, and with the appearance in two volumes of *Plays Pleasant and Unpleasant* in 1898, Shaw began the practice of publishing his plays with long prefaces. These were designed not, as suggested by some unkind critics, to instruct prospective members of the audience what to think about the plays before they saw them in the theater, but rather to explain the background of the ideas from which the plays had sprung. Thus, there is more overt discussion of politics and economics in the prefaces than in the plays themselves, and no assessment of Shaw as a political writer can ignore the direct contribution that the prefaces make, as contrasted with the indirect contribution to the controversies of the plays themselves.

It was also in the 1890s that Shaw took his first steps as a politician in practice as well as in theory. He participated in local government, and his letters during this period give evidence of the amazing way

---

3. Preface to 1893 Edition, *Widowers' Houses, Collected Plays with Their Prefaces*, 1:46.

in which he was able, at the same time, to pursue the parallel careers of playwright and vestryman, or councillor. Eyebrows were raised among some of Shaw's fellow dramatists at what they considered the unliterary content of some of his plays. Shaw defended himself with spirit. To one he explained that his plays, far from being born out of an inward-looking concern with the theater itself and essentially theatrical values, had been written in the afternoons after mornings spent in council meetings, listening to "h-less orators,"[4] a comment which was saved from being patronizing by its truth.[5] He had earlier told William Archer when the latter had criticized *Widowers' Houses* that he had collected rents and philandered widely, in contrast to the limited experience of Archer. He concluded by dismissing his friend as a "sentimental Sweet Lavendery recluse."[6] The jibe was double-barreled. As well as taunting Archer with having no experience of the real world, he managed to relate this to Archer's admiration for the nonpolitical dramatist Pinero by using the title of one of his sentimental comedies, *Sweet Lavender*.

Another critic to whom Shaw replied with spirit was Henry Arthur Jones. Jones was also a successful dramatist of the day and ranked with Pinero as a pillar of the "serious" drama of the 1890s. Nobody tried harder to be a great playwright than did Jones, and Shaw praised his work much more than that of Pinero, although Pinero won greater admiration from other critics and the public. Shaw thought more highly of Jones because he tried to direct some of his works to genuine society itself rather than to the specialized hothouse of what Pinero referred to in *The Second Mrs Tanqueray* as "this little parish of St. James's." Yet Jones thought that Shaw was not enough of a literary man and too much of a politician. Shaw replied. He was a politician, he explained crisply, because he believed in efficiency and did not concern himself merely with narrow abstract "literary" values. It was because he was a politician that he could go to the heart of matters which left other dramatists mouthing platitudes. In other words, it was because he was a politician that his plays were about something, and therefore better plays.[7]

Shaw's active career in politics as a member of an elected body lasted for six years. In 1897 he was elected as vestryman of St. Pancras, and he served until 1903. In 1906, he was defeated in an election for the London County Council. If the 1890s have been described as the years of his most active concern with the Fabian

---

4. That is, they did not aspirate words such as "hat" and "high," but pronounced them as "at" and "igh." Since Received Pronunciation does aspirate the sound "h," this pronunciation marks the speaker as belonging to a lower social class [*Editor*].
5. Letter to Ellen Terry, May 28, 1897, *Collected Letters*, ed. Dan H. Laurence (London: Max Reinhardt, 1965), 1:770.
6. Letter to William Archer, December 14, 1892, *Collected Letters*, 1:373.
7. Letter to Henry Arthur Jones, December 24, 1894, *Collected Letters*, 1:461.

Society, it is not to be supposed that he gave up involvement with politics thereafter. Even though in the early years of the new century, from 1901 with *Man and Superman* to 1914 with *Pygmalion*, he was deeply immersed in the theater, writing (and often producing) ten plays which rank with his most important work, as well as others of lesser value that are nevertheless clever and entertaining, he continued to contribute to the work of the Fabian Society by providing pamphlets, lectures, essays, articles, and general advice to all. He drafted election manifestos and programs, advised candidates, and took part in countless meetings of committees and other bodies. He played a leading part in defending the "Old Gang" of the Society against a spirited attack by H. G. Wells. While the merits of the controversy are still a matter for discussion, it was Shaw's power of argument and his matchless platform personality that discomfited the petulant Wells and finally carried the day. Yet Shaw was not merely of value to the Society when at the center of the stage. His work in preparing *Fabianism and the Empire* is a most striking example of his great contribution to the Society. Edward Pease, its secretary, wrote that "Bernard Shaw has accomplished many difficult feats, but none of them, in my opinion, excels that of drafting for the Society and carrying through the Manifesto called *Fabianism and the Empire.*"[8]

In some flights of fancy from time to time, Shaw would consider himself as remote from the preoccupations of ordinary life. "My kingdom was not of this world," he once said. "I was at home only in the realm of my imagination, and at my ease only with the mighty dead."[9] He was never further from the truth. In his work for the Fabian Society and in his political activity generally, he was never simply the literary man who had strayed by accident into politics. Poetic socialist he may have been, but he always had an eye not so much to what was theoretically desirable as to what was practically possible, to what could be done and what, therefore, should be done. Thus, in a Fabian election manifesto in 1892, he advised the workers how to vote to secure the election of the best candidate or, if all the candidates were bad, to see that the least bad was elected. (There were no Labour candidates at this time.) Shaw advised firmly against any sulking if an elector's whole program could not be adopted: "Every working man must try to get as much of the Labor program as he possibly can staked in his constituency at the election; but if he only succeeds in getting half-an-inch of it staked, he must vote and agitate for that half inch as resolutely as if it were the whole."[1]

8. Quoted in Michael Holroyd, *Bernard Shaw: The Pursuit of Power, 1898–1918* (London: Chatto & Windus, 1989), p. 44.
9. Preface to *Immaturity* in *Prefaces by Bernard Shaw* (London: Odhams Press, 1938), p. 680.
1. Bernard Shaw, *The Fabian Election Manifesto*, Fabian Tract no. 40 (London: Fabian Society, 1892), p. 14.

On another occasion, Shaw expressed himself with some force on the need for compromise in politics. He castigated Joseph Burgess who, after refusing to compromise in an election, lost:

> When I think of my own unfortunate character, smirched with compromise, rotted with opportunism, mildewed by expediency, blackened by ink contributed to Tory and Liberal papers, dragged through the mud of Borough Councils and Battersea elections, stretched out of shape with wire-pulling, putrefied by permeation, worn out by 25 years pushing to gain an inch here or straining to stem a back-rush there, I do think Joe might have put up with just a speck or two on those white robes of his for the sake of the millions of poor devils who cannot afford any character at all because they have no friends in Parliament. Oh, these moral dandies! these spiritual toffs! these superior persons! Who is Joe anyhow that he should not risk his soul occasionally like the rest of us?[2]

While Shaw managed to combine the two activities of playwright and politician, bringing energy to the discharge of either task to an extent that would have involved full-time commitment on the part of anyone else, his concern for politics during this period did not end with his work for the Fabian Society, nor indeed with his campaigning against the censorship of plays, which also took up a great deal of his time. An idea that was widespread at one time and, indeed, survives today, is that Shaw's plays were merely propagandistic or proseletyzing in intention. They were concerned to illustrate political problems, but in personal and dramatic rather than in directly crusading terms. Thus, the interest in "dirty money," involving as it does fundamental questions about the individual's integrity and his or her relationship to society, had intense personal relevance and power in the limited dramatic sense, as well as having the more lasting effect of, it was hoped, persuading those who had seen the play to think more deeply about the social implications that it suggested. Thus, the question, merely momentary in its theatrical interest, of whether Trench, in *Widowers' Houses*, should take the money of the wealthy landlord, Sartorius, or whether Major Barbara in the later play should, in effect, connive at her wealthy father's buying the Salvation Army, would lead to the fundamental question of whether the whole of society should be radically transformed.

In the years after the 1914–18 war, with his local-government period well behind him and never to be resumed, and no longer an active member of the Fabian Society, Shaw's direct concern with the

---

2. Quoted in Hesketh Pearson, *G.B.S.; A Full Length Portrait* (New York and London: Harper & Brothers, 1942), p. 156.

political world may have declined, but his interest continued to be as lively and provocative as ever. This showed itself in articles, lectures, letters to the press, and continual private discussion with friends and acquaintances concerned with the Labour movement. During this period, he made three principal statements on the politics of the time. The longest were *The Intelligent Woman's Guide to Socialism and Capitalism* and *Everybody's Political What's What?*. These two treatises, published in 1928 and 1944, respectively, were attempts by Shaw to set down, in reasonably manageable form, the basis of his political faith and his advice on how the aspirations of that faith could be converted into an effective program of political reform of government and management of the economy. They were written with outstanding lucidity and, even today, when changes in society cannot fail to affect the unfolding of Shaw's argument, the force of his prose makes the exposition of complicated problems still fascinate readers because of his control of the subject and the combined vigor, polish, and wit of his rhetoric.

The third exposition of socialist principles which Shaw published in this period was an article contributed to the supplementary volumes of the *Encyclopaedia Britannica* published in 1926, "Socialism: Principles and Outlook."[3] An unusual note is struck at the beginning. Shaw states directly that socialism, in its simplest and most direct form, consists of the abandonment of private property (although not of personal property) and its transformation into public property. What is unusual and novel in Shaw's exposition is the forthright declaration that "a complete moral *volte-face*"[4] is involved in the total transformation of beliefs, policies, and practices that is required. In Shaw's vocabulary, the words "moral" and "immoral" had always had special connotations. When he declared himself to be a consciously and deliberately "immoral" playwright, he was trying to shock his readers by suggesting that there was in his attitude something of impropriety or even indecency. In fact, he was seeking to convey that morality was not a question of right and wrong, or otherwise of ethical values, but simply a question of what society was prepared to accept. However, when he uses the world "moral" in the *Encyclopaedia Britannica* article, he employs it in the ethical rather than the customary sense. His attitude here is not far from that in the peroration to *The Intelligent Woman's Guide* when, explaining that what he submits is the true meaning of the term "lady," he defines the real lady as the person who gives more to her society than she takes from it.[5] In this article, Shaw tended to combine and, possibly, to confuse

---

3. *Encyclopedia Britannica*, 13th ed. (New York, 1926), 31: 572–75.
4. About face [*Editor*].
5. *The Intelligent Woman's Guide to Socialism and Capitalism* (London: Constable, 1928), p. 463.

the idea of political and economic organization with that of personal
and social rectitude.

The article, which is less than four thousand words long, begins
with a fairly familiar explanation of Shaw's analysis of the development of capitalism and the type of society that emerged in the nineteenth century, first in Britain and then in other developed countries.
He lays special emphasis on the cardinal position of private property
in a capitalist system and the importance attached to "the play of
free contract and selfish interests . . . no matter what anomalies it
may represent." There is an explanation of the growth of the rentier
class, the middle class that grows as an ancillary to the possessing
classes, and of the way in which lower elements of society become
supporters of those whom they would be expected to oppose, simply
because, being parasitic on those others, they have to recognize that,
to a large extent, their own well-being must depend on the continuing prosperity of those who are already much better off than they
themselves. At the same time, competition among employers frequently has the effect of causing overproduction, and there follow
cycles of "booms" and "slumps," when continuing employment cannot be guaranteed to the "proletariat." It is remarkable how closely
some of this refers to developments more than half a century after
the words were written. In addition, Shaw analyzes the extent to
which the nominal owners and therefore directors of large concerns
have to employ middle-class managers, rather on the lines of Man-
gan, presented in *Heartbreak House* as something like a Napoleon of
industry who, while admitted in the government as "a practical business man," is kept going by his traveling expenses alone. Here, too,
Shaw was able to foresee the growth of a "managerial" society.

"The end of the first quarter of the 20th century," contends Shaw
in his *Encyclopaedia Britannica* essay, "finds the political situation
in Europe confused." He thought it threatened dangerous remedies
and the abandonment of previously sacrosanct institutions of parliamentary democracy. Writing before the advent of Hitler in Germany,
he mentions coups d'état and dictatorships in Italy, Spain, and Russia. The loss of faith in capitalism and the realization of the decline
of "the moral plausibility of capitalism" were nevertheless not balanced by "the gain of any widespread or intelligent faith in socialism." Not surprisingly for one who would later depict disillusioned
trade unionists in the characters of Boanerges in *The Apple Cart* and
old Hipney in *On the Rocks*, he had no faith in trade unionism as
the answer to the questions posed by capitalism. Crisply, he sums
up with the comment that "the trade union driving force aims at
nothing more than capitalism with Labour taking the lion's share."

In 1938, there appeared the first and most uncompromising criticism of Shaw on the grounds that, while he attacked the capitalist

system from a professedly socialist standpoint, he did not, in effect, propose any serious or substantial change in the system. Thus, Christopher Caudwell (Christopher St. John Sprigge) devoted to Shaw the first essay in a compilation of pieces on representative writers and thinkers, *Studies in a Dying Culture*. The essay on Shaw was called "A Study of the Bourgeois Superman." Briefly, Caudwell's thesis is that Shaw, while understanding the nature of capitalist society and, because he had read Marx, able to "attack destructively all bourgeois institutions," was never able to give an effective and satisfactory answer to the question of what should be done. While he showed in such works as *Widowers' Houses*, *Mrs Warren's Profession*, and *Major Barbara* the iniquity of "tainted money," he compromised, resisted the idea of "proletarianism" which he had found in Marx, and "adhered to Fabianism with its bourgeois traditions and its social respectability." [6]

A second writer, Erich Strauss, in *Bernard Shaw: Art and Socialism*, published in 1942, also criticized Shaw from, apparently, the standpoint of a convinced Marxist. [7] In the preface to the book, Strauss explained that his study of Shaw had turned out differently from what he had originally intended. He had begun with the idea of illustrating the gradual abandonment of socialism by Shaw the dramatic artist, as distinct from Shaw "the theoretical Socialist." He had found that the book did not proceed in that way. Instead he discovered that all Shaw's work, dramatic as well as nondramatic, was dictated and shaped by his socialism, but that, as Strauss went on to show in the book, there was a gradual disillusion with some aspects of Shaw's socialist faith and a feeling that it would not work in practice. According to Strauss, therefore, Shaw's dissatisfaction with what attempts had been made to introduce socialist solutions to the problems of Britain and of the world led him to confuse an indictment of capitalist democracy with attacks on the essential nature of democracy itself. This caused him to look with increasing favor on the emerging dictatorships of the interwar years, to sound warnings in *The Apple Cart*, and to express the ideas of the old trade unionist, Hipney, in *On the Rocks*:

> Adult suffrage: that was what was to save us all. My God! It delivered us into the hands of our spoilers and oppressors, bound hand and foot by our own folly and ignorance. It took the heart out of old Hipney; and now I'm for any Napoleon or Mussolini or Lenin or Chavender that has the stuff in him to take both the people and the spoilers and the oppressors by the scruffs of their silly necks and just sling them into the way they

6. Christopher Caudwell, *Studies in a Dying Culture* (London: John Lane, Bodley Head, 1938), p. 14.
7. Erich Strauss, *Bernard Shaw: Art and Socialism* (London: Gollancz, 1942), p. 108.

should go with as many kicks as may be needful to make a thorough job of it.[8]

The attitude of Hipney goes some way toward justifying Strauss's
original idea that Shaw the dramatist had abandoned socialism, but
Shaw, when he read the book and wrote to the young author about
it, did not take up this aspect of the matter. He complimented
Strauss on his book but noted that he had fallen into the error of
identifying the statements of characters with their creator's own
ideas. Thus, he said,

> As a Socialist it is my business to state social problems and to
> solve them. I have done this in tracts, treatises, essays, and pref-
> aces. You keep asking why I do not keep repeating these prop-
> ositions and principles Euclidically in my plays. You might just
> as well ask me why I don't wear my gloves on my feet or eat jam
> with a spade. And when you make all these thoughtlessnesses
> the basis of a tragedy of ambition (a blind lust which I have
> never felt in my life), disappointment, failure and despair, your
> book gets out of all relation to the facts, much more to the poetry
> of my life and work.[9]

A third book, in which Shaw's political position was criticized from
roughly the same standpoint as the previous two, was published in
1950, the year of Shaw's death. This was the Marxist Alick West's
"A Good Man Fallen among Fabians." His title was the well-known
aphorism that Lenin used to sum up his idea of Shaw's political
views. In accordance with that opinion, West, as the two previous
writers had done, commended Shaw's acceptance of Marx's analysis
and criticism of the way in which capitalism had developed during
the nineteenth century, but felt that he had failed to take his views
to their logical conclusion of espousing and advocating a full assault
on capitalism in order to destroy it and to replace it by a fully Socialist
or Communist system.

West's attack on Shaw comes to a climax in his analysis of *Major
Barbara*, the last play with which he deals. He finds Shaw's dramatic
art most impressive in the way the second act shows Undershaft, the
munitions manufacturer, as the embodiment of the capitalist system,
in direct contrast to the values of the spirit personified by his daughter, Barbara. Unfortunately, in his opinion, Shaw destroys the force
of his drama by giving Undershaft a contradictory double role. He is
not simply the embodiment of all that is worst in nineteenth- and

---

8. *On the Rocks, Collected Plays with Their Prefaces*, 6: 719. This speech may be compared
   with that of Lord Summerhays in *Misalliance* when he tells Tarleton that "to make Democracy work, you need an Aristocratic democracy. To make Aristocracy work, you need a
   Democratic aristocracy." *Misalliance, Collected Plays with Their Prefaces*, 4: 169.
9. Letter to Erich Strauss, August 4, 1942, *Collected Letters* (London: Max Reinhardt, 1988),
   4: 633.

twentieth-century capitalism, against which Shaw launches eloquent criticism in the preface to the play. He is also made a kind of hero or savior because of his power to destroy capitalism with the benevolent "welfare-statism" of his policy toward his employees in the model village community surrounding the factory visited by Barbara and the other characters in the final act. Shaw justifies this by giving Undershaft the statement that poverty is the worst of all crimes and all ills and that the first duty of everyone is to combat it, both on his own account and, insofar as he can, for the benefit of others.

For West, "neither in the play *Major Barbara* nor in the preface will Shaw face the fact that it is the working class that must have the power to use against the capitalist class." Shaw, in West's view, was right to dream of a socialist future, but he would not take the step of advocating or supporting a full revolutionary move toward that future. Thus, "Shaw's compromise with capitalism, his ridicule of the true idealist as well as of the false, is the logic of his Fabianism, of his abandonment of the hope of socialism as he had dreamed it. It is the defeated admission that his vision is an impractical dream. But it is not the vision itself."[1] For West, as for others of his particular cast of political outlook, Shaw was a good man and right in essence, but his goodness (that is, the acuteness of his political vision) failed to have the right practical effect because he fell among Fabians.

There are two other important aspects of the political Shaw. The first concerns the personal application of his general approach to political themes in the plays. It was his habit, and in this he was probably not very different from other literary artists, to model characters in his plays on real people. Some of the identifications are well known: Sidney Webb was the model for Bluntschli in *Arms and the Man*, and T. E. Lawrence (of Arabia) was the model for Private Napoleon Alexander Trotsky Meek in *Too True to be Good*. A fascinating gallery might be made up of the portraits of twentieth-century prime ministers who appear in his plays.[2] Admittedly, neither Balfour nor Asquith is clearly recognizable in the composite Balsquith in *Press Cuttings*, but both Asquith and Lloyd George are caricatured with some penetration as Lubin and Joyce Burge, respectively, in *Back to Methuselah*. Neither Bonar Law nor Baldwin came into Shaw's focus, but he seized on the many-sided personality of Ramsay MacDonald to create the prime minister Joseph Proteus in *The Apple Cart*, the real-life model for whom was immediately apparent to

---

1. Alick West, *A Good Man Fallen among Fabians* (London: Lawrence and Wishart, 1950), p. 133.
2. In a letter to Molly Tompkins, October 19, 1924, Shaw wrote very disparagingly of British politicians following a general election: "For sheer coarse savage bloody-mindedness it would be hard to beat the orations of Birkenhead, Lloyd George and Churchill. For good sense, unaffected frankness and educated mental capacity give me Trotsky all the time." *To a Young Actress*, ed. Peter Tompkins (London: Constable, 1960), p. 78.

everyone who saw the play, with the single exception of MacDonald himself. Chavender in *On the Rocks* and Sir Orpheus Midlander in *Geneva* make up a composite picture clearly based on Sir Austen Chamberlain, who, in fact, never became prime minister although holding other high offices, including that of foreign secretary, the position of Sir Orpheus in *Geneva*.

Perhaps the single and most important conclusion that emerges from this portrait gallery is of Shaw's conviction that the burden placed on prime ministers is ridiculously excessive, combining as it does the immensely demanding task of supervising the entire business of government with the requirement for regular attendance at sittings in the House of Commons. As Chavender puts it, "I was in the House yesterday until three in the morning; and my brains are just so much tripe."[3] Shaw made it clear that he did not consider the holders of the most important office in the country as anything but capable men; it was simply his view that impossible demands were made upon them. King Magnus in *The Apple Cart* was clearly the most able man in the country, but he had time to be so, and his energies were not sapped by the demands of the party game. This cannot be taken too far, of course. Magnus, as Charles II in *"In Good King Charles's Golden Days"*, may have represented Shaw's ideal of the philosopher-king, but neither could serve as the model for an effective ruler in late twentieth-century conditions.

The second important aspect relates to Shaw's deeper thoughts on the development of Western society.[4] There is very great irony in looking into the subject of Shaw and politics at the beginning of the last decade of the century, when the hold of Socialism (or Communism) over a considerable part of central and eastern Europe is disappearing. Indeed, it is possible to go further. Taking a broader view, it could be argued that the nineteenth century, following the American and French revolutions, was a period of the advance of society in contrast to, if not at the expense of, the individual. Shaw, born in the middle of the century, was able to take his part in the various political movements of the time which pointed in the direction of the nonconservative regimes of the twentieth century in, for example, the Britain of Labour governments, the America of the

---

3. *On the Rocks, Collected Plays with Their Prefaces*, 6: 637.
4. With the greater attention that he paid to international affairs, the later years of his life saw some diminution in Shaw's concern with domestic developments (although *Everybody's Political What's What?* is an important exception). He did write the occasional newspaper article, however, and a good example of his comment on topical developments was in relation to the social-insurance plans produced by Sir William Beveridge in 1942. See "What Would Marx Say about Beveridge?" written in connection with the sixtieth anniversary of the death of Marx, *Daily Herald* (March 10, 1943). For a lucid commentary on Shaw's political development in his later years, see Edmund Wilson, "Bernard Shaw at Eighty," in *The Triple Thinkers* (London: John Lehmann, 1952), p. 158.

Franklin D. Roosevelt years, and the extreme Socialism or Communism of those countries where the experiment is now being rejected. The latter part of the present century has thus seen movement in the direction opposite to that of a hundred years ago. Yet, the position is by no means so simple. When Shaw went to Russia in 1932, he spoke of Lenin as having instituted a great experiment in social organization and added that "if that experiment in social organization fails, then civilization falls, as so many civilizations have fallen before."[5] Shaw did not live to see the end of Stalin, whom he praised with such unqualified superlatives, and, of course, he did not foresee the present collapse, or near collapse, of the Lenin-Stalin experiment and the efforts being made by Gorbachev to bring the state back to life. It is unlikely that he would have been too greatly disturbed. He was nothing if not evolutionist. As, at the end of *Back to Methuselah*, he could see the whole of human life and the entire race as an experiment which could fail and be replaced by another experiment, so he could envisage one political experiment failing and being replaced by another.

Yet his assessment of the development of human society was always optimistic. He had what he called a religious sense, "to be working for things outside yourself," and he would have applied himself to helping to build a world out of the wreckage. Indeed, in the present circumstances, it is not hard to imagine him working, not for a return to a totally unbridled market economy, but for a third force. This would combine the best of individual-centered capitalism and the best of society-centered Socialism, in much the same way that Ibsen foresaw a new force emerging from the conflict between the elements represented by the antagonists in *Emperor and Galilean*. The synthesis would be truly egalitarian, or even Marxian, in its technical and philosophical development.

Thus, despite Shaw's most enthusiastic championing of the Soviet experiment, to prove him wrong in this respect is not to establish that the whole of his political thinking should be rejected. Shaw always condemned the way in which capitalism tended to usher in an idolatry of richness and idleness which inverted previous ideas of social morality. His views have been echoed most impressively in the recent past by a writer who, while not paying any direct debt to Shaw, is the most Shavian in style and content of modern commentators on economic problems—John Kenneth Galbraith. He has remarked on the decay beneath the prosperous surface of some of the outwardly successful Western economies. In his words, "While the only evident remedy under socialism is to move towards the market, so

5. Dan H. Laurence, ed., *Platform and Pulpit* (London: Hart-Davis, 1962), p. 217.

the only possible solution for us is a larger, more compassionate role for the state."[6] At the same time, as Shaw's plays continue to hold the stage for their unique combination of sound sense and witty fun, so may some of his politico-economic writings, touched as they are by much of the same blend of gaiety and intelligence, still command interest and attention.

SALLY PETERS

Shaw's Life: A Feminist in Spite of Himself†

By his seventieth birthday, Bernard Shaw was one of the most famous people in the world. Yet despite intense scrutiny, perhaps no other figure of his stature and visibility has been so thoroughly misunderstood. The only Nobel laureate also to win an Academy Award (for the screenplay of *Pygmalion*), he was recognized as much for his wit and his eccentric personality as for his writings. Certainly the celebrity made unfailing good copy as he voiced opinions on everything from European dictators to childraising. But for too long he insisted on caricaturing himself as a clown and buffoon. Late in life, he lamented that he had been all too persuasive, the overexposed G.B.S. figure trivializing views of both man and artist. Then, too, there had always been an undercurrent of antagonism toward the self-proclaimed genius who insisted on the satirist's right to skewer societal foibles—that insistence marked him as guilty of a disconcerting detachment from the mass of his fellow human beings according to his detractors, a detachment noticeable in the personal sphere as well.

In addition to his own part in misleading critics and would-be biographers, Shaw managed to elude attempts to understand him simply because of the enormity of the task. Not only was he the author of some five dozen plays, his mountain of writings includes five completed novels, a number of short stories, lengthy treatises on politics and economics, four volumes of theatre criticism, three volumes of music criticism, and a volume of art criticism. Add to that total well over a hundred book reviews and an astonishing correspondence of over a quarter of a million letters and postcards.

Then there was the sheer length of the life. G. K. Chesterton's *George Bernard Shaw* preceded his subject's death by a full forty

6. J. K. Galbraith, "Assault on Ideology," *Weekend Guardian* (London), 16–17 December 1989, p. 16.
† From *The Cambridge Companion to George Bernard Shaw*, ed. Christopher Innes (Cambridge: Cambridge University Press, 1998), pp. 3–23. Copyright © 1998 by Cambridge University Press.

years. As Shaw steadfastly outlived his contemporaries, he noisily called attention to his façades, while quietly destroying correspondences and prevailing over biographers. Always needing to control, where his biography was concerned, Shaw was obsessive, coercing, directing, managing. Both Archibald Henderson, North Carolinian mathematician and three-time authorized biographer, and Hesketh Pearson, a long-time friend, more or less willingly submitted. After the death of Frank Harris, Shaw earned the widow's gratitude by completing his own biography, admittedly "quite the oddest" task of his life (Frank Harris, *Bernard Shaw* [Garden City, NJ, 1931], p. 419). When American professor Thomas Demetrius O'Bolger proved both independent and curious, Shaw blocked publication of O'Bolger's work. Although Shaw made clear that his early life was less than idyllic, not until after his death did much darker intimations of family life appear—in the works of St. John Ervine, B. C. Rosset, and John O'Donovan.

A wealth of information about Shaw's life is now available. Dan H. Laurence has edited the massive four-volume *Collected Letters* (London, 1965–88), while individual collections abound. There are correspondences to admiring women such as Florence Farr, Ellen Terry, Mrs Patrick Campbell, and Molly Tompkins; and to men such as Frank Harris, Lord Alfred Douglas, German translator Siegfried Trebitsch, and actor-playwright Harley Granville Barker. Currently, an ongoing ten-volume project includes the correspondences with H. G. Wells, with film producer Gabriel Pascal, and with Fabian Socialists Sidney and Beatrice Webb. Shaw's diaries, edited by Stanley Weintraub, cover the period of 1885–97, the two volumes offering a snapshot of Shaw's activities, rather than a journal of intimate thoughts and feelings.

A plethora of reminiscences and memoirs abound—everyone from Shaw's cook, secretary, and neighbors to the famous and once famous have recorded glimpses of the man. Serious biographical studies include the thoughtful analysis of critic William Irvine, now a half century old. More recently biographer Margot Peters has spotlighted the actresses in Shaw's life, weaving a richly detailed narrative. In another vein, both Daniel Dervin and Arnold Silver have invoked Freudian analysis to explain Shaw, Dervin citing unresolved Oedipal feelings and narcissism, Silver finding "homicidal tendencies." Michael Holroyd, meanwhile, has followed the interpretations of previous biographers, disappointing scholars.

Although many bright Irish Protestant boys endured difficult circumstances, it was the relatively unknown Bernard Shaw who in 1889 loudly proclaimed: "My business is to incarnate the Zeitgeist"[1]

1. Spirit of the age [*Editor.*]

(Collected Letters, vol. I, p. 222). Certainly no other playwright has exercised exactly his influence on society. How did Shaw circumvent the fate that seemed to have decreed that he live and die a clerk in Dublin?

Exploring the many contradictions Shaw presented reveals another Shaw, his real nature intimately but disjunctively connected with his art. Far more enigmatic and complex than the fabricated G.B.S. image, the real Shaw was a man whose relation to the feminine—in himself and others—hailed from a highly extravagant inner life. As he struggled heroically against his own ambivalences, the artist emerged triumphant. Nurtured too in such rich soil was Shaw the feminist, not only by the standards of the nineteenth century but also by today's criteria as we approach the twenty-first century. What was the nature of the man that eluded detection for so long?[2]

Bernard Shaw was born in Dublin on July 26, 1856, the third child and first son of Lucinda Elizabeth Gurly Shaw (Bessie) and George Carr Shaw. As a member of the much resented Protestant ascendancy, the Shaws laid claim to a relatively high rung on the ladder of prestige. Bessie, the motherless daughter of a country gentleman, displeased both her father and her very proper aunt when she married a matrimonial adventurer nearly twice her age. George Carr Shaw, a civil clerk turned wholesale corn merchant, boasted of his kinship to a baronet. But the family had more pretensions than money. "I was a downstart and the son of a downstart," wailed Shaw (Preface to *Immaturity*, p. x).[3] Yet he held to the unverified research of Alexander Macintosh Shaw that the Shaws were descended from Macduff, slayer of Macbeth: "It was as good as being descended from Shakespear, whom I had unconsciously resolved to reincarnate from my cradle" (p. xii). Indeed Shaw spent a lifetime in rivalry with his

---

2. For a full spelling out of the ideas in this essay, see Sally Peters, *Bernard Shaw: The Ascent of the Superman* (New Haven: Yale University Press, 1996).

3. Quotations are from the following: *Bernard Shaw: Collected Letters*, ed. Dan H. Laurence, 4 vols. (New York: Dodd, Mead, 1965, 1972, New York: Viking, 1985, 1988); *The Bodley Head Bernard Shaw: Collected Plays with Their Prefaces*, ed. Dan H. Laurence, 7 vols. (London: Max Reinhardt, The Bodley Head, 1970–74); *The Collected Works of Bernard Shaw*, Ayot St. Lawrence edition, 30 vols. (New York: William H. Wise, 1930–32); *Bernard Shaw: The Diaries, 1885–1897*, ed. Stanley Weintraub, 2 vols. (University Park: Pennsylvania State University Press, 1986); *Bernard Shaw: The Drama Observed*, ed. Bernard F. Dukore, 4 vols. (University Park: Pennsylvania State University Press, 1993); Bernard Shaw, *Everybody's Political What's What?* (New York: Dodd, Mead, 1947); *Fabian Feminist: Bernard Shaw and Woman*, ed. Rodelle Weintraub (University Park: Pennsylvania State University Press, 1977); Frank Harris, *Bernard Shaw* (New York: Garden City, 1931); May Morris, "Morris As I Knew Him," in *William Morris: Artist, Writer, Socialist, Volume the Second: Morris as a Socialist*, pages ix–xl; (1936, rpt. New York: Russell and Russell, 1966); Bernard Shaw, Preface to *Doctors' Delusions*, in *Collected Works*, vol. XXII; Bernard Shaw, Preface to *Immaturity*, in *Collected Works*, vol. 1; *Bernard Shaw: Platform and Pulpit*, ed. Dan H. Laurence (New York: Hill and Wang, 1961); *Bernard Shaw: The Road to Equality: Ten Unpublished Lectures and Essays, 1884–1918*, ed. Louis Crompton (Boston: Beacon Press, 1971); Bernard Shaw, *Sixteen Self Sketches* (London: Constable, 1949); *Bernard Shaw and Mrs Patrick Campbell: Their Correspondence*, ed. Alan Dent (New York: Knopf, 1952).

literary "father," fashioning a dialogue with his powerful precursor that extends through the puppet play *Shakes versus Shav*, written the year before his death.

Behind the Shaw family façade of snobbery and pretense lurked the reality of daily humiliations incurred by both parents. George Carr Shaw boasted of his teetotalism but slipped away to drink in solitary and morose fashion. His embarrassing alcoholism led to the family's banishment from the home of the baronet, Sir Robert Shaw of Bushy Park. Even more portentously for the young Shaw, the drunken father tried to throw his son into a canal. The sudden terrible recognition of his father's fallibility was aggravated by Bessie Shaw's response: contempt for her husband and a refusal to comfort her young son. The man claimed to be marked for life by that disillusioning incident. Quite early the boy learned that his father's drunkenness had to be "either a family tragedy or a family joke," thereby embracing a polarized approach to life (Preface to *Immaturity*, p. xxvi).

Bessie Shaw offered her own humiliations. For she defied the Shaw family creed by singing in Roman Catholic churches and entertaining Catholic musicians in her home. Even more devastating for her son was the *ménage à trois* formed with her voice teacher, George J. Vandeleur Lee, who moved in with the family when Shaw was ten, and soon arranged for them all to share a cottage in rural Dalkey, outside Dublin. Although Shaw insisted that it was an innocent arrangement, his preoccupation with his mother's virtue suggests that he feared otherwise. Meanwhile the influence of the mesmeric Lee on Shaw proved profound and lifelong.

Late in life Shaw claimed to reveal "a secret kept for 80 years": the shame he endured in attending the Central Model Boys' School with the sons of Catholic tradesmen (*Sixteen Self Sketches*, p. 20). As a result he was ostracized by the sons of Protestant gentlemen. In recalling his shame and schoolboy difficulties, Shaw omits a crucial piece of information—that he was subjected to taunts because of a highly visible effeminacy. That effeminacy was the reason he was later chosen to play Ophelia in a production of *Hamlet* at the Dublin English Scientific and Commercial Day School.

Although there was always money for alcohol, George Carr Shaw had no money to give his son a university education and Shaw never forgave his father for sending him to work at age fifteen. Becoming an ill-paid clerk for a land agency was one of the few acceptable forms of employment for a gentleman's son; the lucrative retail trade was contemptuously dismissed. Despite himself, the adolescent Shaw proved so competent that after the cashier absconded with office funds the young stopgap landed the job. Later transferred to make room for his employer's nephew, the incensed Shaw claimed he had resigned to follow his self-perceived destiny as Shakespeare's heir; "For London as London, or England as England, I cared nothing. If my subject had been science or music I should have made for Berlin or Leipsic. If painting, I should have made for Paris . . . But as the English language was my weapon, there was nothing for it but London." (*Preface to Immaturity*, p. xxxviii).

There was another incentive for Shaw to leave his native land—reunion with his mother. For three years earlier Bessie Shaw had abandoned her son and husband to follow Lee to London. She took her eldest daughter Agnes, and sent for daughter Lucinda Frances (Lucy). Shaw arrived in England just a few days after Agnes had died from consumption, moving in with his mother and sister. Bessie was teaching singing and Lucy was trying to make a career singing in *opéra bouffe*. Both women rebelled against their gender-defined roles and were crucial in Shaw's sympathy with the plight of the independent woman. But it was his mother's assertion of female power and her defiance of assigned female roles concerning sexuality, respectability, and career fulfillment that most affected Shaw. When Lee began forcing his attentions on Lucy, Bessie took the "Method," his yoga-like approach to teaching voice, and set up shop herself. It was a more radical move than that of Eliza in *Pygmalion* (another Elizabeth) who only threatened to appropriate Higgins's method of voice articulation. In *Pygmalion*, Shaw explores the intersection of male artistic creation and female self-creation.

During the next nine years, Shaw contributed virtually nothing to his own support, although he made desultory and mostly abortive attempts at finding employment. His first meager pay came from acting as ghostwriter for Lee. His brief buzzings as a weekly pseudonymous music critic for the soon defunct *Hornet* would evolve into the sparkling witticisms and musical perceptions of "Corneto di Bassetto" for *The Star* and of G.B.S. for *The World*: his music criticism would culminate with *The Perfect Wagnerite* (1898), his reading of Wagner's *Ring*. He became a book reviewer for the *Pall Mall Gazette* (1885–88) and an art critic for *The World* (1886–90). He also established himself as a theatre critic, being seemingly omnipresent in that capacity during a stint for the *Saturday Review* (1895–98).

In 1880, the budding critic had not hesitated to launch an attack on the powerful and preeminent actor-manager Henry Irving for his "mutilation" of Shakespeare (a theme Shaw would continually return to even as he denounced "Bardolatry," unconditional admiration of the Bard). His last piece of dramatic criticism would be a May 1950 defense of his own drama of ideas against an attack by playwright Terence Rattigan. The nonagenarian drove home the point: "my plays are all talk, just as Raphael's pictures are all paint, Michael Angelo's statues all marble, Beethoven's symphonies all noise" (*The*

Drama Observed, vol. IV, p. 1524). Meanwhile, in the intervening seven decades, Shaw produced some fifteen hundred pages of vigorous prose, peppered with classical, literary, and biblical allusions. Not content merely to review, he campaigned for his vision of the theatre and proselytized for his theories of art; he offered practical advice on stage technique and acting, celebrated the intensity of puppets, and analyzed the relation of the cinema to the theatre. His pieces are so interlaced with provocative commentary on social, moral, and artistic issues that they offer a lens into the very fabric of his society—everything from diet to the penal code. In various guises, he ponders male/female relations in a restrictive society: "I cannot for the life of me see why it is less dishonorable for a woman to kiss and tell than a man"; and "Can any sane person deny that a contract 'for better, for worse' destroys all moral responsibility?" Married people should be "as responsible for their good behavior to one another as business partners are" (*The Drama Observed*, vol. II, p. 629; vol. III, p. 1036). Outfitted with sound judgment, discriminating taste, and an unfailing wit, Shaw produced the finest body of dramatic criticism since William Hazlitt.

But before the mature journalist and critic emerged there was a time of apprenticeship. He spent his days at the British Museum Reading Room learning his craft. His evenings were occupied with the myriad societies he joined—debating societies, literary societies, political societies. Already he had set himself to the task that would occupy him for more than seven decades: fashioning himself into political and social activist, cultural commentator and satirist, playwright and prophet.

Shaw's development as a playwright cannot be understood apart from his socialism, a cause for which he labored for more than sixty-five years. One September evening in 1882, he heard the American orator Henry George speak on land nationalization and the importance of economics suddenly flashed on him. A few months later, after struggling with the French translation of the first volume of *Capital*, he underwent a "complete conversion" to Marx (*Sixteen Self Sketches*, p. 58). Shaw, who felt compelled to polarize life's possibilities, found Marx's dialectic of history psychologically appealing. Now with a mission in life, Shaw brought the gospel of Marx to the people, speaking in streets and parks, in halls and drawing rooms. Like his hero Sidney Trefusis in *An Unsocial Socialist* (1883), his fifth novel, written during this time, Shaw saw his calling as that of "saviour of mankind" (*Collected Works*, vol. V, p. 110).

The flirtation with Marx was brief. In May 1884, intrigued by the pamphlet *Why are the Many Poor?* he turned up at a meeting of the newly formed Fabian Society. The name was derived from the Roman general Fabius Cunctator, for the Fabians were attracted to

what was believed to be his battle strategy against invading Carthag-
inian general Hannibal. The Fabian credo declared: "For the right
moment you must wait, as Fabius did most patiently, when warring
against Hannibal, though many censured his delays, but when the
time comes, you must strike hard, as Fabius did, or your waiting will
be in vain, and fruitless."

As the socialist group struggled to define itself and to reconcile its
visionary and practical elements, Shaw contributed A *Manifesto*,
Fabian Tract no. 2, which wittily declared that "Men no longer need
special political privileges to protect them against Women, and that
the sexes should henceforth enjoy equal political rights." Thanks to
Shaw, the equal rights of women were firmly established as a Fabian
principle from the outset. Meanwhile the pamphleteer was in his
glory as he turned out tract after tract on socialism.

Believing that human nature is "only the raw material which Society manufactures into the finished rascal or the finished fellowman"
(*The Road to Equality*, p. 96), Shaw collaborated with staunch
Fabian friends like Sidney Webb, Sydney Olivier, and Graham Wal-
las ("the Three Musketeers & D'Artagnan") to forge a better society
(*Collected Letters*, vol. II, p. 490). Everywhere he preached that
human potential was being stymied and depraved by inequality.
Challenged by hecklers or socialists of other stripes, the accomplished platform speaker demolished the opposition with his devastating wit.

Although devoted to socialism, Shaw was no Utopian, one of the
four chief strains of socialist thought in the nineteenth century, along
with the Fabian, Marxist, and Christian Socialist. Unlike artist-poet-
socialist William Morris, Shaw feared a "catastrophic policy for
simultaneously destroying existing institutions and replacing them
with a ready-made Utopia" (*Road*, p. 31). He sought a revolution that
would be "gradual in its operation" (*Road*, p. 35). The Fabian policy
of "permeation," of infiltrating key organizations, fits perfectly with
his psychological need to overturn the *status quo* covertly.

As a critic and platform speaker, Shaw was now a highly visible
figure in Victorian London. Four of the five novels he had produced
methodically during days spent at the British Museum Reading
Room were serialized in little magazines. *Cashel Byron's Profession*,
his fourth novel (1883), based on his own acquaintance with the
boxing ring, was also published in book form, and to some popular
acclaim. In 1901, to protect the novel from theatrical piracy, he
transformed it into a play himself. Written in blank verse in one
week, it emerged as *The Admirable Bashville*. However, the satiric
view of Victorian morality and sentimentality that characterized the
novels doomed the author to remain essentially unsuccessful as a
novelist.

The novels, all autobiographically revealing, document Shaw's early feminist sympathies. In the conclusion of *Immaturity*, Harriet Russell advises Shaw's hero, the jejune Robert Smith, that marriage is "not fit for some people; and some people are not fit for it" (*Collected Works*, vol. I, p. 437). Shaw explores that view further in *The Irrational Knot*, the title a reference to the matrimonial knot. The pregnant Marian Conolly has had a romance, left her husband, and refuses to return even after he tells her she "may have ten romances every year with other men. . . . Be anything rather than a ladylike slave and liar" (*Collected Works*, vol. II, p. 349). Similarly *Love Among the Artists* praises unconventional women who place their professional identities before domesticity. *Cashel Byron's Profession* wittily overturns cultural stereotypes on two fronts: Cashel, boxing champion supreme and Shaw's first vital genius, cheerfully gives up his career to marry Lydia Carew, who claims she wants him for eugenic purposes—*her* intellect and *his* physique. In *An Unsocial Socialist*, Shaw playfully satirizes his hero as a political firebrand who, at novel's end, has met his match in the down-to-earth woman who will marry him and tame him. Throughout the novels, Shavian barbs are aimed at Victorian hypocrisy surrounding love and marriage.

Shaw's growth as a writer during his apprenticeship period was paralleled by the crafting of the persona eventually known as G.B.S. Part of that persona involved an array of seemingly idiosyncratic personal interests and habits. Probing them uncovers a psychological minefield.

Shaw's conversion to vegetarianism in 1881 was more than a trendy cheap alternative to the badly boiled eggs he ate at home. His most famous pronouncement was to a packed meeting of the newly formed Shelley Society where he trumpeted that he was, like Shelley, "a Socialist, Atheist, and Vegetarian" (*Sixteen Self Sketches*, p. 58). It was not mere showmanship because for Shaw vegetarianism had links to the artistic, the political, and the religious. Not only did it fuel his great energy, vegetarianism was necessary in his quest for "fragility" (*Collected Letters*, vol. II, p. 27). Fighting his appetite and watching his weight scrupulously, he attacked meat-eating as a form of cannibalism; it was repugnant to his nature—the higher nature. He invested food and eating with ritualistic meaning, embracing vegetarianism the way saints embrace vigils and fasts. Avoiding alcohol, tea, and coffee, feasting on wheatmeal porridge and lentils, he became a missionary whose creed was celebrated with barley water.

He longed, like his Don Juan, to escape the tyranny of the flesh with its eternal counter-pull to the rank crawling underground world of weasels, stoats, and worms that made him shudder, the stupid "forces of Death and Degeneration" (*Collected Plays*, vol. II, p. 661).

From the mire of such a dread world arose his militant antivivisectionism. Shaw explicitly equated experiments on animals with those on human beings. The butcher uses animal bodies as an end, the vivisectionist as a means, and both kill animals in the service of human desires. Shaw's seeming high-minded stand may have issued from a buried fear that the hand that smote the rabbit could well smite him. In his outrage at vivisection, Shaw never incriminated Lee or called him vivisector. Yet Lee experimented on cadavers and the heads of birds in his effort to locate the secret of bel canto. Lee's dark secrets were all too closely associated with Bessie, his star pupil.

Shaw suffered from a bout of smallpox in May 1881. He claimed to be unblemished but it left his chin and jaw pockmarked, marks concealed by the famous beard that he then nurtured for the first time. His psychological scars were deeper and not so easily concealed. He launched a lifelong campaign against doctors as well as against the vaccination that failed to give him full protection. The one-hundred-page 1911 Preface to *The Doctor's Dilemma* and the 1931 collection of articles known as *Doctors' Delusions* are major prose examples of doctors as perpetrators. The theme of victimization appears as early as an 1887 book review attacking vivisection and as late as comments in *Everybody's Political What's What?* (1944). In his hatred of the medical profession and scientific medicine, he specifically attacked Edward Jenner, Louis Pasteur, and Joseph Lister. The three men had one thing in common: their fame rested on controlling micro-organisms.

Shaw's hatred stemmed from a peculiar sense of being assailed by an unseen world of germs, which he evidenced in a virulent hypochondria. At the same time, he scoffed at that concept of total health known as *mens sana in corpore sano*,[4] the belief of Victorian intellectuals that training the body resulted in a vigorous mind. For Shaw, who longed for the power to will one's destiny, only the reverse would do: "it is the mind that makes the body and not the body the mind" (Preface to *Doctors' Delusions*, p. xiv and *Everybody's*, p. 247; see also "The Revolutionist's Handbook," *Collected Plays*, vol. II, p. 795).

In his drama, Shaw learned to take the materials of his life and transform the virulent into the playful. In *The Philanderer* (1893), he satirizes the vivisector in the character of Dr. Paramore, whose reputation rests on discovering a microbe in the liver that means certain death. When his discovery cannot be confirmed, he is inconsolable, even though it means perfect health for his misdiagnosed patient. Four decades later, in *Too True to be Good* (1931), Shaw satirizes the doctor who cures no disease while blaming the microbe. Comically, Shaw has the microbe appear on stage and lament

4. A healthy mind in a healthy body [*Editor*].

that humans infect microbes, but Shaw was dead serious.

In the early 1880s Shaw immersed himself in boxing, which interested him as both a science and an art. In 1883, having acquired some reputation as a boxer, the author of *Cashel Byron's Profession* entered his name in the Queensberry Amateur Boxing Championships in both the middleweight and heavyweight ("Any Weight") divisions. Although he was not given the chance to compete, The Fighting Irishman from the British Museum carefully preserved the program. His fascination for the sport as a trial of skill never waned as he commented and analyzed in articles and letters, always disdaining the slug fest. Shaw implied that boxing was a reenactment of primitive rites, a reaching back into Greek origins with its celebration of the male body. In *Cashel Byron's Profession*, Shaw reveals his masculine ideal—and reverses the usual voyeurism of gazing at a female—as Lydia is dazzled by the sight of Cashel's body, whose "manly strength and beauty" is compared to the Hermes of Praxiteles (*Collected Works*, vol. IV, p. 38). Meanwhile in the drama, Shaw's characters use their fists or threaten to use them in *How He Lied to Her Husband* (1904), *Major Barbara* (1905), *The Fascinating Foundling* (1909), *Overruled* (1912), *The Millionairess* (1934), and *Shakes Versus Shav* (1949).

Shaw's most visible eccentricity was his adoption of the clothing system of German health culturist Dr. Gustav Jaeger, who touted the hygienic effects of wearing wool. In 1885, with the insurance money from his father's death, the desperately shabby Shaw ordered new clothes. Embracing Jaegerism, he decked himself out in the knitted one-piece wool suit that buttoned up to the neck and along one side, so that he looked something like a gymnast. Eventually he would give up the extreme style of the combination for more conventional tailoring, but his favorite outfit resembled a Norfolk jacket with knee breeches. It was no mere affectation. Nor was it simply part of the attack on the unhealthy and irrational in dress launched by contemporary dress reformers like Edward Carpenter and Henry S. Salt. Shaw's wool clothes were a way to fight the dirt of life. With wool the pores could breathe. Wool let out body dirt and secretions while protecting against contamination in the external world. Carrying his woolen bedsheets with him when he traveled, pulling on gloves to keep his hands clean in the streets, wearing digital socks, garbed in the yellowish red suit, the scrupulously clean Shaw was an immaculate walking mannequin, an elaborate advertisement for the hygienic way of life.

Despite his unflagging intellectual commitment to feminism, deep ambivalences colored his personal relations with women. Pursued all over London by the most advanced women—actresses, artists, and intellectuals—Shaw nevertheless kept his virginity until age

twenty-nine. Then he surrendered it to Jane (Jenny) Patterson, a
tempestuous Irish widow some fifteen years his senior, and his
mother's close friend. A long and stormy affair followed during which
Shaw treated her as a mere convenience, while the jealous Jenny
stole his mail, stalked him, threw violent tantrums, or pleaded
pathetically for time with her young lover.

Undeterred, Shaw flirted with abandon and charmed women all
over London. He admitted to trying to impress Eleanor Marx, the
youngest daughter of Karl Marx, who confided in him her most intimate feelings, including those concerning her unhappy relations
with common law husband Edward Aveling. Having engaged the
affections of the irrevocably married orator and social activist Annie
Besant, he fled in terror after she surprised him by drawing up a
pseudo-marriage contract. He contentedly listened while writer
Edith Bland told tales of husband Hubert's infidelities but refused
to go any further than tea and talk with his friend's wife, thereby
infuriating her. He acted as confidant and advisor to Kate Salt, whose
marital difficulties turned out to stem from her lesbianism. He stole
actress Florence Farr from William Butler Yeats, only to avoid her
once she was divorced from her absent husband. He moved in with
the newly married May Morris (daughter of the great William Morris), destroying her marriage to Henry Halliday Sparling; years later
May scoffed as Shaw blamed the result on a violated "Mystic
Betrothal" between the two of them ("Morris," p. xxvii). All along his
path were strewn the broken hearts of innumerable young Fabian
women. But except for Jenny Patterson, his love affairs remained
platonic.

While the relationship with May Morris was Shaw's most roman-
ticized in-the-flesh love affair, his most ethereal romance took the
form of his correspondence with Ellen Terry, the famous paper
courtship between the fledgling playwright and the world-renowned
actress. During the years 1895–1900, Shaw wooed her entirely
through the mails. In Ellen, nine years his senior, he found a woman
of great sympathy and understanding, a woman to whom he could
reveal many of his deepest fears and longings. He wanted her for his
plays, but shied away from meeting her so that she might admire the
epistolary persona he so artfully created. Although Ellen thought
otherwise, as far as Shaw was concerned, the correspondence was a
completely satisfactory love affair.

The Quintessence of Ibsenism (1891), Shaw's exposition of Ibsen,
contains a chapter titled "The Womanly Woman." There Shaw
decries the "reckless self-abandonment" that transforms woman's
passionate sexual desire into the "caresses of a maniac," a description
that suggests more than his revulsion toward Jenny Patterson's feverish passion (*Collected Works*, vol. XIX, p. 38). It also reveals his own

deep antipathies toward sex. Intellectually, however, he harbored no qualms in asserting a strong feminism. In order to emancipate herself, Shaw thought the Womanly Woman must repudiate "her womanliness, her duty to her husband, to her children, to society, to the law, and to everyone but herself" (p. 44).

Both his tangled personal relations with women as well as his feminist sympathies are evident very early in his drama. The playwright emerged with *Widowers' Houses* (1892), originally conceived in 1884 as a collaboration with drama critic William Archer, and based on the French formula Shaw derided shortly after in the *Saturday Review* as "Sardoodledom." Shaw's bitter satire on slum-landlordism, with its resonances to his Dublin experience in the land agency, scandalized critics. They especially detested its heroine, the darkly melodramatic Blanche Sartorius, who beats her maid.

The offstage drama surrounding his first play had its own scandalous side since Shaw's heroine was based on Jenny Patterson. Moreover, Florence Farr, who played Blanche, was being squired around town by Shaw. One evening, a screaming, swearing Jenny burst in while Shaw was visiting Florence. A "shocked and upset" Shaw determined to be finished with Jenny (*Diaries*, vol. II, p. 902). That final real-life scene is dramatized as the triangular opening scene of *The Philanderer* (1893), Shaw's second play. Leonard Charteris, the philanderer, is portrayed as cool, collected, and in control, exactly what his creator was not.

Shaw's third Unpleasant Play, *Mrs Warren's Profession* (1893), reveals his feminist stance as he portrays the successful brothel-keeper as making a practical career choice in a society that underpays and undervalues women. From Mrs Warren's perspective, marriage is prostitution: "The only way for a woman to provide for herself decently is for her to be good to some man that can afford to be good to her. If she's in his own station of life, let her make him marry her; but if she's far beneath him she cant expect it" (*Collected Plays*, vol. I, p. 314).

Shaw's dissatisfaction with the British ideal of marriage was lasting. In the 1911 Preface to *Getting Married* (1908)—the play itself offering more than a dozen views of marriage—he calls the difference between marriage and prostitution simply the "difference between Trade Unionism and unorganized casual labor" (*Collected Plays*, vol. III, p. 501). In writing the play, Shaw was influenced by the proddings of actress Janet Achurch and Fabian Beatrice Webb, as well as the less than respectable career moves of his mother and his sister.

The Lord Chamberlain denounced *Mrs Warren's Profession* as "immoral and otherwise improper for the stage," refusing to license the play. However to those men "surprised to see ladies present" at a private performance of the play given by the Stage Society, Shaw declared in a 1902 preface to the play that it was written for women and that it had been performed and produced mainly through the determination of women (*Collected Plays*, vol. I, p. 253).

Two other Shaw plays were to be banned. *The Shewing-Up of Blanco Posnet* (1909), which the playwright called "a religious tract in dramatic form," shocked the censor into declaring it blasphemous because of the way Posnet, an accused horse thief and convert to Christianity, refers to God (*Collected Plays*, vol. III, p. 674). Shortly after the banning, Shaw flagrantly flouted the censor with *Press Cuttings* (1909). He created two characters whose satirical names were instantly recognizable, thereby brazenly violating the code which forbade offensive representations of living persons on the stage. Shaw protested that his General Mitchener was not the late Lord Kitchener and that Prime Minister Balsquith (who first appears on stage cross-dressed as a suffragette) was neither Lord Arthur Balfour nor Liberal politician Herbert Henry Asquith.

Shaw's three banned plays amounted to 10 percent of the thirty plays completely banned by the censor between 1895 and 1909, out of some eight thousand plays submitted for licensing. In the one-hundred page Preface to *The Shewing-Up of Blanco Posnet*, Shaw spells out the case against stage censorship, one battle in his long struggle against all forms of censorship—including the censorship of social behavior. In his view, "much current morality as to economic and sexual relations" was "disastrously wrong" (*Collected Plays*, vol. III, p. 698).

Despite his reservations about marriage, in 1898 he married Charlotte Payne-Townshend, a wealthy Irishwoman who had led a largely social life in London since her arrival twenty years earlier from County Cork. Having been thrown together with her in a country house rented one summer by the Webbs, the eligible philanderer immediately began wooing the receptive Charlotte. Characteristically, he also retreated from her for close to two years. But then his health broke down and with it, he claimed, all objection either to his own death or to his marriage. Charlotte's first important role as wife was nurse to the bridegroom, who proceeded to suffer a series of accidents that kept him on crutches or in a wheelchair into the second year of their marriage. Sex was out and Shaw confided that the marriage was never consummated. Safe from pursuing women, the married playwright became the successful playwright.

Man and Superman (completed 1902) offers glimpses of Shaw's view of his own marriage. John Tanner warns the poet Octavius that after a week of marriage he would find even the glamorous Ann Whitefield no more inspiring than a plate of muffins. Don Juan wants to flee to heaven to escape sexual demands; there the women are so dowdy they "might be men of fifty," that is, middle-aged and sexually indistinguishable, like Charlotte (*Collected Plays*, vol. II, p. 683).

Shaw, having long associated the Don Juan myth with himself, used his play as a vehicle to elevate his ambivalent feelings toward women to a cosmic plane. The pursuing woman and the retreating philosophical Don Juan are inversions that reverse the cultural stereotype of passive women and active men. Nevertheless, Shaw reinforces the conventional dichotomy of woman as body, man as mind. As the Life Force courses through the determined Ann—a vitalist genius like Cashel Byron—she becomes nothing less than Woman Incarnate relentlessly seeking her mate for the sake of the children she will bear. In so doing, Shaw integrates the Don Juan myth into Creative Evolution, his private evolutionary myth, both myths depending on the power of sex.[5]

Like Blake, Shaw created his own system so he would not be enslaved by another man's. Socialism and philosophy, biology and metaphysics, merged into the religious-philosophical theory of Creative Evolution that he was to dramatize in *Back to Methuselah* (1918–20). The term declared Shaw's affinity to Henri Bergson's identically titled book, *Creative Evolution*. But before Bergson had published his discourse on the *élan vital*, Shaw had already incorporated what he called the Life Force into *Man and Superman*, for Bergson's book did not appear until 1907.

Celibate himself, Shaw's abiding interest in human sexuality is evidenced in his drama, in Creative Evolution, and in his consuming interest in the science of eugenics. His concerns, which focus on the need for the human race to evolve, are epitomized in the figure of the superman. Like his view of himself, Shaw saw his superman as saint, artist, and genius—the complete outsider. Many of the supermen Shaw admired—such as Shakespeare, Goethe, Michelangelo—were considered by certain of Shaw's contemporaries to be examples of homosexual geniuses. Shaw was also influenced by the view of his friend Edward Carpenter, the homosexual poet and reformer who believed that the artist's very homosexuality was the source of his genius.

The youth in Dalkey had dreamed of amours on the plains of heaven; the man worshipped female beauty. Fascinated and inspired by women, the artist created the most powerful female characters on the English stage since Shakespeare—even while believing that "[n]o fascinating woman ever wants to emancipate her sex: her object is to gather power into the hands of Man, because she knows that

---

5. On the role of myth in the structure of *Man and Superman*, see my essay "Ann and Superman: Type and Archetype," in *Fabian Feminist*. Reprinted in *George Bernard Shaw: Modern Critical Views* and *George Bernard Shaw's Man and Superman: Modern Critical Interpretations*, both ed. Harold Bloom (New Haven: Chelsea House, 1987).

she can govern him" (*Collected Letters*, vol. II, p. 260). His heroines variously overturn custom, care not a whit for propriety, or pretend to be docile and submissive while joyously insisting on their status as fully fledged human beings.

To Ellen Terry, Shaw billed *Candida* (1894) as "THE Mother Play" (*Collected Letters*, vol. I, p. 641). His heroine is worshipped by both her husband, the Reverend James Mavor Morell, and the effeminate poet Marchbanks. Candida encompasses three female roles raised to exaltation—domestic maid, enchantress, angel—and the play exposes patriarchal assumptions concerning love and marriage when she gives herself to "the weaker of the two," the tearful Morell (*Collected Plays*, vol. I, p. 591). Shaw later contended that it was meant as a "counterblast" to Ibsen since in the typical doll's house "it is the man who is the doll," a view representing his own experience at least (*Collected Plays*, vol. I, p. 603).

Lady Cicely Waynflete (created with Ellen Terry in mind), a woman of the managing type like Mrs Warren, is the sole woman in *Captain Brassbound's Conversion* (1899), where she instructs a brigand and overpowers everyone she meets. With God's work still to be done, Barbara Undershaft, in *Major Barbara*, agrees to marry her "dear little Dolly boy," but ideology more than love plays Cupid (*Collected Plays*, vol. III, p. 184). Lina Szczepanowska, the valiant aviator and acrobat in *Misalliance* (1909), wears male garb and triumphantly eschews female roles—especially bourgeois marriage—affirming her independent womanhood in one of the finest bravura pieces in Shaw. Similarly Joan wears clothes that reflect her true role—leading soldiers for God—and rises to lyricism as she expresses her need for unfettered freedom, even at the cost of her earthly body (*Saint Joan*, 1923). Millionairess Epifania Ognisanti di Parerga Fitzfassenden is a judo expert who talks like a man and uses her fists on her passionless bridegroom (*The Millionairess*, 1934). Meanwhile female creations like Mrs George in *Getting Married* (1908) and Hesione Hushaby in *Heartbreak House* (1917) are drenched in a seemingly supernatural sexuality. In Shaw's comic universe, women are more than equal to the ineffectual men around them.

Given Shaw's outspokenness on gender issues and his depiction of strong women in his artistic works, it is not surprising that women sought his political backing. In 1912 when actress Lena Ashwell, president of the female Three Arts Club, asked him to speak on equal rights for professional women, he readily agreed. But he was not always so agreeable where the Woman Suffrage Campaign was concerned. Although Shaw was in sympathy with the suffragettes' goal, he tailored the role he played to fit his own agenda. Privately to his sister, Lucy Carr Shaw, he insisted that women were better off speaking for themselves and, besides, his views on the subject were well known (*Collected Letters*, vol. II, p. 904). Publicly he exaggerated his reluctance, declaring that men at public meetings "brought forward between petticoats . . . looked so horribly ignominious and did it so much worse" than women (*Fabian Feminist*, p. 229). There were other ways to help. With his assistance, American actress and feminist Elizabeth Robins succeeded in getting her suffrage play, *Votes for Women!*, produced at the Royal Court Theatre in 1907.[6]

Shaw was often prompted by events. In addition to numerous comments on the subject, he penned half a dozen essays devoted to woman suffrage. When Sir Almroth Wright posited a specifically feminine mind as a case against woman suffrage, Shaw countered that woman's mind is "exactly like Man's mind" (*Fabian Feminist*, p. 244). In an address in March 1913, he attacked the practice of forcible feeding of suffragettes, expanding the issue of woman's rights beyond suffrage to a more inclusive "commonsense" issue. He asserted that "the denial of any fundamental rights" to a woman is really "a violation of the soul" and an attack "on that sacred part of life which is common to all of us" (*Fabian Feminist*, p. 235). In May 1913, after the government had attempted to suppress *The Suffragette*, the organ of the Woman's Social and Political Union, he protested the action. A few weeks later he wrote three newspaper pieces remonstrating against the government's barbaric treatment of suffragettes, whom he referred to as martyrs.

But Shaw also annoyed suffragettes by suggesting that what was needed was a "coupled vote," every vote cast to be for a pair consisting of a man and a woman so that there would be an equal number of men and women in the elected body. A decade after women had been enfranchised in England, he returned to the idea of the "coupled vote" in the Preface to *"In Good King Charles's Golden Days"* (1939), writing that women, as he had predicted, had used their vote "to keep women out of Parliament" (*Collected Plays*, vol. VII, p. 208).

Feminists might disagree with his assessment of the way women used the vote; nevertheless Shaw still subscribed to the belief he had uttered in 1907 during a rare appearance at a meeting of the National Union of Women's Suffrage Societies: "I deny that any social problem will ever be satisfactorily solved unless women have their due share in getting it solved. Let us get this obstacle of the

---

6. On Shaw's reluctance, Margot Peters sees Shaw as feeling emasculated by the movement as well as disagreeing with both the guerrilla tactics and the conservative politics of Emmeline and Christabel Pankhurst; see *Bernard Shaw and the Actresses* (Garden City, New York: Doubleday & Co., 1980), p. 314. Katherine E. Kelly traces Shaw's differences with the suffragettes and sees a fear of female power and of feminization; see "Shaw on Woman Suffrage: A Minor Player on the Petticoat Platform," in *The Annual of Bernard Shaw Studies, 14: 1992: Shaw and the Last Hundred Years*, ed. Bernard F. Dukore (University Park: Pennsylvania State University Press, 1994), pp. 67–81.

political slavery of women out of the way and then we shall see all set to work on the problems—both sexes together with a will" (*Fabian Feminist*, p. 254).

Shaw, as always, preferred to lead his own movement, not to march under someone else's banner. He saw his work as that of guiding the Fabians toward a new society to benefit both women and men. And, as is suggested below, he also actively pursued his own covert agenda for gender and sexual tolerance.

Shaw's feminist comment that "a woman is really only a man in petticoats" has often been noted. The ignored second half of his aphorism is just as striking. Writing that "a man is a woman without petticoats," he makes the petticoats the essential mark of gender (*Platform and Pulpit*, p. 174). That is, he confers on woman the signifying power of gender, thereby reversing the way gender was determined in his phallocratic society. Similarly—and cryptically—in the Preface to *Saint Joan*, Shaw writes that "it is not necessary to wear trousers and smoke big cigars to live a man's life any more than it is necessary to wear petticoats to live a woman's" (*Collected Plays*, vol. VI, p. 35).

Decades earlier, during a noisy scandal in 1889 involving a male bordello, Shaw wrote a carefully worded letter to the editor of *Truth* under the banner of "moral responsibility." Well aware that "men are loth to meddle" because they might be suspected of acting in their own personal interest, he nevertheless spoke out against the "principle of the law" that inflicted "outrageous penalties" upon consenting adults (*Collected Letters*, vol. I, pp. 230–32). The letter, which showed familiarity with both current and historical views on homosexuality, was never published.

Shaw's stands on the subject remained progressive. He became an early member of the British Society for the Study of Sex Psychology, a membership he kept so quiet that it has escaped the notice of his previous biographers. Established in 1914 to educate the public on issues of sex, the Society was specifically dedicated to reforming the laws on homosexuality. Significantly, the nucleus of the Society was composed of former members of the Order of Chaeronea, a secret society formed in the 1890s by literary and professional men to work for homosexual liberation. Only a few of the Order's members have been conclusively identified.

There is a pattern of evidence in Shaw's life, including his preoccupation with questions of heredity, genius, and "inversion," that suggests that he secretly viewed himself as a "noble invert"—an ascetic artist whose gifts were linked to a homoerotic source. Of his many friendships with men, the closest was with Harley Granville Barker, twenty-one years his junior, a young genius whose gifts he extolled.

Shaw entered into a triumphant theatrical partnership with Barker and John Eugene Vedrenne at the Royal Court Theatre from 1904 to 1907. Brilliant productions from Euripides to contemporary drama, especially Shaw, were mounted. Until then, despite success overseas, Shaw had only a coterie following. Now his work accounted for 70 percent of the Royal Court performances and established him as a successful playwright, even as he cast, directed, and staged his own plays.

Shaw's association with Barker proved an extraordinarily productive one as the men wrote plays in virtual dialogue with one another, themes of one playwright resonating in the work of the other. Shaw plays written during the Court Theatre years were *John Bull's Other Island, How He Lied to Her Husband, Major Barbara, The Doctor's Dilemma*. As the friendship continued, the plays continued to flow: *Getting Married, The Shewing-Up of Blanco Posnet, Misalliance, The Dark Lady of the Sonnets, Fanny's First Play, Androcles and the Lion, Overruled*, as well as several playlets and his prose tract *Common Sense about the War*. Having written *Pygmalion*, he fell in love with his own creation one pleasant afternoon as he read it to Mrs Patrick Campbell, for whom he had created Eliza Doolittle. As Shaw raved about Stella, London buzzed with gossip. But the resurrected Don Juan image was a sham—the much too public indiscretions only a game and so carefully revealed to Ellen Terry for *her* pleasure (*Collected Letters*, vol. III, p. 111).

Then disaster struck. Barker was swept off his feet by Helen Huntington, wife of the American millionaire, Archer M. Huntington. He divorced actress Lillah McCarthy, the two having fallen in love a decade earlier playing John Tanner and Ann Whitefield during the first production of *Man and Superman*. Jealous of Barker's relationship with Shaw, Helen Huntington forbade all contact between the two men. Losing Barker was a tragedy for Shaw. Feeling "suicidal," he began writing *Heartbreak House* (*Bernard Shaw and Mrs Campbell*, p. 209). Captain Shotover's warning to the cultured leisure class was also a warning to Barker, whom Shaw thought seduced by luxury into a drifting existence: "Navigation. Learn it and live; or leave it and be damned" (*Collected Plays*, vol. V, p. 177). *The Secret Life*, Barker's haunting and subtle drama (published 1922), can be read as his melancholy response to Shaw's plea—sometimes only the unattainable can content one and sometimes irrevocable loss brings relief. Although Shaw futilely hoped that the two could reconcile, Barker was a lost cause and his creative life was submerged. Not even T. E. Lawrence (Lawrence of Arabia), a mutual friend whose help Shaw enlisted, could rescue Barker from what Shaw viewed as a life of damnation with Helen.

As wishfulness, longing, and didacticism merged, more and more in his drama Shaw turned to allegory, a form he perfected with *Heartbreak House*. Indeed the play may be the premier example in twentieth-century drama of didactic intention shaping art. Openly amenable to fantasy, in allegory Shaw had a flexible forum to state his beliefs unhampered by the demands of character psychology, as in plot-structured works, or the strictures of negative statement, as in satire.[7]

Shaw's longing for a bodiless ethereal realm is the most startling characteristic of *Back to Methuselah*, the huge allegory he called his "Metabiological Pentateuch." *In the Beginning* opens in the Garden of Eden with Adam, Eve, and the Serpent, the very first *ménage à trois*. It is the Serpent who reveals the guilty secret of human sexuality to a stricken Eve; his laughter makes the Fall a dirty joke. In *The Gospel of the Brothers Barnabas*, set in the first years after World War I, Creative Evolution is posited as promising the longevity needed to advance the human race. In *The Thing Happens*, two unexceptional characters from the former play are the seeming rulers of the British Islands in the year 2170 and an African woman "the real president" (*Collected Plays*, vol. V, p. 477). By 3000 AD, *The Tragedy of an Elderly Gentleman*, the seemingly emotionless, soulless longlivers outnumber the shortlivers, who are highly susceptible to discouragement. Finally, in the year 31,920 AD, *As Far as Thought Can Reach*, human beings hatch from eggs, quickly advance beyond the physical, spend hundreds and hundreds of years in contemplation, and long for life without flesh, "the vortex freed from matter . . . the whirlpool in pure intelligence" (*Collected Plays*, vol. V, p. 630).

In *Saint Joan*, Shaw's next play, he turned from imagining an elusive bodiless future to portraying a historical figure, specifically a figure who had been both elevated and denigrated in the various tellings of her story. Cutting through the carapace of legend, Shaw depicts Joan as a spiritual heroine and an "unwomanly woman." She is both practical and passionate by nature, a woman whose virginity stems from strength, not from mere Victorian purity. As she exercises her individual will and insists on her private vision, she becomes a conduit of evolutionary thought and behavior.

Joan bears striking parallels to the playwright. Like her creator, she was almost drowned by a terrible father, unflinchingly fights hypocrisy, is a vital genius, is the rare Galtonic visualizer (one whose mind's eye is like a magic lantern), and has been forced to live precariously among those who persecute the superior individual. Shaw's self-identification with his androgynous heroine—martyred for

7. For a structural analysis of *Heartbreak House* as allegory, see Sally Peters, "*Heartbreak House*: Shaw's Ship of Fools," *Modern Drama* 21, 3 (1978), pp. 267–86.

revealing her true feelings—results in a play where tragic overtones are tempered by the satiric wit and the generically comic form. The play opens as farce but steadily darkens until the epilogue of Shaw's irreverent divine comedy. Then Joan's brief return to earth signals the comic turn, as those who praise her vanish at the prospect of her resurrection. Only in some future time will saints—and geniuses—be safe on "this beautiful earth" (*Collected Plays*, vol. VI, p. 208).

Saint Joan resulted in a canonization of sorts for the playwright, who received the Nobel Prize for 1925, but, refusing the money, transferred the funds to the newly created Anglo-Swedish Literary Foundation. Meanwhile there was creative silence while Shaw labored on *The Intelligent Woman's Guide to Socialism and Capitalism*. Then Barker published *His Majesty*, his last play, and Shaw responded with *The Apple Cart*, and his own impotent king. Remarkably, Shaw's career stretched forward another two decades. Addressing the International Congress of the World League for Sexual Reform, the ascetic speaker elicited a laugh when he presented himself as an expert on sex. He visited Russia and met Stalin, Gorki, and Stanislavsky. He met Ghandi. He wrote a prose fable, *The Adventures of the Black Girl in Her Search for God* (1932), and made his first visit to America the following year. He wrote a dramatic eugenic fable, *The Simpleton of the Unexpected Isles* (1934), too blithely satirized the European dictators in *Geneva* (1936, final revision 1947), and again wrote his own brand of history with *"In Good King Charles's Golden Days."* As late as *Farfetched Fables* (1948), he was still wedding allegory and eugenics in his drama.

The world-famous Shaw lived half his life in the tiny village of Ayot St. Lawrence. There he spent his days writing in the little hut that revolved to catch the sun. He wrote virtually to the end of his days with a mind clear and unclouded by age. To celebrate his ninety-fourth birthday, he wrote *Why She Would Not*. He was working on a rhyming picture guide to Ayot St. Lawrence at the time of his death, the result of a fall in his garden. On his death bed, he spoke of Barker whose death four years earlier had prompted a public written tribute from the ancient playwright.

He remained a vegetarian, an antivivisectionist, an antivaccinationist, a wool-wearer, a eugenicist, a Fabian, and a feminist. Whatever Shaw's personal unhappiness, the extraordinarily productive life featured an upward trajectory, as he imposed his will and exercised his fancy on seemingly intractable materials, spinning out glorious comedies and enduring parables. Always his vision of the stage was as the apex of human endeavor, a place of beauty and spirituality. Believing that the fates of artists, homosexuals, and women are intertwined, insisting that all great art is didactic, he valiantly worked for a society unblemished by the inequalities of class or gender. "This is the true joy in life, the being used for a purpose recognized by yourself as a mighty one" (*Collected Plays*, vol. II, p. 667).

JEAN REYNOLDS

From Pygmalion's Wordplay†

A New Speech

> HIGGINS   But you have no idea how frightfully interesting it is to take a human being and change her into a quite different human being by creating a new speech for her.

Shaw's *Pygmalion* is a play about language. It was Jacques Derrida, not Eliza Doolittle, who declared that "the problem of language has never been simply one problem among others" (*Grammatology* 6). But Eliza, imprisoned in poverty by her "Lisson Grove lingo" (687)[1] could have made that statement herself—as could Shaw, who used his literary gifts to transform himself from a shy Dublin clerk into one of the towering figures of modern letters.

Shaw's literary output was driven by his reformer's conviction that the world urgently needs a "quite different human being" and a "new speech" (734). In a 1908 letter to G. K. Chesterton, Shaw warned, "Dont forget that the race is only struggling out of its dumbness, and that it is only in moments of inspiration that we get out a sentence. All the rest is padding" (*Letters* 2: 762). *Everybody's Political What's What?* (1944) declares "you cannot have a new sort of world without a new sort of Man" (2). In *The Case for Equality* (1913), Shaw spoke of the urgent need "to grapple with the enormous problems of our modern civilization—problems that demand from you the largest scope of mind, the most unhesitating magnanimity, the most sacred recognition of your spiritual and human equality with every person. . . . To solve them, you need a new sort of human being" (*Practical* 133).

Shaw's efforts to create this "new sort of human being" through language are the subject of this book. *Pygmalion*—the Shavian myth of creation—spotlights the pitfalls and triumphs that await anyone who creates a new identity through language. But "it is characteristic of language to be overlooked," as critic Catherine Belsey has noted

---

† From Pygmalion's *Wordplay: The Postmodern Shaw* (Gainesville: University Press of Florida, 1999). Reprinted by permission of the University Press of Florida.
1. Shaw, *Collected Plays with Their Prefaces*, 4. Subsequent quotations from *Pygmalion* are from this edition. Page numbers appear in the text.

(42), and few of the many critics who have written about *Pygmalion* have considered its linguistic issues in depth.[2]

Yet "the problem of language" is evident throughout the play. As Eliza's command of "new speech" grows, she is both empowered and alienated, admired and rejected. Despite her dazzling success at the embassy reception, Eliza remains a "disclassed" flower girl who will never be completely accepted in British society (787). Even Henry Higgins, her creator, is ambivalent about the transformation he has wrought: She is both a "consort for a king" and "a common idiot" (779–80).

Shaw, who called himself "The Complete Outsider" (*Complete Plays* [CP] 3:36), repeatedly struggled with the linguistic issues that preoccupy him in *Pygmalion*. In his twenties he made the decision to reinvent himself—a shy Irishman with little money and formal education—as a brilliant and entertaining critic and reformer. The results were mixed: Flaunting his wit, brilliance, and outrageous opinions, he both enlightened and offended readers who didn't know what to make of him. The British and American public came to know both a rollicking, playful Shaw who drafted hilarious self-interviews for newspapers and a profound, reverent Shaw who wrote thoughtful essays about churchgoing and theology. But readers who thought they could tell which was the "real" Shaw were quickly disabused. "Do not be deceived, ladies and gentlemen," he warned in a filmed interview. "When a man is playing the simple, unaffected human being, he is pretending as hard as he can" (Wolper). Shaw declined to explain himself, to the continuing befuddlement of the public. In 1898 he sighed, "The only reproach with which I became familiar was the everlasting 'Why can you not be serious?' " (*CP* 1:26).

But Shaw could not be "serious" because he was the harbinger of a new age that was losing its philosophical, psychological, and theological moorings. Shaw, it is true, grew up in an Enlightenment milieu—"I was born in Dublin in 1856, which may be taken as 1756 by London reckoning," he wrote (*Auto* 1:14). But his passionate interest in Shelley, Wagner, and Marx—themselves prophets of postmodernism—thoroughly reshaped his thinking and led him to a new synthesis of art and ideas. As a result, Shaw rejected the old dichotomies of aesthetics versus advocacy, imagination versus intellect, and seriousness versus play. For example, in an 1885 letter to Macmillan protesting the rejection of his novel *An Unsocial Socialist*, Shaw wrote, "Your reader, I fear, thought the book not serious—perhaps because it was not dull" (*Letters* 1:111).

This comprehensiveness is one important postmodern character-

2. For a discussion of sociolinguistic issues in *Pygmalion*, see Lynda Mugglestone, "Shaw, Subjective Inequality, and the Social Meanings of Language in *Pygmalion*." See also John A. Mills, *Language and Laughter*; and Fred Mayne, *The Wit and Satire of Bernard Shaw*.

istic of Shavian "new speech." Shaw's far-ranging intellect had too much vitality to be contained within the boundaries of traditional thinking. Full of paradox and inconsistency, his prose is alternately radical and conservative, reverent and blasphemous, humorous and grave. Eric Bentley, one of the most insightful Shavian critics, explained that Shaw tried "to salvage as much as possible both in orthodox and free-thinking attitudes to life. Both/And: such is the Shavian inclusiveness" (xvi).

This "Shavian inclusiveness" has a linguistic dimension that twentieth-century readers have been slow to discover. Shaw rejected the commonsense notion that language is a simple nomenclature system, with each word representing a small chunk of reality. Independent of Saussure, Shaw intuited the semiotic principle that all experience is mediated by language, which classifies, evaluates, and even invents the phenomena we experience. Much of the freshness of Shavian "new speech" arises from Shaw's struggle to "include the excluded"—to make readers and listeners aware of ideas suppressed in everyday language. *The Quintessence of Ibsenism*, for example, debunks romantic and religious notions of marriage by exposing its economic advantages to society.[3] Shaw's prose writings "include the excluded" in similar ways to generate insights into politics, economics, marriage, criminal justice, theology, poverty, and other subjects. These insights will provide the focus for the first two chapters of this book. Chapter 1 will examine the philosophic and political origins of the "Shavian inclusiveness" and its relationship to Shaw's reformer's mission.

* * * In postmodern fashion, the "Shavian inclusiveness" destabilizes everything it touches, including its creator. Rejecting logocentrism—belief in fixed essences—Shaw constantly explored new possibilities for both the world and himself. In his prose works he skillfully used language to create a multitude of identities: clown, sage, saint, devil's advocate, and others. Shaw was "fathered" more by his teeming imagination than by George Carr Shaw, the hapless alcoholic who was his father and namesake. Significantly for this study, "the absent father" is a Derridean metaphor for writing, the artistic medium that Shaw used to reinvent himself through his "new speech." * * *

Shaw—ahead of his time linguistically as well as politically—startled readers accustomed to the self-effacement of traditional essayists. Victorians did not know what to make of his performative, hyperbolic, witty, profound, and paradoxical style. Shaw's flamboyant mouthpiece, G.B.S., created a superhuman reputation for his

---

3. Shaw employed the same strategy in his *Plays Unpleasant*, which link the "good" money used for tuition and church collections to the "tainted" money paid to slumlords and prostitutes.

creator—as well as bewilderment for readers who did not know what to make of this "quite different human being." Puns were common: Discussing his meatless diet, Shaw wrote, "A vegetarian is not a person who lives on vegetables, any more than a Catholic is a person who lives on cats" (*Delusions* 153).[4] Shaw coined the words "Listerious" and "Listerics" (*Everybody's Political What's What?* 292) to gibe at some of the nonsense associated with antiseptic theory; the Shavian coinage "Comstockery" (referring to the censor Anthony Comstock) is listed in the 1993 *American Heritage Dictionary*. Shaw joked that his father was a "downstart" (*EPWW* 158), condemned Darwin for his theory of "Unnatural Selection" (Ohmann 27), and accused British playgoers and critics of "Bardolatry" (*The Complete Prefaces* 1:80).

Even when discussing a "serious" subject, like his abstinence from alcohol, Shaw managed to sound outrageous, as in "The Chesterbelloc" (1908). The essay itself, as the title suggests, is a whimsical discourse on "a very amusing pantomime elephant, the front legs being that very exceptional and unEnglish individual Hilaire Belloc, and the hind legs that extravagant freak of French nature, G. K. Chesterton" (74). But Shaw's description of himself is just as fanciful:

> If ever there was a man wasted by excess, I am that man. The Chesterbelloc, ministered to by waiters and drinking wretched narcotics out of bottles, does not know what a real stimulant is. What does it know of *my* temptations, *my* backslidings, *my* orgies? How can it, timidly munching beefsteaks and apple tart, conceive the spirit-struggles of a young man who knew that Bach is good for his soul, and yet turned to Beethoven, and from him fell to Berlioz and Liszt from mere love of excitement, luxury, savagery, and drunkenness? Has Chesterton ever spent his last half-crown on an opera by Meyerbeer or Verdi, and sat down at a crazy pianet to roar it and thrash it through with an execution of a dray-horse and a scanty octave and a half of mongrel baritone voice? . . . Far from being an abstinent man, I am the worst drunkard of a rather exceptionally drunken family; for they were content with alcohol, whereas I want something so much stronger that I would as soon drink paraffin oil as brandy. Cowards drink alcohol to quiet their craving for real stimulants: I avoid it to keep my palate keen for them. (*Portraits* 79–80)

Puzzled by Shaw's stylistic extravagance, critics often failed to realize that Shaw stood in a long tradition of rhetoricians who appreciated the transformative power of language—Empedocles, Cicero, Quin-

---

4. G. B. Shaw, *Doctor's Delusions, Crude Criminology, and Sham Education* (London, 1950) [*Editor*].

tilian, Ramus, Vico, Petrarch, and others. Giambattista Vico, attacking Cartesianism in 1709, drew a connection between eloquence and citizenship congruent with Shaw's call for "a new sort of human being": "Two things only are capable of turning to good use the agitations of the soul, those evils of the inward man, which spring from a single source: desire. One is philosophy, which acts to mitigate passions in the soul of the sage, so that those passions are transformed into virtues; the other is eloquence, which kindles these passions in the common sort, so that they perform duties of virtue" (Bizzell and Herzberg 722).

Shaw was introduced to classical rhetoric as a child. Although he often disparaged his own knowledge of Greek and Latin, he had excelled in classical rhetoric as a boy: "I at once rose to the head of the First Latin Junior," he recalled (*Sketches* 40). Years later he remembered studying Juvenal's satires and Cicero's essays; his Wesleyan School awarded him a "first class" for one of his original essays. Much of Shaw's dazzling wordplay—its variety, persuasiveness, and fluency—originates in the "old speech" of ancient Greece and Rome.

What was "new," at least to his public, was Shaw's break with Enlightenment rationalism, Christian reverence, and Victorian modesty. Bertolt Brecht called Shaw a "literary exhibitionist" (Kaufmann 15); Anthony Abbott described Shaw as "perhaps the most persistent self-advertiser in the history of English literature" (95), and Louis Kronenberger said that Shaw was "a showman of ideas" (x). Michael and Mollie Hardwick said of Shaw, "We suspected something of the charlatan about him" (v–vi). To the bewilderment of his public, Shaw flaunted his knowledge and opinions shamelessly. His Preface to *Mrs Warren's Profession* indicts the British moral sense: "[I]t seems impossible to root out of an Englishman's mind the notion that vice is delightful, and that abstention from it is privation" (*CP* 1:117). In the Preface to *On the Rocks* he declared, "I have seen too many newspapers suppressed and editors swept away, not only in Ireland and India but in London in my time, to be taken in by Tennyson's notion that we live in a land where a man can say the thing he will. There is no such country" (*CP* 3:199). In the Preface to *Androcles and the Lion* Shaw explained, "I am no more a Christian than Pilate was, or you, gentle reader" (*CP* 2:159). The 1908 Preface to *The Sanity of Art* announces, with typical Shavian anticlimax, that "it is necessary for the welfare of society that genius should be privileged to utter sedition, to blaspheme, to outrage good taste, to corrupt the youthful mind, and, generally, to scandalize one's uncles" (*CP* 1: 288).

Many of Shaw's contemporaries were shocked by such declarations, especially his shameless self-aggrandizement. In an 1894 letter to Henry Arthur Jones Shaw wrote, "You will at once detect an enormous assumption on my part that I am a man of genius" (*Letters* 1: 462). It was this "immodest" Shaw who wrote in the *Saturday Review* (1898), "With the single exception of Homer, there is no eminent writer, not even Sir Walter Scott, whom I despise so entirely as I despise Shakespear when I measure my mind against his" (*Drama Observed* 3: 1060). He claimed that in *Widowers' Houses* he had invented "such a heroine as had not been seen on the London stage since Shakespear's *Taming of the Shrew*." And, he added, "my shrew was never tamed" (*Portraits* 20).

Shaw's bragging gave the British public ample grounds to denounce his "insolent Shavian advertising," as one editorial writer called it (Bentley 131). The 1938 Preface to *Pygmalion* contains this arrogant statement: "I well know how hard it is for a man of genius with a seriously underrated subject to maintain serene and kindly relations with the men who underrate it" (*CP* 2:263). In the Preface to *Immaturity*, Shaw again presents himself as a superior individual as he describes his quest for his identity: "this finding of one's place may be made very puzzling by the fact that there is no place in ordinary society for extraordinary individuals" (*CP* 3:11). And Shaw made these egotistical self-comparisons in the Postscript to *Back to Methuselah* (1944): "Like Shakespear I had to write potboilers until I was rich enough to satisfy my evolutionary appetite. . . . Like Shakespear again, I was a born dramatist" (310). The Preface to *Three Plays for Puritans* contains this combination of arrogance and modesty: "Were I to tell the truth about myself I must needs seem vainglorious: were I to tell less than the truth I should do myself an injustice and deceive my readers" (*CP* 1:71). Shaw bragged in the Preface to *The Irrational Knot* that he never played the role of "a peasant lad setting his foot manfully on the lowest rung of the social ladder. I never climbed any ladder: I have achieved eminence by sheer gravitation" (*CP* 1:179).

The "Great Man Stunt" (*CP* 2:309) was so successful that G.B.S. became a kind of *doppelganger*[5] whom Shaw struggled to control. In "The Chesterbelloc" Shaw tried to reassure his readers about G.B.S.: "The whole point of the creature is that he is unique, fantastic, unrepresentative, inimitable, impossible, undesirable on any large scale, utterly unlike anybody that ever existed before, hopelessly unnatural, and void of real passion. Clearly such a monster could do no harm, even were his example evil (which it never is)" (*Portraits* 73). But the "freak" (*Portraits* 73) Shaw had created refused to submit, to the bewilderment of readers still immersed in Enlightenment rationalism.

Shaw confused his public still further with declarations of appar-

5. German: double [*Editor*].

ent modesty. He told Archibald Henderson that there was nothing remarkable about his speaking ability: It was just "ordinary self-possession" (137). In *Everybody's Political What's What?* he wrote, "I dare not claim to be the best playwright in the English language; but I believe myself to be one of the best ten and may therefore be classed as one of the best hundred" (47). The Preface to *Three Plays for Puritans* contains this disclaimer: "It does not follow, however, that the right to criticize Shakespear involves the power of writing better plays. And in fact—do not be surprised at my modesty—I do not profess to write better plays." (*CP* 1:80). The effect of such public humility, however, was greater confusion. The question "What is Shaw *really* like?" raged throughout his lifetime, and Shaw never offered a satisfactory answer.

But modest or monstrous, Shaw produced a gargantuan body of writings that, half a century after his death, reveal his intuitive awareness of the dawning of a new intellectual era. In traditional prose, as Fred Mayne notes in *The Wit and Satire of Bernard Shaw*, "Both form and content are the outcome of the artist's attempt to achieve inner harmony by establishing a state of equilibrium between himself and society" (103). But Shaw, a revolutionist who strove to disrupt his readers' assumptions about both society and themselves, had little reason to desire "equilibrium." The traditional "conformist, 'transparent' text," as Eagleton calls it (309), had little appeal for one of the greatest stylists of modern times. Jacques Barzun described Shaw as "a one-man Ministry of All the Talents, a superior organism with more feelers, limbs, and sense than normal manhood affords" (248). Shaw's style, Barzun noted, goes far beyond mere verbal showiness: "It is not the number of his words but the load they carry that is staggering. . . . Let any doubter reread the 80 page Preface to *Blanco Posnet* on the Censorship of Plays and simply *count the subjects*. There has been no tour de force like it since Macaulay's Parliamentary speeches, where thirty historical allusions flash in a paragraph. Yet there is this difference, that Shaw does not merely decorate a proposition, but makes his way from point to point through new and difficult territory" (250).

Predictably, Shaw's flamboyant style displeased Victorians who believed that words are useful enough in their own place—as instruments in the pursuit of truth—but, like proper Victorian ladies, should never call attention to themselves. As a master craftsman, Shaw did not attempt to subordinate his skill to his message. Kenneth Burke, discussing the "categorical appeal of literature," observed that the *"artist's means are always tending to become ends in themselves"* (*Counter-Statement* 53–54)—exactly what happened when Eliza's phonetics project got out of hand, and Higgins found himself with an "artificial duchess" instead of a shop girl on his hands. Geoffrey Hartman notes that "so much of language is *not* resolvable as meaning that literature becomes a way of subverting what it cannot stem: the drive toward containing language within meaning" (xi).

Like postmodernists after him, Shaw recognized that not even scientific terminology separates meaning from message. With his keen awareness of the connection between language and knowledge, Shaw perceived that scientific jargon was just as artificial as literary language. He offended liberal Victorians and Edwardians by attacking scientists who affected an objectivity that no human could ever achieve. Shaw realized that even the most impressive demonstration of scientific skill was inexorably bound to the slippery medium of language: As Derrida was to declare years later, "There is nothing outside of the text" (*Grammatology* 158). In the Preface to *The Doctor's Dilemma* (1911), Shaw disparaged scientists "who are mostly trained not to believe anything unless it is worded in the jargon of those writers who, because they never really understand what they are trying to say, cannot find familiar words for it, and are therefore compelled to invent a new language of nonsense for every book they write" (*CP* 1:407).

"Impostor for impostor," Shaw told Henderson, "I prefer the mystic to the scientist—the man who at least has the decency to call his nonsense a mystery, to him who pretends that it is ascertained, weighed, measured, analyzed fact" (769). In *Everybody's Political What's What?* Shaw recalled, "I once said in public (I was proposing the health of Albert Einstein) that religion is always right and science always wrong" (295). Henry Higgins, a phonetics scientist with a "Miltonic mind" (776), exemplifies the conundrum: Try as it might, science cannot extricate itself from the creative forces of language—forces that resist even the most determined efforts to bring them under control.

But Shaw's traditionalist contemporaries, less attuned to the powers of language, had little appreciation for his critique of science. Instead of listening to and learning from Shaw, they dismissed him as ignorant and reactionary. Martin Price notes that attacks on rhetoric recur "in each age that feels heightened confidence in its approach to truth by a more direct and less fallible means"—an apt description of the Victorian age in England (1). Shaw's friend William Archer, echoing many Victorians, denounced "the whole exaggerative and falsifying apparatus . . . in the convention of rhetoric" (Meisel 71).

Yet even this post-Enlightenment uneasiness about rhetoric was not really new. Both Plato and Aristotle warned their followers about the deceptions of rhetoric; further doubts arose with Locke's emphasis on acquiring knowledge through empirical observations and Descartes' either/or brand of logic—both antithetical to Shaw, with his no-limits intellect. Two thousand years after Plato and Aristotle, critics still abound who declare that an author can be serious or popular, never both.[6] The ancient questions about language are still as controversial as ever: Is rhetoric a distraction or an aid in the pursuit of truth? Should verbal showmanship be admired or distrusted? Do words accurately represent reality—or distort it? Shaw, with his passion for vivid language, complex ideas, and penchant for "both/and" thinking, exploded the limits of such dualistic reasoning.

Even today, long after the passing of Shaw's Victorian critics, his enjoyment of wordplay and paradox creates difficulty for many readers, as Harry Morrison's *The Socialism of Bernard Shaw* (1989) demonstrates. Because Morrison often misses the irony in Shavian "new speech," he can offer only a confused reading of Shaw's prose: "Although there is evidence in his writings that Shaw did favor extermination of 'undesirables' by revolutionary regimes, even that such eliminations be effectuated in lethal gas chambers (and *that*, incidentally, before the advent of Hitler on the scene), we can document his opposition to Hitler's anti-Jewish program as a 'bee in Hitler's bonnet' that he ought to abandon. He did come on strong, however, in support of the practice, by victorious revolutionary governments, of liquidating opponents" (95).

Two pages later, however, Morrison explains that it isn't clear, after all, what Shaw really believed about political extermination: "But wait! As we know, Shaw's philosophy was much like Mark Twain's comment on New England weather. If you abhor what he has been quoted as saying, wait a minute! In a Preface to a book written by his friends and fellow Fabians, Sidney and Beatrice Webb, entitled *English Prisons Under Local Government*, he has much to say on the subject of how to correct the cruelty-impulses that seem to infect some people" (97).

To illuminate the unique, perplexing, and captivating Shavian style that has confused and exasperated so many readers, this study will focus on four far-ranging issues. One is the paradoxical nature of Shaw's "new speech," which both empowers and displaces its practitioners, including Eliza and Shaw himself. Two of Shaw's prose works are especially helpful in understanding his complex philosophy of language. One, *The Quintessence of Ibsenism* (first published in 1891), examines how language both sustains and undermines established power structures—a compelling issue in Shaw's career as a social reformer. The other is Shaw's 1889 speech "Acting, by One Who Does Not Believe in It," which explores the contradictions inherent to role-playing.

6. In *Clearing the Ground*, newspaper columnist Sydney J. Harris advocated taxing "popular works of entertainment" to subsidize "the serious arts."

G.B.S., Shaw's ebullient alter ego, deserves particular attention because he exposes the turbulent process by which a "quite different human being" is created through language. Shaw recognized that the world could not become a better place until it was inhabited by better people. The logical first step was for Shaw to transform himself from a diffident Irish youth into a dynamic and brilliant public figure. Eschewing the self-effacement of traditional authors, Shaw invented G.B.S. and allowed him to romp at will in his prose works. But like Higgins, with his love/hate relationship with Eliza, Shaw was ambivalent about the extraordinary person he had created through language. In a self-drafted 1901 interview, Shaw described G.B.S. as "one of the most successful of my fictions, but getting a bit tiresome, I should think" (*Sketches* 89). He did, however, confess to finding G.B.S. useful in "saying something that needs saying and can be best said in the G.B.S. manner" (89). My study will argue that Shaw's struggle with G.B.S. echoes the creative conflicts in *Pygmalion*—and our own uncertain attempts to remake ourselves. Jacques Derrida wrote, "A text is not a text unless it hides from the first comer, from the first glance, the law of its composition and the rules of its game" (*Dissemination* 63). Derrida's juxtaposition of "law" and "game" offers important clues to an understanding of both Shaw's difficulties and his triumphs.

These creative conflicts open up still another avenue for studying Shaw's prose, this time a psychological one. Traditionalist critics tend to consider Shaw "unpsychological." His penchant for performance erects obstacles in the quest for the "real" human being that, according to conventional psychology, lies hidden behind the masks of role-playing. Often such critics are Freudians who believe that childhood trauma determines adult character and behavior: They generally take a negative view of Shaw's struggle to reinvent himself, diagnosing an inferiority complex and arguing that Shaw overcompensated for his inadequacies by conjuring up imaginary plots and characters totally subject to his control. Arnold Silver's *Bernard Shaw: The Darker Side*, dealing at length with both Shaw's troubled family and *Pygmalion*, is a notable example of Freudian criticism.

But there are other schools of psychology, and Shaw himself, while familiar with Freudian theory, was interested in developing alternatives: In the Preface to *Major Barbara* (1907), he called himself "a professor of natural psychology" (*CP* 1:265).[7] Like Silver and other critics sympathetic to Freudian theory, I will be analyzing *Pygmalion*, but from a vantage point more compatible with Shaw's far-ranging thinking: post-Jungian archetypal psychology, which emphasizes myth, imagination, and creativity rather than causes and

7. In "Shavian Psychology," R. F. Dietrich suggests one possibility for a psychological system based on Shaw's writings.

origins. It is especially relevant to *Pygmalion*, which spotlights Eliza's transformation rather than returning to her childhood memories of Lisson Grove in the Freudian manner.

The chief contemporary theorist of archetypal psychology is James Hillman, a prolific and iconoclastic writer. Hillman is well grounded in the Romantics, who strongly influenced Shaw with their emphasis on beauty, imagination, and spirituality. Coleridge, for example, was the first modern thinker to discriminate between "fancy"—mere recollections of sensory experiences—and "imagination," which he associated with creativity and intuitive knowledge. (Aristotle, by contrast, had little regard for the imaginative faculty, placing it next to brute sensation; Jacques Lacan assigned the "imaginary order" an inferior position in his psychological topography.) Blake's "Marriage of Heaven and Hell"—as Shaw himself noted in the Preface to *Plays Pleasant*—has strong connections to the uncommon Shavian religious outlook (*CP* 1:74).[8] Shaw's 1892 essay "Shaming the Devil about Shelley" offers ample evidence of Shelley's importance to Shavian thought. James Hillman—like Shaw and these Romantic thinkers—emphasizes the imaginative faculty and its power to create a new identity and a new world, thereby offering a provocative alternative to Freudian theory.

Erich Fromm, a psychologist with Marxist sympathies, is another source of insights into Shaw, who was powerfully influenced by Marx's writings. Fromm's summation of Marx's psychology sounds as if it had been written for Shaw: "The dynamism of human nature is primarily rooted in this need of man to express his faculties toward the world, rather than in his need to use the world as a means for the satisfaction of his physiological necessities" (*Crisis* 66). Here, for comparison, is Shaw's statement of life's purpose, from the Epistle Dedicatory to *Man and Superman*: "This is the true joy in life, the being used for a purpose recognized by yourself as a mighty one; the being thoroughly worn out before you are thrown on the scrap heap; the being a force of Nature instead of a feverish selfish little clod of ailments and grievances complaining that the world will not devote itself to making you happy" (*CP* 1:161–62).

This complex Shavian psychology, strongly influenced by both Marx and the Romantics, generated the artistic philosophy that Shaw frequently promulgates in his writings. Shaw's compulsion to explain himself, especially in his dramatic prefaces, has created numerous difficulties for critics. By writing lengthy prefaces, Shaw seemed to suggest that his plays are incomplete and insufficient, lacking the fullness of meaning he intended for them—a particular

---

8. See Irving Fiske, "Bernard Shaw and William Blake." Shaw said of this essay, "This is one I would have published and circulated as widely as if I had written it myself" (Kaufmann 9).

problem for New Critics, who advocate a close reading of texts with minimal resort to supplemental and clarifying materials. (A deconstructionist might say that Shaw's plays are *absent* and his prefaces are *supplements*.) Even Shaw's contemporaries rejected the explanations he provided for them. A. B. Walkley, reviewing *Man and Superman* in 1907, noted, "If Mr Shaw's play were a real play there would be no need to explain the action-plot by laborious reference to the idea-plot. The one would be the natural garment of the other; or rather the one would be the flesh of which the other was the bones" (Meisel 444).

But Shaw insisted that he did indeed write "real plays." His Preface to *Three Plays by Brieux* asserts that a playwright must "pick out the significant incidents from the chaos of daily happenings, and arrange them so that their relation to one another becomes significant, thus changing us from bewildered spectators of a monstrous confusion to men intelligently conscious of the world and its destinies. This is the highest function that man can perform, the greatest work he can set his hand to" (*CP* 1:544).

And Shaw challenged theatrical tradition still further by rejecting the idea that his plays were unified and complete entities. Shaw explained to American playwright Paul Green, "My plays are interludes, as it were, between two greater realities. And the meaning of them lies in what has preceded them and in what follows them. The beginning of one of my plays takes place exactly where an unwritten play ended. And the ending of my written play concludes where another play begins. It is the two unwritten plays they should consider in order to get light upon the one that lies between" (125–26). A postmodernist might say that Shaw's "unwritten plays" are *supplements* that convert the *absence* of the published plays into *presence*. And Shaw boasted that even the playwright's craft was *absent* from his plays: "I avoid plots like the plague" (Henderson, *Table-Talk* 76): He declared that his dramas were "no more constructed than a carrot is constructed" (77). The second half of this book will apply these complex terms—*supplement, presence,* and *absence*—to Shaw's writings, Eliza, and G.B.S.

Before exploring these issues, however, I must address three potential objections to the use of postmodern thought as an instrument for understanding Shaw. First, a significant time block separates Shaw from Jacques Derrida, who was born in 1930 and could not have influenced Shaw, who died in 1950.

Second, Shaw's political and social agenda is inconsistent with present-day intellectual skepticism. In a 1908 letter published in the *Freethinker*, Shaw emphasized the importance of affirmation: "But neither Secularists nor anyone else can live on negations, any more than vegetarians can live on mere abstention from meat. . . . The clearing away of false solutions is not a clearing away of problems: quite the contrary: it brings you face to face with them. Denial has no further interest: you must begin to affirm" (*Agitations* 118).

Most seriously, one can question whether insights from recent literary theory have any relevance to Shaw's mission. Deconstructionist freeplay can expand and illuminate a literary text, but it seems to offer little help in understanding the complexities of Shaw's ideas. Shaw, it is true, occasionally sounds like a postmodern nihilist, as in this statement from the Epistle Dedicatory to *Man and Superman*, describing his view "of the existing relations of men to women": "It is a view like any other view and no more, neither true nor false, but, I hope, a way of looking at the subject which throws into the familiar order of cause and effect a sufficient body of fact and experience to be interesting to you, if not to the playgoing public of London" (*CP* 1:157).

But Shaw's apparent skepticism here is only part of a larger discourse that advocates a passionate search for truth that sounds old-fashioned to postmodernist ears. Shaw complains that the works of Dickens and Shakespeare do not include "any portrait of a prophet or worthy leader; they have no constructive ideas; they regard those who have them as dangerous fanatics: in all their fictions there is no leading thought or inspiration for which any man could conceivably risk the spoiling of his hat in a shower, much less his life" (*CP* 1: 159). Shaw, always a writer with a purpose, seems to have little in common with Jacques Derrida, who, according to Patricia Bizzell and Bruce Herzberg, "does not concern himself with language as purposeful discourse" (1167).

But Derrida—in spite of widespread misunderstanding—is no more a nihilist than Shaw was. In a 1981 interview conducted by critic Richard Kearney, Derrida declared, "Deconstruction certainly entails a moment of affirmation. Indeed, I cannot conceive of a radical critique which would not be ultimately motivated by some sort of affirmation, acknowledged or not. Deconstruction always presupposes affirmation, as I have frequently attempted to point out. . . . I do not mean that the deconstructing *subject* or *self* affirms. I mean that deconstruction is, in itself, a positive response to an alterity which necessarily calls, summons or motivates it. Deconstruction is therefore vocation—a response to a call" (118).

The goal of deconstruction is often misunderstood to be frivolous and bizarre literary interpretation. But Derrida is not a literary critic; he usually analyzes philosophical and political texts that encompass many important issues. He told Richard Kearney, "I am not sure that deconstruction can function as a literary *method* as such. I am wary of the idea of methods of reading" (124). Bizzell and Herzberg notwithstanding, Derrida is profoundly interested in "purposeful discourse," especially in critiquing the far-reaching ways in which logocentrism—the belief in stable essences—has shaped cultural attitudes toward speech and writing. Derrida's critique of logocentrism leads him to conclude that "the problematic of *writing*," which he traces to Plato and beyond, is "one of the key factors in the deconstruction of metaphysics" (Kearney 109). Although Shaw held many Platonist values, including the desire to unite wisdom and power, he, like Derrida, rejected Plato's idea of splitting eternal essences from temporal appearances. Derrida's analysis of Western distrust of writing, especially its performative and self-creative capability, illuminates the charges of manipulation and deception that Shaw's public voiced about Shavian "new speech."

And Shaw undertook a critique, or "deconstruction," of logocentrism in both *Pygmalion* and his prose writings before Derrida was born.[9] Higgins's logocentrism, combined with his fascination for language, makes him a useful focal point for a deconstructionist reading of the play. The following exchange, in which Higgins makes a distinction between Eliza's surface qualities and the more important essence within her, exemplifies his logocentrism:

> LIZA   When you feel lonely without me, you can turn the [gramophone] on. It's got no feelings to hurt.
> HIGGINS   I cant turn your soul on. Leave me those feelings; and you can take away the voice and the face. They are not you. (775)

But Higgins, despite his Platonism, is also a sophist who uses language manipulatively, as Eliza recognizes: "Oh, you are a devil. You can twist the heart in a girl as easy as some could twist her arms to hurt her." (775) Earlier, in Act II, Mrs Pearce made the same observation: "[T]here's more ways than one of turning a girl's head; and nobody can do it better than Mr Higgins" (691).

Pygmalion, constantly debating the uses of language and the problem of essences versus appearances, often anticipates Derridean deconstruction. Even Shaw's marriage of drama and philosophy is echoed in Derrida, whose 1994 book *Specters of Marx* uses Shakespeare's *Hamlet* to explain Marxism. The closeness between Shaw's and Derrida's thinking is clearly visible in a 1971 interview in which Derrida uses terms reminiscent of Shaw, who often attacked "ide-

---

9. Derrida is certainly not the only postmodern to have critiqued Western metaphysics. In *The Order of Discourse*, Michel Foucault writes, "Ever since the sophists' tricks and influence were excluded and since their paradoxes have been more or less safely muzzled, it seems that Western thought has taken care to ensure that discourse should occupy the smallest possible space between thought and speech. Western thought seems to have made sure that the act of discoursing should appear to be no more than a certain bridging between thinking and speaking—a thought dressed in its signs and made visible by means of words, or conversely the very structures of language put into action and producing a meaningful effect" (Bizzell and Herzberg 1163).

alism" in his prose writings: "It is the matrix of idealism. Idealism is its most direct representation, the most constantly dominant force" (*Positions* 51). Like Shaw, Derrida is especially interested in the ways in which logocentric language reinforces established power structures. Far from indifferent about "purposeful discourse," Derrida is—like Shaw—firmly grounded in the realities of human discourse.

A thoughtful reading of Derrida and Shaw reveals that they are often intrigued by the same issues. Like Derrida, Shaw was interested in the ways in which texts resist their creators' authority—another problem explored in *Pygmalion,* as Higgins struggles without success to control the "artificial duchess" he has created. In "Novels of My Nonage"—the Preface to the 1901 edition of *Cashel Byron's Profession*—Shaw noted, "I was to find later on that a book is like a child: it is easier to bring it into the world than to control it when it is launched there" (*CP* 1:92). The cinema version of *Pygmalion* itself is a prime example. Although Shaw's contract with Gabriel Pascal gave him final control of the script, his insistence that Eliza married Freddy, not Higgins, was ignored when the end of the play was filmed.

And Act II of *Pygmalion* shows Henry Higgins struggling with another problem important to Derrida—the tendency of language to "disseminate" meanings different from what the writer intended:

> HIGGINS   You know, Pickering, that woman [Mrs Pearce] has
> the most extraordinary ideas about me. Here I am, a shy, dif-
> fident sort of man. I've never been able to feel really grown
> up and tremendous, like other chaps. And yet she's firmly
> persuaded that I'm an arbitrary overbearing bossing kind of
> person. I cant account for it. (705)

In *The Quintessence of Ibsenism,* Shaw explores the linguistic issue of "dissemination" at some length:

> When Ibsen, by merely giving the rein to the creative impulse
> of his poetic nature, had produced *Brand* and *Peer Gynt,* he was
> nearly forty. His will, in setting his imagination to work, had
> produced a great puzzle for his intellect. In no case does the
> difference between the will and the intellect come out more
> clearly than in that of the poet, save only that of the lover. Had
> Ibsen died in 1867, he, like many another great poet, would
> have gone to his grave without having ever rationally understood
> his own meaning. Nay, if in that year an intellectual expert . . .
> had gone to Ibsen and offered him the explanation of *Brand*
> which he himself must have arrived at before he constructed
> *Ghosts* and *The Wild Duck,* he would perhaps have repudiated
> it. . . . It is only the naif who goes to the creative artist with

absolute confidence in receiving an answer to his "What does this passage mean?" That is the very question which the poet's own intellect, which had no part in the conception of the poem, may be asking him. . . . Just so do we find Ibsen, after composing his two great dramatic poems, entering on a struggle to become intellectually conscious of what he had done. (*Selected* 236)

Not even Shaw himself was immune to such puzzlements. In the Postscript to *Back to Methuselah* he explained that when writing a play, "Sometimes I do not see what the play was driving at until quite a long time after I have finished it; and even then I may be wrong about it just as any critical third party may" (307).

Still another reason for bringing Shaw and Derrida together is that Shaw demonstrates that "deconstruction"—the exposure of contradictory and subversive elements within a text and an ideology—is hardly a new practice, although the term itself did not exist until Derrida coined it. Derrida himself insisted, "No matter how novel or unprecedented a modern meaning may appear, it is never exclusively *modernist* but is also and at the same time a phenomenon of repetition. . . . [T]he most hidden and forgotten archives can emerge and constantly recur and work through history" (Kearney 113).

Shaw's prose contains many examples of deconstruction. In the Preface to *Major Barbara* (1907), for example, he "deconstructs" Christianity—exposes its hidden, discordant components—by contrasting its "retrograde element" (*CP* 1:249) to the true teachings of Jesus. Shaw demonstrates that Christianity disseminates both a "hocus-pocus of innocence and guilt, reward and punishment, virtuous indignation and pardon" (276) and an authentic spiritual message: "the Christian formula that all men are children of one father" (267).

Nor is Shaw trivialized by this link to Derrida, who has devoted himself to making philosophy meaningful to young people in the French school system. Like Shaw, Derrida has never erected barriers between "real life" and philosophy. Derrida told Kearney, "Every week I receive critical commentaries on deconstruction which operate on the assumption that what they call 'post-structuralism' amounts to saying that there is nothing beyond language, that we are submerged in words—and other stupidities of that sort" (123). What deconstruction does attempt, according to Derrida, is "to show that the question of reference is much more complex and problematic than traditional theories supposed" (123). Derrida's goal of exposing the chinks in "serious" discourse is closely akin to Shaw's.

But it does not follow, as some commentators have assumed, that Derrida discounts the possibility or necessity of searching for truth.

Allan Bloom's attack on deconstruction in *The Closing of the American Mind* is typical of contemporary misunderstanding of Derridean thought:

> it is the last, predictable stage in the suppression of reason and the denial of the possibility of truth in the name of philosophy. The interpreter's creative activity is more important than the text; there is no text, only interpretation. Thus the one thing most necessary for us, the knowledge of what these texts have to tell us, is turned over to the subject, creative selves of these interpreters, who say that there is both no text and no reality to which the texts refer. A cheapened interpretation of Nietzsche liberates us from the objective imperatives of the texts that might have liberated us from our increasingly low and narrow horizon. (379).

Derrida—Bloom notwithstanding—is not an irrationalist. In 1989, replying to widespread misunderstandings of his writings, Derrida explained, "the concept of text or of context which guides me embraces and does not exclude the world, reality, history. . . . [The] text is not a book, it is not confined in a volume itself confined to the library. It does not suspend reference—to history, to reality, to being. . . . [The] value of truth . . . is never contested or destroyed in my writings, but only reinscribed in larger, more stratified contexts" (Norris, *Postmodernism* 44–45).

Moreover, Shaw can help clarify Derridean thought. Shaw's "new speech" offers many opportunities to apply postmodern insights to contemporary problems. William Barrett, author of *Irrational Man*, has complained that much twentieth-century philosophy is over-specialized and academic. He cites "the extraordinary preoccupation with technique among modern philosophers, with logical and linguistic analysis, syntax and semantics; and in general with the refining away of all content for the sake of formal subtlety" (6). Shaw, a superb rhetorician with an impressive command of "logical and linguistic analysis, syntax and semantics," can hardly be called "over-specialized and academic." This study will offer a defense of deconstruction against charges of irrelevance brought by such critics as John R. Searle and John M. Ellis.

One further argument can be made for bringing together Shavian "new speech" and Derridean deconstruction: They have a common ancestor in Karl Marx. Shaw's lifelong admiration for Marx is well known. In a 1905 biographical letter to Archibald Henderson, Shaw described his discovery of Marx: "from then on I was a man with some business in the world" (*Letters* 2:486). Shaw never changed his estimation of Marx's importance. In 1942 he told Nancy Astor that *Das Kapital* is "one of the world's bibles" (*Letters* 4:643); in a 1948 letter to Eric Bentley, Shaw described himself as "a confirmed Marxist" (*Letters* 4:823). Shaw was strongly influenced by Marx's insights about language, philosophy, and politics, especially Marx's attack on Western metaphysics—what Shaw called "idealism" and I am calling "seriousness."

Derrida too has thoroughly studied Marx, whose name often appears in Derrida's writings and interviews. According to Michael Ryan, author of *Marxism and Deconstruction*, "Derrida follows Marx as a critic of metaphysics" (43). In 1994 Derrida published *Specters of Marx: The State of the Debt, the Work of Mourning, and the New International*, which explores the continuing importance of Marx's ideas more than a century after his death. Citing "the Marxist memory and tradition of deconstruction" Derrida explains that he is heavily indebted to Marx (92–93).

One central objective underlies these postmodern issues: taking Shaw off the shelf to assert his continuing timeliness. In the nearly five decades since Shaw's death, his reputation has suffered from a sense that his achievements belonged to an earlier time with little connection to ours. A 1913 Shavian warning about Ibsen's reputation sounds prophetic of Shaw himself: "the most effective way of shutting our minds against a great man's ideas is to take them for granted and admit he was great and have done with him" (*CP* 1:581–82). In 1921 Shaw wrote, "I see there is a tendency to begin treating me like an archbishop. I fear in that case that I must be becoming a hopeless old twaddler" (Bentley 132). Eric Bentley notes that D. H. Lawrence, G. K. Chesterton, and T. S. Eliot were already making Shaw sound dated by the end of World War I. But today there is a growing awareness among critics that postmodern thought—refusing, like Shaw, to be "serious"—holds the promise of new insight into Bernard Shaw and his writings. Such critics as Stanley Weintraub, J. L. Wisenthal, and R. F. Dietrich have already begun to apply contemporary thought to Shaw,[1] and a previous study of mine explored the connections between *Pygmalion* and Derridean deconstruction.[2]

Ironically, Shaw himself was uncertain whether future generations would be interested in his writings. His will directed the National Trust to dispose of his home, Ayot St. Lawrence, if his literary reputation began to diminish after his death. Of course exactly the opposite has happened: Interest in Shaw constantly leads to new productions of his plays (including a 1995 staging of *Pygmalion* in Moscow),[3] a wealth of primary and secondary scholarship,

1. See Stanley Weintraub, "The Avant-garde Shaw"; J. L. Wisenthal, "Having the Last Word"; and R. F. Dietrich, "Deconstruction as Devil's Advocacy."
2. Jean Reynolds, "Deconstructing Henry Higgins, or Eliza as Derridean 'Text'."
3. An English-language review by Svetlana Magidson appeared in *Moscow News* (no. 34, September 1–7, 1995).

and the need to continue assessing his achievements. I am convinced
that scholars have only begun to explore Shaw's connections to contemporary philosophy, linguistics, and psychology.

The Shavian Inclusiveness

HIGGINS   This is an age of upstarts. Men begin in Kentish Town
with 80 £ a year, and end in Park Lane with a hundred thousand.
They want to drop Kentish Town; but they give themselves away
every time they open their mouths. Now I can teach them—

Eric Bentley's phrase "the Shavian inclusiveness" offers a useful
starting point for a study of Shavian postmodernism. Jacques Derrida—like Shaw, powerfully influenced by Karl Marx—consistently
rejects traditional dualistic "either/or" thinking. Deconstruction,
focusing on the marginal and repressed elements in a text, offers
many insights into Shavian "new speech," which encompassses an
astonishing range of styles, roles, and rhetorical devices.

Pygmalion can be called an "inclusive" play: A more conventional
dramatist than Shaw might not have included an "upstart" like Eliza
Doolittle in a drama about gentlemen like Higgins and Pickering.
Eliza is a marginal person, startlingly out of place beside the pillars
of St. Paul's Church in Covent Garden, where Higgins first sees her.
But Shaw, marginal himself because of his Irish origins and radical
thinking, was just as unconventional. Regarding himself as "a
sojourner on this planet rather than a native of it," he pondered life
from the vantage point of an alien (*CP* 3:35). In *Mainly about Myself*
(1898) he vividly described his outsider status. * * *

Shaw used his outsider status to advantage, writing both dramatic
and nondramatic works that—like *Pygmalion*—critique contemporary ideologies by exposing what Michael Ryan calls their "gestures
of exclusion" (3). Shaw's prose often explores political, social, economic, and religious ideas overlooked by other writers of his day: the
necessity of women's rights, the failure of Britain's criminal justice
system, the sins of science, and the absurdity of religious orthodoxy.
In his Preface to *Misalliance,* Shaw explained that alien and rejected
ideas are essential to "progressive enlightenment [which] depends
on a fair hearing for doctrines which at first appear seditious, blasphemous, and immoral, and which deeply shock people who never
think originally, thought being for them merely a habit and an echo"
(*CP* 2:38). This "Shavian inclusiveness" is a hallmark of Shaw's
thought.

Shaw's interest in margins and their problems—things excluded
and included—links him to Jacques Derrida, who is preoccupied
with the seemingly extraneous features in a text or ideology that sub-

tly undermine its primary message. According to Derrida, "Every culture and society requires an internal critique or deconstruction as an essential part of its development. . . . Every culture is haunted by its other" (Kearney 116). This "otherness," so pervasive in Shavian prose, is a vital component of deconstruction, as Derrida explains: "Deconstruction is not an enclosure in nothingness, but an openness towards the other" (Kearney 124). In a 1994 interview, Derrida noted that "otherness" is a prerequisite rather than a detriment to dialogue, community, and national unity: "Once you take into account this inner and other difference, then you pay attention to the other and you understand that fighting for your own identity is not exclusive of another identity, is open to another identity. And this prevents totalitarianism, nationalism, egocentrism, and so on" (*Deconstruction in a Nutshell* 13–14).

Like psychoanalysts, deconstructionists attach great significance to the unspoken, unnoticed "others" that are often repressed and denied. They make a sharp break with the traditional Western metaphysics, which, heavily influenced by Plato, seeks to differentiate and banish everything that does not fit its system. In *The Realm of Rhetoric*, Chaim Perelman explains that Plato "recognized a cleansing role in dialectic—the technique Socrates used to refute his opponent's opinions insofar as he was able to bring out their internal inconsistencies. As soon as they contradict themselves, opinions cannot be simultaneously admitted, and at least one of them has to be abandoned for the sake of truth" (Bizzell and Herzberg 1072).

Shaw, with his "both/and" habit of mind, often exposes such metaphysical "cleansing." In the *Quintessence of Ibsenism*, for example, he tells the story of a contemporary woman, Marie Bashkirtseff, who has shocked Britain with her "unfeminine" intellect and independence. Her critics, Shaw points out, simply deny that she is a woman at all: He quotes one who wrote, "She was the very antithesis of a true woman" (*Selected* 224).

Shaw's prose challenges Platonist metaphysics in still another way, by showing how it smoothly absorbs differences and conflicts into a false appearance of harmony. Christopher Norris points out "that power of logocentric thinking to absorb all differences into itself by viewing them as mere stages or signposts on the way to some grand conceptual synthesis" (*Derrida* 231). A prime example appears in the Preface to *Saint Joan*, in which Shaw shows that contemporary thinkers dismiss religion as an early, inadequate source of knowledge that has been superseded by science, rather than considering the possibility that religion may still have something to offer the modern world.

Shaw's penchant for both/and thinking is clearly visible in *Pygmalion*. Despite her outsider status, Eliza, along with her Angel

Court neighbors, is a vital part of English social structure. Like Eliza's dustman father, members of Eliza's class perform distasteful but essential services for the rich. Higgins and his fellows use both strategies mentioned earlier to "cleanse" themselves from the less desirable elements of society. First, the lower classes are banished from view: out of sight, out of mind. Although a small army of workers is required to maintain the standard of living depicted in *Pygmalion*, only a housekeeper, a dustman and a parlormaid are seen onstage. Second, the poor are denied the status of human beings, as in this exchange from Act II of *Pygmalion*:

> PICKERING [*In good-humored remonstrance.*] Does it occur to you, Higgins, that the girl has some feelings?
> HIGGINS [*Looking critically at her.*] Oh no, I dont think so. Not any feelings that we need bother about. (694–95)

Most important, the poor are stereotyped as morally weak. Moments after *Pygmalion* begins, Mrs Eynsford-Hill suspects that Eliza is a prostitute and buys a bunch of flowers in hopes of confirming her suspicions. * * * Freddy's sister Clara protests her mother's injustice to him: "Really, mamma, you might have spared Freddy that" (672). But Clara does not take offense at the insult directed at another member of her own sex: Eliza is beneath her notice.

Despite the scorn repeatedly heaped on Eliza and others of her class, they perform another vital function that goes beyond their menial services to the rich: They help classify British social structure. Eliza's "Lisson Grove lingo" so clearly defines her social position that when she masters upper-class speech, guests at the embassy reception have no clue to her origin. And it is here, with Eliza's "new speech," that British class ideology breaks down, or "deconstructs." Genteel speech, supposedly a natural acquisition of the well bred, isn't "natural" at all—nor is it a reliable social indicator. Although the embassy guests seem homogeneous, they are a jumbled lot: Their ranks include both "upstarts" who have mastered refined speech and aristocrats who never learned to speak it. Of the latter Higgins complains, "theyre such fools that they think style comes by nature to people in their position; and so they never learn" (746–47).

And Higgins himself is seriously flawed. Despite his social standing and "Miltonic mind," he is boorish and manipulative, with as little respect for his peers as for members of Eliza's class. He airily suggests an arranged marriage for Eliza, who retorts, "We were above that at the corner of Tottenham Court Road. . . . I sold flowers. I didn't sell myself" (750). At the end of the play she tells Higgins, "I had only to lift up my finger to be as good as you" (781). Eliza has discovered the fallacy of British social-class ideology.

Marxist critic Kenneth Burke defines an ideology as an "inverted genealogy of culture, that makes for 'illusion' and 'mystification' by treating ideas as *primary* where they should have been treated as *derivative*" (*Rhetoric* 104). Ideologies naturalize events and relationships, creating the impression of inevitability by concealing their causes and origins in order to deter questions, doubts, and critical thinking. Critic Patricia Waugh says this process is accomplished through the medium of "everyday language" by "power structures through a continuous process of naturalization whereby forms of oppression are constructed in apparently 'innocent' representations" (11).

The insults that Higgins directs at Eliza are linguistic evidence of the "naturalization" process that British class structure has undergone: He can throw epithets at her with no fear of reprisal or contradiction. Eliza's low status seems "primary"—the unchangeable result of heredity—even though it is actually "derivative," resulting from economics, education, demographics, and other social phenomena. Higgins's phonetics game of guessing people's origins in Act I drives the point home: Speech patterns are the product not of genes or inborn character, but geography.

In "Karl Marx and 'Das Kapital'" (1887), Shaw recounts a similar process—the establishment of gold as a "natural" medium of exchange: "The soap-maker. . . . finds it troublesome to estimate the value of his ware not only in nails, but in candles, gloves, bread, and every separate ware used by him. So does the nail-maker; and so do all the other exchangers. So they agree upon a suitable ware, such as gold, in which each can estimate the value of his ware. Gold can then be bought for wares; and all wares can be bought for it. Gold becomes money; and values become prices. Money then becomes the customary expression of the "natural price of all things." In the Robinson Crusoe age, before division of labor and exchange, labor seemed the natural price; when wares were exchanged and bartered, wares seemed the natural price" (*Karl Marx* 130).

Such naturalizations reinforce ideologies by concealing the discords simmering within them. Burke's description of an ideology, focusing on the conflicts beneath its surface harmony, sounds much like Derridean deconstruction: "An ideology is not a harmonious structure of beliefs or assumptions; some of its beliefs militate against others, and some of its standards militate against our nature. An ideology is an aggregate of beliefs sufficiently at odds with one another to justify opposite kinds of conduct" (*Counter-Statement* 163).

This commonality between Burke, Shaw, and Derrida should not be surprising, since all three have a Marxist background, and the critiquing of ideologies is a Marxist activity. Shavian critics have tended to underestimate Shaw's debt to Marx because they focus only on the failed socialist economics of *Das Kapital*.[4] Bernard Dukore, describing the myopic views of several of these critics, explains, "To Marxist critics like [Alick] West, Christopher Caudwell, and E. Strauss, Shaw is a bourgeois playwright who is not as radical as he thinks. Before and after 1917, they denounced his Fabian-inspired plays as unsocialistic, for they fail to dramatize the class struggle, vilify capitalists, applaud the moral preeminence of the working class, and present exemplary socialists with whom audiences of workers might identify" (xviii). Actually, Marx's ideas helped form many features of Shavian "new speech": Shaw's passion for social change, his attraction to people and problems outside mainstream thinking, his hatred of idealism, and his ability to break through surface harmony to expose the discord underneath.

Reading *Das Kapital* in 1882 changed Shaw's whole life. Biographer and friend Hesketh Pearson said that Marx "directed [Shaw's] energy, influenced his art, gave him a religion, and, as he claimed, made a man of him" (52). Shaw himself told Pearson that discovering Marx "was the turning-point in my career. Marx was a revelation. His abstract economics, I discovered later, were wrong, but he rent the veil. He opened my eyes to the facts of history and civilisation, gave me an entirely fresh conception of the universe, provided me with a purpose and a mission in life" (51).

*   *   *

---

4. Shaw's socialism is discussed in Paul A. Hummert, *Bernard Shaw's Marxian Romance*; Harry Morrison, *The Socialism of Bernard Shaw*; and Eric Bentley, *Bernard Shaw*.

On *Mrs Warren's Profession*

ANONYMOUS

[Review of *Mrs Warren's Profession*]†

'The lid' was lifted by Mr Arnold Daly and 'the limit' of stage indecency reached last night in the Garrick Theater in the performance
of one of Mr George Bernard Shaw's 'unpleasant comedies' called
Mrs Warren's Profession.

'The limit of indecency' may seem pretty strong words, but they
are justified by the fact that the play is morally rotten. It makes no
difference that some of the lines may have been omitted and others
toned down; there was superabundance of foulness left. The whole
story of the play, the atmosphere surrounding it, the incidents, the
personalities of the characters are wholly immoral and degenerate.
The only way successfully to expurgate *Mrs Warren's Profession* is to
cut the whole play out. You cannot have a clean pig stye. The play
is an insult to decency because—

It defends immorality.

It glorifies debauchery.

It besmirches the sacredness of a clergyman's calling.

It pictures children and parents living in calm observance of most
unholy relations.

And, worst of all, it countenances the most revolting form of
degeneracy, by flippantly discussing the marriage of brother and sister, father and daughter, and makes the one supposedly moral character of the play, a young girl, declare that choice of shame, instead
of poverty is eminently right.

These things cannot be denied. They are the main factors of the
story. Without them there would be no play. It is vileness and degeneracy brazenly considered. If New York's sense of shame is not
aroused to hot indignation at this theatrical insult, it is indeed in a
sad plight.

[There follows a summary of the story of the play.]

† From an unsigned review in the *New York Herald* (October 31, 1905), p. 3. Reprinted in
T. F. Evans, ed., *George Bernard Shaw, The Cultural History* (London: Routledge, 1997).

Does not this literary muck leave a bad taste in the mouth? Does it not insult the moral intelligence of New York theater-goers and outrage the decency of the New York stage?

There was not one redeeming feature about it last night, not one ray of sunshine, of cleanliness, to lighten up the moral darkness of situation and dialogue; not the semblance of a moral lesson pointed. As Letchmere says of his family in *Letty*,[1] 'We are rotten to the core', and the same might be said of the characters in *Mrs Warren's Profession*.

The play was well acted from a technical standpoint by Mr Daly as Frank, Miss Shaw as Mrs Warren, and others of the cast; but while that is ordinarily cause for praise in a performance, it constituted an added sin to last night's production, for the better it was acted the more the impurity and degeneracy of the characters, the situations and the lines were made apparent. There were a few slight excisions made in the play as written, but what was left filled the house with the ill odor of evil suggestion, where it was not blatantly immoral.

After the third act Mr Daly came before the curtain and made a speech in which he rather floundered as though he had forgotten what was committed to memory. He said that the play should only be seen by grown up people who could not be corrupted. Children might be kept to the old fashioned moral illusions, including Santa Claus and Washington.

'We have many theaters', he went on, 'devoted to plays appealing to the romanticist or child—New York has even provided a hippodrome for such. But surely there should be room in New York for at least one theater devoted to truth, however disagreeable truth may appear.

'This play is not presented as an entertainment, but as a dramatic sermon and an exposé of a social condition and an evil, which our purists attempt to ignore, and by ignoring, allow it to gain strength. If Mr Comstock devoted half the energy and time to providing soft beds, sweet food and clean linen to the poor of New York that he does to the suppression of postal cards, we would have less immorality, for the logical reason that virtue would be robbing vice of its strongest features and attractiveness—comfort and health.

'It is a strange but true thing that everybody who has written to the newspapers, asking that this play be suppressed, has concluded the letter with the quaint statement, "I know the play should be suppressed, although, of course, I have not read the book". God has gifted these mortals with strange powers, indeed.

---

1. A play by A.[rthur] W.[ing] Pinero, produced in 1903 [*Editor*].

'If public opinion forces this theater to close and this play to be withdrawn, it will be a sad commentary indeed upon twentieth century so-called civilization and our enlightened new country'.

Then Mr Daly retired amid vociferous applause from the double distilled Shawites present and the speculators who had tickets for sale for to-night—if there is to be any to-night for the play.

TRACY C. DAVIS

Apprenticeship as a Playwright†

*   *   *

Shaw's third full-length play was considered unproducible for very different reasons. *Mrs Warren's Profession* deals with the sociological dimensions of sexual prostitution, questioning just what the precise nature of prostitution is in a society where women have so few economic choices. Shaw refused to comply with the Victorian conventions for writing about bad women and dispensing with their ruined souls, mixing up the brothel keeper Mrs Warren's reconciliation with her university-educated daughter Vivie both structurally and circumstantially, and portraying Vivie's decision to make an absolute break from her mother because living idly on her wealth would make her complicit with the reprehensible exploitation that propelled her mother into prostitution in the first place. The play is about the women and men behind the gorgeous magdalens and sallow wretches of the stage and literature. The Lord Chamberlain, official licensor of drama in England, refused to sanction the play for performance. It was eventually seen by a private audience at the Stage Society in 1902 and in an ill-fated American production in 1905, but did not overcome the licence prohibition in Britain or France for several decades.

For Victorians prostitution was a topic almost as urgent, taboo, and politically heated as AIDS is in the 1990s. The spread of venereal disease made prostitution of urgent concern to the military, resulting in several Contagious Diseases Acts allowing the routine forced examination and hospitalization of women in proximity to various barracks towns. The taboo on discussing prostitution in polite society resulted in an ingenious set of theatrical codes allowing "a woman with a past" and "a fallen woman" to precisely signal indiscretions without having to mention sex. Shaw is even more circumspect. He

† From *George Bernard Shaw and the Socialist Theatre* (Westport, CT: Greenwood Press, 1994), pp. 44–55. Copyright © 1994 by Tracy C. Davis. Reprinted by permission of the publisher.

never uses the word prostitute or even a synonym. Mrs Warren communicates her chosen profession by describing how, when she was
young, her sister Lizzie simply vanished until she serendipitously
reappeared at the bar where Mrs Warren was employed: "One cold,
wretched night, when I was so tired I could hardly keep myself
awake, who should come up for a half of Scotch but Lizzie, in a long
fur cloak, elegant and comfortable, with a lot of sovereigns in her
purse" (*Collected Plays with their Prefaces* 3: 66). This is sufficient
to communicate to Vivie that her aunt was a prostitute and her
mother an instant recruit. Later, Mrs Warren's advancement to
becoming an owner of many houses on the Continent is signaled by
Vivie, who calls attention to the unspeakability of the "two infamous
words that describe what my mother is"—brothel keeper—which she
scrawls but never utters (*CPP* 3: 94–99).

The subject of prostitution was highly relevant to millions of Victorian women whose financial means were insufficient to allow them
to survive in comfort or even provide what was necessary for basic
sustenance. Prostitutes were very visible and available everywhere
except the most reform-oriented family suburbs, at prices that
matched virtually every pocketbook. It is the latter point that Shaw
takes up most vigorously in the play. Instead of trying to justify Mrs
Warren's choices or dramatize the consequence of her infamy, he
puts the subject forward like a writer of Fabian tracts, emphasizing
the similarities between prostitution and other types of business
speculations, with the consequences of poor pay and high unem-
ployment. He condemns the economic system where women find
their best (and perhaps only) avenue to riches (and perhaps survival)
through their sexuality. Mrs Warren's stepsisters perished by making
respectable choices, one the victim of lead poisoning and the other
the wife of an alcoholic labourer whose eighteen shillings a week was
insufficient to support three children. Lizzie was wiser.

> MRS WARREN   When she saw I'd grown up good-looking she
> said to me across the bar "What are you doing there, you little
> fool? wearing out your health and your appearance for other
> people's profit!" Liz was saving money then to take a house
> for herself in Brussels; and she thought we two could save
> faster than one. . . . where can a woman get the money to save
> in any other business? . . . Of course, if youre a plain woman
> and cant earn anything more; or if you have a turn for music,
> or the stage, or newspaper-writing: thats different. But nei-
> ther Liz nor I had any turn for such things: all we had was
> our appearance and our turn for pleasing men. Do you think
> we were such fools as to let other people trade in our good
> looks by employing us as shopgirls, or barmaids, or waitresses,

when we could trade in them ourselves and get all the profits instead of starvation wages? Not likely. (*CPP* 3: 67)[1]

For Mrs Warren, prostitution is a business decision, not a lustful fall: she goes into it as an exercise of choice, not a consequence of seduction.

Shaw sets up for discussion the conflicts prostitution creates among women, pitting the working-class pragmatist Mrs Warren against the analytically minded mathematician Vivie has become in ignorance of her mother's livelihood and friends. Vivie does not make moral judgements, and acknowledges the wisdom of her mother's decision. What she cannot live with is the fact that her mother continues to pursue and expand her businesses despite her wealth, and that her own allowance is from the fruits of this trade. Even her Cambridge University scholarship—the one aspect of her support not devolving from prostitution—came from an equally heinous enterprise. Her mother's business partner cuts her to the quick with this revelation: "Do you remember your Crofts scholarship at Newnham? Well, that was founded by my brother the M.P. [Member of Parliament] He gets his 22 per cent out of a factory with 600 girls in it, and not one of them getting wages enough to live on" (*CPP* 3: 83–84). By never having questioned the sources of her wealth and advantages, Vivie finds herself just as reprehensible as her mother and the Croftses.

This is precisely the anagnorisis[2] Trench reached in *Widowers' Houses*: Trench and Vivie each encounter male investors utterly comfortable with their complicity in degrading the powerless, and realize that they too gain by accepting profits other than from their own labour. The difference is that Trench is squeamish on moral grounds while Vivie sees the matter more systemically. She resolves to break from the whole system, including all remnants of "family." Vivie accepts a partnership in the actuarial office of Honoria Fraser and devotes herself to work. Presumably this profession is Shaw's deliberate choice: actuaries statistically predict calamity, but they do not directly profit from or deal with its occurrence. Vivie becomes part of the competent administrative middle class Fabians needed for bringing about social change.

The social and educational advantages that qualify Vivie to take her place with Honoria are silently counterpointed to Mrs Warren's partnership with Lizzie years before. Vivie writes to Honoria announcing that she is penniless and Honoria unquestioningly takes her in, a circumstance not unlike the brothel keeper's relationship

---

1. Compare the poem by Thomas Hardy, "The Ruined Maid," *The Norton Anthology of English Literature*, 7th ed., vol. II (New York: W. W. Norton, 2000), p. 1938 [*Editor*].
2. Recognition leading to denouement [*Editor*].

to new recruits. The apt similarities that J. Ellen Gainor discovers between mother and daughter would astound and appall Vivie:

> Both first went into partnership with another woman already established in the business, who showed them the desirability, profitability, and suitability for themselves of the field. And both women operate within the patriarchal structure, Vivie and Honoria organizing their office along traditional hierarchical lines, with a male clerk and with no mention of their partnership as in any way distinct from that of other businessmen's, and Mrs Warren, enmeshed in a capitalist, profit-making network recognized by, but not discussed in, good society.[3]

Vivie can take up a respectable occupation which relies on her intellectual capacities, but the mentoring relationship between Honoria and Vivie, like Mrs Warren and her "girls," is salient even though Shaw refrains from having them say so.

Shaw does not portray Vivie as an unequivocal heroine. She rejects the sensuality, frivolity, and pretence of her mother's life and friends but proclaims her similarities with respect to devotion to work and making more money than is strictly necessary. As Germaine Greer asks, "The mystery remains—what is prostitution? What is it more than practicing upon sexuality for gain? It need not involve indiscriminacy, or even sexual intercourse, or even money, but simply gain."[4] She sees this as a failing in Shaw's analysis:

> It is not vice at its worst or virtue at its best which exploits men and women, but the profit motive, which is indifferent to ethics and has no sex at all. Shaw could get no nearer the correct etiology of whoredom than the feeble Fabian diagnosis that women were overworked, undervalued and underpaid so that they were powerfully tempted to a way of life falsely represented as easier.[5]

Greer reflects first-and second-wave feminists' concern with meticulously documenting the interconnectedness between prostitution and marriage. Frank Gardner's hopeless suit for Vivie's hand reverses the usual situation, for he would be "kept" by Vivie and (he presumes) her mother's money. The effect rendered by Shaw is substantially comic rather than political. Ultimately, *Mrs Warren's Profession* is not about sex or even sexual politics. Prostitution is a metaphor for the Fabian "law of rent": all capitalist production is like rent in that it produces a differential advantage of one social

3. J. Ellen Gainor, *Shaw's Daughters: Dramatic and Narrative Constructions of Gender* (Ann Arbor: University of Michigan Press, 1992), p. 38.
4. Germaine Greer, "A Whore in Every Home," in *Fabian Feminist: Bernard Shaw and Woman*, ed. Rodelle Weintraub (University Park: Pennsylvania State University Press, 1977), p. 165.
5. Ibid., p. 166.

group over another, and the exercise of this control is at everyone's expense.

On documentary criteria, *Mrs Warren's Profession* adds a new perspective to Victorian discussions of prostitution. Josephine Butler's campaigns against the "instrumental rape" of the Contagious Diseases Acts claimed much attention in the 1880s and resulted in repeal in 1886. Just as Butler's Ladies' National Association was settling this old offence, William Stead's sensational newspaper articles likened London to a modern Babylon, where the purchase of young girls was as pervasive and reprehensible as the eighteenth-century slave trade. This provided a focus for more politically conservative reformers who believed there was a "white slave trade" among Britain, Europe, the Middle East, and North America.[6] By comparison, Shaw's evidence and tactics are mild and fulfill his preference for "pure philosophy" over "mere news."[7] His artistic achievements, apart from refining his skill at plotting and dialogue writing, include inventing a modified type of the stage prostitute (Mrs Warren) and rejecting moral stances, which for a British dramatist was revolutionary.

*   *   *

---

6. Shaw supported Stead's stance until it was revealed that he had misrepresented the facts. Stead was convicted. See Judith R. Walkowitz, *City of Dreadful Delight: Narratives of Sexual Danger in Late-Victorian London* (Chicago: University of Chicago Press, 1992).
7. Weintraub, *The Unexpected Shaw*, p. 127.

On *Man and Superman*

G. K. CHESTERTON

[Review of *Man and Superman*]†

I wrote last week some rambling remarks about how often scientific men treat from the outside, as oddities, things which they could treat from the inside as ordinary human tendencies. And, oddly enough, I find this very error in the best book that is likely to come out for some time, Mr Bernard Shaw's new play, *Man and Superman*. To attack the play would require a volume, and to praise it a library: I have no intention of doing either. It is concerned, as most people know, with the idea that a man and a woman marry, or should marry, chiefly to produce the higher type—the Superman. The hero is an anti-marriage philosopher, who is forced into marriage by the Life-force, and seems to me, I admit, to be simply doing artificially what most people do naturally. But I do not want to write about that now. The passage that reminded me of the scientists comes in the delightful 'Revolutionist's Handbook' at the end of the play. It is too long to quote, but the keynote may be given in the sentence: 'The modern gentleman who is too lazy to daub his face with vermilion as a symbol of bravery employs a laundress to daub his shirt with starch as a symbol of cleanliness'. Now, I should put this exactly the other way round. I should say that the same noble instinct to pay a ritual respect to others which we obey when we wear white linen might be seen in the savage when he paints his face a beautiful red. He thinks the gentleman a savage. I simply think the savage a gentleman. He says, 'Look at this vermilion and this starch. We have always been barbarous'. I say, 'Look at this starch and this vermilion. We have always been civilized'.

It is the same, of course, throughout the passage. Mr Shaw says that our medical cures are as much hocus-pocus as the old necromancy or miracle. I should say rather that most of our cures are what theirs were and professed to be, faith cures. He would think modern national feeling as brutal as that of a tribe: I should say the tribe had

† From the *Daily News* (August 22, 1903), p. 8.

all the folly and all the heroism of a nation. But the real difference between us requires a broader statement.

I feel that in this fascinating and delightful play Mr Shaw has betrayed and embodied at last his one mistake. He has always prided himself on seeing things and men as they are. He has never really done so: as one might have guessed from his not admiring them. The truth is that he has all the time been silently comparing humanity with something that was not human, with a monster from Mars, with the Wise Man of the Stoics, with Julius Caesar, with Siegfried, with the Superman. But that is not seeing things as they are. It is not seeing things as they are to think first of a Briarius with a hundred hands and then see man as a cripple. It is not seeing things as they are to think first of an Argus with a hundred eyes and then look at the man in the street as if he were a man with one eye. It is not seeing things as they are to imagine a demi-god of complete mental clarity and then see all men as idiots. And this is what Mr Shaw has always secretly done. When we really see men as they are, we do not criticise, but worship; and very rightly. For a creature with miraculous eyes and miraculous thumbs, with strange dreams in his skull and a queer tenderness in his heart for this place or that baby, is really a stupendous and splendid thing. It is the quite arbitrary and priggish habit of comparison that makes us look down on ordinary things; not the facts of the case. It is the fact that every instant of conscious life is an unimaginable marvel. It is the fact that every face in the street has the incredible unexpectedness of a fairy tale. Mr Shaw, in the tone of this play, falls in some degree at least into the great weakness of his master, Nietzsche, which was the strange notion that the greater and stronger a man was, the more he would scorn common men. The greater and stronger a man is, the more he would feel an inclination to worship a periwinkle. That Mr Shaw finds democracy a failure, patriotism an imposture, love a debauch, chivalry a lie, family feeling a fiction, all this does not convince me (though there is a truth in all of it) that he has seen things as they are. But suppose I were to meet Mr Shaw in the street, and he did not see me because he was looking at his feet. And suppose as I drew near I heard him murmuring to himself, 'What are these two beautiful and industrious beings that I see always when I look at the ground, advancing, first one and then the other? What reason have they for serving me? What fairy godmother bade them come trotting out of elf-land when I was made? What god of the borderland have I to propitiate with fire and wine lest they suddenly run away with me? Let me erect an altar to the God of Legs'. Very likely Mr Shaw would run into a lamp-post. But I should know he was seeing things as they are.

And here comes in what is perhaps the most interesting of all the

bewilderingly interesting things that Mr Shaw talks about in 'The
Revolutionist's Handbook' appended to this play—the question of
'progress'—'this goose-cackle about progress' as he calls it. He says
that it is overwhelmingly probable that there has been no progress
since the Greek age. Without going adequately into that side issue,
I will admit it is highly possible that there has not. But then comes
in the most interesting and abysmal difference between the deduc-
tions we draw. Mr Shaw says: 'Man as he is, never will nor can add
a cubit to his stature by any of its quackeries'. Therefore, Mr Shaw
infers, let us breed some bigger, braver, wiser animal with all speed,
for the present condition is unbearable. I say 'If man will not progress
he will stop as he is, in which state I find him very delightful'. This
is not because I have any illusions about what he is. It is simply a
matter of taste—like being fond of cats. But what Mr Shaw has to
understand is that there is such a thing as being fond of humanity.
Not wishing to make it better, like a Sunday school teacher. Not
thinking it the only rational object of service, like a positivist philosopher. Not being sorry for its brute pains, like any decent man with
a dying rat. But being powerfully and incurably fond of the old unaltered, fighting, beer-drinking, creed-making, child-loving, affectionate, selfish, unreasonable, respectable man. That is Christianity; that
is democracy; and they can neither of them be failures, for they are
purely spiritual and no one can reckon what difference they have
made to the spirit. The whole issue is whether we see in this two-
legged man a positive marvel or a negative result. Whitman loved
him; Nietzsche detested him. Christ, when He was founding a
Universal Church, chose, and that Church chose after Him, for its
head neither the brilliant Paul nor the mystic John, but a fool, a
boaster, a coward, a liar, a snob, a denier of the truth—in short, an
ordinary man. And upon that rock He has built His Church, and the
gates of hell shall not prevail against it.

It would seem odd to compare Mr Shaw to the meanest sort of
Christian apologists. But this way of speaking of human improvement affects me very much in the same way as the attempts that the
religious sometimes make to badger the sceptic into a faith in immortality. One set of people says, 'If there be a hereafter, we are lost'.
Mr Shaw says, 'If there be no Superman, we are lost'. I beg respectfully, and without undue egoism, to state that I am not lost. I hope
and think there is a future for the soul; I hope and think there is a
future for the race; I hope there will be a Superman—it might be
fun. But nothing will induce me to say that a child or a brass band
or a baked potato are bad because there are not other things that
would be good. If the Superman descends on us I think it will be
while we are praising these things—while we are on the crest of the
ancient ecstasies. And if he does not, I shall not lose much sleep.

He may be impossible; that does not touch what interests me most. I am not impossible; that is sufficiently extraordinary.

JOHN A. BERTOLINI

Fatherhood and the Self, or the Philosophy of Comedy†

In *Caesar and Cleopatra*, Shaw had confronted one of the main elements that defined how he conceived of his playwrighting self: his relationship to Shakespeare. He dealt with the burden of Shakespeare's influence by writing a play that seemed to precede Shakespeare's Cleopatra play (and his Caesar play for that matter). Shaw also took certain structural motifs, like the putting on of Cleopatra's robe and crown and her helping Antony with his armor, and copied them, but in reverse order, as if to claim sameness (that is equality) and difference (that is originality) in the contest with Shakespeare. Even more important was Shaw's characterization of Caesar and his figuration of himself in that characterization. Shaw portrayed Caesar in such a complex way, constantly juxtaposing Caesar's exceptional ideals with his human foibles, not merely to show that heroes are human, but rather in order to make Caesar's ethics subject to the closest scrutiny, so that audiences may not applaud his abjuration of vengeance in a complacent way, but accept them as they may in full awareness of the difficulties, dangers, and consequences of such an ethic.

Presenting an issue in such a way will become gradually crucial to Shaw's conception of drama, until he repudiates the notion that any one character in his plays is right about any given problem, and states that repudiation as a principle of his dramatic art in the Epistle Dedicatory to *Man and Superman*, where he says of his various characters: "They are all right from their several points of view; and their points of view are, for the dramatic moment, mine also." The way in which Shaw undercuts Caesar's claim on the audience's admiration by emphasizing his tendencies toward vanity and posturing while simultaneously emphasizing Cleopatra's growing maturity had been rehearsed in *Arms and the Man* in Shaw's characterization of Bluntschli as an apparently wise, practical realist, superior to the romance-sodden idealists, Raina and Sergius Saranoff, but in reality

† From *The Playwrighting Self of Bernard Shaw* (Carbondale: Southern Illinois University Press, 1991), pp. 27–57. Copyright © 1991 by the Board of Trustees, Southern Illinois University. Reprinted by permission of the publisher.

an adventure-loving romantic who succeeds in suppressing his true self only part of the time.

In *Man and Superman*, Caesar will be replaced by Tanner as the character who seems to espouse Shaw's principles only to trip over their implementation, especially when Ann Whitefield places an obstacle in his path. And Caesar the author who allows the Library of Alexandria to burn as a figuration of Shaw the writer ambivalent about writing will be replaced by Tanner the author who thinks books will be his only children only to find out that he had mistaken his destiny. In place of Cleopatra the deflator of Caesar's enlarged self-image, Ann Whitefield will play the other side of the true author, always in possession of the knowledge that gives her control over others, knowledge that she keeps secret or reveals in order to maneuver Jack Tanner into the positions she requires for the fulfillment of her will. Moreover, insofar as Shaw cites Shakespeare as a precedent for the innovative reversed love chase whereby Don Juan instead of pursuing women is pursued by them (as if Shaw really needed any precedent besides Mozart-Da Ponte),[1] Shaw continues his competition with Shakespeare into the sphere of romantic comedy. In the Epistle Dedicatory, Shaw remakes Shakespeare's heroines in Ann's image: "In Shakespear's plays the woman always takes the initiative" (Rosalind, Mariana, Helena). In doing so, Shaw repeats the strategy he used in rewriting Shakespeare's *Antony and Cleopatra* as *Caesar and Cleopatra*; he claims equality (my heroine resembles Shakespeare's) and he claims originality (Shakespeare's heroines resemble Ann). But Shaw feels less anxious about his status vis-à-vis Shakespeare, after having written *Caesar and Cleopatra*.

Man and Superman as a whole eludes both comprehensive understanding and simple analysis for several reasons. For one thing its very bigness repels categorical analysis, notwithstanding the apparent straightforwardness of its "trumpery story of London life" (as Shaw with calculated deprecation put it). For another thing, it is the most allusive of all Shaw's plays, invoking as it does almost the history of comic drama and requiring the reader (audience) to recall such disparate inspirations as Aristophanes' *The Birds*, Molière's *The Misanthrope*, and Sheridan's *The Duenna*, not to mention the philosophical underpinning of the play from Nietzsche and Schopenhauer, or the whole Don Juan tradition in literature.[2] Yet, for all its bigness, the play has a unifying theme that I take to be generation in the largest sense and more specifically fatherhood—fatherhood of all kinds, spiritual, biological, and philosophical, literary, political. Shaw's central preoccupation with generation and fatherhood, I

---

1. Mozart composed the score and Da Ponte the libretto for the opera *Don Giovanni* [*Editor*].
2. Don Juan is the archetypal rake: aristocratic, hedonistic, amoral [*Editor*].

believe, can account not only for the dramaturgy of the play but also for its extraordinarily allusive dimension, and hence the unity of purpose that went into the making of the play.

The Epistle Dedicatory

The Epistle Dedicatory ostensibly explains to Arthur Bingham Walkley how *Man and Superman* came into being with its peculiar characteristics as a Don Juan play. Shaw first proffers the explanation that Walkley asked him why he did not write a Don Juan play, as if it were somehow remiss of Shaw not to have done so, or else that it were natural that he should have done so. Shaw goes on to assign responsibility for the play to Walkley, calling it "your play" and even asserting that Walkley must "justify its influence on the young," as if the play functioned in a parent-model way. In one sense, Shaw presents Walkley as the real author of the play, a shadow version of Shaw himself. He refers to Walkley and himself thus: "As twin pioneers of the New Journalism of that time, we two, cradled in the same new sheets, began an epoch in the criticism of the theatre."

In his picture of their relationship, Shaw conjoins an image of himself and Walkley as twin babies to an image of them as parents of a new era. The conjunction of the newborn and the generation of a new epoch in the first paragraph of the Epistle Dedicatory rehearses the themes of *Man and Superman* in a broad way. More subtly, Shaw portrays himself as one who evades responsibility for the product of his imagination: Walkley is the one, Shaw asserts, who knew "the force you set in motion." Moreover, Shaw dramatizes his composition of the play as a divining of Walkley's wishes rather than as producing something out of his own imagination: "But what did you want? Owing to your unfortunate habit—you now I hope, feel its inconvenience—of not explaining yourself, I have had to discover this for myself. . . . I took it that you demanded a Don Juan in the philosophic sense."[3] For the remainder of the Epistle Dedicatory,

---

3. Shaw habitually represents his writer's role as that of passive amanuensis to the life force. Cf. the Postscript to *Back to Methuselah*, where Shaw says: "I do not regard my part in the production of my books and plays as much greater than that of an amanuensis or organ-blower. An author is in the grip of Creative Evolution, and may find himself starting a movement to which in his own little person he is intensely opposed. When I am writing I never invent a plot: I let the play write itself and shape itself, which it always does even when up to the last moment I do not foresee the way out. Sometimes I do not see what the play was driving at until quite a long time after I have finished it; and even then I may be wrong about it just as any critical third party may." Clearly, Shaw has Milton's "celestial patroness, who deigns / Her nightly visitation unimplored, / And dictates to me slumb'ring, or inspires / Easy my unpremeditated verse" (*Paradise Lost*, IX, 21–24). In the Epistle Dedicatory he pictures himself as simply interpreting the mysterious Walkley's wishes. Shaw's general critical principle here seems to anticipate D. H. Lawrence's more famous formulation: "The artist usually sets out—or used to—to point a moral and adorn a tale. The tale, however points the other way as a rule. Two blankly opposing morals, the artist's and the tale's. Never trust the artist. Trust the tale. The proper function of the

Shaw wavers between assigning responsibility for the play to Walkley and accepting it himself.

The point I am driving at is that the Epistle Dedicatory enacts a drama within Shaw the author that is analogous to the drama within Tanner. In the course of the play, Tanner does everything he can to escape becoming a father until he discovers "a father's heart" within himself, while in the course of the Epistle Dedicatory, Shaw discovers his author's identity. Shaw's fictive ambivalence toward his own creation grows more pronounced as he continues the letter to Walkley. After explaining the kind of Don Juan the twentieth century has forced him to write, Shaw forgets Walkley's role temporarily and starts referring to his own role in the delineating of Don Juan's character and in the writing of the play: he speaks of "my attempt to bring him [Don Juan] up to date," and of his "thrusting into my perfectly modern three-act play a totally extraneous act in which my hero, enchanted by the air of the Sierra, has a dream." For the moment, then, the play and the character of Don Juan, are now Shaw's creation. But almost immediately after, Shaw reverts to presenting his role as secondary, claiming that he has "no control" "over the essence of the play." He portrays himself as a mere *distiller* of the dramatic substance *propounded* by Walkley: "I am merely executing your commission." Furthermore, when Shaw eventually summarizes the nature of his Don Juan, he makes both Walkley and himself the parents of Don Juan within the same sentence: "And so *your* Don Juan has come to *birth* as a stage projection of the tragic-comic love chase of the man by the woman; and *my* Don Juan is the quarry instead of the huntsman" (italics mine). The singularity of the sentence epitomizes the ambiguous sense of the play's parentage, which Shaw elegantly conveys. The Epistle Dedicatory seems to ask: Who has generated the play, Walkley or Shaw? Who is its real father?

From this point on, Shaw stops blaming Walkley for the play's existence, and strengthens his acceptance of responsibility for the play; hence, references to his having "made my Don Juan a political pamphleteer." By the end of the Epistle, Shaw has fairly well dispensed with Walkley altogether: he laments that, amid the loud reactions to *Man and Superman*, Walkley's "voice should be dedicated to silence." What produces Shaw's change of attitude, as I see it, is a twofold defining: first Shaw defines his conception of literature, and then he defines his Don Juan as a writer, an author: Shaw ascribes the generation of literature to "the struggle of life to become divinely conscious of itself"; and in the Act III dream sequence, when

---

critic is to save the tale from the artist who created it." See *Selected Literary Criticism*, ed. Anthony Beal (New York: Viking Press, 1966), 297; the quotation comes from "The Spirit of Place," in *Studies in Classic American Literature*, 1924.

Don Juan finally defines how he conceives of existence and the purpose of life, Shaw makes him use the same language Shaw himself had used: "I tell you that as long as I can conceive something better than myself I cannot be easy unless I am striving to bring it into existence or clearing the way for it. . . . That is the working within me of Life's incessant aspiration to higher organization, wider, deeper, intenser self-consciousness, and clearer self-understanding."

The paradoxical and ineffable quality of such striving whispers beneath the spatial metaphor that seeks to express it. Centrifugal in its nature, the force seems to expand in all directions from within the person of Don Juan. Simultaneously the image connects Don Juan with Goethe's Faust, who starts in a high-vaulted, narrow Gothic chamber and ends with a project to beat back the sea from the land, to open free living space for the millions, he whose salvation lay in continual striving, never asking the moment to linger. Shaw has imbued his Don Juan with Faustian striving.[4]

In defining the nature of his Faustian Don Juan, Shaw also creates his own sense of himself as a writer-father, of his generative powers as an author. One of his best jokes in the Epistle Dedicatory is his defense of the Revolutionist's Handbook as part of the volume *Man and Superman*. He informs Walkley that he has given him Tanner's political "pamphlet in full by way of appendix" (the dead metaphor in "appendix" revives when we realize that Shaw thinks of his work as a living organism), and goes on to explain:

> I am sorry to say that it is a common practice with romancers to announce their hero as a man of extraordinary genius, and then leave his works entirely to the reader's imagination; so that at the end of the book you whisper to yourself ruefully that but for the author's solemn preliminary assurance you should hardly have given the gentleman credit for ordinary good sense. You cannot accuse me of this *pitiable barrenness*, this feeble evasion. I not only tell you that my hero wrote a revolutionists' handbook: I give you the handbook at full length for your edification if you care to read it. (italics mine)

Shaw's assertion here of his authorial fecundity might seem to suggest authorial maternity rather than paternity, but elsewhere in *Back to Methuselah*, Part II, Shaw makes Franklyn Barnabas apply the idea of barrenness conditionally to Adam: "If he had killed Eve he would have been lonely and barren to all eternity."

A further defense of the Revolutionist's Handbook leads Shaw to formulate a central principle of his dramatic art, a principle that emphasizes his identity as the father-author:

4. Faust receives power and riches in this world in exchange for damnation in eternity [*Editor*].

And in that handbook you will find the politics of the sex question as I conceive Don Juan's descendant to understand them. Not that I disclaim the fullest responsibility for his opinions and for those of all my characters, pleasant and unpleasant. They are all right from their several points of view; and their points of view are, for the dramatic moment, mine also. This may puzzle the people who believe that there is such a thing as an absolutely right point of view, usually their own. It may seem to them that nobody who doubts this can be in a state of grace. However that may be, it is certainly true that nobody who agrees with them can possibly be a dramatist, or indeed anything else that turns upon a knowledge of mankind. Hence it has been pointed out that Shakespear had no conscience. Neither have I, in that sense.

The father-author accepts responsibility for his children-characters by asserting their right to be discrete selves and not merely mouthpieces for Shaw's opinions. Shaw goes further by implicitly disclaiming the notion that any one character expresses Shaw's own point of view, or even that any one character is right in his opinions. Shaw as dramatic artist is not a propagandist for a particular point of view.[5] The authenticity of Shaw's feelings in this regard comes through shiningly in his subsequent estimation of the significance and worth of his dramatic productions:

I first prove that anything I write on the relation of the sexes is sure to be misleading; and then I proceed to write a Don Juan play. Well, if you insist on asking me why I behave in this absurd way, I can only reply that you asked me to, and that in any case my treatment of the subject may be valid for the artist, amusing to the amateur, and at least intelligible and therefore possibly suggestive to the Philistine. Every man who records his illusions is providing data for the genuinely scientific psychology which the world still waits for. I plank down my view of the existing relations of men to women in the most highly civilized society for what it is worth. It is a view like any other view and no more, neither true nor false, but, I hope, a way of looking at the subject which throws into the familiar order of cause and effect a sufficient body of fact and experience to be interesting to you, if not to the playgoing public of London.

That Shaw by this stage of the argument in the Epistle Dedicatory conceives of himself as a writer-father comes out clearly but oddly in the kinds of images he uses to describe his past and also explains

5. In "Don Juan, Freud and Shaw in Hell: A Freudian Reading of *Man and Superman*," *Shaw Review* 22 (1979), 58–78, Daniel J. Leary argues that the speeches of the characters represent "conflicting aspects of the dramatist's psyche" (63). I am indebted to this excellent article in many ways.

why he feels compelled to acknowledge his literary forebears. For example, he describes Henry Straker as "an intentional dramatic sketch of the contemporary *embryo* of Mr H. G. Wells's anticipation of the efficient engineering class," and he ascribes the idea for Mendoza Ltd. "to a certain West Indian colonial secretary, who, at a period when he and I and Mr Sidney Webb were *sowing our political wild oats* . . . recommended Webb . . . to form himself into a company" (italics mine). The inventory Shaw then draws up of his artistic and literary fathers—"Bunyan, Blake, Hogarth and Turner (these four apart and above all the English classics), Goethe, Shelley, Schopenhauer, Wagner, Ibsen, Morris, Tolstoy and Nietzsche"—has been made possible by Shaw's discovery and acceptance of his own identity as a generative writer. When Shaw later wrote a foreword to a popular edition of *Man and Superman* (1911), he revealed the imaginative centrality of generativeness in his play. He wrote summarily of the Don Juan in Hell scene's significance as follows: "The third act, however fantastic its legendary framework may appear, is a careful attempt to write a new Book of Genesis for the Bible of Evolutionists."

It is as if Shaw's sense of connectedness with a literary tradition enables him to write the play *Man and Superman*, to become a fully mature author himself. His apprenticeship has ended; he is no longer Eugene Marchbanks. He is willing to write a work that competes with Goethe's *Faust* in its attempt to present an account in dramatic form and in cosmic terms of the purpose of human existence, the direction of human destiny. Moreover, having been generated himself by writing, he can now generate writing that in turn generates other texts. In that sense the Epistle Dedicatory[6] generates the first two acts of *Man and Superman*, where Tanner tries frantically to evade his destiny to become a husband and father, which in turn generates the dream sequence of Act III, where Tanner sees his connectedness with his "famous ancestor" (as Ann so labels Don Juan), just as Shaw sees his connectedness with his literary ancestors.

The dream sequence in turn again makes possible the fourth act where Tanner magnificently surrenders after a frenzied struggle and embraces fatherhood. The play ends with Ann's soothing, proud-motherish, consolatory gesture, "Never mind her, dear. Go on talking." Her suggestion then generates the Revolutionist's Handbook, which is, of course, Tanner "talking." Therefore, the very structure of the volume *Man and Superman* embodies the concept of generation in a kind of genetic chain of texts, a chain that does not, however, exactly break, or end, or even form itself into a circle. Before

6. Shaw's calling the piece an Epistle Dedicatory rather than a Preface (making *Man and Superman* unique among Shaw's plays in this regard) stresses the continuity between his play and Restoration drama.

dividing itself into a second part (Maxims for Revolutionists), the Revolutionist's Handbook offers this concluding reflection of Tanner's on writing's efficacy in the real world:

> It is idle for an individual writer to carry so great a matter further in a pamphlet. A conference on the subject is the next step needed. It will be attended by men and women who, no longer believing that they can live forever, are seeking some immortal work into which they can build the best of themselves before their refuse is thrown into that arch dust destructor, the cremation furnace.

The "great matter" is the breeding of the Superman which, for Shaw, if not for Tanner (who is more literal-minded), is shorthand for the necessity of changing the world for the better. In short, the next link in the chain of generating texts that makes up *Man and Superman* must be forged by men and women in life. The emphatic position occupied by this passage, ending the discursive section of the Revolutionist's Handbook (section X, The Verdict of History), before Tanner delivers himself of the Maxims for Revolutionists, is significant in two ways: it explicitly points the points reader and audience toward reforming the world; and it adumbrates the destruction versus creation theme that runs all through the play, climaxes in the third-act debate between Don Juan and the Devil, and resolves itself (after a fashion) in the marriage of Jack and Ann at the end of the play. How much of himself Shaw invests in this passage can easily be seen if it is compared to the famous passage in the Epistle Dedicatory, where Shaw vehemently articulates a personal and categorical view of life:

> This is the true joy in life, the being used for a purpose recognized by yourself as a mighty one; the being thoroughly worn out before you are thrown on the scrap heap; the being a force of Nature instead of a feverish little clod of ailments and grievances complaining that the world will not devote itself to making you happy. And also the only real tragedy in life is the being used by personally minded men for purposes which you recognize to be base. All the rest is at worst mere misfortune or mortality: this alone is misery, slavery, hell on earth; and the revolt against it is the only force that offers the poor artist, whom our personally minded rich people would so willingly employ as pandar, buffoon, beauty monger, sentimentalizer and the like.

Shaw's perfervid[7] declaration here of a view of life testifies to the single-minded intensity of his courage in confronting life. The deliberately awkward construction of "the being . . ." removes the

7. Ardent [*Editor*].

personal from consideration in the long view of life, as does the generous scorn of "feverish little clod of ailments and grievances." What we normally think of as the evils of the day, Shaw diminishes grandly with "All the rest is at worst mere misfortune or mortality," the alliteration acting as an equalizer so that death becomes poor luck. What arouses Shaw's passion is the abuse of human beings by other human beings, the disregarding of Kant's categorical imperative never to treat people as means, but always as ends. Even here, however, Shaw's implicit exhortation is not to the exploiters but to the exploited not to let themselves be exploited; direct evil, in other words, is dismissed. Shaw's sense of the artist's responsibility could not be more clearly articulated and the ability to articulate his view of the artist's function as he never had before comes from the act of writing *Man and Superman*, the play which creates Shaw's identity as father-author.

The Frame Play: Act I

By "frame play" I mean Acts I, II, and IV, the story of how Jack Tanner came to marry Ann Whitefield. But "frame play" clearly misnames the three acts that surround the Don Juan in Hell scene, for the frame is larger than the picture itself. The three acts are a frame only in the sense that they border the dream sequence, and I call them so only for convenience of reference. The frame play, then, has an elegant skeletal structure: Ann Whitefield pursues Jack Tanner until he agrees to marry her. But there is a more hidden structure that becomes palpable by means of certain details that form themselves into a pattern that makes possible Jack's consenting to be Ann's husband, or rather, to father any child Ann might have.

The play begins with the death off stage of a father, Mr. Whitefield, and the presence on stage of a mock-father, Roebuck Ramsden. The plot progressively shows Tanner filling in the father's place left vacant by Mr. Whitefield, and the defeat of all rival claimants to the position of father.

As a parody father, Roebuck Ramsden appears as a figure of mechanical strength, of hard foursquareness: Shaw's description of him emphasizes his polished, bald head (which can *"heliograph orders to distant camps"*) and his feet (in slippers, but his boots are ready for him on the hearthrug); his iron-grey hair is arranged symmetrically on the sides of his face; he seems to have an authoritative bearing, a quality which Shaw mockingly singles out: *"he is marked out as a president of highly respectable men, a chairman among directors, an alderman among councillors, a mayor among aldermen."* Ramsden's identity as a father-figure comes out in several other ways. For example, he greets Octavius, with *"fatherly liking and welcome"*;

he seems to have been, like Mr. Whitefield, a substitute father for Octavius after his real father's death. From the very beginning of the play we are made conscious of a vacuum left by dead fathers. At first, we think Ramsden will fill that vacuum, later that Hector Malone, Sr., will.

Only gradually do we realize that Jack Tanner is destined to take the place of the absent fathers, for Ramsden is only a mock-father. He surrounds himself in his study with busts of his political fathers (as if some of their patriarchal luster will rub off on him),[8] John Bright and John Spencer, and with a portrait of Richard Cobden. But there is in his study another portrait that has symbolic implications, "*a family portrait of impenetrable obscurity.*" This portrait counterpoints both the busts of the recognizable political fathers, and the absent fathers, Mr. Robinson and Mr. Whitefield. The unidentifiable ancestor creates an appetite for an identifiable father, an appetite which the play will force us to feel can only be satisfied by Tanner, especially after he has figuratively overcome all the other potential fathers in the play.

Two successive questions structure the entire first act: who will become the guardian of Ann Whitefield (i.e., who will take her father's place) and who is the father of Violet's baby. Jack Tanner resolves the first question when he finally gives in (after frantic resistance) to the idea of acting as joint guardian with Ramsden. The chief reason he articulates for his adamant reluctance is analogous to Shaw's development of his own persona in the Epistle Dedicatory: there Shaw starts by avoiding the assumption of responsibility for his own work, and here Tanner refuses to accept responsibility for Ann because of his anxiety that he will have no real authority or control over her: "All she wants with me is to load up all her moral responsibilities on me, and do as she likes at the expense of my character. I cant control her; and she can compromise me as much as she likes. I might as well be her husband."

Tanner's last words here are, of course, prophetic, but the passage is more significant because of the theme of responsibility it contains. In Shaw's imagination that theme connects with reading and writing books. For example, in the Epistle Dedicatory, Shaw almost repeats Tanner's expressed fears about Ann, when Shaw talks about the creation of Ann's character in terms of his relationship with his wife: "I find in my own plays that Woman, projecting herself dramatically by my hands (a process over which I assure you I have no more real control than I have over my wife), behaves just as Woman did in the plays of Shakespear." Like Tanner looking at Ann's behavior, Shaw

---

8. The busts also link him with his infernal alter ego, the father of Dona Ana, the commander who likes being a statue because of the admiration he receives in that form. Thus, Ramsden's secret vanity is revealed.

insists that his characters have a life and will of their own that he can hardly control.

In the first act, the idea of evading responsibility connects with books in a very specific way. Tanner decides to test his authority over Ann by asking her to read his Revolutionist's Handbook. Ramsden immediately forbids her to read it and Tanner insists that Ann must choose whom she will obey, that is, to whose authority she is responsible. Mrs. Whitefield interjects at this impasse: "It is rather hard that you should put the responsibility on Ann. It seems to me that people are always putting things on other people in this world."[9] Her admonishment chastens Jack into stopping his resistance to the guardianship: "I let myself in for it; so I suppose I must face it. [*He turns away from the bookcase, and stands there, moodily studying the volumes.*]" Tanner's rueful contemplation of the books equals his attitude toward his responsibility for Ann; Shaw, by means of the stage action, therefore, enforces the subtextual connection between responsibility and books. Moreover, Tanner's professed reason for accepting his responsibility, his advising Ann's father not to name Ramsden as Ann's guardian, acknowledges implicitly his part-authorship in the writing of Mr. Whitefield's will. Of course, in Act IV he will find out that the "will" was really Ann's, for she told her father that she wanted Jack to be her guardian.

Tanner's assumption of a guardian's responsibility pushes him closer to self-discovery and accepting his destiny, as is indicated by the great and subtle comic business that follows Tanner's moody contemplation of the books. Ann, rejoicing in her victory, refers to Tanner as "Jack the Giant Killer."[1] The stage directions tell us that Ann speaks this line as "*She casts a glance at Tanner over her shoulder.*" And, in a wonderful staging echo, Tanner gives his reaction, also "[*over his shoulder, from the bookcase*] I think you ought to call me Mr Tanner." Jack's attempt to flatten Ann's flirtatious gesture at once conceals and reveals his dismay. But Ann quells him at once by threatening to call him "after your famous ancestor, Don Juan." Her ploy produces the desired result; Tanner gives in out of desperation to the name she wants to call him by (a foreshadowing of his ultimate surrender to her will): "I capitulate. I consent to Jack. I embrace Jack. Here endeth my first and last attempt to assert my authority." He speaks better than he knows, for marrying Ann is

9. In Act IV, Mrs. Whitefield again admonishes Jack about placing responsibilities on the wrong person, only this time it is herself: "So if you marry her, dont put the blame on me."

1. A. M. Gibbs points out in his excellent essay on *Man and Superman* that the play abounds in paternal figures for Tanner to defeat, and he notes particularly how Ann's calling Tanner "Jack the Giant Killer" relates to Northrop Frye's archetypal definition of New Comedy as the victory of a young man in love over a blocking figure, usually a father, or an older guardian of some kind. See *The Art and Mind of Shaw: Essays in Criticism* (New York: St. Martin's Press, 1983), 121–32.

embracing his true self, his destiny to become husband and father, though he needs to dream before he can overcome the psychic obstacles to fulfilling that destiny.

To return to the construction of Act I: the second question governing the structure of the act, who is the father of Violet's baby—like the first question, who is to take the place of Ann's father—creates the sense of a missing father and points to Tanner as a possible substitute. Shaw so constructs the action that first Jack is actually suspected of being the father of Violet's baby. Ramsden, in an attempt to get some public denunciation of Tanner's immoral character, more or less nominates him as the likeliest candidate because of his alleged libertinism ("Ramsden as good as accused me of being the unknown gentleman"). Shaw then makes Tanner assume a series of stances that ironically reveal his suitability to become what he thinks he does not want to become: a parent. First, he proclaims his respect and admiration for the role of parent: he regards Violet's supposed pregnancy, for example, as a heroic risking of "her life to create another life," and as "The fulfillment of her highest purpose and greatest function—to increase, multiply, and replenish the earth" (especially since to do so, according to Tanner, she is turning away from dabbling in the arts). Next, he dares to say with brave complacency, "If I had the honor of being the father of Violet's child, I should boast of it instead of denying it."

What Tanner thinks he is doing here is bearding the ram of conventionality in its own den, whereas he is unwittingly letting us know that fatherhood would make him proud. In what I take to be a reworking of Faust's relationship with Gretchen, Shaw has Tanner declare, as a response to Ramsden's objection to Violet's very apparent lack of remorse, "meaning a weeping Magdalen and an innocent child branded with her shame. Not in our circle, thank you. Morality can go to its father the devil." Tanner's boast is idle, because Violet is married, and would never be so human as to fall into the tragic situation Gretchen finds herself in with Faust because of her too great love for him. Beyond that, Tanner opposes himself to the kind of morality fathered by the devil, and thereby again unconsciously sets himself up as a rival father.

Tanner's wholesale deflation resulting from the revelation of Violet's marriage, the turning of his brave stances into the appearance of posturings, should not detract an iota from the value of his fatherly instincts. He simply misapplies them; that is all—comedically so, but not in any way demeaning to his essential worth. That worth gradually accrues in the duologues[2] with which Shaw intersperses the

2. I borrow the term from Andrew Kennedy, *Dramatic Duologue: The Dialogue of Personal Encounter* (Cambridge Univ. Press, 1983).

ensemble scenes in Act I. For this to be seen, Shaw's scheme for the dialogue of Act I needs to be laid out. The opening duologue of the play between Ramsden and Octavius provides exposition and starts the rhythm of intimate conversation followed by ensemble discussion with increasing numbers of participants.

Act I has four duologues: 1) Ramsden and Octavius; 2) Tanner and Ramsden; 3) Tanner and Octavius; 4) Tanner and Ann. They occur in a sequence of increasing consequentiality, concentration, intensity, and thematic density, the culmination being Tanner's long conversation with Ann, which marks itself off from the other three by being between a man and a woman and by not being (as the first three are) permutations of the possible duologues involving Tanner, Ramsden, and Octavius. Each of the duologues is followed by an ensemble discussion in which the two questions governing plot-structure (who will be Ann's guardian and who is the father of Violet's baby) are dealt with: the ensembles become progressively more heated and more complex, owing both to increased numbers of participants and the introduction of new information. The ensembles are: 1) Ramsden, Tanner, and Octavius; 2 and 3) Ann and her mother added; 4) Violet and Ramsden's sister added. All of the ensembles show Tanner's lack of skill in dealing with large groups of people, where he alternately offends, irritates, and orates. They counterpoint the duologues where he expansively displays his ideas and theories on such crucial matters as the role and nature of the artist or man as destroyer and creator.

Tanner's duologue with Ramsden chiefly demonstrates his easy provoking of Ramsden who responds with such rapid changes of tone and mood, such accelerations of anger, that Tanner seems supremely self-controlled and much the cleverer of the two. Their conversation also shows that one decade's liberal becomes the next decade's conservative, not intentionally, but simply because changes in political thinking outrun even time. Tanner's duologue with Octavius treats weighty matter, namely, the artist's work, which Tanner defines as: "To shew us ourselves as we really are. Our minds are nothing but this knowledge of ourselves; and he who adds a jot to such knowledge creates new mind as surely as any woman creates new man." Tanner here anticipates Don Juan's explanation of the purpose of Nature in evolution, striving toward greater self-knowledge, and echoes Shaw in the Epistle Dedicatory when he proposes that art results from Life's struggle "to become divinely conscious of itself." That Tanner, all through his duologue with Octavius, talks about how Ann wants to marry him, only accentuates our perception of Tanner's need for self-knowledge. But more importantly, Tanner has connected the artist's work with a parent's creation of new life. He must understand by the end of the play that the two activities help life equally in its struggle toward greater self-understanding, so that finally he can marry Ann.

Of Tanner's three duologues, the last one with Ann dramatizes with greatest clarity the essential confusions and anxieties that prevent him from seeing that he should get married, all of which he must dream through in order to resolve. In the Don Juan in Hell scene, Tanner makes the Devil into his main antagonist, the one who prevents Tanner's dream-self, Don Juan, from realizing his true self which Don Juan believes is destined to heaven. Hence, in the Act I duologue with Ann, Tanner casts her in the role of devil: he begins by addressing her as, "My dear Lady Mephistopheles"; he says she was "diabolically clever at getting through [a boy's] guard and surprising his inmost secrets"; with himself as Faust in mind, he says, "You lured me into a compact by which we were to have no secrets from one another"; he exclaims, "What a devil of a child you must have been"; and finally he confesses, "I never feel safe with you: there is a devilish charm—." Jack calls Ann many things in the play, but none with the same insistence he shows when speaking to her as if she were the Devil. He explains the reason he stopped being intimate with her as his discovery of his individual identity: "It happened just then that I got something I wanted to keep all to myself instead of sharing it with you. . . . My soul."[3] As long as Tanner conceives of Ann as diverting him from his true purpose in life, as the Devil diverts man (according to Tanner's dream-self, Don Juan), he cannot marry her. When he dreams of Dona Ana pursuing him to heaven to find a father for the superman, he can.

Aside from the idea of Ann as devil, however, the Tanner-Ann duologue contains further matter that will become important in the Don Juan in Hell scene, namely, the theme of destruction versus creation. Tanner sees himself as a destroyer of false creeds and idols, and Ann pleads that she sees no "sense in destruction," for, as she puts it, she is "too feminine" to do so. Tanner argues that she confuses "construction and destruction with creation and murder," but Ann insists that no woman will ever agree with him about the cleansing capacities of destruction. The essential debate between Don Juan and the Devil is whether man is a destroyer or a creator; hence it can be seen that the residue from Tanner's duologue with Ann furnishes the basic material for the dream sequence.

---

3. Tanner persists in associating Ann with the Devil in Act II, where he says to Straker, "Why the devil should she [Ann] come with me?" and to Ann, "What the devil do you mean by telling Rhoda that I am too vicious to associate with her?" Tanner does not use the Devil's "name to secure additional emphasis" (as the Commander does) with any other character.

Act II

The theme of self-discovery connects itself with the act of writing even in the seemingly slight second act, which in terms of plot presents Straker revealing to Tanner that Ann wants to marry him and Tanner's ensuing flight. As in Act I the thematically important material resides in the duologue between Ann and Tanner. The elaborate comedy of the act revolves around Ann's maneuverings to get herself a ride in Jack's car in place of Rhoda. By a series of brilliant contrivances, mainly happy deceptions, she gets her will: for example, by playing on Jack's antipathy toward parental authority, she provokes from him an outburst against mothers.[4] Tanner's outburst seems like his usual riding of a hobbyhorse, but it is actually his emotional conviction that children must become independent of parental authority in order to become themselves: "The man who pleads his father's authority is no man: the woman who pleads her mother's authority is unfit to bear citizens to a free people."

Tanner inevitably connects self-discovery with birth, and in Shaw's imagination the two are intertwined with the act of writing. Therefore, the nexus completes itself when Tanner urges Ann to break her chains: "learn to enjoy a fast ride in a motor car. . . . Come with me to Marseilles. . . . You can write a book about it afterwards. That will finish your mother and make a woman of you." Tanner knows that writing not only grants autonomy but kills the parent as well; what he does not know is that he is talking about himself as much as about Ann. His curious blindness to his true self and destiny is reflected in the subplot (as Shaw has contrived it) by means of Hector Malone, Jr.'s position in his marriage to Violet. Because she does not want their marriage revealed, Hector is forced to pretend that he does not know who Violet's husband is; that is, that he does not know who he himself is. As a hidden father, he is a double for Tanner.

Act III

Tanner's certainty that Ann wants him for a husband produces an anxiety attack and he frantically flees hoping to escape time: he

4. Shaw's staging of this scene for the 1907 revival of the play with Robert Loraine and Lillah McCarthy expresses Ann's perfect control of Tanner. Shaw wrote to Harley Granville-Barker about the scene: Loraine "wanted to deliver the great speech about the tyranny of mothers, enthroned in the motor car, with Lillah somewhere under the wheels with her back to the audience. I immediately saw the value of the idea and put Lillah in the car in a fascinating attitude with her breast on the driving wheel, and Loraine ranting about on the gravel." See *Collected Letters: 1898–1910*, ed. Dan H. Laurence (New York: Dodd, Mead, 1972), 690. The car in many ways represents Ann's instinctual drives with which she is consonant, as Tanner is not with his. Hence, her being in the driver's seat, directing their developing relationship, constitutes a perfect theatrical realization of the dramatic text.

orders Straker to drive him away as soon as possible, to break the speed record to Dover or Folkestone if possible. He escapes to a Shavian equivalent of Shakespeare's green worlds, the Sierra Nevada where, like all of Shakespeare's characters who flee thither, he confronts his sexual identity and the necessity of growing up. Because of what he dreams there, he can marry Ann and become a father. Before the dream itself, however, comes his encounter with Mendoza.[5] It is essential for Tanner to meet Mendoza because as a romantic lover he represents what Jack thinks he has overcome in himself, the impulse toward passionate romantic love.

Mendoza seems to be arrested at the Shakespearean *jeune-premier* stage of psychosexual development. Mendoza almost alludes to Orlando when he tells, "I am like a boy: I cut her name on the trees, and her initials on the sod" (the latter action seems to me an innovation in the tradition). He forms a trio with Hector Malone, Jr., and Octavius (Shaw calls the latter two *"Christians of the Amorist sect,"* and gives that as a reason for their getting along so well together), but there is another side to Mendoza: he is incongruously a political thinker as well as an amorist, and he is a writer. Like Tanner he is an orator, an outsider, a rebel against the existing political and social order, who believes that society misdistributes wealth horribly.[6] But unlike Tanner he believes in romantic love, and his writing is not political, it is doggerel love-poetry. Therefore Tanner needs to meet this strange version of himself. Mendoza's oddly split self forces Tanner to confront the contradictions within himself in his dream.[7]

5. Shaw claims in the Epistle Dedicatory that he took over the character of the brigand poetaster from Sir Arthur Conan Doyle, but I think Sheridan's *The Duenna* also influenced the idea for Mendoza's character. For instance there is a main character who is a Jew, named Isaac Mendoza, and who wants to marry a beautiful, young woman named Louisa, who in turn has a jealous brother. The parallels to Mendoza the Jew, his beloved Louisa Straker, and her jealous brother Henry, anxious to defend his sister's honor seem too striking to be merely coincidental. If not deliberate allusion, they would seem to be at least unconscious reworking. If deliberate, then Shaw is having a good deal of fun turning Sheridan's Mendoza, a vain fortune-hunter and mercenary opportunist, with so little regard for his Jewishness that he converts to Christianity for social advantage, into the love-sick brigand who rebels against capitalism's class system and misdistribution of wealth and who is proud of being a Jew.
6. Louis Crompton has suggested that Shaw based Mendoza partly on Milton's Satan, the setting in the Sierras on the Hellscape of *Paradise Lost*, Book I, and that the political debate among the brigands, which Mendoza supervises, on the debate in Hell among Satan and his co-rebels. See Louis Crompton, *Shaw the Dramatist* (Lincoln: Univ. of Nebraska Press, 1969), 86, 238 n. 13. I think Crompton is perfectly right, and I would only add that the topic being debated by Mendoza and his friends—"Have Anarchists or Social-Democrats the most personal courage?"—exquisitely and knowledgeably parodies Satan's staged demonstration of his personal "courage never to submit or yield."
7. Mendoza mirrors Tanner psychically in several ways. For example, like Tanner, but unlike any other character in the play, Mendoza has no parents or relations who are even mentioned. More significantly, for Mendoza as a projection of a suppressed or unacknowledged part of Tanner's psyche, Mendoza dreams at the same time that Tanner does, suggesting that the Don Juan in Hell dream is shared by both. Tanner's encounter with Mendoza seems to me somewhat modeled on the encounter between Moliere's Dom Juan and the Beggar. That mysterious encounter takes place in a forest and culminates in Dom Juan's giving the Beggar money—for the love of humanity, as Dom Juan puts it (III, 2). Dom

Shaw also connects both Mendoza and Tanner with Hamlet. He has Mendoza quote Hamlet's "40,000 brothers / Could not with all their quantity of love / Make up my sum," and he has Tanner call Ramsden "Polonius," and Ramsden reply, "So you are Hamlet, I suppose." As Mendoza reads Tanner a selection of his verses to Louisa, he warns him that the Sierras make one dream of "women with magnificent hair." Tanner demurs at this suggestion, declaring, "They will not make me dream of women, my friend: I am heartwhole," just before he dozes off.

But Tanner is wrong: he will dream of a woman; and he will not be heart-whole until Ann grasps the "father's heart" within him. Moreover, in his dream Tanner splits himself in two in order to argue with himself: the Devil represents the side of himself that is merely cynical, his unconscious suspicion that there is no purpose to life, his destructive self, while Don Juan represents the creator part of himself, the visionary side, the world-betterer. The dream, then, must develop a view of genesis, the purpose of all generation, before Tanner can become personally generative.[8]

The Hell sequence proper begins with the genesis theme: "*Instead of the Sierra, there is nothing: omnipresent nothing. No sky, no peaks, no light, no sound, no time nor space, utter void. Then somewhere the beginning of a pallor, and with it a faint throbbing buzz as of a ghostly violoncello palpitating on the same note endlessly.*" It is utterly characteristic of the musician and music-lover, Shaw, to rewrite Genesis in this way: In the beginning there was death (the pallor) and there was music (the palpitating cello). That duality generates the debate between Don Juan and the Devil on the nature of man: for which read Tanner's internal conflict which keeps him from marriage.

It is often argued that nothing happens in the Don Juan in Hell scene; this is not so. Quite a lot happens: the Commander decides to move from heaven to hell; Dona Ana decides to be twenty-seven instead of an old hag; Don Juan decides to leave hell and seek heaven; and Dona Ana decides to pursue a father for the superman. The drama then resides in working through all the reasons, questions, doubts, and tensions involved in making the decisions. The question Don Juan starts with is: "the enigma on which I ponder in darkness. Why am I here?" He realizes early in the discussion that he neither belongs nor desires to be in hell; he is not comfortable there as he would be were he intentionally damned. And so he announces his decision to go to heaven before the discussion has

---

Juan spends most of the play getting out of paying his debts; the Beggar is the only one he does pay (apart from God, whom Dom Juan is forced to pay with his death). When Tanner meets Mendoza the brigand, Tanner acknowledges that he himself lives "by robbing the poor," hence, he agrees to pay any reasonable ransom Mendoza may require.

8. I derive my argument here from Leary, "Don Juan," 65.

barely begun: "Heaven is the home of the masters of reality: that is why I am going thither." But he stays in hell long enough to debate the merits of heaven versus those of hell because he himself is not quite so certain that heaven is where he should be.

Only as the debate develops does Don Juan clarify for himself why he must seek heaven. As Tanner's dream, the debate represents his arguing with himself about the nature of man: Is he good or evil? A creator or a destroyer? Does life have any purpose or goal? The Devil and Don Juan take opposing sides on these questions. And the powerful persuasiveness of the Devil's arguments shows several things about Shaw as a dramatic artist: he does practice the principle he enunciated in the Epistle Dedicatory, namely, that all his characters are right from their several points of view, including the Devil (which argues that Shaw himself must have felt within himself the force of the Devil's ideas).[9]

Don Juan and the Devil begin by debating what heaven and hell are really like. For the Devil, hell is the lively home of aestheticism, the place where one cultivates a sympathy for beauty and disregards both physical and moral ugliness: "Its [the world's] sympathies are all with misery, with poverty, with starvation of the body and the heart. I call on it to sympathize with joy, with love, with happiness, with beauty—."[1] For Don Juan hell is the home of the unreal, whereas in heaven, "you live and work instead of playing and pretending." He then extends the theatrical metaphor: "If the play still goes on here and on earth, and all the world is a stage, Heaven is at least behind the scenes. But Heaven cannot be described by metaphor."[2] Don Juan desires to go to heaven in order "to escape from lies, and from the tedious, vulgar pursuit of happiness, to spend my eons in contemplation." When Ana objecting asks if there is nothing more than contemplation in heaven, Don Juan replies that "there is the work of helping life in its struggle upward."[3] This is too much for the Devil who sees nothing upward in the history of mankind.

---

9. This is what I think Eric Bentley meant when he called Shaw's happiness a moral achievement. See *In Search of Theater* (New York: Alfred A. Knopf, 1953), 254.

1. Cf. Lord Henry Wotton: "I can sympathize with everything except suffering . . . I cannot sympathize with that. It is too ugly, too horrible, too distressing. There is something terribly morbid in the modern sympathy with pain. One should sympathize with the colour, the beauty, the joy of life." See Oscar Wilde, *The Picture of Dorian Gray*, Ch. 5. That Shaw seems deliberately to be echoing Wilde here confirms the Devil's position as a representative of aestheticism. In addition, Shaw makes Mendoza, the Devil's alter ego, steal one of Wilde's epigrams: "There are two tragedies in life. One is to lose your heart's desire. The other is to gain it." Cf. *Lady Windermere's Fan*, Act III: "In this world there are only two tragedies. One is not getting what one wants, and the other is getting it." The Devil and Mendoza are both versions of the Wildean Dandy.

2. Cf. *St. Joan* on the ineffableness of visionary matters (Sc. V).

3. Cf. Alceste in Molière's *The Misanthrope*, who at the end of the play wants to escape from the vices and injustices of humanity to a desert where he can have honor. For Shaw's Don Juan, heaven represents a similar kind of escape.

He then delivers the longest speech in the play in which he argues that man is essentially a destroyer, that the death instinct in man is paramount. * * *

With this argument the Devil scores a direct hit, the proof of which is that Don Juan is unable to answer it; he evades it, he dismisses it, but he does not answer it. He evades it by decrying the Devil's argument as a cliché ("Pshaw! all this is old"), implying that man is not destructive, merely cowardly. He dismisses it by dispelling the notion of death as an evil: "It is not death that matters, but the fear of death. It is not killing and dying that degrades us but base living and accepting the wages and profits of degradation."[4] The discussion now moves to Don Juan's relationship to women and how that relates to Don Juan's vision of evolution. Essentially, Don Juan views the male-female sexual relationship as follows: "Sexually, man is woman's contrivance for fulfilling Nature's behest in the most economical way." More personally, he explains that, "It was woman who taught me to say 'I am: therefore I think.' And also, 'I would think more; therefore I must be more.' " In order to be more, he must procreate. So, again, Tanner tells himself through Don Juan that he should marry Ann, that marriage will not lead to self-annihilation but rather to self-discovery. Don Juan speaks of Life's throwing him into the arms of woman as a "moment that introduced me for the first time to myself, and, through myself to the world."

Don Juan's conjoining of sexuality with self-discovery provides the unseen (by Tanner) link between marriage and the ideal of the "philosophic man: he who seeks in contemplation to discover the inner will of the world, in invention to discover the means of fulfilling that will, and in action to do that will by the so-discovered means." The dream ends by symbolically representing Tanner's present state: Don Juan leaves to find heaven, and Ana follows him in pursuit of a father for the superman, as Ann is in pursuit of Tanner. Tanner will seek heaven by marrying Ann.

But before Don Juan leaves hell, the Devil scores another direct hit. He suggests, with a devastatingly keen sense of where Don Juan is vulnerable with his belief in "Life's incessant aspiration to higher organization," that evolution is an illusion, that humankind has made no genuine progress (just as Tanner argues in the Revolutionist's Handbook, section VII, Progress an Illusion), that the movement of history is only a pendulum swinging back and forth, that life is only "an infinite comedy of illusion," that "there is nothing new under the

---

4. Cf. the passage from the Epistle Dedicatory where Shaw defines "the true joy in life." Here Shaw lets Don Juan speak in a voice very similar to his own—signaled I believe by Don Juan's exclamation, "Pshaw!" Shaw's personal commitment to this idea is also signaled by his reference to the potential for such exploitation the writer particularly faces.

JOHN A. BERTOLINI

sun." Moreover, the Devil prefers to be his own master, rather than serve some "blundering universal force" (a Shavian version of Satan's "Non serviam").[5]

Once again, Don Juan barely answers the Devil's arguments. In fact, his final rationale for going to seek heaven is curiously tentative, as if he is not sure of what he is doing, a lack of ease that matches Tanner's disquiet after the dream. Don Juan says, "But at least I shall not be bored. The service of the Life Force has that advantage, at all events." Whether these lines are a final taunt to the Devil about the boredom of hell or not, they do not communicate any fervor on Don Juan's part as he departs for heaven. Also, Don Juan has to ask directions to the frontier between heaven and hell—directions provided, or rather, explained by the Commander (of all people): "Oh the frontier is only the difference between two ways of looking at things. Any road will take you across if you really want to get there." In subtext, the Commander's line seems a final dig at Don Juan, suggesting that no one in his right mind would want to go to "the most angelically dull place in all creation," but it also hints perhaps that Don Juan has needed to argue himself into going, and therefore is not really quite so sanguine about it as he appears.

Shaw maintains a dramatic ambivalence about the visionary idealism of Don Juan's move to heaven through the reactions of the Devil, the Commander, and Dona Ana. The Devil warns: "Beware of the pursuit of the Superhuman: it leads to an indiscriminate contempt for the human." Thus, Tanner can be heard voicing his own unconscious doubts about his vision. The Commander in his military and vanitous fashion translates the concept of the Superhuman into something to be admired because "it's a fine cry" that would help win battles and because "there's something statuesque about it." In this way, he at least partly fulfills the Devil's prediction. Ana, however, restores the balance of ambivalence when she ends the dream sequence by crying out exultantly to the universe that her work as woman is not yet done: "a father for the Superman." Reality awakens Tanner from his dream with "*a live human voice crying* 'Automobile,'" echoing Ana's cry with the visualization of Ann's instinctual drive to marry Tanner. Hector tells Tanner that Ann "tracked you at every stopping place: she is a regular Sherlock Holmes."

Act IV

In the final act, Shaw gathers together all the play's major themes, motifs, and preoccupations, bringing them to a kind of resolution that maintains a precarious balance. He begins Act IV by introducing

5. Latin: I will not serve.

a new character, Hector Malone, Sr., in order to replay the Oedipal struggle between Tanner and Ramsden from Act I. Shaw contrives the action in such a way that a father (Malone, Sr.) reads a love note from his son's wife inviting the son to visit her and decides to go in his son's place—an inversion of Tanner's replacing the dead father in Act I. When the son, Hector Malone, Jr., finds out about the imposture, he practically assaults his father (Shaw describes Hector as *"making for his father"*), as Tanner seemed about to do to Ramsden, when Tanner took Mr. Whitefield's will out of his pocket instead of a revolver. But Hector succeeds in totally obliterating his father by "disowning" him: "He is no father of mine." The calamitous prospect of losing his son, however, makes Malone, Sr., renounce all claims to authority over his son, and especially to having a say in his son's choice of a wife. In short, he loses the Oedipal battle, and Hector gets to keep Violet.

The real dispute between Senior and Junior is over who has the right to be Hector Malone. When Violet's billet-doux,[6] addressed to Hector Malone, is taken and read by Malone, Sr., Malone, Jr., reacts virulently to the usurpation of his name and therefore his identity. Really, he is asserting his right to his father's name, his right to a father's identity, for which Shaw's metaphor is the right to read and interpret what one reads. Once Senior realizes that Junior is determined to be independent of his father, financially and otherwise, the father surrenders to his parental protective instincts and assumes an attitude of complete dotage towards his son. The thought of Hector's leaving him, having to work, to endure hardship, is unbearable to him. In other words, Shaw shows "a father's heart" in action as a preparation for Tanner's becoming a father.

The prerequisite for Tanner's so becoming is the defeat of all mock-fathers, the defathering of rival claimants, and Malone, Sr., is the last of a series comprised of Mr. Whitefield, Ramsden, and (for Tanner's dream self, Don Juan) the Commander. The Commander had renounced his fatherhood upon meeting Ana again in hell: "In this place . . . the farce of parental wisdom is dropped. Regard me, I beg, as a fellow creature, not as a father." Even before his appearance, his paternal potency had already been somewhat diminished not only by Don Juan's having run him through with a sword, but also by Ana's account of his statue's fate in the world above:

> It has been a great expense to me. The boys in the monastery school would not let it alone: the mischievous ones broke it; and the studious ones wrote their names on it. Three new noses in two years, and fingers without end. I had to leave it to its fate at last; and now I fear it is shockingly mutilated. My poor father!

6. Personal or love letter [*Editor*].

Such symbolic castration, however obscured by humor, was one of the main destructive activities of the boy Tanner. Ann reminds him: "You ruined all the young fir trees by chopping off their leaders with a wooden sword. You broke all the cucumber frames with your catapult." Tanner's youthful phallic violence has its counterpart in the aggression of the "mischievous boys" who denosed and defingered the Commander's statue (Tanner defended himself against Ann's accusation of destructiveness by claiming that he was only "mischievous"), just as his writer's destiny to become an Oedipus of political and social thought has its counterpart in the actions of "the studious ones" who "wrote their names on" the statue.

Before filling the vacuum left by all the dead, absent, or impostor fathers, Tanner replays his Act I blunder about Violet's supposed illegitimate child. In this instance, he mistakenly thinks Hector Malone, Jr., believes in the reform of the marriage laws, that Hector like Tanner himself rebels courageously against conventional morality. Instead, Hector turns out to be so conventional as to be the husband of Violet, and Tanner calls him a "moral impostor." In short, this episode previews the final transformation of Tanner, the supposed social reformer who is discovered to be a husband.

All of Act IV (as indeed the whole play) has prepared for Tanner's anagnorisis,[7] the recognition of his love for Ann, his husbandness, above all his fatherness. His final duologue with Ann not only completes their series of duologues (one per act, including Don Juan and Dona Ana), but also sums up almost the whole literary tradition of the gay couple from Shakespeare (Rosalind and Orlando, Beatrice and Benedick) and Molière (Alceste and Celimene) through Congreve (Mirabell and Millamant) and Sheridan (Sir Peter and Lady Teazle) to Wilde (Lord Goring and Mabel Chiltern). Shaw cited Shakespeare's example as moral support for his own portrayal of woman as the real pursuer in the love chase. And clearly Rosalind and Helena are models for Ann in this regard. But Rosalind is also a model for Tanner in the way that she has to vent all her skepticism regarding romantic love before she can surrender fully to her impulse toward Orlando's manhood. Alceste, the misanthrope, in his detestation of the politesse that makes societal relationships possible, as well as in his maladroit application of his principles to human relations fathers Tanner equally as much as his nominal ancestor, Don Juan, while Celimene influences Ann's coquettishness. Likewise Millamant's perception of marriage as threatening her individual freedom, privacy and dignity, Shaw adapts to Tanner, making him fear that he will "dwindle" into a husband ("I will become a thing that has served its purpose"). The name-calling and sarcasm of Tan-

7. Recognition leading to denouement [*Editor*].

ner's exchanges with Ann derive plainly from Beatrice and Benedick (and from Kate and Petruchio before them) as well as from Lady Teazle and Sir Peter, though Shaw never allows Ann and Tanner to be as coarsely cruel as their Shakespearean predecessors sometimes are. Rather he finds in Mabel Chiltern and Lord Goring a model for the genial sexual charm that pervades the sexy courtship of Ann and Tanner.

Shaw's putting his play squarely in the tradition of stage comedy has a reason beyond that of mere literary borrowing or influence. For he comes in this play, as I have tried to show, to a vital sense of himself as an author—as a writer of the genre, comedy. Shaw called *Man and Superman* a Comedy and a Philosophy; he might have called it the philosophy of comedy, for that is what the play is in its intense self-consciousness: its allusive awareness of the tradition to which it belongs; its attempt to examine human nature from an evolutionary and cosmic perspective; and above all its representation of the metaphysics of marriage, the teleological view of sexual relations. The philosophy of the play as a whole, but most especially of the last duologue between Tanner and Ann, derives largely from Schopenhauer's 1844 essay, "The Metaphysics of Sexual Love," an appendix to *The World as Will and Idea* (as has been amply demonstrated).[8] * * *

Schopenauer's reliance on the drama both for his vocabulary in these passages and his use of comedy matter to illustrate his theories make apparent why Shaw found his essay so useful. It is a piece of writing that generates *Man and Superman*: its explicit analysis of comedy's defining principle, to wit, the conflict between the evolutionary aims of the species and the personal desires of individuals, becomes not merely the philosophical underpinning of the play's conclusion, but more significantly part of Tanner's consciousness: "What we have both done this afternoon is to renounce happiness, renounce freedom, renounce tranquility, above all renounce the romantic possibilities of an unknown future for the cares of a household and a family." Shaw tells us in the Epistle Dedicatory that he has made his hero one who "does actually read Schopenhauer," which suggests that Tanner has read Schopenhauer's characterization of "almost all comedies," which in turn suggests a meta-consciousness on Tanner's part of his own nature as a dramatic character, that is, the progenitor of writing merges with Tanner the begotten by writing.

Tanner's becoming conscious of himself as a progenitor of children, therefore, embodies both Shaw's affirmation of himself as

8. See Crompton, *Shaw the Dramatist*, 84–90, and Maurice Valency, *The Cart and the Trumpet: The Plays of George Bernard Shaw* (New York: Oxford Univ. Press, 1973), 217–22. Shaw first read Schopenhauer's essay in 1888.

author-father as well as double exposing Tanner's sexual impulse toward Ann with his impulse to be generative. * * * [Extract from *Man and Superman*: dialogue between Tanner and Ann follows.]

*   *   *

The impassioned dialogue here manages to do several things at once complexly. First of all, it has two emotional focuses: Tanner's feeling of the "clutch that holds and hurts," as he senses that Scho-penhauer baby taking life from him even as he generously wants to give it—destruction and creation; and Ann's miming of a mother's birth pangs,[9] after she has expressed her own anxiety about moth-erhood, the potential of dying herself in childbirth, as she gives life to the baby: "It will not be all happiness for me. Perhaps death"—destruction and creation. Tanner's reversal of himself when he acknowledges that he does love Ann follows Shaw's parody of the scene in Mozart's and Da Ponte's *Don Giovanni*, where the Statue exhorts the Don to repent thrice and Don Giovanni refuses thrice: Three times Tanner refuses to accept Ann's urging him three times to say yes to marrying her, "Before it is too late for repentance." And then he is "*struck by the echo from the past*" and wonders aloud, "When did all this happen to me before? Are we two dreaming?" Shaw's parody of *Don Giovanni* here fits the emotional intensity of Ann and Tanner in the way it incorporates the death of Don Gio-vanni into their marriage: destruction and creation again.

Shaw's most successful enactment of the creation-destruction dia-lectic lies in the overlaying of Ann and Tanner's duologue with an orgasmic rhythm. Ann's expression of a mother's birth pangs are also an orgasmic lack of control, as is Tanner's abandonment of self-interest after his discovery of his father's heart. That abandonment of self goes beyond Ann's anxieties about dying in childbirth to a longing for death, which she quickly echoes, so that Ann and Tanner become transfigured into Wagner's Tristan and Isolde, each crying, "Lass mich sterben,"[1] at the height of their erotic communion in the Act II love-duet. In his essay "An Unusual Case of Dying Together," Ernest Jones interprets the case of a married couple who died at Niagara Falls in one another's arms as having an unconscious sig-nificance: "The desire to beget a child with the loved one."[2] In view of Tanner's line, "If we two stood now on the edge of a precipice, I would hold you tight and jump," I find Jones' interpretation remark-ably indicative of Shaw's uncanny sense of the confluence of differ-ent desires: the wish to die together at a scene instancing the natural

9. I owe this point to Martin Meisel's famous study, *Shaw and the Nineteenth-Century The-ater* (Princeton: Princeton Univ. Press, 1963), 182.
1. "Let me die" [*Editor*].
2. See *Essays in Applied Psycho-Analysis*, Vol. 1 (London: Hogarth Press, 1951), 16–21.

sublime translates the unconscious desire to beget a child.

Shaw's interweaving of love and death, creation and destruction, at the comic and emotional climax of the play, I believe, reenacts the debate between Don Juan and the Devil about whether man is a destroyer or a creator, and even seems to anticipate Freud's position in *Beyond the Pleasure Principle*, that "the aim of all life is death."[3] But Shaw does not stop there, for he finally answers the Devil's definition of man as a death-lover in two ways: he has Ann mime a death and resurrection by making her swoon and subsequently regain consciousness in time to announce to the company that she has consented to marry Jack; and Shaw has Tanner in his last speech vow to make his marriage work to carry on his writing's influence. He insists that "the copies of Patmore's Angel in the House in extra morocco and the other articles you are preparing to heap upon us, will be instantly sold, and the proceeds devoted to circulating free copies of the Revolutionist's Handbook."[4] Thus books are made to generate books through marriage and the largess of the would-be father, Jack Tanner. Both Ann's reaction to Tanner's speech, calling it "talking," and the final triple-meaning stage direction, "*Universal laughter*," cast a tempering and ironic light on Shaw's and Tanner's evolutionary fervor, but do not destroy their vision of "the life to come."

When Shaw comes to write *Major Barbara*, * * * two years after *Man and Superman*, he is still preoccupied with defining the self. *John Bull's Other Island*, the play which appears in between *Man and Superman* and *Major Barbara*, may have had an external motivation for its existence, namely, Yeats' invitation to write a play for the Abbey, nevertheless, it treats the theme of an Irishman in England who must confront his national heritage and hence, like its neighbor plays, concerns itself with self-definition, but in terms of place of origin and national character, rather than in terms of fatherhood as in its predecessor, or in terms of finding one's life-work as in its successor.

3. Shaw is explicit both in the play and in the Maxims for Revolutionists about the rule of the unconscious. He has Ann say to Octavius in Act IV, "But I doubt if we ever know why we do things." And one of Tanner's Maxims is: "The unconscious self is the real genius."
4. In the earliest editions of the play, it is not Patmore but Tennyson that Tanner scorns as a typical wedding present. Perhaps Tennyson, as one of Shaw's unacknowledged literary fathers (especially the Tennyson who looked forward to "one far-off divine event / To which the whole creation moves" at the end of *In Memoriam*), no longer needed to be mocked so publicly, once Shaw had achieved a secure sense of himself as author-father through the writing of *Man and Superman*.

On *Major Barbara*

MARGERY MORGAN

[Shaw's Blakean Farce]†

Major Barbara has been generally acclaimed as one of Shaw's finest plays. The impact it made on Brecht is indicated by the extent to which it inspired *St Joan of the Stockyards*. Francis Fergusson's account of it as a 'farce of rationalizing',[1] however denigratory in tone, is true to the quicksilver brilliance and buoyancy of the play, as careful analysis cannot be. To attempt such analysis would be misguided if it were not necessary to show that the intellectual intricacy of the dramatic structure is precise, not confused, and that Shaw now handles his ironies with a clarity and control lacking in the comparably ironic *Candida*.

The mainspring of the play seems to have been provided by Shaw's response to Blake, reinforced by a reading of Nietzsche where he is closest to Blake. The dialectical terms of *The Marriage of Heaven and Hell* provide the intellectual perspectives of the drama:

> Without contraries is no progression. Attraction and repulsion, reason and energy, love and hate, are necessary to human existence.

> From these contraries spring what the religious call good and evil. Good is the passive that obeys reason; evil is the active springing from energy.

> Good is heaven. Evil is hell.[2]

† From *The Shavian Playground: An Exploration of the Art of George Bernard Shaw* (London: Methuen & Co Ltd, 1972), pp. 134–57. © 1972 Margery M. Morgan. Bernard Shaw previously unpublished texts © 1972 by The Trustees of the British Museum, Governors and Guardians of the National Gallery of Ireland and the Royal Academy of Dramatic Art.
1. See Francis Fergusson, *The Idea of a Theater*, Anchor Books edition (New York: Doubleday, 1953) pp. 192–94.
2. The self-evident relationship of these quotations from *The Marriage of Heaven and Hell* to *Major Barbara* is objectively confirmed by Shaw's comment in the Preface to *Three Plays for Puritans*: 'Let those who have praised my originality in conceiving Dick Dudgeon's strange religion read Blake's Marriage of Heaven and Hell; and I shall be fortunate if they

Conventional moral distinctions are annihilated as the antinomies prove to be complementary. Like *The Marriage of Heaven and Hell*, *Major Barbara* employs the shock tactics of paradox to induce a more comprehensive understanding of the world. The means used involve insistence on both literal and metaphoric meanings, simple and ironic readings.

Shaw's original intention of calling the play *Andrew Undershaft's Profession* implied the reworking of the pun already employed in *Cashel Byron's Profession* and *Mrs Warren's Profession*, so as to bring out the relation between a trade or occupation and the creed implicit in its pursuit. In each instance (and this also applies to *Widowers' Houses*), practice of the occupation is permitted, or even relied on, by society, while official morality disapproves. On the realistic level, the munitions firm of Undershaft and Lazarus and Bodger's whisky firm represent capitalist enterprise exploiting human weakness for pecuniary gain and producing further social evils, destructive to humanity. In theory, Christians reject war; they are answered by the 'Voice of the Devil' (Blake's phrase) issuing from Andrew Undershaft, in whom Blake's view of Satan and Nietzsche's Dionysus unite to form one of Shaw's most impressive characters. Imaginative vision, it seems, can use the devil as a friend who has important truths to tell: gunpowder, fire and drink have positive value as symbols of elemental power, revolutionary, cleansing, inspirational. Indeed they are symbols in the Coleridgean sense, marked by a translucence of the general in the particular and of the eternal in the temporal; they are true symbols of power for change because, as material objects, they can bring about change. Together they represent the general Blakean category of Energy. Shaw associates with them—as society does—money, capitalist profit (or Illth), which can also be positively seen as a token of natural abundance translated into the commodities of civilization and *human* power, which reason can master and wield.

Certainly nowhere else in Shaw's work do we come so close to the imaginative sense of Blake's propositions:

1. Man has no body distinct from his soul . . .
2. Energy is the only life, and is from the body; and reason is the bound or outward circumference of energy . . .

and, above all, the sense of:

3. Energy is eternal delight.

---

do not rail at me for a plagiarist'. This is the starting-point of I. Fiske's essay, *Bernard Shaw and William Blake* (Shavian Tract No. 2), reprinted in R. J. Kaufmann (ed.), *G. B. Shaw*, pp. 170–78. The link with *Major Barbara* is not noted there.

Undershaft, the manufacturer of armaments, is in a different relation to society from Sartorius, the slum landlord of *Widowers'*
Houses, or Mrs Warren, owner-director of an international chain of
brothels. Whereas those earlier creations remain prisoners of society,
outcasts from respectability, and in presentation are touched with
the pathos of melodrama, the nature of the commodity Undershaft
traffics in puts him in mastery over society and gives him the confidence and authority to set up his sign: 'UNASHAMED', implying a
total rejection of (puritan) guilt on all fronts. In this play Shaw
grasped the basic nature of the threat offered to the intellect by the
actual world: the challenge of undifferentiated force and mass in the
physical universe to the essentially sole and individual; the ruthless
and mindless violence that 'can destroy the higher power just as a
tiger can destroy a man'. But man naturally has a tiger in him, too,
which can match the violence of the elements. Active, aggressive,
this force is translated into social terms under the image of an army.
The literal fact of the Salvation Army is essential to the realistic
fabric of the play. Traditional metaphors of Christian life as warfare
are already implicit in the uniformed figures of men and women,
marching with banners, bearing the sign 'Blood and Fire', to a drum
that beats out a quickened pulse of life. As interpreted through
Cusins, Major Barbara's fiancé, it takes on the more general significance of the Church Militant of a universal religion: organized
humanity, active, purposeful and joyous in its onslaughts against
misery and darkness. The play as a whole demonstrates its theme
by the physical exhilaration and the optimism it generates through
its explosions of condensed thought and the aggressive release of
laughter.

As in *Mrs Warren's Profession,* the basic conflict of opposites is
again enacted within a child-parent relationship: the innocence of
society's dupes is confronted with the disillusion of its exploiters.
But this time the parent and the child are of opposite sexes, and
experience does not simply destroy innocence; it complements it and
produces new strength. The simple dialectical plan, in which Barbara's heavenly counsel and Undershaft's hellish counsel fight it out,
was complicated in the process of writing, when Shaw transformed
the heroine's fiancé from a young man-about-town comparable to
Charles Lomax (for so he is characterized at the beginning of the
longhand version) to a Professor of Greek. I think we can assume
that Cusins was at first envisaged as playing a minor, or choric, role
comparable to Frank's in the earlier play: that of an observer and
commentator who also sets the comic tone of the drama. In his character of observer, the Professor of Greek is qualified to identify for
us the philosophical issues and the mythopoetic analogues as they
arise. His intellectual quality does not entirely obscure the linea-

ments of the clown; but he plays the ironical fool to Lomax's 'natural'. As a more considerable and distinguished member of society, he is also fitted to become one of the main pivots of the dramatic scheme. The extension in the play's significance which has followed from this later conception of the character culminates in a scrap of dialogue inserted as an afterthought in the longhand text of Act III (B.M. Addit. MS. 50616 A–E):

UNDERSHAFT   . . . . Remember the words of Plato.
CUSINS [*Starting.*]   Plato! You dare to quote Plato to me!
UNDERSHAFT   Plato says, my friend, that society cannot be saved until either the Professors of Greek take to making gun- powder, or else the makers of gunpowder become Professors of Greek.

To the opposition between Undershaft and Barbara there has been added an independent opposition between Undershaft and Cusins. Of course, these are various examples of a single basic conflict between idealism and realism. But the placing of the two in the progress of the drama must absolve Shaw from any charge of tau- tology: Barbara, the indubitable protagonist of Act II, subsides into watchfulness in Act III, while Cusins takes over from her, is put to the test and makes the crucial decision; her endorsement of this in the last moments of the play lends strength to the impression that he has indeed been deputizing for her. It is dramatically necessary, after her defeat by Undershaft in Act II, that the initiative should pass from Barbara. Cusins carries the play into its final movement, as he makes his pact with Undershaft. This has the effect of restoring Barbara to her proper centrality, though now in alliance with her former opponents. As the representative of spirituality, she returns to inform and bless the compact between reason and energy and the paradox of good *in* evil, heaven *in* hell. Cusins's function has been to introduce the dialectical synthesis. The reconciliation he proposes between power and service, realism and idealism, corresponds, of course, to the Platonic advocacy of the philosopher-king.

The peculiarly Shavian variety of Ibsenite dramatic structure, imi- tated from the Platonic dialogues, is evident in the verbal debates, rationally conceived and conducted to a great extent—especially in the last act—in abstract terms. This is the drama of ideas in exem- plary form. But there is much more to the play than this. The realism of its settings—the library in Wilton Crescent, the Salvation Army shelter in Canning Town, and the especially topical Garden City[3]—

---

3. The fact that Ebenezer Howard, as originator of the Garden City idea, was an exponent of the Smiles's Self-Help attitude to the working class, drawing the teeth of revolt, is relevant to the interpretation of Shaw's plays. [Samuel Smiles was the author of *Self-Help* (1856), a best-selling manual of economic and social self-improvement (*Editor*).] Perivale St Andrews is still more suggestive of the philanthropy of George Cadbury, founder of

establishes it as a critique of actual society that reveals the spectrum of class and its cruel contrasts, as *Man and Superman* did not. Changes of setting are matched by changes in dramatic style. Wealth, aristocracy and the culture that goes with them play out a comedy of manners in Act I; Dickensian realism verging on melodrama invades Act II, in the Salvation Army Shelter, bare and chill, with its horse-trough as derisive comment on the poorly dressed wretches at their free meal; Act III presents a Utopia designed by contemporary paternalism, and theory reigns there—a front for the Satanic mills that produce the wealth of Wilton Crescent, or that, differently directed, could blow the whole unequal system sky-high. Metaphysically, Perivale St Andrews represents the spiritual cosmos, heaven and hell and the battlefield of the world (in its fort with dummy soldiers), corresponding to the emotional range—touching tragedy and ecstasy—that the play embraces. The action of *Major Barbara* contains thinly disguised versions of folk-lore quests and divine rituals, as well as sharp clashes of personality, to set off the philosophy. The dialectical scheme is strongly supported by mythopoetic patterns and humanized by a rich assortment of characters. The second act in particular with its centrally placed sub-plot, involving Barbara with a character from a sub-group, Bill Walker, is highly exciting in the pace of its symbolically weighted action and the intense sense of crisis it conveys. Energy, one is reminded, is the stuff of drama.

Energy, of course, is the power that Nietzsche called dionysian and regarded as the antithesis of the Socratic poise he defined as apollonian.[4] 'The business of the Salvation Army is to save, not to wrangle about the name of the pathfinder,' declares Cusins. 'Dionysos or another: what does it matter?' The protest was anticipated by Nietzsche himself in the passage from his Preface to *The Birth of Tragedy* already mentioned in relation to *Candida*:

> It was *against* morality, therefore, that my instinct, as an intercessory instinct for life, turned in this questionable book, inventing for itself, a fundamental counter-dogma and countervaluation of life, purely artistic, purely *anti-Christian*. What

---

Bournville. See Warren Sylvester Smith, *The London Heretics* (London: Constable, 1967), p. 248.

4. Louis Crompton has taken up the point of Shaw's debt to Nietzsche and his concept of Dionysus in 'Shaw's Challenge to Liberalism', *Prairie Schooner*, Vol. XXXVII (1963), pp. 229–44, reprinted in R. J. Kaufmann (ed.), op. cit., pp. 88–89 (see Louis Crompton, *Shaw the Dramatist*, pp. 105–2), which I read after writing this chapter in draft. I have let my discussion of the matter stand, as its direction and emphasis are different from Mr Crompton's. I compared Shaw's use of his source in *Major Barbara* with Yeats's in *The Resurrection* in 'Shaw, Yeats, Nietzsche and the Religion of Art', *Komos*, Vol. I (English Department, Monash University, 1967), pp. 24–34.

should I call it? As a philologist and man of words I baptized it, not without some liberty—for who could be sure of the proper name of the Antichrist?—with the name of a Greek god: I called it *Dionysian*.[5]

In fact, Dionysus is mentioned in the dialogue with sufficient frequency to justify entirely the critics Shaw attacked in his Preface for labelling his play as derivative from Nietzschean philosophy. Barbara Undershaft, the evangelist, represents the orthodox Christian attitude that Nietzsche described as 'a libel on life'. Her father, whom Cusins nicknames 'Prince of Darkness' and 'Mephistopheles', as well as 'Dionysos' and 'Machiavelli', challenges her with the 'fundamental counter-dogma and counter-valuation of life':

> Leave it to the poor to pretend that poverty is a blessing: leave it to the coward to make a religion of his cowardice by preaching humility; I had rather be a thief than a pauper. I had rather be a murderer than a slave. I dont want to be either; but if you force the alternative on me, then, by Heaven, I'll choose the braver and more moral one.

In adding to these two the figure of a Professor of Greek, Shaw had supplied his play with a representative of that dispassionate and philosophical Hellenic consciousness upon which Nietzsche saw the originally Asiatic religion of Dionysus as having broken in, at a critical point in the history of civilization. The passage in *The Birth of Tragedy* that supplies the fullest account of this event and its consequences can be related illuminatingly to *Major Barbara*:

> On the other hand, we should not have to speak conjecturally, if asked to disclose the immense gap which separated the *Dionysian Greek* from the Dionysian barbarian. (p. 29)

Already this hints at the rationale of supplying Undershaft with a double opposition in, first, the aptly named Barbara, and then Professor Cusins. The famous essay goes on:

> From all quarters of the Ancient World . . . we can prove the existence of Dionysian festivals, the type of which bears, at best, the same relation to the Greek festivals as the bearded satyr, who borrowed his name and attributes from the goat, does to Dionysus himself . . . the very wildest beasts of nature were let

5. See Chapter 4, p. 77 [of Morgan's work]. I have quoted W. A. Haussmann's translation of *The Birth of Tragedy* (Edinburgh and London: Foulis, 1909), as this version, in manuscript at least as early as 1901, is the one Shaw is most likely to have known when he wrote *Major Barbara*. For the text, see Friedrich Nietzsche, *Complete Works*, ed. Oscar Levy, Vol. I, p. 11. The facts concerning Shaw's early familiarity with Nietzsche's work are discussed in my article, 'Shaw, Yeats, Nietzsche and the Religion of Art', pp. 25–26 and 35.

> loose here, including that detestable mixture of lust and cruelty
> which has always seemed to me the genuine 'witches' draught'.
> (pp. 29–30)

Now Shaw has almost entirely dissociated these forces from his principal characters. They are symbolically represented in the play by
Undershaft's explosives and the wars in which they are used: 'the
men and lads torn to pieces with shrapnel and poisoned with lyddite![6]
. . . the oceans of blood . . . the ravaged crops!'—by 'Bodger's Whisky
in letters of fire against the sky', by the drum that Cusins beats, and
by the Salvation Army motto of 'Blood and Fire!' More directly, they
are present in the physical violence with which Bill Walker disturbs
the shelter, in Act II, and for which he has prepared himself by
drinking gin:

> Aw'm noa gin drinker . . . ; bat when Aw want to give my girl a
> bloomin good awdin Aw lawk to ev a bit o devil in me.

Returning to Nietzsche, we find the immunity of Shaw's principal
characters, the educated and the aristocratic, accounted for:

> For some time . . . it would seem that the Greeks were perfectly
> secure and guarded against the feverish agitations of these fes-
> tivals . . . by the figure of Apollo himself rising here in full pride,
> who could not have held out the Gorgon's head to a more dan-
> gerous power than this grotesquely uncouth Dionysian. It is in
> Doric art that this majestically rejecting attitude of Apollo per-
> petuated itself. (p. 30)

The production note which prepares for Cusins's first entrance on
the stage refers to his 'apalling temper'. The character described is
that of a man who has obtained mastery over his own passions and
thus, according to Socrates, fitted himself for the task of governing
others:

> *The lifelong struggle of a benevolent temperament and a high
> conscience against impulses of inhuman ridicule and fierce impa-
> tience has set up a chronic strain . . . He is a most implacable,
> determined, tenacious, intolerant person who by mere force of
> character presents himself as—and indeed actually is—consider-
> ate, gentle, explanatory, even mild and apologetic, capable pos-
> sibly of murder, but not of cruelty or coarseness.*

Cusins has his proper place in Lady Britomart Undershaft's library.
Its decorum, reflecting her own majestic rejection of all license, is
an essential adjunct to its perfect security; she is herself prepared to
recognize the dependence of the standards of a gentleman upon the
tradition of classical education.

6. Explosive [*Editor*].

The significance of Cusins's crucial decision to accept a director-ship in the Undershaft firm, in order to 'make war on war', can be explored in terms of the rest of the passage from *The Birth of Tragedy*, which grows now even more closely analogous to the play than in its earlier sentences:

> This opposition became more precarious and even impossible, when, from out of the deepest root of the Hellenic nature, sim-ilar impulses finally broke forth and made way for themselves: *the Delphic god, by a seasonably effected reconciliation, was now contented with taking the destructive arms from the hands of his powerful antagonist.* This reconciliation marks the most impor-tant moment in the history of the Greek cult: whenever we turn our eyes we may observe the revolutions resulting from this event. It was the reconciliation of two antagonists, with the sharp demarcation of the boundary-lines to be thenceforth observed by each . . . in reality, the chasm was not bridged over. But if we observe how, under the pressure of this conclusion of peace, the Dionysian power manifested itself, we shall now rec-ognize, in the Dionysian orgies of the Greeks, as compared with the Babylonian Sacaea and their retrogression of man to the tiger and the ape, the significance of festivals of world-redemption and days of transfiguration. Not till then does nature attain her artistic jubilee; not till then does the rupture of the *principium individuationis*[7] become an artistic phenom-enon. (pp. 30–1)

The dramatic crisis, towards which the play moves, is related to the action of Barbara Undershaft, granddaughter of the Earl of Steven-age, daughter of a millionaire capitalist, leaving the established church of the established social order to join the Salvation Army. The inheritance of power (the 'destructive arms') is kept in the family through the resolution and audacity of her fiancé, who makes his pact with 'Dionysos Undershaft', though asserting still: 'I repudiate your sentiments. I abhor your nature. I defy you in every possible way.' The 'transfiguration' which ensues has its appropriate setting in the Garden City of Perivale St Andrews, blueprint for the millen-nium of social welfare, and its individual enactment in Barbara's change of mood: 'She has gone right up into the skies,' says Cusins.

Proleptically,[8] the new festivals are represented in the play before Cusins's decisive gesture is made. He himself is ritually prepared for the crisis by an evening spent with Undershaft (shown in the film version, alluded to in the stage play): 'he only provided the wine. I think it was Dionysos who made me drunk'; by implication, the

7. Principle of individuality [*Editor*].
8. Anticipating the event [*Editor*].

drunkenness was spiritual and inspirational, not crudely orgiastic. And the values the dramatist associates with the Salvation Army are multiple, the morality of the soup kitchen, which Nietzsche-Undershaft rejects, being only tangential to it. The spirit of the Salvation Army, as it has attracted Barbara Undershaft, is itself dionysiac and revolutionary; but it is an enlightened and purified version of older, cruder enthusiasms, which the Hellenistic mind is already able to approve and associate with from the start of the play; for Cusins too, though in pursuit of Barbara, has joined the Salvation Army. In his apologia to Undershaft, he declares:

> I am a sincere Salvationist. You do not understand the Salvation Army. It is the army of joy, of love, of courage: it has banished the fear and remorse and despair of the old hell-ridden evangelical sects: it marches to fight the devil with trumpet and drum, with music and dancing, with banner and palm, as becomes a sally from heaven by its happy garrison. It picks the waster out of the public house and makes a man of him: it finds a worm wriggling in a back kitchen, and lo! a woman . . . It takes the poor professor of Greek, the most artificial and self-suppressed of human creatures, from his meal of roots, and lets loose the rhapsodist in him . . .

In fact the reconciliation of Dionysus and Apollo enacted dramatically in Act III is, in non-dramatic form, imaged from the first, already achieved. Music itself is the sublimation of dionysiac energy. (The full title of Nietzsche's famous essay is, of course, *The Birth of Tragedy from the Spirit of Music*.)

Shaw actually stages the beginning of one triumphal procession and accompanies it with a shadow-play of the supersession of one religion by another. The form in which the climax, in Act II, is presented may be related to another extract from *The Birth of Tragedy*:

> Schopenhauer has described to us the stupendous *awe* which seizes upon man, when of a sudden he is at a loss to account for the cognitive forms of a phenomenon, in that the principle of reason, in some one of its manifestations, seems to admit of an exception. Add to this awe the blissful ecstasy which rises from the innermost depths of man, ay, of nature, at this same collapse of the *principium individuationis*, and we shall gain an insight into the being of the *Dionysian*, which is brought within closest ken perhaps by the analogy of *drunkenness*. It is either under the influence of the narcotic draught, of which the hymns of all primitive men and peoples tell us, or by the powerful approach of spring penetrating all nature with joy, that those Dionysian emotions awake, in the augmentation of which the subjective vanishes to complete self-forgetfulness. So also in the

German Middle Ages singing and dancing crowds, ever increasing in number, were borne from place to place under this same Dionysian power. In these St John's and St Vitus's dancers we again perceive the Bacchic choruses of the Greeks, with their previous history in Asia Minor, as far back as Babylon and the orgiastic Sacaea. There are some, who, from lack of experience or obtuseness, will turn away from such phenomena as 'folk-diseases' with a smile of contempt or pity prompted by the consciousness of their own health: of course, the poor wretches do not divine what a cadaverous-looking and ghastly aspect this very 'health' of theirs presents when the glowing life of the Dionysian revellers rushes past them. (pp. 25–6)

With his presentation of the Salvation Army as a recrudescence of dionysiac fervour, Shaw extended Nietzsche's medieval analogues to the bacchic chorus into modern times. The image suggested in the last lines of Nietzsche's paragraph may have provided the hint for the episode in which Barbara, who has just witnessed the triumph of Undershaft at which her faith, as it seems, has crumbled, remains a still figure amid the animated scene as the Salvation Army band, caught up in the exultation with Undershaft, marches off with music to the great meeting:

> CUSINS [*Returning impetuously from the shelter with a flag and a trombone, and coming between Mrs Baines and Undershaft.*] You shall carry the flag down the first street, Mrs Baines [*He gives her the flag.*] Mr Undershaft is a gifted trombonist: he shall intone an Olympian diapason to the West Ham Salvation March. [*Aside to Undershaft, as he forces the trombone on him.*] Blow, Machiavelli, blow . . . It is a wedding chorus from one of Donizetti's operas; but we have converted it . . . 'For thee immense rejoicing—immenso giubilo – immenso giubilo.' [*With drum obbligato.*] Rum tum ti tum tum, tum tum ti ta—
>
> BARBARA   Dolly: you are breaking my heart.
>
> CUSINS   What is a broken heart more or less here? Dionysos Undershaft has descended. I am possessed . . . Off we go. Play up, there! Immenso giubilo. [*He gives the time with his drum; and the band strikes up the march, which becomes more distant as the procession moves briskly away.*]
>
> MRS BAINES   I must go, dear. Youre overworked: you will be all right tomorrow. We'll never lose you. Now Jenny: step out with the old flag. Blood and Fire! [*She marches out through the gate with her flag.*]
>
> JENNY   Glory Hallelujah! [*Flourishing her tambourine and marching.*]
>
> UNDERSHAFT [*To Cusins, as he marches out past him easing the slide of his trombone.*] 'My ducats and my daughter'!

CUSINS [*Following him out.*]   Money and gunpowder!
BARBARA   Drunkenness and Murder! My God: why hast thou
forsaken me?
*She sinks on the form with her face buried in her hands. The
march passes away into silence.*[9]

The exclamatory dialogue contributes to the excitement; the syntax
of logical speech has little place here. The crescendo of sound is
intensified by the gathering in of themes, the drawing together of
the various symbolic perspectives in which Shaw presents his fable
during the course of the play. Cannon and thunder, elemental and
divine, as well as the strong pulse of life, are to be heard in the
beating drum. But the sense of emotional and mental violence com-
municated at this point comes chiefly from the harshly ironic intersection of moods: exhilaration set against agony. Horror at the
contemplation of destructive power is transformed through identification with that power; pity is rejected for recognition of agony as
a further inverted celebration of violent energy. Shaw had perhaps
remembered that comedy and tragedy alike have been traced back
to the satyr chorus of the Dionysiac festival. There is no doubt that
audiences are infected by the exhilaration. The conventional reaction to the sentimental appeal of a deserted heroine is pressed into
service to give a keener edge to Cusins's brutal denial of sympathy
and emphatic reassertion of unmixed joy. We should like to recoil
from him, but cannot. The experience is a brilliantly conceived vehicle for the loss of self-possession in a transport of irrational feeling.
Shaw is demonstrating something very like a physical law: the superior power of volume of sound, weight of numbers, releasing energy
under the pressure of an intensifying rhythm. And the march
remains a wedding march as the gentle-mannered Cusins confronts
the chagrin of a subdued Barbara with a bridegroom's self-regarding
exultation.

Yet the impression of the single figure in its stillness persists: there
is strength of another kind in this maintained integrity and isolation.
It is the apollonian will in Barbara that holds out now. And with the
shock of recognizing in her final cry, 'My God: why hast thou forsaken me?', the words of the Christian divine saviour, the audience
is returned to thoughtfulness.[1]

'There are mystical powers above and behind the three of us,'
declares Undershaft in the screen version. The shadows of Dionysus
and Apollo are to be glimpsed shiftingly behind Undershaft himself,
Cusins and Barbara, but Barbara alone is the Christ figure of the

9. The text is drawn from Bernard Shaw, *Six Plays* (London: Constable, 1962).
1. Shaw had rehearsed the effect obtained in this scene in Act IV of *John Bull's Other Island*,
   where the stage is divided into two areas, one dominated by the passionate grimness of
   Keegan, the other occupied by a group contorted with mirth at the story of Haffigan's pig.

play,[2] its action represents her ministry, her betrayal and abandonment by her disciples, and her agony; leaving off the uniform of the Army is a kind of death; visiting the munitions factory of Undershaft and Lazarus, she harrows hell. The multiple symbolism of the play's final setting suggests, as Shaw chooses to bring the various implications dramatically to life, Golgotha, in the dummy corpses of mutilated soldiers; the exceeding high mountain of the Temptation; the mount of the Ascension, with a view of the New Jerusalem itself, where Peter Shirley has been given the job of gatekeeper and timekeeper.

Shaw, indeed, introduced a valid criticism of Nietzsche when he identified the Salvation Army not only with the worshippers of Dionysus, but also with the Church Militant of the risen Christ. His representation of Christianity as a variety of dionysiac religion corrects Nietzsche's exaggeration of its 'subjective' quality, which made possible his over-schematic view of the opposition between Christianity and Dionysus-Antichrist. The Preface to *Major Barbara* distinguishes between true Christianity and Crosstianity, the religion of negation, of sin and guilt, suffering and death, submission and deprivation. Within the play, a process of redemption is enacted through a bargaining for souls and a vicarious sacrifice. It is a redemption of Christianity itself. Undershaft does not destroy the Salvation Army; he is ready partly to identify himself with it, more ready to identify it with himself, as, in order to win Barbara, he buys it with his cheque to Mrs Baines, the Commissioner. Barbara's spiritual pilgrimage takes her through disillusion and despair to a rebirth of hope and a new vision. Her private emotional experience enforces the recognition that 'the way of life lies through the factory of death', that destruction has its proper place in a healthy scheme of things, and even religion and morality must change in order to survive.[3] Her spiritual death and resurrection contain the promise of a new social order: the money for which she was betrayed bought the freedom of Bill Walker's soul. What this freedom implies is given rational definition in Cusins's declaration of his own new-found purpose:[4]

> I now want to give the common man weapons against the intellectual man. I love the common people. I want to arm them against the lawyers, the doctors, the priests, the literary men, the professors, the artists, and the politicians, who, once in authority, are more disastrous and tyrannical than all the fools,

2. She is the daughter of Britomart, which being interpreted is 'the sweet virgin', and, when the play opens, she does not know her father.
3. Among the best-known lines in the play are Undershaft's ' . . . you have made for yourself something that you call a morality or a religion or what not. It doesnt fit the facts. Well, scrap it. Scrap it and get one that does fit.'
4. There are here some parallels of thought and idea with Yeats's *Calvary*, also indebted to Nietzsche.

rascals and impostors.[5] I want a power simple enough for common men to use, yet strong enough to force the intellectual oligarchy to use its genius for the general good.

The purging of obsolete and unworthy elements in Barbara's Christian faith is accompanied by revision of its liturgy. This process begins in Act I, when the household, except for Stephen, is seduced from family prayers to the more original and vital form of service conducted by Barbara in the drawing room. It opens to the strains of 'Onward, Christian Soldiers, on the concertina, with tambourine accompaniment'. The emblematic sword, which Undershaft has referred to as the sign of his works, is already at least as appropriate as the cross in the insignia of Barbara's religion; and Shaw certainly expected his audience to supply the remembrance of Christ's words, 'I came not to send peace but a sword.' Cusins's excuse to Lady Britomart is unserious in manner and may easily be taken as simple camouflage; but rejecting, as it does, the terms of the General Confession, it at least calls into question the common sense of perfectionism and the morality of self-abasement and excessive emphasis on guilt:

> . . . you would have to say before all the servants that we have done things we ought not to have done, and left undone things we ought to have done, and that there is no health in us. I cannot bear to hear you doing yourself such an injustice, and Barbara such an injustice. As for myself, I flatly deny it: I have done my best.

Undershaft later proposes a revision in the Church Catechism to admit that 'Money and gunpowder' are the 'two things necessary to Salvation'. His account of the works of mercy follows from an identification of the deadly sins with the burdensome material necessities of 'Food, clothing, firing, rent, taxes, respectability and children.' Stephen, in Act I, supplies the address of the Undershaft business as 'Christendom and Judea'. This serves as a warning note of a half-hidden movement in the play from the Old Testament (and ancient Greek) morality of just exchange to the New Testament morality of forgiveness and love. In effect, these are reconciled through the rejection of false and facile interpretations of the New Testament admonitions. Cusins's point of agreement with Undershaft, 'forgiveness is a beggar's refuge. I am with you there: we must pay our debts,'[6] is the necessary counterpoise to that repudiation of irrational

---

5. The Platonic view seems to have been adopted in order to be abandoned.
6. Cf. Bill Walker: 'Let wot Aw dan be dan an pide for; and let there be a end of it.' This is one point where the professor can appropriately point out that the modern Cockney thinks and acts like an ancient Greek. But Bill's attempt to buy his way out of obligations to practise the virtues of mercy and forbearance is no denial of those virtues. (Cusins and Barbara do not cease to value them, and indeed they are implied in Shaw's blueprint for

guilt in Act I (quoted above). Cunningly Undershaft confounds his daughter in answering her charge, 'Father do you love nobody?', by carrying the meaning of love to the extreme of 'Love your enemies':

UNDERSHAFT   I love my best friend.
LADY BRITOMART   And who is that, pray?
UNDERSHAFT   My bravest enemy. That is the man who keeps me up to the mark.[7]

Cusins's admiring response to this, 'You know, the creature is really a sort of poet in his way', does more than acknowledge the Socratic unfolding of neglected truth in a paradox; it conveys a recognition of beauty in the healthy ambivalence of strong emotions, an admission very necessary in the lover of Barbara that aggression need not be ugly and mean. His repudiation of beggarly forgiveness prepares for her new version of the Lord's Prayer:

I have got rid of the bribe of bread. I have got rid of the bribe of heaven. Let God's will be done for its own sake: the work he had to create us to do because it cannot be done except by living men and women. When I die, let him be in my debt, not I in his; and let me forgive him as becomes a woman of my rank.[8]

This is so different from conventional humility, it could unkindly be termed arrogance and found unattractive.[9] For the most part, Shaw manages to endear us to a heroine whose actual living counterpart might well repel us. He does so by suffusing the portrait with his own warm appreciation of the type and setting it off by contrast with a minor sketch of a more conventionally admirable woman.

Orthodox Christianity has a truer representative in Jenny Hill, the Salvation Army lass, than in Barbara Undershaft, and Jenny's Christian spirit is a sublimation of her womanly nature. Jenny is the natural victim of the bullying male; turning the other cheek in response to Bill Walker's assault, offering forgiveness instead of revenge and treating her suffering as matter for joy. She merits her place in the triumphal band, bearing her tambourine, for she has positive qualities that Shaw admires: genuine courage and cheerfulness and industry in the cause she has at heart; this is a credible instance of

---

the millennium, as presented in the last act of the play.) This is just a stage in the process of his rehabilitation.
7. Cf. Blake's 'Opposition is true friendship'. Shaw is certainly fulfilling Blake's promise: 'NOTE. This Angel, who is now become a Devil, is my particular friend: we often read the Bible together in its infernal or diabolical sense, which the world shall have if they behave well.' (*The Marriage of Heaven and Hell*.) But Shaw may also have had Burke in mind: 'He who wrestles with us strengthens our nerves and sharpens our skill. Our antagonist is our helper.' (*Reflections on the Revolution in France*.)
8. Cf. *The Marriage of Heaven and Hell*: 'God only acts and is in existing beings and men.'
9. Yet it is a repellent quality, an aggressiveness, far from unfamiliar in the militant virgin saint of Christian tradition.

the 'worm . . . in the back kitchen' become a woman, a daughter of the Highest. But Jenny's morale (she is only eighteen) is fed by her admiration of Barbara, and there are weaknesses in her that lessen her appeal. Her conventional expressions of piety often strike a false note; her insistence on *love* is too facile; her pity is equally sentimental. Neatly, Shaw demonstrates something unpleasant in her excessive sympathy; Barbara's sense of the ridiculous, like Undershaft's antagonisms, conveys a truer respect for human dignity, for the independence and privacy of the soul:

> BILL [*With sour mirthless humour.*]   Aw was sivin anather menn's knees at the tawm. E was kneelin on moy ed, e was . . . E was pryin for me: pryin camfortable wiv me as a cawpet. Sow was Mog. Sao was the aol bloomin meetin. Mog she says 'Aw Lawd brike is stabborn sperrit; bat down urt is dear art.' Thet was wot she said. 'Downt urt is dear art!' An er blowk thirteen stun four!—kneelin wiv all is wight on me. Fanny, ain't it?
>
> JENNY   Oh no. We're so sorry, Mr Walker.
>
> BARBARA [*Enjoying it frankly.*]   Nonsense! of course it's funny . . .
>
> JENNY   I'm so sorry, Mr Walker.
>
> BILL [*Fiercely.*]   Downt you gow being sorry for me: youve no call . . . Aw downt want to be forgive be you, or be ennybody . . .

If Shaw was concerned to attack the morbid sentimentality of late Victorian Christianity, he was—he needed to be—ready likewise to attack the womanly ideal associated with it. The imbalance between Jenny's emotional and intellectual development has made her the dupe of society, unawake to realities, assisting the millionaire's daughter in collecting the pennies of the indigent in her tambourine, as the wealthy good-for-nothing Lomax takes them in his hat. There is an analogy to be drawn between her and Barbara, who, with the same power of work and need to expend herself in a cause, has to be cured of a similar blindness to things as they are, saved from an equal frittering away of her quality in a cause unliberated from a capitalist economy. Certainly G.B.S. does not repudiate wholesale the Christianity that Barbara and Jenny share; it is its vulnerability and self-betrayal that he rejects. So, in the symbolic structure of his play, he has replaced Christ by the Female Warrior, an androgynous type presiding over the new religion. In the setting aside of the old interpretation of woman's role, along with other forms of masochism, an ideal of sexual equality is implied.

The whole play is flagrantly concerned with money. The first scene, set in the luxurious and stately library of the house in Wilton Crescent and dominated by the opulent physical presence of Lady

Britomart, laps us round in an atmosphere of womblike security. The unreality of material need and adversity, in this context, comes through all the more clearly for Lady Britomart's talk of economy. If it were anxious talk, the whole effect would be destroyed; but there is no anxiety in Lady Britomart's make-up: she is the abundant and never-failing earth-mother of the peak of the golden year. In explaining to Stephen their financial situation, she is merely eliciting the moral approval she thinks due to her; she knows the easy and comfortable solution to her problems—such as they are!—and will apply it quite unscrupulously and without false pride; for she is free of the personal uncertainty that needs to worry about pride. In the first few minutes of the dialogue, we learn of the money available: the Lomax millions (though Charles will not inherit for ten years); the 'poverty' of the Earl of Stevenage on 'barely seven thousand a year'[1] and her own personal income, enough to keep one family in its present luxury. The date is 1906,[2] and the value of the pound is high. Anyway, Shaw has thoughtfully provided a cost-of-living index within the play: thirty-eight shillings a week[3] is the standard wage paid by that model employer, Andrew Undershaft; in the first scene itself, her mother's standard of 'poverty' can be measured against the reference to Barbara discharging her maid and living on a pound a week—a gesture with more of eccentricity about it than real asceticism, for she still lives in Wilton Crescent and, when we see her, is the perfect representative of physical well-being—plump with nourishment, rosy-cheeked and 'jolly' with health, brisk with energy. The immediate prospect is, perhaps, a little more serious for Sarah Undershaft and Charles Lomax, 'poor as church mice' on £800 a year, as they are less richly endowed by nature. But there is always the comforting thought of the unseen providence who has only to be supplicated: the absent father, 'rolling in money', 'fabulously wealthy'. Not a hint of the uncertainties of great wealth creeps into the dialogue, no shadow of sudden losses and bankruptcies, only of the chances of picking up a fortune. In every generation since the reign of James I some foundling has succeeded to the vast Undershaft inheritance; and 'they were rich enough to buy land for their own children and leave them well provided for', apart from the main bequest. Through the centuries the wealth has been accumulating without a break, it seems. This play is certainly not haunted by the Malthusian nightmare.[4]

1. Approximately $11,000 [Editor].
2. January 1906 is the date given in the preliminary directions to Act I of the published (stage) version. No year is given in the original longhand MS. The first performance of the play at the Court Theatre took place on November 28, 1905.
3. Thirty-eight shillings (nearly £2) is approximately $3.50 [Editor].
4. The economic principle that the increase in population tends to outstrip that of the means of living [Editor].

In this respect, its world is that of folklore and fairy tale, of Dick Whittington and Jack and the Beanstalk; a world of inexhaustible hoards of treasure, where straw can be spun into gold and geese lay golden eggs; a world ruled over by luck and indulgent to its favourites: the young, the beautiful, the cheerful, the quick-witted and, not least, the hopeful stranger who carries off the prize from the legitimate heir. The conditions of the will made by Charles Lomax's father establish the genre: 'if he increases his income by his own exertions, they may double the increase.' They reveal a principle of economic distribution that could be called natural, though it is also familiar in Christian terms: 'To him that hath shall be given'; the proposition is that the naturally endowed are fittest to control the resources of civilized society. *Major Barbara*, in its unfolding, extends the principle beyond economic bounds: power to the strong; authority to the commanding.

The fictional situations on which Shaw's plays turn are often absurd and fantastic. Their remoteness from credible actuality works curiously in alliance with the excessively rational element. The arbitrariness of the fable, as an excuse for the play, is flaunted: Shaw is not dramatizing a story with a moral, but creating a dramatic image of his conflicting emotions and ideas. The blatant casuistry with which Cusins matches the doubtful relevance of the test—claimants for the Undershaft inheritance must prove that they are foundlings—communicates the dramatist's sense of logic as a game, his mind's self-delight in its own free play, and a scorn for the plodding literalist. More seriously, it communicates his sense of the slipperiness of all attempts to interpret life rationally. Casuistry is a common element in fairy tales. But the foundling motif is not without serious significance.[5] In relation to Shaw's own psyche, the foundling figure is here interestingly linked with the images of providential bounty and the blueprint for a benevolent paternalism.

The conversion of Barbara, on which the play turns, is essentially conversion to the acceptance of wealth.[6] As part of Shaw's campaign against idealism, or more precisely 'Impossibilism' as it was currently termed among the Fabians, *Major Barbara* sets itself against false pride in unrealizable commodities. Beyond the temptation to refuse tainted money lies the more pernicious temptation to keep out of the marketplace altogether. The position from which Cusins has begun to emerge in pursuit of Barbara, when the play begins, represents the negation from which he and Barbara have to be saved: the retirement of the intellectual, poet, or saint, possible only as a

5. It may be noted here that Lady Britomart and the foundling had had fairly recent theatrical precursors in Wilde's Lady Bracknell and the child mislaid in a handbag. T. S. Eliot, remembering *The Importance of Being Earnest* in *The Confidential Clerk*, recognized that it was a farce on classical themes.
6. But this wealth connotes more than money or power; it is fullness of life, too.

form of privilege (Oxford—surely it is Oxford?—being in 1906 no more an exposed position in society, no less comfortable than Wilton Crescent, as Lady Britomart's acceptance of Cusins recognizes; scholars are gentlemen, and 'nobody can say a word against Greek'). Shaw uses Cusins's intellectual clarity to make explicit, near the end of the play, the realist's view of selling the soul in compromise with the world:

> It is not the sale of my soul that troubles me: I have sold it too often to care about that. I have sold it for a professorship. I have sold it for an income. I have sold it to escape being imprisoned for refusing to pay taxes for hangmen's ropes and unjust wars and things that I abhor . . .

Before we reach this point, our acceptance of the statement as a truism has been prepared by Shaw's confrontation of the Faustian theme of the bargain with its connotations in the central Christian myth.

Undershaft as Mephistopheles, *Doppelgänger*[7] to Cusins's Faust, is presented as a sham villain in a sham conflict. He is more like Cusins than at first appears probable, the stage 'heavy', but intellectualized, no more dionysiac in temperament and character than Cusins, the self-confessed apollonian. The two together provide the play with twin foci of ironic consciousness, mutually comprehending; undershaft merely reveals to Cusins what he already knows, in order to elicit admission of the knowledge: intellectually they are from the start equally free of illusions. They watch each other's manœuvring for the winning—or betrayal—of Barbara; they may talk of rivalry, but the total view they present is more like complicity.

It is in Act II, where Undershaft and Cusins observe the working out of the subplot, or inset play, involving Barbara and Bill Walker, that Shaw concentrates awareness of the Christian analogues:[8] the price received by Judas for the betrayal of Christ and the sanctified bargain of the Redemption, the sacrifice which ransoms human souls. The act begins with the frauds, the minor characters of Rummy Mitchens and Snobby Price ('Snobby's a carpenter,' says Rummy, so preparing for our recognition of the fullness of Bill Walker's pun: 'Wot prawce selvytion nah? Snobby Prawce! Ha! ha!').[9]

7. German: Double [*Editor*].
8. Mrs Glenys Stow has pointed out to me that Shaw's description of the set for Act II, if followed closely, would give a cruciform design dominating the action. Furthermore, the shed to one side, the horse-trough to the other are potentially suggestive of a Bethlehem (waiting for the 'rough beast' of 'The Second Coming'?) [a poem by W. B. Yeats (*Editor*)]; or the shape and stone colour of the horse-trough could suggest to the eyes a tomb, even more than a manger: the extremes of the messianic life of earth.
9. His full name is Bronterre O'Brien Price, commemorating the Dublin Chartist, editor of *The Poor Man's Guardian*. (Incidentally, Bronterre> Brunty> Brontë+ Romola + Shirley suggests that Shaw's mind was running on women novelists and women of genius in general.)

Both are unscrupulous in their readiness to benefit from the providence of the Salvation Army. (Rummy and Lady Britomart, it seems,
are sisters under their skins.) They epitomize a natural way of regarding wealth, opposed to Peter Shirley's and Bill Walker's legalistic
way. Peter talks conscientiously in terms of paying for what he gets
and being himself paid a just price for what he gives. Bill, attempting
legalistically to buy the natural freedom of his soul, throws his sovereign on the drum, where it is followed by Snobby Price's cap;
Snobby, the instinctive, unregenerate socialist, is a parasite on legality, as well as the self-justified petty thief preying on such master-
thieves as Undershaft and Bodger. Barbara, alluding to Bill's 'twenty
pieces of silver' and suggesting that her father need contribute no
more than another ten 'to buy anybody who's for sale', gives the
gesture its ironic ambiguity: in the miniature play, the ostensible
object of the bargain is Bill's soul and Barbara is both tempter and
cheapjack working up the bidding—'Dont lets get you cheap,' as she
works up the collection at Army meetings; the greater price paid for
Barbara herself, in the cheque handed over to Mrs Baines by Undershaft, cancels out Bill's payment and is the token of his release from
his bond;[1] the second payment is not only a magnified reflection of
the first, but its sacramental transfiguration.

The folk law, to which the Undershaft tradition adheres, bears a
genuine relation to the mythology at the centre of the play and to
the ritual of the Dionysiac festivals in which Attic drama is believed
to have originated, ritual celebrations of the rebirth of God in a divine
foundling. In the present Shavian context, official Christianity is certainly reborn as natural religion after the symbolic 'death' of Barbara.
(Cf. Proserpine's descent into the Shades.) But there is also present
the suggestion of a foundling Apollo inheriting from Dionysus.[2] The
transmutation of this into the fairy-tale of the boy from Australia
who takes up the challenge and proves himself worthy of the kingdom and the hand of the princess, that traditionally go together, does
much to save *Major Barbara* from pretentiousness. It might limit its
power to disturb, if the ironic ambiguity of the end of the play was
not realized—a realization important also to the success of the play
in performance (for, without the edge such an interpretation
gives, Act III, so exciting to read, could well fall dramatically flat

---

1. Another modern dramatic model comes to mind here: Yeats's Countess Cathleen pledging
   her soul in exchange for the lesser souls bought by the devils.
2. Cf. Note 1 to Gilbert Murray's 'Excursus on the Ritual Forms Preserved in Greek Tragedy',
   in Jane Harrison, *Themis* (Cleveland: Meridian Books, 1962), p. 341: 'It is worth remark-
   ing that the Year-Daimon has equally left his mark on the New Comedy. The somewhat
   tiresome foundling of unknown parentage who grows up, is recognized, and inherits, in
   almost every play of Menander that is known to us, is clearly descended from the foundling
   of Euripidean tragedy who turns out to be the son of a god and inherits a kingdom'. Jane
   Harrison herself (ibid., p. 443) suggests that Apollo and Dionysus 'are Kouroi and Year
   Gods caught and in part crystallized at different stages of development'.

after Act II—as it did when the play was first produced at the Court
Theatre).

Major Barbara is no exception to the tendency of Shaw's plays to
reflect the pantomime form of fairy-tale, or mythological material,
while relying on the fundamental unity in such different forms of
imaginative construct. Britomart, Barbara and Undershaft are
Edwardian incarnations of Demeter, Persephone and Dis/Minos
(more easily recognizable as such in the years just following Arthur
Evans's first exhibition of finds from the Knossos site[3] than their
counterparts in Candida had been); but also there is a touch of that
sham villain, the demon king, about Undershaft, and in the grouping
of Britomart and Barbara an intriguing resemblance to the association of the pantomime Dame with the Principal Boy. In the course
of the play, a number of references are made to Barbara's self-evident
likeness to her mother. The most broadly comic is assigned to Lady
Britomart herself in the opening scene:

> Ever since they made her a major in the Salvation Army she has
> developed a propensity to have her own way and order people
> about which quite cows me sometimes. It's not ladylike: I'm sure
> I don't know where she picked it up.

The whole of this scene is an emphatic demonstration of Lady Britomart's matriarchal domination of her son, Stephen. She accuses
him of fiddling first with his 'tie', then with his 'chain', and the objects
are certainly emblematic of his relations with her. The trick is later
repeated in her scene alone with Undershaft:

> LADY BRITOMART   Andrew: you can talk my head off; but you
> cant change wrong into right. And your tie is all on one side.
> Put it straight.
> UNDERSHAFT [Disconcerted.]   It wont stay unless it's pinned
> [he fumbles at it with childish grimaces].

Here Andrew takes on the aspect of Jove in a nineteenth-century
classical burlesque, bullied by his consort. The parental reconciliation which seems implied in the last act denotes more than the
acceptance by society of an unpalatable truth, the reconciliation
between power and the 'incarnation of morality'. When Undershaft
has won his daughter, his wife sweeps in to appropriate the empire

3. Evans paid his first visit to Crete in 1893, and A. C. Merrian published 'Discoveries in
Crete' in The Nation (August 1894), p. 81. Excavations at Knossos began in 1900 and
continued until 1905. An article by M. Galloway, 'Labyrinth of Crete', appeared in The
Nineteenth Century (July 1901), pp. 96–102, and a note by Evans himself, 'Labyrinth and
the Palace of Knossos' in The Athenaeum (July 26, 1902), p. 132. An exhibition of repro-
ductions of the Knossos finds was held in London in 1903. (See Cornhill [March 1903],
pp. 319–32). From all this the prominence of a mother-goddess in Cretan worship was
made very clear, one of her names perhaps being Britomart (known to Pausanias).

he has built up.[4] The last glimpse we are given of Barbara represents her clutching *'like a baby at her mother's skirt'*.

In retrospect, the action of the play, initiated by Lady Britomart, can be seen as the working-out of her purpose: to absorb and assimilate the potentially hostile forces, adding them to her own strength. Nations are revitalized in this way; and who else but Britannia at her most imperial have we here? But the persistent victory of the mother over her children, her power always to *contain* them, is more ambiguous in its value. Barbara claims to take a less narrowly domestic and material view than her mother—

> I felt like her when I saw this place—felt that I must have it—that never, never, never could I let it go; only she thought it was the houses and the kitchen ranges and the linen and china, when it was really all the human souls to be saved . . .

—but she is equally possessive, and her similar tendency to treat men as children implies that the pattern will continue in the next generation. She addresses her fiancé invariably by the pet name of 'Dolly' (Lady Britomart, with the formality of her period, calls him reprovingly 'Adolphus'); even when he has seemingly passed the test of manhood by accepting Undershaft's challenge, he remains to Barbara 'Silly baby Dolly', and she can cry exultantly: 'I have my dear little Dolly boy still; and he has found me my place and my work.' The child keeps the doll, the mother keeps the child, the Stevenages maintain their ascendancy through the instrumentality of the strangers they annex.[5] The Earl of Stevenage, Lady Britomart claims, suggested the inviting of Andrew to Wilton Crescent. Whether we take this eponymous ancestor of the conventionally philistine Stephen[6] to be a smokescreen or an actual presence in the background, the sense of ulterior motivation remains, and the sense of a consciousness, like the author's, foreseeing and embracing the whole dramatic development. Bill Walker warns Cusins of the fate before him, as he relates his own experience of Barbara to what may be in store for her 'bloke':

> Gawd elp im! Gaw-aw-aw-awd elp im! . . . Awve aony ed to stend it for a mawnin: e'll ev to stend it for a lawftawm.

---

4. Cf. the ostentatious ease and *sang-froid* with which the attractive, but indolent, Sarah seats herself on the cannon.
5. Cf. Shaw's letter to the *Evening Standard* (Nov. 30, 1944), concerning *Candida*: 'the play is a counterblast to Ibsen's *Doll's House*, shewing that in the real typical doll's house it is the man who is the doll.'
6. Stephen, of course, is the name of the first martyr and thus both this character and his grandfather, the Earl of Stevenage, form part of the mythological machinery of *Major Barbara* as a play about the emergence of a new religion and a new cultural epoch. It may be appropriate to observe here that Undershaft's first name brings him also within the fold of Christianity. One wonders who decided to give his son the name of the first martyr.

Martin Meisel has classified Barbara's wooing of Bill Walker's soul as an example of the reversed love-chase (in which the woman is the pursuer). Certainly it offers a reflection of, or insight into, Cusins's fate. It is in relation to Bill that we chiefly see demonstrated Barbara's capacity for chivvying and bullying, and Shaw leaves us in no doubt of the hidden pressures on her side: her self-confidence is the manner of her class, the product of money, of social prestige and the habit of authority, the certainty of police protection and support. What subdues Bill, before ever Barbara appears to him, is the information that she is an earl's granddaughter; when her millionaire father turns up, he involuntarily touches his cap; the brute force and skill of Todger Fairmile, already won over to Barbara's faith, are her final weapons.

Male vulnerability to the woman's ethic of respect for weakness, shame and guilt is recognizably caricatured in the boastful 'Snobby' Price, whose official confession, 'how I blasphemed and gambled and wopped my poor old mother', is balanced by his private admission to Rummy, 'She used to beat me', and who runs out the back way when his mother arrives at the gate. Bill's blow to Jenny Hill's face is his repudiation of this ethic; making reparation for the act, in preference to being forgiven, is the next stage in his discovery of a morality that does not rob him of his self-respect and self-responsibility. Class distinction no longer cows him when he has paid his debt. Before his exit, near the end of Act II, he is able to take his leave of the desolate Barbara with the magnanimity and good humour of an equal, restored to freedom. He checks his instinctive gesture towards his cap, and he does not take the hand she puts out to him—that would be acceptance of middle-class manners, and Bill can now afford, as he prefers, to keep proudly to his own: 'Naow mellice. Sao long, Judy.'[7] It is a recognition of an integrity in her that matches his own. Her 'Passion', as well as her betrayal by the rest, has thus played its part in saving his soul—from guilt, gloom, slavery and negativism.

Fergusson's critique of *Major Barbara* refers to the Wilton Crescent setting of Act I as though it was retained throughout the play. His interpretation of it as 'the London version of the bourgeois world's' appearing to Shaw 'as stable and secure as the traditional cosmos of the Greeks or Elizabethans', is not simply an affront to Lady Britomart's aristocratic breeding; it disregards the extent to which Shaw has fantasticated the locale through the characters he

7. I owe the observation of this nice point of stage business to my colleague Mr Dennis Douglas. The film of *Major Barbara* included a shot of Bill Walker as a newly prosperous citizen of Perivale St Andrews, thus confusing what is clear in the play: that Bill, at least, achieves a kind of heroism and is not bought up and assimilated to the Establishment. Cusins, who understands and sympathizes with Bill, need not be assimilated either; but he has a life-long siege to withstand.

gathers there and the dialogue they speak, not least by introducing 'Salvation' music among the games of the young people. In fact, the play destroys any possible illusion that this is a naturalistic interior and not a richly furnished stage to accommodate the superhuman stature of Lady Britomart and Andrew Undershaft, sprung from the gutter to become secular master of the world. But Fergusson's mistake can be related to the impression other critics have got from the end of the play. Alick West, seeing in it Shaw's capitulation to bourgeois values and decisive desertion of Marxist socialism, ended serious consideration of Shavian drama, in *A Good Man Fallen Among Fabians*, at this point. Indeed there are sections of Marcuse's 1966 Preface to *Eros and Civilization* on the actualities of our 'advanced industrial society' which it is useful to place beside the situation Shaw has brought his characters to, in Perivale St Andrews. Marcuse is concerned with the difficulty, in an affluent society, of breaking 'the fatal union of productivity and destruction, liberty and repression' and learning 'how to use the social wealth for shaping man's world in accordance with his Life Instincts, in the concerted struggle against the purveyors of Death':

> The very forces which rendered society capable of pacifying the struggle for existence served to repress in the individuals the need for such a liberation . . . In the affluent society, the authorities are hardly forced to justify their dominion. They deliver the goods; they satisfy the sexual and the aggressive energy of their subjects. Like the unconscious, the destructive power of which they so successfully represent, they are this side of good and evil, and the principle of contradiction has no place in their logic.

Only in the name of Undershaft and perhaps the Wedding Chorus that reminds us that *Major Barbara* is, like *Widowers' Houses*, in part a marriage play, does Shaw take sexual energy into account. Otherwise Marcuse's diagnosis is uncannily close to the terms in which Shaw has resolved the philosophical dilemma of his play. Undershaft has successfully induced Barbara to abandon the principle of contradiction for the faith that 'There is no wicked side: life is all one', and the question must be asked, whether she has truly gone *beyond* good and evil, or whether the unity of vision beyond moralistic duality has been achieved at the cost of a vital distinction. Perhaps she and Cusins *have* lost their way and been subtly tricked by the older generation ('The odds are overwhelmingly on the side of the powers that be,' Marcuse remarks).[8] The political Preface to *Eros and Civilization* takes a historical perspective:

---

8. 'As to the triumph of Undershaft,' wrote Shaw to Gilbert Murray, 'that is inevitable because I am in the mind that Undershaft is in the right, and that Barbara and Adolphus, with a

This situation is certainly not new in history: poverty and exploitation were products of economic freedom; time and again, people were liberated all over the globe by their lords and masters, and their new liberty turned out to the submission, not to the rule of law but to the rule of the law of the others. *What started as subjection, by force soon became 'voluntary servitude', collaboration in reproducing a society which made servitude increasingly rewarding and palatable. The reproduction, bigger and better, of the same ways of life came to mean, ever more clearly and consciously, the closing of those other possible ways of life which could do away with the serfs and the masters, with the productivity of repression.*[9] (My italics.)

I do not think Shaw was confused or uncertain, but fully conscious of the perilous ambiguity of the situation. The last line of his text is an alert.

> UNDERSHAFT [*to Cusins*] Six o'clock to-morrow morning, Euripides.

And the undercutting of the dramatic resolution in the reduction of Cusins and Barbara in the last moments is functional in referring the problem back to the audience. It implies a recognition (which Brecht later shared) that the true resolution of socialist drama belongs not in the work of art but outside it in society. Cusins's choice is a resolution in terms of plot; as a total structure of ideas the play remains a paradox in which antitheses retain their full value and cannot be resolved away. The many churches in Perivale St Andrews are not only confirmation of the comparative mythology built into the play; they represent rival visions and issues undecided. There is nothing static about this New Jerusalem: snobbery and the sense of hierarchy survive, but they are confronted by the principles of the William Morris Labor Church. Barbara is aware that the efficient industrial society, however prosperous, is not the fulfillment of her vocation but its opportunity. Her purity of intention, what the nineteenth century called 'character' and what *On the Rocks* was to call 'conscience', is relied on still to find its way through a perspective of infinitely proliferating ironies. Singleness of purpose is necessary to action; but conversely, Shaw's drama now implies, the purity of the action needs to be safeguarded by a matching scepticism, an understanding of things that has moved beyond the defensive self-

---

great deal of his natural insight and cleverness, are very young, very romantic, very academic, very ignorant of the world. I think it would be unnatural if they were able to cope with him.' Letter of October 7, 1905, published in Gilbert Murray, *Unfinished Autobiography* (London: Allen and Unwin, 1960), pp. 155–57.

9. The text is quoted from the Sphere Books edition of Herbert Marcuse, *Eros and Civilization* (London: Sphere Books, 1969; Boston: Beacon Press, [1966]), pp. 11–13.

irony of *Candida* to become a well-forged weapon of assault against 'the purveyors of Death'.

STANLEY WEINTRAUB

Four Fathers for Barbara†

G.B.S. was seldom as specific about the real-life models for characters in his plays as he was for *Major Barbara* (1905). He would title it "Murray's Mother-in-Law," he teased Gilbert Murray, and he made it clear that not only was Murray's stuffy mother-in-law, Lady Rosalind Howard, Countess of Carlisle, the play's dowager Lady Britomart but that Murray himself—a young Australian-born professor of Greek—was the model for Adolphus Cusins. (To make Cusins's identification obvious, Shaw not only borrowed from Murray's own version of *The Bacchae* the lines Cusins quotes from Euripides but prefaced his indebtedness.) Major Barbara herself, it later became known, was modeled after Murray's wife, Lady Mary, and the vivacious young American actress Eleanor Robson. "I want to see if I can make a woman a saint," he had confided to her, and wooed her for the cast of the first production in the epistolary manner with which he usually had such success. "I can't connect Barbara with anyone but you," Shaw wrote, "and am half tempted to take the play right up into the skies at the end because there is a sort of desecration in your marrying even your poet."[1] But Miss Robson chose to continue her American tour with the sentimental and successful *Merely Mary Ann*, and G.B.S. reluctantly found someone else for the role. Later she became the bride of United States Steel magnate August Belmont. It was almost as if she had married Andrew Undershaft.

G.B.S. identified Undershaft, Barbara's father, with no immediate prototype, although he suggested—more seriously this time—that he thought the character so overshadowed the rest of the cast that the play might well be called *Andrew Undershaft's Profession*. The profession itself was crucial for Shaw, although he used it to symbolize all antisocial sources of wealth, for no profession endorsed by Mammon—not even Mrs. Warren's well-known one—had such potential for negative dramatic impact. Three imposing figures in the armaments industry apparently were in Shaw's mind, as well as at

---

† From *The Unexpected Shaw: Biographical Approaches to G.B.S. and His Work* (New York: Frederick Ungar, 1982).
1. Shaw to Elinor Robson, July 4, 1905, in Elinor Robson, *The Fabric of Memory* (New York: Farrar, Strauss and Cudahy, 1957), p. 39.

least one more prototype forgotten everywhere but at Ayot St. Lawrence,[2] where one of Shaw's friends and neighbors soon would be Stage Society playwright Charles McEvoy. McEvoy's father had supported the Confederate side in the American Civil War and by the close of the war had established a factory in the South for the manufacture of torpedoes and high explosive.[3] The gentle, humane McEvoy, of benign appearance but barbarous occupation, must have appealed to Shaw's sense of dramatic paradox.

There was a different, more sardonic, kind of paradox Shaw then could turn to in Swedish arms maker and inventor of dynamite Alfred Nobel. More a sufferer from *Schuldkomplex*[4] than Undershaft (whose industrial motto, "Unashamed," nevertheless implies a moral dilemma), he elected in his last years to "make war on war" by endowing an international peace prize, first awarded in 1901, five years after his death. A complex man, Nobel had his intellectual and humanitarian side, which resulted in his other annual awards; Shaw himself received the one for literature in 1926. Before the posthumous Nobel Prizes however, Alfred Nobel was known for his activities in international finance and for the armaments firm he had inherited from his father and built up to enormous size through his hardheadedness in selling weapons and patents, like Undershaft, to all comers regardless of politics. His own politics belied his business practices. An ardent Social Democrat, he was, to his liberal friends, "the gentle Bolshevik," but he earned millions by selling weapons to nations all over the world, many of which desired nothing more than to suppress any form of social democracy; and his motto "My home is where my work is, and my work is everywhere" would have pleased the motto-loving Undershaft.[5]

Nobel alone might explain the character of a dealer in death who can quote Plato and espouse humanitarian principles, but there was also another reputation available to Shaw. Munitions entrepreneur Sir Basil Zaharoff, a man of mystery to millions of Europeans, not only sold to all comers and even arranged, for his even vaster profit, the large lines of credit necessary (in both cases like Shaw's unashamed arms dealer), he came, like Undershaft, from origins resembling the most romantic Victorian cheap fiction. Barbara's father is an abandoned East End orphan of mysterious origins. The goateed Sir Basil (whose eventual name was almost certainly neither that of his mother nor father) was born in 1849, probably in the brothel quarter of Constantinople, but rumor had him originating all over Europe, one version even claiming that he was an orphan from the

2. The village which the Shaws had made their home [*Editor*].
3. Archibald Henderson, *George Bernard Shaw* (Cincinnati: Stewart and Kidd, 1911), p. 380.
4. Guilt complex [*Editor*].
5. Louis Crompton, *Shaw the Dramatist* (Lincoln: University of Nebraska Press, 1969), pp. 115–16.

slums of Whitechapel. By the early 1900s he was notorious as the Prince of Blood and Steel (Undershaft is called the Prince of Darkness and claims to Barbara that the Salvation Army's motto might be his own—"Blood and Fire"). In the 1890s he had formed a munitions-making partnership with Sir Hiram Maxim of the famous machine gun, and soon merged with Vickers, manufacturers of naval cannon. In the wars of the period—Japan and China, Turkey and Greece, Britain and the Boers, Russia and Japan, Bulgaria and Serbia—Zaharoff and his agents were on the scene selling to both sides and often accused of having provoked the conflicts for the firm's advantage. Regularly, he put his political affiliations to use, via shares he controlled in firms in which many who owned stock were influential in English public life, the Admiralty and the Army. To the end of his life, although he became a Knight Commander of the Bath, he was a public figure of undiminished secretiveness and mystery, having influenced a venal press in his client countries so effectively that it is not surprising that hardly any of his extensive press dossier is even remotely accurate. This underside of his career helps explain Undershaft's outburst to his naive and nearly forgotten son Stephen—*"with a touch of brutality,"* Shaw notes in the preliminary stage directions:

> The government of your country! *I* am the government of your country: I, and Lazarus. Do you suppose that you and half a dozen amateurs like you, sitting in a row in that foolish gabble shop, can govern Undershaft and Lazarus? No my friend, you will do what pays us. You will make war when it suits us, and keep peace when it doesn't. You will find out that trade requires certain measures when we have decided on those measures. When I want anything to keep my dividends up, you will discover that my want is a national need. When other people want something to keep my dividends down, you will call out the police and military. And in return you shall have the support and applause of my newspapers, and the delight of imagining that you are a great statesman. Government of your country! Be off with you, my boy, and play with your caucuses[6] and leading articles and historic parties and great leaders and burning questions and the rest of your toys. *I* am going back to my counting-house to pay the piper and call the tune.

And then there was the portly and unprepossessing Fritz Krupp, inheritor of the Krupp munitions dynasty, which he ruled from 1887 to 1902, building the cannonmakers of Essen into a world industrial power that sold arms from Chile to China, under the firm's unofficial motto *"Wenn Deutschland blüht, blüht Krupp"* (When Germany

---

6. Group which meets to ensure victory of a favored political candidate [*Editor*].

flourishes, Krupp flourishes).[7] Undershaft, like all of his dynasty, has taken, on the instruction of his predecessor, the name of the firm's founder. As Lady Britomart tells the story,

> The Undershafts are descended from a foundling in the parish of St. Andrew Undershaft in the city. That was long ago, in the reign of James the First. Well, this foundling was adopted by an armorer and gun-maker. In the course of time the foundling succeeded to the business; and from some notion of gratitude, or some vow or something, he adopted another foundling, and left the business to him. And that foundling did the same. Ever since that, the cannon business has always been left to an adopted foundling named Andrew Undershaft.[8]

Through this aspect of his play, Shaw, with brilliant, almost miraculous, foreshadowing, prepared the way for life to follow art. Aided by special governmental decrees (even one from Hitler later, in 1943), the Krupps had followed the strictest rules of primogeniture, endowing the whole of family wealth and power upon the eldest son. Siblings, when necessary, were absorbed into the firm, but only as drab underlings. All the world knew in 1905, as Shaw wrote his play, that the Krupp dynasty lacked a male successor. After Fritz Krupp's death in 1902, the succession had fallen awkwardly (as there was no male heir) to his daughter Bertha, with a younger sister, Barbara, disinherited. In 1905 both were approaching marriageable age. Barbara, Shaw could not help having observed with a fine sense of irony, might have been named for the patron saint of armorers and artillerymen. Shaw, after all, wanted a saint for his play.

Barbara is substituted for Bertha. Deliberately? In the play there is a weak son in addition to the two sturdier sisters, who complains, "I have hardly ever opened a newspaper in my life without seeing our name in it. The Undershaft torpedo! The Undershaft quick-fires! The Undershaft ten-inch! The Undershaft disappearing rampart gun! The Undershaft submarine! And now the Undershaft aerial battleship!" So too the headlines about the Krupps and their products, although Shaw can have been nothing less than uncanny in his foreshadowing of several weapons still to be turned out at Krupp arsenals, one the secret U-1, already under way and under wraps at Kiel. Further, the discussion in Act III about the Undershaft nursing home, libraries, schools, insurance and pension funds, and building

---

7. William Manchester, *The Arms of Krupp* (Boston: Little, Brown, 1968), p. 179.
8. Lady Britomart tells her son Stephen that Undershaft considers his company one of two successful institutions in history in which the mode of continuing the leadership was by adoption. The Antonine emperors adopted their successors—a key to their success, according to Undershaft. The Undershaft solution is Shaw's commentary on the difficulty of bequeathing talent and drive (as well as money) to one's natural heirs.

societies bears a resemblance to Krupp paternalism in Essen. As a foreign visitor to the *Konzern* reported in the days of Fritz Krupp,

> Everywhere the name of Krupp appears: now on the picturesque marketplace, on the door of a mammoth department store, then on a bronze monument, now on the portals of a church . . . over a library, numerous schoolhouses, butcher shops, a sausage factory, shoemakers' shops and tailoring establishments, over playgrounds and cemeteries. . . . There is a German beer garden close to each park, and over each of them is written plainly, "Owned by Friedrich Krupp."[9]

Far more uncanny, however (for there were modest English equivalents to this industrial paternalism known to Shaw), is the parallel between what is to happen to Barbara Undershaft—her eventual marriage to the professorial Adolphus Cusins and his thereupon preparing to become, even in name, the next Andrew Undershaft—and what *does* happen in 1906 to Barbara Krupp's sister, Bertha.[1] Cusins himself may have been named to suggest consanguinity, as Murray's father had married, in Australia, where it was legal—the law was changed in England only in 1907—his deceased wife's sister, furnishing Shaw the "orphan" option the play requires in Act III. In Shaw's original 1905 manuscript he had been "Dolly" Tankerville, which would have been uncanny enough, as the Undershaft factory town turns out implements of war. A last-minute change of name kept Shaw from anticipating the tank, invented and first used in 1916. In the play Cusins promises rather to become, in our 20/20 hindsight, something else seemingly out of a crystal ball. Handpicked for Barbara's sister as consort by the Kaiser was a scholarly, obscure diplomat, Gustav von Bohlen und Halbach. And as a dramatic conclusion to the nuptials *Seine Majestät* announced that "To ensure at least an appearance of continuity of the Essen dynasty" (*damit wenigstens eine äusserliche Fortführung der Essener Dynastie ermöglicht ist*), henceforth the bridegroom would take the name of Krupp and the right to pass it and the armaments empire that went along with it to his eldest son. The huge instrument giving legality to the procedure, with royal red wax seal seven inches in diameter, reaffirmed "the special position of the House of Krupp" (*die besondere Stellung des Hauses Krupp*), but, the Kaiser added (as might Andrew Undershaft himself), it was up to the bridegroom to prove himself *"ein wahrer Krupp"*—a real Krupp.[2] Had *Seine Majestät* taken the idea from Shaw? German newspapers (G.B.S. was popular there) had

9. Manchester, *The Arms of Krupp*, p. 206.
1. After whom her husband sentimentally named the big 420-mm cannon used in France in 1914.
2. Ibid., pp. 29–32.

been full of reports of the play. If so, it may be the most amazing case of life utilizing art in our time. But in any case, the possibility that Shaw in the play was, among other things, satirizing Krupp dynastic problems cannot be overlooked.[3]

That Shaw knew what he was doing when he thought in terms of Krupp became obvious two years after *Major Barbara* was produced, when for a German edition of *The Perfect Wagnerite* G.B.S. added lines about the mythic Alberich of *The Rhinegold*. Each would-be Alberich in real life, Shaw wrote,

> discovers that to be a dull, greedy, narrow-minded money-grubber is not the way to make money on the modern scale; for though greed may suffice to turn tens into hundreds and even thousands, to turn thousands into hundreds of thousands requires economic magnanimity and will to power as well as to pelf.[4] And to turn hundreds of thousands into millions, Alberic must make himself an earthly Providence for masses of work-men, creating towns, and governing markets. . . . Consequently, though Alberich in 1850 many have been merely the vulgar Manchester factory-owner portrayed in Friedrich Engels's *Condition of the Working Classes*, in 1876 he was well on the way towards becoming Krupp of Essen, or Cadbury of Bournville, or Lever of Port Sunlight.

As the last line makes clear, even beyond the four dealers in death there were—at a farther remove—other likely "fathers" for Barbara, not dealers in cannon but in chocolate [Cadbury (Editor)] and soap [Lever (Editor)]. But there was also a dealer in the stuff of arma-ments—steel. Shaw's curious statement in 1900 that he thought that "Mammon can be developed into a socialist power, whereas Jehovah makes any such change of mind possible,"[5] sounds like an antici-pation of the Undershaft philosophy (as well as the Alberich lines); and it has been suggested that indeed it is, and that Shaw had indus-trialist Andrew Carnegie in mind. J. P. Morgan had just purchased Carnegie's factories for an estimated hundred million dollars in order to form U.S. Steel, and Carnegie's ventures in philanthropic uses of the staggering sum had led him to the writing of "The Gospel of Wealth," in which he wrote in Bunyanesque cadences[6] that his gos-pel "but echoes Christ's words. It calls upon the millionaire to sell

---

3. Shaw was also satirizing, like Wilde in *The Importance of Being Earnest*, the Victorian dramatic cliché of foundlings recovering their identities, fortunes and finances.
4. Ill-gotten gains [*Editor*].
5. David Bowman, "Shaw, Stead and the Undershaft Tradition," *Shaw Review* XIV (January 1971), p. 29.
6. Which Shaw must have recalled when he wrote, in the preface to *Major Barbara*: "I do not call a Salvationist really saved until he is ready to lie down cheerfully on the scrap heap, having paid scot and lot and something over, and let his eternal life pass on to renew its youth in the battalions of the future."

all he hath and give it in the highest and best form to the poor by administering his estate himself for the good of his fellows, before he is called upon to lie down and rest upon the bosom of Mother Earth." Shaw's response, in a new prefatory note to a reissue of his pamphlet "Socialism for Millionaires" (1901) was that "a Millionaire Movement" had taken place, "culminating in the recent expression of opinion by Mr. Andrew Carnegie that no man should die rich." Only in this way, Shaw thought, could Mammon develop into a socialist power, when traditional inheritance formulas were eschewed. English editor and crusader W. T. Stead reported Carnegie's ideas as to how this could be done in a way that seems to foreshadow the Undershaft scheme of disinheriting one's children— the basic plot device of *Major Barbara*:

> Carnegie laid it down as a fundamental principle upon which the partnership should be conducted that when a partner dies his estate should be settled up within thirty days, and his interest in the business acquired by the remaining partners, and also that no son or child of any of them should have a share in the concern or a voice in its management. This policy has been rigidly observed down to the present. The consequence is that the partnership from time to time has been refreshed and invigorated by infusions of new blood, and the active managers have been young and energetic men.

Stead also provided a link with the Salvation Army aspect of Shaw's play, suggesting that there were passages in Carnegie's exhortations which might lead one to predict that the industrialist "might even become a strong supporter of the social scheme of the Salvation Army." But it was a hint Shaw did not need, for one of his earlier writings had even sketched out what seems the germ of the West Ham Shelter act (II) of the play, with its salvationists and the grudgingly saved:

> The solitary rough is not brave. He is restless and shamefaced until he meets with other roughs to keep him in countenance. He especially dreads that strange social reformer, the Hallelujah lass. At first sight of her quaint bonnet, jersey, and upturned eyes, he rushes to the conclusion that chance has provided him with a rare lark. He hastens to the outskirts of her circle, and after a few inarticulate howls, attempts to disconcert her by profane and often obscene interjections. In vain. He may as easily discontent a swallow in its flight. He presently hears himself alluded to as "that loving fellow creature," and he is stricken with an uncomfortable feeling akin to that which prompted Paul Pry's protest, "Don't call me a phoenix: I'm not used to it." But the Hallelujah lass is not done with him yet. In another minute

she is praying, with infectious emotion, for "his dear, precious soul." This finishes him. He slinks away with a faint affectation of having no more time to waste on such effeminate sentimentality, and thenceforth never ventures within earshot of the Army except when strongly reinforced by evil company or ardent spirits. A battalion of Hallelujah lasses is worth staying a minute to study. . . . As long as they speak strenuously, they consider themselves but little about lack of matter, which forces them to repetitions which, it must be confessed, soon become too tedious for anyone but a habitual Salvationist to endure. . . . [7]

Also a wealthy industrialist, and even less related to armaments than Carnegie, was the Englishman George Cadbury, whose community-planning work Shaw knew well. Perivale St. Andrews, the utopian community built by Undershaft for the workers in his factories, seems based in part upon the model town movement which Cadbury championed and which pioneered the decentralization of industries about planned communities complete to company-sponsored schools and municipal services. Cadbury had been a poor boy and was a self-made man. A Quaker and a humanitarian who believed in providing people with jobs rather than charity, he was the inverse of Undershaft in choosing to enter the chocolate business (in which the company is still eminent) rather than heavy industry. By the turn of the century his community-planning ideas were attracting wide attention, but the Boer War had begun, and he turned his wealth and energies to campaigning for peace.

Shaw was also aware of the paternalistic factory towns of the north, such as Saltaire, begun in 1850 by Sir Titus Salt; and even closer to home was Jonathan Thomas Carr's housing estate, Bedford Park, at the Turnham Green Station of the Metropolitan Railway on the western edge of London. Begun as a speculation by Carr, it offered such attractive features as churches, shops, club, and tavern as well as a variety of house-and-garden designs within the frame of a single architectural style, Queen Anne Revival. As Shaw realized from his artistic and literary acquaintances who gravitated there, Bedford Park was a triumph of planning over monotony, an oasis with just enough of an Aesthetic atmosphere to make the middle-class mind uneasy.

Cadbury's real successor, however—the direct progenitor of Andrew Undershaft's planned community—was Shaw's friend Ebenezer Howard. A high-minded dreamer less practical than Cadbury yet less imaginative than Carr, Howard had nevertheless founded the Garden City movement in 1898 and counted Shaw among his earliest supporters. Shaw even gave the movement the benefit of

7. Ms draft of article, probably 1880s (Texas).

some of his most benevolent satire in *John Bull's Other Island* (1904), the immensely popular comedy about Ireland and Anglo-Irish manners which he wrote just before beginning *Major Barbara*:

> BROADBENT   Have you ever heard of Garden City?
> TIM [*Doubtfully.*]   D'ye mane Heavn?
> BROADBENT   Heaven! No: it's near Hitchin. If you can spare half an hour I'll go into it with you.
> TIM   I tell you what. Gimme a prospectus. Lemmy take it home and reflect on it.
> BROADBENT   You're quite right: I will. [*He gives him a copy of Ebenezer Howard's book, and several pamphlets.*] You understand that the map of the city—the circular construction—is only a suggestion.
> TIM   I'll make a careful note of that. [*Looking dazedly at the map.*]
> BROADBENT   What I say is, why not start a Garden City in Ireland?
> TIM [*With enthusiasm.*]   Thats just what was on the tip of my tongue to ask you. Why not? [*Defiantly.*] Tell me why not.
> BROADBENT   There are difficulties. I shall overcome them; but there are difficulties. . . . [8]

Town-planners such as Howard, and company-town planners on the order of his predecessor Cadbury almost certainly were in Shaw's mind when he completed *John Bull* and began his new play, in which Undershaft's pollution-free factory community of Perivale St. Andrews *"lies between two Middlesex hills, half climbing the northern one. It is an almost smokeless town in white walls, roofs of narrow green slates or red tiles, tall trees, domes, companiles, and slender chimney shafts, beautifully situated and beautiful in itself."* Surveying the Undershaft domain, Cusins remarks half in elation, half in disappointment, "Not a ray of hope. Everything perfect! wonderful! real! It only needs a cathedral to be a heavenly city instead of a hellish one." But as Cusins quickly learns, Perivale St. Andrews has, in addition to the libraries, schools, building funds, community ballrooms, and banqueting facilities, several churches prudently provided by Undershaft, one ironically a "William Morris Labor Church."[9] But the most important church of all to Undershaft's Utopia may be one physically not in Perivale St. Andrews at all. In East London is the

8. *John Bull's Other Island*, Act I.
9. On which is the motto around the dome: "NO MAN IS GOOD ENOUGH TO BE ANOTHER MAN'S MASTER." There actually was a Labour Church Union at the turn of the century, founded in 1891 in Manchester by John Trevor, who attempted, as did Christian Socialism, to combine the social and religious rebellions against the Establishment into one movement. There was even a William Morris Labour church in Leek, Staffordshire. By 1895 there were fourteen congregations in the Labour Church Union, but the concept never caught on in London and did not survive the 1914–18 war.

Church of St. Andrew Undershaft, erected 1520–32. It is called Undershaft—after an earlier church on the same site—according to the chronicler and antiquary John Stow because in the early days of its existence "an high or long shaft, or Maypole, was set up there, in the midst of the street, before the south side of the said church."[1] As it rose higher than the steeple, the church on the corner of St. Mary Axe, Leadenhall Street, became known as St. Andrew Undershaft, distinguishing it from the numerous other London churches dedicated to the popular St. Andrew.[2]

On one occasion during the reign of the first Elizabeth, Stow records, a puritanical cleric named Sir Stephen (here one may usefully recall Undershaft's mediocrity of a son, of the same name) preached against the shaft as a profane source of happiness, accusing the inhabitants of the parish of St. Andrew Undershaft of sacrilegiously setting up for themselves an idol, the proof being their addition to the name of the church—"under that shaft." Stow further writes, "I heard his sermon at Paul's cross, and I saw the effect that followed." What followed was that the parishioners, eager to assert their religious orthodoxy, pulled down their beloved Maypole, hacked it into pieces, and put it to the pyre.[3] Blood and fire.

Shaw's play has been called his *Divine Comedy*—in brief, because its pervasive religious aspect includes three acts possibly divisible allegorically into Dante's Hell, Purgatory, and Paradise.[4] If the genealogy of Major Barbara's father ironically recalls the conflict at the great shaft of Cornhill between bleak, negative orthodoxy and the small-scale but positive juxtaposition of divine and materialistic happiness represented by the paradox of the Maypole and the Mass merging at St. Andrew Undershaft—a literal *Divine Comedy* in itself—it may be that Shaw intended it so. Certainly his christening of Barbara's father suggests, as does the entire density of allusion in the drama, that he had thoroughly done his homework. Yet had Shaw's Undershaft solved the spiritual problem in his armaments-dependent Utopia? "Try your hand on my men," he confidently invites Barbara as they tour his "City of God": "Their souls are hungry because their bodies are full." And Barbara is ensnared by that temp-

---

1. John Stow, *A Survey of London* (1658), Henry Morley, ed. (London, 1890), p. 163. The first time attention was called to Stow's account was in S. Weintraub, *Shaw Review* II (1958), p. 22.
2. Undershaft has clearly meant to suggest particular relevance to his vale-situated company town through the St. Andrews of its name. The first of Shaw's "Saint Barbara's" many forefathers may thus be a saint himself, the St. Andrew of the lost Gospel (alluded to by tradition), who gave the playwright his excuse to title part of his preface "The Gospel of St. Andrew Undershaft", and who had special significance to Shaw's audience as (with St. George) one of the two patron saints of Britain.
3. Ibid.
4. Joseph Frank, "*Major Barbara*: Shaw's *Divine Comedy*," PMLA LXXI (1956): 61–74. In an irony which very like escaped G.B.S. it is St. Bernard who, when Dante reaches the heavenly zone, assumes the role of guide and reveals to the poet the final aim of man.

tation, as has been her husband to be. It is not without reason that Cusins earlier had labeled Undershaft "Mephistopheles-Machiavelli," for ironic Faustian overtones are not merely in the Satanic mills which nourish the heavenly city but permeate the play.

There was, one must also own, a real Stratford St. Andrew Rectory, a house in Suffolk rented by the Webbs where Shaw in 1896 spent a long summer holiday. The skein of association in creativity is labyrinthine—Barbara's Salvation Army assistant, Jenny Hill, for example, recalls the music hall comedienne of the same name Shaw may have remembered who sang (shades of East Ham!) "The City Waif" and who died at forty-six in 1896. That Shaw's capacious subconscious stored the Stratford St. Andrew location is apparent by its postal address of "near Saxmundham," for Andrew Undershaft in Act II is asked to match a gift to the Salvation Army by Lord Saxmundham, who had been Horace Bodger the distiller until his benefactions to restore a crumbling cathedral were recognized—a bit of history Shaw borrowed from the Guinness brewing family, as he took Bodger's "letters of fire across the sky" illuminated sign (in Barbara's agonized description) from the pioneering one for Dewar's Whisky.

Four fathers for Barbara? The four armorers are but a beginning, in a play inspired not only by people and events Shaw saw around him but by the *Republic* of Plato, the *Bacchae* of Euripides, the *Pilgrim's Progress* of Bunyan, *The Prince* of Machiavelli, the *Marriage of Heaven and Hell* of Blake, the *Emperor and Galilean* of Ibsen, and the *Ring* of Wagner.[5] In visualizing so many threads drawn together, we not only achieve an insight into a remarkable creative process but through that insight realize a sense of the ramifications of a single dramatic personality. A character with such complex origins cannot be one from whom we can extract simple answers. Although much can be learned about Shaw's intentions within various levels of meaning from Barbara's many forefathers—not only from the four dealers in death—*Major Barbara* resists simplification and remains the most complex of Shaw's plays. Decades after he wrote *Man and Superman*, with its structure of preface, play, mythic play within the play, appendix purportedly written by one of the characters, and aphoristic fireworks of an appendix to that appendix, Shaw boasted that he had put all of his intellectual goods in the shop window in that play.[6] He had put even more into *Major Barbara*, but not with such shop-window obtrusiveness. In the paradoxes of Barbara's many fathers is the intellectual center of Shaw's most profound work for the theatre.

5. Also, unless the echo is no more than that, the *Past and Present* of Carlyle, in which a "Plugson of Undershot" is the owner of a firm located in the parish of "St. Dolly Undershot." Julian Kaye, who notes this in *Bernard Shaw and the Nineteenth-Century Tradition*, suggests that the "Dolly" might have further echoed in Shaw via Adolphus "Dolly" Cusins.
6. Preface, *Back to Methuselah*.

A final, postplay irony brings together Saints Barbara and Andrew—for a World War II air raid blotted out the buildings on the opposite corner of Leadenhall Street and St. Mary Axe, leaving the Church of St. Andrew Undershaft relatively unscathed. The bomb very possibly was manufactured by Krupp.

On *Pygmalion*

J. ELLEN GAINOR

The Daughter in Her Place†

In the late extravaganza *Too True to Be Good* (1932), Shaw explicitly addresses and condemns the type of mother/daughter relation characterized at the end of *Major Barbara*. The daughter here tries to escape the clutches of her over-protective, infantilizing mother, exclaiming,

> No woman can shake off her mother. There should be no mothers: there should be only women, strong women able to stand by themselves, not clingers. . . . Mothers cling: daughters cling: we are all like drunken women clinging to lamp posts: none of us stands upright. . . . If only I had had a father to stand between me and my mother's care. (509)

Shortly thereafter, she presents her goals for the future:

> I have the instincts of a good housekeeper: I want to clean up this filthy world and keep it clean. There must be other women who want it too. Florence Nightingale had the same instinct when she went to clean up the Crimean war. She wanted a sisterhood; but there wasnt one. . . . I want a sisterhood. Since I came here I have been wanting to join the army, like Joan of Arc. It's a brotherhood, of a sort. (511–12)

Although we are to see the narrowness of the young woman's interests—particularly as she wants those who do not join her "strangled" (511)—her remarks merit attention for their complex fusion of themes. She rejects her mother and longs for a father figure to intercede and support her. She relies on a feminine, domestic metaphor ("housekeeper") to ground herself and describe her larger social inclinations. She expresses interest in a "sisterhood," a communion of women in which there is no place for the older women, the mothers (and for which there is no model anywhere in Shaw, who avoids

† From *Shaw's Daughters: Dramatic and Narrative Constructions of Gender* (Ann Arbor: The University of Michigan Press, 1991), pp. 224–39.

any female bond more compelling than the luncheon date between Grace and Sylvia in *The Philanderer*). And the only image she can find for the sisterhood she desires is male: the army. Compressed in these speeches is Shaw's division of female experience, the gulf that separates younger from older women and strips any sense of conti-nuity or purpose from the matriarchs. Through "The Patient" (as Shaw designates her throughout), Shaw reinforces an essentially domestic role for women, although they may be motivated to bring their domestic experience into the larger social sphere. That larger world exhibits its own patriarchal structure clearly, yet the young woman cannot conceive of entering it without emulating men and male institutions; she has no idea what a female structure in the larger sphere could be.

The fusion of the domestic with a (re) movement for a woman into a professional domain similarly characterizes the epilogue to *Pyg-malion*, although Shaw does not portray the transition with as much revolutionary fervor as he does in *Too True*. This may in part be because Eliza's separation is from a paternal, rather than maternal, figure, and Shaw clearly presents this division as negligible—the Col-onel still oversees Eliza's and Freddy's business, while Eliza contin-ues "to meddle in the housekeeping at Wimpole Street" (123–24).

Different critics organize the progress of Shaw's writing in various ways. Arthur Ganz, for example, sees the marriage of Ellie Dunn and Captain Shotover as "the culmination of a line of impassioned father-daughter relationships" (193), while Eric Bentley seems to suggest that the character named Pygmalion in *Back to Methuselah* demonstrates the ultimate result of attempts at human creation (83). Bentley also depicts "the 'education of Eliza' " as "a caricature of the true process" (86), although he does not explain, or give examples of, what that "true process" might be like. But Bentley's remark suggests why *Pygmalion* strikes me as the logical end point for this study, in that the play both exposes and exploits the subgenre Shaw has been creating: that which revolves around the intricacies of the father/daughter, teacher/pupil/lover relation. In *Pygmalion* the playwright demonstrates a better balance between the central male and female characters, calling into question the extent of Higgins's impact on Eliza and the relative power each brings to their relationship.

Pygmalion is a favorite target for Shavian and drama critics gen-erally, and it has particularly attracted biographical and psychoana-lytic readings. Arthur Ganz groups the romance with other works in which Shaw projects himself as a young female: "When he wrote a play about a flower girl who in acquiring a new speech acquires a new soul, Shaw was dramatising a central action of his life" (6). Arnold Silver expresses a similar theory: "Shaw could sympathetically speed her on this journey [to selfhood] because in certain important respects Eliza's fairy-tale career paralleled his own" (185). Maurice Valency feels "Shaw himself had learned upper-class English ways in somewhat the same manner as Eliza" (323). Philip Weissman constructs a more elaborate interpretation, seeing in Shaw's difficult childhood and subsequent need of a mother figure the impetus for the creation of Eliza. Shaw's rapport with Mrs. Patrick Campbell[1] informed the drama, for he served as a teacher/director for her, while she mothered him. Weissman maintains that the idea for *Pygmalion* was a logical outgrowth of Shaw's work on *Caesar and Cleopatra*. "In his 'unconscious drama' he was recasting Caesar as the West End gentleman, Henry Higgins. . . . Similarly, he transformed Cleopatra into Pat Campbell as the East End donna, Eliza Doolittle" (163).

These various interpretations, each of which strikes me as plausible and ingenious, represent attempts to contain and explain the sustained power struggles and complex nexus of pseudofamilial relations in the play. What intrigues me, however, is not what lies behind Shaw's portrayals, but the implications and (subtextual) thrust of the action of these characters. Clearly he uses established dramatic structures to spin out variations on his theme. *Pygmalion* follows patterns of paternal pedagogy, maternal marginalization, and emotional complication found elsewhere. But Shaw introduces key distinctions in this drama found in none of the related pieces. One singular difference is Eliza's active entrance into the teacher/pupil situation. Unlike Cleopatra, who learns from Caesar during his colonial invasion of her land, or Barbara, whose growth is integrally connected to her biological tie to her father, or Dorothea, who as a child has no control over the behavior of adults who take her education as their personal responsibility, Eliza independently chooses to seek out Higgins's tutelage.

By invoking the Pygmalion myth in his title, Shaw clearly asks his audience to be aware of the idea of human creation and formation and to think about the problems inherent in the drive to mold an ideal being. Yet as with the depiction of Undershaft in *Major Barbara*, the attractiveness and power of a character or situation may conflict with the authorial desire to expose that very magnetism. Shaw's work does not distance his audience with the methods of alienation later developed by Brecht to avoid this problem. Rather, he seems to rely on an informed, thoughtful audience's "self-alienation." It must subsequently disengage itself from the seductive quality of the characters by realizing how and why Shaw's work evolved the way it did, and ideally engage in a Fabian-like attempt to resolve similar struggles in the real world differently. Yet equally

---

1. Mrs. Patrick Campbell played Eliza Doolittle to Herbert Beerbohm Tree's Henry Higgins [*Editor*].

possible is the sense that this is a critical rationalization for the conflicts the audience may face between the immediate impact of the work and its later feeling that Shaw's intention must have been different, given his sociopolitical position. This speculative spiral is irresolvable, however; surely it is too much to expect complete coherence, particularly if *Pygmalion* emerged from the depths of psychological and emotional conflict so many critics suggest.

It is intriguing that Shaw conflates two seemingly separate myths in the play, the Pygmalion story and a fairy-tale plot that overtly resembles *Cinderella* in its transformation of ragged young woman to "princess," but also more subtly invokes *Snow White*. The French feminist critic Hélène Cixous shows the connection between these male-authored myths—a connection that fits the Shavian rendition peculiarly well:

> One cannot yet say of the following history "it's just a story." It's a tale still true today. Most women who have awakened remember having slept, *having been put to sleep.*
> *Once upon a time . . . once . . . and once again.*
> Beauties slept in their woods, waiting for princes to come and wake them up. In their beds, in their glass coffins, in their childhood forests like dead women. Beautiful, but passive; hence desirable: all mystery emanates from them. It is men who like to play dolls. As we have known since Pygmalion. Their old dream: to be god the mother. The best mother, the second mother, the one who gives the second birth. (66)

Through Mrs Higgins's censure of Pickering and her son, Shaw expresses his understanding, parallel to Cixous's analysis, of the "artist-men": "You certainly are a pretty pair of babies, playing with your live doll" (68). Shaw's fairy-tale allusions make the connection even more apt. Shaw also includes strategic references to the Snow White tale, which features in many versions the famous glass coffin, and, more important, the queen's magic mirror and her poisoned apple.

In the well-known Grimm version of the tale, the evil queen, stepmother to Snow White, disguises herself as an old peddler to seek out the young princess, who is hiding from her in the forest at the home of the dwarfs. She brings with her an apple, half of which has been poisoned. She tricks Snow White into sharing the apple with her, by breaking it in two and safely eating the unadulterated portion. The poisoned bite that Snow White takes becomes lodged in her throat as she falls into a deathlike sleep. In *Pygmalion*, Shaw casts Higgins in the stepmother role, as he tries to seduce Eliza into staying to learn to talk like a duchess:

> HIGGINS [*snatching a chocolate cream from the piano, his eyes suddenly beginning to twinkle with mischief*] Have some chocolates, Eliza.

LIZA [*halting, tempted*]   How do I know what might be in them?
Ive heard of girls being drugged by the like of you. [*Higgins
whips out his penknife; cuts a chocolate in two; puts one half
into his mouth and bolts it; and offers her the other half.*]

HIGGINS.   Pledge of good faith, Eliza. I eat one half: you eat
the other. [*Liza opens her mouth to retort: he pops the half
chocolate into it*]. You shall have boxes of them, every day.
You shall live on them. Eh?

LIZA [*who has disposed of the chocolate after being nearly choked
by it*]   I wouldnt have ate it, only I'm too ladylike to take it
out of my mouth.

Eliza's room in Higgins's house also contains a full-length mirror,
the first one she has ever encountered. In the Snow White tale, the
stepmother learns from the magic mirror of Snow White's
whereabouts as well as of her own loss of superior beauty. Although
Shaw does not use this prop as exactly, he does imbue it with the
evil connotations of the fairy-tale (from Eliza's viewpoint), and it does
become a vehicle for self-appraisal and self-recognition. After Eliza's
bath in act 2, she sees an unrecognizable self in the mirror for the
first time. Reflecting her puritanical upbringing, she feels the vision
of her naked body is indecent, and she covers it with a towel (52).[2]
Yet it also reveals her physical beauty, and thus the mirror "tells" the
same news as in the fairy-tale. The mirror reappears in the last scene
of act 4, moreover, to demonstrate Eliza's disenchantment with the
image of herself created by Higgins. Dressed in the clothes Pickering
has provided, surrounded by the furnishings Higgins has procured,
Eliza rejects her reflection as she severs the tie with Wimpole Street,
sticking her tongue out at the mirror princess who has achieved Higgins's ideal as she exits her room for the last time, leaving fairy land
behind (85).

   Shaw's association of Higgins with the evil stepmother adds a dark
tone to *Pygmalion*—one that contrasts with the fairy godmother
transformation of the slavey Cinderella. This shading in the play
finds its strongest evidence in the repeated threats to Eliza's sexual
and physical safety. Martin Meisel centers this action in "the seduction scene of the second act," where "everyone suspects Higgins'
designs" (175–76). But the theme is introduced much earlier, in the
opening scene of the play, with her first "terrified" and "hysterical"
insistence of her respectability and the fear of losing her "character"
(15). Eliza's concerns operate on two levels here: not only does she
fear a loss of reputation (meaning actually the acquisition of one as

2. The analysis here draws on Shaw's final, definitive edition of the play, published after his
   work on the film version, and incorporating several scenes (including the bath and mirror
   sequences) not in the original edition.

a loose woman) and legal livelihood, but her speech also foreshadows the larger issue of Eliza's loss of self—the transformation into a new identity and "character" created by Higgins.

From her act 1 protestation that "I'm a good girl, I am" (17) through her act 5 taunt to Henry, "Wring away. What do I care? I knew youd strike me some day" (108), Eliza consistently expresses concern for her physical and moral well-being at the hands of her teacher and surrogate father Higgins. Both Higgins and the bystanders at Covent Garden identify the former with teaching (19–20), and Shaw establishes the didactic nature of the drama in its brief preface (9). But he explicitly fuses paternal and pedagogical roles with the threat of physical violence early in act 2:

> MRS PEARCE   Dont cry, you silly girl. Sit down. Nobody is going to touch your money.
>
> HIGGINS   Somebody is going to touch *you*, with a broomstick, if you don't stop snivelling. Sit down.
>
> LIZA [*obeying slowly*]   Ah-ah-ah-ow-oo-o! One would think you was my father.
>
> HIGGINS   If I decide to teach you, I'll be worse than two fathers to you. (30)

Higgins, of course, is actually one of three fathers for Eliza, the other two being Colonel Pickering—another teacher from whom she "learnt really nice manners" (97)—and "the regulation natural chap," Alfred Doolittle. These three men represent the social spectrum of patriarchy, each with his own mode of keeping Eliza "in her place." Doolittle, who knows nothing of the didactic arrangement under which Eliza will stay at Wimpole Street, arrives at the house to arrange the "sale" of his daughter for five pounds, acting out the exchange of women in patriarchal culture. He makes the Victorian assumption that Higgins's job, as the prospective husband in this burlesqued exchange, will be to "improve Eliza's mind" and suggests that the most efficacious method will be "with a strap" (52).

Unbeknownst to Doolittle, of course, Higgins manipulates their conversation so that the member of "the undeserving poor" (48) will reveal his class differences and prejudices. Eliza, from the same class origins, is a victim of both class and sex discrimination, and Shaw draws parallels between these two forms of injustice in the play. Although Eliza repeatedly asserts her essential similarity to the upper classes, with whom she shares self-respect and human feelings, Higgins maintains a stance in opposition to her beliefs.

> PICKERING [*in good-humored remonstrance*]   Does it occur to you, Higgins, that the girl has some feelings?
>
> HIGGINS [*looking critically at her*]   Oh no, I dont think so. Not

any feelings that we need bother about. [*Cheerily*] Have you, Eliza?

LIZA   I got my feelings same as anyone else. (34)

Through Higgins's infantilization of Eliza, treating her as a child and talking about her as if she weren't present or able to understand, Shaw creates a parallel between issues of class and sex: discrimination toward the poor and toward women (who are tantamount to children) appear very similar. By erasing detectable class difference in Eliza through speech education, Higgins believes he will be endowing her with the humanity she lacks. The issue of Eliza's sex, however, does not enter into Higgins's equation in any considered way. Speech training and gender programming go hand in hand with Higgins's method, and thus as Eliza learns Henry's speech, she also absorbs the masculine context from which it evolved.

Late in the play, Henry delivers the first of his "creation" speeches, fulfilling his Pygmalion image: "I have created this thing out of the squashed cabbage leaves of Covent Garden" (97). Eliza clarifies this creative, educational process, highlighting the masculine nature of his precepts: "I was brought up to be just like him, unable to control myself, and using bad language on the slightest provocation" (97). In other words, Higgins has reared Eliza in his own image, a male image. Significantly, language, the instrument of male paternity, is the medium through which Eliza assumes her resemblance to Higgins. As Mrs Higgins observes:

> MRS HIGGINS   You silly boy, of course she's not presentable. She's a triumph of your art and of her dress maker's; but if you suppose for a moment that she doesnt give herself away in every sentence she utters, you must be perfectly cracked about her.
>
> PICKERING   But dont you think something might be done? I mean something to eliminate the sanguinary element from her conversation?
>
> MRS HIGGINS   Not as long as she is in Henry's hands.
>
> HIGGINS [*aggrieved*]   Do you mean that *my* language is improper?
>
> MRS HIGGINS   No, dearest: it would be quite proper—say on a canal barge; but it would not be proper for her at a garden party. (67)

Mrs Higgins opposes the masculine realm of the canal barge to the more feminine location, the garden party, and shows that Eliza speaks her teacher's masculine language. Eliza confirms this, speaking of both the class and sexual nature of language:

> You told me, you know, that when a child is brought to a foreign country, it picks up the language in a few weeks, and forgets its own. Well, I am a child in your country. I have forgotten my own language, and can speak nothing but yours. Thats the real break-off with the corner of Tottenham Court Road. (99)

In act 4, after Eliza's triumph, when she expresses anger and frustration over the men's insensitivity to her dominant role in the success, Higgins remarks, "Youre not bad-looking: it's quite a pleasure to look at you sometimes—not now, of course, because youre crying and looking as ugly as the very devil; but when youre all right and quite yourself" (82). The subtext of his comment, "when you behave in a feminine fashion—that is, crying or being temperamental—you are 'not yourself,' not the creature I made," comes through clearly. When in act 5 Eliza asserts her independence Higgins exclaims triumphantly—in the same manner in which Shaw's avuncular persona instructed "his" Dorothea—"By George, Eliza, I said I'd make a woman of you; and I have. I like you like this" (108–9). Her attainment of Higgins's sense of "womanhood" allows her access to male identity: "Now youre a tower of strength: a consort battleship. You and I and Pickering will be three old bachelors instead of only two men and a silly girl" (109).

In shorter form, Shaw reinforces the paternal education of Eliza by creating a parallel scenario for Clara Eynsford-Hill in his "sequel" (5), the prose epilogue that follows the play. Clara becomes Eliza's legal sister through the latter's marriage to her brother Freddy Eynsford-Hill, and spiritual sister through her education into moral, socially conscious humanity. Clara, "who appeared to Higgins and his mother as a disagreeable and ridiculous person, and to her own mother as in some inexplicable way a social failure, had never seen herself in either light" (118), not, at least, until she read H. G. Wells and Galsworthy. Clara, Shaw tells us, formed "a gushing desire to take her [Eliza] for a model" (119), but experienced quite a shock when she learned "that this exquisite apparition had graduated from the gutter in a few months time" (119).

> It shook her so violently, that when Mr H. G. Wells lifted her on the point of his puissant pen, and placed her at the angle of view from which the life she was leading and the society to which she clung appeared in its true relation to real human needs and worthy social structure, he effected a conversion and a conviction of sin comparable to the most sensational feats of General Booth. (119)

Thus Clara, through male literary paternity, similarly achieves a laudable social stature, having taken the authors' precepts to heart and having substituted them as her models. In the process, of course,

Clara leaves her mother's conventional views and her circle at Large-lady Park.

> It exasperated her to think that the dungeon in which she had languished for so many unhappy years had been unlocked all the time, and that the impulses she had so carefully struggled with and stifled for the sake of keeping well with society, were precisely those by which alone she could have come into any sort of sincere human contact. (120)

Clara, another princess locked away, learns from Galsworthy of the potential that lay within her all the time. By negative association with her mother and her mother's circle, these unspecified "impulses" take on masculine qualities.

The maternal rejection presented in this sequel also continues a matriarchal theme from the main drama. Eliza is another of Shaw's orphan characters, having been brought up in a motherless home: "I aint got no mother. Her that turned me out was my sixth step-mother. But I done without them" (34). Higgins offers his house-keeper, Mrs Pearce, as a maternal substitute for the girl: "You can adopt her, Mrs Pearce: I'm sure a daughter would be a great amuse-ment to you" (34), and indeed entrusts this older woman with all domestic matters relating to Eliza's stay, including those feminine matters of hygiene inappropriate for him to supervise. Shaw estab-lishes Mrs Pearce as a parallel character to Higgins's mother (Mor-gan 172), a domineering, scolding, condescending woman, who is the object of Henry's continual rebellion. As such, the mothers are both ineffectual teacher figures; their "boy" Henry never carries out their instructions, particularly with regard to his pupil, Eliza:

> Then might I ask you not to come down to breakfast in your dressing-gown, or at any rate not to use it as a napkin to the extent you do, sir. And if you would be so good as not to eat everything off the same plate, and to remember not to put the porridge saucepan out of your hand on the clean tablecloth, it would be a better example to the girl. You know you nearly choked yourself with a fishbone in the jam only last week. (42–43)

The women's failure as teachers corresponds to Higgins's patriarchal belief in pedagogy as a masculine occupation. This also accounts for his surprising reaction to Eliza's notion of being an elocution instruc-tor. As the "assistant to that hairyfaced Hungarian" (108), Eliza would place herself in the traditionally feminine position of inferi-ority, appropriating male privilege while maintaining a feminine identity. This prompts Higgins's threat to "wring your neck" (108). But when Eliza realizes her ability to perform independently, to mirror her teacher/father instead of compete with him via feminine affiliation with another male, his response is altogether different. Eliza cries,

> Aha! Now I know how to deal with you. What a fool I was not to think of it before! You cant take away the knowledge you gave me. You said I had a finer ear than you. . . . I'll advertize it in the papers that your duchess is only a flower girl that you taught, and that she'll teach anybody to be a duchess just the same in six months for a thousand guineas. (108)

Her discovery elicits his above-quoted exclamation of pleasure with the woman he has "made," a woman who to his eyes resembles a man like himself. This characterological mirroring corresponds to the physical mirror emblem that runs through the play. Higgins's mirror reflects Higgins in Eliza, a correlation he confirms at the end of act 4, after the passage quoted earlier about her not being "herself" when she, essentially, does not project his image of her. He tells her, "You go to bed and have a good nice rest; and then get up and look at yourself in the glass; and you wont feel so cheap" (82).

The disparagement of Eliza, calling her, "cheap" and a "dirty slut" (38) again has class connotations, with a heavily sexual undertone. Mrs Pearce echoes Higgins's defamation of Eliza, and as his minion she enters into the darker mythic subplot discussed earlier. Higgins informs Eliza in act 2, "If you're naughty and idle you will sleep in the back kitchen among the black beetles, and be walloped by Mrs Pearce with a broomstick" (36). Despite Higgins's numerous threats of physical violence, he never actually hurts Eliza, mental and emotional cruelty notwithstanding. Instead, Shaw projects onto Mrs Pearce the physical, sexual violation of Eliza that Henry suppresses throughout, in a lesbian "rape" scene added to the original script at the time it was filmed (1938).[3]

Higgins insists that Mrs Pearce "bundle her off to the bath-room" (37) to clean her as a first step toward respectability. This action fits neatly with the mythic "rebirth" of Eliza, for bathing has always been symbolically associated with the remission of sin and rebirth in the Western Christian tradition.[4] Mrs Pearce conducts Eliza to "a spare bedroom" on "the third floor." Eliza had "expected to be taken down to the scullery" (38), but she begins her transformation by a physical elevation that metaphorically parallels her expected rise in social stature. She is told "to make [herself] as clean as the room: then [she] wont be afraid of it" (38)—a simile that counters the previous elevation metaphor with its continuation of the girl's dehumaniza-

---

3. Arnold Silver [in *Bernard Shaw: The Darker Side* (Stanford, 1992)] also reads this sequence as a rape scene, but he makes no mention of the lesbian content (270–72).
4. Note the parallel context of sin from which Clara emerges in the epilogue.

tion. Eliza associates cleanliness with death; however, the metaphoric, sexual sense of death remains perhaps subtextual:

> LIZA   You expect me to get into that and wet myself all over!
> Not me. I should catch my death. I knew a woman did it every
> Saturday night; and she died of it. . . . (*weeping*) . . . Its not
> natural: it would kill me. Ive never had a bath in my life. (38)

Mrs Pearce counters with inducements and slurs: "Well, dont you
want to be clean and sweet and decent, like a lady? You know you
cant be a nice girl inside if youre a dirty slut outside" (38). The
reasoning is the twisted logic of upper-class male seducers of lower-
class women in eighteenth and nineteenth century romance: submit,
succumb, and receive the outer embellishments of higher social
status. The ambiguity of the term *slut*, which can mean either a
physically dirty or morally questionable woman, stands out strongly;
Eliza's claims of being a "good girl" are thrown into question by the
alternative, sexual connotation of the label. This indeterminacy res-
onates with the link between physical cleanliness and sexual purity
that is inverted by the scene's subtext into physical cleanliness and
sexual defloration.

Despite Eliza's cries of protest, she is ordered to "take off all [her]
clothes" (39).

> Mrs Pearce puts on a pair of white rubber sleeves . . . then takes
> a formidable looking long handled scrubbing brush and soaps it
> profusely with a ball of scented soap. Eliza comes back with noth-
> ing on but the bath gown . . . a piteous spectacle of abject terror
> . . . Deftly snatching the gown away and throwing Eliza down on
> her back . . . she sets to work with the scrubbing brush. Eliza's
> screams are heartrending. (39–40)

The blatancy of these stage directions implies Shaw's cognizance
of their implications. The phallic brush and cleansing ball are applied
with the clinical coldness of the bath/laboratory's rubber gloves.
That Eliza should be thrown on her back to be "cleaned," which in
a bathtub would literally lead to drowning, cements the rape imagery,
highlighting for the reader the symbolic interpretation over the literal. Using a female surrogate for the male rapist, Shaw again conceives of this lesbian encounter in a heterosexual context, in keeping
with the late Victorian/Edwardian medical paradigm for a lesbian
relation. But perhaps more important, he transfers the onus of sexual
violence onto a woman, thereby safeguarding the gruff geniality of
Higgins and insuring his respectability at the same time that he fulfills the dark threat to Eliza that the play's opening dialogue foreshadows.

The film version, which facilitated the inclusion of this scene, graphically follows the outline of Shaw's directions, and creates a profoundly disturbing atmosphere on screen. At the start of the bath scene, Mrs Pearce wraps herself in a sheet/apron (instead of the printed "sleeves") and promptly corners Eliza in the bathroom, trying to talk her into removing her clothes. She finally pushes Eliza out into the adjacent bedroom to change into a robe, leaving Mrs Pearce alone. At this point, ominous music begins quietly, and almost like the witch whose broomstick has been alluded to earlier, she begins to mix bath salts in a tub that quickly foams with the appearance of a bubbling cauldron. Mrs Pearce looks toward the bedroom door with a determined glint in her eye and picks up the scrubbing brush and soap. After another brief tangle getting Eliza to remove the robe—the camera having cut to Mrs Pearce draping the bathroom mirror with a towel—Eliza is seen in the tub, screaming and struggling with Mrs Pearce, who, like Blanche before her, has the other woman by the hair, grabbing hold of it to keep Eliza submerged in the bathwater. Interspersed with her genuinely "heartrending" screams, Eliza cries, "I've never done this kind of thing before, really I haven't . . . No, Mrs Pearce, no, don't . . . stop it . . . this has never happened to me before . . . oh help, help . . . I've never been . . . stop it . . . help."[5] Amid her screams, the camera cuts to a shot of Higgins and Pickering at the foot of the stairs below. They are staring up at the sound of the cries, and they exchange a bemused look. Higgins shrugs and turns back into his study, while Pickering remains, smirking. The camera cuts back to Eliza, still screaming, eyes shut (to keep out soap), hand groping along the tile wall of the tub. Her hand grasps hold of a handle, and suddenly the shower head above explodes with a cascade of shooting water. This ejaculatory conclusion to the scene clearly literalizes the subtextually heterosexual paradigm controlling the attack on Eliza.

Although the actors, screenwriters, and directors[6] must be credited for the overall production, Shaw's close involvement with the film implicates him in its creation and impact as well.[7] The thrust of this scene in particular is patently clear; the "innocuous" bath barely masks the reality of female violation conveyed by the dialogue and action.

When Eliza reenters Higgins's study, Shaw provides a description for her as he would for a new, as yet unnamed character: "a dainty and exquisitely clean young Japanese lady in a simple blue cotton

5. All dialogue comes from the soundtrack to the film version, readily available on videocassette.
6. The film was directed by Anthony Asquith and Leslie Howard, who also played Higgins.
7. For a detailed discussion of Shaw's involvement in the making of the film, see Costello [Donald P. Costello, *The Serpent's Eye: Shaw and the Cinema* (Notre Dame, 1965)] (50–82). The film was a tremendous box office success, and Shaw claimed major responsibility for this.

kimono" (50–51), and indeed she is unrecognized by the other characters, with the exception of Mrs Pearce, who has conducted the transformation. Significantly, Eliza cannot "see" herself in the mirror after the bath; she cannot confront the new self that has been robbed of all vestiges of her old identity, including a symbolic virginity.

When she finally comes into her own at the end of the play, Higgins observes that she has "had a bit of [her] own back" (102), meaning a little revenge on him, but also suggesting another interpretation. She has chosen to return to a life independent of Higgins and Pickering, thus reasserting some of the original identity she had lost while at Wimpole Street. She declines Higgins's offer to "adopt [her] as [his] daughter and settle money on [her]" (105), his attempt to formalize the structure that has defined their relationship to date. Needless to say, his earlier suggestion that Mrs Pearce adopt Eliza has long been forgotten, and Eliza expresses no indebtedness to the housekeeper for any of her learning. Ultimately, Mrs Pearce emerges as an alter image for Eliza: what she might become were she to stay in Higgins's household, for the older woman has never been able to break free of the hold Higgins has over her (104).

Eliza's announcement, "I'll marry Freddy, I will, as soon as I'm able to support him" (107), seems a refreshingly feminist twist on the usual pattern of young female pupils' marrying men inferior in some way to their paternal teacher. But Shaw's "sequel" undermines this assertiveness, by showing Eliza's financial dependence on Pickering and emotional involvement with Higgins for years to come. Thus in the narrative resolving the conflicts of the play, Shaw reasserts literary control over the more balanced voices of the drama and removes the power Eliza seems to gain in her fight for independence. Eliza may not "like" her father-figures all that much (124), but Shaw makes it clear in his closing sentence that for her, they will always be "godlike" (124).

ERROL DURBACH

Pygmalion: Myth and Anti-Myth in the Plays of Ibsen and Shaw†

London at 11.15 p.m. Torrents of heavy summer rain. Cab whistles blowing frantically in all directions. Pedestrians running for shelter into the portico of St Paul's church (not Wren's cathedral but Inigo Jones's church in Covent Garden vegetable market).

We are reminded instantly of the classical origins of the Pygmalion myth when the curtain rises on Shaw's play to reveal, miraculously, a Grecian temple within the modern context of costermongers, flower girls, and opera-goers. Indeed, Inigo Jones's Palladian church would seem the perfect milieu for the Ovidian[1] myth of mysterious transformation—even in modern dress—for Shaw's stagecraft is a perfect fusion of the rational and the marvellous, the secular and the divine. Despite a temperament typically embarrassed by ancient notions of divinity, Shaw discovers in the natural phenomenon of a London storm all the portents of supernatural awe. Eliza Doolittle has only to enter and bump into Freddy when *"a blinding flash of lightning, followed instantly by a rattling peal of thunder, orchestrates the incident"*; and as St Paul's anachronistic clock strikes the second quarter, Professor Higgins hears in it *"the voice of God, rebuking him for his Pharisaic want of charity to the poor girl."* But for all the promise of its mythical ingredients in act 1, the play cannot be seen to recapitulate the specific narrative incidents of the original myth; and although Shaw retains the basic metaphorical idea of a metamorphosis, he empties the process of all its mystery and insists upon the commonplace nature of the transfiguration: "Such transfigurations," he writes in the epilogue, "have been achieved by hundreds of resolutely ambitious young women." And, finally, he deliberately demythologizes the romantic implications of Ovid's tale. The modern Pygmalion does *not* fall in love with and marry the modern Galatea; and Shaw provides a highly unsatisfactory reason for this radical alteration of the traditional myth. Eliza, he says, does not really care for Higgins: "Galatea never does quite like Pygmalion: his relation to her is too godlike to be altogether agreeable."

What is so unsatisfactory about this rationalization is not its frustration of romance—there is, after all, no good reason why Galatea

---

† From *George Bernard Shaw's* Pygmalion, ed. Harold Bloom (New York: Chelsea House, 1988), pp. 87–98.

1. Publius Ovidius Naso (43 B.C.E.–18 C.E.) collected a number of myths of transformation (e.g., human to animal) in *Metamorphoses*. *Pygmalion* is based on his story of Venus's transformation of a beautiful statue to a living woman [*Editor*].

should love Pygmalion—but Shaw's eccentric remark that Pygmalion is *godlike*, and therefore inaccessible or disagreeable. This suggests so crucial a misreading of Ovid as to make it almost irrelevant to invoke a classical source for Shaw's play; for what Shaw has failed to keep distinct (in his epilogue, at any rate) is the important difference between the Artist-as-Creator who carves a paradigm of female perfection and the God-as-Creator who transfigures cold stone into living flesh. In Ovid, Pygmalion merely provides the form for Galatea. It is the Goddess, Venus, who blesses her with life—and there is nothing whatever of Venus in Professor Higgins. In the work of the Pre-Raphaelites—Shaw's nineteenth-century predecessors in the treatment of this myth—the distinction between Pygmalion and Venus, Artist and God, remains very clear and unambiguous: there is no embarrassed rationalization of divinity, no attempt to disguise the presence of Venus beneath the trappings of modern scepticism. In his *Earthly Paradise* (1868–70), for instance, William Morris provides an authentic Ovidian account of the metamorphosis; and Edward Burne-Jones[2] depicted the major stages of the myth in a series of four sumptuous paintings which he completed in 1879. In the first, a melancholy Pygmalion turns his back on the external world to contemplate the world of art—the living women outside carefully balanced by the hard sculptural forms in the studio; in the second, he carves Galatea—hard, cold, monumental, and dead in her exquisite beauty; in the third, a gorgeous Botticellian Venus descends in a flutter of doves and a glow of rose-petals to depetrify the marmoreal beauty; and, in the final panel, Pygmalion worships the living woman on his knees. The series would surely have graced Shaw's lovely Pre-Raphaelite setting for the third act—the Morris and Burne-Jones room in Mrs Higgins's Chelsea flat, a pictorial reminder, perhaps, of the last age in which it was still possible for the myth of Pygmalion to flourish. But Shaw's Galatea flings slippers at the head of her Pygmalion; and Shaw's Pygmalion is asexual to the point of having nothing better to offer his Galatea than a strictly celibate form of female bachelorhood in his domestic employ. If Ovid is no feasible source for Shaw's play, then neither, it would seem, is the Brotherhood.

The most notable treatment of the myth in pre-Shavian *drama*, however, is the *Pygmalion and Galatea* which W. S. Gilbert wrote in 1871—a curious blend of sentimental idealism declining sadly into a form of equally sentimental cynicism. What is significant about this piece is not its probable influence on Shaw—he may or may not have known it—but Gilbert's peculiarly Victorian definition of the myth (which Shaw would most certainly have rejected) and his pecu-

2. A Pre-Raphaelite painter [*Editor*].

liarly post-Romantic definition of the anti-myth (which Shaw would most certainly have deplored). It is a rather nasty little play; but, in a comparative context, it provides an essential bridge between the authentic Classicism of the Pre-Raphaelites and Shaw's demythological view. The basis of the myth in Gilbert's play is, again, the metamorphosis; and in the absence of the embarrassing Goddess, he leaves his Galatea to cope with the difficulty as best she may. In the circumstances she does pretty well:

> I felt my frame pervaded by a glow
> That seemed to thaw my marble into flesh;
> Its cold hard substance throbbed with active life,
> My limbs grew supple, and I moved—I lived!
> Lived in the ecstasy of new-born life!
> Lived in the love of him that fashioned me!
> Lived in a thousand tangled thoughts of hope,
> Love, gratitude—thoughts that resolved themselves
> Into one word, that word, Pygmalion! (*Kneels to him.*)

The Goddess Venus we recognize in this passage as the transforming power of love, which is surely a charming secular explanation of divinity in terms of ordinary human passion—until Galatea, still on her knees, defines the special nature of her love:

> A sense that I am made *by* thee *for* thee;
> That I've no will that is not wholly thine:
> That I've no thought, no hope, no enterprise
> That does not own *thee* as its sovereign;
> That I have life, that I may live for thee,
> That I am thine—

Here she is again—the Victorian domestic paragon, the Angel in the House,[3] the chauvinist definition of ideal womanhood, a piece of property without the shred of a sense of self, on her knees before a sovereign master. One searches, in vain, for a hint of irony in Gilbert's lines. And it is precisely *this* image of the Victorian Galatea that Higgins so vehemently rejects:

> I think a woman fetching a man's slippers is a disgusting sight: did I ever fetch your slippers? I think a good deal more of you for throwing them in my face. No use slaving for me and then saying you want to be cared for: who cares for a slave?

I have the sense, though, that Gilbert's distasteful manipulation of the myth is inherent even in Ovid, and that the Burne-Jones alternative—Pygmalion on his knees before Galatea—is really no more

---

3. Title of a poem sequence by Coventry Patmore (1854–1861) which enshrines the Victorian ideal of woman as serving man in the form of the domestic "angel" [*Editor*].

acceptable as a human statement. The Pygmalion of book 10 of the *Metamorphoses* is the model, it seems to me, of the neurotic idealist—the man for whom reality is so unendurable, so imperfect, that he turns towards forms of the imperishable to assuage the human wound. "Disgusted with the faults which in such full measure nature had given the female mind," writes Ovid, "he lived unmarried." Pledged to a life of celibacy, fearful of sex and death, he can love only symbolic images of immutable perfection; and his romantic solution to perishable mortality is to carve a statue "giving it a beauty more perfect than that of any woman ever born. And with his own work he falls in love." There is a crucial turning away from life in the Pygmalion myth, an impossible demand for perfection as the precondition for any human attachment, and a definition of sexual love as that which seeks satisfaction in imperishable and therefore dead forms. The type and the temperament are familiar, even outside the context of the myth; and they express themselves in identical metaphors. Othello, for instance, just before he smothers Desdemona, compares her to "monumental alabaster" (5.2.5)—for the statue is a tangible symbol for the "cunning'st pattern of excelling nature" (5.2.11), pure Neoplatonic form, both dead and deathless, supremely inhuman and therefore supremely desirable. "I'll kill thee," he says, "and love thee after" (5.2.18). What I am suggesting, in other words, is that the Pygmalion myth—the metamorphosis of dead stone into flesh and blood—contains also the germ of its anti-myth: that form of Romantic idealism that stands in danger of changing living flesh into stone. What Pygmalion most desires is a living doll, Hoffmann's Coppelia, or that ghastly automaton with which Cassanova copulates in the closing sequences of Fellini's film. This is the dead end of neurotic Romanticism. If Gilbert's Galatea evades this aspect of the anti-myth, it is only because *she* rather than Pygmalion is the neurotic—the perfect woman unable to tolerate an imperfect world, unable to understand the adulterous implications of her love for an already married Pygmalion, and—above all—terrified of an existence in which all living things must, by their very nature, die. In the closing moments of the play she reverses the process of transfiguration and recedes into the imperishable security of stone.

By far the most impressive gallery of frozen and petrified Galateas in pre-Shavian drama, however, are those women of Ibsen's late plays: Mrs Borkman chilled to the bone in a suffocatingly heated room, Rebekka West draped in the white shroud of her wedding veil, and—above all—the Lady in White who appears in *When We Dead Awaken*, that living allegory of Life sacrificed to an inhuman Art. Realism, here, strains against its own boundaries to create a dramatic symbol of living death, a sculptural form invested with attenuated breath:

Her face is pale and drawn, as if it were frozen: her eyelids are lowered, and her eyes seem without sight. Her dress hangs down to her feet in long straight close fitting folds. A large shawl of white crêpe covers her head, arms, and the upper part of her body. She keeps her arms folded over her breast. She carries herself stiffly, and her walk is staid and measured.

This woman, Irena, is Ibsen's last and most powerful indictment of the idealist, the Artist-as-Creator, who chooses perfection of the work above all else and who, in dissociating this ideal from the passions of life, merely desecrates his art and dehumanizes his living muse—Irena, his model. Professor Rubek, Ibsen's Pygmalion, is the greatest sculptor of his generation; and he has used Irena's naked beauty as the inspiration for his masterwork—the statue of a divine woman awakening from earthbound mortality into a resurrected state of eternal purity and joy. But, terrified of desecrating his sublime artwork by the reality of sexual desire, he has repressed all passion for Irena to a clinical impersonality; and the folly of denying their love for each other, which is the human source of his creativity, recoils upon him as an act of self-destruction. He has wrenched the soul from a living being to create his ideal—and Irena, in "dying," has destroyed his creative capacity for ever. She can no longer inspire. He can no longer sculpt. And while each is indispensable to the other's awakening from the living death, both are powerless to effect the resurrection. A single indictment re-echoes from play to play in Ibsen's versions of the anti-myth—Galatea's cry against Pygmalion's essential lovelessness: Rosmer's freezing of Rebekka's joy, Borkman's murder of Ella Rentheim's power to love, Rubek's sacrifice of Irena's soul. For if the creative principle which turns stone into flesh in the Ovidian myth is Venus—Goddess of love and erotic desire—then the discreative principle in the anti-myth is the denial of Venus, the flight from sexuality, the sacrifice of human realities to ascetic ideals. Leo Lowenthal in *Literature and the Image of Man* sees Ibsen as the spokesman of a disenchanted nineteenth-century idealism, a critic of moribund values which no longer serve the liberal impulse. Ideals no longer motivate creative acts; they merely conceal their opposites. For when art becomes a defence against life rather than a heightening of it, then the creative justification of the artist merely degenerates into an excuse for human fallibility and weakness. In *When We Dead Awaken*, writes Lowenthal,

> a comparison with the Greek legend might help to point up the character of Rubek, the sculptor. . . . In this tale, inanimate material is released for the development of a human being, but Ibsen's drama displays a reverse process. . . . The egoism of the artist . . . transforms human relations and men themselves into

objects to be used for his own purposes; they have value for him only when they serve his ambitions.

There's a faint echo here of Eliza Doolittle's Galatean cry against Higgins—

> Ive won your bet for you, havnt I? Thats enough for you. I don't matter, I suppose. . . . Why didn't you leave me where you picked me out of—in the gutter? You thank God it's all over, and that now you can throw me back again there, do you? . . . Whats to become of me? Whats to become of me?

—and of Higgins's contemptuous retort:

> How the devil do I know whats to become of you? What does it matter what becomes of you?

One fact of which we may be quite certain in finding analogues to Shaw's *Pygmalion* is that he read Ibsen with enthusiasm and intelligence, producing the first major analysis of Ibsen's drama in English: *The Quintessence of Ibsenism.* "Ibsenism," nowadays, has acquired certain extremely pejorative connotations; and I leave it to others to defend Shaw against charges of reducing Ibsen to a shrill propagandist. But if "Ibsenism" may be stretched slightly to imply a severe indictment of death-dealing idealism, the neurotic Romantics and the transcendentalists, then it is not surprising that Shaw should have found in Ibsen a spokesman for his own ideas about the moral and spiritual values of his society. *Pygmalion*, I think, is a very Ibsenian play—not merely a charming comedy of manners, but more importantly a comedy of morals and the spiritual life; and I'd like to look briefly at Professor Higgins as a Pygmalion-idealist figure who probably has more in common with the spirit of positive Ibsenism than he does with his Ovidian prototype.

Teaching the play, I often find that students develop a strong antipathy to Higgins and tend to see him as another Rubek: selfish, vain, sexually ascetic, and (taking the cue from Shaw's description of him) *"violently interested in everything that can be studied as a scientific subject, and careless about himself and other people, including their feelings"* True enough, he embodies much of the negative spirit of Pygmalion: a ruthless professionalism in which doing something superlatively well in the interest of his art takes precedence over all human considerations, a sexlessness which prompts his contemptuous dismissal of all women (except his mother) as idiots, and an obsession with the creation of empty social forms. This Pygmalion may not carve ideal beauty out of stone, but he does fashion ladies out of the crushed cabbage-leaves of Covent Garden and duchesses

out of draggle-tailed guttersnipes—which is to say that the Phone-
tician-as-Artist is essentially concerned with the metamorphosis of
social classes, with the transfiguration of working-class caterpillars
into aristocratic butterflies. In this, of course, he is miraculously
successful—with one important reservation. Galatea's sculptor, as
I've suggested, is *not* godlike. He may provide the form, call it what
you will—princess, duchess, consort—but mere form, like the
statue, is shape without substance, a social role without those qualities of soul that make it live. Act 3 is a glorious comic exposé of the
myth, in which an exquisitely dressed Eliza, every inch a lady of the
middle classes, reveals the grotesque disparity between social form
and spiritual content. She discourses in elegant tones on horren-
dously inelegant topics:

> My aunt died of influenza: so they said. . . . But it's my belief
> they done the old woman in. . . . Why should she die of influ-
> enza? She come through diphtheria right enough the year
> before. I saw her with my own eyes. Fairly blue with it, she was.
> They all thought she was dead; but my father he kept ladling
> gin down her throat till she came to so sudden that she bit the
> bowl off the spoon.

Blessed by Venus? Not bloody likely. "She's a triumph of your art
and of her dressmaker's," says Mrs Higgins—and in this she is perfectly correct. But she goes even further in her condemnation of the
Professor's playing (as she calls it) "with your live doll." For she
regards the metamorphosis, the gift of social mobility from the gutter
to the middle class, as a foolish disservice to the flower girl which
will ultimately disqualify the lady from earning her own living. Pygmalion, in other words, is charged with the creation of a futile and
useless thing fit for nothing, as Eliza-Galatea herself laments, but a
form of marital prostitution: "I sold flowers. I didnt sell myself. Now
you've made a lady of me I'm not fit to sell anything else. I wish youd
left me where you found me." Shaw tempts us to read the play as
anti-myth, a parable of the indifferent destruction of a working-class
girl by educating her and refining her out of her class; and my
students, who tend to romanticize the gutter and who scorn middle-
class values, inevitably succumb to this fragment of the Shavian
argument.

This anti-mythic reading, I imagine, derives in part from faulty
syllogistic reasoning. "All socialists are unalterably opposed to an
effete aristocracy of duchesses and princesses and consorts; Shaw is
a socialist; and therefore he must disapprove deeply of Higgins's
brand of social metamorphosis." Such an argument, however,
ignores Shaw's claim in the preface that "the reformer we need most
today is an energetic phonetic enthusiast: that is why I have made

such a one the hero of a popular play." In 1914 this must have sounded unforgivably facetious—as if the reformation of English pronunciation could possibly save England from catastrophe. But there are unmistakable political undertones, in both the preface and the play, to Shaw's idea of the heroic reformer; and I would argue that Higgins-as-Pygmalion is not only an artist and teacher but an idealist of the political life, a reformer of the moral life, and a socialist of the soul. His idealism, indeed, has much in common with those moral-political aspirations of Ibsen's heroes—of Rosmer, for example, whose life's quest it is to free society from its spiritual limitations, "to win over minds and desires. To make men noble all around you— in wider and wider circles." Higgins expresses the idealism behind his own program of social transfiguration in very similar Ibsenist terms:

> But you have no idea how frightfully interesting it is to take a human being and change her into a quite different human being by creating a new speech for her. It's filling up the deepest gulf that separates class from class and soul from soul.

This is the most articulate definition of the metamorphosis in Shaw's play, and the process is inextricable from the Ibsenist vision of a revolution of the human spirit. Rosmer, of course, can effect this revolution only by destroying all joy in Rebekka, only by requiring proof of her ennoblement in an act of suicide. But Higgins's achievement is *not* anti-mythic; and although he obviously shares the asceticism and the coldness of his prototype (to which he contributes his own peculiar vituperative ill manners), his justification of such behaviour reveals the spiritual socialism that underprops all his actions:

> The great secret, Eliza, is not having bad manners or good manners or any other particular sort of manners, but having the same manner for all human souls: in short, behaving as if you were in Heaven, where there are no third-class carriages, and one soul is as good as another.

An equality of souls in a classless paradise—these are the ideal ends to which a phonetic education is the means. But the gulf between the guttersnipe and the lady is not merely a matter of pronunciation. It is the gulf between the garbage in which poverty cannot afford morality and the moneyed middle class in which morality inhibits the natural depravity of the human animal. "You see," says Higgins, "we're all savages, more or less. We're supposed to be civilized and cultured—to know all about poetry and philosophy and art and science, and so on; but how many of us know even the meanings of these names?" And Shaw, it seems to me, endorses this anti-

Romantic vision of society in which savagery and culture, amorality and morality, are constantly opposed. Eliza's transformation from the gutter to the drawingroom is surely her salvation as a social being—not because Shaw despises the working class but because he despises third-class carriages, poverty, the savagery that the gutter breeds, and the moral horror engendered by the dustheap.

The exemplar of gutter-morality in *Pygmalion* is, of course, Alfred Doolittle who is of the dust, dusty; and this play of marvellous transformations traces the double metamorphosis of Eliza from flower girl to princess, and of her father from garbageman to gentleman. The deep economic gulf that separates class from class, in Doolittle's case, is fortuitously filled (as he tells Mrs Higgins) by

> this here blasted three thousand a year that shoves me into the middle class. . . . Intimidated: thats what I am. Broke. Bought up. Happier men than me will call for my dust, and touch me for their tip; and I'll look on helpless, and envy them. And thats what your son has brought me to.

Like Eliza, he cries that he's been ruined, tied up and delivered into the hands of middle-class morality, his happiness destroyed forever by enforced upward mobility. Again—echoes of the anti-myth. But those who believe that the pursuit of happiness is an inalienable human right would do well to inquire carefully into Doolittle's definition of the term. As one of the undeserving poor, he lives in squalor with his common-law wife, drinks away his money, and thinks nothing of prostituting his daughter for the price of a Saturday-night spree.

> I'm undeserving; and I mean to go on being undeserving. I like it; and thats the truth. Will you take advantage of a man's nature to do him out of the price of his own daughter what he's brought up and fed and clothed by the sweat of his brow until she's growed big enough to be interesting to you two gentlemen? Is five pounds unreasonable? I put it to you; and I leave it to you.

The politics of poverty are unassailable. But because Shaw finds them irresistible is no argument that he endorses them. The scene may be funny, but it's morally foul. Alfred Doolittle, transfigured into a gentleman of means and lecturer for the Moral Reform World League, may not be a happy man—but happiness, after all, is not one of Shaw's primary values when its corollary is poverty and the moral savagery that it promotes. Doolittle's first gesture as a victim of the middle classes is to marry the woman with whom he's been living, however reluctantly, and undertake the support of his daughter. The transformation may be painful, but a sentimental hankering after the amoral happiness of the dust-heap must be balanced against the life of moral responsibility and self-respect. This is what Higgins must persuade Eliza to understand:

> If you cant stand the coldness of my sort of life, and the strain of it, go back to the gutter. Work til youre more a brute than a human being; and then cuddle and squabble and drink til you fall asleep. Oh, it's a fine life, the life of the gutter.

If money can close the gulf between class and class, between savagery and morality, and change one species of human being into another, then what force is it that can close the gulf between soul and soul to create a *spiritual* democracy? It is this mystery that lies at the heart of the myth—the force that Ovid calls Venus, and for which the modern temperament must seek more secular analogies. Colonel Pickering has helped to shape the "lady" with the nice manners, and Higgins has created what he disparagingly calls the "artificial duchess" in the hired tiara; but the self-possessed Eliza of act 5 cannot possibly be defined by these empty social forms. She has acquired an identity, a sense of self, quite distinct from the shapes into which her Pygmalion has moulded her; and Higgins acknowledges his error in supposing that her autonomy is still dependent on his will or that all her ideas and words are of his creating. He may be able to turn Eliza on as a phonographic mechanism made to speak correctly, but, as he says, "I cant turn your soul on. Leave me those feelings; and you can take away the voice and the face. They are not you." The essential Galatea, the living soul who asserts her independence of sculptural form, is that most creative and innovative contribution to the myth in modern dress—a reinterpretation of Ovid, and a rejection of W. S. Gilbert's Victorian tableau of the dependent creature whose integrity is subservient to her creator's. In this, it seems to me, *Pygmalion* is a genuinely Ibsenist play in the very best sense of the word. For the English champion of Ibsen could not possibly have read *A Doll's House* without recognizing it, not as a shrill feminist tract, but as the most articulate parable of spiritual transformation in late nineteenth-century drama. The narrative events of Nora's metamorphosis may find no direct parallels in Ovid—but the spirit of the myth is dramatically enacted in the literal transfiguration of a doll into a self-reliant and responsible free spirit. Nora may embody many of the anti-mythic qualities of Rebekka West and the Lady in White; but Ibsen knows that no woman of flesh and blood can possibly be petrified without her willing acquiescence in the process of destruction. Bedecked in her Neapolitan fancy-dress, pirouetting and flattering and tittilating, Nora plays the willing capitulant to the social and sexual roles imposed upon her by male sovereignty; and the difficult recognition of her status as some

northern Coppelia turns *A Doll's House* into a tragedy of moral education and spiritual self-discovery—a tragedy, because the death of
the doll, the destruction of a secure and macaroon-filled paradise,
and the grievous loss of her children are the consequences of accepting freedom and self-respect as the primary conditions of life. The
Nora who takes off her fancy-dress, who transfigures herself from
doll into woman, is a heroic paradigm of the liberated spirit in
Ibsen—the self-creating being who discovers in her own spiritual
strength that vivifying force which Ovid called Venus. The God in
Ibsen is the God within, just as in Burne-Jones's third panel the
ethereal Goddess appears (by chance or design?) as the exact likeness
of the living Galatea. Modern existential psychology, no doubt, could
translate *Venus* into any number of terms: the authentic self, the
autonomous being. But Shaw, eschewing both existentialism and
divinity, has his own peculiar pseudo-theological vocabulary in
which to express the idea of *Venus*. What in other contexts he refers
to as the Life Force, he expresses in this play through Higgins's sense
of a self-sufficient integrity: "I can do without anybody. I have my
own soul: my own spark of divine fire." Eliza, like Nora, discovers
precisely this: a *divine fire* which turns dead form into living flesh by
defining herself in the face of a stronger and potentially destructive
personality. She emerges from the conflict as a fine and independent
Galatea, who has only to accept herself transfigured in order to be
free; and, at the end of the play, she rises to the occasion:

> I can do without you: don't think I can't. . . . Oh, when I think
> of myself crawling under your feet and being trampled on and
> called names, when all the time I had only to lift my finger to
> be as good as you, I could just kick myself.

And to this assertion of genuine spiritual democracy, Higgins ecstat-
ically responds: "By George, Eliza, I said I'd make a woman of you;
and I have. I like you like this."

In this godlike claim, of course, Higgins is arrogantly in error. He
had said no such thing. He had promised to create the lady, the
princess, the duchess, the consort—but only Eliza can create the
woman. The divine prerogative is hers. The cockney feathers of the
flower girl, the finery of the doll's dressmaker, and the diamond tiara
of the artificial duchess finally yield, like Nora's fancy-dress, to that
sunny and self-possessed young woman who will open a flower shop
not far from the Victoria and Albert Museum—and who would surely
deny that Norwegian housewives are incapable of heroic transfigurations, or that only princesses merit souls.

George Bernard Shaw:
A Chronology†

1856	Born George Bernard Shaw, July 26, in Dublin, Ireland
1876	Publishes first music criticism
1878	*Passion Play* (unfinished)
1879	*Immaturity* (published 1930)
1882–83	*Cashel Byron's Profession* (published 1886; subsequently revised)
1884	*Today* serializes *An UnSocial Socialist*
1885–92	*Widowers' Houses* (performed 1892; first public performance 1907)
1886	Publishes first art criticism
1898	*The Gadfly, or The Son of the Colonel* (adaptation; unfinished)
1889	*Un Petit Drame* (unfinished); *Fabian Essays*
1889–90	*The Cassone* (unperformed)
1891	*The Quintessence of Ibsenism* (subsequently revised)
1893	*The Philanderer* (first performed 1898; first public performance 1907)
1893–94	*Mrs Warren's Profession* (first performed 1902; first public performance 1925)
1894	*Arms and the Man* (first performed 1894); *Candida: A Mystery* (first performed 1895; first public performance 1904)
1895	*The Man of Destiny* (first performed 1897)
1895–96	*You Never Can Tell* (first performed 1898; first public performance 1900)
1896–97	*The Devil's Disciple: A Melodrama* (first performed 1897)
1898	*The Perfect Wagnerite; Caesar and Cleopatra: A History* (first performed 1899; first performed in public in England, 1907)
1899	*Captain Brassbound's Conversation: An Adventure*

† Significant historical events are included for context and appear in boldface type.

(first performed 1899; first performed in public, 1902)

1900   *Love Among the Artists*

1901   **Death of Queen Victoria; Accession of Edward VII;**
     The Admirable Bashville, or Constancy Unrewarded
     (first performance 1902; first professional perfor-
     mance 1903)

1901–1903 *Man and Superman: A Comedy and a Philosophy* (first
     performed 1905; first performed in public 1905; first
     performed in entirety 1915)

1904   *John Bull's Other Island; How He Lied to Her Husband*

1905   *The Irrational Knot; Major Barbara*

1906   *Passion, Poison, and Petrification, or The Fatal Gazo-*
     gene; Our Theatres in the Nineties (Shaw's criticism
     for *The Saturday Review* 1895–98); *The Doctor's*
     Dilemma

1906–1907 *Dramatic Opinions and Essays*

1907   *The Interlude at the Playhouse/The Inaugural Speech:*
     An Interlude

1908   *Getting Married: A Conversation*

1909   *The Shewing-Up of Blanco Posnet: A Sermon in Crude*
     Melodrama (first performed 1909; first public perfor-
     mance 1921); *The Glimpse of Reality: A Tragedietta*
     (first performed 1927; first professional performance
     1927); *Press Cuttings; The Fascinating Foundling*
     (first performance 1909; first public performance
     1928)

1909–10 *Misalliance*

1910   **Accession of George V;** *The Dark Lady of the Son-*
     nets: An Interlude

1911   *Fanny's First Play: An Easy Play for a Little Theatre*

1912   *Androcles and the Lion: A Fable Play* (first performed
     1913); *Overruled: A Demonstration*

1912–13 *Pygmalion* (first performed 1913; first performed in
     England 1914)

1913   *Great Catherine (Whom Glory Still Adores); Beauty's*
     Duty (unfinished); *The Music Cure: A Piece of Utter*
     Nonsense (first performed 1914)

1914–18 **First World War**

1914   *Common Sense About the War*

1915   *O'Flaherty, VC: A Recruiting Pamphlet* (first per-
     formed 1917, on the Western Front; first profession-
     ally performed 1920)

1916   **Easter Rising in Dublin**

1916   *The Inca of Perusalem: An Almost Historical Come-*

	dietta; *Augustus Does His Bit: A True-to-Life Farce* (first performed 1917; first professional performance 1919)
1917	*Annajanska, The Wild Grand Duchess/Annajanska, The Bolshevik Empress: A Revolutionary Romancelet* (adapted from Gregory Bessinoff)
1918–20	*Back to Methuselah: A Metabiological Pentateuch* (first performed 1922–23)
1919	*Heartbreak House* (first performed 1920)
1920	**Treaty of Versailles; formation of League of Nations**
1921–22	*The War Indemnities* (unfinished)
1922	**Publication of James Joyce, *Ulysses*; T. S. Eliot, *The Waste Land***
1922	*Jitta's Atonement* (adapted from Siegfried Trebitsch; first performed 1923)
1923	*Saint Joan: A Chronicle Play*
1926	*Translations and Tomfooleries*
1927	*The Yahoos* (unfinished)
1928	*The Intelligent Woman's Guide to Socialism and Capitalism; The Apple Cart: A Political Extravaganza* (first performed in Polish in Warsaw, 1929; first performed in England 1929)
1929	**Stock market crash; the great depression**
1931	*Music in London 1890–94: Criticisms contributed Week by Week to the World; Immaturity; Pen Portraits and Reviews; Too True To be Good: A Political Extravaganza* (first performed 1932); *Doctors' Delusions: Crude Criminology: Sham Education*
1932	*What I Really Wrote About the War; The Adventures of the Black Girl in Search of God*
1933	*Village Wooing* (first performed 1934); *On the Rocks*
1934	*Short Stories, Scraps and Shavings; Prefaces; The Simpleton of the Unexpected Isles: A Vision of Judgment* (first performed 1935); *The Six of Calais*
1934–35	*The Millionairess* (first performed in Germany 1936; first performed in England 1936)
1935	**T. S. Eliot, *Murder in the Cathedral***
1935	*The Garden of the Hesperides* (unfinished); *The Girl with the Golden Voice* (unfinished)
1936	**Accession and abdication of Edward VIII; accession of George VI**
1936–39	**Spanish Civil War**
1936	*Geneva* (subsequently revised; first performed 1938); *Arthur and Acetone* (unfinished)

1937   *London Music in 1888–89 As Heard by Corno di Bas-*
              setto (Shaw's pseudonym); *Sequence for the King's*
              People (unfinished); *Cymbeline Refinished*
1939–45   **Second World War**
1939   *"In Good King Charles's Golden Days": A True History*
              That Never Happened
1944   *Everybody's Political What's What?*
1945–47   *Buoyant Billions: A Comedy of No Manners* (first per-
              formed in Germany 1948 as *Zu Viel Geld*; first per-
              formed in England 1949)
1948–50   *Farfetched Fables*
1949   *Sixteen Self Sketches; Shakes Versus Shav*
1950   *Why She Would Not: A Little Comedy* (unfinished) Die
              at Ayot St Lawrence, November 2, 1950

Selected Bibliography

BIBLIOGRAPHY

Laurence, Dan H., ed. *Bernard Shaw: A Bibliography*. Oxford: Clarendon Press, 1983.
Weintraub, Stanley, ed. *George Bernard Shaw: A Guide to Research*. Pennsylvania: Pennsylvania State University Press, 1992.

BIOGRAPHY

Holroyd, Michael. *Bernard Shaw*. Vol. 1, *The Search for Love, 1856–1898*; vol. 2, *The Pursuit of Power, 1898–1918*; vol. 3, *The Lure of Fantasy, 1918–1950*; vol. 4, *The Last Laugh*—vol. 4 & 5: *The Shaw Companion*. London: Chatto & Windus, 1988–1992.
———. *Bernard Shaw* (abridged and revised, one-volume definitive edition). London: Chatto & Windus, 1997.
Laurence, Dan H., ed. *Bernard Shaw: Collected Letters*. London: Reinhardt, 1965–1988.
Shaw, George Bernard. *Sixteen Self Sketches*. New York: Dodd, Mead, 1949.
Weintraub, Stanley, ed. *Shaw: An Autobiography, Selected from His Writings*. 2 vols. London: Max Reinhardt, 1970–71.

CRITICISM

Adams, Elsie, ed. *Critical Essays on George Bernard Shaw*. New York: G. K. Hall, 1991.
Bentley, Eric. *Bernard Shaw: A Reconsideration*. Norfolk, Conn.: New Directions Books, 1947.
———, ed. *Shaw on Music*. New York: Applause, 1995.
Berst, Charles A. *Bernard Shaw and the Art of Drama*. Urbana: University of Illinois Press, 1973.
Bertolini, John A. *The Playwrighting Self of Bernard Shaw*. Carbondale: Southern Illinois University Press, 1991.
Chesterton, G. K. *George Bernard Shaw*. London: John Lane, 1909.
Corrigan, Felicitas. *The Nun, the Infidel and the Superman*. London: John Murray, 1985; rept. as *Friends of a Lifetime: The Nun, the Infidel and the Superman*, 1990.
Costello, Donald P. *The Serpent's Eye: Shaw and the Cinema*. Paris, France: Notre Dame, 1965.
Crompton, Louis. *Shaw the Dramatist: A Study of the Intellectual Background of the Major Plays*. Lincoln: University of Nebraska Press, 1971.
Davis, Tracy C. *George Bernard Shaw and the Socialist Theatre*. Westport, Conn.: Greenwood, 1994.
Dietrich, Richard F. *Portrait of the Artist as a Young Superman; A Study of Shaw's Novels*. Gainesville: University of Florida Press, 1969.
Dukore, Bernard F. *Bernard Shaw, Director*. London: Allen and Unwin, 1971.
———. *Bernard Shaw, Playwright: Aspects of Shavian Drama*. Columbia: University of Missouri Press, 1973.
———, ed. *The Collected Screenplays of Bernard Shaw*. London: George Prior, 1980.
Gainor, J. Ellen. *Shaw's Daughters*. Ann Arbor: University of Michigan Press, 1991.
Gainz, Arthur. *George Bernard Shaw*. New York: Grove, 1983.
Gibbs, A. M. *Shaw: Interviews and Recollections*. Basingstoke: Macmillan, 1990.
Gordon, David J. *Bernard Shaw and the Comic Sublime*. Basingstoke: Macmillan, 1989.
Harris, Frank. *Bernard Shaw*. New Jersey: Garden City, 1931.

Holroyd, Michael. *Genius of Shaw: A Symposium.* New York: Holt, Rinehart and Winston, 1979.

Hugo, Leon. *Edwardian Shaw: The Writer and His Age.* Basingstoke: Macmillan, 1999.

———. *Bernard Shaw: Playwright and Preacher.* London: Methuen, 1971.

Innes, Christopher, ed. *The Cambridge Companion to George Bernard Shaw.* Cambridge: Cambridge University Press, 1998.

Laurence, Dan H., ed. *Shaw's Music.* 3 vols. London: Reinhardt, 1981.

Meisel, Martin. *Shaw and the Nineteenth-Century Theater.* Westport, Conn.: Greenwood, 1976.

Morgan, Margery. *The Shavian Playground: An Exploration of the Art of George Bernard Shaw.* London: Methuen, 1972.

———. *George Bernard Shaw.* Windsor, Berkshire: Profile Books, 1982.

———. *File on Shaw.* London: Methuen Drama, 1989.

Pascal, Valerie. *The Disciple and His Devil.* London: Joseph, 1971.

Patch, Blanche Eliza. *Thirty Years with G.B.S.* London: Victor Gollancz, 1951.

Pearson, Hesketh. *Bernard Shaw: His Life and Personality.* London: Collins, 1942.

Pearson, Hesketh. *G.B.S.: A Full-Length Portrait, and A Postscript.* New York: Harper, 1950.

Peters, Margot. *Bernard Shaw and the Actresses.* Garden City, New York: Doubleday, 1980.

Peters, Sally. *Bernard Shaw: The Ascent of the Superman.* New Haven, Conn.: Yale University Press, 1996.

Reynolds, Jean. *Pygmalion's Wordplay: The Postmodern Shaw.* Gainesville: University Press of Florida, 1999.

Roy, R. N. *George Bernard Shaw's Historical Plays.* Delhi: Macmillan, 1976.

Rusinko, Susan, ed. *Shaw and Other Matters: A Festschrift for Stanley Weintraub on the Occasion of His Forty-Second Anniversary at The Pennsylvania State University.* Susquehanna University Press; Selinsgrove, PA: Associated UP, 1998.

Shaw, Bernard. *Bernard Shaw on Photography.* Salt Lake City: Gibbs Smith, 1989.

———. *Fortissimo: Moments from the Music Reviews of Bernard Shaw.* Hastings: Pickpockets, 1994.

———. *Major Critical Essays: The Quintessence of Ibsenism, The Perfect Wagnerite, The Sanity of Art.* London: Constable, 1972.

Silver, Arnold. *Bernard Shaw: The Darker Side.* Stanford: Stanford University Press, 1982.

Valency, Maurice Jacques. *The Cart and the Trumpet: The Plays of George Bernard Shaw.* New York: Oxford University Press, 1973.

Weintraub, Stanley. *Journey to Heartbreak.* London: Routledge and Kegan Paul, 1971.

———. *The Unexpected Shaw: Biographical Approaches to G.B.S. and his Work.* New York: Frederick Ungar, 1982.

———, et al. *Shaw: Seven Critical Essays.* Toronto: University of Toronto Press, 1971.

JOURNALS

The Annual of Bernard Shaw Studies. Pennsylvania: Pennsylvania State University Press.

The Independent Shavian. New York.

The Shavian: The Journal of the Shaw Society. Stone, Staffordshire: The Shaw Society.

MRS WARREN'S PROFESSION

Mudford, Peter. *"Mrs. Warren's Profession." The Shavian: The Journal of the Shaw Society* 6.5 (Spring 1987): 4–10.

Salih, Sabah A. "The *New York Times* and Arnold Daly's Production of *Mrs. Warren's Profession." The Independent Shavian* 26.3 (1988): 57–60.

Sterner, Mark H. "The Changing Status of Women in Late Victorian Drama." *Within the Dramatic Spectrum.* Ed. K. V. Hartigan. Lanham, MD: University Press of America, 1986, pp. 199–212.

Wiley, Catherine. "The Matter with Manners: The New Woman and the Problem Play." *Women in Theatre.* Ed. James Redmond. Cambridge: Cambridge University Press, 1989, pp. 109–27.

MAN AND SUPERMAN

Bloom, Harold, ed. *George Bernard Shaw's* Man and Superman. New York: Chelsea House, 1987.

Bryden, Mary. "Coils of the Cobra: The Predatory Woman of Shaw and Beckett." *New Comparison: A Journal of Comparative and General Literary Studies* 7 (Summer 1989): 160–71.

Emmett, V. J. "Roebuck Ramsden's Study: Shaw as Philosophical Conservative." *Journal of Irish Literature* 11.3 (September 1982): pp. 103–8.

Gibbs, A. M., ed. *Bernard Shaw:* Man and Superman *and* Saint Joan: A Casebook. Basingstoke: Macmillan Education, 1992.

Sterner, Mark H. "*Man and Superman:* Drama as Clash between Social and Spiritual Exigencies." *Text and Presentation.* Ed. K. V. Hartigan. Lanham, MD: University Press of America, 1989, pp. 141–48.

MAJOR BARBARA

Albert, Sydney P. "The Mood of Barbara Revisited: Shaw, Jevons, and the Syllogism." *The Independent Shavian* 32.2–3 (1994): 29–36.

Bloom, Harold, ed. *George Bernard Shaw's* Major Barbara. New York: Chelsea House, 1988.

Dukore, Bernard F. "Shaw's 'Big Three' (*Major Barbara, John Bull's Other Island* and *Man and Superman.*" *Shaw: The Annual of Bernard Shaw Studies* 4 (1984): 33–67.

Hoeveler, Diane Long. "Shaw's Vision of God in *Major Barbara.*" *The Independent Shavian* 17 (1979): 16–18.

Rogers, M. E. "The Machiavellian Tendencies of Adolphus Cusins." *Shaw: The Annual of Bernard Shaw Studies* 12 (1992): 261–70.

Weintraub, Stanley. "Bernard Shaw in Darkest England: G.B.S. and the Salvation Army's General William Booth." *Shaw: The Annual of Bernard Shaw Studies* 10 (1990): 45–59.

Zimbardo, Rose A. *Twentieth-Century Interpretations of* Major Barbara: A Collection of Critical Essays. Englewood Cliffs, N.J.: Prentice-Hall, 1970.

PYGMALION

Amkpa, A. "Drama and the Languages of Postcolonial Desire: Bernard Shaw's *Pygmalion.*" *Irish University Review: A Journal of Irish Studies* 29.2 (Autumn–Winter 1999): 294–304.

Berst, Charles A. Pygmalion: *Shaw's Spin on Myth and Cinderella.* New York: Twayne, 1995.

Bloom, Harold, ed. *George Bernard Shaw's* Pygmalion. New York: Chelsea House: 1988.

Loewe, Frederick. *My Fair Lady: a Musical Play in Two Acts.* London: Max Reinhardt, 1958.

Mugglestone, Lynda. "Shaw, Subjective Inequality, and the Social Meanings of Language in *Pygmalion.*" *Review of English Studies: A Quarterly Journal of English Literature and the English Language* 44. 175 (August 1993): 373–85.

Reynolds, Jean. "Deconstructing Henry Higgins, or Eliza as Derridean 'Text.' " *Shaw: The Annual of Bernard Shaw Studies* 14 (1994): 209–17.

Sparks, Julie A. "An Overlooked Source for Eliza? W. E. Henley's London Types." *Shaw: The Annual of Shaw Studies* 18 (1998): 161–79.

Starks, Lisa S. "Educating Eliza: Fashioning the Model Woman in the '*Pygmalion* Film.' " *Post Script: Essays in Film and the Humanities* 16.2 (Winter–Spring): 44–55.

Vesonder, Timothy G. "Eliza's Choice: Transformation Myth and the Ending of *Pygmalion.*" *Fabian Feminist.* Ed. Rodelle Weintraub. Pennsylvania: Pennsylvania State University Press, 1977.